KB055021

한국 인권문제

국제사면위원회 방한 및 대응 2

한국 인권문제

국제사면위원회 방한 및 대응 2

| 머리말

일제 강점기 독립운동과 병행되었던 한국의 인권운동은 해방이 되었음에도 큰 결실을 보지 못했다. 1950년대 반공을 앞세운 이승만 정부와 한국전쟁, 역시 경제발전과 반공을 내세우다 유신 체제에 이르렀던 박정희 정권, 쿠데타로 집권한 1980년대 전두환 정권까지, 한국의 인권은 이를 보장해야 할 국가와 정부에 의해 도리어 억압받고 침해되었다. 이런 배경상 근대 한국의 인권운동은 반독재, 민주화운동과 결을 같이했고, 대체로 국외에 본부를 둔 인권 단체나 정치로부터 상대적으로 자유로운 종교 단체에 의해 주도되곤 했다. 이는 1980년 5 · 18광주민주화운동을 계기로 보다 근적인 변혁을 요구하는 형태로 조직화되었고, 그 활동 영역도 정치를 넘어 노동자, 농민, 빈민 등으로 확대되었다. 이들이 없었다면 한국은 1987년 군부 독재 종식하고 절차적 민주주의를 도입할 수 없었을 것이다. 민주화 이후에도 수많은 어려움이 있었지만, 한국의 인권운동은 점차 전문적이고 독립된 운동으로 분화되며 더 많은 이들의 참여를 이끌어냈고, 지금까지 많은 결실을 맺을 수 있었다.

본 총서는 1980년대 중반부터 1990년대 초반까지, 외교부에서 작성하여 30여 년간 유지했던 한국 인권문제와 관련한 국내외 자료를 담고 있다. 6월 항쟁이 일어나고 민주화 선언이 이뤄지는 등 한국 인권운동에 많은 변화가 있었던 시기다. 당시 인권문제와 관련한 국내외 사안들, 각종 사건에 대한 미국과 우방국, 유엔의 반응, 최초의 한국 인권보고서 제출과 아동의 권리에 관한 협약 과정, 유엔인권위원회 활동, 기타 민주화 관련 자료 등 총 18권으로 구성되었다. 전체 분량은 약 9천여 쪽에 이른다.

2024년 3월

한국학술정보(주)

| 일러두기

· 본 총서에 실린 자료는 2022년 4월과 2023년 4월에 각각 공개한 외교문서 4,827권, 76만 여 쪽 가운데 일부를 발췌한 것이다.

· 각 권의 제목과 순서는 공개된 원본을 최대한 반영하였으나, 주제에 따라 일부는 적절히 변경하였다.

· 원본 자료는 A4 판형에 맞게 축소하거나 원본 비율을 유지한 채 A4 페이지 안에 삽입하였다. 또한 현재 시점에선 공개되지 않아 '공란'이란 표기만 있는 페이지 역시 그대로 실었다.

· 외교부가 공개한 문서 각 권의 첫 페이지에는 '정리 보존 문서 목록'이란 이름으로 기록물 종류, 일자, 명칭, 간단한 내용 등의 정보가 수록되어 있으며, 이를 기준으로 0001번부터 번호가 매겨져 있다. 이는 삭제하지 않고 총서에 그대로 수록하였다.

· 보고서 내용에 관한 더 자세한 정보가 필요하다면, 외교부가 온라인상에 제공하는『대한민국 외교사료요약집』1991년과 1992년 자료를 참조할 수 있다.

| 차례

머리말 4

일러두기 5

A.I.(국제사면위원회) 보고서 및 대응활동, 1991. 전2권 (V.1 1-9월) 7

A.I.(국제사면위원회) 보고서 및 대응활동, 1991. 전2권 (V.2 10-12월) 305

정 리 보 존 문 서 목 록					
기록물종류	일반공문서철	등록번호	2019040021	등록일자	2019-04-09
분류번호	736.21	국가코드		보존기간	영구
명 칭	A.I.(국제사면위원회) 보고서 및 대응활동, 1991. 전2권				
생 산 과	국제연합과	생산년도	1991~1991	담당그룹	
권 차 명	V.1 1-9월				
내용목차					

0001

관리번호 91-13

분류번호	보존기간

발 신 전 보

번 호 : WUK-0018 910104 1945 FK 종별 : 지급

수 신 : 주 영 대사. 총영사

발 신 : 장 관(국연)

제 목 : A.I 대책

1. 귀지 A.I 발간 Newsletter 1월호에 아태지역의 1990년 인권상황이 게재된바, 이중 한국관계 부분 기사에 대하여 관계부처는 귀관 공보관 명의 반박서한을 발송, 이를 동 뉴스레터에 게재하는 방안을 검토중임.

2. 상기관련, 반박서한 필요 여부 및, 발송시 차기 뉴스레터에 게재될수 있는지 여부에 관한 귀견 보고바라며, 기타 적절한 대응책에 관한 귀견바람.

(국제기구조약국장 문동석)

일반문서로 재분류 (1991.12.31.)

검 토 필 (1991. 6.30.)

보안통제	

앙고재	91년 1월 4일	과	기안자 성명		과 장		국 장		차 관	장 관
			송영완				전결			

외신과통제

0002

A.I.의 91.1월호 Newsletter중 한국인권 관련사항

o 대만소재 A.I. 지부는 한국내 구속노조원 석방을 위한 A.I. 캠페인 지원 목적으로 유인물등 제작

o 파키스탄의 A.I. 지부도 불란서, 이태리소재 A.I. 지부와의 연합하에 한국내 양심수선정 및 석방운동 전개

o 홍콩 A.I. 회원도 한국, 수단, 이디오피아의 양심수 석방탄원서 송부중

o 한국에서는 양심수가 공산주의 신념을 버리지 않는한 무기한 구금될 수도 있음. 또한 북한과의 불법접촉의 혐의가 있는 자는 구속됨.

o 1988년도에 한국에서는 일부 양심수가 사면조치로 석방되었으나, 89년에 새로이 300여명이 불법방북, 북한인접촉, 북한서적 출판, 배포등의 혐의로 구속됨.

* 북한은 중국, 라오스, 미얀마, 스리랑카등과 더불어 A.I.의 접촉 자체가 불가능한 국가임.

0003

관리 번호	91 -24

	분류번호	보존기간

발 신 전 보

번 호 : WUK-0037 910108 1716 CG 종별 :

수 신 : 주 영 대사 . 총영사

발 신 : 장 관 (국연)

제 목 : A.I. 대책

연 : WUK - 0018

연호, 지급보고 바람. 끝.

(국제기구조약국장 문동석)

1991. 6. 30 에 예고문에 의거 일반문서로 재분류됨

앙고재	91년 1월 8일	유엔과	기안자		과 장		국 장		차 관	장 관
			송영완		(서명)		(서명)			(서명)

보안통제	외신과통제
(서명)	

0004

관리번호	91-31

원 본

외 무 부

종 별 :

번 호 : UKW-0046 일 시 : 91 0109 1400

수 신 : 장관(국연,구일)

발 신 : 주 영 대사

제 목 : A.I.대책

대: WUK-001(827)

1. 대호, 아측 반박서한의 차기 뉴스레터 게재 가능성 관련, A.I. 의 VANDALE 한국담당관은 A.I. 내 담당부서 및 사무총장등과 협의한후, 당관에 통보해 주겠다고함.

2. VANDALE 담당관의 사견으로는 뉴스레터의 한정된 지면에 비추어 아측서한이 사실관계에 관한 정정이나 새로운 사실(예컨데 양심수석방 또는 인권관련법개정) 홍보에 관한 간략한 내용이라면 게재 가능성이 있을것이나 인권상황에 관한 입장표명이나 논평은 게재되는데 어려움이 있을 것이라고함.

3. A.I. 측 입장 및 당관의견등 추보 위계임.끝

(대사 오재희-국장)

예고: 91.12.31 일반

일반문서로 재분류(1991.12.31.)

검 토 필(1991. 6.30.)

국기국 구주국

PAGE 1

91.01.10 07:34

외신 2과 통제관 BW

0005

연
오
(동)

관리 번호	91 -38

원 본

(要 樺 付)

외 무 부

종 별 : 지 급

번 호 : UKW-0053 일 시 : 91 0110 1400

수 신 : 장관(국연,구일,정홍,해신)

발 신 : 주 영 대사

제 목 : A.I.대책

대: WUK-0018,0063

연: UKW-0046

1. 연호, 당지 A.I. 본부의 VANDALE 한국담당관은 내부협의를 거쳐 A.I. 측입장을 아래와 같이 통보해옴.

가. 91.1. 뉴스레터의 한국관련 부분을 재검토해본 결과, 5 페이지의 "공산주의자 무기한 구금" 부분이 오류임을 발견하였음. 따라서 91.2. 뉴스레터에 정상기사를 게재할 방침임. 정정기사 문안은 아직 확정되지 않았지만 기본적으로 "1989 법개정으로 공산주의자의 무기한 구금을 허용하는 법규정은 없어졌다" 는 내용이 담길것임.

나. 아측서한의 뉴스레터 게재 가능성에 대해서는 정부의 반박 또는 논평을뉴스레터에 게재하지 않는것이 A.I. 의 입장임. 다만, 아측서한의 내용상 홍보가 필요하다고 인정할 경우 A.I. 의 별도문서(영국정 723-282(90.3.6) 첨부서류와 유사한 형식)로 배포하는 것은 고려해 볼수 있음.

2. 상기에 비추어 대호(WUK-0063) 조치를 그대로 시행할지에 대한 본부지침회시바람. 끝

(대사 오재희-국장)

예고: 91.12.31 일반

일반문서로 재분류 (1991 12 .31

검 토 필(1991. 6 .30.)

503-7045

국기국 구주국 정문국 공보처

PAGE 1 91.01.11 07:26

외신 2과 통제관 FE

0006

아국인권신문제

주 영 대 사 관

영국(정) 723- 24 1991. 1. 10.

수신 : 장관

참조 : 국제기구조약국장

제목 : 인권서한

당지 국제사면위(A.I.)의 1990 위원회는 별첨 서한을 당관에 송부, 홍성담의 석방을 탄원하였음을 보고합니다.

첨부 : 동 서한 . 끝.

1991. 1. 10

주 영 대 사

00877

0007

AMNESTY INTERNATIONAL Glasgow 1990

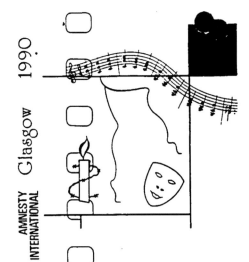

Contact Address
Amnesty 1990 Campaign
Room 5 (Basement)
235 George St
Glasgow G2
Tel Nº 041-227 5556
(Answering Machine)

15 December 1990

The Ambassador
Embassy of the Republic of Korea
4 Palace Gate
London W8 5NF

Your Excellency,

Appeals for the release of HONG SONG DAM

As you are no doubt aware there is international concern about the continued imprisonment of Korean artist Hong Song Dam. Amnesty International considers him to be a prisoner of conscience, imprisoned solely for the peaceful expression of his ideas through his art.

I am sending you copies of petitions appealing for his immediate and unconditional release. These petitions were signed by Members of the European Parliament in Strasbourg, and signatories include Members of the European Parliament representing all parties and all member states of the European Community. Claude Cheysson, former Foreign Minister of France, is a signatory to the petition, as is Max Gallo, the French author and M.E.P. The petition was also signed by a delegation from the University of Marmara in Turkey during their visit to the European Parliament.

I respectfully request that these petitions be sent to your government in Korea as evidence of the concern felt in Europe about the fate of Hong Song Dam.

Yours respectfully and sincerely,

Hazel M R Mills

Hazel M. R. Mills M.A.

Amnesty International 1990 Committee

0008

Cultural Prisoners of Conscience
1990—Fighting for Cultural Freedom

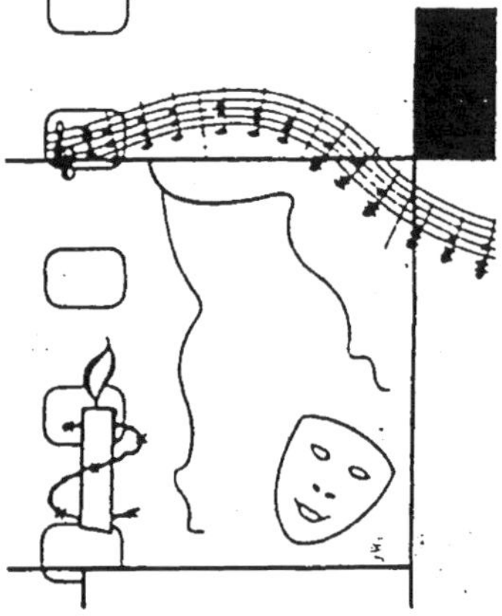

We, the undersigned, call upon the government of Vietnam to release Nguyen Chi Thien. He is a poet who has been in and out of prison since 1958 for "writing romantic poetry to discredit the government". He was last re-arrested in 1979 after passing a manuscript of his poetry to staff at the British Embassy. This collection was published as "Testament of a Vietnamese".

We, the undersigned, call upon the government of South Korea to release Hong Song Dam. He is a South Korean artist of international repute. He was arrested in 1989 under charges of espionage and has been sentenced to 7 years in prison. We have reason to believe that he has been tortured. His actual "crime" was to paint a mural on a wall and send a picture of it to fellow artists in North Korea.

We, the undersigned, call on the government of Malawi to release Jack Mapanje. He was arrested in 1987 for an undisclosed crime, and he has never been brought to trial, or the terms of his imprisonment disclosed. This arrest followed the banning of his poem collection "Of Chameleons and Gods".

NAME	ADDRESS	SIGNATURE
E.P Wolfjer	Berg Wartier 10 Venray	[illegible]
ROGER BARTON	MEP for Sheffield	[illegible]
Maibaum G.	Mordenstr. 5 Köln 40	[illegible]
David Morris	MEP Mid + West Wales	[illegible]
Llew Smith	S-G Wales (M.E.P)	[illegible]
Quistorp	MEP 1-Berlin-31	Quistorp
Canavarro	MEP - Portugal	[illegible]
Colom i Naval	M.E.P.	[illegible]
Joanna Roe	MEP.	[illegible]

AMNESTY INTERNATIONAL

0009

Cultural Prisoners of Conscience

1990—Fighting for Cultural Freedom

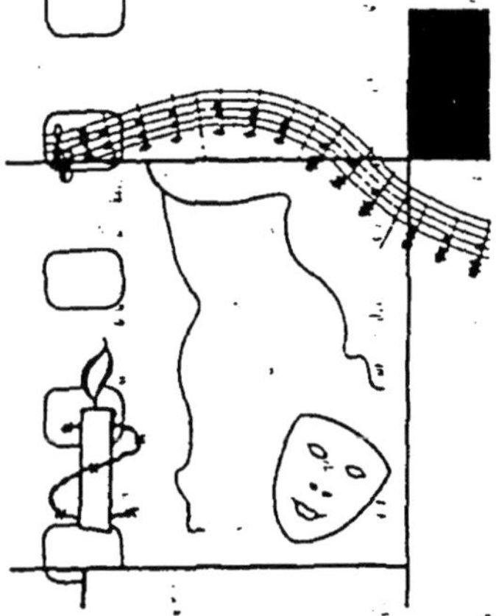

We, the undersigned, call upon the government of Vietnam to release Nguyen Chi Thien. He is a poet who has been in and out of prison since 1958 for "writing romantic poetry to discredit the government". He was last re-arrested in 1979 after passing a manuscript of his poetry to staff at the British Embassy. This collection was published as "Testament of a Vietnamese".

We, the undersigned, call upon the government of South Korea to release Hong Song Dam. He is a South Korean artist of international repute. He was arrested in 1989 under charges of espionage and has been sentenced to 7 years in prison. We have reason to believe that he has been tortured. His actual "crime" was to paint a mural on a wall and send a picture of it to fellow artists in North Korea.

We, the undersigned, call on the government of Malawi to release Jack Mapanje. He was arrested in 1987 for an undisclosed crime, and he has never been brought to trial, or the terms of his imprisonment disclosed. This arrest followed the banning of his poem collection "Of Chameleons and Gods".

NAME	ADDRESS	SIGNATURE
Yeşim Sümerkan	University of Marmara ISTANBUL/TURKEY	Y. Sümerkan
Cim ADAM	MEP Northumbria	
WAYNE DAVID.	S. Wales Euro. Office. 199 Newport Rd, Cardiff	
Rosmini Fadiné	67 la Canebière 13001. MARSEILLE	
LYNDON HARRISON	2. Stanley St. Chester	
Alex Smith M.E.P.	35 KIRKLAND ROAD IRVINE SCOTLAND KA11 1BP	
Annemarie Goedmakers	MEP: Rijnbandijk 161, 4041 AV KESTEREN The Netherlands	
DESAMA Cl.	MEP 161 E, rue du Paradis, 4821 DISON – BELGIUM	
Joop de Vries	MEP European Parliament	

AMNESTY INTERNATIONAL

0010

Cultural Prisoners of Conscience

1990—Fighting for Cultural Freedom

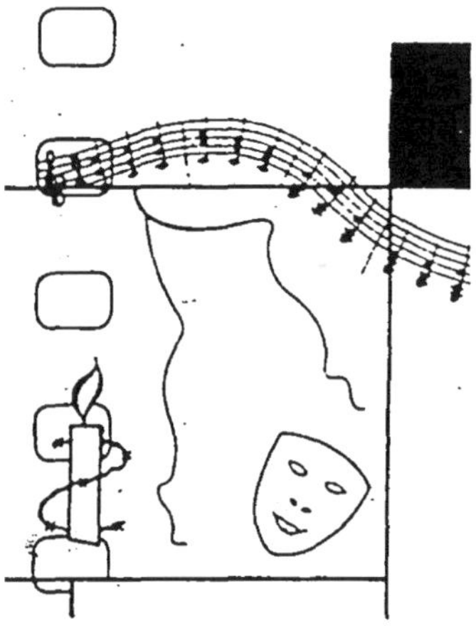

We, the undersigned, call upon the government of Vietnam to release Nguyen Chi Thien. He is a poet who has been i and out of prison since 1958 for "writing romantic poetry to discredit the government". He was last re-arrested in 1979 after passing a manuscript of his poetry to staff at the British Embassy. This collection was published as "Testament of a Vietnamese".

We, the undersigned, call upon the government of South Korea to release Hong Song Dam. He is a South Korean artist of international repute. He was arrested in 1989 under charges of espionage and has been sentenced to 7 years in prison. We have reason to believe that he has been tortured. His actual "crime" was to paint a mural on a wall and send a picture of it to fellow artists in North Korea.

We, the undersigned, call on the government of Malawi to release Jack Mapanje. He was arrested in 1987 for an undisclosed crime, and he has never been brought to trial, or the terms of his imprisonment disclosed. This arrest followed the banning of his poem collection "Of Chameleons and Gods".

NAME	ADDRESS	SIGNATURE
Christine Crawley	MEP. Birmingham East	C.M.Cr
J. ROBERT de [illegible]	[signature] M.E.P.	
Pauline Green	MEP London North	[signature]
[signature]	MEP, Huizen, Nederland	WJ van Velzen
M H Hindley	MEP Lancs East	HINDLEY
[signature]	MPE - Asturias, Spain	GARCIA ARIAS
[signature]	MPE France	BOMBARD
Martine BURON	MPE France	BURON
Michael ELLIOTT	MEP U.K.	[signature]

AMNESTY INTERNATIONAL

0011

Cultural Prisoners of Conscience

1990—Fighting for Cultural Freedom

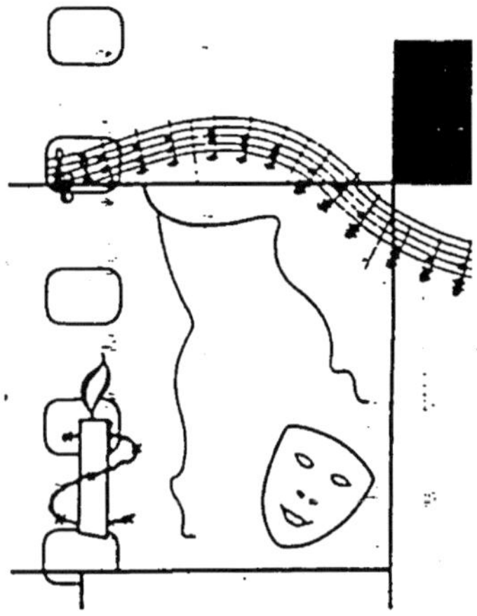

We, the undersigned, call upon the government of Vietnam to release Nguyen Chi Thien. He is a poet who has been in and out of prison since 1958 for "writing romantic poetry to discredit the government". He was last re-arrested in 1979 after passing a manuscript of his poetry to staff at the British Embassy. This collection was published as "Testament of a Vietnamese".

We, the undersigned, call upon the government of South Korea to release Hong Song Dam. He is a South Korean artist of international repute. He was arrested in 1989 under charges of espionage and has been sentenced to 7 years in prison. We have reason to believe that he has been tortured. His actual "crime" was to paint a mural on a wall and send a picture of it to fellow artists in North Korea.

We, the undersigned, call on the government of Malawi to release Jack Mapanje. He was arrested in 1987 for an undisclosed crime, and he has never been brought to trial, or the terms of his imprisonment disclosed. This arrest followed the banning of his poem collection "Of Chameleons and Gods".

NAME	ADDRESS	SIGNATURE
Aldo CUNHA OLIVEIRA	ACORES — PORTUGAL	[signature]
Huguette FUGIER	A. I. France	H Fugier
ROGALLA	[illegible] Rogalla 4630 BOCHUM	[signature]
BARROS MOURA	Rua dos Soeiros, 327-5º, 1500 LISBOA	[signature]
TORRES COUTO	RUA BUENOS AIRES Nº 11 LISBOA	[signature]
B. H. SOLE	CITY HALL - BRADFORD - UK	[signature]
Janey Buchan	EUROPEAN PARLT.	[signature]
GALLO MAX	PARIS	[signature]
Ahmet Ciftci	GA school of Journalism Ankara	[signature]

AMNESTY INTERNATIONAL

0012

Cultural Prisoners of Conscience

1990—Fighting for Cultural Freedom

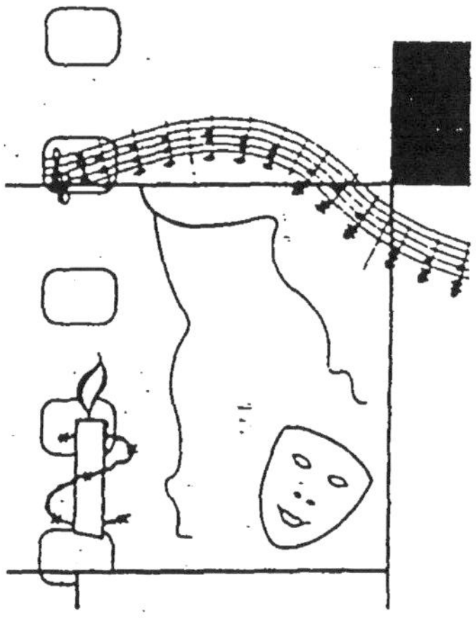

We, the undersigned, call upon the government of Vietnam to release Nguyen Chi Thien. He is a poet who has been in and out of prison since 1958 for "writing romantic poetry to discredit the government". He was last re-arrested in 1979 after passing a manuscript of his poetry to staff at the British Embassy. This collection was published as "Testament of a Vietnamese".

We, the undersigned, call upon the government of South Korea to release Hong Song Dam. He is a South Korean artist of international repute. He was arrested in 1989 under charges of espionage and has been sentenced to 7 years in prison. We have reason to believe that he has been tortured. His actual "crime" was to paint a mural on a wall and send a picture of it to fellow artists in North Korea.

We, the undersigned, call on the government of Malawi to release Jack Mapanje. He was arrested in 1987 for an undisclosed crime, and he has never been brought to trial, or the terms of his imprisonment disclosed. This arrest followed the banning of his poem collection "Of Chameleons and Gods".

NAME	ADDRESS	SIGNATURE
Aslan Gündüz	University of Marmara İstanbul	[signature]
Ertuğ Yaşar	University of Marmara / Ist. / Turkey	Ertuğ Yaşar
Beatrix Seral	Socialist Group. European Parliament	[signature]
Ocarcio HORALES	SOCIALIST GROUP E. P.	[signature]
Alvaro MARIN AENLLE	" " "	[signature]
WILLAME Estelle	Rue des Déportés 32 - 6700 ARLON Belgium	[signature] 12/6/90
Seyhan Bakuzyol	University of Marmara ISTANBUL TURKEY	[signature] 12/6/90
Funda Gökalın	University of Marmara ISTANBUL TURKEY	[signature] 12.6.1990

AMNESTY INTERNATIONAL

0013

Cultural Prisoners of Conscience

1990—Fighting for Cultural Freedom

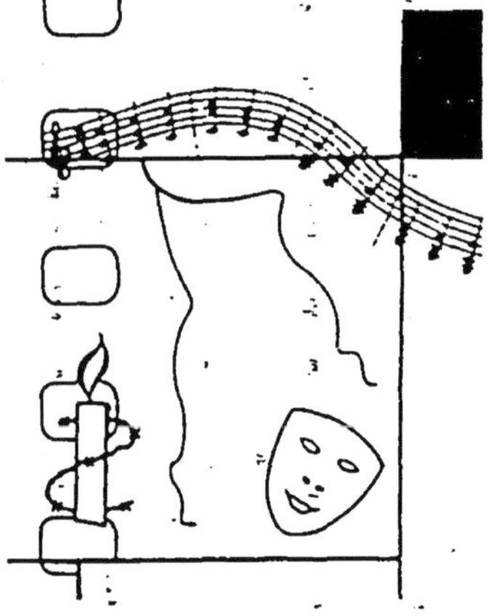

We, the undersigned, call upon the government of Vietnam to release Nguyen Chi Thien. He is a poet who has been in and out of prison since 1958 for "writing romantic poetry to discredit the government". He was last re-arrested in 1979 after passing a manuscript of his poetry to staff at the British Embassy. This collection was published as "Testament of a Vietnamese".

We, the undersigned, call upon the government of South Korea to release Hong Song Dam. He is a South Korean artist of international repute. He was arrested in 1989 under charges of espionage and has been sentenced to 7 years in prison. We have reason to believe that he has been tortured. His actual "crime" was to paint a mural on a wall and send a picture of it to fellow artists in North Korea.

We, the undersigned, call on the government of Malawi to release Jack Mapanje. He was arrested in 1987 for an undisclosed crime, and he has never been brought to trial, or the terms of his imprisonment disclosed. This arrest followed the banning of his poem collection "Of Chameleons and Gods".

NAME	ADDRESS	SIGNATURE
Zeyno D. DAVUTOĞLU	Cinnah cad. 34/1 Çankaya, Ankara 06690 TURKEY	
Ayşegül Kandaş	Oyak Sitesi 35/3 Yeni Levent İstanbul TURKEY	[signature]
Bent Hansen	Tåsingegade 47 Kopenhagen Denmark	[signature]
Johannes van der Klaauw	Rue Berckmans 9 1060 Brussels	[signature]

AMNESTY INTERNATIONAL

0014

Cultural Prisoners of Conscience

1990—Fighting for Cultural Freedom

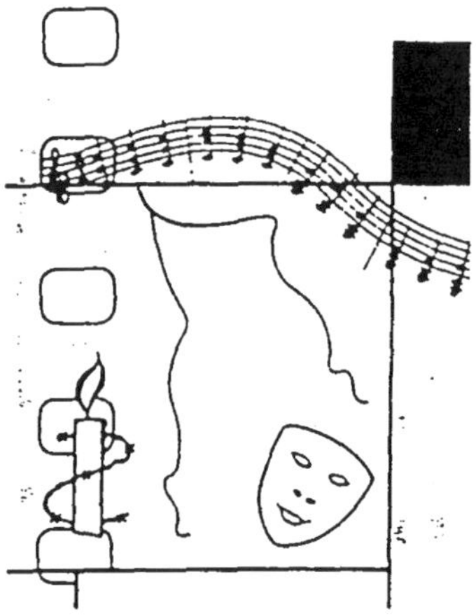

We, the undersigned, call upon the government of Vietnam to release Nguyen Chi Thien. He is a poet who has been in and out of prison since 1958 for "writing romantic poetry to discredit the government". He was last re-arrested in 1979 after passing a manuscript of his poetry to staff at the British Embassy. This collection was published as "Testament of a Vietnamese".

We, the undersigned, call upon the government of South Korea to release Hong Song Dam. He is a South Korean artist of international repute. He was arrested in 1989 under charges of espionage and has been sentenced to 7 years in prison. We have reason to believe that he has been tortured. His actual "crime" was to paint a mural on a wall and send a picture of it to fellow artists in North Korea.

We, the undersigned, call on the government of Malawi to release Jack Mapanje. He was arrested in 1987 for an undisclosed crime, and he has never been brought to trial, or the terms of his imprisonment disclosed. This arrest followed the banning of his poem collection "Of Chameleons and Gods".

NAME	ADDRESS	SIGNATURE
A. POLLACK	177 Lavender Hill SW11 5TE	[signature]
Michael Wood	Committee Secretariat, European Parliament	[signature]
A. Oostlander	4, rue de Parlement Brux	[signature]
L. Gadouche	Parlement Européen Bureau femmes Groupe Vert	[signature]
D Reed	1 Avenue du Haut Pont, Bruxelles 1060	[signature]

AMNESTY INTERNATIONAL

0015

Cultural Prisoners of Conscience

1990—Fighting for Cultural Freedom

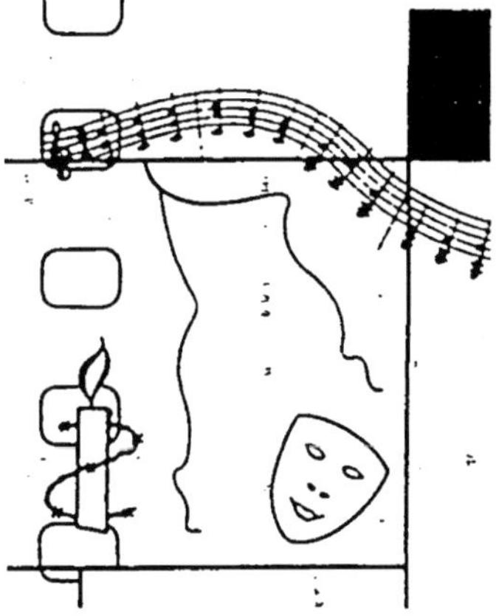

We, the undersigned, call upon the government of Vietnam to release Nguyen Chi Thien. He is a poet who has been in and out of prison since 1958 for "writing romantic poetry to discredit the government". He was last re-arrested in 1979 after passing a manuscript of his poetry to staff at the British Embassy. This collection was published as "Testament of a Vietnamese".

We, the undersigned, call upon the government of South Korea to release Hong Song Dam. He is a South Korean artist of international repute. He was arrested in 1989 under charges of espionage and has been sentenced to 7 years in prison. We have reason to believe that he has been tortured. His actual "crime" was to paint a mural on a wall and send a picture of it to fellow artists in North Korea.

We, the undersigned, call on the government of Malawi to release Jack Mapanje. He was arrested in 1987 for an undisclosed crime, and he has never been brought to trial, or the terms of his imprisonment disclosed. This arrest followed the banning of his poem collection "Of Chameleons and Gods".

NAME	ADDRESS	SIGNATURE
Berat Bir	University of Marmara EC Institute - Istanbul - TURKEY	[signature]
PÖHLMANN, Mariya	EP - Soc. group	[signature]
ENGMANN, Jytte	EP - Socialist Group	[signature]
Leenaars, Riänne	EP - Socialist group	[signature]
DIEULANGARD Emmanuelle	PE. GROUPE SOCIALISTE	[signature]
MARET	[illegible]	[signature]

AMNESTY INTERNATIONAL

0016

관리 번호	91 -43

	분류번호	보존기간

발 신 전 보

번 호 : WUK-0076 910112 1203 FK 종별 :

수 신 : 주 영 대사 ~~총영사~~

발 신 : 장 관 (국연)

제 목 : A.I. 뉴스레터 대응

대 : UKW-0046, 0053

연 : WUK-0018, 0063

1. 대호 A.I. 뉴스레터의 아국 인권상황 왜곡관련, A.I.측 오류의 지적 및 아국정부의 관심 표명을 위하여 A.I.측 관계자를 접촉, 다음 입장을 전달하고 결과 보고바람.

가. 그간 한국정부는 A.I. 측이 국내인권상황과 관련하여 보인 관심에 대하여 작년도 관계자의 방한조사활동시에도 각종 필요한 자료를 제공하는 등 적극적으로 협조하고자 노력해 왔음.

나. 그러나 이에도 불구하고 이미 89년도에 개선된 상황을 전세계에 배포되는 뉴스레터에 왜곡 보도한 것은 이해하기 어려우며 이에 대해 유감을 표명함.

다. 향후 여사한 오류가 발생하지 않기를 희망하며 A.I. 측의 한국내 인권개선에 대한 보다 정확한 이해를 기대함.

2. 이와관련, 연호 공보관 명의 서한은 뉴스레터 게재 또는 별도 문서 배포 여부와 관계없이 A.I 측에 별도로 송부하기 바람. 끝.

1991.6.30 에 예고문에 의거 인반문서로 재분류됨

(국제기구조약국장 문동석)

앙 고 재	91년 7월 12일	국연 과	기안자		과 장		국 장	차 관	장 관
			윤미환		(서명)		전결		(서명)

보안통제	외신과통제

0017

A.I.대외비

A.I.측 입장 (Vandale 한국담당관이 아측에 통보)

91. 1. 14.

ㅇ 91.1. 뉴스레터의 한국관련 부분을 재검토해본 결과, 5페이지의 "공산주의자 무기한 구금" 부분이 오류임을 발견하였음. 따라서 91.2. 뉴스레터에 정정기사를 게재할 방침임. 정정기사 문안은 아직 확정되지 않았지만 기본적으로 "1989 법개정으로 공산주의자의 무기한 구금을 허용하는 법규정은 없어졌다"는 내용이 담길것임.

ㅇ 아측 서한의 뉴스레터 게재 가능성에 대해서는;정부의 반박 또는 논평을 뉴스레터에 게재하지 않는 것이 A.I.의 입장임. 다만, 아측 서한의 내용상 홍보가 필요하다고 인정할 경우 A.I.의 별도 문서로 배포하는 것은 고려해 볼 수 있음.

0018

관리 번호	91 -67

기 안 용 지

분류기호 문서번호	국연 2031 - 122	(전화:)		시 행 상 특별취급	
보존기간	영구·준영구. 10. 5. 3. 1	장 관			
수 신 처 보존기간					
시행일자	1991. 1. 16.				

보조기관	·국 장	전 결	협조기관		문서통제 검열 1991. 1. 17 통제관
	과 장				
기안책임자		송영완			발송인

경 유		발신명의	발송 1991. 1. 17 외무부
수 신	법무부장관		
참 조	법무 실장		
제 목	A.I. 의 아국인권상황 왜곡에 대한 반박		

1. A.I. 는 91년 1월호 Newsletter에서 아국의 인권상황과 관련, "한국에서는 양심수가 공산주의 신념을 버리지 않는한 무기한 구금될 수도 있음"이라고 왜곡 기재하는등 아국의 인권상황에 대한 그릇된 인식을 갖게 할 우려가 있는 내용을 게재한 바 있습니다.

2. 이와관련, 당부는 1.9. 주영대사를 통하여 A.I. 본부에 동 Newsletter 의 오류를 지적하고 동 왜곡

//계속...

0019

(2)

내용의 정정을 강력 요청한 바, A.I. 측도 아국인권상황에 대한 오류를 시인하고 정정기사를 91.2월호 Newsletter 에 게재할 방침임을 알려왔습니다.

3. 또한 당부는 1.12. 주영대사관 담당관으로 하여금 A.I. 측 관계자를 접촉, A.I. 측의 아국인권상황 왜곡보도에 대한 아국정부의 유감을 전달하고 향후 여사한 오류가 발생하지 않도록 A.I. 측의 한국 인권 상황에 대한 정확한 이해를 촉구토록 지시하였습니다.

4. 이와 함께, A.I. Newsletter 의 한국관련 부분중 아래 오류를 지적하는 서한을 주영대사관 공보관 명의로 작성, A.I. 측에 전달토록 하였음을 알려드립니다.

o 간첩등 국가전복을 기도한 실정법 위반자를 양심범으로 표현하고 있음.

o 공산주의자가 전향을 하지 않아도 재판에의해 확정된 형기만 복역하면 출소함.

- 89.5.16 보안검찰법 제정 전까지는 "보안감호"라 하여 출소후에도 행동의 제한을 받았음.

//계속...

0020

(3)

- 동법 제정으로 "보안감호"제도가 폐지되어 주거제한이

  철폐되고 이들의 해외여행까지 허용됨.

o 북한에서 간행된 책자를 소지하였다하여 무조건 처벌되는

  것이 아니고 명백히 대남 적화혁명을 선동하는 내용의

  표현물만 금지됨.

  - 89년 10월말 현재 114종의 북한원전 책자가 시판되고 있음.

첨 부 : A.I. Newsletter 91.1월중 한국관련부분. 끝.

1991. 6. 30. 에 예고문에
의거 일반문서로 재분류

0021

(5-2)

1. Amnesty Int'l은 1월 Newsletter 3-6면 (총 8면)에서 아시아, 태평양 지역의 1990년 인권상황을 다루고 있는바 한국관련 내용이 있어 이를 발췌 송부합니다.

2. 한국 관련 사항

- 사진 2매 게재
- 기사 내용
  - 구속 노조원 및 양심수등 인권관련 A I의 캠페인, 리프렛 제작등 활동
  - 반공법 위반자 구속문제
  - 북한은 아직도 A I의 접근 자체가 불가능한 국가중 하나임.

끝.

0022

(5-3)

AMNESTY INTERNATIONAL

AI CROSSES MILLION MARK: Movement gains strength: see page 8

NEWSLETTER JANUARY 1991 VOLUME XXI NUMBER 1

AI's mandate is as relevant in the Asia/Pacific region today as it was 30 years ago. Thousands of prisoners of conscience are detained by governments across the political spectrum. Torture is widespread. Extrajudicial execution and "disappearance" are everyday occurrences. The death penalty is retained and imposed by most of the countries in the region.

The language of human rights violations is an international language. Prisoner of conscience, "disappearance", extrajudicial execution, and unfair trial, are words in common usage across the world. Human rights violations in the Asia/Pacific region also have local terminologies. Extrajudicial executions are known as "encounter" killings in India and as "salvaging" in the Philippines. In Myanmar torturers use the "iron road" - they roll an iron bar or a bamboo cane up and down their victim's shins until the skin comes off.

Human rights violations often occur when governments are faced with armed opposition. Throughout the Asia/Pacific region ethnic and nationalist tensions have erupted into protracted and bitter conflict. AI has frequently received reports of the torture and killing of prisoners by governments and by armed opposition groups in the context of armed conflicts. AI unequivocally condemns any such abuses, whoever the perpetrators. International law clearly states that no matter what circumstances they face, governments must never resort to torture and extrajudicial execution.

This region, the most populous in the world, encompasses some of the richest and poorest countries on earth. The last decade has seen widespread political upheaval, leading to increased respect for fundamental human rights in some countries — and a deterioration in others. All too often governments which came to power pledged to end human rights abuses have failed to do so.

The challenge for the 1990s is to build human rights awareness in the broadest sense of the term: to ensure that no government can cloak its illegal activities in secrecy; that the rights of even the poorest citizens are upheld; and to build a truly international movement capable of taking action against human rights violations wherever they occur.□

ASIA AND THE PACIFIC

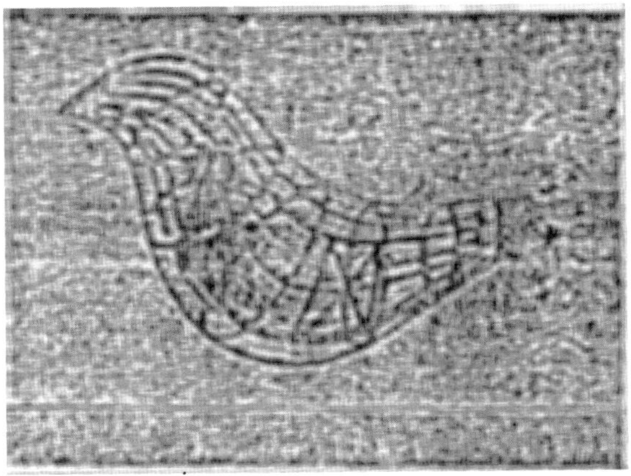

Building a human rights movement

0023

In South Korea the Yong Nam University group gathers signatures on a petition to the Sri Lankan Government

Newsletters are regularly published in Korean, Japanese, Urdu, Tamil and Thai. Future priorities include increasing the number of AI publications available in Chinese, and producing Bengali and Hindi versions of the International Newsletter. Groups in Taiwan are working on a Chinese version of the *Prisoner of the Month* appeal, and have produced leaflets and action materials for recent AI campaigns on behalf of imprisoned trade unionists and for human rights in South Korea. A number of international human rights standards, particularly the Universal Declaration of Human Rights, have been translated and distributed throughout the region.

Key to the development of an effective multilingual program is the regional publications and distribution service, the Asia Distribution Service (ADS), based in Hong Kong. ADS hopes to provide a wide range of translation and distribution services and eventually plans to offer facilities to produce and distribute cassette tapes, videos and publicity materials specially tailored for the Asia/Pacific region.

Human rights education plays an indispensable role in mobilizing people to participate in the [illegible] AI groups use street theatre, seminars and exhibitions to raise public awareness of human rights issues. In Pakistan, the Lahore group produces plays on human rights themes, which tour in shanty towns and rural areas. The Madaripur group in Bangladesh organized seminars and information stalls to coincide with International Women's Day, 1990. The group collected 10,000 signatures on an appeal for women prisoners of conscience, and translated an *AI Newsletter* article on Women and Human Rights into Bengali for mass circulation.

In Pakistan, 1989 saw AI groups established in Lahore, Karachi and Islamabad. They are already publishing AI informational leaflets and action documents in Urdu. The Pakistani press provides sympathetic coverage of human rights issues and has helped AI groups to emphasise the global nature of human rights concerns. The Lahore group has adopted a prisoner of conscience in South Korea and is working with groups in France and Italy to help secure his release.

In June 1989 the Beijing massacre focused national and international attention on China. AI Hong Kong responded by working night and day to provide AI information to the media and general public. Later in the year, the section undertook a demanding program of assistance to Vietnamese asylum seekers, a major focus of AI's refugee work. In cooperation with AI's London-based International Secretariat, the Hong Kong section raised AI's concerns about the screening process with the Hong Kong Government and protested about the forcible return to Viet Nam of over 50 asylum-seekers in December 1989. At the same time, AI members in Hong Kong continued to send appeals on behalf [illegible] South Korea, Sudan and Ethiopia.

0024

There is no monopoly on oppression by any one political system in the region. In Viet Nam "propaganda against the socialist system" continues to be punishable by imprisonment. In Indonesia writing or teaching deemed to be contrary to the official *Pancasila* ideology was the "crime" committed by scores of prisoners of conscience. In South Korea prisoners of conscience may be held indefinitely upon failure to "renounce" communist beliefs they may never have acknowledged holding - or for owning a book that was published in North Korea.

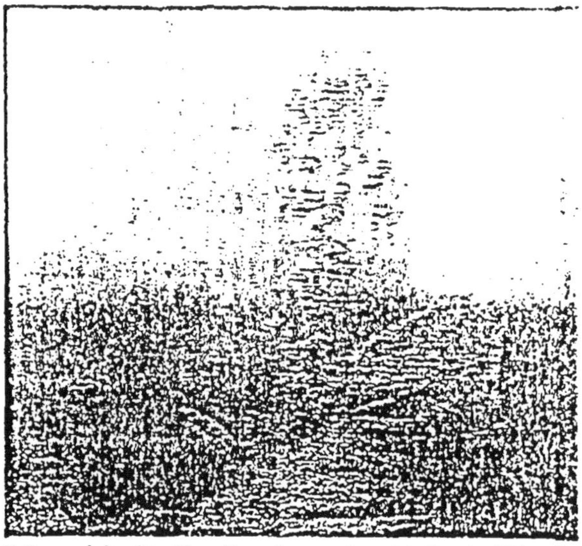

Father and daughter Kang Hee-sul were released during the 1990 action on South Korea, and sent AI the following message: "We won! Thank you for your encouragement."

Human rights violations in Asia and the Pacific

South Koreans suspected of any unauthorized connection with North Korea face imprisonment.

Several such prisoners were released in 1988 under amnesties granted by President Roh Tae-woo. 1989, however, saw a new [illegible] tional security, with over 300 people taken into custody for offences such as printing or distributing North Korean books, making unauthorized visits to North Korea or trying to contact North Koreans to discuss reunification.

AI has been denied access to research its concerns in several countries in the region. China, Laos, Myanmar (Burma), Sri Lanka and North Korea have remained closed to AI. India denied access to AI delegations for over a decade. AI action has moved forward even on "closed" countries, however, as persistent research has produced substantial information about human rights violations in these countries. AI has published several major reports on a broad range of human rights issues in China - and sustained action for the release of prisoners of conscience and an end to torture and the death penalty. Myanmar, too, has been the subject of several reports, continuing work for individual prisoners and concerted, worldwide membership action.

0025

관리번호 91-75

주 영 대 사 관

영국(정) 723- 004 1991.1.16.

수신 : 장관

참조 : 국제기구조약국장

제목 : A.I. 뉴스레터 대응

연 : UKW-0152

연호 당관 공보관 명의 반박서한을 별첨 송부합니다.

첨부 : 동 서한 사본 1부. 끝.

발송 1991. 1. 1. 주영대사관

1991.6.30에 예고문에 의거 인반문서로 재분류됨

주 영 대 사

접수	1991. 1. 18	231	
처리과			

0026

EMBASSY OF THE REPUBLIC OF KOREA
4 PALACE GATE
LONDON W8 5NF

16th January, 1991

Dear Secretary General,

I would like to express my satisfaction with the recent cooperative working relationship between Amnesty International and the Korean Government on the subject of human rights in my country.

With this close cooperation in mind, I would like to point out that part of Amnesty International's Newsletter dated January 1991, Volume XXI, describing the Korean situation is misleading.

Firstly, we do not hold in custody "indefinitely" those who have Communist beliefs, even though they fail to give up such beliefs. They are imprisoned for a period fixed through the normal judicial process. The new law passed in 1989 rules that they shall not be discriminated against after their release in any aspect of basic human rights because of their beliefs, and that they shall also be allowed to travel abroad.

Secondly, those who possess books published in North Korea shall not be punished unless their content is explicitly seditious in favour of Communist revolution. You may be interested in noting the fact that 114 kinds of books from North Korea were on sale to the public as of October 1989.

Thirdly, we dispute the standards by which "prisoners of conscience" are classified. It seems to us that Amnesty International applies the concept rather generously to Communist activists threatening our national security in violation of relevant laws.

.../

0027

It would be appreciated if you would give full consideration to the above. I sincerely hope that our view is duly communicated to your members around the world.

Yours sincerely,

Byung Ho Suh
Press and Cultural Attache

Mr Ian Martin,
Secretary General,
Amnesty International,
1 Easton STreet,
London WC1X 8DJ.

0028

관리 번호 91-69

원 본

외 무 부

종 별 : 지 급

번 호 : UKW-0152 일 시 : 91 0117 1100

수 신 : 장관(국연,해신,정홍,구일)

발 신 : 주 영 대사

제 목 : A.I.뉴스레터 대응

대:WUK-76

연:UKW-2259(90.11.30)

1. 당관 조참사관은 1.14(월) 대호 내용에 따라 A.I. 아태지역 과장 MR. DEREK EVANS 에게 아국 정부의 유감을 표명하고, 금후 그러한 오류가 발생하지 않도록 유의해 줄것을 요망하였음

2. MR.EVANS 는 한국정부의 입장을 충분히 이해하고 A.I. 로서도 금번 오류를 당황스럽게 생각한다고 말하면서 금후 이러한 일이 재발하지 않도록 최대한 주의를 기울이겠다고 말했음. 동인은 또한 91.2 월 뉴스레타에 문제의 내용을 정정 게재하고 한국정부에 동 뉴스레터 1 부를 적절한 형식으로 전달하겠다고 약속했음

3. 당관 공보관 명의 서한은 1.16(수) I.MARTIN A.I. 사무총장 앞으로 발송한 바, 동 서한사본 파편 송부함. 끝

(대사 오재희-국장)

91.6.30 까지

1991. 6. 30 에 예고문에 의거 일반문서로 재분류됨

국기국 구주국 정문국 공보처

PAGE 1 91.01.17 23:52

외신 2과 통제관 CF

0029

관리 번호	91 -70

원 본

외 무 부

종 별 :

번 호 : UKW-0161 일 시 : 91 0117 1800

수 신 : 장관(국연)

발 신 : 주 영 대사

제 목 : A.I.협조 요청사항

연: UKW-2259(90.11.30)

1.16(수) 당지 A.I. 의 VANDALE 한국담당원은 연호 7 항 A.I. 협조사항을 상기시키고, 그중 특히 국가보안법 저촉자 관련자료의 입수 가능성에 관심을 표명했는바, 검토 조치해 주시기 바람. 끝

(대사 오재희-국장)

예고: 91.6.30 일반

1991.6.30 에 예고문에 의거 일반문서로 재분류됨

국기국

PAGE 1

91.01.18 07:23

외신 2과 통제관 FE

0030

3708

기 안 용 지

분류기호 문서번호	국연 2031 -	(전화:)	시 행 상 특별취급	
보존기간	영구·준영구. 10. 5. 3. 1	장	관	
수 신 처 보존기간				
시행일자	1991. 1. 23.			

보조기관	국 장	전 결	협조기관		문서통제 검열 1991. 1. 23
	과 장				
기안책임자		송영완			발송인 1991. 1. 23 외무부

경 유 수 신 참 조	주영대사	발신명의	
제 목	A.I. 인권관련 서한 대책		

1. 국제사면위 회원들이 90년도 3/4분기중 아국에 보내온 석방탄원서한을 검토한 결과 홍성담, 장의균, 방양균, 김명식, 유원호, 임수경, 문규현 등 7명이 주요 석방요구 대상자로 분석되었습니다.

2. 상기인들에 관한 설명자료를 별첨 송부하오니 A.I. 측에 적의 설명바라며 A.I. 회원들에 의한 불필요한 서한발송을 자제해 주도록 요청하시기 바랍니다.

첨 부 : 상기 설명자료 1부. 끝.

0031

관리번호 91-99

기안용지

분류기호 문서번호	국연 2031 - 167	(전화:)	시행상 특별취급	
보존기간	영구·준영구. 10. 5. 3. 1	장 관		
수신처 보존기간				
시행일자	1991. 1. 23.			
보조기관 국장	전결	협조기관		문서통제
과장				1991. 1. 28
기안책임자	송영완			발송인 1991. 1. 28 외무부
경유 수신 참조	주영대사	발신명의		
제목	A.I. 협조요청 자료송부			

대 : UKW-2259, 0161

연 : 국연 2031-2677 (90.10.30)

1. 대호, A.I측 요청자료를 별첨 송부합니다.

2. 법무부는 6공화국 출범후 국가보안법 각조항별 적용하의 구속자 및 형사소추 통계자료는 없고 다만 보안법 위반 구속자수 통계만 작성 가능함을 알려왔는 바, A.I.측에 적의 설명바라며 A.I.가 기관심표명한 14건의 개별사안은

//계속...

0032

(2)

연호 자료를 참조하여 A.I. 측에 가급적 구두로 설명하시기 바랍니다. (동 사안에 관한 설명자료를 서면으로 작성, 전달함은 부적절할 것으로 판단됨)

첨 부 : 1. 보안법위반 구속자수 통계 1부

2. 인권규약 아국가입문서 사본 각 1부

3. 아국정부가 A.I.와 의견을 달리하는 사안 설명문 1부. 끝.

일반문서로 재분류 (1991 . 12. 31.

검 토 필(1991. 6. 30.)

0033

관리 번호	91-91

	분류번호	보존기간

발 신 전 보

번 호 : WUK-0157 910124 1936 DA 종별 :

수 신 : 주 영 대사·총영사

발 신 : 장 관 (국연)

제 목 : A.I. 협조자료 송부

대 : UKW-2259, 0161

1. 대호자료, 1.23. 파편 송부함.

2. 상기자료의 A.I. 대표단이 방한중 아측에 구두로 요청한 바 있는 북한형법 해설서(영문판) ~~및 이규익편 홍보책자(영문판)~~는 2월중순경 발간시 추송예정임. 끝.

(국제기구조약국장 문동석)

일반문서로재분류(1991.12.31.)

검 토 필(1991. 6.30.)

앙 고 재	91년 1월 24일	유엔과	기안자		과 장		국 장		차 관	장 관
			송영완		(서명)		전결			(서명)

보안통제	외신과통제
(서명)	

0034

152

관리번호	91 —111

원 본

외 무 부

종 별 :

번 호 : UKW-0270 일 시 : 91 0130 1400

수 신 : 장관(국연,해신,정홍,구일)

발 신 : 주 영 대사

제 목 : A.I.뉴스레터 대응

연: UKW-0152

연호, A.I. 의 91.2 월 뉴스레터에 아래와 같이 정정기사 게재되었음.(마지막 페이지 말미 BOX). 동 뉴스레터 금파편 송부함.

-아 래-

SOUTH KOREA: IN ISSUE NO. 1, PUBLISHED JANUARY 1991, IT IS STATED THATPRISONERS OF CONSCIENCE WHO DO NOT RENOUNCE THEIR COMMUNIST BELIEFS MAY BE DETAINED INDEFINITELY. THE PUBLIC SECURITY LAW, WHICH ALLOWED FOR SUCH DETENTION, WAS REPEALED IN 1989. HOWEVER, POLOTICAL PRISONERS HELD UNDER NATIONAL SECURITY LEGISLATION, INCLUDING PRISONERS OF CONSCIENCE, HAVE BEEN DENIED THE BENEFIT OF MEASURES SUCH AS RELEASE ON PAROLE, UNLESS THEY AGREE TO BE "ANTI-COMMUNIST". 끝

(대사 오재희-국장)

예고: 91.6.30 일반

1991.6.30 에 예고문에 의거 일반문서로 재분류

국기국 구주국 정문국 공보처

PAGE 1

91.01.31 07:36

외신 2과 통제관 BT

0035

관리번호 91-115

원 본

외 무 부

종 별 :

번 호 : UKW-0276 일 시 : 91 0131 1200

수 신 : 장관(국연,사본:법무부장관)

발 신 : 주 영 대사

제 목 : A.I. 인권관련 자료

대: 국연 2031-3708,167(91.1.23)

국연 2031-2677(90.10.31)

대호 국제사면위(A.I)에 제공 또는 구두 설명하기 위한 인권관계 자료는 그양이 방대하고 법집행에 관한 전문적 내용을 포함하고 있는 바, 문제의 사안들에 대한 아측 입장을 관계전문가의 시각에서 영문자료로 작성, 제공하여 주지않는한 인권단체의 이해를 증진 시키는데 한계가 있을 것으로 사료되오니 관계부처와 협의, 적절한 대책을 강구해 줄 것을 건의함. 끝

(대사 오재희-차관)

예고: 91.12.31 일반

일반문서로 재분류(1991 12.31.)

검 토 필(1991. 6. 30.)

국기국 차관 법무부

PAGE 1

91.02.01 07:29

외신 2과 통제관 FE

0036

분류번호 91-123

주 영 대 사 관

영국(정) 723-007 1991. 1. 30.

수신 : 장관

참조 : 국제기구조약국장

제목 : A.I. 뉴스레터 대응

연 : UKW-0270

연호 A.I. 뉴스레터를 별첨 송부합니다.

첨부 : 동 뉴스레터 1부. 끝.

발송 1991. 1. 31 주영국대사관

1991. 2 접수 4337 결재(공람)

주 영 대 사

1991. 6. 30. 에 예고문에 의거 인반문서로 재분류됨

0037

AMNESTY INTERNATIONAL
NEWSLETTER
FEBRUARY 1991 VOLUME XXI • NUMBER 2

BRAZIL

Street children activist threatened

WOLMER do Nascimento, Rio de Janeiro coordinator of Brazil's National Street Children's Movement, went into hiding and sent his family to stay at an undisclosed location after he and his two young children repeatedly received written and oral death threats in early November.

In late November he received Federal Police protection on orders from the Justice Minister.

Wolmer do Nascimento founded a refuge for street children in Duque de Caxias, one of Rio's most violent suburbs. Recently he has denounced the role of police, judges, businessmen and politicians in supporting death squads. He says that these "extermination groups" killed 184 children in the area during the first five months of 1989.

Local and state authorities have apparently been slow to investigate or prosecute suspected death squad members. Although President Collor called in September for full investigation of all killings of children, human rights groups in Brazil said little progress had been made by the end of 1990.

Despite receiving police protection, Wolmer do Nascimento continued to stay away from Duque de Caxias and the refuge there. Frightened by news of the threats to Wolmer do Nascimento and his children, some of the street children who had frequented the refuge abandoned it.

As a result of an urgent action appeal, Wolmer do Nascimento reports that more than 1,000 letters from AI members expressing concern about his safety arrived at his Rio office.□

TURKEY

Torture and killing in the southeast

THERE have recently been large-scale detentions throughout southeast Turkey where government troops are carrying out counter-insurgency operations against guerrillas of the Kurdish Workers' Party (PKK). The PKK have been carrying out armed attacks in the region since 1984.

The security forces have evacuated dozens of villages along the Syrian border, in an attempt to deprive the guerrillas of shelter and food. Villagers with no history of political activity have been interrogated, often under torture, usually on suspicion of having provided shelter for guerrillas.

On 8 September almost the entire population of Çizmeli village, near Siirt, was taken into custody. While most were released within a short time, Abit Ekinci remained in incommunicado detention in Eruh Gendarmerie Headquarters for 20 days. "My hands were bound, my clothes were removed and I was suspended from the ceiling by my arms", he said. "I was beaten constantly, and subjected to *falaka* (beating on the soles of the feet). I was given electric shocks three times. My testicles were bound with string and squeezed. My hands and neck were burned with cigarettes. The soles of my feet were slit with a razor and salt rubbed in. They forced me to sign a statement." Abit Ekinci was charged with sheltering Kurdish guerrillas and committed to Diyarbakir Prison.

A similar operation was conducted in the village of Yeniköy near Mardin following a clash between security forces and guerrillas in mid-November. Twenty-two villagers were detained; several of them later reported that they had been tortured at Mardin Police Headquarters. Of nine people charged and committed to prison, it is reported that one has serious leg injuries and another has broken teeth.

Ibrahim Döner

On 25 November the body of 24-year-old Yakup Aktaş from Derik, a small town in the Mardin area, was returned to his family by the Mardin Gendarmerie who had detained him a week earlier. The autopsy report stated that he had died of a heart attack. However, those who washed the body stated that there were wounds which suggested that he may have died under torture. His family's request for a second autopsy was refused and his body was buried under military supervision.

On 28 September the village of Kayadeler was occupied by troops and members of anti-guerrilla "special teams". They entered the mosque where the men were gathered, and told all of them to go home except for the imam, Ibrahim Döner. Shots were heard and two hours later his body was presented to his brother together with a pistol and a suicide note.

AI appealed to the Turkish Government to initiate investigations into all these incidents, but had not received a response by the end of December.□

CHAD

New government promises reforms

THE Government of President Hissein Habré fell on 30 November 1990 when rebel forces led by Idriss Déby occupied the capital, N'Djamena, without bloodshed and Hissein Habré fled to Cameroon. The new government, in which Idriss Déby became President, promised to introduce multi-party democracy and to protect human rights. One of the last acts of Hissein Habré's Presidential Guards, which AI had previously identified as responsible for gross human rights violations, was to extrajudicially execute over 300 political opponents secretly detained at the presidential palace.

Several hundred other prisoners who had been detained at secret detention centres in N'Djamena were released on 1 December. Many had been tortured. Other prisoners were found in secret detention at a residence of the former Minister of the Interior.

Released prisoners confirmed reports published by AI in March 1990 of a pattern of systematic torture and ill-treatment of political prisoners, in which former President Habré was allegedly directly involved. More than 400 political prisoners from the Hadjerai and Zaghawa communities, arrested in May 1987 and April 1988, were either killed in secret or died in detention as a result of torture, malnutrition, lack of hygiene and medical attention.

AI urged the new government to introduce safeguards to prevent killings of prisoners and to establish an inquiry into the fate of hundreds of political prisoners who "disappeared" in the period since 1982 while President Habré was in power.□

0038

CAMPAIGN FOR PRISONERS OF THE MONTH

Each of the people whose story is told below is a prisoner of conscience. Each has been arrested because of his or her religious or political beliefs, colour, sex, ethnic origin or language. None has used or advocated violence. Their continuing detention is a violation of the United Nations Universal Declaration of Human Rights. International appeals can help to secure the release of these prisoners or to improve their detention conditions. In the interest of the prisoners, letters to the authorities should be worded carefully and courteously. You should stress that your concern for human rights is not in any way politically partisan. In *no* circumstances should communications be sent to the prisoner.

IRAN

Malakeh Mohammadi: ***a journalist and editor aged in her 70s, she was among hundreds of people arrested in April 1983 because of their political activities on behalf of the left-wing Tudeh Party, then a legal organization.***

Malakeh Mohammadi and other leaders of the Tudeh Party were accused of plotting against the Islamic Republic of Iran; many were tortured to force them to confess to espionage and other offences and some were subsequently executed. Some of those who survived, including Malakeh Mohammadi's husband, Mohammed Pourhomozan, were among thousands of political prisoners secretly executed in the latter part of 1988.

Malakeh Mohammadi remained in detention for three and a half years before she was finally tried in 1986. She was not allowed to present any defence and has never been informed of the precise charges against her. She was sentenced to death, but this was later commuted to 20 years' imprisonment. She is alleged to have been tortured during the seven and a half years she has now been held.

Malakeh Mohammadi is held at Evin Prison, together with other women prisoners of conscience, arrested in 1983, from the Tudeh Party and other left-wing groups. All have suffered continuous pressure to renounce their conscientiously-held political beliefs. In August 1990 some accepted offers of temporary release, although nearly all are now said to be back in prison. Malakeh Mohammadi is reported to have declined the offer, as she had no close relatives left alive and had decided to leave prison only when the authorities granted her a full, unconditional release.

■Please send courteous appeals for her immediate release to: His Excellency Hojatoleslam Ali Akbar Hashemi Rafsanjani/President of the Islamic Republic of Iran/ The Presidency/Palestine Avenue, Azerbaijan Intersection/Tehran/ Islamic Republic of Iran.□

RWANDA

Innocent Ndayambaje: ***a 29-year-old economics student at the National University of Rwanda, he was arrested in October 1986 and held incommunicado without charge for three years.***

In March 1990 Innocent Ndayambaje was tried and sentenced by the State Security Court to five years' imprisonment for contravening Rwanda's one-party Constitution.

Under the constitution all Rwandese are obliged to be members of the ruling National Revolutionary Movement for Development (MRND), and the establishment or membership of other parties is a criminal offence.

At his trial Innocent Ndayambaje pleaded not guilty to the charge of contravening the constitution, but admitted to being the sole member of the National Resistance Front (FRONAR) which, he said, aimed to end regional and ethnic injustices in Rwanda. He is a member of Rwanda's minority Tutsi ethnic group.

He was sentenced to five years' imprisonment for his membership of FRONAR and for distributing political tracts in the town of Butare.

AI is concerned that Innocent Ndayambaje did not receive a fair trial: he had no access to legal counsel either before or during his trial and no general right of appeal against his conviction and sentence.

The court's five judges are appointed by Presidential decree and included two soldiers and an official from the President's office; none of them is known to have legal training.

He remains held at Kigali Central Prison. He is apparently not allowed to communicate with his relatives nor to receive visits.

■Please send courteous letters appealing for his immediate release to: Son Excellence Monsieur le Général-Major Habyarimana Juvénal/Président de la République/Présidence de la République/BP 15, Kigali/République Rwandaise.□

CUBA

Esteban González González and six others: ***members of the unofficial Movimiento Integracionista Democrática (MID), Movement for Democratic Integration, they were arrested in Havana in September 1989. In June 1990 they were convicted of "rebellion".***

Esteban González González, a 60-year-old mathematics teacher, founded the MID in early 1989. The movement explicitly rejects any violent activity and advocates a wide range of democratic reforms, including the establishment of a pluralistic government, thus challenging the monopoly of the Communist Party, the only legal party in Cuba.

After their arrest, the seven men were held in State Security headquarters for several months without access to legal counsel.

For at least the first month they were reportedly held in small cells with constant artificial light and were allowed no fresh air or exercise.

They were transferred to prison in December 1989 but are believed to have had access to legal counsel only in May 1990 when the prosecution presented the results of its investigations to the court. The seven were accused of possessing and disseminating "counter-revolutionary propaganda"; seeking funds and recognition from international sources; planning a campaign of civil disobedience; and wanting to change the political and social system and to restore capitalism. Esteban González was sentenced to seven years' imprisonment; Arturo Montané Ruiz, Manuel Mora, Edgardo Llompart Martín and Manuel Regueiro Robaína received sentences ranging from three to six years' imprisonment and Isidro Ledesma Quijano was given three years' "restricted liberty", rather than imprisonment, on grounds of ill-health. The imprisoned men are serving their sentences in Combinado del Este Prison.

■Please send courteous letters appealing for the release of the six imprisoned men to: His Excellency Dr Fidel Castro Ruz/President of the Republic/Ciudad de la Habana/Cuba.□

PRISONER NEWS

AI learned in November 1990 of the release of 43 prisoners under adoption or investigation. AI took up 150 cases.

RELEASED

AI has learned that Ladji Traoré, prisoner of the month in October 1990, was released in November 1990 without charge or trial.

Stop press

The following reports are now available from AI:

Colombia: AI is concerned about human rights violations against members of indigenous communities in Caldas department in central Colombia and the apparent lack of progress in the official investigations into these abuses.
(Index No. AMR 23/61/90)

Sierra Leone: AI has received reports that 12 people were sentenced to death in Sierra Leone earlier this year after being convicted of murder and armed robbery. Although death sentences have not been carried out in recent years in non-political cases, AI is concerned that the execution of six men for treason in 1989 may herald a return to the use of the death penalty.
(Index No. AFR 51/01/90)

0039

FOCUS amnesty international

Women in the front line

AI has received numerous reports of women being tortured while in police custody in Turkey.

Nevruz Türkdoğan was treasurer of the Women's Association for Democracy in Turkey. While distributing a journal in Ankara on 15 September 1990, she and her husband were detained by police.

Despite informing the police that she was two and a half months pregnant, Nevruz Türkdoğan testifies that she was repeatedly beaten for three days. She miscarried on 19 September. She was then taken to Ankara Numune Hospital. On 20 September she was unconditionally released by Ankara State Security Court.

Please send courteous letters urging an impartial and independent investigation into allegations of torture and ill-treatment of Nevruz Türkdoğan, insisting that those responsible be brought to justice. Send appeals to: Abdülkadir Aksu/Minister of Interior/Içişleri Bakanlığı/06644 Ankara/Turkey□

A pregnant woman detainee is punched in the stomach by police officers. An elderly woman is raped in front of her family by armed soldiers. A young girl is detained and sexually humiliated by government officials. A wife is tortured by interrogators to force her husband to "confess". A mother is shot dead by soldiers simply because her son is suspected of political activities. A daughter is threatened with death by government agents because she asks after her "disappeared" father.

The list of such gross human rights violations against women is endless. Many are targeted because they are strong — because they are political activists, community organizers, or persist in demanding that their rights or those of their relatives are respected. Others are targeted because they are seen as vulnerable — young women who can easily be sexually abused or humiliated, frightened mothers who will do anything to protect their children, or pregnant women fearful for their unborn babies, women who can be used to get at men, or refugee women, isolated and vulnerable in unfamiliar surroundings.

This report details human rights violations which are primarily suffered by women as well as a range of human rights abuses that women have experienced alongside men and children. By focusing on human rights violations committed against women, AI hopes to mobilize international support for the protection of women and, by extension, for all members of the societies in which they live.

This report records the experiences of women who have survived human rights violations. It also tells the stories of many who did not survive. The violations have occurred, and continue to occur, in every region of the world and under every system of government.

These pages do not contain a comprehensive account of all human rights violations against women, merely an indication of the type of atrocities women have suffered and therefore what must be prevented from happening to anyone in the future. Nor is this a survey of all violations of women's human rights. It covers only those human rights violations which fall within AI's strictly defined mandate: to seek the release of prisoners of conscience — men and women detained solely for their beliefs, colour, sex, ethnic origin, language or religion, who have neither used nor advocated violence; to work for prompt and fair trials for all political prisoners and to oppose the death penalty, extrajudicial executions and torture without reservation. AI covers a limited spectrum of rights, but not because it ignores the importance of other rights. It believes that there is a close relationship between all human rights but recognizes that it can achieve more by working within set limits.

0040

Women's human rights, like those of men and children, are proclaimed in the Universal Declaration of Human Rights — the individual freedoms basic to human life. These include freedom of conscience, expression and association, freedom from arbitrary arrest and detention, freedom from torture, the right to a fair trial, and freedom from extrajudicial killing. These rights have been trampled on by governments around the world. Whatever the circumstances, however deep the economic, social or political crisis a government may face, there can never be a valid excuse for contravening fundamental human rights.

Women are primarily the victims of certain abuses. Rape, frequently used as a form of torture, is most often inflicted on women detainees. The United Nations (UN) Convention against Torture and Other Cruel, Inhuman or Degrading Treatment or Punishment prohibits "any act by which severe pain or suffering, whether physical or mental, is intentionally inflicted" for purposes such as obtaining information or punishing, intimidating, or coercing a person. No government official should be permitted to commit or tolerate rape and other forms of sexual attack.

No government official should be permitted to commit or tolerate rape and other forms of sexual attack

Women are particularly vulnerable to rape between the time of arrest and arrival at official detention centres. In some countries law enforcement officials or military personnel have committed rape and other sexual abuses without having officially arrested the victim. However, confinement in an official place of detention does not necessarily protect women from rape or other sexual abuses. Many have reported that prison guards have raped them, attempted to rape them, or threatened them with rape.

For women who are pregnant at the time of detention, additional suffering often accompanies human rights abuses. They risk injury to the foetus, miscarriage and the prospect of giving birth in harsh prison conditions. The women who become pregnant as a result of rape in custody face yet a further set of traumas.

Women also suffer from sexual humiliation, threats of rape and verbal abuses intended to degrade them. All of these violate their basic human rights by subjecting them to cruel, inhuman or degrading treatment or punishment.

Women from all walks of life have been targeted for human rights abuse. In some cases, the reasons are connected with a woman's occupation or peaceful, legitimate activities. Governments detain or direct violent attacks against women who are physicians, lawyers, journalists, trade unionists, teachers, human rights activists, political activists, community organizers and members of many other professions. In other cases, women's human rights are violated because of their ethnic origin or religious beliefs.

Some women are subjected to human rights violations merely because they happen to be the wives, mothers, daughters or friends of people whom the authorities consider to be "dangerous" or "undesirable". These women are threatened, held as substitutes for their relatives, tortured or even killed as governments attempt to exert their will over those closely connected in some way with the women.

The leading human rights activists in many societies are prisoners' relatives: often wives and children, endlessly in the front line, campaigning for the prisoner's release, confronting government officials, trying to get information, trying to care for the prisoner. Prisoners' families bear the burden of providing assistance of all sorts — from daily meals, medicine and clothing, through to raising funds to pay legal fees, ransoms, or to publicize the case.

In many African countries a strong tradition of family or community solidarity has protected prisoners in vulnerable situations. This has led some governments deliberately to exploit family relations, by imprisoning, threatening and harassing prisoners' relatives. In Guinea, under the rule of the late President Sékou Touré, wives were pressurized by the state to divorce their imprisoned husbands.

Embarca ment Taleb ould Husein, a radio announcer in Laayoune in the Western Sahara, was taken from her home by plainclothes police officers in September 1979 and has not been seen since. She left behind a 13-year-old daughter.

She is one of hundreds of people who have "disappeared" in the south of Morocco and the Western Sahara, many of whom were arrested because they or their relatives were suspected of opposing Moroccan rule of the Western Sahara territory and sympathizing with the Polisario Front armed opposition organization.

Evidence suggests that many of the "disappeared" in Morocco are still alive and confined in secret detention centres.

Please write courteous letters, in French if possible, urging that Embarca ment Taleb ould Husein be released immediately and unconditionally unless charged with a recognizably criminal offence and given a fair trial. Send appeals to: SM Le Roi Hassan II/Office de SM le Roi/Palais Royal/Rabat/Morocco□

Countless women are forced to live in the shadow of another person's "disappearance". A woman may suddenly become her family's sole source of support just at the time when she is facing the absence of a close relative and is trying to locate the "disappeared" victim. She may be effectively widowed by her husband's "disappearance", yet unable to claim state or other benefits because her husband has not been declared dead, officially or legally. Members of the National Coordinating Committee of Widows of Guatemala, an Indian group known as CONAVIGUA, have denounced their government's attitude to providing compensation. The group has repeatedly alleged that government compensation is granted only if a widow attributes her husband's death to opposition guerrilla forces and if she ceases to pursue investigation into her husband's death or "disappearance".

Relatives of the "disappeared" face additional, emotional suffering in many cultures. Women often refuse to give up hope and search for years for husbands and children who have "disap-

0041

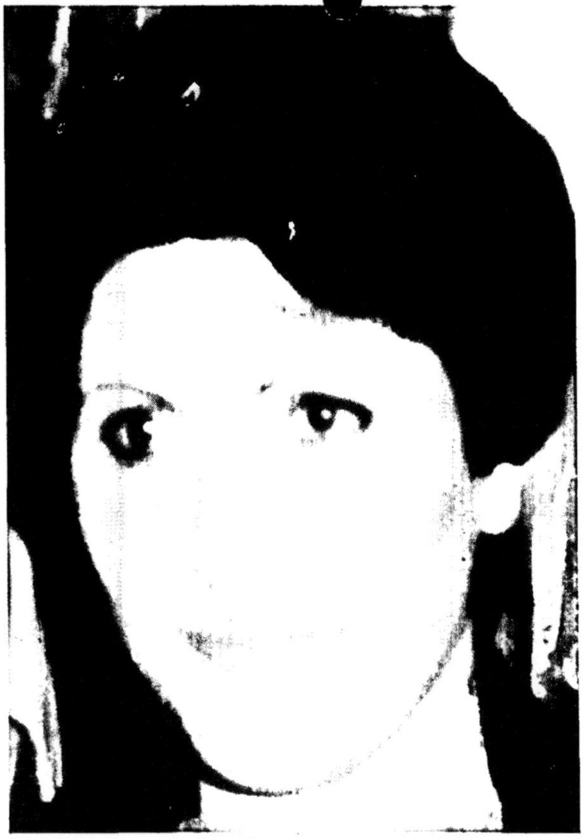

Wafa' Idriss is one of at least 77 women arrested in Syria between August 1977 and February 1988 who remain in detention without charge or trial.

Hundreds of women have been arrested in Syria since 1985 because of their relationship to men sought by the security forces, or because of their own peaceful political activities.

Torture of political prisoners is systematic in Syria. It is carried out during interrogation to extract "confessions" and information, and to punish detainees.

Reports of rape by members of the security forces are numerous.

Please write courteous letters expressing concern at widespread reports that women have been subjected to severe torture and sexual abuse while in detention and asking that the 77 women be released immediately unless charged with a recognizably criminal offence and given a prompt, fair trial. Send appeals to: His Excellency 'Abd al-Halim Khaddam/Vice-President/Office of the President/Presidential Palace/Damascus/Syrian Arab Republic□

peared", even though relatively few victims of "disappearance" survive this inhuman violation. But unless or until they reappear, or their bodies are found, their families suffer years of uncertainty, unable properly to mourn their loss and thus perhaps to lay their grief to rest.

In areas of civil turmoil or armed conflict, women are often subjected to brutal treatment simply because they live in a particular location or belong to a particular ethnic group. They are often caught in the crossfire between armed opposition groups and government forces, living under the threat of violence from both sides.

AI, as a matter of principle, condemns the torture and killing of prisoners by anyone, including opposition groups. It does not, however, treat such groups as though they had the status of governments. Nor does it address them unless they are certain of the essential attributes of a government, such as control over substantial territory and population. It is, after all, governments which have jurisdiction to determine criminal responsibility and to bring to justice those responsible for violent attacks on government authorities, security forces, and civilians. The state's exercise of such lawful authority, however, must conform to international standards of human rights and observe norms safeguarding fundamental human rights provided in domestic law.

Many governments do not maintain these norms. The rape of peasant women, either while in formal custody or when held by soldiers during counter-insurgency operations, is a common phenomenon in many countries. Governments often are complacent in the face of such abuse. Legal officials in Peru's Ayacucho department told AI representatives in 1986 that rape by government troops operating in rural areas was to be expected. In late September 1990, a Peruvian woman and her 17-year-old daughter were detained in a military base and repeatedly raped by a number of soldiers. Both women were subsequently released but warned not to report the rape. They have requested anonymity lest they face reprisals. Effective investigations into cases of rape in Peru are not known to have taken place nor have the perpetrators been brought to justice.

Women refugees and asylum-seekers have also been the victims of sexual abuse by police, soldiers or other government agents. Many of these women lack the support systems which would be provided in their own communities or by their close relatives. With few resources to protect them from abuse or to provide the means of redress, they become victims of a range of violations.

Cultural or social circumstances sometimes render women particularly isolated by the human rights violations they experience. They may choose not to report humiliating assaults by government authorities, fearing reprisals from their own families, traumatic social repercussions, or further attacks by government officials.

Women who choose not to remain silent in the face of human rights violations inflicted upon them may face barriers such as official tolerance of the injuries caused to them. If they are from disadvantaged social or economic groups, they may find that official channels of communication are closed to them. Law enforcement officials may not listen, and they may have no place to turn.

During the past decade, increasing numbers of women have spoken out for human rights protection. They have stated publicly and clearly what they and other members of their communities have suffered. They have also organized community and national groups to protest against human rights abuses. In some countries their vulnerability to such abuse has increased as they have assumed public leadership roles and spoken out about the special measures needed to protect women's human rights. Despite this, they continue to make their demands heard. The Committee of Mothers and Relatives of Political Prisoners, and Victims of Political Assassination and Disappearance, known as COMADRES, has been prominent for many years in the struggle to protect human rights in El Salvador. The COMADRES continue their work today, despite repeated threats against members of the group and violent attacks such as the October 1989 bombing of their San Salvadore offices.

Some women are subjected to human rights violations because of their relationship to people whom the authorities consider "dangerous"

The following month, soldiers raided the offices and arrested nine COMADRES activists. Some of those arrested later said that they had been blindfolded, handcuffed, and beaten in detention.

The Mutual Support Group for the Appearance of Our Relatives Alive, known as GAM, has been a target of violence in Guatemala. GAM members press government authorities to account for those who "disappear".

Several GAM leaders, including Rosario Godoy de Cuevas, were abducted and killed in 1985, apparently by government agents.

Other GAM members are now the target of threats. The group's leader, Nineth Montenegro de García, has received so many death threats that human rights activists worldwide have sent appeals on her behalf to the Guatema-

0042

lan authorities on a number of occasions. Her mother, whose house was strafed with machine-gunfire in July 1990, also appears to be at risk from government forces or people associated with them. The bullets recovered from the attack reportedly were of a calibre known to be used by the military.

Women have played prominent roles in South African human rights organizations such as the Detainees' Parents Support Committee and the Black Sash. Despite decades of repression, women activists have continued to mobilize against mass detentions, torture, and the injustices perpetuated by *apartheid*.

Noma India Mfeketo attended the 1985 International Women's Congress in Nairobi, representing the United Women's Congress and the Federation of South African Women. Her international prominence, however, did not protect her when she returned home: she spent nine months in detention without charge or trial in 1987 and was again detained for several months in 1988 and 1989. Like many of her colleagues, she was detained solely for the peaceful exercise of basic human rights.

© Maggie Murray/Format

Woman and child in refugee camp. Refugee women are particularly vulnerable to human rights abuses

Susan Aniban of Task Force Detainees, a human rights group in the Philippines, was reportedly detained and tortured in November 1988. Numerous women human rights workers there have been subjected to such ill-treatment.

Turkish officials detained several members of a women's organization in January 1990, after a police raid on the offices of the Association of Democratic Women in Ankara. They were reportedly interrogated under torture.

The perseverance of women like these in the face of such persecution, along with the courage of many other men and women who continue to fight for human rights, has yielded significant results in recent years. More information is now available to the international community about what is happening to women worldwide than ever before. The momentum to end patterns of abuse has increased as more women have joined efforts to publicize the facts and to press for change.

The international campaign is expanding and accelerating on behalf of women who struggled for their rights and did not survive, on behalf of women now struggling to survive, and on behalf not only of women but of all people who ought never to have to face human rights violations. Human rights activists are demanding that protections guaranteed under international treaties become a reality in all countries.

The international human rights covenants, The UN Convention against Torture, the UN Convention on the Elimination of All Forms of Discrimination against Women, and many other agreements, establish minimum standards of government responsibility.

If governments ignore their responsibilities to any sector of society — whether to women, to the young, or to members of ethnic or religious minorities — then no one's human rights are safe.□

Maria Nonna Santa Clara, a social worker in Naga City, and her colleague, Angelina Llenaresas, "disappeared" on 26 April 1989. They had been visiting a woman in Santa Cruz, who said later that she saw them being followed by three unknown men after leaving her house. Eye-witnesses reported seeing Maria Nonna Santa Clara later the same day shouting for help from a military jeep in Naga City.

Military authorities have denied all knowledge of the whereabouts of the two women, despite substantial evidence that they were responsible for their abduction. The family of Maria Nonna Santa Clara, and others involved in trying to clarify her fate, have received death threats which they believe to have come from military sources.

Please write courteous letters urging the government to take prompt action to establish the whereabouts of Maria Nonna Santa Clara and her colleague, and to bring to justice those responsible for their "disappearance". Send appeals to: President Corazon Aquino/Malacanang Palace/Manila/Phillipines□

0043

IRAQ

Widespread abuse follows invasion

WIDESPREAD human rights abuses were perpetrated by Iraqi forces following the invasion of Kuwait on 2 August 1990. These include the arbitrary arrest and detention without trial of thousands of civilians and military personnel; systematic torture; the imposition of the death penalty and the extrajudicial execution of hundreds of unarmed civilians, including children; and the "disappearance" of hundreds of detainees, many of whom are feared dead. The abuses were detailed in a report published by AI in December 1990*.

AI takes no position on the conflict in the Gulf. The organization is concerned, however, about human rights violations taking place in that context.

AI's report contained numerous testimonies from former detainees, who said they were held incommunicado without charge or trial and tortured throughout their detention. No less than 38 methods of torture are cited in the report which concluded that the brutality of the treatment inflicted on detainees appeared designed to terrorize the population at large and to discourage people from expressing, in whatever form, their opposition to the Iraqi presence in Kuwait.

Families were given no official notification of the arrest or place of detention of the detainees, who therefore effectively "disappeared" in custody, and remained ignorant of their fate and whereabouts until they had either been released or executed. The bodies of those executed were either found in the streets of Kuwait City, or were dumped outside their homes.

From about mid-August, a pattern of extrajudicial executions emerged, whereby, according to one source, "the Iraqis would bring the detainee back to his home and ask his family to identify him. Once he had been identified, the Iraqis would shoot him in the back of the head, right in front of his family". Children were among those who died in this manner.

Iraq also extended the scope of the death penalty in August, shortly after the invasion. However, AI has concluded that ostensibly criminal offences, such as looting, were used by the Iraqi authorities as a pretext to execute individuals who had taken part in opposition activity against Iraqi forces in Kuwait.

In December, AI called on the Iraqi Government to implement a series of recommendations, including: granting immediate access to the International Committee of the Red Cross to enable it to provide protection to prisoners and civilians in Kuwait; releasing immediately and unconditionally all prisoners of conscience; investigating all reports of torture, extrajudicial executions and "disappearances"; and taking immediate steps to ensure that no further torture, executions or other abuses are carried out.

Iraq/Occupied Kuwait: Human rights violations since 2 August is available from AI sections or the International Secretariat.□

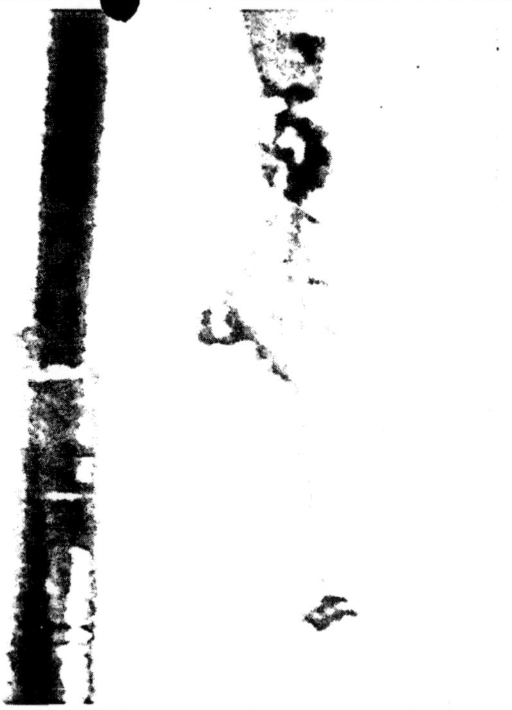

This body, left hanging from a crane in Kuwait City, was said to be that of an Iraqi soldier executed for looting on 16 August

REPUBLIC OF YEMEN

Eight granted clemency to mark AI's visit

THE Yemeni Government told an AI delegation in November 1990 that the country would accede to the United Nations Convention against Torture and Other Cruel, Inhuman or Degrading Treatment or Punishment. Eight political prisoners under sentence of death since 1985 were granted clemency in honour of AI's visit. The government also assured AI that it would review the cases of all untried political detainees currently held.

AI's delegates, led by the Secretary General, met the President and Vice-President, and the Ministers of Foreign Affairs, Interior and Justice, with whom they raised AI's concerns in Yemen, including cases of sentenced political prisoners and untried detainees, irregularities in arrest and detention procedures, and the continued use of the death penalty and of shackles in prisons. In addition, the Secretary General addressed the Yemeni Parliament. He welcomed the recent positive human rights developments in the country but drew attention to AI's outstanding concerns.

AI was publicly invited to visit the country by the President of Yemen in February 1990.□

JORDAN

Prisoners freed by royal pardon

EIGHT prisoners were released in September and November 1990 following royal pardons granted by King Hussein bin Talal. One had been sentenced to death and the others to lengthy terms of imprisonment after unfair trials by the Martial Law Court for political offences involving violence, including an attempt on the life of the King.□

VENEZUALA

Grave of Caracas victims exhumed

IN November, a judge ordered the exhumation of unmarked graves believed to contain the remains of a number of those who died in Caracas between 27 February and 10 March 1989, when hundreds were killed by members of the security forces.

A forensic anthropologist visited the country between 26 and 30 November as an AI delegate to monitor the investigations and gather information on the location of the burial site, the recovery of the bodies and their identification. Several bodies were recovered to be analysed by local forensic experts.

The victims' relatives welcomed the developments but, together with human rights monitors, continued to call for full investigatios into the killings — the circumstances of several of which suggested the victims were extrajudicially executed. However, little progress had been reported by the end of 1990.□

MAURITANIA

Reports of torture

OVER 1,000 people, including at least three former prisoners of conscience, were arrested in Mauritania's capital, Nouakchott, and in Nouadhibou in November and December 1990. They were detained in military barracks in the Nouakchott area. A government official said they had been detained in connection with a conspiracy to overthrow the government, but none of them is known to have been formally charged with any offence. AI has received reports that at least 15 of them may have died in custody as a result of torture. All the detainees belong to the black Hal-pulaar ethnic group, which the authorities suspect of opposing the government. There have been widespread arrests, torture, "disappearance" and extrajudicial executions of Hal-pulaar people, particularly in the south of the country, since April 1989.□

0044

SAUDI ARABIA

Women detained for driving

ON 6 November 1990 a women's demonstration took place in Riyadh in protest at the country's traditional prohibition against women driving cars. Dozens of women drove cars in convoy along a main thoroughfare in Riyadh. Forty-nine women who took part were detained for some hours, but were released.

Salih al-'Azzaz, a prominent writer and journalist, was also arrested on suspicion of being one of the organizers of the demonstration. He was reportedly taking photographs of the demonstration at the time of his arrest. He was reportedly held incommunicado at the *Mabahith al-'Amma* (General Intelligence) Headquarters in the 'Ulaisha district of Riyadh, and was only allowed family visits at the end of December. AI considers him a prisoner of conscience and has called for his immediate and unconditional release.

A week after the demonstration the ban on female drivers was formally made law. The law states that anyone violating the prohibition for women to drive is liable to an unspecified punishment.□

UNITED KINGDOM

Broadwater Farm case to go to appeal

THE United Kingdom Government announced in December the referral of the case of Engin Raghip to the Court of Appeal. Engin Raghip is one of three young men serving life sentences for the murder of a policeman during a 1985 riot at the Broadwater Farm public housing estate in London. The government based its decision on new evidence concerning psychological testing.

AI has consistently urged the government to review all the Broadwater Farm cases in which convictions were based solely on confessions. The organization had received many allegations that confessions had been obtained through coercion and in the absence of a lawyer. In the February 1987 trial three juveniles were acquitted of murder after the judge criticized police conduct in the interrogation of two of them. At a subsequent disciplinary hearing the officer leading the murder investigation was found guilty of denying a 13-year-old boy access to a lawyer during three days of detention. Another police officer still faces disciplinary charges over the boy's interrogation.□

AI delegation visits India

AN AI delegation visited Delhi from 10 to 17 December 1990 to attend the World Congress on Human Rights. While there, they sought meetings with government officials, including Prime Minister Chandra Shekhar. Such meetings had been approved in principle by the previous government which resigned in November 1990.□

AMNESTY INTERNATIONAL NEWSLETTER is published every month in four languages to bring you news of AI's concerns and campaigns worldwide, as well as in-depth reports. Available from Amnesty International (address below)

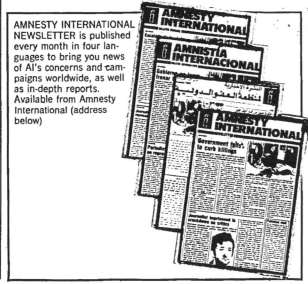

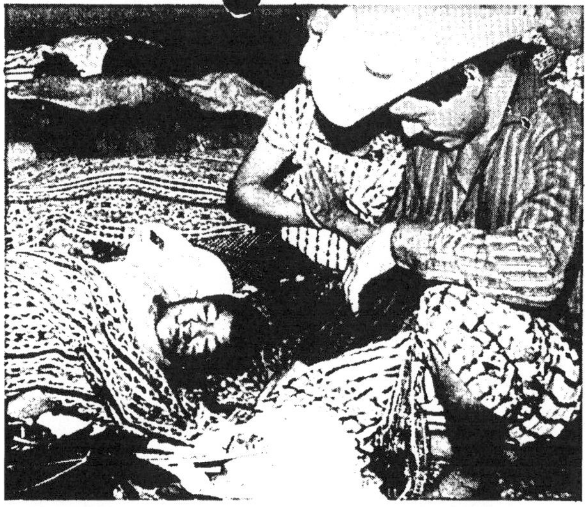

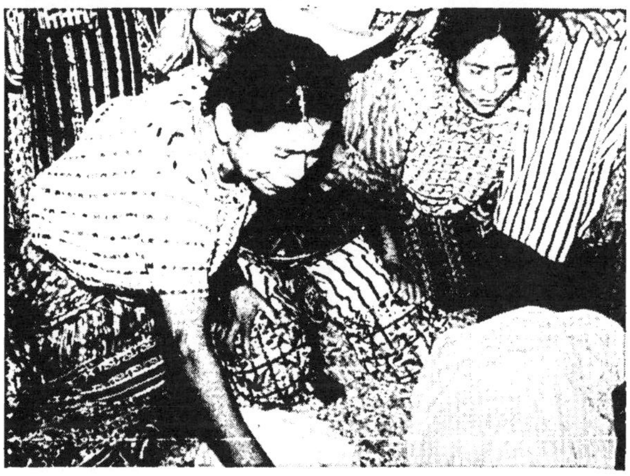

Relatives grieve over the bodies of the dead

GUATEMALA

Army kills fifteen civilians

AT least 15 people, three of them children, were reportedly killed and 19 others, including several children, were wounded when soldiers opened fire on a crowd of unarmed villagers at a military base in Sololá Guatemala on the evening of 2 December 1990.

According to eyewitness reports, the events leading to the killings began when soldiers from the base, who were allegedly drunk, broke into a villager's house, tried to rob him and reportedly opened fire and wounded him. A crowd of some 1,500 went to the base to protest and were fired on by soldiers.

Survivors interviewed in hospital by local and international press and human rights groups insist that the crowd was peaceful and unarmed and that the soldiers opened fire when leaders of the protest asked to speak to the base commander.

Military personnel initially claimed that the villagers had provoked the incident. However, after widespread national and international expressions of outrage, military spokesmen announced that two soldiers, one said to have provoked the initial incident at the villager's home, the other the base commander had been detained.

AI has asked the government to say whether there will be an inquiry into the killings, and urged that any findings be made known promptly, that any criminal acts committed be referred to the tribunals and that steps be taken to ensure adequate medical care for the injured, the security of all witnesses to either incident, and appropriate compensation for victims' relatives.□

SOUTH KOREA: In Issue No. 1, published January 1991, it is stated that prisoners of conscience who do not renounce their communist beliefs may be detained indefinitely. The Public Security Law, which allowed for such detention, was repealed in 1989. However, political prisoners held under national security legislation, including prisoners of conscience, have been denied the benefit of measures such as release on parole, unless they agree to be "anti-communist".

AMNESTY INTERNATIONAL, 1 Easton Street, London WC1X 8DJ, United Kingdom. Printed in Great Britain by Flashprint Enterprises Ltd. London.
Available on subscription at £7 (US$12.00) for 12 issues. ISSN 0308 6887

법 무 부

인권 2031-1931 503-7045 1991. 2. 9.

수신 외무부장관

참조 국제기구조약국장

제목 국제사면위 관련 협조 요청

1. 국제사면위 회원들이 '90 4/4분기 동안 각 부처에 보내온 특정인 석방탄원 편지를 검토한 결과 3/4분기 대상자 이외에 김성만, 이면제, 김진엽 등 3명이 주요 석방요구 대상자로 분석되었습니다.

2. 동인들에 대한 설명자료 및 양심수라는 주장에 대한 당부입장을 별첨과 같이 송부하오니 동 내용이 국제사면위 본부측에 적의 설명될 수 있도록 조치하여 주시기 바랍니다.

첨 부 : 관련자료 1부. 끝.

법 무 부 장 관

0046

공 란

공 란

공 란

양심수 주장에 대하여

ㅇ 국제사면위원회는 폭력을 사용하거나 옹호하지 않음에도 신념, 피부색, 성별, 인종적 기원, 언어, 종교를 이유로 구금된 자를 양심수로 정의하는 것으로 알고 있음

ㅇ 그러나 그러한 정의도 대상을 판단함에 있어서 명확한 개념이 되고 있지는 아니함. 즉 신념이나 종교를 이유로 구금된 자라고 한다면 어떤 신념이나 종교를 가지고 있다는 사실만으로 구금된 자를 말하는 것인지 아니면 그 뿐만 아니라 어떤 신념이나 종교에 입각한 행동이 비폭력적인 경우에도 모두 양심범에 해당한다는 것인지 명백하지 아니함. 예를들면 공산주의 사상을 가지고 있다거나 기독교를 믿고 있다는 사실만으로 구금된 자를 말하는 것인지 아니면 그 뿐만 아니라 공산주의 사상에 입각하여 공산주의 국가를 위해 비폭력적인 간첩행위를 하는 경우, 또는 종교적인 이유로 군복무를 거부하거나 기도만을 주장하다 유아를 죽게 만드는 경우에도 모두 양심범에 해당한다는 것인지 명백하지 아니함

0050

o 국제사면위원회의 정의가 만약 전자를 의미한다면 대한민국에는 신념, 피부색, 성별, 인종적기원, 언어, 종교만을 이유로 구금된 자는 없음

o 즉 아국은, 단순히 어떤 사람이 공산주의사상을 가지고 있다는 이유로 또는 특정종파를 믿는다는 이유로, 피부가 검다는 이유로, 여자라는 이유로 구금을 한 사실은 없음

o 그러나 국제사면위원회의 정의가 후자를 의미한다면, 즉 어떤 사람이 신념이나 종교에 따라 적극적 또는 소극적 행위를 한 경우에 그 행위가 비폭력적인 한 즉각 석방되어야 할 양심수라는 견해에는 전혀 수긍할 수가 없음

o 왜냐하면 어떤 신념이나 종교에 따라 행해 진 행위가 비록 비폭력적이라고 할 지라도 앞에서 설명한 바와 같이 폭력적 행위에 못지 않게 어떤 국가나 사회, 그리고 다른 개인에게 큰 피해와 고통을 줄 수 있기 때문임

0051

○ 또한 국제사면위원회의 양심수라는 개념이 어떠한 국가나 사회에 있어서도 적용될 수 있는 인류의 보편적 양식에 기초한 것이라고 믿기 때문에 더욱 후자의 견해는 수긍할 수가 없는 것임

○ 그리고 어떤 신념이나 종교에 근거하여 행해진 적극적, 소극적 행위에 대해 법적 제재를 가하는 범위는 그 나라의 역사, 환경, 전통, 가치, 윤리등에 따라 차이가 있을 수 있으며, 결국 그 내용은 그 나라의 국민 총의에 바탕을 둔 헌법과 법률로 나타난다고 할 것임

○ 지금까지 국제사면위원회에서 양심수로 거론된 사람들을 보면 단순히 그들이 어떤 신념과 의사를 가지고 있다는 이유만으로 구금된 사람은 없음. 그들은 그 신념과 의사를 이유로 적극적 행위에 까지 나간 것이며 그것이 실정법을 위반하게 된 것임. 즉 북한을 위해 국가기밀을 수집하는 등 간첩행위를 한다거나 몰래 북한을 왕래한다거나 폭력혁명을 선동하는 유인물을 제작, 배포하는 등의 실정법위반 행위를 한 것이며, 따라서 재판결과에 따라 처리되어야 할 것임.

0052

o 만약 이들이 즉각 석방되어야 할 양심수라고 주장한다면 그것은 각국이 가지고 있는 공산주의자들의 활동에 관한 규제법률, 출입국에 관한 법률, 집회에 관한 규제법률 등에 위반된 사람들이 모두 사상이나 이행, 의사 표현의 자유에 대한 신념에 따른 행동을 한 사람들이므로 즉각 석방되어야 한다는 주장과 마찬가지라 할 수 있을 것임

0053

5486

기 안 용 지

분류기호 문서번호	국연 2031 -	(전화:)	시 행 상 특별취급	
보존기간	영구·준영구. 10. 5. 3. 1	장		관
수 신 처 보존기간				
시행일자	1991. 2. 18.			

보조기관	국 장	전 결	협조기관		문서통제 (1991. 2. 18 통제관)
	과 장				
기안책임자		송영완			발송인 (1991. 2. 18 외무부)
경 유 수 신 참 조	주영대사		발신명의		
제 목	A.I. 대응 설명자료 송부				

연 : 국연 2031-3708 (91.1.23)

1. A.I. 회원들이 90년도 4/4분기중 아국정부에 보내온 인권관계 서한을 검토한 결과 연호 3/4분기 대상자 이외에 김성만, 이면제, 김진엽등 3명이 주요 석방요구 대상자로서 분석되었습니다.

2. 동인들에 관한 법무부 설명자료를 별첨 송부하오니 A.I. 측에 적의 설명바라며 A.I. 회원들에 대한 불필요한 서한발송을 자제해주도록 요청하시기 바랍니다.

첨 부 : 상기자료 1부. 끝.

0054

주 영 대 사 관

영국(정) 723- 13 1991. 2. 20.

수신 : 장관

참조 : 국제기구조약국장

제목 : A.I. 뉴스레터 대응

연 : 영국(정) 723-004 (91.1.16)

대 : 국연 2031-167, 3708(91.1.23)

1. 연호 반박서한에 대하여 국제사면위(A.I)의 M.Smart 연구부장이 당관에 보낸 답신을 별첨 송부합니다.

2. 동 답신 3번째절의 "substantial written comments"라 함은 당관이 제공한 대호자료를 의미하는 것임을 참고하시기 바랍니다.

첨부 : 동 서한 1부. 끝.

검 토 필(1991. 6. 30.)

주 영 대 사

0055

amnesty international

INTERNATIONAL SECRETARIAT,
1 Easton Street, London WC1X 8DJ,
United Kingdom.

Ref.: TG ASA 25/91.04

Mr Byung Ho Suh
Press and Cultural Attache
Embassy of the Republic of Korea
4 Palace Gate
London W8 5NF

15 February 1991

Dear Mr Suh,

Thank you for your letter of 16 January. Amnesty International also appreciates the positive atmosphere in which views have recently been exchanged with your government and it is our wish that future communication between us is held in the same spirit.

We note your clarification on the Social Surveillance Law passed in 1989 after the repeal of the Public Security Law. Amnesty International regrets the error in the January 1991 issue of the Amnesty International Newsletter and has published a correction in the February 1991 issue, a copy of which I enclose for your reference. We hope the correction makes it clear that our present concern relates to the fact that political prisoners held under national security legislation, including prisoners of conscience, have been denied the benefit of measures such as release on parole, unless they agree to be "anti-communist".

Last week we received substantial written comments from your Ministry of Justice which appear to relate to the other points you made in your letter about Amnesty International's decision to consider some prisoners in the Republic of Korea as prisoners of conscience. We shall be writing to the Ministry of Justice as soon as we have had their comments translated and we shall send you a copy of our letter for your information.

Yours sincerely,

Malcolm Smart
For the Secretary General

cc. Counsellor Cho Sang Hoon

☎ (44)(71) 413 5500 Telegrams: Amnesty London WC1 Telex: 28502 FAX: 956 1157

0056

Amnesty International is an independent worldwide movement working impartially for the release of all prisoners of conscience, fair and prompt trials for political prisoners and an end to torture and executions. It is funded by donations from its members and supporters throughout the world. It has formal relations with the United Nations, Unesco, the Council of Europe, the Organization of African Unity and the Organization of American States.

관리 번호	91 -183

원 본

외 무 부

종 별 :

번 호 : UKW-0496 일 시 : 91 0222 1900

수 신 : 장관(국연)

발 신 : 주 영 대사

제 목 : A.I.면담

대: 국연 2031-167(91.1.23)

1. 당관 황서기관은 금 2.22(금) A.I. 의 VANDALE 한국담당연구원을 면담, 대호 14 개 사안에 대하여 설명하였는 바, 동 연구원은 개별사안 각각에 대하여 A.I. 가 기 수집한 자료들과 비교분석해 보겠다고 말함.

2. 동 14 개 사안(15 명죄수)을 양심수(PRISONER OF CONSCIENCE)로 간주하느냐는 질문에 대하여, 동 연구원은 70 년대말 박기래를 양심수로 지정한바 있으며, 다른 사람들에 대해서는 아직 결정한바 없다고 말함. 끝

(대사 오재희-국장)

예고: 91.12.31 일반

검 토 필(1991. 6. 30.)

국기국 차관 1차보

PAGE 1

91.02.23 08:16

외신 2과 통제관 BW

0057

자체 문제

법무부 인권과

19 . . .

아래 문건을 수신자에게 전달하여 주시기 바랍니다.

제 목 :

수 신 : 국제엠네스티 송영란 서기관님
(수신처 FAX NO: 720-2686)

발 신 : 법무부 인권과

표지포함 총 ____ 매

0058

공 란

공 란

공 란

[illegible]한 H1-345 S03 사회(1770)

全敬煥.李哲熙씨등 특별감형　　　　　　[illegible] 91. 2. 20.

政府,1천8백78명에 사면,감형단행　　　　　　17:00

[illegible].[illegible]씨도사면 '良心囚'포함안돼

남파간첩등 公安사범 27명만 감형.가석방

全.李씨 刑期절반복역으로 곧 가석방될듯

(서울=聯合)정부는 20일 5共비리로 구속수감중인 全斗煥前대통령의 친동생 全敬煥씨와 '李.張사건'의 李哲熙씨의 형량을 낮추고 남파간첩을 포함한 공안사범 10명을 가석방하는등 모두 1천8백78명에 대해 특별사면.감형조치를 오는 25일을 기해 단행키로 했다.

6共들어 4번째로 취해진 이번 특별사면.감형대상에는 밀입북사건으로 구속된 文益煥목사와 文奎鉉신부,徐敬元의원,林秀卿양,任鍾晳군등 재야에서 주장하는 이른바 '양심수'와 민생침해 사범들은 포함되지 않았다.

이번 조치로 5共비리로 구속됐다 특별가석방으로 풀려난 [illegible]서울시장과 [illegible]서울시교육감및 美대사관 사제폭발물 투척사건의 [illegible]씨등 6명을 비롯한 일반형사범,공안사범 [illegible]

남파간첩으로 미전향한 李인중씨를 비롯한 공안사범 6명등 모두 5백65명이 감형됐다.

또 미전향 간첩인 무기수 유한욱씨등 5명을 포함한 공안사범 10명과 모범수.모범소년원생 3백82명등 모두 3백99명은 특별 가석방.가퇴원으로 풀려나게 됐다.

주요 감형대상자인 全敬煥씨(48.영등포교도소수감)는 지난 89년5월 징역 7년형 확정으로 지금까지 2년8개월을 복역해왔으나 잔여형기의 2분의1이 감형됨에 따라 [illegible]1개월이 남게 됐으며,징역 15년이 확정돼 지금까지 8년9개월을 복역한 李哲熙씨([illegible].안양교도소 수감)도 형량이 3년2개월로 줄어 들게 돼 두 사람 모두 감형된 형량을 기준으로 형기의 2분의1을 복역,빠르면 석탄절,늦어도 연말까지는 가석방이 가능할 것으로 보인다.

이와 함께 각각 징역 3년6월과 징역 3년이 확정됐다 지난해 8월 특별가석방된

정부는 이에앞서 지난 88년2월 제13대 대통령취임기념 특별사면.복권조치를 취한 것을 비롯,88년12월20일 '11.26 대통령특별담화'에 따른 특별사면,90년 4월12일

0062

[illegible]시장과 [illegible] 유감[illegible] 잔여형기는 자동면제된다.

정부는 이에앞서,지난 88년2월 제13대 대통령취임기념 특별사면,복권조치를 취한 것을 비롯,88년12월20일'11.26 대통령특별담화'에 따른 특별사면,90년 4월12일 [illegible] 특별사면 등 [illegible] 차례의 사면 감형조치를 취했었다.

특별사면.감형은 국무회의의 의결을 거쳐 대통령의 재가를 통해 취해지는 조치로 사면대상자들은 나머지 형의 집행이 면제되어 형기를 모두 복역한 것으로 간주되며,특별감형의 경우는 무기수는 징역 20년 또는 징역 25년으로,유기수는 나머지 형기의 2분의 1이 감경된다.

또 특별 가석방된 사람은 가석방이 취소되지 않고 잔여형기가 지나면 형집행을 마친 것으로 간주된다.

법무부 관계자는"이번 사면은 제13대 대통령의 취임3주년을 맞아 취해지는 조치로 잘못을 뉘우친 수형자들을 사회에 복귀시켜 새 출발의 기회를 부여하고 국민화합과 국정쇄신위기를 쇄신하려는데 그 목적이 있다"고 밝히고"그러나 정부가 현재 모든 역량을 동원해 범죄와의 전쟁을 수행하고 있는 현실을 감안,강도살인.가정파괴 등 민생침해사범에 대해서는 은전의 대상에서 제외했다"고 강조했다.

이 관계자는 또"공안사범의 경우 10년이상 복역한 무기수중 고령에 질병이 있거나 행형성적이 우수한 6명과 미전향 간첩이지만 30년이상 복역한 70세이상 고령질병자 5명 등 모두 21명에 대해서는 인도적 차원에서 특별감형및 형집행정지,특별가석방 조치를 취했다"고 밝히고"그러나 명일빌딩사건으로 구속수감중인 소위'시국사범'들에 대해서는 특별히 고려할 만한 사정이 없어 사면.감형 대상에서 제외시켰다"고 말했다.

특별사면.감형.형집행 정지된 주요인사및 공안사범들은 다음과 같다.

△특별사면

△[illegible]△[illegible]△[illegible](25.특수공무집행방해등.미대사관 사제폭탄[illegible] 투척사건)△朴[illegible](23.".")△片[illegible](25.".")△金[illegible](25.".")△洪[illegible](26.".")

△특별감형(괄호안은 감형된 형량)

△[illegible]△[illegible]△차주섭(61.남파간첩.징역 25년)△金재목(68.재일북괴공작원 포섭간첩.징역 20년)△장중갑(67.지리산 빨치산.징역 20년)△李연[illegible](75.남파간첩.징역 20년)△朴기래(63.재일교포간첩관련.징역 20년)△정시일(51.재일교포간첩관련.징역 20년)

△형집행정지

▲유한욱(73.무기.남파간첩)▲許영철(70.".")▲방재순(73.".")▲金우택(71.".")▲장호(70.".")(끝)

0063

관리번호 91-204

주 영 대 사 관

영국(정) 723-15 1991. 2. 27.

수신 : 장관

참조 : 국제기구조약국장

제목 : 인권문제탄원

1. 국제사면위 영국지부(A.I. British Section)가 당관에 보내온 홍성담 석방탄원 서명록과 이에대한 당관의 답신을 별첨 송부합니다.

2. 상기와 관련, A.I. 본부의 Ms. Francois Vandale 한국담당 연구원은 한국정부가 기 재공한 홍성담 설명자료를 검토해 보았지만 홍성담이 양심수 (prisoner of conscience) 라는 A.I. 의 입장에는 변함이 없다고 말했음을 참고하시기 바랍니다.

발송 1991. 2. 28 주영국대사관

첨부 : 1. 홍성담 석방탄원 서명록

2. 당관 답신. 끝.

전	
접수일시 1991. 3. 2	748
처리과	

주 영 대 사

검토필(1991. 6. 30.)

0064

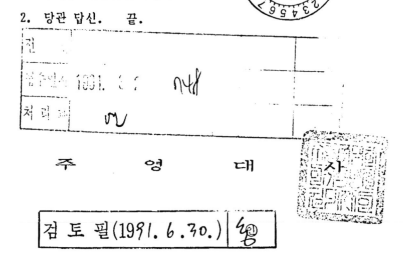

EMBASSY OF THE REPUBLIC OF KOREA
4 PALACE GATE
LONDON W8 5NF

26th February, 1991

Mr David Bull
Director
Amnesty International (British Section)
99-119 Rosebery Avenue
London EC1R 4RE.

Dear Mr Bull,

I write to acknowledge receipt of your letter of 21st February 1991, addressed to Ambassador Oh, enclosing petitions with regard to the case of Hong Song-Dam.

The Korean governments's position on the case has been provided to the International Secretariat of Amnesty International on two occasions (August 1990 and January this year).

It would be appreciated if you would liaise with the Secretariat for any information you might need on the case.

Yours sincerely,

Sang Hoon Cho
Counsellor

0065

AMNESTY INTERNATIONAL

Amnesty International British Section
99-119 Rosebery Avenue, London EC1R 4RE
Tel: 071-278 6000 Fax: 071-833 1510 Telex: 917621 AIBS
Nobel Peace Prize 1977 UN Human Rights Prize 1978

21 February 1991

His Excellency Mr. Jay Hee Oh
Embassy of the Republic of Korea
4 Palace Gate
W8 5NF

Your Excellency,

Petitions for the release of Hong Song-Dam

Please find enclosed petitions calling for the immediate release of Hong Song-Dam, artist of international repute who is in jail for sending colour slides of his paintings to North Korea, and who is understood to have been tortured following his arrest in 1989. We believe him to be a prisoner of conscience detained for expressing his right to freedom of expression.

Please forward these petitions from the people of Glasg ow and Bristol to your government.

Yours sincerly,

David Bull
Director Amnesty INternational (British Section)

tb:cl

0066

Amnesty International is a worldwide movement working impartially for the release of all Prisoners of Conscience, fair and prompt trials for all political prisoners and an end to torture and executions. It is independent of any government, political opinion or religious creed and is voluntarily financed. Amnesty International has formal relations with the United Nations, UNESCO, the Council of Europe, the Organisation of African Unity and the Organisation of American States.

관리 번호	91-229

	분류번호	보존기간

발 신 전 보

번 호 : WUK-0488 910313 1803 FK 종별 :

수 신 : 주 영 대사 . 총영사

발 신 : 장 관 (국연)

제 목 : A.I. 대응 활동

대 : UKW-0496

연 : 국연 2031-5486 (91.2.18)

1. A.I. 회원들의 진정서 송부와 관련, A.I.측 관계관을 접촉, 기송부한 자료를 참고하여 주거론되는 인사의 범법사실을 구두로 설명하고 무분별한 범법자 석방 탄원을 자제해 주도록 촉구하고 3.22.한 결과 회보바람.

2. 특히 A.I.측이 소속회원들에게 아국내 구속자들의 석방을 탄원토록 하고 있으나, 전세계에서 가장 혹독한 인권탄압이 자행되고 있는 북한에 대하여는 그 폐쇄성으로 인한 정보 부재를 이유로 10-15만 내외의 정치범 석방을 위한 조치를 전혀 취하지 않는등 형평을 잃고 있음을 지적하고, 분단 및 남북대립 이라는 특수한 상황하에서도 꾸준히 인권신장을 위해 최선의 노력을 경주하고 있는 정부입장을 적극 설명바람. 끝.

(국제기구조약국장 문동석)

검 토 필(1991. 6. 30.)

앙 고 재	91년 3월 13일	UN과	기안자		과 장		국 장		차 관	장 관
			송영완							

보안통제	외신과통제

0067

관리 번호	91 —250

원 본

외 무 부

종 별 :

번 호 : UKW-0694　　　　일 시 : 91 0318 1800

수 신 : 장관(국연,구일,기정)

발 신 : 주 영 대사대리

제 목 : A.I.사무총장 면담

대: WUK-0488

1. 소직은 3.18(월) A.I. 사무총장 IAN MARIN 과 면담, 대호 A.I. 회원들의진정서 송부와 관련, 최근 A.I. 회원이 석방 요구하는 인사들의 범법 사실을 설명하고, 이에대한 아국정부의 입장을 아래와 같이 전달함

0 이들은 자유민주주의 체제를 전복코자 간첩행위 또는 폭력 혁명 선동을 하여 실정법을 위반한 자 이었음을 강조

0 한국이 국가안보의 위협을 받고 있는 세계 유일의 분단국임에도 불구하고, 우리 정부는 관계법령(형법, 형소법, 사회보호법) 정비, 구속자의 석방, 행형제도의 개선, 인권규약 가입등 가능한 모든 방법을 통하여 인권신장을 위하여 노력해 왔음을 감안, 차후 A.I. 회원들의 무분별한 진정서 송부를 자제할 것을 강하게 요청

0 이와관련 세계에서 가장 혹독한 인권탄압이 있는 북한에 대하여 수많은 정치범 석방을 위하여 A.I. 가 아무런 조치를 취하지 않은것은 크게 형평을 잃는처사라고 첨언

2. 이에대하여 MARTIN 사무총장은 그간 한국정부가 A.I. 측 자료제공 요청에 대하여 적극적인 협조를 해준데 대하여 사의를 표하고, 회원에 대한 인권관련서한 발송 자제 요청에 대하여는 A.I. 의 존재 이유와 관련되는 문제라고 하면서 난색을 표하였으며, 북한의 인권문제에 대하여는 구속자 석방을 위하여 많은 서한을 발송하였으나, 아무런 답신이 없어, 더 이상의 진전이 되지 않았다고 설명함. 또한 동 사무총장은 A.I. 측과 대사관측이 대화하는 기회를 자주 갖는것은쌍방의 이해를 위하여 크게 도움을 주는 것으로 생각한다고 발언함. 끝

(대사대리 최근배-국장)

91.12.31. 까지

검 토 필(1991. 6. 30.)

국기국　차관　1차보　2차보　구주국　청와대　안기부

PAGE 1　　　　91.03.19 08:48

외신 2과 통제관 FE

0068

A.I. 대응활동

91.3.20

91. 3. 19.
국제연합과

1. A.I. 사무총장에 대한 아국입장 전달

o 주영대사대리는 3.18(월) A.I. 사무총장 Ian Martin과 면담하고 A.I. 회원들의 진정서송부 문제를 제기, 무분별한 진정서 송부를 자제해 줄 것과 최근 A.I. 회원의 석방탄원 대상인사들의 범법사실을 설명하고 특히 하기 아국입장을 강조함.

- A.I. 회원들이 석방을 주장하는 장기복역수들은 자유민주주의 체제를 전복코자 간첩행위 또는 폭력혁명 선동을 하여 실정법을 위반한 자들임.
- 한국이 국가안보의 위협을 받고있는 세계 유일의 분단국임에도 불구하고, 우리정부는 관계법령(형법, 형소법, 사회보호법) 정비, 구속자의 석방, 행형제도의 개선, 인권규약 가입등 가능한 모든 방법을 통하여 인권신장을 위하여 노력해 왔음을 감안, 차후 A.I. 회원들의 무분별한 진정서 송부를 자제할 것을 강하게 요청
- 세계에서 가장 혹독하게 인권을 탄압하고 있는 북한에 대하여 A.I.가 정치범 석방 요구등 시급히 요망되는 조치를 취하지 않는 것은 크게 형평을 잃는 처사임.

o 이에 대하여 Martin 사무총장은 하기 요지로 언급함.

- 그간 한국정부가 A.I.측의 자료제공 요청에 대하여 적극적인 협조를 해준데 대하여 사의를 표함.
- A.I. 회원에 대한 인권관련 서한발송 자제 요청은 A.I.의 존재 이유와 관련되는 문제이므로 수락키 어려운 요청임.

/

0069

- 북한의 인권문제와 관련, A.I. 회원들이 북한당국에 의해 적법절차를 거치지 않고 구속된 구속자 석방을 위하여 많은 서한을 발송하였으나, 아무런 답신이 없어 더이상의 진전이 되지 않고 있음.
- A.I.측과 한국대사관측이 대화하는 기회를 자주 갖는 것은 쌍방의 이해를 위하여 크게 도움을 주는 것으로 생각함.

2. A.I.에 대한 북한인권문제 제기

o 소련 극동지역 체그도문 벌목장서 만여명의 북한인들이 합숙생활을 하며 벌목작업을 하고 있는 바, 북한당국이 동 합숙소에 보위부 요원을 파견하여 탈출자를 고문, 처벌하는등 비인도적 행위를 자행하고 있다는 내용의 소련 모스크바뉴스 최근호(3.10.자) 보도내용 관련, 주영대사관에 A.I.측 인사 접촉시 하기 내용 요청토록 지시(3.19)
  - 상기 보도내용을 알고 있는지 탐문
  - 필요시 자료전달등으로 A.I.측의 관심을 유도
  - A.I.측이 불필요한 아국문제에 대한 관심 경주보다는 심각한 북한 인권문제를 보다 적극적으로 다루어 줄 것을 요청

0070

1S070

기 안 용 지

분류기호 문서번호	국연 2031-	(전화 :)	시 행 상 특별취급	
보존기간	영구 · 준영구. 10. 5. 3. 1.	장 관		
수 신 처 보존기간				
시행일자	1991. 4. 22.			
보조기관 국 장	전 결	협조기관		문 서 통 제
과 장				심열 1991. 4. 24 통 제 관
기안책임자	송 영 완			발 송 인
경 유 수 신 참 조	법무부장관	발신명의		1991. 4. 23
제 목	설명자료 요청			

영국소재 Amnesty International은 주영대사관을 통하여 홍근수 목사(91.2.20. 구속) 및 이삼렬 교수(91.3.6. 구속)의 체포에 관하여 문의하는 서한을 송부하여 왔는 바, 동 서한에 대한 회신작성에 참고코자 하니 동 구소자들의 범죄사실, 사법처리 현황, 아국정부입장을 포함한 설명자료를 조속 당부로 송부하여 주시기 바랍니다.

첨 부 : A.I 서한 1부. 끝.

1505－25(2－1) 일(1)갑 190㎜×268㎜ 인쇄용지 2 급 60g/㎡
85. 9. 9. 승인 "내가아낀 종이 한장 늘어나는 나라살림" 가 40－41 1989. 6. 8

0071

관리번호 91-507

외 무 부

종 별 :

번 호 : UKW-1129　　　　일 시 : 91 0522 1700

수 신 : 장관(국연,국기,구일,정이,해신,기정)

발 신 : 주 영 대사

제 목 : 국제사면위 직원 면담

연: UKW-0961, 1061

대: WUK-0856(1), 국연 2031-15785(2)

1. 당관 이서기관은 91.4.29-5.4 간 IPU 총회에 참석한 A.I. 한국담당관 MISS F.VANDALE 를 5.21(화) 접촉, 대호 (1) A.I. 의 북한 체류기간중 활동내용 및 차후 처리방향등을 문의하였는 바, 동인은 A.I. 의 활동내용 및 북한인권에 관한 평가는 적절한 절차를 거쳐 91.7. 판 NEWSLETTER 지 (A.I. 기관지)에 게재될 것이라고 하면서 91.6 월말경 그 내용을 미리 당관에 알려주겠다고함.

2. 이 서기관은 지난 5.10. 국회에서 통과된 국가보안법 개정안 및 아국 및 북한의 인권상황에 대한 대호(2) FREEDONM HOUSE 의 보고서를 인용하면서, 아국 정부의 인권보장을 위한 제도적 장치 구축노력과 인권상황에 대한 타인권기관의 긍정적인 평가를 강조하였음.

3. 이에 VANDALE 은 사견임을 전제로, 자신도 88 년도 이후 한국의 인권이 전반적으로는 개선되는 느낌을 받았으나, 앞으로도 아국정부가 사회 각방면에서 인권 상황이 더욱 개선될 수 있는 조치를 취해주기를 바란다고 언급함. 끝

(대사 이홍구-국장)

예고: 91.12.31 일반

일반문서로 재분류 (1991.12.31.)

검토필(1991.6.30.)

국기국 공보처　차관　1차보　2차보　구주국　국기국　정문국　청와대　안기부

PAGE 1　　　　91.05.23　05:58

외신 2과　통제관 CF

0072

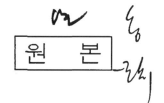

관리 번호	91-557

원 본

외 무 부

종 별 :

번 호 : UKW-1168 일 시 : 91 0530 1600

수 신 : 장관(국연,정홍,해기)

발 신 : 주 영 대사

제 목 : 국가보안법 위반자 관용조사

대: AM-0107

연: 영국(정) 723-185(91.2.28),-25(91.3.25)

1. 국제사면위(A.I) F.VANDALE 한국담당관은 5.28(화) 대호 국가보안법 위반자에 대한 특별관용조치(5.25. 자)에 대하여 환영의 뜻을 표하면서, A.I. 본부의 자료정리 및 A.I. 회원에게 석방탄원 편지의 발송을 자제토록 하기위하여, 관용조치 대상자(258 명) 의 명단을 요청하여 왔는 바, 이에대한 자료 송부바람.

2. 동 담당관은 또한 연호 체포된 7 명의 노조관련자중 박창수의 사망과 관련, 사인 및 사명경위에 대하여 문의하였는 바, 관련자료 회시바람. 끝

(대사 이홍구-국장)

예고: 91.12.31 일반

일반문서로 재분류(1991.12.31.

검 토 필(1991. 6. 30.)

국기국 외정실 공보처

PAGE 1

91.05.31 06:29

외신 2과 통제관 FM

0073

관리 번호	91 -563

외 무 부

종 별 :

번 호 : UKW-1177 일 시 : 91 0531 1600

수 신 : 장관(해신,정홍,국연,아일)

발 신 : 주 영 대사

제 목 : 서승 유럽방문

대: WUK-1011

대호 국제사면위 F.VANDALE 한국담당관에 확인한 바, 서승은 유럽제국의 A.I. 국별지부 연례회의(매년 4 월경 개최) 의 초청 결정에 따라, 개별지부의 지원하에 유럽각국을 방문중인 것으로 알고 있다고 말함. (91.5 월초 영국방문). 끝

(대사 이홍구-국장)

예고: 91.12.31 일반

일반문서로재분류(1991 .12.31.

검 토 필(1991. 6.30.)

공보처 차관 1차보 아주국 국기국 문협국 청와대 안기부

PAGE 1 91.06.01 03:49

외신 2과 통제관 CF

0074

발 신 전 보

분류번호	보존기간

번 호 : WUK-1038 910601 1146 WG 종별 :

수 신 : 주 영국 대사. 총영사

발 신 : 장 관 (국연)

제 목 : A.I. 활동

1. A.I.는 5.28. 창립 20주년을 맞아 세계각국의 양심수중 30명을 선정, 이들의 석방운동을 전개하기로 했다고 하는 바, 대상자중 한국인 김성만도 포함되어 있다 함.

2. 동 관련 신문기사를 별첨 FAX 송부하니 참고바람. 끝.

WUK(F)- 46

(국제기구조약국장 문동석)

보안통제	

앙고재	91년 6월 1일	UN과	기안자 성명		과 장	국 장		차 관	장 관
			송영완			전결			

외신과통제

0075

WUK(F)-46 10601 1140

中央日報

1991. 5. 31. 금, 27면

국제赦免위원회 창립 30주년

세계 良心囚30명 석방운동

세계 최대의 인권보호단체인 국제사면위원회가 28일 창립30주년을 맞이했다.

이날을 맞아 국제사면위원회는 세계 각국에서 복역중인 수만명의 良心囚가운데 30명을 선정, 올연말까지 이들에 대한 대대적인 석방운동을 벌이기로 했다.

국제사면위원회의 피터 더피의장은 28일 국제사면위원회 프랑스지부에서 가진 기자회견을 통해 이같은 계획을 발표하고 『정치적 반대자들을 투옥하고 있는 나라들은 더이상 이를 정당화하려는 핑계를 대지말고 이들을 즉각 석방하라』고 촉구했다.

국제사면위원회가 선정한 30명의 양심수 가운데는 韓國人 1명도 포함돼 있다. 지난86년 간첩죄로 대법원에서 死刑이 확정된뒤 현재는 無期囚로 복역중인 金成萬씨(33·구속당시 在美유학생).

지난해 3·1절 특사로 풀려난 徐勝씨(가운데 안경낀 사람). 국제사면위는 창립 30주년을 맞아 徐씨를 초청했다.

韓國 무기수 金成萬씨 1명포함

해당국에 항의서한등 발송

국제사면위원회는 이날 배포한 자료에서 「金씨 본인의 自白이외에 그가 간첩으로 활동했다는 어떠한 증거도 재판과정에서 제시된게 없으며 그 자백도 가혹한 고문에 의해 강요된 자백이었다고 본인은 밝히고 있다」면서 「국가의 정책에 반대하고, 그것을 숨기지 않았다는 이유로 평생을 감옥에 붙잡아두는 일은 용납될 수 없으며, 그는 즉각 석방돼야 한다」고 밝혔다.

이들 30명가운데는 金씨이외에도 反體制詩를 썼다는 이유로 30년째 감옥생활을 하고 있는 越南人, 단지 출국을 희망했다는 이유만으로 15年刑을 선고받은 蘇聯人, 아무런 사법절차도 없이 구금돼 獄苦를 치르고 있는 이스라엘 점령지역거주 팔레스타인人, 한 記者의 체포에 반대했다고 10년째 옥살이를 하고 있는 中國人등 각국에서 자행되고 있는 대표적인 인권침해 사례들이 포함돼 있다.

국제사면위원회는 이들의 석방을 위해 런던본부와 전세계 44개국지부가 총동원돼 해당국 관계기관에 항의서한을 끊임없이 발송하고, 필요할 경우 조사단을 파견하며, 해당국대사관에서 항의시위를 벌이고, 각국 언론기관을 통해 국제적인 여론을 환기시키는등 할수있는 모든 방법을 동원할 계획이다.

한편 국제사면위원회는 창립30주년을 맞아 지난 20년간 사상범으로 복역하다 지난해 2월 석방된 徐勝씨(45·徐俊植全民聯 인권위원장의 친형)를 초청했다. 지난71년 「在日교포 유학생 간첩단사건」으로 구속돼 무기징역을 선고받고 복역해오다 사상전환을 하지 않고 석방된 첫케이스로 풀려난 徐씨는 이날 국제사면위원회 프랑스지부에서 그동안 자신의 석방을 위해 애써준 사면위원회측 관계자들과 감격적인 인사를 나누었다.

『국제사면위원회활동이 거둔 대표적 결실가운데 하나로 평가돼 이번에 초청된것 같다』고 말한 徐씨는 『지금도 大田교도소에서는 51명의 사상범이 남아있다』면서 이들의 조속한 석방을 희망했다.

지난 61년 英國人변호사 피터 베넨슨씨에 의해 창립돼 그동안 세계각국의 양심수석방과 고문금지·死刑제도 폐지등 人權분야에서 괄목한 성과를 거둬온 국제사면위원회는 지난77년 그 공로를 인정받아 노벨평화상을 수상하기도 했다. 그동안 이 단체가 석방노력을 기울여온 양심수만도 4만2천명에 달하고, 지난30년동안 총9백22회에 걸쳐 각국에 조사단을 파견하기도 했다. 현재 이 단체의 회원과 기부자등은 전세계1백50개국에 걸쳐 1백10만명에 이르고 있는데 특히 여기에서 발행되는 「국제사면위원회연례보고서」는 전세계 인권상황에 관한 최고의 참고서로 평가되고 있다.

【파리=裵明福특파원】

0076

원 본

외 무 부

종 별 :

번 호 : UKW-1187　　　　일 시 : 91 0603 1700

수 신 : 장관(국연,해기,기정)

발 신 : 주영대사

제 목 : A.I.30주년 기념 발간물

대: WUK-1038

A.I. 30주년을 맞이하여 A.I.'S 30TH ANNIVERSARY APPEALCASES 라는 보고서를 발간하였는바, 이중아국 관련사항(김성만 관련) 별첨 FAX 보고함.

첨부: UKWF-0245.끝

(대사 이홍구-국장)

국기국　구주국　안기부　공보처

PAGE 1　　　　91.06.04 05:08 BU

외신 1과 통제관

0077

UKW (F) - 0845　　　DATE: 10603 1700

수 신 : 장 관 (

발 신 : 주 영 국 대 사

제 목 : UKW-1187 첨부물

KIM SONG-MAN　　　SOUTH KOREA

"I am a person who wishes the independence of our nation and democracy. I think that this ideal can be realized in a socialistic country. I was interrogated and tortured mercilessly at the Agency for National Security Planning. During the interrogation and torture I was even forced to write a suicide letter addressed to my parents in order to disguise my possible death by suicide. The press widely published my forced confession as though it was true. I only long for the day we can enjoy our independence from under the slavish submission to a foreign power. Even if all the world does not believe me I know that God knows the truth".

For expressing such views, Kim Song-man was sentenced to death in South Korea in January 1986. His sentence was commuted three years later to life imprisonment. He is in jail today because he was labelled a North Korean spy.

Unauthorized meetings with North Koreans are punishable in South Korea under the National Security Law, as is the publication of views said to benefit North Korea. Kim Song-man admitted at his trial that he had visited the embassies of North Korea in East Berlin and Budapest on two occasions, but he denied having been recruited as a North Korean agent. He said he had confessed to being a spy because he had been "tortured mercilessly" and that he had met North Koreans merely to find out about the possibilities for Korean reunification. Apart from his confession, obtained while he was held incommunicado by the Agency for National Security Planning, no evidence was produced at his trial that he had gathered or sent intelligence to North Korea. The national secrets he was accused of passing to North Korea were in fact copies of his own pamphlets calling for the withdrawal of US troops from South Korea.

Kim Song-man was born in 1957. He comes from a Christian family; his grandfather founded the Evangelical Church in Korea. In his student days in Seoul he was active both in politics and the Christian Student Association. In June 1982 he went to the United States and enrolled at the Western Illinois University to study political science.

Kim Song-Man did not agree with the political state of affairs in South Korea, nor did he keep his opposition secret. He wrote pamphlets critical of government policies and he visited the embassies of North Korea. The authorities of South Korea may not like such behaviour, but to torture and then to sentence a man to spend the rest of his life in prison for such actions is wrong. Kim Song-man should be freed immediately.

0078

주 영 대 사 관

영국(정) 723-587   1991. 6. 10.

수신 : 장관

참조 : 국제기구조약국장

제목 : A.I. 30주년기념 발간물

연 : UKW-1187

연호 A.I. 발간물 "30th Anniversary Appeal Cases" 전문을 별첨 송부합니다.

첨부 : 상기 발간물 1부. 끝.

발송 1991. 6. 11 주영대사관

주 영 대

선 결			결재		
접수일시	1991. 6. 13	번호			
처리과	32937				

0079

30th

ANNIVERSARY APPEAL CASES

0080

SITA VALLES

ANGOLA

Sita Valles was suspected of being a leading figure in a 1977 coup attempt in Angola. She "disappeared" and it is feared that she died or was killed in custody.

On 27 May 1977 members of a faction of the ruling party, the *People's Movement for the Liberation of Angola (MPLA)*, attempted to overthrow by force the Government of President Agostinho Neto. This faction was led by Nito Alves, former Minister of the Interior. The coup failed but seven senior government officials were captured and killed before government forces regained control. Sita Valles and her husband, José van Dúnem, said to be one of the leaders of the attempted coup, went into hiding in a suburb of the Angolan capital, Luanda. In June 1977 they were arrested by members of the *Angolan Directorate for Information and Security (DISA)*.

President Neto said at first that clemency would be shown towards those involved in the attempted coup. Soon after, however, he announced that retribution would be swift. In July 1977, Special Military Tribunals were set up. The proceedings, verdicts and sentences of these tribunals were kept secret. In August 1977 President Neto announced that some leaders of the coup had been executed by firing squad, but gave no names.

The secret executions continued between July 1977 and March 1978. There were reports that hundreds of people were executed without trial, on the orders of either the Special Military Tribunal or simply security police officials. Unofficial sources suggest that the government entrusted the *DISA* not only with interrogating detainees, but also with deciding upon their fate and executing them. There were also reports that ambulances took intended victims away from prison at night.

Only those directly involved in the killings will ever know the final number executed. Edgar Ademar Valles, Sita Valles' brother, was among the victims of the last executions, reported to have taken place in Luanda in March 1978.

Some relatives, especially those of soldiers involved in the coup, were informed of executions. They were told prisoners had been tried, sentenced and executed. Many others, however, were given no information, and if they were, the information was not always reliable. One woman reassured by an official that her husband was still alive was advised by prison guards that she was wasting her time taking food and medicine as her husband had been executed.

In July 1979, the *DISA* was dissolved by President Neto, apparently because of "excesses" it had committed. A number of its officers suspected of torture and killings were arrested. They were all released without charge a few months later and many retained their jobs.

In December 1979 about 200 of those jailed for their part in the 1977 coup were released. By mid-1980 it was reported unofficially that all those involved had been released. There has been no news of Sita Valles since her arrest in June 1977. It is feared that she was one of the hundreds of people killed in custody in the year following the coup attempt.

No government has the right to make people "disappear" or to execute them without trial. The families of Sita and Edgar Ademar Valles, and hundreds of others who "disappeared", have the right to know what has happened to their relatives.

0081

CAPTAIN MADAM DOGO ABOUBAKAR CAMEROON

In November 1989 Captain Madam Dogo Aboubakar was reportedly tortured because a radio, a copy of the Qur'an and prayer beads were found in his cell. He was apparently denied medical treatment and is believed to have died on 3 December 1989. Up to now the government has not confirmed his death or explained the circumstances in which it occurred.

Another man, Adjutant Pagoré, also reportedly died in the same jail in the same month. The two were among 30 political prisoners who were said to have been severely beaten and tortured for being found with possessions forbidden to political prisoners. These included religious materials, radios and even spoons.

The men were held at Nkondengui Prison in Yaoundé, the capital of Cameroon. Captain Madam Dogo, a former officer in the gendarmerie, had been denied all contact with his family and the outside world for five years. He was serving a life sentence in connection with an unsuccessful coup attempt in April 1984.

The bodies of the two men who died were apparently not returned to their families. No official enquiry is known to have been held and the Cameroon Government has not responded to Amnesty International's inquiries about these deaths.

After the attempted coup, about 275 people were convicted in secret and unfair trials held before special military courts. Over 50 people were sentenced to death and executed.

In April 1990, President Paul Biya announced that all those still held in connection with the 1984 coup attempt would be released. However, at least 61, possibly more, are believed to be still serving their sentences at Nkondengui Prison. At least 16 others who were acquitted or never tried remain in detention. Of those held in connection with the 1984 coup attempt, 26 are known to have died in prison.

Conditions at Nkondengui Prison are known to be harsh. Many prisoners have died there in recent years from malnutrition, disease and medical neglect. At times during 1987 and 1988, as many as four or five prisoners are said to have died in the prison each day. For two months in late 1989, political prisoners are also said to have been put on a diet of maize gruel and salted water. However, due to their isolation from other prisoners and the outside world, it is difficult to confirm such reports.

In 1986, Cameroon acceded to the United Nations Convention Against Torture and other Cruel, Inhuman and Degrading Treatment or Punishment. In 1989, the year Captain Madam Dogo died, Cameroon ratified the African Charter on Human and Peoples' Rights. Under Cameroonian and international law, the allegations of torture against Captain Dogo and others in Nkondengui Prison should be fully investigated. Those responsible for torture or ill-treatment of prisoners should be brought to justice.

0082

WANG XIZHE PEOPLE'S REPUBLIC OF CHINA

Wang Xizhe was jailed by the Chinese authorities nine years ago. He was sentenced to 14 years' imprisonment for belonging to a "*counter-revolutionary group*" and for his involvement in "*counter-revolutionary propaganda and incitement*".

Wang Xizhe was a political activist in China's *Democracy Movement* in the late 1970s. He edited unofficial journals critical of official policies. Although critical, they called for democratic reform under the leadership of the Communist Party.

Wang Xizhe first came to prominence as one of three co-authors of a huge wall newspaper which appeared in Guangzhou City in November 1974. Almost 100 metres long, the poster attracted attention in China and around the world. By March 1977 the three authors, including Wang Xizhe, had been arrested and jailed. They were released in January 1979.

In November 1979 another journal editor, Liu Qing, was arrested for publishing the trial transcripts of Wei Jingsheng, a political prisoner who had been sentenced to 15 years in jail. In response, Wang Xizhe wrote an "open letter" to the Chinese authorities criticizing the arrest of Liu Qing and defending the constitutional right to publish trial transcripts.

After Liu Qing was arrested the authorities announced that all journals must have a recognized organization to accept responsibility for them. In response, Wang Xizhe and others formed the *National Association of Democratic Journals.*

On 20 April 1981 Wang Xizhe was arrested at his workplace, a factory in Guangzhou. The police also seized more than 300 of his documents. He was brought to trial on 28 May 1982. The charges against him were derived from his "open letter", articles he had written and his association with another activist, Xu Wenli. The authorities were later to jail Xu Wenli because they said he was the leader of a "*counter-revolutionary*" group aimed at "*destroying the one-party dictatorship*".

At first Wang Xizhe's jail sentence was spent labouring in a workshop in a prison camp in Guangdong province. As a political prisoner, he was later segregated from other inmates. His family were refused permission to see him before the trial; his wife is now allowed to see him twice a year. The visits are supervised, no longer than 45 minutes, and they are forbidden to talk about why he is in jail.

The 1989 student demonstrations in Tiananmen Square, Beijing, did not mark the beginning of the *Democracy Movement* in China. Neither did it mark the beginning of the repression of people who call for political change. Wang Xizhe is just one of many who have been imprisoned since the late 1970s because of their non-violent political activities.

0083

ALIRIO DE JESÚS PEDRAZA BECERRA — COLOMBIA

Alirio de Jesús Pedraza Becerra, a lawyer and human rights worker, was last seen on the night of 4 July 1990. Eye-witnesses watched eight men in plain clothes, with automatic guns and rifles, seize Dr Pedraza at about 10pm as he was leaving a baker's shop in the *"La Campiña"* shopping centre in Bogatá's Suba district.

Dr Pedraza was an active member of the Political Prisoners Solidarity Committee (CSPP) and had just participated in one of their meetings when he was abducted. Now he has "disappeared", as have others who work for human rights in Colombia.

At the time of his "disappearance" he was working on behalf of a number of trade unionists in Cali, a large city in the southwest of the country. His clients were charged with belonging to a guerrilla organization. Dr Pedraza was particularly concerned because they said they had been tortured while in detention by soldiers of the army's 3rd Brigade in Cali. The charges against the trade unionists were dropped but Dr Pedraza was pursuing inquiries about the accusations of torture when he "disappeared".

Those who seek to protect human rights in Colombia are frequently at risk. Dr Daniel Libreros Caicedo was another lawyer who worked on the case of the trade unionists in Cali. He was stopped from boarding a plane at Cali's airport by 3rd Brigade soldiers who detained him for several days. He later told friends that he was ill-treated during his detention.

Other members of the Political Prisoners Solidarity Committee have received death threats. Three weeks after Dr Pedraza's "disappearance", an active member of the CSPP received an anonymous death threat. It was in the form of an invitation to her own funeral. Another woman, a committed human rights worker in Medellín, received a phone call telling her that she would suffer the same fate as Dr Pedraza if she did not stop working on behalf of prisoners.

Dr Pedraza's wife and seven-year-old son fear that he may be dead. They do not know whether they will ever see him again. Families of the "disappeared" often suffer years of uncertainty, not knowing whether the victims are alive or dead.

Despite such pressures, the Political Prisoners Solidarity Committee and other human rights organizations continue to work for those whose rights are threatened.

0084

ESTEBAN GONZALEZ GONZALEZ — CUBA

In July 1990 Esteban González González was sentenced to seven years in jail after a Cuban court found him guilty of "rebellion". The charge was based on his membership of an illegal political party, the *Movement for Democratic Integration* (MID).

On the night of 23 September 1989 security agents arrived at Esteban González's house. By 3am they had searched the house and said that they had found the *"illegal and counter-revolutionary"* documents which were later used in evidence against him. He was arrested and taken to State Security Headquarters. The next day six others, also said to be members of the MID, were arrested.

Esteban González is the founder and leader of the MID which advocates political reform in Cuba. Its demands include elections for a multi-party political system. This challenges the position of the Cuban Communist Party, the only legal political party. The MID also calls for respect for human rights. It explicitly rejects the use of violence and has declared, *"We prohibit and repudiate any terrorist activity among our members"*.

The seven MID members were held for several months without access to defence lawyers, and were not tried until 20 June 1990. The charge of "rebellion" states, among other things, that *"anyone who attempts to change the economic, political and social regime shall be liable to between seven and 15 years in jail"*. Esteban González was sentenced to seven years' imprisonment, one MID member was sentenced to three years' house arrest for health reasons, and the others to between three and six years' imprisonment. The imprisoned men are believed to be held in Combinado del Este Prison in Havana.

Esteban González, now 60 years old, was a mathematics teacher at a pre-university night school and a member of the unofficial *Cuban Commission of Human Rights and National Reconciliation*. He also set up a prisoners' support group called the *Cuban Pro-Amnesty Group* (not connected with Amnesty International). This group seeks an amnesty for all political prisoners in Cuba and calls for the death penalty to be abolished.

Esteban González had been in trouble with the Cuban authorities before, earlier in the year. He and others were planning to hold a demonstration when Soviet President Gorbachev visited Cuba, calling on him to support their work, but before he arrived they were arrested. After being held for three days, they were released with written warnings telling them that if they did not stop their "counter-revolutionary activities", other measures would be taken against them.

To criticize the way your country is run should not be an offence. Esteban González and the six other men detained, did not call for violence in support of their views. They are detained because they wanted political choice and free elections.

0085

FEBE ELÍSABETH VELÁSQUEZ EL SALVADOR

On 25 October 1989 a journalist asked Febe Elísabeth Velásquez if she was frightened of being killed because of her work as a trade unionist in El Salvador. She replied that she didn't want to die, but had to be prepared for attacks on her life. Six days later, she was killed by a bomb which destroyed the union headquarters where she worked. Nine others died in the blast.

Febe Velásquez first experienced the dangers of being a trade unionist in El Salvador when she was 19 years old. In 1985 she was a union official in the factory where she worked. During that year she was detained and tortured by the security forces. There was a public outcry in El Salvador and Febe Velásquez became known as a woman who would stand up for the rights of working people.

She later became the secretary-general of FENASTRAS - the *National Federation of Salvadorean Workers.* Over the past 10 years, FENASTRAS has often been referred to by official government sources as a terrorist front organization for the armed opposition group, FMLN - the *Farabundo Marti Front for National Liberation.* FENASTRAS is a legally recognised organization which denies such accusations. This did not stop attacks on FENASTRAS. In 1989 alone their office was bombed three times and repeatedly raided by security forces.

In August 1990 Sara Cristina Chan-Chan Medina, a photographer working with FENASTRAS, was seen being arrested by members of the Air Force. She has not been seen since and the authorities deny holding her - she has "disappeared". In September 1989, 64 trade unionists and supporters were arrested during a FENASTRAS demonstration. Many detained by the police say they were tortured.

Worse was to come. On 31 October 1990 the leaders of FENASTRAS were meeting in their offices in San Salvador when a bomb exploded. Ten people including Febe Velásquez died and thirty were wounded. The government claimed the bomb exploded inside the office and therefore must have belonged to the organization. Witnesses, however, say that it was placed by two unknown individuals just inside the perimeter wall surrounding the office.

Human rights workers who investigated the killings concluded that the attack was the work of individuals linked to the military or security forces. They also believe that the bombing may have been in retaliation for an FMLN mortar attack on the Armed Forces Headquarters the previous day.

Despite assurances from President Cristiani that the attack would be investigated exhaustively, little progress has been made. The government has blamed the lack of progress on FENASTRAS's unwillingness to assist in investigations. However, FENASTRAS and human rights organizations have called for those responsible to be brought to justice ever since the attack took place. They have also repeatedly asked the government to make public the results of a preliminary investigation carried out by the governmental Special Investigative Unit over a year ago.

0086

MULUGETTA MOSISSA ETHIOPIA

Mulugetta Mosissa and his pregnant wife, Namat Issa, were imprisoned without trial 10 years ago. In 1989 Namat Issa and her son, who was born in prison, were released. Mulugetta Mosissa is still in prison.

He is held in Ethiopia's main torture centre in the capital, Addis Ababa. It is known as the "third police station", or *Maekelawi* in the Amharic language.

Mulugetta Mosissa and his family were arrested in February 1980 with hundreds of other members of the Oromo ethnic group. They were apparently suspected of links with the Oromo Liberation Front (OLF), an armed opposition group, but no evidence of their involvement has ever been produced. Mulugetta Mosissa has not been charged or tried for any offence.

Mulugetta Mosissa, now aged about 46, is an economics graduate of the National University of Addis Ababa. At the time of his arrest in 1980 he was a senior official of the Ethiopian Grain Board. His wife was an official in the Ministry of Foreign Affairs.

The authorities gave no explanation for their arrests. Neither did they explain why they arrested other Oromo people, including the Minister for Law and Justice, although it was probably because they were suspected of links with the OLF. The OLF advocates independence for the Oromo people, and has mounted armed opposition to government forces in parts of west and east Ethiopia.

Many of the Oromos detained in 1980 were released in September 1989, the 15th anniversary of the revolution which overthrew Emperor Haile Salassie's government. Those released included Mulugetta Mosissa's wife, and their son, Amonsissa, who spent the first nine years of his life in prison with his mother.

The Ethiopian authorities have given no reason why Mulugetta Mossisa was detained, nor why he was not released with other Oromo prisoners in 1989. Several other Oromo political prisoners remain in detention, untried, in Addis Ababa.

Mulugetta Mosissa was severely tortured in the first months of his detention. Conditions in the *Maekelawi* are much harsher than in the Central Prison, where his wife and son were kept for the nine years of their captivity. During that time they were never allowed to meet.

Mulugetta Mosissa has been in jail for over 10 years. He has had no trial. He is apparently in jail because he is an Oromo who held a prominent position in government. He should be released without further delay.

0087

JOAQUÍN ELEMA BORINGUE — EQUATORIAL GUINEA

In September 1988, Joaquín Elema Boringue, a former army sergeant, was sentenced to death for attempting to assassinate the President of Equatorial Guinea. He was sentenced by five soldiers appointed as judges for the three-day trial. The only evidence of guilt was his own "confession", made after torture, and a plan of the Presidential Palace which he had drawn two years previously, on the orders of a senior officer.

Joaquín Elema Boringue was arrested with about 40 others suspected to be supporters of an opposition party based outside the country. Equatorial Guinea is officially a one-party state.

Joaquín Elema Boringue had no access to a lawyer until a few hours before his trial. At the trial he retracted his confession and told of the torture that had made him sign a piece of paper without even reading it. When the plan of the Presidential Palace was produced in court, Joaquín Elema Boringue pointed out that a superior officer had ordered him to draw it in 1986. The drawing was not found when Joaquín Elema Boringue was arrested, it appears that it had merely been taken from military files and produced in court.

Joaquín Elema Boringue was tried with Francisco Bonifacio Mbá Nguema, who was also charged with attempting to kill the President. The evidence to support the charge against Francisco Bonifacio Mbá Nguema was that he was found in possession of the Frederick Forsyth novel, *"The Dogs of War"*, which is a novel about a coup in an African state, often said to refer to Equatorial Guinea. He was also said to have planned to place a bomb aimed at the President. No evidence of any bombs or plans for attacks were produced in court. Nevertheless, the two men were found guilty of attempting to kill the President.

Another man arrested at the same time was later released. However, he did not escape the torture subjected upon Joaquín Elema Boringue and others, which he described as follows:

> *"With a stick placed between knees and elbows they hang you up. They ill-treat the bare parts of your body, most of all the feet. They also introduce your head in a bucket of water mixed with detergent. Your head remains there until you lose consciousness and swallow the dirty water."*

He also describes whippings, electric shocks applied to the genitals and prisoners being crushed under sacks of cement which their interrogators walked on.

The death sentences were commuted eventually to 20 years' imprisonment. Joaquín Elema Boringue and five others are still in prison, sentenced after blatantly unfair trials. They are prisoners of conscience, they should be freed immediately.

0088

ANDREAS CHRISTODOULOU GREECE

Andreas Christodoulou's religious convictions will not allow him to perform military service. He is in jail today because of those convictions.

Military service is compulsory for all fit, young men in Greece. The Greek authorities do not provide them with the option of serving their country in non-military ways. Their only choice is between the military for 15-21 months, unarmed military service for twice as long, or prison for three years.

In November 1989 Andreas Christodoulou had to choose between joining the military or being tried by a Military Court Martial. He chose to stand by his convictions.

He was tried before a Military Court Martial in Athens in November 1989. At the trial he was sentenced to four years in jail.

Andreas Christodoulou was born in Hanover, Federal Republic of Germany, in 1970. At the age of six he returned with his parents to Greece. He has a sister, Angeliki aged 18 and a brother Giorgos, 26. As a result of a severe illness when he was a baby Georgios is now cared for in a special institution. The Christodoulou family have had financial problems since Andreas was imprisoned, as he had previously helped them with money for his brother's care.

Before his imprisonment Andreas Christodoulou had worked as a mechanical engineer in an industrial plant for two years. Later, he became an assistant accountant.

His unwillingness to join the military was because of his religious beliefs. He is a member of the Jehovah's Witness religious sect which was founded in the USA in 1872. There are over 400 Jehovah Witnesses imprisoned in Greece for their refusal to serve in the military. Most are serving four year sentences, which are usually reduced to three years.

The United Nations Commission on Human Rights has recognized conscientious objection to military service as "a legitimate exercise of the right of freedom of thought, conscience and religion" and has called on governments to introduce alternative service for conscientious objectors, which should be "of a non-combatant or civilian character, in the public interest and not of a punitive nature".

Andreas Christodoulou doesn't have to be in jail. If the Greek authorities offered a civilian alternative to military service he could be benefiting society rather than being isolated from it.

0089

ARCHANA GUHA INDIA

The Indian police arrested Archana Guha in the middle of the night on 17 July 1974. She was then the headmistress of a Junior High School. She was arrested in place of her brother whom the police believed to be involved in a left-wing armed opposition group - the *Naxalites*. Archana Guha was taken to the Calcutta Police Headquarters where she says she was tortured over the next 27 days. She later described how five policemen tied her hands and feet and slung her from a pole. Her feet were beaten, her hips were kicked and her feet were burned with cigarettes. She was threatened with rape and told that her family would also be tortured if she did not cooperate.

She was never charged or brought to trial. Nor was she brought before a magistrate within 24 hours of arrest, as Indian law requires. Nevertheless, she remained in jail under the Maintenance of Internal Security Act for three years. She was released in May 1977. The torture she had suffered three years earlier caused paralysis of her legs and she left jail in a wheelchair.

Soon after her release Archana Guha began court proceedings to bring her torturers to justice. She had to be carried into court to identify the officer in charge of her investigation and the four other police officers who had tortured her.

Thirteen years later the officers have still not been brought to justice. Two of the five accused are now said to be dead. Another cannot be traced. The officer in charge, who has since been promoted, has used every legal avenue to stay out of the courts. Although some delay was caused by Archana Guha's travel abroad for medical treatment, the main cause was delaying tactics used by the police officer's lawyers. Legal proceedings were halted for more than two years because the accused police officers claimed that Archana Guha's lawyers should be barred from defending her. Their case was rejected by the Supreme Court.

Even though she had still not been able to give evidence in court, the Calcutta High Court quashed her case in 1988 on the grounds that it had then exceeded the time limit on criminal cases - seven years. However, an appeal judge re-opened her case in March 1990 on the grounds that those accused of the torture had

"at every stage taken steps which prolonged and intended to frustrate the proceedings".

Since then a further array of applications for "stay orders" has meant that the police officers Archana Guha says tortured her have still not been brought to trial. Nor have those still in the police force been suspended from their duties.

0090

DR THOMAS WAINGGAI INDONESIA

Dr Thomas Wainggai, 53, lived in Irian Jaya, a province of Indonesia he believes should be independent. In early September 1989 he was sent to prison for 20 years for this belief. His appeal against sentence was rejected. Thirty six others, including his Japanese-born wife Teruko, were sentenced to terms of between two and eight years in jail for sharing his belief that Irian Jaya should be independent.

The court found Dr Wainggai guilty of subversion. His crimes were said to include *"harbouring feelings of antipathy towards the Indonesian State, conceiving the idea of a West Melanesian State and gathering people to implement his plan."* Not even the Indonesian Government suggested that Dr Wainggai had used or advocated violence in support of his views. In fact, one month before he was sentenced, the regional military commander in Irian Jaya said that Dr Wainggai's group was *"...not an armed movement. It is really nothing more than a diplomatic group. He had got together a few people to act as functionaries for a new state, but he hadn't got to making any laws."*

Dr Wainggai was arrested on 14 December 1988 at a public ceremony which he had organized to proclaim Irian Jaya the independent state of "West Melanesia". Beforehand he had written to the United Nations and over a dozen national governments setting out his case for independence. At the ceremony some 60 people, sang songs, said prayers and a flag was unfurled. However, military trucks arrived before the ceremony was over. The soldiers detained all those present, forced them onto the trucks and drove them to a military camp for interrogation.

About half the people detained were later released without charge. Thirty-seven were arrested and most were charged with subversion - a crime punishable by death. A woman who had helped to sew the flag used in the ceremony was sentenced to two years in jail.

Crowds of several hundred people tried to attend the public hearings of Dr Wainggai's trial. The authorities reacted by shifting the trial to a military base, and trying to keep the trial secret. The trial was not reported in the Indonesian press and a foreign journalist was asked to leave Irian Jaya after writing about the case. At one hearing, attended by hundreds of people, soldiers fired their weapons in the air to disperse the crowd. After the trial, the judges are said to have destroyed some of the most important evidence, including the text of the constitution for the proposed new state, and letters asking for the support of UN member states. The trial of Teruko Wainggai, a Japanese national, was conducted entirely in Indonesian, a language she does not understand well.

International human rights conventions guarantee the right of all to express their beliefs peacefuly. Dr Wainggai was arrested for his beliefs. He did not call for the use of violence. He has been in prison since December 1988 and faces another 17 years in jail.

0091

TRIFA SA'ID MUHAMMAD   IRAQ

Trifa Sa'id Muhammad was 14 years-old when the Iraqi authorities tried to poison her to death.

Since 1980, there have been a number of reports about the use of poison by the Iraqi authorities on political opponents. There has been much news about the chemical bombing of whole villages of Kurdish civilians, but little is known about how often the poisoning of individuals is carried out.

It is known, however, that Trifa was poisoned in November 1987. She is still sick as a result. At the time she lived in the town of Marga in the Iraqi province of Sulaimaniya. On the day she was poisoned she was at the house of a member of the *Patriotic Union of Kurdistan*, a banned movement in conflict with the Iraqi authorities.

During a meal, an agent of the Iraqi security forces laced a yoghurt drink with the rat poison, thallium. Ten people at the meal were poisoned. Three of the victims died within hours of drinking the yoghurt. One of the dead was Trifa's 60 year-old grandmother.

The seven survivors suffered a prolonged range of symptoms including vomiting, fever, neurological disorders and loss of hair. Because of poor transport and bad weather, Trifa was not able to seek medical help for three months. The roads were bad or were blocked by snow. When she was finally treated, Trifa said:

> *"I didn't know I was poisoned as well. After three days my hair began to fall and at the same time I felt weakness in my legs and I walked as if I were drunk. After seven days all my hair was lost and when I walked the problems in my knees were so bad that I fell after a few steps."*

Isolated attacks on small groups of Kurds by Iraqi authorities were combined with massive operations against Kurdish communities throughout Iraq. They happened immediately after a ceasefire was declared in the Iran-Iraq war in August 1988. 57,000 Kurds living in Iraq crossed the border into Turkey. Many, when questioned, gave accounts of chemical and armed attacks which had killed their friends and relatives. The total number of isolated killings using poison may never be known.

0092

NASRIN RASOOLI IRAN

Nasrin Rasooli was killed by the Iranian authorities because she was a supporter of a political organization which opposed the government. She was one of thousands of people who suffered a similar fate soon after the end of the Iran-Iraq war in 1988.

Nasrin Rasooli was born in 1958 and was a physics graduate. She was arrested in 1981 for supporting the *People's Mojahedine Organization of Iran*, before it became involved in armed opposition to the Iranian authorities. At the time of Nasrin Rasooli's arrest, it was a legally recognized political organization.

In Iran in the early 1980s, people suspected of political opposition were arrested in their thousands, often arbitrarily. Torture was systematic, prisons were overcrowded and insanitary. After two years in detention, Nasrin Rasooli became mentally ill. By 1986 her condition had deteriorated seriously, and she was released. Apparently, she was neither charged or tried.

The war between Iran and Iraq ended in August 1988. With an end to hostilities the Iranian authorities turned their attention to the domestic scene, executing thousands of political prisoners. Because the executions were carried out in secret, it is impossible to say exactly how many people were killed. Horrifying pictures were smuggled out of the country showing half-buried bodies in shallow mass graves.

The names are known of over 2,500 people who are said to have been executed between July 1988 and January 1989. Many were prisoners who had been sentenced to prison terms after unfair trials, or had been detained for years without charge or trial. Others, like Nasrin Rasooli, were former prisoners who were rounded up and executed, apparently without any charge or trial.

The Iranian authorities have never admitted that executions took place on this scale. Many relatives still do not know if missing members of their families were among those killed, or do not know where the bodies are buried.

Public attention has moved away from these mass executions, but the Iranian authorities must not be allowed to remain silent about such gross violations of the right to life. The fate of Nasrin Rasooli should be made known.

0093

'ABD AL-RA'UF GHABIN

ISRAEL AND THE OCCUPIED TERRITORIES

'Abd al-Ra'uf Ghabin, a bookshop owner, was arrested by Israeli security forces on 30 August 1990, in the Beach Refugee Camp in the Gaza Strip. He was taken to the interrogation wing of the Gaza prison where he was apparently tortured.

The reason for his detention was that the security forces believed him to be a member of an outlawed political organization, the *Popular Front for the Liberation of Palestine (PFLP)*, a faction of the *Palestine Liberation Organization.* He was also accused of distributing leaflets and is currently held in administrative detention, without charge or trial.

After 18 days in detention he was brought before a judge, but there was no lawyer present. His detention was extended by another 70 days. It wasn't until 24 September 1990 that he saw a lawyer. Two days later, he made a signed statement to another lawyer. In that statement he said:

> *"I was interrogated every day, Saturdays excepted, starting on 30 August 1990 until 18 September 1990...During the interrogation I was beaten 4 to 6 times - on my head, abdomen, genitals - usually with a fist."*

He also said that during the same period he was only allowed to sleep on Friday and Saturday nights, and for one other period of two hours. The rest of the week he was ordered to sit on a chair. Except for when he ate or slept, his hands were handcuffed behind his back. On one occasion he says he was told that he was to be allowed some extra sleep in a cell:

> *"But when I entered the cell, a soldier did not let me sleep and told me to sit up."*

Throughout his interrogation, 'Abd al-Ra'uf Ghabin denied that he was a member of the *PFLP* or that he had distributed any leaflets. His lawyer has complained about his alleged torture to the Israeli authorities.

In October 1990, 'Abd al-Ra'uf Ghabin was transferred to Ramallah prison on the West Bank, then to Ashkelon prison inside Israel, and finally back to Gaza. On 22 October he was issued with a six-month administrative detention order and was transferred to the Ketziot detention centre in southern Israel where he remains. On 27 December 1990 he appealed against the order. The judge confirmed the order, but reduced it by approximately six weeks and ordered that he be released on 22 February 1991.

'Abd al-Ra'uf Ghabin had been detained for five weeks by the Israeli authorities two years earlier, seemingly for his part in the filming of a television documentary about the Gaza Strip.

Under Israeli law, lawyers can be prevented from visiting detainees for up to 18 days. In Amnesty Internatioal's (AI) experience, such prolonged periods of incommunicado detention can facilitate torture or ill-treatment. AI believes that all detainees should be given prompt access to lawyers, relatives and independent doctors.

0094

'ALI MUHAMMAD AL-QAJIJI LIBYA

'Ali Muhammad al-Qajiji was sentenced to spend his life in prison because he was said to be a member of a political organization banned in Libya. He has been in jail since 1973. He was first sentenced to 15 years in jail, later increased to life imprisonment. In November 1974 Colonel Mu'ammar al-Gaddafi, the country's leader, said in a speech that people like 'Ali Muhammad al-Qajiji would stay in jail,

"until they are well again ... and this may take 10, 20 or even 50 years".

'Ali Muhammad al Qajiji has now spent 18 years in jail and there is no sign that he will be released in the near future.

'Ali Muhammad al-Qajiji was a student when he was arrested in April 1973, soon after the declaration of the "Popular Revolution" which introduced popular committees as the country's primary administrative units. Between 300 and 400 people were arrested for alleged membership of illegal political parties at that time. After 10 months of investigations the majority of those arrested were released. Those still in jail include people like 'Ali Muhammad al-Qajiji who were said to be members of the *Islamic Liberation Party (ILP).* They were accused of plotting to overthrow the government.

There was no suggestion at their trials that they believed in the use of violence in support of their cause.

Membership of an illegal organization is an offence punishable by death under two laws: Law 71 of 1972 and Law 80 of 1975. At least four ILP members arrested with 'Ali Muhammad al-Qajiji have since been executed in Libya.

In March 1988 Colonel Mu'ammar al-Gaddafi made world news when he drove a tractor through the walls of a jail in Tripoli and officially set free 400 political prisoners. Amnesty International welcomed these releases and called for the release of all prisoners of conscience. However, 'Ali Muhammad al-Qajiji and others remained in prison. Amnesty International believes that about 500 political prisoners, including prisoners of conscience such as 'Ali Muhammad al-Qajiji, are currently held. How much longer must 'Ali Muhammad al-Qajiji and all the prisoners of conscience remain in Libyan jails?

0095

MAMADOU BÂ MAURITANIA

Twelve-year-old Mamadou Bâ and his younger brother, Abdoulaye, were looking after the family's sheep and goats when members of the Mauritanian National Guard slit their throats and left them to die. They had been tending their animals in the valley of the Senegal river, which marks the border between Mauritania and Senegal. The sole reason for their deaths seems to be the colour of their skin and the language they spoke.

These killings, in June 1989, were connected with a Mauritanian policy of forcing black Mauritanians to move to Senegal. This policy began in April 1989 when inter-communal violence erupted in both Senegal and Mauritania. In Mauritania both Senegalese and black Africans, including black Mauritanians, were also being targeted for attacks and killings.

Thousands of Senegalese living in Mauritania returned to Senegal. A similarly large number of Mauritanians returned from Senegal to Mauritania as a result of a repatriation program agreed between the two governments.

By the end of April, arrests were made in Senegal of some of those involved in the killings, and much of the violence there ended. In Mauritania, however, few arrests were made. With fewer Senegalese in the country, the violence became increasingly targetted at black Mauritanians, particularly at members of one ethnic group, known locally as the *"Hal-Pulaar"* (Fula speakers), or elsewhere as the *Peul* or *Fula*. What had begun as mob violence increasingly developed into state security force violence.

In May 1989 the National Guard carried out mass expulsions of black Mauritanians to Senegal. Thousands of people were expelled, after being detained for weeks or months. Some were tortured while in detention. Others, like Mamadou Bâ and his brother, were killed out of hand by the security forces.

Witnesses saw units of the Mauritanian security forces surrounding villages of black Mauritanians in the Senegal river valley and forcing the villagers into boats across the river, having taken their land and cattle. Farmers and cattle-herders who resisted were either arrested of killed.

Like many young boys in this area, Mamadou and Abdoulaye Bâ drove their animals into the bush. They were pursued there and killed by the National Guard. Since then, no investigations of their killings or hundreds of similar incidents have taken place. Mauritanian officials justify expulsions by saying that most black Mauritanians are, in fact, Senegalese. However, there are many reports of National Guardsmen ripping up official identity cards of black Mauritanians. Whatever their nationality, there can be no justification for any government to allow the torture, detention and killing of people just because of the colour of their skin, or the language they speak.

0096

VERA CHIRWA MALAWI

Vera Chirwa has been in jail since 1981 because she thinks Malawi should be governed differently. Her husband, Orton Chirwa is imprisoned for the same crime. For the first two years of their imprisonment their son, Fumbani, was also jailed without charge or trial.

Vera and Orton Chirwa were originally sentenced to death for the crime of treason. After an international outcry about the unfairness of their trial, the Life-President of Malawi, Dr Hastings Kamuzu Banda, commuted these sentences to life imprisonment. However, on at least one occasion he has said that he was too lenient on the Chirwas and has suggested that they should be executed. In 1991 they are serving their 10th year in prison.

Vera Chirwa, like her husband, had trained as a lawyer in Britain in the 1950s. They both played a leading role in the campaign for Malawi's independence in 1964. Orton Chirwa was a founder and the first President of the Malawi Congress Party, which has ruled Malawi since independence. When Dr Banda returned to Malawi in 1960 after years of political exile, Orton Chirwa stood down for him. Orton Chirwa continued, however, to play a leading role in the party and after the 1961 elections he held many political positions. By the time of independence from Britain in 1964, he was a leading cabinet minister in the government.

Within weeks of independence there was a major dispute about domestic and foreign policy which resulted in the resignation or dismissal of six leading cabinet ministers, including Orton Chirwa. All six went into exile abroad. Vera and Orton Chirwa went to Tanzania with their son, Fumbani.

They lived there for 17 years. While there, Vera Chirwa was a visiting lecturer in law at the University of Zambia in Lusaka. Orton Chirwa formed a new political party, the Malawi Freedom Movement, in exile. Life-President Banda has regularly issued threats against Malawian politicians in exile.

In January 1982 *Malawi Radio* announced that Vera and Orton Chirwa, and their son, Fumbani, had been arrested on 24 December 1981. Accounts of their arrest differ. The authorities say they entered the country in secret in order to overthrow the government. The Chirwas say they were visiting sick relatives in eastern Zambia when they were forcibly abducted by Malawi security officials and taken into Malawi.

In May 1983 Vera and Orton Chirwa finally came to trial. They were convicted of treason. They were tried before a traditional court. An appeal court later agreed that their first trial was, among other things "wrong in law". However, for unstated reasons, the appeal court upheld the death sentence on both Vera and Orton Chirwa. They were unfairly tried, are in jail for the expression of non-violent political beliefs and should be set free immediately.

0097

JOSÉ RAMÓN GARCÍA GÓMEZ MEXICO

José Ramón García left his home for a political meeting on 16 December 1988 but never arrived. Since then, his whereabouts remain unknown.

José Ramón García was a leading member of the Workers' Revolutionary Party in Mexico at the time of his "disappearance" and had been active in a campaign publicizing claims of electoral fraud in the July 1988 presidential elections. He was said to have been under investigation by the state government authorities for his political activities. A vehicle, believed to belong to the security forces, was seen by witnesses outside his home in Cuautla, in the state of Morelos, shortly before his "disappearance".

His "disappearance" was the first to occur under the current administration of President Carlos Salinas de Gortari, who took office in July 1988. President Salinas set up a commission of inquiry and appointed a special prosecutor to investigate the case. However, legal representatives for the family complained that the local police were reluctant to carry out a proper inquiry. The special prosecutor himself was reported to have focused his investigations on the theory that José Ramón García staged his own abduction.

At least 500 "disappearances" were reported in Mexico during the 1970s and 1980s. In spite of repeated calls for a full investigation into the circumstances surrounding their "disappearance" successive governments have failed to account for the fate of the victims or bring those responsible to justice.

At least six "disappearances" have been reported since José Ramón García's "disappearance" in 1988.

0098

MOHAMED SRIFI MOROCCO

The authorities produced left-wing leaflets and a duplicating machine in court as evidence that Mohamed Srifi and over 170 others accused with him wanted to overthrow the Moroccan monarchy.

Mohamed Srifi was sentenced to 30 years jail although there was no convincing evidence that he believed in the violent overthrow of the authorities. He simply believed that Morocco should have a different political structure.

Mohamed Srifi was born in Tangiers in 1952. At the time of his arrest in 1974 he was studying Spanish literature at the Faculté des Lettres at Rabat University. He was also a member of *Ila'l-Amam ("Forward")*, a Marxist organization which is outlawed in Morocco.

Mohamed Srifi went into hiding to avoid arrest in 1972. For two years, he and other members of *Ila'l-Aman* produced and distributed leaflets which called for the creation of a people's republic of Morocco.

In November 1974 Mohamed Srifi was arrested and taken to the Derb Moulay Cherif detention centre in Casablanca. He remained in the detention centre for over a year without charge or trial. During that time he was tortured.

In January 1977 he was finally brought to trial. The prosecution argued that by calling for a people's republic he was calling for the violent overthrow of the Moroccan monarchy. The leaflets and duplicating machine were produced as evidence against him. An Amnesty International observer at the trial said there was no evidence produced which backed the charges that Mohamed Srifi or any of the others had ever suggested using violence. The trial was blatantly unfair. Defence lawyers were intimidated and not allowed to talk to defendants in court during the hearings. Neither did the judge allow Mohamed Srifi to describe the torture he suffered while in the Derb Moulay Cherif.

It can be dangerous for defendants to complain about the fairness of their trials in Morocco. Mohamed Srifi and those tried with him received an extra two years' sentence because they protested in court about the fairness of their trial.

Mohamed Srifi's fiancée received a 5-year sentence at the same trial. From 1978 onward they were allowed to visit each other. Later they got permission to marry, but continued to serve their sentences apart. Mohamed Srifi is one of eight remaining prisoners of his group. The others were either released on expiry of their sentence or after an amnesty.

Mohamed Srifi is serving his sentence in the Kenitra Central Prison in Casablanca. His only crime was expressing his peaceful political views; he should be free.

0099

AUNG SAN SUU KYI MYANMAR

Aung San Suu Kyi is considered a political threat by the military government of Myanmar, formerly known as Burma. For this reason she has been confined to her own home since 19 July 1989.

Aung San Suu Kyi is a part of the political history of Myanmar. She is the daughter of Aung San, considered to be the father of Myanmar independence. She is also the General Secretary of the *National League for Democracy* (NLD).

The NLD is the largest legally recognised political party in Myanmar. It won more than 80% of the votes in the May 1990 elections. However, it is the military authorities, who staged a coup in September 1988, who hold power, and not the NLD. Before and during the military coup, hundreds of peaceful demonstrators were killed by security forces. Martial Law introduced shortly after the coup included laws banning "political gatherings".

Beginning in June 1989 the NLD and other opposition parties organized rallies in defiance of Martial Law. The NLD also held memorials for students killed by the military and rallies at which Aung San Suu Kyi called for non-violent resistance to Martial Law. She was joined in these calls by the NLD chairperson, a retired military officer, General Tin U.

General Tin U and Aung San Suu Kyi always insisted that the gatherings they organized should be non-violent. But their activities throughout June and early July 1989 were met by the military authorities with a wave of arrests.

On 19 July Aung San Suu Kyi and other party leaders called off a Martyrs' Day March planned for that day. There were reports of lines of troops blocking the route. Truck loads of more troops were said to be standing by. Aung San Suu Kyi was worried and called off the march because of:

> *"the very big troop presence and because we have heard that some hospitals have made preparation to receive extra patients".*

When Aung San Suu Kyi returned to her home she found 11 truck loads of troops outside her house. They remained there all night and all the next day. On 21 July 1989 a military government spokesperson confirmed that both General Tin U and Aung San Suu Kyi were under house arrest.

Despite her party's election victory in May 1990 Aung San Suu Kyi is still under house arrest. Contacts with her family are extremely limited. She has struggled peacefully against an oppressive military government which has often resorted to the use of violence. She should be set free and allowed to express her non-violent political views freely and to organize peaceful political assemblies.

0100

AUGUSTINE EKE NIGERIA

Augustine Eke was 14 years' old when he was arrested in 1984. In 1988, he was sentenced to death. He was convicted of taking part in an armed robbery. A senior legal official later said,

> "the whole trial was full of procedural irregularities and overt bias... the evidence of the identification of the dependants should have been summarily rejected by the tribunal as it was a complete sham".

A sham it may have been, but Augustine Eke and ten others sentenced to die at that trial are still on death row in Kirikiri prison near Lagos.

Augustine Eke's ordeal began as he was buying shoe laces. He and 12 others were identified by two men already in police custody. They were all arrested. Whilst awaiting trial, one of the others, a youth, died in prison. Apparently, he died because of poor prison conditions and lack of proper medical attention.

At the trial, the two main accused, the ones who had identified Augustine Eke and the others, claimed that they had been beaten and threatened by the police. They told the court that they had been forced into identifying the other defendants. Both men were subsequently deported to neighbouring Benin in an exchange of prisoners: it is believed that this may have taken place in May 1988, before sentence was passed.

The trial continued and Augustine Eke and the others were convicted almost entirely on the basis of the identification evidence, later described as a "sham". There were other irregularities: on one occasion one of the prosecution witnesses, a police officer, apparently changed his testimony after an unexplained and abrupt adjournment while he was giving evidence.

Cases of armed robbery are not tried in the ordinary courts in Nigeria. They are heard by the special Robbery and Firearms Tribunals from which there is no right of appeal. Anyone found guilty of taking part in an armed robbery, whether or not it resulted in death or injuries, must be sentenced to death. Since the reintroduction of these special courts in 1984 at least a thousand people are known to have been executed.

A hopeful sign for Augustine Eke and the others was when the Federal Minister of Justice assured Amnesty International that they would not be executed. Since then, however, the Military Governor of Lagos State announced in July 1990 that he would not commute the sentences. In December 1990 one of the 12, Mohammed Ibrahim, died in prison, apparently from pulmonary tuberculosis.

The death penalty is the ultimate cruel and degrading punishment. That it can irrevocably take away the lives of innocent people is just one of the many arguments against its use. A 14-year-old when arrested, Augustine Eke has been on death row for three years although the evidence against him was described as a "sham".

0101

FIDEL INTUSCA FERNANDEZ PERU

Fidel Intusca Fernandez has described how, during one week in August 1990, he found himself a victim both of an armed group and of the Peruvian authorities. He was abducted by one and tortured by the other.

Fidel Intusca is a miner in the San Juan de Lucanas mine in the Department of Ayacucho, Peru. On the evening of 2 August 1990 the mine was raided by a group of 30 armed men. Fidel Intusca later said that he presumed they were members of the *Sendero Luminoso*, "Shining Path", armed opposition group. Fidel Intusca and other workers in the mine were forced to load a lorry with explosives. The armed men then forced him to drive the lorry out of the mine area to make their escape. He was later set free and allowed to return to the mine in the lorry. However, his ordeal did not end there.

Four days later, on 6 August, he and another worker from the mine were told that they had to make a statement about the incident at the local military base at Puquio. They went to the base with two trade union officials and two representatives from the mining company. Fidel Intusca and his colleague made their statements and were allowed to leave.

The six men left the base at Puquio and started back to the mine. They had not gone far when, the men say, they were halted by hooded and armed soldiers. The soldiers wanted Fidel Intusca. The union officials, the company representatives and the other mine worker were apparently allowed to continue their journey back to the mine. Fidel Intusca was taken away, but later escaped.

At a press conference Fidel Intusca described how he had been taken back to a military base and tortured. He had been hung from the ceiling and beaten; submerged in water until he thought he was about to drown; and burned on the back and neck. He also told journalists that he had been told he was going to be killed.

Fidel Intusca's detention and torture has been denounced to the military and civilian authorities in Peru by local human rights organizations who have called upon the Peruvian authorities to make sure no harm comes to him or his family.

What happened to Fidel Intusca is an example of how ordinary people in Peru are "caught between two fires": at risk of serious human rights violations at the hands of the security forces, and of abuses such as torture and killings by armed opposition groups.

0102

MARIO RAÚL SCHAERER PRONO PARAGUAY

Mario Raúl Schaerer Prono died after being arrested by the Paraguayan police in April 1976. The authorities say he was killed in a "shoot-out". The evidence of eye-witnesses, however, supported reports that he was tortured to death.

Now that former President Stroessner is no longer in power in Paraguay, Mario Schaerer's family can finally ask the courts to prosecute those responsible for torturing Mario Schaerer to death. If there are convictions, it will help show that torturers can be brought to justice, even though many years have passed since their crimes.

On the night of 5 April 1976 security police surrounded Schaerer's house. He was inside with his wife Guillermina Kanonnikoff and a friend, Juan Carlos da Costa. The security police said they believed the three people in the house to be part of a fledgling armed opposition movement. The police moved in and opened fire. Juan Carlos da Costa was killed in the attack. Police authorities claimed that there was return of fire and that Mario Schaerer was mortally wounded at that time.

Mario Schaerer and his wife escaped before they were captured. They fled to the school where they both worked as teachers. They were looked after by Canadian nuns. The next morning, the priest who ran the school felt obliged to inform the police of the couple's whereabouts. When questioned later, both the nuns and the priest testified that when Mario Schaerer arrived his only injury was to his foot.

They were taken to the security police headquarters, *Departamento de Investigaciones, (DIP-C)*. Guillermina Kanonnikoff, who was pregnant, was pulled along the floor by her hair and forced to watch as her husband was beaten. The next morning she saw her husband being taken to another building in the centre. She then heard his screams. When she next saw him he was unable to stand unsupported and had injuries to his face.

The next time she saw him, he was being dragged into the officers' mess by two men in civilian clothes. She says that at that time he looked barely alive. At least two other prisoners at the centre saw Mario Schaerer alive that day. The next day, police authorities handed over Mario Schaerer's body to relatives. They were told that he had died as a result of wounds received in a "shoot-out".

Guillermina Kanonnikoff did not find out about her husband's death until four months later. She was told by the then Minister of Interior, Sabino Montanaro, that,

"it was necessary to kill Mario Schaerer because he was a danger to the peace and tranquillity which the country enjoyed..."

In April 1989 she began court proceedings in an attempt to bring to justice those responsible for her husband's torture and death. Senior officials in the Stroessner government such as Pastor Coronel, the head of the *DIP-C* and General Britez Borges, Chief of Police, were charged and placed in custody. At the end of 1990, those proceedings were continuing.

0103

MARIA NONNA SANTA CLARA PHILIPPINES

Maria Nonna Santa Clara's family do not know where she is. They fear that they will never see her again.

On 26 April 1989 she "disappeared" with a colleague, Angelina Llenaresas. Both women worked at an Ecumenical Centre for Research and Development in Naga City in the middle of the Philippines. The centre services grassroots organizations in the region. Maria Nonna Santa Clara was a social worker and Angelina Llenaresas a voluntary worker at the centre.

Cases of "disappearance" have been increasing in the Philippines since late 1987. Many of the victims have been involved in a wide range of lawful non-governmental organizations. The military authorities have publicly accused these organizations of being "fronts" for the outlawed Communist Party of the Philippines and its armed wing, the New People's Army. However, they have produced no proof of these allegations and organizations such as the Ecumenical Centre for Research and Development vigorously deny them.

On the day they "disappeared" Maria Nonna Santa Clara and Angelina Llenaresas visited a woman in the village of Santa Cruz. She said later that when the two young women left her house, she noticed they were being followed by three men. Other local residents say that they later saw two women being accosted by men in plain clothes. Between 4.30 and 5pm that day, two church ministers saw a woman shouting for help from inside a military jeep as it drove past. When shown the photograph of Maria Nonna Santa Clara, they were certain that she was the woman in the jeep.

Maria Nonna Santa Clara's family made frantic enquiries at detention centres in the area, but were unable to find her. Nine days after her "disappearance" her family heard that two women had been taken to the headquarters of the Regional Command at Camp Bagong Ibalon in Legaspi City. They made the long trip to the camp only to be told that the military authorities knew nothing about their daughter. However, when they enquired at the Military Intelligence Group office inside the camp, a staff member said that two unknown women had recently been brought to the office.

Maria Nonna Santa Clara's family and others trying to help her are now in danger. They have received anonymous death threats thought to come from members of the military. Despite this, new witnesses have come forward to say they saw members of the Philippines military taking Maria Nonna Santa Clara and Angelina Llenaresas away in the jeep.

The military deny all knowledge of the whereabouts of Maria Nonna Santa Clara and Angelina Llenaresas. However, several witnesses have clearly identified individual military officers who were seen with both women after they "disappeared". The Government of the Philippines should conduct an immediate enquiry into the fate of two women who were simply trying to help their community.

0104

ZAHRA' HABIB MANSUR AL-NASSER SAUDI ARABIA

Zahra' Habib Mansur al-Nasser died in custody, apparently after having been tortured by the Saudi police. The torture is said to have happened after she was arrested for having a Shi'a prayer book and a picture of Ayatollah Khomeini.

Before her death, Zahra' al-Nasser lived with her husband in the village of Awjam in the Eastern Province of Saudi Arabia. In July 1989 she and her husband had travelled to the Sayyida Zainab Shrine in Damascus, Syria. The shrine is a Shi'a place of worship.

On 15 July, on their way home via Jordan, they were stopped and searched at the Saudi border check-point by police officers. The police found Zahra' al-Nasser with two holy objects - the book and the picture.

Zahra' al-Nasser and her husband were detained at the checkpoint for three days. She was in good health at the time of her arrest. On 18 July when her husband was released Zahra' al-Nasser's dead body was delivered to her family. It is said to have been severely bruised and to have borne marks of torture. The Saudi authorities provided no explanation for her death, and no official enquiry into its cause or circumstances is known to have been carried out.

Torture in Saudi Arabia is not uncommon. In the early days of detention the most common methods used are *falaqa*, beating on the soles of the feet, *tas hir*, sleep deprivation, *ta'liq*, hanging by the wrists and beatings all over the body.

Amnesty International called for a full and independent inquiry into Zahra' al Nasser's death. The Saudi authorities did not reply.

0105

Sékou Mary was alive when the Gambian authorities handed him over to the Senegalese security forces. Soon afterwards, his dead body was delivered to his home in the village of Kabiline. The people who saw Sékou Mary's body say he had been beaten to death.

Sékou Mary, known as Agnocoune, lived in Kabiline in southern Senegal with his two wives and 10 children. On 24 June 1990 he and two close relatives fled the village. They had heard that the security forces were coming to question them about other members of the family, who were said to be involved with armed government opponents fighting for the independence of southern Senegal's Casamance region.

It seems that Sékou Mary and the two others had good cause to be frightened. When the security forces arrived in the village they ill-treated several villagers and shot dead 45-year-old Famara Mary, a close relative of Sékou Mary.

Fearing for their lives, Sékou Mary and the two others fled across the border to The Gambia. On 26 September 1990, they were arrested together with seven others by the Gambian authorities and charged with entering the country without a permit. They were remanded to await trial in Banjul's Mile 2 Prison. However, no trial took place. On 12 October the 10 men were handed over to Gambian immigration officers at Jiboro. The Gambian authorities must have known these men could be in danger if they were returned to their own country. Nevertheless, they were taken to a quiet part of the border and forcibly expelled from The Gambia.

Sékou Mary was so frightened that he returned to The Gambia. On 23 October 1990 he was again arrested by Gambian authorities, and held for a short time in Brikama police station. Then he was summarily handed over to the Senegalese security forces, who took him to the gendarmerie station in the town of Diouloulou, where he was apparently beaten to death.

It is not known whether Sékou Mary had been involved with the armed rebels. The soldiers who sought to question him apparently believed that other relatives were involved, but not Sékou Mary.

Since 1982 advocates of independence or autonomy for the Casamance region in the south of Senegal have been in conflict with the Senegalese Government. Their organization, the *Mouvement des forces démocratiques de la Casamance*, (MFDC) the Movement of Casamance's Democratic Forces, which stresses Casamance's separate identity, has dramatically increased its armed activities against government forces since May 1990. In response, government forces are reported to have arrested many suspected MFDC supporters and have been accused of using torture and committing extrajudicial executions on an unprecedented level.

International law states that no asylum-seeker should be returned to a country where their life or freedom would be threatened on account of their race, religion, nationality, membership of a particular social group or political opinion. When the Gambian authorities handed over Sékou Mary to the Senegalese security forces they must have known that he was in danger. Yet they still chose to expel him.

0106

STANZA BOPAPE SOUTH AFRICA

Johannes Maisha "Stanza" Bopape "disappeared" after he and a collegue were arrested by security police on 9 June 1988. They were detained under Section 29a of the Internal Security Act, which allows the police to hold uncharged detainees indefinitely incommunicado and in solitary confinement for interrogation. Many political detainees have been tortured, in some cases resulting in death, while held under such legislation in South Africa. Both detainees were taken to the security police headquarters at John Vorster Square in Johannesburg.

Stanza Bopape was aged 28 at the time of his arrest. He was General Secretary of the local black Civic Association in Mamelodi Township near Pretoria and a staff member of the Community Resource and Information Centre (CRIC) in Johannesburg. CRIC had previously been the target of arson attacks and other CRIC staff had previously been detained for political reasons. Stanza Bopape had previously been detained for two weeks and allegedly tortured in October 1980, when he was a high school student. In 1985, he was detained without charge for six weeks and was held in custody again from August 1986 until June 1987, when charges then brought against him were dropped.

The police say Stanza Bopape escaped from a van four nights after his arrest while he was being taken under police guard from Johannesburg to Vereeniging, 60 kilometres away. They say the van had to stop because of a flat tyre, and that Stanza Bopape escaped while the police were changing a wheel.

Former detainees, human rights activists and others have questioned the police version of events. They note that Stanza Bopape apparently had three police guards when he allegedly escaped and that Section 29 prisoners are routinely handcuffed and kept in leg-irons while being transported. Further doubts were raised by the failure of the police to inform Stanza Bopape's family or lawyer until three weeks after his alleged escape, or to question his family or friends to see if they knew of his whereabouts. In fact, the police had told Stanza Bopape's lawyer on 17 June that he was still in detention, although when they announced his "escape" on 4 July, they said it had occurred on 12 June.

South Africa's Minister of Law and Order said in June 1990 that an *"intensive investigation"* into Stanza Bopape's "disappearance" was *"continuing unabated"*, but none of Stanza Bopape's relatives or friends say they have heard from him since his alleged escape, and he is not known to have arrived in any neighbouring country. Amnesty International remains concerned that Stanza Bopape may have died or been killed in security police detention and that this was covered up by those responsible.

0107

KIM SONG-MAN SOUTH KOREA

"I am a person who wishes the independence of our nation and democracy. I think that this ideal can be realized in a socialistic country. I was interrogated and tortured mercilessly at the Agency for National Security Planning. During the interrogation and torture I was even forced to write a suicide letter addressed to my parents in order to disguise my possible death by suicide. The press widely published my forced confession as though it was true. I only long for the day we can enjoy our independence from under the slavish submission to a foreign power. Even if all the world does not believe me I know that God knows the truth".

For expressing such views, Kim Song-man was sentenced to death in South Korea in January 1986. His sentence was commuted three years later to life imprisonment. He is in jail today because he was labelled a North Korean spy.

Unauthorized meetings with North Koreans are punishable in South Korea under the National Security Law, as is the publication of views said to benefit North Korea. Kim Song-man admitted at his trial that he had visited the embassies of North Korea in East Berlin and Budapest on two occasions, but he denied having been recruited as a North Korean agent. He said he had confessed to being a spy because he had been "tortured mercilessly" and that he had met North Koreans merely to find out about the possibilities for Korean reunification. Apart from his confession, obtained while he was held incommunicado by the Agency for National Security Planning, no evidence was produced at his trial that he had gathered or sent intelligence to North Korea. The national secrets he was accused of passing to North Korea were in fact copies of his own pamphlets calling for the withdrawal of US troops from South Korea.

Kim Song-man was born in 1957. He comes from a Christian family; his grandfather founded the Evangelical Church in Korea. In his student days in Seoul he was active both in politics and the Christian Student Association. In June 1982 he went to the United States and enrolled at the Western Illinois University to study political science.

Kim Song-Man did not agree with the political state of affairs in South Korea, nor did he keep his opposition secret. He wrote pamphlets critical of government policies and he visited the embassies of North Korea. The authorities of South Korea may not like such behaviour, but to torture and then to sentence a man to spend the rest of his life in prison for such actions is wrong. Kim Song-man should be freed immediately.

0108

DR USHARI AHMED MAHMOUD   SUDAN

Dr Ushari Ahmed Mahmoud is a campaigner for human rights. He lives in a country which needs such skills. Because of his work, he has been detained without trial since July 1989.

At the time of his arrest Dr Mahmoud was a lecturer at the university in the Sudanese capital, Khartoum. As with many others currently held in Sudan, the government has given no reason for his detention. However, it seems that he was detained because of a report he wrote in October 1987. He had already been jailed for two short periods by a previous government because of this report.

The report focused on a 1987 massacre in Al-Daien in the province of Darfur. Hundreds of unarmed civilians belonging to the Dinka ethnic group were murdered by pro-government militias from the Rizeigat ethnic group. Dr Mahmoud was detained and questioned for several hours when the report was published. Nine months later he was detained again, this time for two weeks. When released, he was forbidden to travel abroad.

In June 1989 the elected civilian government of Prime Minister Sadiq al Mahdi was overthrown in a military coup. In the wake of the coup, many political leaders, trade unionists, academics and lawyers were arrested and detained. By 8 July 1989 Dr Mahmoud found himself in jail again. Once again, it appears the reason was the report he had written about the Al-Daien massacre.

After his arrest he was taken to Kober prison in Khartoum. While there he was visited by a government minister who reportedly threatened him with indefinite detention if he did not retract the Al-Daien report. Dr Mahmoud refused to do so and as a result was moved to Shalla prison in Darfur province.

Conditions at Shalla prison are very harsh. In April 1990 a smuggled letter from a detainee held there spoke of prisoners almost dying of thirst in the scorching desert heat. Whole days would pass without water and the air was full of swarms of flies attracted by the open prison sewers.

On 13 March 1990 the Sudanese Head of State, Lieutenant-General Omar Hassan al-Bashir, publicly announced that all political prisoners in Sudan had been released. Three days later, 71 political prisoners still detained in Shalla prison made it clear that this was not so: they managed to get publicity for an open letter to the Head of State. They denounced their continuing detention without trial, the use of torture against many of them and the prison conditions in which they were all kept.

Dr Mahmoud was in Shalla prison at the time the open letter was publicized. He is still there today, living proof that whatever the government says, political prisoners continue to be locked away in Sudan.

0109

GHASSAN NAJJAR

SYRIA

In April 1980 Ghassan Najjar took part in a one-day strike protesting against the State of Emergency then in force in Syria for 17 years. It remains in force today. Along with many others Ghassan Najjar was later arrested.

The strike was supported by doctors, lawyers and engineers. As well as an end to the State of Emergency, it called for the abolition of state security courts and the release of all untried detainees.

Official reaction was quick and harsh. Hundreds of people, including 68 members of the Engineers' Association, were arrested. The Councils of the Medical, Engineers' and Bar Associations were dissolved by Presidential decree. Like most of those detained, Ghassan Najjar is still in prison without charge or trial.

Ghassan Najjar was born in Aleppo in 1938. He received a degree in mechanical engineering from the University of Istanbul in 1963. He is married and has four children. At first he was held in *al Qal'a* civil prison in Damascus. When this prison was closed in September 1984 he was moved to *'Adra* civil prison near Damascus.

In July 1984 his family became very worried when they heard that he had been moved to hospital for emergency treatment. He had apparently been beaten by prison guards in an attempt to force him to end a hunger-strike. The hunger-strike was in protest about his continuing detention. His treatment at the hospital was said to be for a spinal injury.

In October 1986 his family heard that Ghassan Najjar was suffering from a fractured spine, a damaged heart muscle and stomach ulcers. His psychological state was described as very poor. Repeated appeals about his detention and health from both his family and organizations abroad have had no response from the Syrian authorities.

Ghassan Najjar has been detained without charge or trial for 11 years. His crime was to take part in a peaceful public protest about the abuse of emergency powers.

0110

VYTHIALINGAM SKANDARAJAH — UNITED KINGDOM

After Vythialingam Skandarajah's home in Sri Lanka was bombed and he was detained at a police station where he was brutally ill-treated, he decided that, as a Tamil, it was no longer safe for him to live in the country.

Vythialingam Skandarajah left Sri Lanka in June 1987. He intended to apply for asylum in Canada, but his flight schedule included a stop-over in London, United Kingdom (UK), where he was questioned by immigration officers. He applied for political asylum in the UK, as it appeared he would not be allowed to continue his journey. He was held in detention while his application for asylum was considered. His assylum claim was refused. His lawyers contested the Home Office decision to expel Vythialingam Skandarajah - both in the High Court and in the House of Lords - but these courts could only adjudicate on the way the decision was made and could not consider the merits of his asylum claim. He therefore had no effective right of appeal against refusal of asylum in the UK before he was expelled.

Vythialingam Skandarajah had explained to UK authorities that his life would be in danger if he returned to Sri Lanka but he and four other Tamils were expelled to Sri Lanka on 10 February 1988.

His lawyers continued to pursue his case and following his return to Sri Lanka lodged an appeal against refusal of asylum. Vythialingam Skandarajah made his way home to Jaffna. At that time,the Indian Peace Keeping Force (IPKF) were responsible for security of the area. The IPKF were attempting to combat the Liberation Tigers of Tamil Eelam (LTTE), an armed separatist group fighting for an autonomous Tamil state.

One morning soon after his return, Vythialingam Skandarajah was on his way to the local market when he was detained by members of the IPKF. He had been "identified" as being involved with the LTTE and he was taken by truck to an IPKF camp in Jaffna where he was questioned about the LTTE. He describes what happened during the questioning as follows:

> *"They began to club me. They used plastic pipes filled with something, I think, sand. This makes them flexible but very heavy. It hurt terribly. I wept a lot and screamed. I told them I could not have anything to do with the LTTE because I had been in England."*

He reports that in the next seven days he was beaten and questioned on three different occasions. Throughout his questioning Vythialingam Skandarajah denied any connection with the LTTE. Despite this he was kept with six others in a cell measuring 9 feet by 10 feet for ten more weeks until his family finally managed to secure his release.

In March 1989, when his appeal was finally determined in the UK, it was found that Vythialingam Skandarajah and the four Tamils expelled with him were entitled to asylum. They eventually returned to the UK in October 1989. When Vythialingam Skandarajah is asked what he thinks of the treatment he received in Britain he says:

"We went through every test in the land - all the courts - and still we were sent back to suffer again".

0111

DALTON PREJEAN USA

Dalton Prejean, a black mentally retarded juvenile offender, was executed by electric chair in Louisiana on 18 May 1990. The State Govornor denied clemency despite a recommendation by the Louisiana Board of Pardons and Paroles that the death sentence should be commuted to life imprisonment.

Dalton Prejean was convicted in May 1978 of the murder of a white police officer who was shot when he stopped a car in which Dalton Prejean and three others were present. Only 17 at the time of the crime, Dalton Prejean was under the influence of drugs and alcohol.

At his trial Dalton Prejean's mental abilities were questioned. He was reported to have a mental age of 13. However, his lawyer failed to tell the jurors at the sentencing hearing that Dalton Prejean had a documented history of mental illness, including a diagnosis of schizophrenia and a history of childhood neglect and abuse. Nor were they told that medical specialists had previously recommended that he receive long term inpatient hospitalization when he had been convicted of a killing when he was only 14. Dalton Prejean never received that treatment because there was no official funding available at the time.

Dalton Prejean was the fourth juvenile offender executed in the USA since the death penalty was reintroduced in the 1970s. The USA is one of only seven countries which permit the execution of juvenile offenders. The execution of an offender under the age of 18 at the time of the crime contravenes international human rights standards, including the International Covenant on Civil and Political Rights which the USA has signed but not ratified.

As of September 1989 there were 32 prisoners under sentence of death in Louisiana, 17 of whom were black. Nineteen, including eight who were black, have been executed in the State since 1977. Dalton Prejean was convicted and sentenced to death by an all-white jury after the judge had changed the trial venue to a predominantly white area and the prosecutor had excluded prospective black jurors.

The death penalty is the ultimate form of cruel and inhuman punishment or treatment. It should never be used. The jurors at Dalton Prejean's sentence hearing had to decide between life imprisonment without parole or the death penalty. Without knowing all the facts, they chose the death penalty. Appeal and clemency avenues failed to reverse this. This is just one example of why the death penalty should be abolished.

0112

NIKOLAY SHUST USSR

Nikolay Shust has been jailed twice within the last four years because he has religious objections to being conscripted into the military in the Soviet Union.

Nikolay Shust first refused to be conscripted in late 1987 and was jailed in November of that year. He was sentenced to three years' imprisonment but as is now common in such cases, he received some remission and was released in July 1989.

Within months of his release he was again sent his call-up papers for active duty in the military. Nikolay Shust had already shown that his religious convictions meant more to him than the threat of a jail sentence and once again he refused to be called up.

On 24 October 1990 he was sentenced to two years' imprisonment by a court in the city of Mozyr for *"evasion of regular call-up for active military service"* under Article 77 of the Belorussian Criminal Code. He is now serving his sentence in an unknown corrective labour colony somewhere in the Mogilyov area of Belorussia.

The USSR Constitution describes military service as the *"honourable duty"* of every Soviet male citizen. Conscription is obligatory for every able-bodied man between the ages of 18 and 27.

In the same month that Nikolay Shust was given a second prison sentence for refusing to be called-up, a new USSR law on Freedom of Conscience and Religious Organizations came into force. This new law granted religious believers many rights previously denied them. It did not, however, introduce a civilian alternative to military service.

At the time of writing, Amnesty International knows of some 16 young men, mostly Jehovah's Witnesses, serving prison sentences for refusing military service in the USSR.

There is news from the USSR which shows that attitudes to religious conscientious objectors may be improving. On 14 February 1991 the official news agency, TASS, announced that the USSR parliament would soon consider legislation which would provide for alternative non-military service for those unable to perform military service because of their religious or other beliefs.

Attitudes towards concientious objectors in the USSR may be improving, but as the law stands people like Nikolay Shust face the possibility of being called-up for military service, and perpetually jailed for each refusal.

0113

CRISANTO MEDEROS VENEZUELA

Crisanto Mederos, a 38-year-old painter and poet and a member of the Christian Social Party, was apparently killed in his home by soldiers on 3 March 1989.

His death occurred in the context of widespread disturbances following austerity measures introduced by the Venezuelan Government after the refinancing of the country's external debt through the International Monetary Fund. On 27 February 1989 hundreds of people took to the streets in protest and there was widespread looting. The following day the government suspended a wide range of constitutional guarantees, imposed a curfew and transferred responsibility for law and order to the armed forces.

The night Crisanto Mederos died a group of soldiers burst into his mother's home and made everyone lie on the floor while they searched the house. They then went next door to Crisanto Mederos' house. The family heard a shot. One of Crisanto Mederos' brothers heard a soldier asking for a plank of wood, but when his mother tried to go next door to see her son, a soldier threatened to kill her. Neighbours later described seeing the soldiers leaving Crisantos' home carrying a bulky object on a plank.

The next day the family heard that Crisanto Mederos was dead. They went to the morgue where they found his body. A note tied to the thigh indicated that the body was unidentified and should not be handed over. The death certificate stated that the cause of death was due to *"bullet wounds in the neck"*. Underneath was written, *"disregarded curfew, found in the street"*. No mention was made of a deep wound in his forehead said to look as if he had been hit with the butt of a weapon.

The case, initially investigated by a civilian judge but later handed to the military courts, has not been resolved. Those responsible for his death have not been brought to justice.

Crisanto Mederos was one of hundreds of people killed between 27 February and 8 March 1989. Many died in the generalized violence. A number, however, were killed as a result of indiscriminate or deliberate shooting by military or police.

0114

NGUYEN CHI THIEN — VIET NAM

Nguyen Chi Thien has spent more than half his life in detention. He is not a dangerous criminal. He is in detention today because he is a writer and a poet.

Nguyen Chi Thien was born in Ha Noi in 1932. He was first arrested in 1958.
In September 1956, the ruling party decided that the time had come to end its repression of culture. This was the time of the *"Hundred Flowers"* campaign in what was then North Viet Nam, and resulted in the authorized publication of many new journals. "Let a hundred flowers bloom", was the call at that time. The journals contained a broad spectrum of political opinion, and exposed and criticized corruption in the government. In short, there was a relatively free press.

After just over a year of this relative freedom, the government clamped down; all the journals were suspended. The hundred flowers were never to bloom. Not satisfied with closing down the journals, the authorities also decided to "re-educate" many of those who had written or edited the publications. Nguyen Chi Thien and some friends had published a literary magazine during the *"Hundred Flowers"* campaign. In 1958 Nguyen Chi Thien was sentenced to two years' hard labour in a "re-education camp" for his part in the magazine.

He was released in early 1961. By November of that year he had been declared an "underdeveloped citizen" and was back in a "re-education" camp. After his release in September 1964 he managed to remain free until October 1965 when he was sent to yet another "re-education" camp. This time he was detained for almost 13 years. The reasons for this period of detention remain unclear.

When he was released in 1978, he returned to his home town of Hai Phong where he continued to write poetry and teach English and French to private students. His poetry remained political and critical of the government. He was arrested again in April 1979. He had passed a manuscript of his poems to a foreign diplomat in Ha Noi. These were published abroad in 1984 under the title *"Flowers from Hell"*. It was not until May 1988 that the Vietnamese authorities acknowledged his detention. They said that he was awaiting trial.

Nguyen Chi Thien is held at Ba Sao Camp, deep in the mountains in the province of Ha Nam Ninh, about 70 kilometres south of Ha Noi. He has now been held continuously without trial for the past 12 years. His only crime has been to write openly about his feelings about the way his country is governed. He should be freed immediately.

0115

분류번호	보존기간

발 신 전 보

번 호 : WUK-1136 910615 1516 FO 종별 :

수 신 : 주 영국 대사. ~~총영사~~

발 신 : 장 관 (국연)

제 목 : A.I. Newsletter

91년 1월-6월(91.2월호 제외)까지의 A.I. Newsletter 각 1부 최선파편 송부바람. 끝.

(국제기구조약국장 문동석)

보안통제	

앙고재	91년 6월 15일	과	기안자 성명		과 장		국 장		차 관	장 관

외신과통제

0116

91 -628

기안용지

분류기호 문서번호	국연 2031 - 1555	(전화:)	시 행 상 특별취급	
보존기간	영구·준영구. 10. 5. 3. 1	장 관		
수 신 처 보존기간				
시행일자	1991. 6. 15.			

보조기관	국 장	전 결	협조기관		문서통제
	과 장				1991. 6. 17
기안책임자		송영완			발 송 인

경 유		발신명의	
수 신	법무부장관		
참 조	검찰국장		
제 목	노조관련자 사망 경위		

국제사면위(Amnesty International) 한국담당관은 주영 대사관측에 노조관련 구속자중 박창수의 사인 및 사망경위를 문의 하여 온 바, 국제사면위에 설명코자 하니 동 관련자료를 송부하여 주시기 바랍니다.

검 토 필(1991. 6. 30.)

첨 부 : 주영대사관 전문 사본 1부. 끝.

일반문서로 재분류(1991.12.31.)

0117

주 영 대 사 관

영국(정) 723- 611 1991. 6. 18.

수신 : 장관

참조 : 국제기구조약국장

제목 : A.I. News Letter

대 : WUK-1136

대호 A.I. News Letter 91.1 - 7 관 각 1부를 별첨 송부합니다.

첨부 : 동 News Letter. 끝.

발송 1991. 6. 18 주영국대사관

주 영 대

34783

0118

AI CROSSES MILLION MARK
Movement gains strength: see page 8

AMNESTY INTERNATIONAL
NEWSLETTER
JANUARY 1991 VOLUME XXI • NUMBER 1

INDIA

Torture and killing rise in Punjab

SYSTEMATIC torture, as well as extrajudicial killings and some "disappearances" from police custody continue to be reported in Punjab. This Indian state, where armed opposition groups are demanding an independent Sikh state ("Khalistan"), has been under direct rule from the union government in New Delhi since May 1987. Sikh groups have been responsible for politically motivated killings of hundreds of police, members of the security forces and civilians. The security forces have persistently been accused of executing political activists in staged "encounters", even after the government announced in April 1990 that a 30 August 1989 police order offering awards for the "liquidation" of "terrorists" had been withdrawn.

Several thousand people are estimated to be detained in Punjab. Important legal safeguards to protect detainees have been suspended or weakened under preventive detention laws and the Terrorist and Disruptive Activities (Prevention) Act. In other cases safeguards are simply ignored and people are arbitrarily detained. Unacknowledged and incommunicado detention, sometimes at secret locations, has facilitated a pattern of torture, and police have sometimes flaunted High Court orders to trace "disappeared" detainees.

Women have been increasingly subjected to ill-treatment and torture. Gurmeet Kaur and Gurdev Kaur were tortured in August 1989 during interrogation about their husbands' whereabouts. They were beaten and had wooden bars rolled up and down their legs. Other common methods of torture include forcing the legs apart to cause pelvic injury and hanging people from the ceiling upside-down. Electric shocks have also been used.

Political prisoners have allegedly been killed while in police custody. Such cases are difficult to investigate, as police officials often deny knowledge of arrests, or claim that a person "escaped" or died in "encounters" with the police.

Many "disappearances" remain unresolved. Baldev Singh, for example, was only 15 years old when arrested in October 1988. Although his twin brother was released, relatives have been unable to establish Baldev Singh's fate or whereabouts. In August 1990 relatives wrote to AI asking for assistance in tracing him.

Human rights abuses were widespread in Punjab under the Congress government and continued under the National Front coalition government. AI is calling on the new government in India to halt human rights violations and investigate past abuses.□

GUATEMALA

Candidates urged to protect human rights

AN AI delegation visited Guatemala in October 1990. At the first press conference the organization has ever held in the country, the delegation released an open letter calling on the candidates in the November presidential elections to outline the steps they would take to improve the human rights situation in Guatemala. The press conference drew attention to AI's recent report on abuses against street children* and received major coverage in the local press and on Guatemalan radio and television.

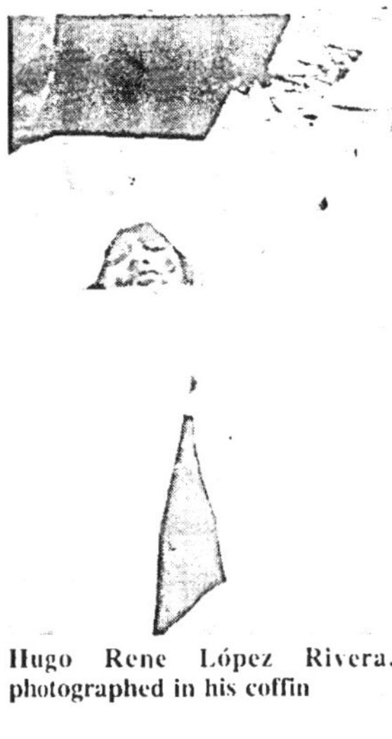

Hugo Rene López Rivera, photographed in his coffin

The delegation also met with government officials, local human rights groups, independent organizations and victims of recent abuses. In particular the delegates sought information about the ongoing investigation into the case of 13-year-old street child Nahamán Carmona López who died in hospital in March after a brutal attack by the police. Four policemen were arrested and charged in connection with the crime and the evidence against them includes compelling eye-witness accounts.

However, out of thousands of cases of human rights violations reported in Guatemala in recent years, AI knows of only one instance in which criminal charges have led to convictions against security force personnel. In 1988 six policemen were convicted and imprisoned for the 1987 kidnapping and murder of two Quetzaltenango agronomists. Despite strong forensic evidence linking them to the crime, they were released in July 1990 after an appeal court overturned their convictions.

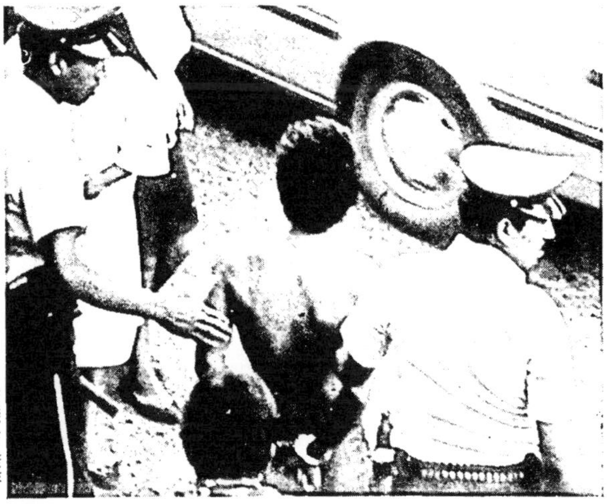

The 16-year-old street child pictured above was beaten after being taken away by police officers. The case was not recorded on police files

AI's delegation also took testimony concerning the attempted abduction on 14 October of a young girl who is the sole survivor and key witness to the abduction of five street children in June. Two of the other victims have "disappeared," and two were found dead, horribly mutilated.

Another street child, eight-year-old Hugo René López Rivera, was found dead on 25 October, showing signs of a savage beating, haemorrhaging and strangulation. Hugo López was one of the street children who found Nahamán Carmona unconscious in the street, and thinking he was dead, put white crepe paper over him, customary when children die in Guatemala. Since the fatal police attack on Nahamán Carmona, any street children believed by the police to have information about the circumstances of his death have been repeatedly harassed, interrogated and sometimes beaten.□

**Guatemala: Extrajudicial Executions and Human Rights Violations against Street Children (AMR 34/37/90).*

0119

CAMPAIGN FOR PRISONERS OF THE MONTH

Each of the people whose story is told below is a prisoner of conscience. Each has been arrested because of his or her religious or political beliefs, colour, sex, ethnic origin or language. None has used or advocated violence. Their continuing detention is a violation of the United Nations Universal Declaration of Human Rights. International appeals can help to secure the release of these prisoners or to improve their detention conditions. In the interest of the prisoners, letters to the authorities should be worded carefully and courteously. You should stress that your concern for human rights is not in any way politically partisan. In *no* circumstances should communications be sent to the prisoner.

U Ba Thaw, serving 20 years' imprisonment with hard labour in Myanmar

MYANMAR

U Ba Thaw: ***a 62-year-old writer and a leading member of the National League for Democracy, a legal political party, he is serving a sentence of 20 years' imprisonment with labour.***

U Ba Thaw is understood to have been arrested in early 1989. A former naval officer, he is one of Myanmar's best known novelists and was also president of the Writers' Union. His novels recount his experiences in the navy and his most recent book is about a shipwreck which took place over 30 years ago.

On 5 October U Ba Thaw was brought before a military tribunal on charges of inciting members of the armed forces to join the democracy movement. He was found guilty and sentenced to 20 years' imprisonment with hard labour.

Since July 1989 military tribunals presided over by military officers have systematically interned the leadership and many rank and file activists of the pro-democracy movement in Myanmar. Defendants brought before them are stripped of their rights. The tribunals may refuse to call "unnecessary" witnesses and do not have to produce prosecution witnesses. The minimum sentence they may impose is three years' imprisonment with hard labour; the maximum is death. The decision of the military tribunal is final. No appeal against sentence is allowed. Many of those convicted by military tribunal are prisoners of conscience.

U Ba Thaw is in Insein Prison, Yangon, and is said to be held in solitary confinement. He suffers from chronic spondilitis, an arthritic-like condition of the spine which causes pain and stiffness. It is not known whether he is receiving medical treatment for this condition.

■Please send courteous appeals for his immediate and unconditional release to: General Saw Maung/Chairman/State Law and Order/Restoration Council/ Yangon (Rangoon)/Union of Myanmar (Burma).□

BURKINA FASO

Seni Konanda and Sié Souleymane Coulibaly: ***the president of the National Association of Burkinabè Students (ANEB), and an ANEB executive committee member respectively, they have been held without charge or trial since their arrest following student protests in May 1990.***

At the beginning of May ANEB presented a number of demands to the university authorities, including the right to use rooms at the university for ANEB meetings. When this was refused, students occupied rooms at the university in protest. The police and army intervened and 10 students were dismissed from the university.

More than 40 students were arrested when police dispersed further demonstrations to demand negotiations with the university authorities and the reinstatement of the dismissed students. Although many were subsequently released, four are still held in incommunicado detention in Ouagadougou, either at security service and police headquarters or at the *Conseil de l'Entente* building which is used as a detention centre. Eight other students were forcibly conscripted into the army and are held at Pô, Dedougou and Koudougou. None of the students has been charged with any offence. They have been denied visits since their arrest and their families have not been informed of their individual whereabouts in prison or army barracks. AI regards all 12 as prisoners of conscience.

Reports of torture followed the arrests in May and a medical student, Boukary Dabo, died in detention, probably as a result of torture or ill-treatment.

The government has not responded to calls for an investigation into his death.

■Please send courteous appeals for the immediate release of Seni Konanda, Sié Souleymane Coulibaly and other students detained since May 1990 to: Président Blaise Compaoré/Présidence du Faso/Ouagadougou/Burkina Faso.□

SYRIA

Mufid Mi'mari: ***a 43-year-old teacher, he has been held without charge or trial since 1980 for suspected membership of the prohibited Communist Party Political Bureau (CPPB).***

Mufid Mi'mari was arrested on 15 March 1980 under State of Emergency legislation in force in Syria since 1963. He was transferred from Kafr Sousseh Prison to a detention centre in Damascus in February 1986, where he was interrogated by *Idarat al-Amn al-Siyassi* (Department of Political Security). He was reportedly held in solitary confinement and tortured to force him to renounce his affiliation to the CPPB. AI issued urgent appeals on his behalf in April 1986.

The CPPB was founded in 1973 after a split within the Syrian Communist Party. Its members have been arrested because of the party's non-violent opposition to the present government's policies and particularly to Syria's intervention in Lebanon since 1976. In October 1980 prominent members of the CPPB, including Riad al-Turk, the party's First Secretary, were arrested after the signing of Syria's Treaty of Friendship and Cooperation with the Soviet Union and attempts by Syrian political forces to form a coalition opposed to the government.

Over 200 members of the CPPB have been arrested since 1980. Some were released after short periods, but most remain in detention without charge or trial.

Mufid Mi'mari is currently reported to be held in Saidnaya Prison, near Damascus.

■Please send courteous letters appealing for the immediate release of Mufid Mi'Mari to: His Excellency Khaled al-Ansari/Minister of Justice/Nasr Street/Damascus/Syrian Arab Republic□

0120

AI's mandate is as relevant in the Asia/Pacific region today as it was 30 years ago. Thousands of prisoners of conscience are detained by governments across the political spectrum. Torture is widespread. Extrajudicial execution and "disappearance" are everyday occurrences. The death penalty is retained and imposed by most of the countries in the region.

The language of human rights violations is an international language. Prisoner of conscience, "disappearance", extrajudicial execution, and unfair trial, are words in common usage across the world. Human rights violations in the Asia/Pacific region also have local terminologies. Extrajudicial executions are known as "encounter" killings in India and as "salvaging" in the Philippines. In Myanmar torturers use the "iron road" - they roll an iron bar or a bamboo cane up and down their victim's shins until the skin comes off.

Human rights violations often occur when governments are faced with armed opposition. Throughout the Asia/Pacific region ethnic and nationalist tensions have erupted into protracted and bitter conflict. AI has frequently received reports of the torture and killing of prisoners by governments and by armed opposition groups in the context of armed conflicts. AI unequivocally condemns any such abuses, whoever the perpetrators. International law clearly states that no matter what circumstances they face, governments must never resort to torture and extrajudicial execution.

This region, the most populous in the world, encompasses some of the richest and poorest countries on earth. The last decade has seen widespread political upheaval, leading to increased respect for fundamental human rights in some countries — and a deterioration in others. All too often governments which came to power pledged to end human rights abuses have failed to do so.

The challenge for the 1990s is to build human rights awareness in the broadest sense of the term: to ensure that no government can cloak its illegal activities in secrecy; that the rights of even the poorest citizens are upheld; and to build a truly international movement capable of taking action against human rights violations wherever they occur.□

ASIA AND THE PACIFIC

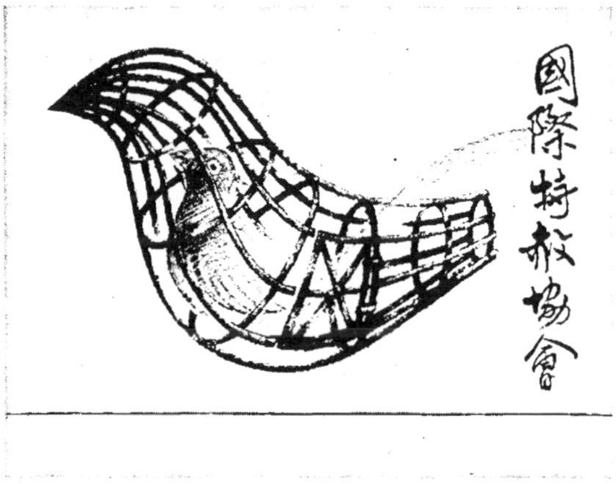

Building a human rights movement

AI members in the Asia/Pacific region work on behalf of men and women wrongfully imprisoned all over the world. The barriers of language and culture have not obstructed their efforts. When Reverend Tshenuweni Simon Farisani, a South African prisoner of conscience and Dean of the Lutheran Church, went on hunger strike in early 1987, the Japanese section appealed to people all over Japan to write to the South African authorities. Dean Farisani was released some months later: he himself has acknowledged how the vast correspondence from Japan contributed to this. Since no one at his prison could read Japanese, the authorities translated thousands of letters, at considerable expense, only to discover that they all demanded "release Dean Farisani".

In their efforts to secure the release of their adopted prisoners, AI group members write letter after letter to government officials, judges, prison officers - anyone who might be able to help. At the same time, members seek to publicize the prisoner's plight in the local press, approach embassies, or ask influential people to sign petitions and support protests. To ensure their impartiality and independence, each group works only on behalf of prisoners held in countries other than their own.

Does it work? AI does not claim credit for the release of any prisoner. But once a prisoner of conscience is "adopted", AI never gives up its efforts. And sometimes, even when there is no official response, the results can be rewarding. Two prisoners released in 1975 from the National Prison in Ho Chi Minh City (then Saigon) said afterwards: "We could always tell when international protests were taking place... the food rations increased and the beatings inside the prison got less... but when the letters stopped, the dirty food and repression started again."

AI members also take part in national and international campaigns to draw attention to human rights abuses in specific countries. These often highlight practices such as widespread detention without trial, torture, the death penalty, and extrajudicial executions.

AI's campaign against human rights violations in Brazil took place between September 1988 and February 1989. In Japan, members from 23 groups swamped the Brazilian authorities with appeals urging an end to the torture and extrajudicial executions of peasants involved in land disputes. The Japanese groups produced an informational leaflet and rapidly distributed all 7,000 available copies.

Across the Asia/Pacific region such efforts are being carried out as part of the worldwide movement to put pressure on governments to stop human rights abuses. Today there are well-established AI sections in Hong Kong, India, Japan, New Zealand and Australia, active groups in seven countries and individual members and supporters in another seven.

AI is by no means the only representative of the broader human rights movement in the region. Women's groups have raised the banner of rights for women; the cause of children is championed by activists in many countries; the environment, housing and development issues have all been supported, often at great personal risk, by men and women all over the region. Some of them came into contact with AI because they became prisoners of conscience, and some have gone on to enlist others in the international struggle for human rights.

In 1965 the Indian Government detained human rights activist Mridula Sarabhai. She was adopted by AI as a prisoner of conscience. During her first months in jail, she received cards from AI members all over the world which helped give her the hope and courage to bear her incarceration. In September 1968, after her release, she helped establish the first AI group in India.

Ten years later AI India launched a campaign to persuade the Indian government to ratify the International Covenant on Civil and Political Rights and the International Covenant on Economic, Social and Cultural Rights, agreements which give legal force to the principles enshrined in the Universal Declaration of Human Rights. Over 3,000 signatures were collected on a petition urging ratification. On 10 April 1979, during the course of the campaign, India acceded to the two covenants. A delegation from the section was invited to visit the prime minister and present the AI petition.

AI in India has continued to grow and members participate in appeals against human rights violations across the world. The Indian section played a leading role in AI's 1987 campaign for human rights in Kampuchea (now Cambodia); groups all over the country collected signatures on a petition, which was presented to the Kampuchean Embassy in New Delhi. In June 1988 the Indian section lobbied the British Embassy about human rights concerns in the UK following the publication of the AI Report: *Killings by Security Forces in Northern Ireland.*

To support their worldwide campaigning work, AI members need to raise money for postage, stationery, the printing of campaign materials and the dozens of minor expenses incurred in the course of an action. Throughout the region, AI groups sell t-shirts, handicrafts and greeting cards. Groups in Hong Kong participate in sponsored walkathons, and artists in New Zealand have donated their work to a charity auction for AI. Concerts promoting human rights work have been held in the Philippines, New Zealand, India and Japan. The Japanese Section persuaded 28 famous Japanese artists to contribute to the "Freedom 80s Poster Exhibition", which toured the country in a second-hand bus driven by volunteers.

The challenge to developing AI's campaigning program is complicated by the enormous number of languages spoken throughout the Asia/Pacific region. In order to reach the vast audiences, information and campaigns have to become completely multilingual. Funds are seldom available for extended translation work, but a grassroots volunteer effort throughout the region is making substantial inroads.

Newsletters are regularly published in Korean, Japanese, Urdu, Tamil and Thai. Future priorities include increasing the number of AI publications available in Chinese, and producing Bengali and Hindi versions of the International Newsletter. Groups in Taiwan are working on a Chinese version of the *Prisoner of the Month* appeal, and have produced leaflets and action materials for recent AI campaigns on behalf of imprisoned trade unionists and for human rights in South Korea. A number of international human rights standards, particularly the Universal Declaration of Human Rights, have been translated and distributed throughout the region.

Key to the development of an effective multilingual program is the regional publications and distribution service, the Asia Distribution Service (ADS), based in Hong Kong. ADS hopes to provide a wide range of translation and distribution services and eventually plans to offer facilities to produce and distribute cassette tapes, videos and publicity materials specially tailored for the Asia/Pacific region.

Human rights education plays an indispensable role in mobilizing people to participate in the worldwide movement. AI groups use street theatre, seminars and exhibitions to raise public awareness of human rights issues. In Pakistan, the Lahore group produces plays on human rights themes, which tour in shanty towns and rural areas. The Madaripur group in Bangladesh organized seminars and information stalls to coincide with International Women's Day, 1990. The group collected 10,000 signatures on an appeal for women prisoners of conscience, and translated an *AI Newsletter* article on Women and Human Rights into Bengali for mass circulation.

In South Korea the Yong Nam University group gathers signatures on a *petition to the Sri Lankan Government*

A growing understanding of human rights issues and the relaxation of political restrictions in some countries has resulted in a substantial increase in AI's membership base in the Asia/Pacific region. The easing of constraints on freedom of association, expression and assembly in Nepal after a months-long protest movement seeking political change coincided with a surge of interest in AI. Several new groups have been formed in Nepal, including a women's group in Kathmandu, and campaigning activities are under way on a wide range of issues. The Biratnagar group distributed over 10,000 pamphlets calling for the abolition of the death penalty, and published and sold a collection of poems on capital punishment.

Shortly after martial law was lifted in Taiwan two AI groups were formed in the capital, Taipei. In March 1990 they set up information stalls and collected thousands of signatures on a petition to end human rights violations against women in countries across the world.

In Malaysia, a committee has been formed to register AI as a Malaysian organization, and a constitution was submitted to the authorities in accordance with the requirements of Malaysian law. More than 70 international members have held an inaugural meeting and are waiting for permission from the authorities to form official AI groups.

In Pakistan, 1989 saw AI groups established in Lahore, Karachi and Islamabad. They are already publishing AI informational leaflets and action documents in Urdu. The Pakistani press provides sympathetic coverage of human rights issues and has helped AI groups to emphasise the global nature of human rights concerns. The Lahore group has adopted a prisoner of conscience in South Korea and is working with groups in France and Italy to help secure his release.

Although the imposition of evening curfews in Karachi make it difficult for the group there to hold public meetings, the members continue to send letters to the government of Sudan, appealing for the release of two prisoners of conscience, and have recently published articles on AI's work in national newspapers and medical magazines.

The death penalty, the promotion of ratifications of international human rights instruments and refugee concerns are the main issues on which AI members can address their own governments. AI's 1989 worldwide campaign to abolish the death penalty provided an opportunity for AI's membership to organize a range of activities directed towards their own and other countries.

AI groups in the Philippines sent hundreds of letters to government officials and the media in Jamaica, Grenada, Singapore and Taiwan, citing arguments for the abolition of the death penalty and urging governments to halt executions and abolish the death penalty.

While the campaign was in progress, the Philippine Government called for the reintroduction of the death penalty. In a public hearing conducted by the Senate committee on constitutional amendments and revision of laws and codes, representatives of AI and the Philippine Alliance of Human Rights Advocates cited the lack of conclusive evidence that executions have any deterrent effect. *The Manila Chronicle* published letters from AI groups in the Netherlands which also argued against the restoration of the death penalty. Such intervention by AI groups worldwide contributed to the Senate Committee's decision to defer debate on the issue until 1991.

In June 1989 the Beijing massacre focused national and international attention on China. AI Hong Kong responded by working night and day to provide AI information to the media and general public. Later in the year, the section undertook a demanding program of assistance to Vietnamese asylum seekers, a major focus of AI's refugee work. In cooperation with AI's London-based International Secretariat, the Hong Kong section raised AI's concerns about the screening process with the Hong Kong Government and protested about the forcible return to Viet Nam of over 50 asylum-seekers in December 1989. At the same time, AI members in Hong Kong continued to send appeals on behalf of prisoners of conscience in South Korea, Sudan and Ethiopia.

AI members often seek to enlist the support of political leaders in human rights work. Members of Australia's national parliament have formed an all-party group to focus on human rights issues and have lobbied their government on such issues, and on AI concerns throughout the world, since 1974. Not all Australian political leaders have given

Krishna Prasad Bhattarai, Prime Minister of Nepal and a former prisoner of conscience, lights the AI candle during the closing ceremonies of the membership training workshop in July 1990. The meeting was attended by representatives from all 11 AI groups and groups in formation in Nepal

AI their unqualified support; in 1981 Queensland's State Premier accused the organization of being "an arm of communist propaganda".

In May 1990 an all-party AI group was formed in the Japanese parliament. AI's Secretary General Ian Martin attended the press conference held to announce the group's formation. Forty Members of Parliament joined immediately, and membership has since doubled.

Outside of formal government structures, several initiatives in the past decade have helped to establish mechanisms for the regional protection and promotion of human rights. In 1983, 37 non-governmental organizations from a dozen countries attended a meeting coordinated by the Law Association for Asia and the Western Pacific (LAWASIA). This meeting established the Asian Coalition of Human Rights Organizations (ACHRO), which aims to strengthen the work of individual organizations and enhance their capacities for human rights activism.

The Asian Human Rights Commission (AHRC) was founded in December 1984. The AHRC is an independent body that seeks to promote greater awareness of human rights in the Asia region, and mobilize public opinion to obtain relief and redress for the victims of human rights violations.

In acknowledgment of the growing influence of the Asia/Pacific region in the worldwide fight to end human rights abuses, AI representatives from around the world will meet in Japan for their next International Council Meeting (ICM). The 1991 ICM, the first to be held in Asia, will be attended by AI members from more than 70 countries.□

Father and daughter Kang Hee-sul were released during the 1990 action on South Korea, and sent AI the following message: "We won! Thank you for your encouragement."

Human rights violations in Asia and the Pacific

There has been little evidence of any trend towards an end to the detention of prisoners of conscience in the Asia/Pacific region. The release of thousands of long-term prisoners of conscience and other political prisoners has been confirmed in several countries over the past decade, but the Asia/Pacific human rights community must respond each day to new arrests. AI members in the region and around the world work towards the release of all prisoners of conscience - including those who have spent decades wrongfully imprisoned and shamefully forgotten.

There is no monopoly on oppression by any one political system in the region. In Viet Nam "propaganda against the socialist system" continues to be punishable by imprisonment. In Indonesia writing or teaching deemed to be contrary to the official *Pancasila* ideology was the "crime" committed by scores of prisoners of conscience. In South Korea prisoners of conscience may be held indefinitely upon failure to "renounce" communist beliefs they may never have acknowledged holding - or for owning a book that was published in North Korea.

The human rights catastrophes which reach the world's headlines - the slaughter of demonstrators in front of the television cameras or the extrajudicial execution or "disappearance" of thousands - overshadow international attention on the very real personal tragedies of prisoners of conscience. Yet the systematic efforts of a prison regime to break a prisoner's will may be paralleled in the outside world by the destitution, hunger and illness of their families. The deaths of children left without support by the imprisonment of their parents continues to be a cost borne by prisoners of conscience.

The deaths of thousands or tens of thousands are also a part of the Asia/Pacific region's longstanding human rights panorama. For much of the 1980s bitter conflict in Sri Lanka provided the backdrop for thousands of "disappearances" and extrajudicial executions, facilitated by the wide powers bestowed on the security forces under a nationwide state of emergency in force almost continually since 1983. These violations by government forces reached unprecedented levels in 1989, as the security forces sought to suppress the armed opposition group *Janatha Vimukhti Peramuna*.

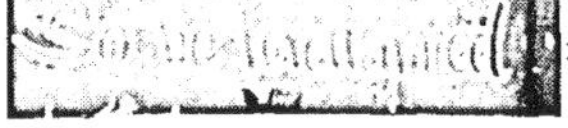

Abbas/Magnum

In Malaysia the death penalty is mandatory for convicted drug-traffickers. Billboards in airports and cities provide graphic warnings of the penalties for conviction. At least 97 men and women have been executed for drug- trafficking in Malaysia during the last five years

AI concerns in the Asia/Pacific region are long-term concerns. Torture in Afghanistan was already widespread and a focus for AI action before Soviet forces invaded the country in 1979. Information was particularly difficult to obtain, but it became clear, as AI disclosed in a major report in 1986, that prisoners in the custody of the Afghan State Information Services were routinely tortured, often in the presence of Soviet personnel.

Soviet forces withdrew from Afghanistan in early 1989, but armed conflict - and gross human rights abuses - have continued. Increasingly, AI has been concerned in Afghanistan not only by the actions of government forces but also by the treatment of prisoners by the opposition Mujahideen, who operate in and exercise control over different parts of the country.

Human rights emergencies across the region have demanded immediate action. The mass movements calling for fundamental human rights which swept China and Myanmar at the end of the 1980s were suppressed by the killing or imprisonment of thousands of people. In June 1989, following the army's deployment in the streets of Beijing, AI appealed to the Chinese authorities to prevent further arbitrary killings and to issue instructions to troops not to resort to the use of lethal force against peaceful protestors. The year before, similar appeals were made to the authorities in Myanmar (then Burma), when thousands of non-violent demonstrators were shot down.

Armed conflict, either domestic or with international dimensions, provided the context of severe human rights abuses throughout the decade. In the Indian state of Jammu and Kashmir, thousands of people have been arrested, and dozens of unarmed civilians deliberately and arbitrarily killed by government forces, in connection with measures to suppress a violent campaign for independence from India.

Since the mid-1970's armed opposition to the Government of Bangladesh in the remote Chittagong Hill Tracts has provided the context for widespread arbitrary arrests, torture and extrajudicial execution of unarmed tribal people. Throughout the 1980s AI documented these violations.

In 1989 armed conflict erupted on the island of Bougainville in Papua New Guinea, when a group sought secession for the island and compensation for environmental damage resulting from copper mining. The government declared a state of emergency which gave the security forces wide powers of arrest, detention and seizure. AI documented torture, ill-treatment and extrajudicial execution by government counter-insurgency forces.

Human rights abuses continue even in countries where new governments have promised to stop them. The fall of Ferdinand Marcos in the Philippines in 1986 raised hopes of an end to the country's record of torture, "disappearances" and extrajudicial executions. The new government, headed by President Corazon Aquino, repeatedly stated its commitment to protecting human rights, but it has failed to do so. In 1989 alone there were over 200 apparent extrajudicial executions, dozens of "disappearances", and persistent reports of torture.

In Pakistan the Government of Benazir Bhutto, in office from December 1988 until August 1990, also pledged itself to protecting human rights. All death sentences were commuted and most political prisoners who had been convicted by special military courts were released under an amnesty. However, the persecution of members of the Ahmadiyya religious group continues. Ahmadis may be imprisoned for up to three years simply for calling themselves Muslims or for engaging in Muslim religious practices. The Hudood Ordinances, under which women can be subjected to punishments which AI regards as cruel and degrading, are still in force.

Suppression of religious belief is widespread in the Asia and Pacific region. Buddhist and Christian clergy are among the prisoners of conscience held in Viet Nam. In China, since 1949, Protestants, Roman Catholics and Tibetan Buddhists have been tried and imprisoned, in some cases for over 20 years, for refusing to join the official "patriotic" religious organizations. 1989 saw a new crackdown on members of underground church groups.

Ideological repression has dominated the region for decades. Over one million Indonesians were arrested in the aftermath of an abortive coup attempt in 1965, because they were suspected of having links with the banned Communist Party, the PKI. Although most were released in the late 1970s, hundreds of thousands of these former PKI prisoners, most of whom were never tried, are still subject to stringent restrictions. They must undergo "ideological screening" before being permitted to vote or to enter certain professions, and many are under house arrest or unable to leave their village or city.

Thousands of prisoners endured years of hard labour in Vietnamese "re-education" camps because of their association with the previous administration. Most were released in major amnesties in 1988 but at least 100 are reportedly still detained. In a positive step the Vietnamese Government recently announced that it intended to phase out these camps.

South Koreans suspected of any unauthorized connection with North Korea face imprisonment. Several such prisoners were released in 1988 under amnesties granted by President Roh Taewoo. 1989, however, saw a new wave of arrests in the name of national security, with over 300 people taken into custody for offences such as printing or distributing North Korean books, making unauthorized visits to North Korea or trying to contact North Koreans to discuss reunification.

Torture has also been a longterm focus for AI's work. Since 1975, when Indonesian forces invaded East Timor and claimed it as Indonesia's 27th province, there have been repeated reports of serious human rights violations. In 1985 AI launched a campaign based on 10 years' research into widespread killing and torture by Indonesian troops in East Timor. Since 1989, despite a heavily publicized "opening" of the island to tourism and commerce, reports of unfair trials, torture in police and military custody, political killings and "disappearances" continue. AI presented information about human rights violations in East Timor to the UN Special Committee on Decolonization in August 1990, in the belief that the Committee's discussion should be informed by an understanding of the human rights situation in the territory. In 1987 AI brought the widespread practice of torture in Kampuchea (now Cambodia) to world attention.

AI has been denied access to research its concerns in several countries in the region. China, Laos, Myanmar (Burma), Sri Lanka and North Korea have remained closed to AI. India denied access to AI delegations for over a decade. AI action has moved forward even on "closed" countries, however, as persistent research has produced substantial information about human rights violations in these countries. AI has published several major reports on a broad range of human rights issues in China - and sustained action for the release of prisoners of conscience and an end to torture and the death penalty. Myanmar, too, has been the subject of several reports, continuing work for individual prisoners and concerted, worldwide membership action.

Recently, some governments have shown a greater willingness to discuss human rights with AI or allow access to their country. In 1989 AI visited Viet Nam for the first time in 10 years, and had constructive contact with the government about a range of human rights issues. In 1990, a new Indian government agreed in principle to receive an AI delegation and to consider whether AI can have access to the Punjab and other areas in which human rights violations have been reported.□

The death penalty

The extreme cruelty of the death penalty was clearly illustrated in Indonesia with the execution in February 1990 of four men who had spent over two decades under sentence of death for alleged involvement in the 1965 coup attempt. None of them were allowed to see their relatives before being shot.

The Indonesian Government sought to justify the long delay in carrying out the February executions on the grounds that the four were required as "material witnesses" in other trials. However, there have been no trials related to the 1965 coup attempt for over 10 years. AI believes political considerations lie behind these and other recent executions. The use of the death penalty in Indonesia has escalated sharply in recent years.

The death penalty is in force throughout most of the region. In China unofficial sources allege that hundreds of people were executed after the Beijing massacre in June 1989. Judicial proceedings in China are swift and summary, with verdict and sentence often decided before the trial.

China: Policemen prepare to shoot Wang Guiyuan and Zhou Xiangcheng, who were convicted of arson during protests in Chengdu which followed news of the massacre in Beijing. They were executed on 8 July 1989

1989 saw a three-fold increase in executions in Taiwan since the previous year; over 69 people were put to death. Executions continued at the same rate in 1990.

In Myanmar over 100 people have been sentenced to death since July 1989. The youngest of the condemned prisoners was just 17 years old when his sentence was handed down by a military tribunal.

Three juveniles have been executed in Pakistan during the last decade. In Bangladesh Mohammed Selim was executed in 1986 at the age of 17, although the government disputed his age.

The world trend towards harsher penalties for drug-trafficking has been evident in Asia. In Singapore and Malaysia the death penalty is mandatory for possession of a specified amount of drugs. In 1987 alone 14 people, one of them a 69-year-old woman, were executed in Malaysia for drug-trafficking.

There has also been progress. The death penalty has been abolished in Australia, New Zealand, the Philippines and Cambodia, and its scope has been reduced in Nepal. In New Zealand the Minister of Justice is empowered to refuse to extradite a person to another country if the laws of that country allow the suspect to be sentenced to death or executed.□

0124

IRAN

Human rights violations continue

ON 5 December 1990 AI published a 64-page report entitled *Iran: Violations of Human Rights 1987-1990*. The report stresses that a pattern of serious and widespread human rights abuses continues. They include huge numbers of executions for both political and criminal offences; the imprisonment of prisoners of conscience; grossly unfair trials in political and capital cases; torture; and the use of cruel, inhuman and degrading punishments.

The report examines the wholesale secret execution of political prisoners in the latter part of 1988. In many cases, the authorities have still not informed victims' families of their deaths, or where they were buried.

AI has recorded the names of over 2,500 prisoners alleged to have been executed, and believes the true total was far higher. In December 1988 the organization asked the authorities for information about 325 of these alleged victims. It has received no response. The authorities, in fact, have consistently failed to reply to requests for information on specific cases: they say simply that violations do not take place.

Many hundreds of prisoners of conscience have been detained in Iran, often without charge or trial. The report describes how over 20 people who had signed an open letter criticizing the lack of rights and freedoms in Iran were arrested in June 1990. Several of them were elderly, some had serious health problems, and it was feared that they might all be tortured to force them to make televised "confessions". In August AI asked the Iranian authorities for permission to observe their trial, but no reply has been received.

Other prisoners of conscience in Iran are serving prison sentences imposed after unfair trials before Islamic Revolutionary Courts. These trials often consist of little more than the pronouncement of sentence. Defendants may never even be informed of the precise charge against them. They have no legal representation and no right to appeal.

Unfair trials have also resulted in thousands of executions since the Iranian Revolution in 1979. In 1989 alone, over 1,100 people convicted of drug-trafficking by Islamic Revolutionary Courts were hanged.

The past two years have seen what appears to be a pattern of political killings of Iranian opposition activists in exile. In at least two of these cases, police investigations have revealed evidence that Iranian Government agents were involved.

AI has called on the Iranian Government to honour its commitments under the international human rights treaties to which it is bound, and to implement effective safeguards to protect human rights.□

DEATH PENALTY

Further advances to abolition in Africa

THE death penalty was abolished in two more African countries - Sao Tome and Principe and Mozambique - in September and November 1990 respectively.

Both countries abolished the death penalty when they revised their constitutions to introduce multi-party political systems.

In Sao Tome and Principe no one was ever convicted of "mercenarism" (being a mercenary), the only crime punishable by death after the death penalty was introduced in 1979. Very few people in the islands' close-knit community were reported to be in favour of capital punishment.

Mozambique introduced the death penalty, also in 1979, in an attempt to deter guerrilla attacks and extended it in 1983 to other crimes. A total of 78 people were sentenced to death and executed: the last death sentences were carried out in May 1986.□

STOP PRESS

Peru: AI has received reports from Huanta province, Ayacucho department, that on 22 August 1990 soldiers and members of civil defence groups detained and shot dead 16 members of the Iquicha peasant community. The dead included women and children.
(*Index No. AMR 46/66/90*)

South Africa: The practice of detention without charge or trial continues in South Africa, and has resulted in serious human rights violations. This report contains a statement submitted by AI in October 1990 to the UN Special Committee Against *Apartheid*, outlining AI's concerns, submitting information about specific cases and urging the government to repeal legislation providing for indefinite incommunicado detention.
(*Index No. AFR 53/70/90*)

Sudan: Over 250 prisoners of conscience, including 19 health professionals, are detained in Sudan. Prisoners routinely suffer ill-treatment and torture: one doctor reportedly died as a result of torture after being held for a month in a secret detention centre. This report focuses on the arrests, torture and ill-treatment of health workers, and examines allegations of torture that have been corroborated by medical evidence.
(*Index No. AFR 54/35/90*)

Prisoners tortured and killed in Senegal

SINCE May 1990 a marked increase in violent opposition in Senegal's southern region of Casamance has been accompanied by disturbing reports of human rights violations by government forces. Abuses include both torture - reported sporadically throughout the 1980s in Casamance - and the extrajudicial executions of prisoners. The victims, mainly Casamance villagers, were apparently suspected by the authorities of launching attacks on government and civilian targets.

In September 1990 soldiers searching the village of Kanaw gathered the male inhabitants, forced them to lie down and beat some of them. Five men were taken away and shot. Their bodies were found later in a rice field.

The use of torture is reported to have increased, both in military barracks and at police stations run by the Gendarmerie. Between May and November at least 10 people were reported to have died from torture. At least one victim was handed over to Senegalese police by the Gambian authorities. Sékou Mary (known as Agnocome) fled to the Gambia in June 1990. In September he was arrested in the Gambia and forced to return to Senegal: he managed to escape arrest and return to the Gambia, but was again detained and this time delivered directly to Senegalese officials. He died a few days later, apparently after severe beatings while in Gendarmerie custody.

AI has appealed to the Senegalese Government to issue clear instructions to the security forces that the killing and torture of prisoners are forbidden by both Senegalese and international law. AI's appeals to the authorities to investigate reports of extrajudicial executions and torture have not yet received a positive response.□

USSR

Legal rights for religious believers

IN October 1990 the USSR parliament passed a new law regulating the activity of religious bodies and granting rights denied under previous legislation.

Hundreds of religious believers have been imprisoned in the past for seeking to exercise these rights.

The "Law on Freedom of Conscience and Religious Organizations" came into force on 9 October. It guarantees religious citizens equality in all areas of public life and declares all religions equal before the law. Religious bodies may now apply to become legal entities by submitting their statute for registration and may then own property, establish religious and charitable institutions and engage in publishing, printing and manufacturing activity for religious purposes.

There is no obligation for a congregation to register.

Past stringent regulations required believers to register and in doing so to give up rights such as evangelizing, charitable works, teaching religion to children, controlling the content of their sermons and appointing their own clergy. Unregistered churches were illegal, and their members subject to disruption of religious services, job dismissal, fines, searches and even long periods of imprisonment. Those printing and distributing their own religious material were also liable to imprisonment.

However, the new law does not provide for a civilian alternative to military service for conscientious objectors, although proposals are to be submitted to the next session of parliament. In November AI knew of at least 16 young men imprisoned as conscientious objectors in the USSR, the majority of whom had refused military service on religious grounds.□

0125

PERU

New wave of abuses

A temporary lull in reported human rights violations since President Alberto Fujimori came to power in July has been followed by a considerable upsurge in "disappearances" and extrajudicial executions, including two massacres. In spite of his stated intentions to respect and promote human rights and to establish a national human rights commission, the President has not implemented specific measures.

On 22 August 16 peasants from the Iquicha community, near Uchuraccay, Huanta province, Ayacucho department, were reportedly killed by soldiers and *ronderos* (civil defence groups under military command), in what appears to have been extrajudicial executions. This incident occurred after Iquicha's community leaders refused to accept a demand made by the military and the *ronderos* to cooperate in a planned confrontation with *Sendero Luminoso*, an armed opposition group active in the area. Three days after the confrontation took place 50 soldiers and some 100 *ronderos* reportedly detained and shot dead 16 members of the community, including women and children.

In mid-October the beaten and bullet-ridden bodies of 18 people were found in a mass grave in the district of San Pedro de Cachi, Huamanga province, Ayacucho department. Nine of the bodies are reported to be those of a group of peasants, detained on 22 September by soldiers from the Castropampa military base and *ronderos*. The authorities had denied any knowledge of their detention.□

AMNESTY INTERNATIONAL NEWSLETTER is published every month in four languages to bring you news of AI's concerns and campaigns worldwide, as well as in-depth reports. Available from Amnesty International (address below)

Detained: (from left to right) Kenneth Matiba and Charles Rubia, and George Anyona

KENYA

Critics of one-party rule imprisoned

TWO prominent advocates of a multi-party system for Kenya, Kenneth Matiba and Charles Rubia, and a former prisoner of conscience, Raila Odinga, have been held under indefinite administrative detention orders since July, when the latest crackdown on critics of President Daniel arap Moi's government began.

Four other government critics - including George Anyona, a former member of parliament, and Edward Oyugi, a professor of educational psychology - are in prison facing possible 10-year sentences for "sedition". Their trial is scheduled for early 1991. At least 20 others, some of whom have been released on bail, are also awaiting trial and could face long terms of imprisonment for alleged possession of a "seditious publication" (such as *Africa Confidential*, a widely-read newsletter published in London) or a banned publication.

Several of those arrested since July 1990 are reported to have been tortured or ill-treated. They include Koigi wa Wamwere, an exile opposition leader with asylum in Norway, who appeared under arrest in Nairobi in mysterious circumstances in October 1990. He was charged with treason, a capital offence, together with two prominent lawyers. They were denied access to legal representatives and allege that they were tortured. No date has been set for their trial, in which five of their relatives will also appear on charges of concealment of treason.□

Over a million members!

AI's membership has now topped the one million mark. Information compiled from the available membership figures for 1990 show that there are now more than 1,100,000 members, subscribers and regular doners in over 150 countries.

SYRIA/LEBANON

Reports of extrajudicial executions

AT least 30 supporters of General Michel Aoun were reportedly extrajudicially executed following their capture by Syrian troops on 13-14 October 1990.

The killings occurred after a military assault by a joint force of Syrian troops and Lebanese Army soldiers was launched on 13 October against forces supporting General Aoun. General Aoun had been in opposition to the Lebanese Government of President Elias Hrawi. General Aoun's forces were effectively defeated after fighting in which combatants from both sides were killed and which resulted in General Aoun seeking refuge in the French Embassy in Beirut.

Many of the victims of the alleged extrajudicial executions were said to be soldiers from General Aoun's ranks who were stripped and had their hands tied behind their backs before being shot at close range. Some reports indicated that civilians, including children, were also extrajudicially executed by Syrian forces in villages considered sympathetic to General Aoun. Those killed apparently include 10 members of one family in the village of Deir Wahash.

AI called on the Lebanese Government to initiate an official inquiry into these allegations and to take measures to prevent any further killings. It urged the Syrian authorities to investigate the specific role of their troops in these incidents. AI also called on the Lebanese and Syrian authorities to ensure the safety of prisoners in their custody.□

Papua New Guinea

Between early 1989 and March 1990 government security forces faced armed opposition on the island of Bougainville. They responded with torture, ill-treatment and extrajudicial executions. AI's new report *Papua New Guinea: Human Rights Violations on Bougainville** focuses on 19 cases of extrajudicial execution or death after torture, and a further 50 cases of ill-treatment or torture by the security forces.
(Index No: ASA: 34/05/90)

AMNESTY INTERNATIONAL, 1 Easton Street, London WC1X 8DJ, United Kingdom. Printed in Great Britain by [illegible] Enterprises Ltd. London.
Available on subscription at £7 (US$12.00) for 12 issues. ISSN 0308 6887

AMNESTY INTERNATIONAL
NEWSLETTER
FEBRUARY 1991 VOLUME XXI • NUMBER 2

BRAZIL

Street children activist threatened

WOLMER do Nascimento, Rio de Janeiro coordinator of Brazil's National Street Children's Movement, went into hiding and sent his family to stay at an undisclosed location after he and his two young children repeatedly received written and oral death threats in early November.

In late November he received Federal Police protection on orders from the Justice Minister.

Wolmer do Nascimento founded a refuge for street children in Duque de Caxias, one of Rio's most violent suburbs. Recently he has denounced the role of police, judges, businessmen and politicians in supporting death squads. He says that these "extermination groups" killed 184 children in the area during the first five months of 1989.

Local and state authorities have apparently been slow to investigate or prosecute suspected death squad members. Although President Collor called in September for full investigation of all killings of children, human rights groups in Brazil said little progress had been made by the end of 1990.

Despite receiving police protection, Wolmer do Nascimento continued to stay away from Duque de Caxias and the refuge there. Frightened by news of the threats to Wolmer do Nascimento and his children, some of the street children who had frequented the refuge abandoned it.

As a result of an urgent action appeal, Wolmer do Nascimento reports that more than 1,000 letters from AI members expressing concern about his safety arrived at his Rio office.☐

TURKEY

Torture and killing in the southeast

THERE have recently been large-scale detentions throughout southeast Turkey where government troops are carrying out counter-insurgency operations against guerrillas of the Kurdish Workers' Party (PKK). The PKK have been carrying out armed attacks in the region since 1984.

The security forces have evacuated dozens of villages along the Syrian border, in an attempt to deprive the guerrillas of shelter and food. Villagers with no history of political activity have been interrogated, often under torture, usually on suspicion of having provided shelter for guerrillas.

On 8 September almost the entire population of Çizmeli village, near Siirt, was taken into custody. While most were released within a short time, Abit Ekinci remained in incommunicado detention in Eruh Gendarmerie Headquarters for 20 days. "My hands were bound, my clothes were removed and I was suspended from the ceiling by my arms", he said. "I was beaten constantly, and subjected to *falaka* (beating on the soles of the feet). I was given electric shocks three times. My testicles were bound with string and squeezed. My hands and neck were burned with cigarettes. The soles of my feet were slit with a razor and salt rubbed in. They forced me to sign a statement." Abit Ekinci was charged with sheltering Kurdish guerrillas and committed to Diyarbakir Prison.

A similar operation was conducted in the village of Yeniköy near Mardin following a clash between security forces and guerrillas in mid-November. Twenty-two villagers were detained; several of them later reported that they had been tortured at Mardin Police Headquarters. Of nine people charged and committed to prison, it is reported that one has serious leg injuries and another has broken teeth.

Ibrahim Döner

On 25 November the body of 24-year-old Yakup Aktaş from Derik, a small town in the Mardin area, was returned to his family by the Mardin Gendarmerie who had detained him a week earlier. The autopsy report stated that he had died of a heart attack. However, those who washed the body stated that there were wounds which suggested that he may have died under torture. His family's request for a second autopsy was refused and his body was buried under military supervision.

On 28 September the village of Kayadeler was occupied by troops and members of anti-guerrilla "special teams". They entered the mosque where the men were gathered, and told all of them to go home except for the imam, Ibrahim Döner. Shots were heard and two hours later his body was presented to his brother together with a pistol and a suicide note.

AI appealed to the Turkish Government to initiate investigations into all these incidents, but had not received a response by the end of December.☐

CHAD

New government promises reforms

THE Government of President Hissein Habré fell on 30 November 1990 when rebel forces led by Idriss Déby occupied the capital, N'Djamena, without bloodshed and Hissein Habré fled to Cameroon. The new government, in which Idriss Déby became President, promised to introduce multi-party democracy and to protect human rights. One of the last acts of Hissein Habré's Presidential Guards, which AI had previously identified as responsible for gross human rights violations, was to extrajudicially execute over 300 political opponents secretly detained at the presidential palace.

Several hundred other prisoners who had been detained at secret detention centres in N'Djamena were released on 1 December. Many had been tortured. Other prisoners were found in secret detention at a residence of the former Minister of the Interior.

Released prisoners confirmed reports published by AI in March 1990 of a pattern of systematic torture and ill-treatment of political prisoners, in which former President Habré was allegedly directly involved. More than 400 political prisoners from the Hadjerai and Zaghawa communities, arrested in May 1987 and April 1988, were either killed in secret or died in detention as a result of torture, malnutrition, lack of hygiene and medical attention.

AI urged the new government to introduce safeguards to prevent killings of prisoners and to establish an inquiry into the fate of hundreds of political prisoners who "disappeared" in the period since 1982 while President Habré was in power.☐

0127

CAMPAIGN FOR PRISONERS OF THE MONTH

Each of the people whose story is told below is a prisoner of conscience. Each has been arrested because of his or her religious or political beliefs, colour, sex, ethnic origin or language. None has used or advocated violence. Their continuing detention is a violation of the United Nations Universal Declaration of Human Rights. International appeals can help to secure the release of these prisoners or to improve their detention conditions. In the interest of the prisoners, letters to the authorities should be worded carefully and courteously. You should stress that your concern for human rights is not in any way politically partisan. In *no* circumstances should communications be sent to the prisoner.

IRAN

Malakeh Mohammadi: ***a journalist and editor aged in her 70s, she was among hundreds of people arrested in April 1983 because of their political activities on behalf of the left-wing Tudeh Party, then a legal organization.***

Malakeh Mohammadi and other leaders of the Tudeh Party were accused of plotting against the Islamic Republic of Iran; many were tortured to force them to confess to espionage and other offences and some were subsequently executed. Some of those who survived, including Malakeh Mohammadi's husband, Mohammed Pourhomozan, were among thousands of political prisoners secretly executed in the latter part of 1988.

Malakeh Mohammadi remained in detention for three and a half years before she was finally tried in 1986. She was not allowed to present any defence and has never been informed of the precise charges against her. She was sentenced to death, but this was later commuted to 20 years' imprisonment. She is alleged to have been tortured during the seven and a half years she has now been held.

Malakeh Mohammadi is held at Evin Prison, together with other women prisoners of conscience, arrested in 1983, from the Tudeh Party and other left-wing groups. All have suffered continuous pressure to renounce their conscientiously-held political beliefs. In August 1990 some accepted offers of temporary release, although nearly all are now said to be back in prison. Malakeh Mohammadi is reported to have declined the offer, as she had no close relatives left alive and had decided to leave prison only when the authorities granted her a full, unconditional release.

■Please send courteous appeals for her immediate release to: His Excellency Hojatoleslam Ali Akbar Hashemi Rafsanjani/President of the Islamic Republic of Iran/The Presidency/Palestine Avenue, Azerbaijan Intersection/Tehran/Islamic Republic of Iran.□

RWANDA

Innocent Ndayambaje: ***a 29-year-old economics student at the National University of Rwanda, he was arrested in October 1986 and held incommunicado without charge for three years.***

In March 1990 Innocent Ndayambaje was tried and sentenced by the State Security Court to five years' imprisonment for contravening Rwanda's one-party Constitution.

Under the constitution all Rwandese are obliged to be members of the ruling National Revolutionary Movement for Development (MRND), and the establishment or membership of other parties is a criminal offence.

At his trial Innocent Ndayambaje pleaded not guilty to the charge of contravening the constitution, but admitted to being the sole member of the National Resistance Front (FRONAR) which, he said, aimed to end regional and ethnic injustices in Rwanda. He is a member of Rwanda's minority Tutsi ethnic group.

He was sentenced to five years' imprisonment for his membership of FRONAR and for distributing political tracts in the town of Butare.

AI is concerned that Innocent Ndayambaje did not receive a fair trial: he had no access to legal counsel either before or during his trial and no general right of appeal against his conviction and sentence.

The court's five judges are appointed by Presidential decree and included two soldiers and an official from the President's office; none of them is known to have legal training.

He remains held at Kigali Central Prison. He is apparently not allowed to communicate with his relatives nor to receive visits.

■Please send courteous letters appealing for his immediate release to: Son Excellence Monsieur le Général-Major Habyarimana Juvénal/Président de la République/Présidence de la République/BP 15, Kigali/République Rwandaise.□

CUBA

Esteban González González and six others: ***members of the unofficial Movimiento Integracionista Democrática (MID), Movement for Democratic Integration, they were arrested in Havana in September 1989. In June 1990 they were convicted of "rebellion".***

Esteban González González, a 60-year-old mathematics teacher, founded the MID in early 1989. The movement explicitly rejects any violent activity and advocates a wide range of democratic reforms, including the establishment of a pluralistic government, thus challenging the monopoly of the Communist Party, the only legal party in Cuba.

After their arrest, the seven men were held in State Security headquarters for several months without access to legal counsel. For at least the first month they were reportedly held in small cells with constant artificial light and were allowed no fresh air or exercise.

They were transferred to prison in December 1989 but are believed to have had access to legal counsel only in May 1990 when the prosecution presented the results of its investigations to the court. The seven were accused of possessing and disseminating "counter-revolutionary propaganda"; seeking funds and recognition from international sources; planning a campaign of civil disobedience; and wanting to change the political and social system and to restore capitalism. Esteban González was sentenced to seven years' imprisonment; Arturo Montané Ruiz, Manuel Mora, Edgardo Llompart Martín and Manuel Regueiro Robaína received sentences ranging from three to six years' imprisonment and Isidro Ledesma Quijano was given three years' "restricted liberty", rather than imprisonment, on grounds of ill-health. The imprisoned men are serving their sentences in Combinado del Este Prison.

■Please send courteous letters appealing for the release of the six imprisoned men to: His Excellency Dr Fidel Castro Ruz/President of the Republic/Ciudad de la Habana/Cuba.□

PRISONER NEWS

AI learned in November 1990 of the release of 43 prisoners under adoption or investigation. AI took up 150 cases.

RELEASED

AI has learned that Ladji Traoré, prisoner of the month in October 1990, was released in November 1990 without charge or trial.

Stop press

The following reports are now available from AI:

Colombia: AI is concerned about human rights violations against members of indigenous communities in Caldas department in central Colombia and the apparent lack of progress in the official investigations into these abuses.
(*Index No. AMR 23/61/90*)

Sierra Leone: AI has received reports that 12 people were sentenced to death in Sierra Leone earlier this year after being convicted of murder and armed robbery. Although death sentences have not been carried out in recent years in non-political cases, AI is concerned that the execution of six men for treason in 1989 may herald a return to the use of the death penalty.
(*Index No. AFR 51/01/90*)

FOCUS amnesty international

Women in the front line

AI has received numerous reports of women being tortured while in police custody in Turkey.

Nevruz Türkdoğan was treasurer of the Women's Association for Democracy in Turkey. While distributing a journal in Ankara on 15 September 1990, she and her husband were detained by police.

Despite informing the police that she was two and a half months pregnant, Nevruz Türkdoğan testifies that she was repeatedly beaten for three days. She miscarried on 19 September. She was then taken to Ankara Numune Hospital. On 20 September she was unconditionally released by Ankara State Security Court.

Please send courteous letters urging an impartial and independent investigation into allegations of torture and ill-treatment of Nevruz Türkdoğan, insisting that those responsible be brought to justice. Send appeals to: Abdülkadir Aksu/Minister of Interior/İçişleri Bakanlığı/06644 Ankara/Turkey□

A pregnant woman detainee is punched in the stomach by police officers. An elderly woman is raped in front of her family by armed soldiers. A young girl is detained and sexually humiliated by government officials. A wife is tortured by interrogators to force her husband to "confess". A mother is shot dead by soldiers simply because her son is suspected of political activities. A daughter is threatened with death by government agents because she asks after her "disappeared" father.

The list of such gross human rights violations against women is endless. Many are targeted because they are strong — because they are political activists, community organizers, or persist in demanding that their rights or those of their relatives are respected. Others are targeted because they are seen as vulnerable — young women who can easily be sexually abused or humiliated, frightened mothers who will do anything to protect their children, or pregnant women fearful for their unborn babies, women who can be used to get at men, or refugee women, isolated and vulnerable in unfamiliar surroundings.

This report details human rights violations which are primarily suffered by women as well as a range of human rights abuses that women have experienced alongside men and children. By focusing on human rights violations committed against women, AI hopes to mobilize international support for the protection of women and, by extension, for all members of the societies in which they live.

This report records the experiences of women who have survived human rights violations. It also tells the stories of many who did not survive. The violations have occurred, and continue to occur, in every region of the world and under every system of government.

These pages do not contain a comprehensive account of all human rights violations against women, merely an indication of the type of atrocities women have suffered and therefore what must be prevented from happening to anyone in the future. Nor is this a survey of all violations of women's human rights. It covers only those human rights violations which fall within AI's strictly defined mandate: to seek the release of prisoners of conscience — men and women detained solely for their beliefs, colour, sex, ethnic origin, language or religion, who have neither used nor advocated violence; to work for prompt and fair trials for all political prisoners and to oppose the death penalty, extrajudicial executions and torture without reservation. AI covers a limited spectrum of rights, but not because it ignores the importance of other rights. It believes that there is a close relationship between all human rights but recognizes that it can achieve more by working within set limits.

0129

Women's human rights, like those of men and children, are proclaimed in the Universal Declaration of Human Rights — the individual freedoms basic to human life. These include freedom of conscience, expression and association, freedom from arbitrary arrest and detention, freedom from torture, the right to a fair trial, and freedom from extrajudicial killing. These rights have been trampled on by governments around the world. Whatever the circumstances, however deep the economic, social or political crisis a government may face, there can never be a valid excuse for contravening fundamental human rights.

Women are primarily the victims of certain abuses. Rape, frequently used as a form of torture, is most often inflicted on women detainees. The United Nations (UN) Convention against Torture and Other Cruel, Inhuman or Degrading Treatment or Punishment prohibits "any act by which severe pain or suffering, whether physical or mental, is intentionally inflicted" for purposes such as obtaining information or punishing, intimidating, or coercing a person. No government official should be permitted to commit or tolerate rape and other forms of sexual attack.

No government official should be permitted to commit or tolerate rape and other forms of sexual attack

Women are particularly vulnerable to rape between the time of arrest and arrival at official detention centres. In some countries law enforcement officials or military personnel have committed rape and other sexual abuses without having officially arrested the victim. However, confinement in an official place of detention does not necessarily protect women from rape or other sexual abuses. Many have reported that prison guards have raped them, attempted to rape them, or threatened them with rape.

For women who are pregnant at the time of detention, additional suffering often accompanies human rights abuses. They risk injury to the foetus, miscarriage and the prospect of giving birth in harsh prison conditions. The women who become pregnant as a result of rape in custody face yet a further set of traumas.

Women also suffer from sexual humiliation, threats of rape and verbal abuses intended to degrade them. All of these violate their basic human rights by subjecting them to cruel, inhuman or degrading treatment or punishment.

Women from all walks of life have been targeted for human rights abuse. In some cases, the reasons are connected with a woman's occupation or peaceful, legitimate activities. Governments detain or direct violent attacks against women who are physicians, lawyers, journalists, trade unionists, teachers, human rights activists, political activists, community organizers and members of many other professions. In other cases, women's human rights are violated because of their ethnic origin or religious beliefs.

Some women are subjected to human rights violations merely because they happen to be the wives, mothers, daughters or friends of people whom the authorities consider to be "dangerous" or "undesirable". These women are threatened, held as substitutes for their relatives, tortured or even killed as governments attempt to exert their will over those closely connected in some way with the women.

The leading human rights activists in many societies are prisoners' relatives: often wives and children, endlessly in the front line, campaigning for the prisoner's release, confronting government officials, trying to get information, trying to care for the prisoner. Prisoners' families bear the burden of providing assistance of all sorts — from daily meals, medicine and clothing, through to raising funds to pay legal fees, ransoms, or to publicize the case.

In many African countries a strong tradition of family or community solidarity has protected prisoners in vulnerable situations. This has led some governments deliberately to exploit family relations, by imprisoning, threatening and harassing prisoners' relatives. In Guinea, under the rule of the late President Sékou Touré, wives were pressurized by the state to divorce their imprisoned husbands.

Embarca ment Taleb ould Husein, a radio announcer in Laayoune in the Western Sahara, was taken from her home by plainclothes police officers in September 1979 and has not been seen since. She left behind a 13-year-old daughter.

She is one of hundreds of people who have "disappeared" in the south of Morocco and the Western Sahara, many of whom were arrested because they or their relatives were suspected of opposing Moroccan rule of the Western Sahara territory and sympathizing with the Polisario Front armed opposition organization.

Evidence suggests that many of the "disappeared" in Morocco are still alive and confined in secret detention centres.

Please write courteous letters, in French if possible, urging that Embarca ment Taleb ould Husein be released immediately and unconditionally unless charged with a recognizably criminal offence and given a fair trial. Send appeals to: SM Le Roi Hassan II/Office de SM le Roi/ Palais Royal/Rabat/Morocco□

Countless women are forced to live in the shadow of another person's "disappearance". A woman may suddenly become her family's sole source of support just at the time when she is facing the absence of a close relative and is trying to locate the "disappeared" victim. She may be effectively widowed by her husband's "disappearance", yet unable to claim state or other benefits because her husband has not been declared dead, officially or legally. Members of the National Coordinating Committee of Widows of Guatemala, an Indian group known as CONAVIGUA, have denounced their government's attitude to providing compensation. The group has repeatedly alleged that government compensation is granted only if a widow attributes her husband's death to opposition guerrilla forces and if she ceases to pursue investigation into her husband's death or "disappearance".

Relatives of the "disappeared" face additional, emotional suffering in many cultures. Women often refuse to give up hope and search for years for husbands and children who have "disap-

0130

Wafa' Idriss is one of at least 77 women arrested in Syria between August 1977 and February 1988 who remain in detention without charge or trial.

Hundreds of women have been arrested in Syria since 1985 because of their relationship to men sought by the security forces, or because of their own peaceful political activities.

Torture of political prisoners is systematic in Syria. It is carried out during interrogation to extract "confessions" and information, and to punish detainees.

Reports of rape by members of the security forces are numerous.

Please write courteous letters expressing concern at widespread reports that women have been subjected to severe torture and sexual abuse while in detention and asking that the 77 women be released immediately unless charged with a recognizably criminal offence and given a prompt, fair trial. Send appeals to: His Excellency 'Abd al-Halim Khaddam/Vice-President/Office of the President/Presidential Palace/Damascus/Syrian Arab Republic□

peared", even though relatively few victims of "disappearance" survive this inhuman violation. But unless or until they reappear, or their bodies are found, their families suffer years of uncertainty, unable properly to mourn their loss and thus perhaps to lay their grief to rest.

In areas of civil turmoil or armed conflict, women are often subjected to brutal treatment simply because they live in a particular location or belong to a particular ethnic group. They are often caught in the crossfire between armed opposition groups and government forces, living under the threat of violence from both sides.

AI, as a matter of principle, condemns the torture and killing of prisoners by anyone, including opposition groups. It does not, however, treat such groups as though they had the status of governments. Nor does it address them unless they are certain of the essential attributes of a government, such as control over substantial territory and population. It is, after all, governments which have jurisdiction to determine criminal responsibility and to bring to justice those responsible for violent attacks on government authorities, security forces, and civilians. The state's exercise of such lawful authority, however, must conform to international standards of human rights and observe norms safeguarding fundamental human rights provided in domestic law.

Many governments do not maintain these norms. The rape of peasant women, either while in formal custody or when held by soldiers during counter-insurgency operations, is a common phenomenon in many countries. Governments often are complacent in the face of such abuse. Legal officials in Peru's Ayacucho department told AI representatives in 1986 that rape by government troops operating in rural areas was to be expected. In late September 1990, a Peruvian woman and her 17-year-old daughter were detained in a military base and repeatedly raped by a number of soldiers. Both women were subsequently released but warned not to report the rape. They have requested anonymity lest they face reprisals. Effective investigations into cases of rape in Peru are not known to have taken place nor have the perpetrators been brought to justice.

Women refugees and asylum-seekers have also been the victims of sexual abuse by police, soldiers or other government agents. Many of these women lack the support systems which would be provided in their own communities or by their close relatives. With few resources to protect them from abuse or to provide the means of redress, they become victims of a range of violations.

Cultural or social circumstances sometimes render women particularly isolated by the human rights violations they experience. They may choose not to report humiliating assaults by government authorities, fearing reprisals from their own families, traumatic social repercussions, or further attacks by government officials.

Women who choose not to remain silent in the face of human rights violations inflicted upon them may face barriers such as official tolerance of the injuries caused to them. If they are from disadvantaged social or economic groups, they may find that official channels of communication are closed to them. Law enforcement officials may not listen, and they may have no place to turn.

During the past decade, increasing numbers of women have spoken out for human rights protection. They have stated publicly and clearly what they and other members of their communities have suffered. They have also organized community and national groups to protest against human rights abuses. In some countries their vulnerability to such abuse has increased as they have assumed public leadership roles and spoken out about the special measures needed to protect women's human rights. Despite this, they continue to make their demands heard. The Committee of Mothers and Relatives of Political Prisoners, and Victims of Political Assassination and Disappearance, known as COMADRES, has been prominent for many years in the struggle to protect human rights in El Salvador. The COMADRES continue their work today, despite repeated threats against members of the group and violent attacks such as the October 1989 bombing of their San Salvadore offices.

Some women are subjected to human rights violations because of their relationship to people whom the authorities consider "dangerous"

The following month, soldiers raided the offices and arrested nine COMADRES activists. Some of those arrested later said that they had been blindfolded, handcuffed, and beaten in detention.

The Mutual Support Group for the Appearance of Our Relatives Alive, known as GAM, has been a target of violence in Guatemala. GAM members press government authorities to account for those who "disappear".

Several GAM leaders, including Rosario Godoy de Cuevas, were abducted and killed in 1985, apparently by government agents.

Other GAM members are now the target of threats. The group's leader, Nineth Montenegro de García, has received so many death threats that human rights activists worldwide have sent appeals on her behalf to the Guatema-

0131

lan authorities on a number of occasions. Her mother, whose house was strafed with machine-gunfire in July 1990, also appears to be at risk from government forces or people associated with them. The bullets recovered from the attack reportedly were of a calibre known to be used by the military.

Women have played prominent roles in South African human rights organizations such as the Detainees' Parents Support Committee and the Black Sash. Despite decades of repression, women activists have continued to mobilize against mass detentions, torture, and the injustices perpetuated by *apartheid*.

Noma India Mfeketo attended the 1985 International Women's Congress in Nairobi, representing the United Women's Congress and the Federation of South African Women. Her international prominence, however, did not protect her when she returned home: she spent nine months in detention without charge or trial in 1987 and was again detained for several months in 1988 and 1989. Like many of her colleagues, she was detained solely for the peaceful exercise of basic human rights.

© Maggie Murray/Format

Woman and child in refugee camp. Refugee women are particularly vulnerable to human rights abuses

Susan Aniban of Task Force Detainees, a human rights group in the Philippines, was reportedly detained and tortured in November 1988. Numerous women human rights workers there have been subjected to such ill-treatment.

Turkish officials detained several members of a women's organization in January 1990, after a police raid on the offices of the Association of Democratic Women in Ankara. They were reportedly interrogated under torture.

The perseverance of women like these in the face of such persecution, along with the courage of many other men and women who continue to fight for human rights, has yielded significant results in recent years. More information is now available to the international community about what is happening to women worldwide than ever before. The momentum to end patterns of abuse has increased as more women have joined efforts to publicize the facts and to press for change.

The international campaign is expanding and accelerating on behalf of women who struggled for their rights and did not survive, on behalf of women now struggling to survive, and on behalf not only of women but of all people who ought never to have to face human rights violations. Human rights activists are demanding that protections guaranteed under international treaties become a reality in all countries.

The international human rights covenants, The UN Convention against Torture, the UN Convention on the Elimination of All Forms of Discrimination against Women, and many other agreements, establish minimum standards of government responsibility.

If governments ignore their responsibilities to any sector of society — whether to women, to the young, or to members of ethnic or religious minorities — then no one's human rights are safe.□

Maria Nonna Santa Clara, a social worker in Naga City, and her colleague, Angelina Llenaresas, "disappeared" on 26 April 1989. They had been visiting a woman in Santa Cruz, who said later that she saw them being followed by three unknown men after leaving her house. Eye-witnesses reported seeing Maria Nonna Santa Clara later the same day shouting for help from a military jeep in Naga City.

Military authorities have denied all knowledge of the whereabouts of the two women, despite substantial evidence that they were responsible for their abduction. The family of Maria Nonna Santa Clara, and others involved in trying to clarify her fate, have received death threats which they believe to have come from military sources.

Please write courteous letters urging the government to take prompt action to establish the whereabouts of Maria Nonna Santa Clara and her colleague, and to bring to justice those responsible for their "disappearance". Send appeals to: President Corazon Aquino/Malacanang Palace/Manila/Phillipines□

0132

IRAQ

Widespread abuse follows invasion

WIDESPREAD human rights abuses were perpetrated by Iraqi forces following the invasion of Kuwait on 2 August 1990. These include the arbitrary arrest and detention without trial of thousands of civilians and military personnel; systematic torture; the imposition of the death penalty and the extrajudicial execution of hundreds of unarmed civilians, including children; and the "disappearance" of hundreds of detainees, many of whom are feared dead. The abuses were detailed in a report published by AI in December 1990*.

AI takes no position on the conflict in the Gulf. The organization is concerned, however, about human rights violations taking place in that context.

AI's report contained numerous testimonies from former detainees, who said they were held incommunicado without charge or trial and tortured throughout their detention. No less than 38 methods of torture are cited in the report which concluded that the brutality of the treatment inflicted on detainees appeared designed to terrorize the population at large and to discourage people from expressing, in whatever form, their opposition to the Iraqi presence in Kuwait.

Families were given no official notification of the arrest or place of detention of the detainees, who therefore effectively "disappeared" in custody, and remained ignorant of their fate and whereabouts until they had either been released or executed. The bodies of those executed were either found in the streets of Kuwait City, or were dumped outside their homes.

From about mid-August, a pattern of extrajudicial executions emerged, whereby, according to one source, "the Iraqis would bring the detainee back to his home and ask his family to identify him. Once he had been identified, the Iraqis would shoot him in the back of the head, right in front of his family". Children were among those who died in this manner.

Iraq also extended the scope of the death penalty in August, shortly after the invasion. However, AI has concluded that ostensibly criminal offences, such as looting, were used by the Iraqi authorities as a pretext to execute individuals who had taken part in opposition activity against Iraqi forces in Kuwait.

In December, AI called on the Iraqi Government to implement a series of recommendations, including: granting immediate access to the International Committee of the Red Cross to enable it to provide protection to prisoners and civilians in Kuwait; releasing immediately and unconditionally all prisoners of conscience; investigating all reports of torture, extrajudicial executions and "disappearances"; and taking immediate steps to ensure that no further torture, executions or other abuses are carried out.

Iraq/Occupied Kuwait: Human rights violations since 2 August is available from AI sections or the International Secretariat.□

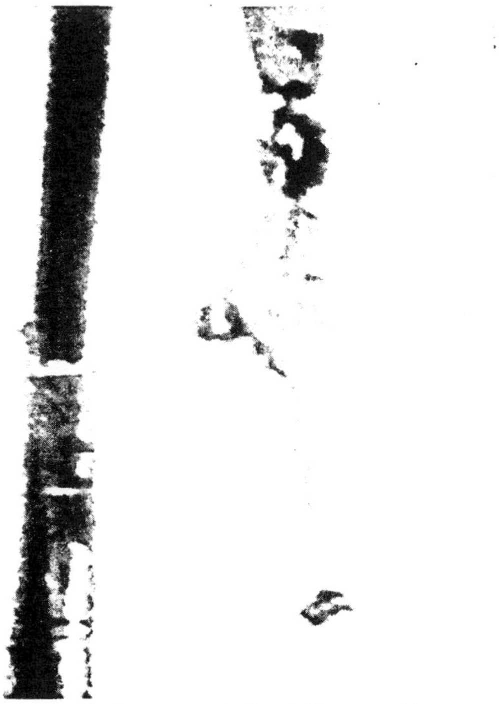

This body, left hanging from a crane in Kuwait City, was said to be that of an Iraqi soldier executed for looting on 16 August

REPUBLIC OF YEMEN

Eight granted clemency to mark AI's visit

THE Yemeni Government told an AI delegation in November 1990 that the country would accede to the United Nations Convention against Torture and Other Cruel, Inhuman or Degrading Treatment or Punishment. Eight political prisoners under sentence of death since 1985 were granted clemency in honour of AI's visit. The government also assured AI that it would review the cases of all untried political detainees currently held.

AI's delegates, led by the Secretary General, met the President and Vice-President, and the Ministers of Foreign Affairs, Interior and Justice, with whom they raised AI's concerns in Yemen, including cases of sentenced political prisoners and untried detainees, irregularities in arrest and detention procedures, and the continued use of the death penalty and of shackles in prisons. In addition, the Secretary General addressed the Yemeni Parliament. He welcomed the recent positive human rights developments in the country but drew attention to AI's outstanding concerns.

AI was publicly invited to visit the country by the President of Yemen in February 1990.□

JORDAN

Prisoners freed by royal pardon

EIGHT prisoners were released in September and November 1990 following royal pardons granted by King Hussein bin Talal. One had been sentenced to death and the others to lengthy terms of imprisonment after unfair trials by the Martial Law Court for political offences involving violence, including an attempt on the life of the King.□

VENEZUALA

Grave of Caracas victims exhumed

IN November, a judge ordered the exhumation of unmarked graves believed to contain the remains of a number of those who died in Caracas between 27 February and 10 March 1989, when hundreds were killed by members of the security forces.

A forensic anthropologist visited the country between 26 and 30 November as an AI delegate to monitor the investigations and gather information on the location of the burial site, the recovery of the bodies and their identification. Several bodies were recovered to be analysed by local forensic experts.

The victims' relatives welcomed the developments but, together with human rights monitors, continued to call for full investigatios into the killings — the circumstances of several of which suggested the victims were extrajudicially executed. However, little progress had been reported by the end of 1990.□

MAURITANIA

Reports of torture

OVER 1,000 people, including at least three former prisoners of conscience, were arrested in Mauritania's capital, Nouakchott, and in Nouadhibou in November and December 1990. They were detained in military barracks in the Nouakchott area. A government official said they had been detained in connection with a conspiracy to overthrow the government, but none of them is known to have been formally charged with any offence. AI has received reports that at least 15 of them may have died in custody as a result of torture. All the detainees belong to the black Hal-pulaar ethnic group, which the authorities suspect of opposing the government. There have been widespread arrests, torture, "disappearance" and extrajudicial executions of Hal-pulaar people, particularly in the south of the country, since April 1989.□

0133

SAUDI ARABIA

Women detained for driving

ON 6 November 1990 a women's demonstration took place in Riyadh in protest at the country's traditional prohibition against women driving cars. Dozens of women drove cars in convoy along a main thoroughfare in Riyadh. Forty-nine women who took part were detained for some hours, but were released.

Salih al-'Azzaz, a prominent writer and journalist, was also arrested on suspicion of being one of the organizers of the demonstration. He was reportedly taking photographs of the demonstration at the time of his arrest. He was reportedly held incommunicado at the *Mabahith al-'Amma* (General Intelligence) Headquarters in the 'Ulaisha district of Riyadh, and was only allowed family visits at the end of December. AI considers him a prisoner of conscience and has called for his immediate and unconditional release.

A week after the demonstration the ban on female drivers was formally made law. The law states that anyone violating the prohibition for women to drive is liable to an unspecified punishment.□

UNITED KINGDOM

Broadwater Farm case to go to appeal

THE United Kingdom Government announced in December the referral of the case of Engin Raghip to the Court of Appeal. Engin Raghip is one of three young men serving life sentences for the murder of a policeman during a 1985 riot at the Broadwater Farm public housing estate in London. The government based its decision on new evidence concerning psychological testing.

AI has consistently urged the government to review all the Broadwater Farm cases in which convictions were based solely on confessions. The organization had received many allegations that confessions had been obtained through coercion and in the absence of a lawyer. In the February 1987 trial three juveniles were acquitted of murder after the judge criticized police conduct in the interrogation of two of them. At a subsequent disciplinary hearing the officer leading the murder investigation was found guilty of denying a 13-year-old boy access to a lawyer during three days of detention. Another police officer still faces disciplinary charges over the boy's interrogation.□

AI delegation visits India

AN AI delegation visited Delhi from 10 to 17 December 1990 to attend the World Congress on Human Rights. While there, they sought meetings with government officials, including Prime Minister Chandra Shekhar. Such meetings had been approved in principle by the previous government which resigned in November 1990.□

AMNESTY INTERNATIONAL NEWSLETTER is published every month in four languages to bring you news of AI's concerns and campaigns worldwide, as well as in-depth reports. Available from Amnesty International (address below)

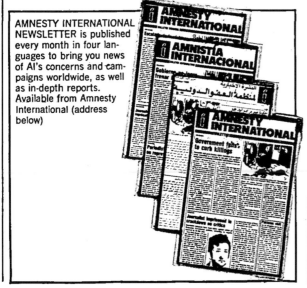

Relatives grieve over the bodies of the dead

GUATEMALA

Army kills fifteen civilians

AT least 15 people, three of them children, were reportedly killed and 19 others, including several children, were wounded when soldiers opened fire on a crowd of unarmed villagers at a military base in Sololá Guatemala on the evening of 2 December 1990.

According to eyewitness reports, the events leading to the killings began when soldiers from the base, who were allegedly drunk, broke into a villager's house, tried to rob him and reportedly opened fire and wounded him. A crowd of some 1,500 went to the base to protest and were fired on by soldiers.

Survivors interviewed in hospital by local and international press and human rights groups insist that the crowd was peaceful and unarmed and that the soldiers opened fire when leaders of the protest asked to speak to the base commander.

Military personnel initially claimed that the villagers had provoked the incident. However, after widespread national and international expressions of outrage, military spokesmen announced that two soldiers, one said to have provoked the initial incident at the villager's home, the other the base commander had been detained.

AI has asked the government to say whether there will be an inquiry into the killings, and urged that any findings be made known promptly, that any criminal acts committed be referred to the tribunals and that steps be taken to ensure adequate medical care for the injured, the security of all witnesses to either incident, and appropriate compensation for victims' relatives.□

SOUTH KOREA: In Issue No. 1, published January 1991, it is stated that prisoners of conscience who do not renounce their communist beliefs may be detained indefinitely. The Public Security Law, which allowed for such detention, was repealed in 1989. However, political prisoners held under national security legislation, including prisoners of conscience, have been denied the benefit of measures such as release on parole, unless they agree to be "anti-communist".

AMNESTY INTERNATIONAL, 1 Easton Street, London WC1X 8DJ, United Kingdom. Printed in Great Britain by Flashprint Enterprises Ltd. London. Available on subscription at £7 (US$12.00) for 12 issues. ISSN 0308 6887

0134

AMNESTY INTERNATIONAL
NEWSLETTER
MARCH 1991 VOLUME XXI • NUMBER 3

SYRIA

Deaths in custody

A Palestinian detained without trial since 1985 is reported to have died in custody in December 1990. Muhammad Dawud (also known as Abu Dawud), a senior member of the Palestine Liberation Organization, was held incommunicado throughout his detention. He is reported to have died in *Fara' Falastin* (Palestine Branch) detention centre in Damascus after having been denied medical treatment for injuries resulting from torture during his detention and from ailments contracted as a result of prolonged detention and poor prison conditions. The Syrian authorities reportedly refused to release his body for burial.

AI is aware of at least three other deaths in custody in questionable circumstances during 1990. No official enquiry is reported to have been carried out into these deaths.☐

ZANZIBAR

Prisoners released

FIFTEEN prominent government opponents detained without charge or trial in Zanzibar since mid-1990, including former Zanzibar Chief Justice Ali Haji Pandu and the former Political Commissar to the police, Machano Khamis, were released on the orders of Tanzania's President in December.

The 15 prisoners of conscience were arrested in the months before last October's general elections and accused of attempting to disrupt the elections. Zanzibar nationalists campaigning for a referendum on the continuing union between Zanzibar and the mainland had called on people not to register for the electoral roll.

Said Shariff Hamad, the unofficial nationalist leader, remains in custody in Zanzibar charged with illegal possession of government documents. His trial is expected soon.☐

(c) Associated Press

Thousands joined a rally in support of democracy in the town of Kavaja, Albania, on 25 December 1990

ALBANIA

Political prisoners pardoned

ON 5 January reportedly 202 political prisoners were pardoned. The authorities stated that when pardons granted to political prisoners between June and December 1990 were included this brought the total number of prisoners pardoned to 393. Three days later it was announced that a further 170 would be pardoned shortly. All those pardoned appeared to have been convicted of "anti-state agitation and propaganda" and "flight from the state" after attempting to exercise their rights to freedom of expression and movement. Another 160 political prisoners were reportedly due to have their sentences reviewed.

The leader of a recently founded Albanian human rights organization was officially informed on 18 January that 120 political prisoners remained detained, in addition to some 150 arrested during anti-government riots in December 1990. Among those released was Henrik Gjoka (Prisoner of the Month in December 1990), who was serving an 11-year sentence after conviction in 1986 on charges of attempting to leave the country illegally.

On 11 December, following mass student demonstrations in Tirana, the communist party decided to legalize independent political parties. However, during the following three days violent anti-government riots took place in several towns and 157 people were arrested and investigated on charges of vandalism, attempted murder, assault and illegal assembly. Reportedly many were tortured and ill-treated following arrest. AI expressed concern about the torture and ill-treatment allegations, and called for legal safeguards for all those arrested, including adequate time to prepare their defence. Within a week of arrest, 26 of the accused had been sentenced to up to 20 years' imprisonment.

A draft constitution published at the end of December proposed lifting the ban on religious activity dating from 1967 and if adopted, would guarantee freedom of conscience. It also would guarantee the rights to freedom of expression, association, assembly and movement and the right to strike. However, these rights would be subject to sometimes restrictive laws. Unlike the existing constitution, it would guarantee Albanian citizens equality regardless of political conviction and decree that a person is innocent until proved guilty by a final court decision. It also would guarantee the right to a defence lawyer throughout criminal proceedings and ban the use of torture and all other forms of inhuman treatment and punishment. It would not, however, abolish the death penalty as AI had earlier urged.☐

PRISONER NEWS

AI learned in December 1990 of the release of 39 prisoners under adoption or investigation. AI took up 237 cases.

0135

CAMPAIGN FOR PRISONERS OF THE MONTH

Each of the people whose story is told below is a prisoner of conscience. Each has been arrested because of his or her religious or political beliefs, colour, sex, ethnic origin or language. None has used or advocated violence. Their continuing detention is a violation of the United Nations Universal Declaration of Human Rights. International appeals can help to secure the release of these prisoners or to improve their detention conditions. In the interest of the prisoners, letters to the authorities should be worded carefully and courteously. You should stress that your concern for human rights is not in any way politically partisan. In *no* circumstances should communications be sent to the prisoner.

TAIWAN

Huang Hua: ***a 52-year-old political activist, he has spent over 21 years in prison for his peaceful political activities and began his fourth term of imprisonment in December 1990 when the Taiwan High Court sentenced him to 10 years' imprisonment for preparing to commit sedition.***

Huang Hua strongly believes that the Government of the Republic of China on Taiwan should abandon its claim to reunify Taiwan and mainland China and should instead declare a "Republic of Taiwan". Such "independentist" views are forbidden under the National Security Law and the Statute for the Punishment of Sedition.

Huang Hua

To promote his views Huang Hua founded the New Nation Movement in 1988 and organised and spoke at rallies throughout Taiwan. The New Nation Movement also supported a number of pro-independence candidates during the parliamentary and local elections of December 1989. During the March 1990 indirect presidential elections Huang Hua campaigned for direct presidential elections. He declared himself a candidate for the opposition Democratic Progressive Party (DPP), although he was not eligible for public office having been deprived of his civil rights when previously convicted of sedition.

Huang Hua ignored several summonses to appear before the Taiwan High Court and went into hiding after a warrant was issued for his arrest in July 1990. He was arrested in November after attending the funeral of a DPP legislator. At his trial he refused to answer the judge's questions and instead explained his political views. When sentencing him to 10 years' imprisonment, the judge said that Huang Hua's "words and actions had overstepped the boundaries of freedom of speech". Huang Hua has refused to appeal against his sentence. He was excluded from the 1 January presidential amnesty because of his previous convictions.

■Please send courteous letters appealing for the immediate and unconditional release of Huang Hua to : President Lee Teng-hui/Office of the President/Chieshou Hall, Chungking S. Road/Taipei/Taiwan/Republic of China.☐

HONDURAS

Rolando Vindel González: ***President of the National Electricity Workers' Union (STENEE), he "disappeared" seven years ago.***

Rolando Vindel González "disappeared" on 18 March 1984 after leaving his home in Tegucigalpa to attend a union meeting, where he was to discuss the union's next move in deadlocked wage negotiations with the state-owned power company. He was seized by a group of heavily armed men, thrown into a vehicle and driven away. Relatives and colleagues searched for him at police and military units around the capital, but his detention was not acknowledged by the authorities. He was never seen again.

Evidence gathered by local human rights groups suggests that the captors were agents of the National Directorate of Investigations (DNI), the investigative arm of the security forces. STENEE alleged that following his abduction Rolando Vindel González was held at three different clandestine detention centres, including a military centre used by United States military to train Honduran and Salvadorian military officers. The Honduran authorities, however, have repeatedly denied that he was ever in custody.

This was not the first time that Rolando Vindel had been detained for his trade union activity. In January 1981 he was held by the DNI on charges of subversion but was released for lack of evidence. After his release he said he had been beaten and tortured with electric shocks and death threats.

On learning of the "disappearance" of Rolando Vindel, in 1984, AI issued urgent appeals. The government of the time replied that the National Congress had ordered an investigation into the case, but to AI's knowledge no findings were ever published.

Rolando Vindel is one of 143 men and women believed to have "disappeared" at the hands of the military and security forces in Honduras since 1981, whose whereabouts and fate have never been clarified. In December 1990 the current Minister of the Interior announced that his government would take steps to investigate past "disappearance" cases. AI sought further details from the government but by the beginning of February 1991 the government had not replied nor made public any information about these investigations.

■Please send courteous appeals asking what steps have been taken to clarify the whereabouts and fate of Rolando Vindel González and the other "disappeared" to: Sr. José Francisco Cardona/Ministro de Gobernación y Justicia/Palacio de los Ministerios, 2o piso/Tegucigalpa/Honduras.☐

USSR

Oleg Gorshenin: ***a 22-year-old pacifist, he is serving an 18-month prison sentence for refusing to perform military service on grounds of conscience.***

Oleg Gorshenin was first arrested on 27 March 1989 in Moscow, after failing to respond to his call-up papers for two years. In a statement to the Soviet authorities he declared that he was a "convinced pacifist", and asked to be permitted to emigrate to any country which did not have compulsory military service, or which made provision for alternative civilian service. Oleg Gorshenin was taken back to his home city of Orsk and sentenced to 18 months' compulsory labour under restricted conditions, but failed to present himself at the place where he was to serve his sentence.

On 19 June 1989 a court tried Oleg Gorshenin *in absentia* and substituted imprisonment for compulsory labour. He went into hiding, and in July that year applied for political asylum at the Belgian Embassy in Moscow. Eventually, in April 1990, he was rearrested and sent to serve his sentence in a corrective labour colony in the Orenburg region.

The United Nations Commission on Human Rights has recognized that conscientious objection to military service is a legitimate exercise of the right of freedom of thought, conscience and religion. In January 1991 AI was working for the release of over 14 conscientious objectors imprisoned in the USSR, most of them Jehovah's Witnesses. A new USSR law on Freedom of Conscience and Religious Organizations came into force on 9 October 1990, but did not provide for a civilian alternative to military service. Proposals for the introduction of such a service are to be submitted to the next session of the USSR parliament.

■Please send appeals for his immediate and unconditional release, and for the introduction of a civilian alternative to military service to: Boris Yeltsin/Chairman of the RSFSR Supreme Soviet/Verkhovny Sovet RSFSR/Krasnopresnenskaya nab.,2/Moscow/USSR.☐

RELEASED

AI learned that Hiram Abi Cobas Nuñez, prisoner of the month in July 1990, was released on 27 November 1990 for health reasons.

0136

FOCUS amnesty international

Addiction to killing

"I'm ready for execution. I already saw the gallows being tested," said the sailor. His wrists were handcuffed as he spoke. Outside the jail a group of journalists kept vigil.

Next morning, at 6.02am, he was dead, one hour later than the usual time for the execution of a condemned man in Malaysia. His hanging had been delayed as a special concession so that he could perform his prayers at dawn — the first of five prayers a Muslim is obliged to perform daily.

The 37-year-old seafarer, a native of Indonesia, died protesting his innocence. Convicted of possessing 937 grams of marijuana and being a member of a drug syndicate, he became the first prisoner in 1990 to join Malaysia's ever-rising toll of those executed in what officials now admit is a deadly failure to stem the country's drugs trade.

Malaysia's anti-drug drive made international headlines in the early 1980s when the country's leaders made the death penalty mandatory for drug-trafficking. Huge billboards warned local citizens and foreign travellers: "Be forewarned: Death for drug traffickers under Malaysian law". By June 1990 the national press reported that 104 convicts had been hanged on drug charges since 1983 and a further 200 were awaiting execution on death row.

Drug abuse and trafficking pose major problems for the world community. In the words of the United Nations (UN) Secretary-General, in a statement made in 1985, "Illicit drugs wherever they are produced or used contaminate and corrupt, weakening the very fabric of society. Increasing worldwide abuse is destroying uncounted useful lives...The suffering of individuals is not the only cost. Illicit drugs and crime go hand in hand. The allure of tremendous profits constitutes a potent attraction to criminals, and drug-trafficking frequently entails other criminal acts, including bribery, larceny, the corruption of public officials and even murder...It must also be stressed that trafficking in illegal drugs represents a heavy toll on many national economies. The cost must be counted in literally billions of dollars traceable to the time lost in the work place, to the substantial burden imposed on judicial and penal systems, and to the treatment and rehabilitation of drug offenders". Although the UN considers drug abuse to be a serious problem, UN bodies have consistently rejected the use of the death penalty as a solution. The death penalty was not among the many measures proposed by the International Conference on Drug Abuse and Illicit Trafficking, held under UN auspices in June 1987. Instead the conference recommended such measures as the prevention and reduction of demand through education and control of drug abuse in the work-place; improved programs for the treatment of addicts; disruption of major trafficking networks through controls over ships and aircraft and surveillance of borders; facilitation of the extradition of alleged traffickers; and forfeiture of the proceeds of trafficking.

An execution in China, where the death penalty is used routinely to punish drug-trafficking
© Pascal G/Agence Vu

Nevertheless, since the 1960s increasing numbers of governments have attempted to tackle the problems of drug-trafficking and drug abuse by introducing the death penalty. In some 24 countries drug-related offences are now punishable by death. Thousands of prisoners convicted of drug offences have been executed.

In countries where the death penalty is provided, there are wide disparities in the way drug offences are actually punished. Some countries have not sentenced anyone to death while others regularly carry out executions. Some national statutes restrict the death penalty to trafficking in poppy-based drugs; others include cocaine and even cannabis, a drug whose use in some countries is treated only as a minor offence. Some statutes attempt to limit the death penalty to the most serious offences by restricting it to cases involving more than a specified amount of drugs, others have no minimum amount or an amount so low that addicts can be punished by death with no specific evidence that they have engaged in trafficking. In some countries prisoners accused of drug-trafficking are sentenced to death and executed under procedures which fall short of international standards for a fair trial.

Ten of the countries which have introduced the death penalty for drug offences have done so in the last decade. In March 1987 Saudi Arabia introduced the death penalty for drug-trafficking and the authorities executed at least 10 people for drug-related offences over the following 12-month period. Mauritius has sentenced four people to death under a law introduced in 1986 providing for a mandatory death sentence for the importation of dangerous drugs. In July 1988 Bangladesh introduced the death penalty for drug-trafficking. In November 1988 the United States of America introduced the death penalty for drug offences under federal law. Federal law now allows the imposition of the death penalty as an optional punishment for people who intentionally kill or order killings while committing drug-related offences.

Huge numbers of executions have been carried out in Iran; over 1,000 executions for drug offences were recorded in 1989 alone. Records for 1990 showed

0137

Public beheading in Saudi Arabia, where the death penalty for drug-trafficking was introduced in March 1987 © Gabriel/Sepia Press

a decline in the number of executions for drug offences reported in the official press, although, at around 400, the number remained very high. The figure rose sharply after a new initiative was launched to combat drug-trafficking at the beginning of September 1990. The mass hangings of convicted drug traffickers which had taken place throughout the previous year resumed, when two groups of 44 and 48 people were hanged publicly within two weeks of each other in the city of Mashhad.

The executions followed an announcement at the end of August by Hojatoleslam Moghtadaie, President of the Supreme Court, that a special system was being set up so that courts could deal with drug-trafficking cases more quickly: the stated aim was to ensure that convicted traffickers would be hanged within 15 days of arrest.

This summary justice is a violation of Iran's obligations under international human rights standards to ensure that all prisoners facing the death penalty receive a fair trial guaranteeing the defendant all necessary safeguards. Many people are sent to their death in Iran as a consequence of speedy, summary trials in which the right to be presumed innocent until proven guilty is seriously undermined.

In China the practice of verdict first, trial second ensures that a defendant in a capital case rarely receives a fair trial. Over 900 death sentences were recorded and more than 600 executions took place in 1990 alone. From 28 December 1990 those convicted of smuggling or selling more than one kilogramme of opium or 50 grammes of heroin will face penalties ranging from 15 years' imprisonment to death. In practice, the death penalty has been used routinely in China to punish drug-trafficking, which is one of the "six evils" to be severely dealt with during a continuing campaign against crime.

In 1989 Egypt carried out its first ever execution for drug-trafficking: Anwar Hussein Kassar Hussein, a 27-year-old Pakistani national, was hanged in a Cairo prison on 6 July. Since the mid-1980s there has been increasing governmental concern about drug abuse in Egypt. 1985 saw the first application of a legal provision introduced in 1966, providing for the death penalty as an optional punishment for exporting, smuggling, producing or processing narcotic substances with the intent of dealing in them: on 7 November 1985 a Lebanese national was sentenced to death *in absentia*. Since then over 50 people have been sentenced to death by Egyptian courts, many of them foreign nationals sentenced *in absentia*. In June 1990, about 30 convicted drug-traffickers were reported to be awaiting execution in Egyptian prisons.

'I remember the one who was executed, Lim Seng, and I hoped by his death there [would] be less narcotics addiction in our country, but today we have more. There is now a Narcotic Command, [a] whole command to deal with narcotics addiction. So therefore the life of that man...has been lost in vain...'

Teodulo Natividad, author of the 1972 Dangerous Drugs Act, Philippines.

The death penalty appears to have been introduced with little consideration of the risks it could entail. These include the risk that traffickers faced with a possible death penalty would more readily kill to avoid capture, increasing the danger to law enforcement officials; the risk that minor traffickers or even drug abusers would suffer the death penalty while those behind the crimes escaped capture and punishment; the risk that increasing the severity of penalties would play into the hands of organized crime, involving hardened criminals prepared to face the attendant dangers. Not only does the introduction of the death penalty pose risks, there is also no evidence that it will deter trafficking more effectively than other punishments, despite this being a widespread justification for its use.

The lack of deterrent effect was cited at the December 1985 meeting of the UN Expert Group on Countermeasures to Drug Smuggling by Air and Sea. The group's report stated, "...in the experience of several experts, the fact that capital punishment appeared on the statute books as the maximum penalty did not necessarily deter trafficking; indeed, in some cases it might make prosecution more difficult because courts of law were naturally inclined to require a much higher standard of proof when capital punishment was possible or even mandatory... The most effective deterrent was assuredly the certainty of detection and arrest."

International experts agree. In an article written in June 1990 Dr Peter Albrecht, the Presiding Judge of the Criminal Court, Basel, Switzerland, argues: "Neither on the basis of crime statistics nor by any other method has it been possible to demonstrate convincingly that the death penalty has a greater deterrent effect than long prison sentences. Nowhere, for example,

0138

Mass hanging of convicted drug-traffickers in Iran, where over 1,000 executions for drug offences were recorded in 1989

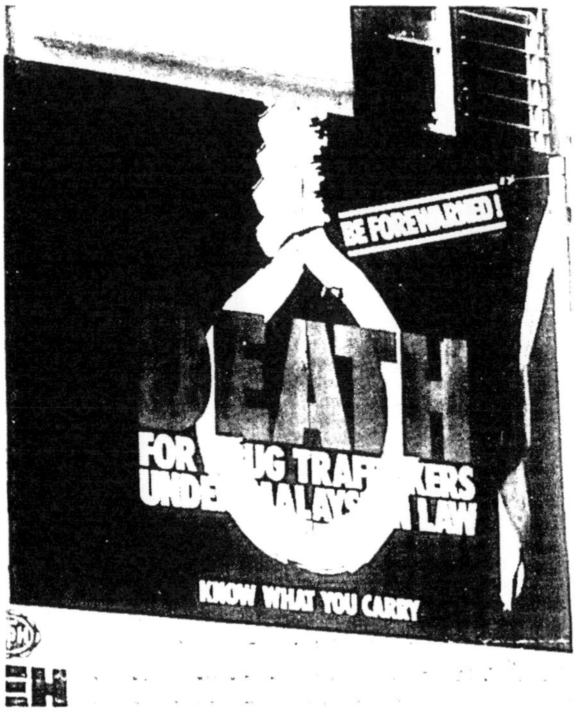

Billboard in Malaysia warning that drug-traffickers will hang. The death penalty, however, has not deterred the drugs trade. *Abbas/Magnum*

has a rise in the homicide rate been observed as a result of the abolition of the death penalty for murder, nor do I personally know of any empirical studies which would indicate that executions have been able to reduce the level of drug abuse.

"In view of the long-recognized criminological evidence that it is the probability of arrest, rather than the nature or severity of the expected punishment, which tends to act as a deterrent, these results can hardly be surprising...However, experience shows that authorities have particular difficulty in arresting and prosecuting drug-traffickers and that the danger of their being apprehended and sentenced is very slight. Hardly ever do big drug dealers appear in court, and in any case, the drug mafia is not intimidated even by the threat of the most severe punishment, in view of the enormous profits to be made in drugs."

Professor Ezzat A. Fattah, a professor of criminology in Canada and a long-standing opponent of the death penalty, has also concluded that the threat of severe punishments is not an effective solution to the problems of drug-trafficking, a view derived from his own experiences as a public prosecutor assigned to narcotics cases in Egypt during the 1950s. In an article written in 1988, he describes the effect of increasing the penalty for drug-trafficking from a maximum of three years' imprisonment to mandatory life imprisonment with hard labour.

"The results of the new drug law were exactly the opposite of what its makers had intended. Drug traffickers came up with many ingenious methods to ply their trade without being detected. The task of drug enforcement officers was rendered not only more difficult but extremely dangerous as well. Smugglers and traffickers were willing to employ violence, even in its ultimate form, to evade detection and to avoid arrest. Instead of reducing the volume of the drug traffic, the new law led to increasing dismissal of marginal cases by the police. Judges became quite reluctant to convict and acquitted accused persons in a very large number of cases either for supposed lack of evidence or despite the evidence on grounds of technicalities. Furthermore, with the increased theoretical risk the price of drugs went up sharply and the prospect of high profits attracted new elements to the illicit drug market...

"The new law did not improve the drug situation in Egypt and in many respects made it much worse. Its application provided an irrefutable proof, if any proof was needed, that harsh punishments are no solution to the drug problem as they have never been the answer to the crime problem."

> ***'The death penalty, in its utter disregard for the value of human life, is subject to the gravest reservations...the well-known objections to this penalty are valid even in the face of the overwhelming problem of drugs. Calling in the executioner to deal...with drug abuse, is a most questionable practice.'***
>
> ***Dr Peter Albrecht, Presiding Judge of the Criminal Court, Basel, Switzerland***

The experience described by Professor Fattah is by no means unique. The futility of the death penalty as a deterrent to drug-trafficking and drug abuse is well-illustrated elsewhere. Malaysia, where the death penalty has been mandatory for almost a decade, has become a crucible for testing the effectiveness of the punishment as the ultimate antidote to illicit drugs.

The statistics for addiction paint a grim picture. In 1970 only 711 addicts were identified in the country. Two decades later, in December 1989, the Home Ministry's *Dadah* (drugs) Treatment and Rehabilitation Division had identified 145,685 addicts throughout the country.

Not only has the increase been staggering, but it has continued regardless of the hangman. Two years after the 1983 decision to make the death penalty mandatory for drug offences, the government's figure for registered addicts stood at 102,807. Fourteen months later it had risen to 111,688. Two years later — and with executions of foreigners as well as local citizens being carried out in a blaze of publicity — the addiction register had gone up to 128,741, an increase of nearly 30 per cent over three years.

The death penalty failed to reduce addiction; nor has it deterred the drugs trade. A 1989 report by the International Narcotics Control Board said that Malaysia was continuing to be affected by growing "transit traffic" involving primarily opium and heroin. Both were being smuggled across the country's northern border or through its western coastline. The report noted, however, that "in trying to come to grips with the drug abuse and trafficking situation, the government has made it clear that it will not compromise in dealing with drug offenders, including foreigners."

The experiment had failed.

0139

Anwar Hussein Kasser Hussein, the first person executed in Egypt for narcotics smuggling, was hanged in a Cairo prison on 6 July 1989

Associated Press

But the executions continue. Of the 104 reported executions, 25 were said to have been of foreigners. These now include Hau Tsui Lin, one of eight Hong Kong citizens executed on 30 May 1990 in Malaysia's biggest mass execution. She became the first foreign woman to hang in Malaysia.

Time after time, when a foreigner has been sentenced to death, press interest has been intense and heads of government have publicly and privately appealed to the Malaysian authorities to show clemency. To date, the pleas have fallen on deaf ears and nationals of Australia, Britain, Indonesia, the Philippines, Singapore, Thailand and Hong Kong have been put to death.

AI has repeatedly urged the Malaysian authorities to stop these killings. It has taken the same stand against the death penalty for all offences in all countries. In *When the State Kills...* a report on the death penalty released worldwide in 1989, AI concluded that despite thousands of executions there is no clear evidence of a decline in drug-trafficking which could be clearly attributed to the threat or use of that penalty.

Even in Malaysia officials are beginning to express doubts about the effectiveness of the death penalty as a deterrent. In June 1990 the Deputy Minister of Home Affairs said that the country's mandatory death penalty for drug-trafficking had failed to curb either the trade or drug abuse and that a new approach to the problem was needed.

In a paper presented at the national Seminar on Drugs Treatment and Rehabilitation in Kuala Lumpur in July 1990, the deputy director of Malaysia's Criminal Investigation Department's anti-narcotics force said the mandatory death sentence had not shown signs of fulfilling its role as a deterrent in the six years since its enforcement. Instead, the number of people detained for trafficking had increased and those detained were usually replaced by other traffickers within a short time. He said: "Our intelligence shows that people were found to be trafficking in *dadah* even when a member of their family has been detained and awaiting trial."

Even as the death penalty is introduced to curb drug-trafficking in some countries, its use is being rejected elsewhere. On 10 April 1985 three men were publicly executed by firing-squad in Nigeria; they had been convicted of drug offences under a decree introduced the year before with retroactive effect. The executions provoked wide-spread protests from intellectuals, religious leaders, newspapers and ordinary citizens. Among the objections made were that death was too harsh a punishment for the offences involved; that killing would brutalize rather than reform; that the death penalty was unfair and not a deterrent. A number of other prisoners were sentenced to death, but there were no further executions in drug cases. In 1986 the decree was amended, removing provision for the death penalty for drug offences. Outstanding death sentences imposed for drug offences were commuted to terms of imprisonment. In 1987 in the Philippines, where drugs offences had been punishable by death since 1972, the death penalty was abolished for all crimes when a new constitution was ratified.□

What you can do

Write to the authorities of the countries below, urging them to stop executing people convicted of drug offences.

Send your appeals to:

Iran: Hojatoleslam Ali Shushtari/Minister of Justice/Ministry of Justice/Park-e Shahr/Tehran/Islamic Republic of Iran

Malyasia: YB Datuk Dr Haji Sulaiman Haji Daud/Minister of Justice/21st Floor/Bangunan Kuwasa/Jalan Raja Laut/Malaysia

China: Lui Fuzhi/Jianchazhanag/Zuigao Renmin Jianchayuan/Beijingshi/Zhonghua Renmin Gongheguo/People's Republic of China

Addiction to killing

The following countries provide for the death penalty in law for drug-related offences:

Bahrain
Bangladesh
Brunei Darussalam
Burma
People's Republic of China
Egypt
Indonesia
Iran
Iraq
Jordan
Kuwait
Malaysia
Mauritius
Qatar
Republic of Korea (South Korea)
Saudi Arabia
Singapore
Sri Lanka
Syria
Taiwan
Thailand
Turkey
United Arab Emirates
United States of America

0140

'Disappearances' continue in the Philippines

MORE than 50 people "disappeared" in the Philippines during 1990. Five were killed by their captors or died in custody shortly after their "disappearance" and at least 15 reappeared after a period in unacknowledged police or military custody. Most were still missing at the end of the year.

In a report published in February AI describes the pattern of "disappearances" in the Philippines in 1990 and the fate of dozens of individual victims. "Disappearances" occurred against a background of armed conflict between government forces and the New People's Army, the armed wing of the outlawed Communist Party of the Philippines. The majority of the "disappeared" were non-combatants: health workers, trade unionists, human rights activists, and peasant organizers.

Several of the victims reappeared in police or military custody weeks or months later, confirming that members of the security forces were responsible for their "disappearance". Soledad Mabilangan, leader of a village youth organization in Samar province, and her friend Alita Bona, who was then three months pregnant, "disappeared" in March 1990 after being detained by soldiers. For more than six weeks military authorities denied having them in custody but in April 1990 an AI delegation found the two women in detention at an army camp.

Some of the "disappeared" are known to have been tortured or killed in custody. In February 1990, three members of a fishermen's organization "disappeared" after being detained by security forces in Bulacan province. Two of the men later escaped and said they had seen their friend, Efren Concepcion, beheaded by his military captors.

Two other young men, who worked with poor farmers in Samar, may have met the same fate. Nestor Loberio and Diomedes Abawag were abducted by suspected members of a military "death squad" in January 1990. Diomedes Abawag's head, bearing signs of torture, was found in the sea a few days later. Nestor Loberio's whereabouts remained unknown at the end of the year.□

JAPAN

Call for abolition of death penalty

IN January AI published a report calling on the Japanese Government to abolish the death penalty, investigate reports that police have ill-treated suspects in custody and introduce further safeguards to prevent ill-treatment of detainees.

Over 80 prisoners are currently under sentence of death, almost half of whom have had their sentences confirmed by the Supreme Court. The government rarely commutes individual death sentences and there has been no general amnesty commuting death sentences since 1952.

The government claims widespread public support for the death penalty "to punish those who commit vicious offences". Death sentences are now imposed only for murder. However, AI believes that support for abolition would increase significantly if people were given the facts about the death penalty: that it is the ultimate cruel, inhuman and degrading punishment. In recent years AI has sought to contribute to the debate on this issue by issuing publications in Japanese.

AI is also concerned that some detention procedures have facilitated police abuse of criminal suspects. The organization has investigated claims of police ill-treatment for several years and in 1989 interviewed several former prisoners who said they were beaten, threatened with long sentences or forced to undergo long interrogation sessions which left them exhausted and confused. Most of these prisoners were acquitted after appeal courts dismissed the evidence against them.

AI recommends that separate authorities should be responsible for interrogation and detention of prisoners.□

ARGENTINA

Pardon for former general

A HIGH-RANKING military officer accused of human rights violations in Argentina has been pardoned before the end of trial proceedings against him.

Former general Carlos Suárez Mason was pardoned by President Carlos Menem on 29 December 1990. He was extradited from the United States in 1988 and was awaiting trial in Argentina on 39 murder charges relating to human right violations.

AI is concerned that Carlos Suárez Mason was pardoned before his trial concluded. The organization believes that failing to proceed with this trial will impede investigations into "disappearances" which occurred in zones under his authority, most of which have never been resolved.

The leaders of the military juntas which ruled Argentina between 1979 and 1983 and other high ranking officers jailed for human rights violations committed while they were in power were also pardoned on 29 December.

Argentina's civilian governments have systematically reduced the scope of investigations into serious human rights violations, which took place under the military juntas. This has helped the military to evade accountability. Many members of the armed forces accused of having perpetrated these abuses were pardoned by civilian governments before being brought to trial for the offences.

AI is concerned that the Argentinian Government's failure to bring to justice those responsible for human rights violations may signal its lack of commitment to preventing the recurrence of the gross human rights abuses which prevailed in the past. The National Commission on Disappeared People documented 8,960 cases of "disappearance" during the years of military rule.□

RWANDA

Unfair trials for alleged rebels

AT the beginning of January 1991 an AI representative observed the trial of 13 prisoners charged in connection with the violent attack in October 1990 on northeast Rwanda by Uganda-based Rwandese exiles. Some 7,000 people were arrested, over 4,000 of whom were released.

The Rwandese authorities had announced on 21 December that 1,566 detainees would be brought to trial, implying that all would be tried before the end of the year. The first trial, of 12 defendants, began on 28 December 1990. It was adjourned until January 1991 because some of the defence lawyers complained that they had not been given sufficient time to study the charges.

AI's observer attended the trial of 13 people on 3 January and concluded that the trial was summary and unfair in many respects. The hearing lasted less than five hours. Although 12 defendants, including a 16-year-old boy, faced capital charges, none was assisted by legal counsel and no witnesses appeared in court. Most of the accused told the court that they were beaten or threatened into making admissions of guilt while in pre-trial custody but the court neither investigated these claims nor ruled such evidence inadmissible. The main defendant, accused of recruiting and training the others as rebels, was sentenced to death. Neither he nor any of the others were accused of taking part in the insurgency. Nine were sentenced to prison terms of between 15 and 20 years, one was acquitted and the 16-year-old and one other received shorter prison sentences.

The court's judges did not appear to be fully independent or impartial. Four out of the five judges were closely linked to the armed forces or the government and only two of them had significant legal training. The judges have been under considerable pressure from the state-owned media to impose death sentences.□

The latest reports

The following reports are now available from AI.

The People's Republic of China: Several prominent political detainees were charged in November 1990 with "counter-revolutionary" offences after being held without charge for over a year. They are among several dozen political detainees who are expected to be tried soon in Beijing for their role in the 1989 pro-democracy movement.
(*Index No. ASA 17/74/90*)

United States of America: AI has received allegations that police in Chicago, Illinois, systematically tortured or otherwise ill-treated suspected criminals between 1972 and 1984. Most of the alleged victims of ill-treatment were black.
(*Index No. AMR 51/42/90*)

Haiti: AI has received reports of abuses similar to those that occurred under previous administrations, including arbitrary arrests, ill-treatment and killings by the police and military forces.
(*Index No. AMR 36/09/90*)

0141

TURKEY

Human rights activists face repression

THE Turkish Human Rights Association, which in 1990 received the Bruno Kreisky Prize for its work, is facing considerable pressure from the authorities.

Several of its officials have been detained and imprisoned and members of the association's regional branches have been prosecuted for producing campaigning material without government consent. The Gaziantep branch has been closed indefinitely by the authorities because of its alleged links with political parties and illegal organizations.

In October Ali Özler was sentenced to six years and eight months' imprisonment for his activities as the chairperson of the Tunceli branch of the association. He is in Erzincan Special Type Prison and has been adopted as a prisoner of conscience by AI.

In October, during the association's annual meeting, Vedat Aydin, a member from Diyarbakir, gave a speech in Kurdish, which was translated by lawyer Ahmet Zeki Okçuoğlu. Although the speech had not advocated violence, both men were immediately detained and remained in custody until their trial in Ankara State Security Court began. They have been charged with "making separatist propaganda", with a possible sentence of 10 years. An AI delegate attended the trial.

In December, lawyer Hüsnü Öndül, secretary of the Ankara branch, was held incommunicado for 10 days and interrogated while blindfolded. Also in December Hasan Hüseyin Reyhan, of the İskenderun branch, was arrested after pressing a complaint against police who he alleged assaulted him when he attempted to interview a client at police headquarters in August. Both lawyers were conditionally released and now face charges of membership of illegal organizations.☐

São Paulo, Brazil, December 1990: A military police officer forces his gun into a street child's mouth. Although suspended from duty for this act, the police officer reportedly continued working during his suspension. Later the children reportedly went into hiding after being detained overnight and beaten by other police officers.

Street children in Brazil are frequently the victims of arbitrary arrest, torture and extrajudicial executions by police officers.☐

UGANDA

Unarmed civilians killed by soldiers

EXTRAJUDICIAL executions of civilians by soldiers have continued to be reported in Uganda, despite arrests and official investigations after some incidents.

Over 100 civilians are believed to have been extrajudicially executed during 1990 by soldiers in rural areas where the army is fighting insurgents. In the east, for example, 13 extrajudicial executions were reported in three separate incidents in Pallisa in late April and early May; in August 16 civilians were burnt to death in Bugondo after they had been forced into a thatched hut which was then set alight; and in September 20 civilians detained in Soroti town were taken to a swamp and battered to death.

The government says it is investigating these and other incidents, but no formal disciplinary action is known to have been taken within the army, and investigations seem to have been entrusted to the army itself rather than to an independent authority. No measures have been announced to prevent extrajudicial executions.

Investigations announced into incidents which took place in rural areas in 1988, notably a Commission of Inquiry set up under the Minister of State for the North, have so far failed to issue reports on their findings. It remains impossible to assess whether these investigations represent genuine attempts to confront problems of human rights in rural areas.

The government acted promptly, however, when in early December 1990 police opened fire without warning on striking students at Makerere University in Kampala, killing two. The police were apparently trying to prohibit a student meeting to consider ending the strike and opened fire when students refused to disperse. The country's two senior police officers were suspended and 27 others were arrested. An independent Commission of Inquiry headed by a Supreme Court judge was established.

The authorities have also acted quickly to punish soldiers accused of committing serious crimes while off-duty. Some have been executed following summary military tribunals which allow no appeal — a gross violation of human rights.☐

AMNESTY INTERNATIONAL NEWSLETTER is published every month in four languages to bring you news of AI's concerns and campaigns worldwide, as well as in-depth reports. Available from Amnesty International (address below)

PERU

Habeas corpus upheld

APPARENTLY for the first time since a pattern of "disappearances" was reported in Peru, a *habeas corpus* petition on behalf of a "disappearance" victim has been upheld in court. A lower court judge has ordered the Minister of the Interior and two police generals to release an unacknowledged detainee.

The petition concerned Ernesto Rafael Castillo Páez, a 22-year-old student last seen on 21 October 1990, when he was reportedly detained by police officers in Villa El Salvador, Lima. Eyewitnesses say that he was handcuffed, forced into the boot of a police car and driven away. However, the authorities denied any knowledge of his detention.

Judge Elva Greta Minaya concluded that the student had been arbitrarily detained by the police and ordered his immediate release. She also denounced serious irregularities at a police station she visited to establish Ernesto Castillo's whereabouts. Police initially failed to produce the register of detentions, and when they did so, the judge found that the records had been altered.

A higher court, the Eighth Correctional Tribunal, upheld the judge's decision and ordered the authorities to reveal Ernesto Castillo's whereabouts. The tribunal also ordered the provincial prosecutor to bring charges against the heads of the two police services involved.☐

AMNESTY INTERNATIONAL, 1 Easton Street, London WC1X 8DJ, United Kingdom. Printed in Great Britain by Flashprint Enterprises Ltd. London.
Available on subscri tion at £7 (US$12.00 for 12 issues. ISSN 0308 6887

AMNESTY INTERNATIONAL

NEWSLETTER APRIL 1991 VOLUME XXI • NUMBER 4

MALI

Children tortured

SCHOOLCHILDREN under 12 were among detainees tortured or ill-treated by police in January in Bamako, Mali's capital city. Many are said to have been beaten, others left outside for long periods in the full heat of the sun and denied water.

Some 240 people, most of them young, were illegally held incommunicado for 10 days without charge or trial. In one case, men, women and children were reportedly held together in one large cell with no toilet or washing facilities and on a diet of bread and water.

Some were pro-democracy activists attacked by police with batons and tear-gas during a peaceful demonstration on 18 January. However, most were arrested on 21 and 22 January after rioting broke out in Bamako. Students protesting at the rumoured arrest of their leader were joined by young onlookers. Cars, government buildings and officials' homes were attacked. At least five people were said to have been killed by the security forces. The unrest spread to other towns. In the southern town of Sikasso, on 28 January, Siaka Traoré, a school pupil, was reportedly shot by the security forces and crushed by an armoured vehicle. On 31 January the government ordered the release of 196 school children and said that 34 other people were to be charged with criminal offences; by late February they had still not been charged.

Several large and peaceful demonstrations in favour of multi-party democracy have taken place in recent months. On 18 January a new Minister of the Interior ordered two pro-democracy organizations and an independent student body to halt all political activity. He subsequently claimed only two people had been arrested. AI called on the government to investigate reports of torture and to take action to protect prisoners.☐

Peaceful demonstrators try to stop a Soviet armoured vehicle in Vilnius, Lithuania, on 11 January 1991. Two days later 13 unarmed demonstrators were killed by Soviet troops. See page 8 © Associated Press

PEOPLE'S REPUBLIC OF CHINA

Dissidents tried in Beijing

THE latest and most public stage in the Chinese Government's suppression of the pro-democracy movement since June 1989, began in November 1990 with the trials of prominent activists.

At least 32 people detained since 1989 had been tried in Beijing by mid-February 1991. Fifteen, mostly student leaders and intellectuals, were sentenced to prison terms ranging from two to 13 years. Six others were "exempted from criminal punishment". By 12 February, the verdicts against at least 11 other defendants had not yet been announced. It is feared that they may have received harsh sentences, as they were charged with offences which in "serious" cases, are punishable by death.

Two of the most prominent dissidents were sentenced to 13 years' imprisonment. Chen Ziming, director of a private research institute in Beijing, and Wang Juntao, an economist and editor, were convicted of "plotting to overthrow the government" and "counter-revolutionary propaganda and agitation" for their role in the 1989 protests. The official media claimed they were the "masterminds" of the protests. The New China News Agency announced their sentences on 12 February, saying they had "shown no willingness to repent". Both are prisoners of conscience.

Another prisoner of conscience, veteran human rights activist Ren Wanding, was sentenced on 26 January to seven years' imprisonment for "counter-revolutionary propaganda and agitation". Since 1988 he had made public appeals for human rights and democratic reforms, but he did not play a major role in the 1989 protests.

AI believes that the dissidents tried recently in Beijing and others convicted previously were denied fair trials. Trial proceedings in China fall far short of international standards and the practice of "deciding on the verdict before trial" is still common. In political cases, the chance of a fair hearing is even more remote than in ordinary criminal cases and the outcome is usually a foregone conclusion.

Hundreds of less prominent individuals have already been tried and jailed since 1989, but very few such trials were publicly reported by Chinese official sources. Some dissidents held in provincial cities have received long prison sentences for the peaceful exercise of their rights to freedom of speech or association. Others may have been tried recently in Beijing and elsewhere without their cases being publicly acknowledged.

Official sources also announced in January 1991 the release of 69 dissidents. Only 15 of the 69 reportedly released were officially identified.☐

AI visits India

AN AI delegation, including the Vice Chairperson of the IEC and the Secretary General, attended the World Congress on Human Rights in New Delhi in December. While in India, they met the Cabinet Secretary, Naresh Chandra, and Foreign Secretary Muchkund Dubey, who re-affirmed the previous government's assurance that AI could visit New Delhi for discusssions with the government. AI was not given access to Punjab, Jammu and Kashmir or the north-east, but the delegation was told that, depending on the security situation in these areas, it might be allowed to do so in the future. AI's delegates also discussed the organization's work, including the protection of human rights in the context of armed conflict, with leading members of most political parties.☐

0143

CAMPAIGN FOR PRISONERS OF THE MONTH

Each of the people whose story is told below is a prisoner of conscience. Each has been arrested because of his or her religious or political beliefs, colour, sex, ethnic origin or language. None has used or advocated violence. Their continuing detention is a violation of the United Nations Universal Declaration of Human Rights. International appeals can help to secure the release of these prisoners or to improve their detention conditions. In the interest of the prisoners, letters to the authorities should be worded carefully and courteously. You should stress that your concern for human rights is not in any way politically partisan. In *no* circumstances should communications be sent to the prisoner.

MYANMAR

Ma Theingee: ***a painter and art teacher in her early 40s, she was arrested on 20 July 1989 with many other leaders of the National League for Democracy (NLD).***

Ma Theingee served as the personal secretary to NLD leader Aung San Suu Kyi. They were both arrested in a mass crackdown on the opposition in Myanmar in July 1989. Aung San Suu Kyi has been held under house arrest since 20 July 1989.

Ma Theingee

Ma Theingee taught art at Yangon's (Rangoon) International School before her arrest. She has also written a book on the tradition of Burmese puppet theatre, which is awaiting publication in Bangkok, and has worked as a translator. She speaks English, French, Japanese and Burmese.

Although many NLD leaders were detained at the time, the party won over 80 per cent of the seats in the May 1990 national parliamentary elections. However, the State Law and Order Restoration Council (SLORC), Myanmar's ruling military authorities, have not yet convened the National Assembly or said when they will do so. Hundreds of political activists remain in prison, held for their opposition to military rule. Four more NLD leaders were detained on 16 January 1991.

Ma Theingee was reportedly sentenced "for breach of existing laws", but AI has no further information about the date of her sentencing or the exact nature of the charges against her. Nor is it clear when and before which court she was tried, though it seems likely that she may have appeared before one of the military tribunals established by the SLORC, whose procedures fall far short of international fair trial standards.

She is believed to be held in solitary confinement in the womens' wing at Insein Prison near Yangon.

■Please send courteous appeals for her immediate and unconditional release to: General Saw Maung/Chairman/State Law and Order Restoration Council/ Yangon (Rangoon)/Union of Myanmar (Burma).□

PRISONER NEWS

AI learned in January 1991 of the release of 67 prisoners under adoption or investigation. AI took up 188 cases.

KENYA

Kenneth Matiba: ***aged 58, a prominent Nairobi businessman and former government minister, he has been imprisoned without charge or trial since 4 July 1990 under Kenya's administrative detention laws, because of his support for a multiparty system in Kenya.***

Kenneth Matiba was one of the most prominent of a number of businessmen, politicians, lawyers and church leaders campaigning in mid-1990 for the reintroduction of multi-party democracy in Kenya, a one-party state since 1982. President Daniel arap Moi suppressed widespread public debate on the issue of multi-party democracy but later proposed reforms to the ruling Kenya African National Union (KANU) and the electoral system.

On 6 June 1990 Kenneth Matiba and Charles Rubia, another former government minister, announced that they intended to hold a rally in Nairobi on 7 July. This was banned by the government and on 4 July Kenneth Matiba, Charles Rubia and Raila Odinga (the son of the former Vice-President of Kenya, Oginga Odinga) were arrested and placed under administrative detention for an indefinite period without charge or trial. Others arrested with

Kenneth Matiba

them, including their lawyer, John Khaminwa, and two other prominent human rights lawyers, were later released.

Kenneth Matiba is held in permanent solitary confinement in Kamiti prison near Nairobi in a cell adjacent to a block used to house mentally-disturbed prisoners. Conditions are harsh, contact with his family is limited to infrequent, brief and supervised visits, and he has very little access to his legal representative. Kenneth Matiba suffers from high blood pressure but is denied medication and adequate medical attention.

■Please send appeals for his release to: His Excellency President Daniel arap Moi/President of the Republic of Kenya/Office of the President/PO Box 30510/ Nairobi/Kenya.□

GREECE

Leonidas Tsaousis: ***21 years old, he is serving a four-year sentence in Avlona Military Prison for refusing to perform military service.***

Leonidas Tsaousis is a Jehovah's Witness. His religious beliefs do not allow him to serve in the armed forces in any capacity. He therefore cannot accept the unarmed military service Greece offers conscientious objectors as an alternative to military service. Unlike most European countries with conscription, Greece does not provide a completely civilian alternative service for conscientious objectors and at any given time holds some 400 Jehovah's Witnesses in prison for their conscientious objection. Most of them receive four-year prison sentences, of which they usually serve three years. AI considers them to be prisoners of conscience.

Before his imprisonment Leonidas Tsaousis studied chemistry and intends to pursue a career in that field once he is released. His parents, who are workers living in Athens, visit him for two hours every Monday. He spends his days in prison reading the Bible and literature.

For many years AI has been urging successive Greek governments to release conscientious objectors and to introduce alternative civilian service of non-punitive length. In 1988 the Greek Government announced a draft law proposing a civilian service double the length of military service. It has not yet been debated by the Greek parliament.

Greece has failed to observe United Nations, Council of Europe and European Parliament resolutions and recommendations which call on member states to implement alternative civilian service of non-punitive length for conscientious objectors.

■Please send courteous appeals for the immediate and unconditional release of Leonidas Tsaousis and the introduction of civilian service of non-punitive length for conscientious objectors to military service to: Prime Minister Constantine Mitsotakis/Office of the Prime Minister/Maximou Palace/ Herodou Atticou Avenue/Athens/ Greece.□

CORRECTION: There was a mistake in the February 1991 Cuba Prisoner of the Month article. The names of the five men imprisoned with Esteban Gonzáles Gonzáles are Arturo Montané Ruiz, Manuel Pozo Montero, Mario Fernández Mora, Edgardo Llompart Martín and Manuel Regueiro Robaína.

0144

amnesty international

HUMAN RIGHTS in the SHADOW OF WAR

Human rights are under increased attack today in many countries as a result of the Gulf conflict. Nothing could make clearer the risk that persistent human rights violations pose to a just and stable world order than this present crisis, which is already claiming a rising toll of war casualties. Whatever its political and military outcome, it is imperative that the war not be allowed to further claim human rights as one of its casualties.

Amnesty International has made repeated appeals over the past decade both to individual governments and to the United Nations to deal constructively and effectively with human rights abuses in all regions of the world. Our concerns have included large numbers of prisoners of conscience in the Soviet Union and other East European countries under former governments; mass "disappearances" in Latin America; widespread extrajudicial executions in a number of African countries; arbitrary arrest and unfair trials in China and other Asian countries, and the increasing use of the death penalty in the USA, among other countries, in the face of a worldwide trend towards abolition.

The Middle East

In the Middle East, throughout the 1980s, we have attempted again and again to focus world attention on the suppression of fundamental human rights in Iraq. We have drawn attention year after year to gross violations in Iran; to the consistent pattern of abuses inflicted on Palestinians detained or killed during the unrest in Israel and the Occupied Territories; to political detainees and the use of torture and the death penalty in Saudi Arabia; to torture and extrajudicial executions in Syria, and to torture and "disappearances" in Morocco. We have published exhaustive reports on our efforts to end torture and arbitrary arrest in Bahrain, Jordan and Egypt. And we appealed repeatedly for respect for fundamental human rights in Kuwait before the Iraqi invasion.

When the governments of the world had a clear opportunity to deal with these grave and compelling issues, they chose not to do so. Governments across the political spectrum failed to pay due consideration to the human rights records of the countries to which they exported military, security and police assistance that could be used to commit further violations. Now, the resolution of these and broader issues is subject to the consequences of war.

The human rights Amnesty International seeks to protect are most at risk when political, military and economic considerations become the overwhelming preoccupation of governments.

States must not be permitted to condone by their selective silence the human rights violations committed by their allies and to condemn violations by others for propaganda purposes. When that happens, the shadow of war is cast far beyond the battlefield, and in distant lands the jailers, torturers and killers sense the slackening of international concern for human rights.

Since the events of 2 August 1990 we have seen this deeply distressing pattern re-enacted. We have documented the human rights violations inflicted on the people of Kuwait by the Iraqi forces — a catalogue of arbitrary detention, torture and extrajudicial killing sadly familiar to anyone who has studied our previous reports on violations in Iraq itself. We have reported the detention and torture of large numbers of Yemeni nationals held in Saudi Arabia — apparently for no other reason than the Yemeni government's position on the Gulf crisis.

Dissident views

Now Amnesty International is receiving reports that people in several other countries who have dissident views about the crisis are being arrested or imprisoned. They include Magdy Ahmed Hussein, an Egyptian journalist and deputy leader

0145

of the Socialist Labour Party who spoke against the war at a Cairo mosque. In Turkey, three Socialist Party members were arrested while trying to mail a US flag to President Turgut Ozal in protest at his Gulf policies — they are to be prosecuted for "insulting the President".

Opposition to the war has begun to surface within the armed forces. In the USA, a soldier was jailed after he refused to help prepare supplies for troops in Saudi Arabia because he had come to object on moral and religious grounds to participating in all wars. He is a prisoner of conscience.

The risk

In times of war, the risk of arbitrary detention escalates. People are detained without charge or trial, with no effective possibility of defending themselves against the authorities' accusations. In Israel and the Occupied Territories, Dr Sari Nusseibeh, a leading Palestinian advocate of a peaceful solution of conflicts in the region, has been arrested and put in administrative detention. He too is a prisoner of conscience.

In the United Kingdom, the detention of more than 50 Iraqi and other nationals pending deportation on national security grounds was contrary to international standards because they were not told specific reasons for their detention and did not have the right to a fair judicial hearing, with legal representation.

Each of these cases is a matter of concern to Amnesty International, but taken together they give rise to great disquiet: the fear is that such measures will be tolerated and eventually become systematic for as long as the war and its aftermath persist. We must prevent this happening.

The preoccupation with this present conflict threatens respect for human rights in a number of other countries because violations there risk being seen as secondary by a world whose attention is rivetted on the Gulf.

We have seen that the violent suppression of peaceful forces for democratic change in Myanmar has continued unabated, as has the practice of torture, "disappearance" and extrajudicial execution in the context of civil war in Sri Lanka. In Mauritania, mass arrests and deaths under torture of black Mauritanians have increased since November 1990 and in neighbouring Mali, children as young as 12 have been tortured after pro-democracy demonstrations in January 1991. In Lebanon, forces of the Syrian army carried out the deliberate killing of captive soldiers and civilians in October 1990. This year in Morocco — following the unrest there in December 1990 — hundreds of people have been sentenced to up to 15 years' imprisonment after trials which were grossly unfair. In China, pro-democracy advocates have been jailed after grossly unfair political trials. Unarmed civilians were shot dead by Soviet troops in Lithuania and there have been increasing fears for the protection of human rights and fundamental freedoms in other areas of the Soviet Union.

Respect

Respect for human rights — recognized by the United Nations Universal Declaration of Human Rights as "the foundation of freedom, justice and peace in the world" — must not be sacrificed to political expediency.

If peace is to emerge from the present conflict, it can only hope to endure if it is built on principles that include a genuine commitment by every government to the universal and impartial protection of the human rights of *all* people.

The challenge for all those working for human rights at this grave moment is to insist on a single standard for human rights worldwide. For its part, Amnesty International will continue to apply its impartial and strictly defined mandate to free all prisoners of conscience, ensure fair trials for political prisoners and oppose torture and executions wherever they occur.

amnesty international
international secretariat
1 Easton Street, London WC1X 8DJ, UK.
AI Index: POL 30/01/91 February 1991

0146

FOCUS amnesty international

Serious and wide-ranging human rights violations, including long-term imprisonment of prisoners of conscience, torture, unfair trials of political opponents, and "disappearances", have been committed in Morocco since the 1960s.

Supporters of legal opposition parties have frequently been tried and imprisoned for peacefully expressing their views. Some have been in prison for over 15 years. "Disappearances" of political opponents were recorded from the 1960s to the 1980s: many of them are still missing. Over 60 military officers, imprisoned after attempts on the life of King Hassan II, were taken in 1973 to a secret detention centre: at least 29 are said to have died as a result of inhuman conditions and the sentences of most of those still held have expired.

On 14 December 1990 a one-day general strike was called by two major trade unions in support of a number of economic and social demands, including a minimum wage and the right to strike. The unions asked their members to remain at home and not to demonstrate, but in some cities, such as Fes and Tanger, serious rioting broke out. Young people smashed cars and attacked shops and luxury hotels: the government said five people were killed but unofficial sources put the number of dead at between 50 and over 100. Hundreds were arrested: by mid-January 1991 over 500 people had been sentenced to prison terms of up to 15 years.

Gross violations of human rights continue. Prisoners of conscience and political prisoners are serving long sentences imposed after unfair trials. Incommunicado *garde à vue* detention is still prolonged. Torture is widespread.

These serious abuses violate international human rights treaties to which Morocco has committed itself. Despite repeated representations to the Moroccan authorities by human rights organizations including AI, and other international bodies, the government has yet to demonstrate its commitment to these ideals. The time for action is long overdue.

A demonstration in the early 1980s by families of political prisoners. Political prisoners do not receive fair trials in Morocco

State vengeance and repression in Morocco

In the 1970s demonstrations against government policies were met by police repression and widespread arrests. Hundreds of arrests among the armed forces followed attempted coups in 1971 and 1972: some of those subsequently sentenced to three years in prison remain in detention.

Further arrests took place of alleged members of opposition groups. Many critics and opponents of the government were brutally tortured before being given summary trials and sentenced to long terms of imprisonment.

Non-violent protests followed by violent reprisals continued in the 1980s. A general strike against price rises led to major confrontations between strikers, demonstrators and the security forces in June 1981. Hundreds of people were reported killed and around 2,000 arrested.

In early 1984 a huge wave of protest spread across most of Morocco, precipitated by the government's announcement of price rises and drastic cuts in education services. The protests started in secondary schools and led to strikes in both schools and colleges. Mass student demonstrations were supported by other social groups, particularly the unemployed.

Most of the demonstrations began peacefully but were met by large-scale police repression, arrests and shootings. Officially, 29 people died and 169 were wounded, but unofficial sources put the number of dead at more than 200 and alleged that several thousand were wounded.

Repression was particularly severe in northern towns where thousands of people, most of them students, were arrested. At the same time, the authorities rounded up those they regarded as political dissidents: many who had not even taken part in demonstrations were detained because of their past or suspected activities. Most were suspected of having left-wing sympathies, although several members of Islamic organizations were also detained.

Over 1,500 of those arrested were eventually brought to trial. Many of the defendants alleged that they had been tortured while held in pre-trial detention in police stations or in secret detention centres such as Derb Moulay Cherif in Casablanca. Most of those tried received up to five years' imprisonment, often after unfair trials. At least 110 of those sentenced are still in prison.

In the waves of arrests and trials in the past 15 years, especially in 1981 and 1984, two groups of people, in particular, have been targeted by the authorities: members of Marxist organizations and, more recently, those belonging to radical Islamic groups. A third group singled out for repression are people of Western Saharan origin (Sahrawis), who were suspected of supporting the armed opposition, the Popular Front for the Liberation of Seguia al-Hamra and Rio de Oro (Polisario Front): AI believes that hundreds of Sahrawis have "disappeared". The Polisario Front and the government have been at war since Morocco annexed the Western Sahara in 1975.

0147

The missing families

In some cases of "disappearance" the whole family is held responsible for the "crime" of one of its members. State vengeance seems to be the only motive.

One notable example of this involved the "disappearance" of eight members of the family of General Mohammed Oufkir, (left), a former minister of the interior and army chief of staff. He died in suspicious circumstances immediately after he reportedly led a coup attempt in 1972. Following his death, his widow and six children, together with a female cousin, "disappeared". Nothing was heard of them for 15 years. Then, in 1987, four of the children escaped from their secret, incommunicado detention. They managed to meet a French lawyer in the garden of a hotel, where they told him of the family's plight. But four days after their escape, they were rearrested.

Now, they are once again held without charge or trial together with the other members of their family at a farm near Marrakech. Only the parents of General Oufkir's wife and a military doctor are allowed to visit them.

In another case, 11 members of the family of Mohammed Lamine el-Leili, one of the first leaders of the Polisario Front, are said to have "disappeared".

The first to "disappear" was his sister, Fatma Ghalia, who was seized in a street in Tan Tan by four men in January 1976. Four weeks later, both his parents were arrested at their house in Tan Tan. A brother, Mohammed Fadel, a student, was arrested soon after in Kenitra. Other members of the family arrested include an uncle, Fadel Mohammed el-Leili, and his sister, Tagla. All remain "disappeared".

Many human rights violations have taken place within the context of the use and abuse of the Moroccan legal system. This remains the situation today. Vaguely worded laws on demonstrations and public assembly have been repeatedly invoked to imprison people involved in non-violent protests. In 1984, for example, they were used to sentence people allegedly involved in anti-government demonstrations; five years later, in 1989, students said to have been involved in protests at university campuses were jailed under such laws for periods ranging from four months to 10 years.

Other laws, regulating associations, the holding of meetings, the press, and membership of illegal organizations, have been used to imprison prisoners of conscience. Hundreds of people have been arrested and sent to prison under these provisions in the past 30 years, particularly members of left-wing groups opposed to the monarchy, and advocates of self-determination for the Western Sahara, such as members of *Ila'l-Amam*, Forward, an illegal Marxist group, and those allegedly belonging to Islamic associations such as *al-Jami'at al-Khayriyya*, the Charitable Association (also known as *al-'Adl w'al-Ihsan*, Justice and Charity).

Real or suspected opponents of the government have frequently been subjected to physical and psychological torture or ill-treatment, particularly while held incommunicado for long periods in pre-trial *garde à vue* detention.

Garde à vue detention allows the police to detain suspects for interrogation without referring their cases promptly to the judiciary and without giving detainees access to lawyers and relatives. In practice, legal time limits on *garde à vue* are commonly exceeded in political cases: the police appear to be able to flout the requirements of the law with total or virtual impunity.

In addition, arrest dates are frequently falsified on official documents by police officers — most notably on the detainee's statement to the police (*procès-verbal*). Detainees are often forced to sign these statements, which can then be used as evidence in any subsequent trial. This is done apparently to conceal the length of time detainees have been held and, on occasion, to cover up the extent to which they may have been subjected to torture or coercion.

The fact that Moroccan law allows for an accused person to be sentenced to up to five years' imprisonment solely on the basis of an uncorroborated confession contained in a statement to the police appears actively to invite — perhaps even to incite — the security forces to torture or ill-treat detainees.

The most common methods they use include beatings with fists, whips or sticks; *falaqa* — beating on the soles of the feet with a stick, often while the victim is suspended; suspension in contorted positions tied to a pole — known as the "aeroplane" (*l'avion, al-tayyara*) and the "parrot" (*le perroquet*) or "chicken" (*al-farrukh*); being hanged from the ceiling by the wrists with just the toes touching the ground, or by the ankles upside-down; immersion of the head in buckets of water, urine or excrement; and the application of electric shocks to sensitive parts of the body.

In addition, detainees have repeatedly been kept manacled for long periods, subjected to threats against their own and their relatives' lives, and deprived of sleep. Members of the security forces appear to be able to commit such torture without any fear of administrative reprisals.

In some secret detention centres, such as Derb Moulay Cherif in Casablanca, political detainees are tortured and ill-treated as a matter of routine.

Convicted political prisoners have also been beaten and ill-treated in various prisons throughout Morocco. Many have been confined in small, damp, windowless cells to the detriment of their health, and denied adequate medical treatment. Since the 1970s political prisoners have launched a series of hunger-strikes, sometimes unlimited and resulting in deaths, in protest at these inhuman conditions.

"Disappearances" in custody have been reported since the 1960s. Since 1975, several hundred people of Western Saharan origin are alleged to have "disappeared" following arrest.

There are more than 400 political prisoners, including many who are or may be prisoners of conscience.

In the past political prisoners have been released in amnesties granted by King Hassan II. AI has welcomed these initiatives, but they are not enough. All prisoners of conscience should be released immediately and unconditionally and major changes to Moroccan law and the practices of the security forces must be introduced to stop the widespread and gross violations of human rights which have persisted for so long in Morocco.

Trade unionists march through Casablanca to celebrate 1 May, Labour Day

Unfair trials

During the trial of seven student activists in 1989 at Oujda, one of the defendants, Ahmed El-Azzouzi, took off his bloodstained shirt to show the court injuries to his back. He alleged that he had received these as a result of torture sustained in police detention.

The judge, however, refused to allow him to be examined by a

0148

A woman collapses with grief outside the house of a prisoner who died during a hunger-strike in 1984. Political prisoners have launched a series of hunger-strikes in protest at harsh conditions. Two prisoners have been on hunger-strike for over five years © Hashi Libération/Gamma

forensic doctor: ignoring the defendant's evidence, the judge said that the wounds could have been self-inflicted. After a summary trial, all seven students were convicted of participating in illegal demonstrations and jailed for 18 months.

Such reports of unfair trials have been received from Morocco for many years. Procedures observed during political trials have consistently contravened international standards for fair trial.

The laws under which political prisoners have been tried are so broadly framed that many have been convicted and sometimes given long jail sentences for nothing more than the non-violent expression of their political beliefs.

Hundreds of political trials have been held in Morocco in the past 30 years. At least 400 political prisoners, including prisoners of conscience, remain in jail. Most of these trials have violated internationally accepted standards for fair trial. Many defendants were sentenced after unfair trials. Several were convicted solely on the basis of confessions extracted under torture while they were held incommunicado in *garde à vue* detention.

Rights of defence have been severely restricted, sometimes to the point where defence lawyers have withdrawn in protest. Defendants have been harassed and prevented from calling witnesses to testify to their innocence, and have been convicted solely on the basis of uncorroborated statements to the police, as is permitted under Moroccan law. Many such statements have been allegedly made under torture but the courts have consistently failed to investigate allegations of torture.

Many political trials have been conducted in a manner which mocks the principle of presumption of innocence guaranteed under Morocco's Criminal Procedure Code and belies any claims by the courts to judicial independence. The accused have often been treated so badly in court that there was no question of them receiving a fair hearing.

In one trial in Casablanca of 71 members of Islamic groups in mid-1984 the proceedings were marked from beginning to end by gross violations of human rights. When most of the defendants were arrested, no warrants were produced and no reasons were given to the victims or their relatives. Moveover, when some of those being sought by the police could not be found, relatives were detained in their place.

Many of the detainees were held in *garde à vue* detention for up to seven months in Derb Moulay Cherif, where they say they were tortured. However, when they came to trial the court refused to order an investigation despite many allegations by the accused that they had been tortured and forced to sign what amounted to confessions while blindfolded and under threat. None had apparently been informed of the charges against them until they appeared before an examining magistrate, in some case months after their arrest.

No evidence was presented by the prosecution indicating that the accused, mostly members of the *Shabiba Islamiyya*, Islamic Youth, had used or advocated violence. Thirteen of the defendants were sentenced to death (seven *in absentia*) and 34 to life imprisonment.

In some cases such as those of the Islamists and of one journalist tried in 1990, defence lawyers walked out of the court when permission to call defence witnesses was refused by the judges.

Abdallah Zaazaa (left) shows scars to his feet caused by torture in Derb Moulay Cherif detention centre in 1974

Torture

Derb Moulay Cherif detention centre in Casablanca is well known to political detainees in Morocco. Here, torture and ill-treatment of prisoners takes place as a matter of routine, either to extract information or confessions, or as a means of intimidation.

A political detainee tried in February 1986 described what had happened to him in Derb Moulay Cherif:

"They started off with psychological torture — 'you will talk even if we have to kill you'. They slapped and kicked me all over while I was blindfold. Next day I experienced my first physical torture (the 'aeroplane') for about 30 minutes.

"Then I was questioned.... That evening, they tried another torture (the 'parrot')... and they stifled me with rags and their hands until I nearly passed out."

Torture of political detainees has also been reported frequently in other detention centres, including Fes, Oujda, Tanger and Tetouan. A detainee in Oujda police station wrote in 1986:

"I was handcuffed and had my feet bound. I was blindfold and put in the 'parrot' position. Then they tortured me in three ways: giving me electric shocks on the sensitive parts of my body; with *falaqa* and blows with a special hose pipe; and by being choked and having dirty water poured in my mouth and up my nose."

Several people have died in custody in circumstances suggesting that they had been tortured or ill-treated.

One such case involved Amine Tahani, a 29-year-old engineer and an official of the National Union of Engineers. He was ar-

0149

Mohammed Alaoui Suleimani

Prisoner of conscience

Mohammed Alaoui Suleimani, a primary school headmaster in Marrakech, has been arrested more than once for his religious views. He is 60 years old and has eight children.

In March 1990 he was sentenced by the Court of First Instance at Salé to two years' imprisonment and a fine of 10,000 dirhams. He was convicted on charges connected with an unauthorized Islamic association, Justice and Charity, founded by Abdessalam Yassine. The sentence was confirmed on appeal in 1990.

He was first arrested in 1972 after he helped to print an open letter from Abdessalam Yassine to King Hassan II. He "disappeared" for 18 months after his arrest. His description of his detention suggests that he was held in Derb Moulay Cherif. He was released, without trial, in Casablanca. He is now held in Salé Prison.□

Prisoner of conscience

Abdallah al-Harif is one of the longest-serving prisoners of conscience in Morocco. He was one of 178 defendants who were tried in 1977 for membership of an illegal organization and endangering the internal security of the state. Eight remain in prison.

In 1969, he completed his studies of metallurgy at the *Ecole des mines* in Paris, returned to Morocco and became a prominent civil engineer in Casablanca. From 1971 he was the Secretary General of the National Union of Engineers, and also an active member of Forward, an illegal Marxist-Leninist movement.

He was arrested in January 1975 and was held incommunicado for one year at the secret Derb Moulay Cherif detention centre in Casablanca, during which time he was severely tortured. At the trial, which took place in 1977, only after several hunger-strikes, Abdallah Al Harif was sentenced to 20 years' imprisonment.

He is serving his sentence at Kenitra Central Prison. In prison, he has been studying economics.□

Tanks patrolling the streets of Casablanca in June 1981 following a general strike against food price rises

rested in October 1985 and shortly after admitted to Averroes Hospital where he died. He had been an asthmatic since childhood and his death was said by the authorities to have been caused by an acute asthma attack.

However, according to other detainees held at Derb Moulay Cherif at the same time, when Amine Tahani was returned from an interrogation session, it was clear to them from his extreme state of distress that he had been tortured or ill-treated.

In response to inquiries by AI, the authorities made available some details of his medical condition in detention to support their finding that he had died from an asthma attack, but neither an autopsy nor a formal inquiry into the full circumstances preceding his death was carried out.

'Disappearances'

Hundreds of people have "disappeared" in custody in Morocco since the 1960s. Most of them "disappeared" before 1987, and the majority are of Western Saharan origin. However, at least 100 Moroccan nationals have allegedly "disappeared" in the past 30 years, including suspected political opponents of the government and the family of General Oufkir, a former minister.

Some of the "disappeared" have been released after years in incommunicado detention without trial or charge. Eight students and others who "disappeared" in 1976 and 1977 were held for eight years in secret detention centres in Casablanca before being freed.

Hundreds of people from the south of Morocco and the Western Sahara are believed to have "disappeared" between 1975, when the former Spanish Sahara was annexed, and 1987. They are thought to have been arrested by the security forces and held in secret jails.

Victims include the very old and very young, although students and educated Sahrawis have been particularly targeted. Sometimes whole families have "disappeared". Protest against "disappearance" in the Western Sahara is muted for fear of similar treatment.

Nearly all Sahrawis held in prolonged detention without trial for political reasons have been denied normal legal processes. In all cases, reports suggest that the victims or their families were suspected by the authorities of supporting the Polisario Front.

Only one group of Sahrawis, the so-called "Meknes Group" of 26 people, mainly students, is known to have been brought before a judge for alleged sympathies with the Polisario Front. They were convicted in 1980 of conspiracy to change the system of government and sentenced to up to five years' imprisonment.

Eighty-eight cases of "disappearances" have been taken up by AI groups and raised countless times with the Moroccan authorities: in response the authorities have simply denied any record of these prisoners.

What you can do

AI is an international campaigning organization, which enrols the support of ordinary women and men worldwide in its actions. Here are some suggestions about what you can do to try to stop further human rights violations in Morocco:

Write to the King

Send a letter to King Hassan II. Explain that you have read about the human rights violations taking place in Morocco, and urge him to institute measures to stop further abuses. Ask him to release all prisoners of conscience and to launch investigations into all cases of torture and "disappearance". Send your letter to: His Majesty King Hassan II/Palais Royal/Rabat/Morocco.□

Death penalty

Although no death sentences have been carried out since 1982, Ahmed Khiari has been facing execution for more than 18 years. He was condemned to death in 1972, at the age of 39, for assassinating Monadi Brahim, a police informer. He was an active member of the resistance against the French before independence and later joined the National Union of Popular Forces (UNFP).

He is not the only prisoner in Morocco who has suffered years of torment in expectation of death. Of the 147 prisoners on death row in Kenitra Central Prison, two have been there since the 1960s. Fifteen are held for political offences; some may be prisoners of conscience. Most were sentenced after unfair trials.

Under the Penal Code the death penalty is applicable for at least 30 crimes. It is currently retained as punishment for crimes including premeditated murder, murder in the course of other crimes, parricide, armed robbery, arson, and certain crimes against the internal and external security of the state and public order, including treason, damaging territorial unity in time of war, and taking up arms for, or inciting, civil war.

The death penalty is also provided for under the Code of Military Justice for crimes such as desertion to the enemy. It is mandatory for attempts on the life of the King.□

0150

EGYPT

Gulf war opponents arrested

STUDENTS, journalists, medical doctors and lawyers were among some 20 people arrested in January and February, apparently for expressing their opposition to the Gulf war. Palestinians and Egyptians with Palestinian connections were also reportedly detained under state of emergency legislation in force since 1981.

Some have been charged with specific offences relating to the preparation of leaflets, or the dissemination of information held to be "hostile to the national interest". Others have been placed in administrative detention and held incommunicado by the State Security Intelligence Police.

AI called on the Egyptian Government to release all those held for the non-violent exercise of their human rights, and to ensure that all detainees were being humanely treated, in accordance with Egypt's obligations under international human rights treaties.□

DJIBOUTI

Torture reported after arrests

DOZENS of prisoners were reportedly tortured by Djibouti security police after over a hundred members of the Afar ethnic group were arrested in connection with an attack on a northern military barracks on 8 January. People demonstrating against the arrests were also detained but most were quickly released. Two soldiers were killed in later attacks for which no organization has yet claimed responsibility.

The government blamed Afar opponents for the attacks. Thirty-five prisoners, including Ali Aref Bourhan, a former Prime Minister, were subsequently charged with "undermining the security of the state" and murder, offences carrying the death penalty which are tried by a special security court with no right of appeal.

AI expressed concern to the government about the torture reports and called for an independent investigation. It urged that detainees be brought before a magistrate without delay and given access to legal representatives, doctors and relatives.□

CUBA

Human rights activists detained

DOZENS of government critics and human rights activists have been detained in Cuba in the past 18 months. Although many were released without charge shortly after arrest, others were held for months before being tried.

In cases that have attracted international attention, non-custodial sentences ranging from a few months to three years' "restricted liberty" have been imposed but the defendants were held for long periods in the Havana State Security headquarters without access to lawyers.

The Secretary-General of the Party for Human Rights in Cuba (PPDHC), Dr Samuel Martínez Lara, was sentenced to three years' "restricted liberty" for "rebellion" in February 1991 after being held for 11 months by State Security. He was denied access to a lawyer for eight months. Eight other members of the PPDHC, including former Secretary-General Tania Díaz Castro who has since renounced her human rights activities, were sentenced to between three months' and one year's "restricted liberty" in November 1990 for "illegal association". Students Jorge Quintana and Carlos Ortega received sentences of three years' and two years' "restricted liberty" in November 1990 after being convicted of "disrespect" for openly criticizing President Fidel Castro.

Relatively heavy sentences have been imposed in less well-known cases on a number of people convicted of "enemy propaganda" whom AI believes may be prisoners of conscience.

Many were arrested outside the capital city and precise details of their cases have proved hard to obtain because of the virtual outlawing of human rights monitoring within the country.

Nine members of the Cuban Committee for Human Rights (CCPDH), in the Province of Villa Clara were convicted in September 1990 on charges of "enemy propaganda" and/or "illegal association", reportedly in connection with their activities on behalf of the committee. Their sentences ranged from one to six years' imprisonment. The CCPDH secretary from Ciego de Avila in Camaguey Province, Felipe Alexis Morejón Rodríguez, was sentenced to two years' imprisonment in June 1990 for "enemy propaganda". Juan Mayo Méndez, a mathematics teacher from Las Tunas Province arrested in January 1990, was sentenced to six years' imprisonment, allegedly for writing anti-government slogans.□

Islamists arrested in Tunisia

OVER 500 members, sympathizers and suspected sympathizers of the unregistered Islamic movement *al-Nahda* have been detained in Tunisia since September 1990. Many of them were released without charge after having been held incommunicado, often beyond the 10-day maximum period allowed in Tunisian law. Others have been sentenced to up to two years' imprisonment for offences such as encouraging and participating in unauthorized demonstrations, belonging to an unauthorized organization and spreading false information.

There have been numerous reports of torture and ill-treatment in incommunicado detention. Monji Jouini, an independent candidate in the 1989 legislative elections, was arrested on 19 December 1990, held incommunicado for 43 days, and released without charge on 30 January 1991. Abdellatif Tlili, detained without trial for 18 months between 1987 and 1989, was arrested again on 21 November 1990, held incommunicado for 42 days, and released without charge on 1 January 1991. Both allege that they were tortured during incommunicado detention, including by suspension in the *poulet rôti* position (suspended on a bar with the hands tied behind the knees), sexual abuse and beating.

Hamadi Jebali, editor of the weekly *al-Fajr*, the newspaper of the Islamic movement *al Nahda*, was sentenced by military court on 31 January 1990 to one year in prison for publishing an article calling for the abolition of military courts in Tunisia. AI has adopted him as a prisoner of conscience. The writer of the article, lawyer Mohammed Nouri, was sentenced to six months' imprisonment and granted bail pending appeal. Both men were charged with defamation of a judicial institution.

The Tunisian Government has denied the torture allegations raised by AI. The organization, however, remains concerned at the increasingly numerous reports of torture and prolonged incommunicado detention.□

Dr Sari Nusseibeh

ISRAEL/OCCUPIED TERRITORIES

Prisoner of conscience detained

DR Sari Nusseibeh, a prominent Palestinian figure in the Israeli Occupied Territories, was administratively detained in January. The Israeli authorities have accused him of being a leading member of the Palestine Liberation Organization and of spying for Iraq.

Dr Nusseibeh stated he had "always been clearly and unequivocally opposed to all forms of violence", including war, and categorically denied having ever engaged in intelligence gathering. He said he believed he had been detained because of his public standing and his support for "achieving peace with Israel through recognition of the rights of the Palestinian people".

The judge who reviewed his detention order reduced his detention period from six to three months.

AI believes that Dr Nusseibeh is a prisoner of conscience, detained for his non-violent political opinions and activities as a leading Palestinian figure. It has called for his immediate and unconditional release.

Some 14,000 other Palestinians, including prisoners of conscience, have been administratively detained since December 1987. Detainees are virtually never given enough information to be able to defend themselves against the authorities' accusations. Those currently held include three other prominent Palestinians known for their public support for peaceful dialogue with Israel.□

0151

USSR

AI calls for inquiry into killings in Vilnius

AI has called for a full and impartial investigation into reports that 13 peaceful, unarmed demonstrators were killed by Soviet troops in the Lithuanian capital of Vilnius on 13 January 1991.

The killings occured after a large crowd had gathered outside the city's television tower that evening to prevent Soviet troops taking over the building.

Eye-witnesses say the demonstrators offered only passive resistance when tanks and soldiers used tear-gas and live ammunition to disperse them.

The Lithuanian authorities list 14 people dead, including one Soviet soldier, and over 160 injured as a result of the operation. Of the dead, one is said to have died from injuries inflicted by explosives and three others were crushed by armoured vehicles. The remaining demonstrators and the soldier died of gunshot wounds.

According to the USSR Minister of Interior Affairs, members of the crowd fired on the soldiers first. President Mikhail Gorbachov announced on 22 January that there would be an investigation into these and other recent deaths in the Baltic republics: six people died of gunshot wounds in Latvia after incidents involving troops on 16 and 20 January.

AI has urged the authorities to ensure that law enforcement officials are aware of, and conform to, international standards regarding the use of force.□

Schoolchildren taking part in a painting competition organized by an AI group in India on 10 December 1990, International Human Rights Day. The theme of the competition was "Human rights in a changing world"

CAMEROON

Journalists convicted under new laws

TWO well-known Cameroonian journalists were convicted in January of publishing an article criticizing the government. Pius Njawe, editor of *Le Messager*, a Douala newspaper, and economist Célestin Monga, author of the article, were charged with showing contempt for the head of state, the courts and members of the National Assembly. Amid countrywide protests against their prosecution, they were convicted on 17 January 1991 of showing contempt for the National Assembly and given suspended prison sentences and fined.

They were convicted under one of several new repressive laws adopted in December 1990. In amendments to the penal code the maximum penalty for showing contempt for the courts or National Assembly members was increased from one to five years' imprisonment, and three new political offences were introduced, all punishable by long prison sentences. These involved spreading false information and incitement to revolt and rebellion.

The government has presented these new laws as reforms which herald a new era of multi-party democracy and political freedom. However, in reality, old repressive laws appear simply to have been replaced with new ones. Broad powers of administrative detention without charge or trial are still retained and a state of emergency may still be imposed by presidential decree without control by the legislature or the judiciary.

There are no safeguards against abuse of emergency powers or against arbitrary and unjust detention. Political trials will no longer be heard by special military tribunals but by another special court, the State Security Court. As before, its members will be appointed by the government and it will allow no right of appeal to a higher, independent court. Press censorship has been tightened, and new laws allowing political parties and activities also place restrictions on both.□

AMNESTY INTERNATIONAL NEWSLETTER is published every month in four languages to bring you news of AI's concerns and campaigns worldwide, as well as in-depth reports. Available from Amnesty International (address below)

GUATEMALA

Mother and baby 'disappear'

MARÍA Tiu Tojín and her one-month-old daughter María Josefa "disappeared" after being detained in August 1990 by the Guatemalan army in El Quiché department, along with a community of 85 peasants, including women and children. The peasants had fled their villages during earlier army counter-insurgency campaigns and did not wish to return to areas under army control; the army customarily accuses such displaced people of collaborating with the guerrillas.

According to witnesses from the group, the military authorities repeatedly accused María Tiu Tojín of being a guerrilla and subjected her to prolonged interrogation. She and her baby were then taken to a military base; the peasants to a displaced persons' centre. Soldiers reportedly told María Tiu's family that she and her baby were detained at the base, but when family members went to search for them there, their detention was denied. It is also reported that after the two "disappeared", soldiers in the area had a baby in their possession. However, there has been no further word of the two, and relatives and witnesses to their arrest who have attempted to locate them have received threats from local military authorities.□

0152

AMNESTY INTERNATIONAL

NEWSLETTER MAY 1991 VOLUME XXI • NUMBER 5

AI visits Niger

AN AI delegation visited the Republic of Niger in February 1991. They discussed the organization's concerns, including political imprisonment, torture and extrajudicial executions, with government ministers. The delegates also collected information about human rights violations in the Tchin-Tabaraden area in May 1990 following an attack by members of the Tuareg community on government buildings. Many Tuareg were arrested, including some who may be prisoners of conscience. AI had received reports of extrajudicial executions and the widespread use of torture resulting, in many cases, in deaths. Government ministers who met AI's representatives denied that the security forces had committed any human rights violations and said that all those arrested had been involved in endangering the security of the state. Shortly before the delegates arrived, 36 untried detainees were released and they were able to meet some of the 44 untried detainees still held.☐

BELIZE

Official inquiry in torture case

THE Prime Minister of Belize, George Price, has appointed a Commission of Inquiry in response to queries from AI and others about the fate of Luis Arturo Arévalo, a Guatemalan reportedly tortured by the Belizean security forces in late October 1990. He was reported to have been subsequently deported to Guatemala where there were grounds to believe he might be subjected to further violations. The Prime Minister has written to those who inquired about the case, informing them of the terms of reference of the inquiry, and promising to inform them of its results.

AI is also monitoring the cases of three Belizeans sentenced to death in 1990 for murder, who were granted retrials in February: two of them because they had given their statements after being beaten by the police. Belize's last execution was in 1985.☐

Free at last: after 16 years of wrongful imprisonment the "Birmingham Six" enjoy their first taste of freedom. Pictured above with UK parliamentarian Chris Mullin (centre) who campaigned for their release, they are, from left to right, John Walker, Patrick Hill, Hugh Callaghan, Richard McIlkenny, Gerard Hunter and William Power. **See page 8**

© Joe St Leger/Irish Times

TURKEY

Detainees die in custody

THERE has been a marked increase in reports of deaths as a result of torture in Turkish police stations. Nine such cases have been reported to AI since 25 November 1990.

Birtan Altunbaş, a medical student at Hacettepe University, Ankara, was taken into custody at the Political Branch of Ankara Police Headquarters on 9 January 1991. The authorities said they suspected him of complicity in political murder. He died on 16 January in Gülhane Military Hospital.

Murat Böbrek, a student detained at the same time, alleged that for four days and nights he heard Birtan Altunbaş's cries and shouts, and that he saw him naked, being made to run up and down between two policemen, a known method of diminishing the traces left by beating on the soles of the feet.

An autopsy was performed the day of Birtan Altunbaş's death, but two months later his family had still not been notified of the results. The government has claimed, to AI, that Birtan Altunbaş died of "heart disease caused by malnutrition". Birtan Altunbaş had been on hunger strike since his arrest — a period of only seven days.

AI believes cases of death in custody under torture are directly attributable to routine breaches of the detention procedure laid down by the Turkish Criminal Procedure Code (TCPC).

A lawyer's presence during interrogation, as required by the TCPC, would prevent ill-treatment and protect the detainees' legal interests. Access by lawyers to detainees throughout the detention period provides not only a safeguard against torture but also protects the police against the possibility of false allegations of ill-treatment.

The Turkish Government continues to assert that lawyers are permitted access to detainees, citing circulars issued by the Prime Minister in 1989 and 1990 which reaffirm this right. However, lawyers were permitted access in only eight of the 271 cases of detention by police and gendarmerie monitored by AI between August 1990 and April 1991. Torture was alleged in most of the cases.

"Yes, it is true that torture continues unabated," said Turgut Kazan, President of the Istanbul Bar Association, in March 1991. "In spite of Turkey's signature of international conventions, nothing has changed. The Prime Minister's circular is being ignored."

AI has copies of documents issued by the Ankara State Security Court Prosecution refusing detainees access to lawyers "on the principle of the secrecy of interrogation".

Access becomes even more important when, as in Turkey, the term of police custody is very long: under the TCPC the maximum term is 15 days, increasing to 30 days in the southeastern provinces under Emergency Powers. In practice, these terms are often exceeded.

A recent such case is that of Erol Özpolat, İbrahim Bingöl, Cavidan Kocaacar and Alp Aslan who were detained in February in Ankara, suspected of participation in political murder. Lawyers were refused access, and all four were held well beyond the 15-day legal maximum — for Erol Özpolat this meant 29 days of incommunicado detention. All allege that they were tortured.☐

0153

CAMPAIGN FOR PRISONERS OF THE MONTH

Each of the people whose story is told below is a prisoner of conscience. Each has been arrested because of his or her religious or political beliefs, colour, sex, ethnic origin or language. None has used or advocated violence. Their continuing detention is a violation of the United Nations Universal Declaration of Human Rights. International appeals can help to secure the release of these prisoners or to improve their detention conditions. In the interest of the prisoners, letters to the authorities should be worded carefully and courteously. You should stress that your concern for human rights is not in any way politically partisan. In *no* circumstances should communications be sent to the prisoner.

CHINA

Father Jin Dechen: ***the 71-year-old Catholic Vicar-General of Nanyang diocese, Henan Province, he was sentenced in July 1982 to 15 years' imprisonment for "counter-revolutionary" offences. He is currently held at the No.3 provincial prison at Yuxian in Henan.***

Fr Jin was first arrested in the late 1950s, when many Catholics were detained for proclaiming their loyalty to the Vatican. The detentions followed the formation of an official Patriotic Catholic Association (PCA), independent of the Church of Rome, intended to bring Catholic affairs under the control of the Chinese Government. Fr Jin was released in 1973, but kept under strict surveillance.

He was arrested again in December 1981, when other Catholics who had already served long prison sentences were detained for refusing to co-operate with the PCA. As well as maintaining his allegiance to Rome, Fr Jin is reported to have spoken out against government policies on contraception and abortion, which contravene Vatican teachings.

The authorities are reportedly prepared to release Fr Jin if he appeals for clemency on grounds such as ill-health. Fr Jin has apparently refused — he is in good health despite his age — and will not admit to any criminal activity to secure his release.

AI continues to receive reports of the arrest and sentencing of Catholics for their activities in the "underground" church. Several were detained after an unofficial Bishops' Conference in Shaanxi Province in November 1989. Two were sentenced to three years' "re- education through labour", and others are believed to have been imprisoned. In December 1990, at least 23 Catholics were arrested after police raided their homes in Hebei Province. Their fate is uncertain.

■Please write courteous letters appealing for Fr Jin Dechen's release to: Minister of Public Security Tao Siju/Gonganbu/Dong Chang'an Jie/Beijingshi/People's Republic of China.☐

CAMEROON

Olivier Nwaha Binya'a: ***a Jehovah's Witness, he has been detained without charge or trial since May 1984 because of his religious beliefs.***

Olivier Nwaha Binya'a appears to be held in indefinite administrative detention without any opportunity to challenge his imprisonment. Jehovah's Witnesses are a Christian denomination which does not support the use or advocacy of violence. Persecution of Jehovah's Witnesses began in Cameroon in the 1960s, mainly because of their refusal to recognize the sovereignty of the state by saluting the national flag or voting in elections. A 1970 presidential decree banning the movement was apparently prompted by the mass abstention by Jehovah's Witnesses from voting in a presidential election. Since 1970 hundreds of Jehovah's Witnesses have been detained without charge or trial for up to five years. In 1983 AI learned of the release of a group of Jehovah's Witnesses who had been held without trial since 1978 and in December 1984 at least 80 Jehovah's Witnesses were arrested in Limbé, southwest Cameroon, after holding an unauthorized religious meeting.

Individual Jehovah's Witnesses have been detained because of their refusal to join Cameroon's ruling party, for many years the only political party allowed to operate in the country. The government of President Paul Biya, who became head of state in 1982, has retained legislation banning the Jehovah's Witness sect. At least four Jehovah's Witnesses were reported to have been detained in 1988; one was released after a short time, but it is not clear whether the others were also subsequently released.

Olivier Nwaha Binya'a is held in Yoko *prison de production* (labour camp) in the centre of Cameroon, which is used mainly for political prisoners and others held in administrative detention. The prison diet is poor and medical treatment inadequate; his health has deteriorated during his seven years in detention.

■Please send courteous letters appealing for his immediate release to: President Paul Biya/Palais de la Présidence/Yaoundé/Cameroon.☐

TUNISIA

Hamadi Jebali: ***a 51-year-old newspaper editor from Sousse, he was sentenced by the military court in Tunis on 31 January 1991 to one year's imprisonment for publishing an article calling for the abolition of military courts in Tunisia.***

The article, entitled "When will military courts, serving as special courts, be abolished?" and written by a Tunisian lawyer, was published on 27 October 1990 in *Al-Fajr* (Dawn), the official newspaper of the non- recognized Islamic group *Hizb al-Nahda* (Renaissance).

Hamadi Jebali was charged with defamation of a judicial institution under the Tunisian Press Code.

Hamadi Jebali

Under the 1975 Press Code, prior authorization by the Ministry of Interior is required to publish any newspaper or periodical. Once authorization is granted, the Press Code requires that the first printed copy of each issue be submitted to the Ministry of Interior which can then intervene to stop distribution. The issue of *Al-Fajr* in which the article appeared was submitted to and apparently approved by the Ministry of Interior. However, the Ministry of Defence decided to prosecute Hamadi Jebali. The Tunisian authorities ordered the newspaper *Al-Fajr* to close until further notice on 8 February 1991.

Hamadi Jebali's sentence was confirmed on 6 March 1991 by the *Cassation* court. This is the only court of appeal for cases tried by the military court, and looks only at points of law and not at facts and findings, thus providing a restricted appeal.

In October 1990, Hamadi Jebali, who is a member of the executive council of *Hizb al-Nahda*, had received a six months' suspended sentence and a fine of 1500 dinars for publishing an article entitled "The people of the State or the State of the People?" in *Al-Fajr* in June 1990. This sentence may be added to the new one year term.

■Please send courteous letters appealing for his immediate and unconditional release to: Son Excellence Président M. Zine El Abidine Ben Ali/Président de la République/Palais Présidentiel/Tunis/Carthage/Tunisie.☐

Prisoner of conscience released

SALIH al-'Azzaz, a prominent writer and journalist, was released uncharged on 4 March. In November 1990 he had been arrested in connection with a protest by women in Riyadh against a ban on women drivers. He was held in solitary confinement in the General Intelligence headquarters in Riyadh and was reportedly tortured.

He had previously been arrested in May 1982, when he was editor-in-chief of *al-Yawm* newspaper, and was held without charge or trial until he was released following an amnesty at the end of 1982.☐

0154

FOCUS amnesty international

AI was launched 30 years ago this month. Today it is an international organization with more than 1,100,000 members, subscribers and regular donors in over 150 countries and territories and with over 4,200 AI volunteer groups in 70 countries.

The fact that AI's work continued for 30 years should not be a cause for celebration, rather a cause for outrage. Now, perhaps more than ever, a worldwide movement dedicated to the protection of human rights is essential. Nothing could make clearer the risk that persistent human rights violations pose to a just and stable world order than the Gulf war.

AI has made repeated appeals over the last 30 years both to individual governments and to the United Nations to deal constructively and effectively with violations of human rights in all regions of the world. Our concerns have included large numbers of prisoners of conscience in the Soviet Union and other East European countries under former governments; mass "disappearances" in Latin America; widespread extrajudicial executions in various African countries; arbitrary arrests and unfair trials in China and other Asian countries, and the increasing use of the death penalty in the USA, among other countries, in contradiction to a worldwide trend towards abolition.

In the Middle East we sought over many years to focus world attention on the suppression of fundamental human rights in Iraq.

Nothing could make clearer the risk that persistent human rights violations pose to a just and stable world order than the Gulf war.

We have repeatedly drawn attention to gross violations in Iran and to the pattern of abuses inflicted on Palestinians detained or killed during the unrest in Israel and the Occupied Territories. We have intervened on behalf of political detainees and victims of torture and the death penalty in Saudi Arabia, campaigned against torture and extrajudicial executions in Syria, and publicized torture and "disappearances" in Morocco. We have also published exhaustive

Candlelit vigil for the "disappeared" by Venezuelan members in 1988

Amnesty International's 30th Anniversary

A cause for outrage not celebration

reports on our efforts to end torture and arbitrary arrests in Bahrain, Jordan and Egypt. And we appealed repeatedly for respect for fundamental human rights in Kuwait before the Iraqi invasion.

When the world's governments had a clear opportunity to deal with these grave and compelling issues, they chose not to do so. Governments across the political spectrum failed to pay due consideration to the human rights records of the countries to which they exported military, security and police assistance that could be used to commit further violations.

Today the governments of the world stand in danger of sabotaging the hope of a new era for human rights — a hope for which millions of ordinary people are struggling, often risking their lives or freedom. Some governments are sabotaging it by the violations they commit directly; others by the selectivity with which they exert their influence. Even those governments which are committed to protecting the rights of their own citizens have other interests to pursue in their foreign relations, and these frequently conflict with their obligation to defend human rights worldwide. Sometimes, human rights concerns become the short-term beneficiary of this self-interest; more often they become the casualty of political expediency.

This is why the existence of a worldwide human rights movement, independent of the political and economic interests of national states, remains so necessary.

The foremost contribution to this movement is made by those men and women who struggle to defend human rights at the local and national level in countries where they are violated daily. Without their courage, persistence and resilience, AI and other international organizations would often know little about the abuses: their struggle requires the strongest possible support across national frontiers. Where no open stand for human rights is feasible, the international human rights movement must proclaim the rights of those who are not permitted to proclaim their own.

AI has been a part of this movement since its foundation in 1961. The organization was born out of a sense of outrage at violations of human rights perpetrated despite the assent of governments to the Universal Declaration of Human Rights. Thirty years on, its members remain outraged. Accounts of prisoners of conscience, unfair trials of political prisoners, torture, "disappearances" after arrest and judicial and extrajudicial executions still arrive at AI's offices every day from different corners of the earth.

There have never been valid excuses for the commission of these gross violations of human rights. The first excuse for the sin of omission — of failure to act against them — is ignorance. The human rights movement acting at local, national, regional and international levels has today deprived governments and most peoples of that excuse. The world has also too often heard governments' excuses that political and economic interests override human rights issues — events already in this decade should have put an end to these excuses once and for all.

In the last decade of the 20th century it is not enough for some people to feel vindicated and others ashamed because of the changes which have improved respect for human rights in some

It is a time to remain outraged by the continuation of gross violations of human rights. And it is a time to act.

countries. It is a time to act to secure those improvements, especially as many are already threatened by new conflicts or the resurgence of old ones. It is a time to remain outraged by the continuation of gross violations of human rights — and to identify the situations which individuals, governments and the international community will be ashamed of tomorrow if we do not act today. We have heard enough excuses; we want action.□

0155

ZAHRA' AL-NASSER

SAUDI ARABIA

Died in custody, apparently as a result of torture

NAHAMÁN CARMONA

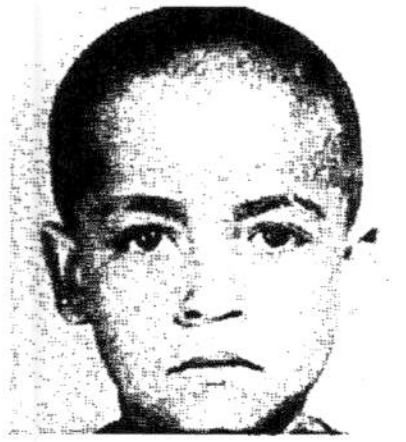

GUATEMALA

Kicked to death by police officers

ARCHANA GUHA

INDIA

Left paralysed after 27 days of torture

AUNG SAN SUU KYI

MYANMAR

Under house arrest because of her non-violent political beliefs

NASRIN RASOOLI

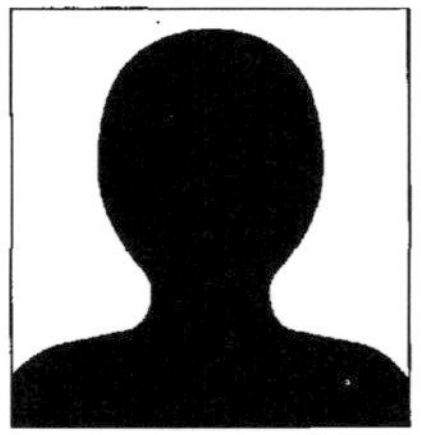

IRAN

Executed for her non-violent political activities

V. SKANDARAJAH

UNITED KINGDOM

Forcibly returned to Sri Lanka, despite the risk of torture

DR THOMAS WAINGGAI

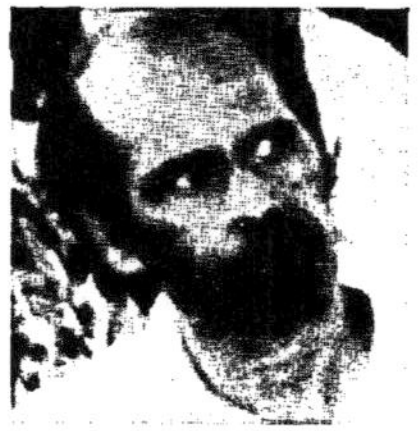

INDONESIA

Imprisoned for advocating independence for Irian Jaya

DR PEDRAZA

COLOMBIA

"Disappeared" in July 1990 while campaigning for human rights

STANZA BOPAPE

SOUTH AFRICA

"Disappeared" in 1990 during his fourth detention in 10 years

ESTEBAN GONZALEZ

CUBA

Jailed for criticizing the political system in his country

MARIA SANTA CLARA

PHILIPPINES

"Disappeared" while working for a community organization

MAMADOU BÂ

MAURITANIA

Killed, aged 12, by government troops because he was black

NIKOLAY SHUST

USSR

Jailed for refusing to perform military service

DALTON PREJEAN

USA

Juvenile offender, executed despite a history of mental illness

FEBE VELÁSQUEZ

EL SALVADOR

A trade unionist killed in a bomb attack on the union headquarters

Stop the suffering

These 30 cases represent some of the tens of thousands of prisoners who have been tortured, unfairly tried, "disappeared", judicially and extrajudicially executed on whose behalf AI has worked over the last 30 years.

MULUGETTA MOSISSA

ETHIOPIA

Jailed for over 10 years because of his ethnic origin

REV LAWFORD IMUNDE

KENYA

Six years' jail for writing opinions in his diary

WANG XIZHE

PEOPLE'S REPUBLIC OF CHINA

Jailed since 1981 for advocating democracy

SITA VALLES

ANGOLA

"Disappeared" in detention after a coup attempt in 1977

MOHAMED SRIFI

MOROCCO

Sentenced to 30 years in jail for his peaceful political views

VERA CHIRWA

MALAWI

Jailed for believing that her country should be run differently

ERHAN TUSKAN

TURKEY

Jailed for publishing political writings in his magazine

FIDEL INTUSCA FERNANDEZ

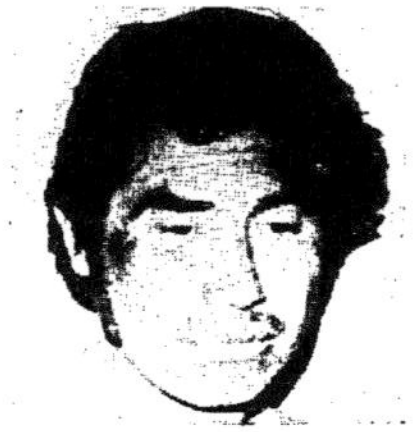

PERU

Tells of his torture by soldiers at a military base

ANDREAS CHRISTODOULOU

GREECE

Jailed for refusing to perform military service

DR USHARI

SUDAN

Jailed for struggling for the human rights of others

'ABD AL-RA'UF GHABIN

ISRAEL

Tells of being beaten during interrogation and deprived of sleep

NGUYEN CHI THIEN

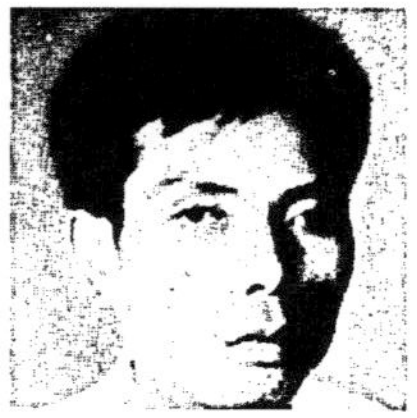

VIET NAM

A poet who has spent half his life in jail for his political verses

JOSÉ RAMÓN GARCÍA

MEXICO

"Disappeared" for publicizing alleged electoral fraud

GHASSAN NAJJAR

SYRIA

Imprisoned for protesting about the abuse of emergency powers

AUGUSTINE EKE

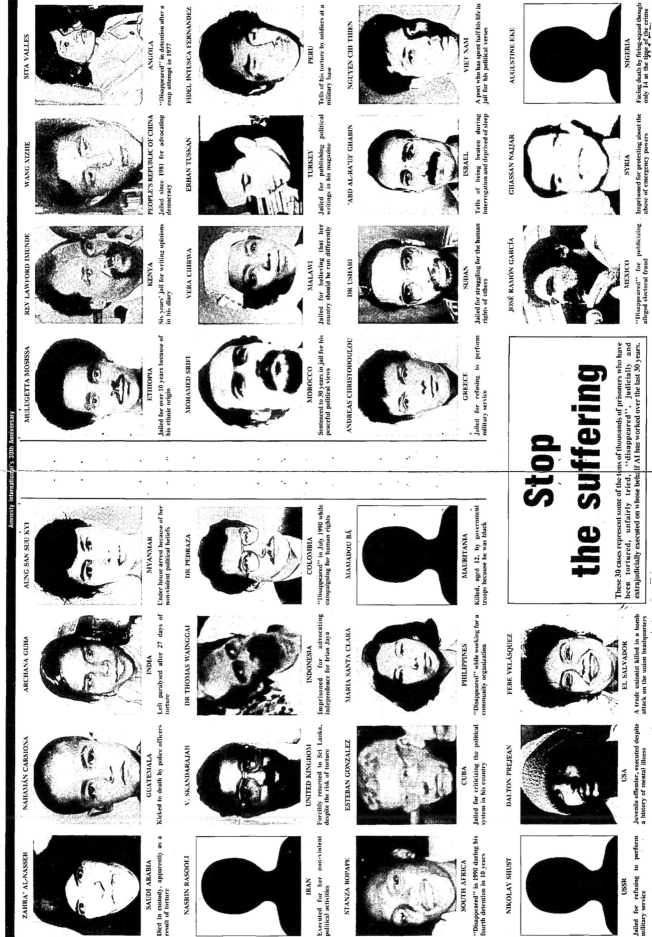

NIGERIA

Facing death by firing-squad though only 14 at the time of the crime

0156

What Amnesty International does

Since 1961 AI has adopted or investigated more than 42,000 prisoners' cases. Each case may involve one individual or many. Of these cases, over 38,000 are now closed.

At the end of November 1990 AI was working on more than 3,000 cases involving more than 4,500 individuals from countries all over the world. These cases concerned the adoption of prisoners of conscience or their investigation as possible prisoners of conscience.

To get emergency help to prisoners and others threatened with torture or death, an Urgent Action network of 50,000 volunteers in 65 countries is ready to organize speedy appeals by electronic mail, telex, fax and express mail. In the first 11 months of 1990 it went into action 764 times to help people in 80 countries. Each Urgent Action can generate several thousand urgent appeals to the authorities within a matter of days.

Of these appeals, 144 were prompted by reports of torture and prisoners urgently in need of medical treatment. Fifty-four appeals were issued in cases of arbitrary arrest, prolonged incommunicado detention, detention without charge or trial or unfair trial. Fifty-eight appeals related to extrajudicial executions, 90 to "disappearances" and 96 were made on behalf of prisoners sentenced to death. Other appeals were issued in cases of deaths in custody, death threats, fear of ill-treatment, conscientious objection and fear of refoulement.

Fifty Medical Actions were launched in 1990 to help prisoners in 28 countries. These actions involve about 8,000 health professionals in 30 countries who appeal on behalf of sick prisoners and those sentenced to death, as well as members of the health professions held as prisoners of conscience.

As well as working on behalf of individuals, AI publishes major documents on human rights violations. In 1990 over 135 reports were published covering issues ranging from "disappearances" in Chile, El Salvador, Morocco and Sri Lanka to extrajudicial killings in Brazil, Guatemala, India and Turkey and torture in Equatorial Guinea and Myanmar.

The organization also sends delegations on country visits to discuss its concerns with government authorities, observe political trials and carry out investigations into human rights abuses.□

Participants in AI's 'Race for Rights' in Coimbatore, India, December 1990. Banners and vehicles carried messages calling for the abolition of the death penalty and for people to join the struggle for human rights

The Ecuador Section holds an exhibition during the Chile campaign in 1988

AI Week concert, one of a series of events organized by Jordanian members in 1990

Delegates at the 1985 annual general meeting in Tanzania during AI's Campaign Against Torture

AI members demonstrate outside the Chinese Consulate in Gdansk, Poland, on 4 June 1990, the anniversary of the Beijing massacre

What you can do

AI doesn't just talk about human rights. It is an activist organization. It asks people to join, to become involved in actitivies and to motivate other people to become active members too.

The people whose cases are described overleaf and others in similar positions need help. All over the world AI has offices where you can find details of what can be done to help the victims of human rights violations. You may sympathise with AI's aims, you may be a member already, you may be an active member, you may be encouraging your friends and colleagues to become active members. Whatever your involvement in AI now think about making this the year you do more.

JOIN

We have offices in 60 capital cities of the world. Write to your nearest office and tell them you want to join.

BECOME AN ACTIVE MEMBER

Maybe you are already a member but have not found the time to get involved in AI's activities. Think about using AI's 30th anniversary year as a reason to find the time to write a letter once a month, to become more involved in your group or help others to get involved in AI's work.

FIND NEW MEMBERS

The more people working for human rights, the greater the pressure on those governments who violate those rights. You may be an active member, but what about your friends and colleagues? Do they know about AI? Ask them to read AI's publications and make sure they know how and where to join.□

UNITED NATIONS COMMISSION ON HUMAN RIGHTS

Commission acts on Iraq

AFTER several years of taking no action on reports of grave and widespread violations in Iraq, the Commission on Human Rights has appointed a Special Rapporteur to investigate the human rights situation there; another Special Rapporteur has been appointed to examine violations committed by Iraqi forces in occupied Kuwait.

The Commission also took a stronger stand in respect of two other countries: Cuba will now come under special scrutiny by a representative of the UN Secretary-General and the Expert on Equatorial Guinea, a country which receives assistance under the UN Advisory Services Program, has been requested to study the human rights situation there.

Another significant development to emerge from the latest session of the Commission was its decision to establish a Working Group on arbitrary detention. This will be the first UN mechanism with a mandate which could allow it to examine cases of prisoners of conscience anywhere in the world. It will fill an important gap in the framework of protection established by the Commission's existing "theme mechanisms".

It was disappointing that a proposed new international instrument on "disappearances" was held over for further study. Another proposed instrument that the Commission will consider next year is a revised draft of the Optional Protocol to the UN Convention against Torture, which would set up an international system of visits to places of detention.

The Commission kept under public review the human rights situation in Afghanistan, El Salvador, Iran and Romania but sent a clear signal that it may terminate special scrutiny of El Salvador and Iran at its next session. Chad, Myanmar, Somalia and Sudan are to be kept under consideration in the confidential 1503 procedure for situations showing "a consistent pattern of gross violations of human rights". Haiti was transferred to the Advisory Services Program and Guatemala was kept under this program for a further year despite AI's appeals for stronger measures.□

Abolishing the death penalty in Africa

FOLLOWING significant moves against the use of the death penalty in Africa in 1990 AI is appealing to all African governments to reduce the use of this uniquely cruel form of punishment as a significant step towards its total abolition. AI is appealing in particular to countries where current constitutional or legal reforms offer opportunities for immediate or early abolition: these include Angola, Burkina Faso, Burundi, Guinea-Bissau and South Africa.

In 1990 Namibia, São Tomé and Príncipe and Mozambique abolished the death penalty in their constitutions, joining Cape Verde which has been abolitionist since its independence in 1975. In South Africa the number of executions carried out in Pretoria declined from 117 in 1988 to 53 in 1989 and a moratorium on executions was declared in 1990. Some countries, while retaining the death penalty in law, have a long-standing tradition of not executing prisoners. Elsewhere, legal amendments have reduced the scope of the death penalty. National human rights groups are becoming increasingly involved in the campaign for abolition.

Despite these positive trends, the use of the death penalty remains widespread. In 1990 a total of 114 political opponents were executed in just three countries, Ethiopia, Nigeria and Sudan after trials behind closed doors. Their trials were unfair in various ways and they had no right to appeal to a higher court against their convictions and sentences. Hundreds of others throughout Africa were sentenced to death for non-political offences — often after faulty police or judicial procedures.

As a contribution to the debate about the death penalty in Africa AI is publishing a report* in May. Taking examples from various countries, it illustrates some of the arguments against the death penalty.□

** Africa: Towards abolition of the death penalty*
(AI Index No. AFR 01/01/91)

USA

Conscientious objectors imprisoned

TWO US soldiers imprisoned for exercising their fundamental right to freedom of conscience by refusing to bear arms or participate in armed conflict have been adopted as prisoners of conscience.

Sergeant George Morse, 25, was sentenced to five months' imprisonment in December 1990 for refusing to help prepare supplies for troops in Saudi Arabia. Lance Corporal Eric Hayes, 25, was convicted on 15 January 1991 on charges of desertion and not reporting for duty. He was sentenced to three years' imprisonment of which he will serve a maximum of eight months. Their prison sentences were the result of their conscientious objection to participating in war.

Captain David Wiggins, a 28-year-old army doctor sent to Saudi Arabia in December 1990, had applied for conscientious objector discharge in February 1990 when he came to the conclusion that the use of military force "is immoral because it leads to an unending cycle of killing and destruction". However, despite a positive recommendation from the investigating officer his application was denied. His attempts to be discharged have led to charges against him and a court martial is pending. AI is concerned that he may not be able to exercise his right to legal representation and to call witnesses at his court-martial, which may take place in Saudi Arabia.

AI has appealed for the immediate and unconditional release of George Morse and Eric Hayes and to ensure that David Wiggins has a fair trial.□

STOP PRESS

Ali Özler, sentenced to six years eight months for various activities carried out as chairperson of the Tunceli branch of the Turkish Human Rights Association and adopted as a prisoner of conscience by AI was conditionally released in early March by the 8th Criminal Appeal Court in Ankara. His case will be retried.□

USSR

Death penalty statistics no longer secret

STATISTICS on the death penalty in the USSR have been made public for the first time since 1934.

Figures on its use from 1985 to 1989 were announced by the Minister of Justice at a news conference on 16 January 1991. These show a progressive decrease in death sentences from 770 in 1985, of which 20 were commuted, to 271 in 1988 with 72 commutations. The 1989 figures indicate a reversal of this trend with 276 death sentences passed and a sharp reduction of commutations to 23. The 1990 figures, provided more recently by the Ministry of Justice report a dramatic increase to 447 death sentences, mostly for murder under aggravating circumstances. Another official source reports that 190 executions took place last year.

AI welcomes the publication of statistics on the death penalty, as well as current proposals to limit its scope. However, it remains concerned that there has been no stay on sentences or executions pending the review of existing legislation.□

CENTRAL AFRICAN REPUBLIC

Pro-democracy activists freed

TWENTY pro-democracy activists, members of the Coordination Committee for the Convening of a National Conference (CCCCN), arrested in the capital, Bangui, on 12 September 1990 were freed on 4 March after an examining magistrate ruled that they had no case to answer.

They had been arrested and charged with endangering the internal security of the state after attending a meeting to plan a national conference to herald the replacement of the country's one-party state by a multi-party political system.

Five members of the CCCCN who were arrested on 13 October 1990 remained in detention. The examining magistrate ruled that they should be brought to trial because they organized an illegal public meeting which degenerated into violence.□

RELEASED

Oleg Gorshenin, prisoner of the month in March 1991, has been released. No further action is required.

0158

0159

UNITED KINGDOM

Birmingham Six released

THE "Birmingham Six", six prisoners given life sentences in 1975 for pub bombings, had their convictions quashed on 14 March. The Irish Republican Army had claimed responsibility for the bombings, which resulted in 21 dead and 162 wounded. The six were convicted on the basis of contested confessions and scientific evidence interpreted as showing traces of explosives on some of the men's hands.

Throughout their 16-and-a-half years in prison the six claimed that they were innocent and that they had confessed after being ill-treated during incommunicado detention. They alleged that during those days they had suffered beatings, verbal threats to themselves and their families, threats involving the use of firearms and mock executions, and deprivation of sleep and food. Their allegations were rejected by the court in the original trial in 1975, as well as by the Appeal Court which heard new evidence in 1988.

The convictions of the "Birmingham Six" were quashed on 14 March 1991 by the Court of Appeal. This followed nine days of hearings during which lawyers for the six revealed new evidence. Most of it had been uncovered during an investigation by the Devon and Cornwall police. On the basis of the evidence, the Director of Public Prosecutions had stated at preliminary hearings in January and February that the testimony of all police officers involved in the case was to be regarded as unreliable, as was the scientific evidence. A lawyer for the six prisoners told the court that eight of the 25 police officers involved in the original investigation had lied and six others had given unreliable testimony to the original trial in 1975. Evidence showed that the officers had fabricated and rewritten notes, forged a custody sheet and altered key details of the timings of interrogations.

The UK government has announced that a Royal Commission would conduct a wholesale review of the criminal justice system.

AI remains concerned about other prisoners serving long prison terms, notably people convicted of serious offences in connection with the disturbances at Broadwater Farm Estate, London, in 1985. In these cases there was a pattern of police misconduct in keeping suspects in incommunicado detention.☐

PRISONER NEWS

AI learned in February 1991 of the release of 88 prisoners under adoption or investigation. AI took up 135 cases.

KUWAIT

Reprisal killings and torture

IN March AI called on the United Nations (UN) and all parties with effective authority in Kuwait to protect Palestinians and other Arabs from reprisal killings, arbitrary arrest and torture in the aftermath of the Gulf War.

Some had been targeted because they were suspected of collaborating with the Iraqi troops, and others apparently on account of their nationality. According to one eye-witness account, a Sudanese national was publicly executed by armed Kuwaiti civilians. Several hundred Palestinians were reportedly arrested and detained following Iraq's withdrawal from Kuwait on 26 February. The Kuwaiti military authorities reportedly expelled scores of them to Iraq, where some were at risk of torture or execution. Several people who were released after being detained for a week or more alleged that they were beaten with canes, rifles or rods, subjected to electric shocks and that cigarettes were extinguished on their bodies during interrogation. These violations were attributed to armed Kuwaiti civilians and members of Kuwait's regular army.

AI has appealed for the protection of Palestinians and others at risk of reprisal killings and other abuses in Kuwait and called for an urgent and independent investigation into allegations of arbitrary arrests and torture. It has urged the UN to ensure that the human rights of all people in Kuwait are protected. AI urged the Kuwaiti Government to grant the International Committee of the Red Cross immediate access to all detainees, and not to expel people to countries where they may face human rights violations. In early March the Kuwaiti authorities had denied that Palestinians were being mistreated.☐

AFGHANISTAN

Political prisoners tortured

HUNDREDS of Afghan political prisoners have reportedly been held without charge or trial for up to nine years. Many have been tortured.

In a report* published in March 1991 AI called on the Afghan Government to end the torture and long-term detention without trial of political prisoners.

The detainees include individuals suspected of involvement in armed opposition or non-violent anti-government activity. They are initially held in isolation cells for periods lasting as long as several months. During their isolation, they are reportedly denied access to legal counsel and family visits and are at risk of systematic torture and ill-treatment.

After the interrogation period, prisoners are transferred to detention centres run by the Ministry of State Security. These include Blocks 1 and 2 of Pul-e-Charkhi Prison near Kabul, where some have been kept indefinitely without charge or trial, denied family visits and outside correspondence.☐

** Afghanistan: Reports of torture and long-term detention without trial (AI Index No. ASA 11/01/91)*

BRAZIL

Rural workers leader attacked

NO less than four leaders of the Rural Workers Union of Rio Maria, Pará, Brazil, have been killed since 1985. The most recent killing occurred on 2 February 1991, when Expedito Roberto de Souza, then president of the union, was shot dead by a gunman near his home.

On 4 March his successor, Carlos Cabral Pereira, was himself attacked. He was shot outside the cemetery where a former president of the Rural Workers Union, João Canuto de Oliveira, was killed by gunmen reportedly hired by a local landowner in 1985.

Carlos Cabral Pereira was wounded in the back, treated in hospital and later discharged. He is now under police protection and a gunman who confessed to the shooting has been arrested.

AI welcomes these actions by the Brazilian authorities. In Brazil, over a number of years, many peasant leaders involved in land or labour disputes have been killed by gunmen allegedly hired by landowners and land claimants. In spite of the notorious, widespread and persistent nature of these killings, the Brazilian authorities have failed to take effective measures to stop them.

AI continues to monitor developments in this case and has called on the Brazilian Government to thoroughly and impartially investigate the incident.☐

AMNESTY INTERNATIONAL NEWSLETTER is published every month in four languages to bring you news of AI's concerns and campaigns worldwide, as well as in-depth reports. Available from Amnesty International (address below)

AI visits Chad

AN AI delegation visited Chad in March, three months after a new government took power. The delegation met the new head of state, Idriss Deby, and other government officials to discuss ways of preventing human rights violations and implementing the new government's slogan "Never again!" — a reference to the torture and killings of thousands of political prisoners by the previous government, headed by Hissène Habré.☐

AMNESTY INTERNATIONAL, 1 Easton Street, London WC1X 8DJ, United Kingdom. Printed in Great Britain by [illegible] Enterprises Ltd. London. Available on subscription at £7 (US$12.00) for 12 issues. ISSN 0308 6887

AMNESTY INTERNATIONAL
NEWSLETTER
JUNE 1991 VOLUME XXI • NUMBER 6

KUWAIT

Wave of abuses in the wake of war

AI has publicly appealed to the Emir of Kuwait to end the wave of arbitrary arrests, torture and killings in the country since the withdrawal of Iraqi forces.

The appeal followed a two-week AI fact-finding visit to Kuwait. The team reported that scores of victims had been killed and hundreds more had been arbitrarily arrested since 26 February. Many were brutally tortured by Kuwaiti armed forces and members of "resistance" groups since 26 February. Most of the victims were Palestinians, among them Jordanian passport holders. They also included Iraqi and Sudanese nationals and members of the "Bidun" community (stateless persons in Kuwait, denied basic civil and political rights).

Victims have been shot in public or tortured and killed in secret. Hundreds were taken from their homes or arrested at check-points, many to be tortured in police stations, schools and other makeshift detention centres.

Savage beatings with sticks, hose-pipes and rifle butts and whippings with electric cables were the most common methods, but AI's team catalogued over a dozen forms of torture, including electric shocks, burning with cigarettes, candles and acid, cutting with knives, biting, threats of execution and of sexual assault. Teams of torturers reportedly worked in relays, maintaining the torture for hours. Daily torture of captives appeared to have been common.

Most of the abuses immediately after the Iraqi withdrawal were said to have been carried out by "resistance" squads, but armed forces personnel have been increasingly cited in later cases. Victims were still being killed and tortured during AI's visit from 28 March to 9 April.

The team also updated information in AI's December 1990 report on violations by Iraqi forces in Kuwait. AI was able to confirm that its report had given an accurate overall picture of the range and intensity of the violations inflicted on the population during the occupation, although it could not confirm the precise number of killings by Iraqi forces during the occupation.

However, on the highly publicized issue in the December report of the baby deaths, AI's team was shown alleged mass graves of babies, but found no reliable evidence that Iraqi forces had caused their death.

In response to AI's appeal, the Kuwaiti Government admitted, on 19 April, that human rights violations had been committed immediately after the withdrawal of Iraqi forces but insisted that such abuses are no longer taking place.□

IRAQ

Appeal to stop the killing

IN April AI appealed to the Iraqi Government in the strongest possible terms to immediately put an end to the mass deliberate killing of unarmed civilians and the summary execution of government opponents and their suspected supporters.

The appeal followed numerous and credible reports received by AI that Iraqi Government forces were committing these and other human rights violations following the recapture of cities and towns in the northern Kurdish and southern Shi'a areas of the country. Some two million Kurds and Arab Shi'a Muslims were forced to flee to Iran and Turkey and tens of thousands more into the United States-occupied region of southern Iraq. Many were reportedly deliberately killed by Iraqi forces as they fled.

In its appeal AI also expressed dismay at reports that Iraqi Kurds who returned to Arbil in northern Iraq following a government announcement of an amnesty for Kurds on 5 April were arbitrarily arrested, summarily executed or subjected to forms of cruel, inhuman or degrading treatment.

In light of these reports, AI also sent urgent appeals to the governments of the United States, Kuwait and Saudi Arabia in April, urging them to ensure that Iraqi refugees then under the control of United States-led coalition forces were guaranteed effective and durable protection against human rights violations by Iraqi Government forces. AI stated that it strongly feared that the refugee population would be at risk of certain torture, "disappearance" or execution if returned to Iraqi Government control.□

A Kurdish mother and her sick child at Isikveren refugee camp on the Turkish border with Iraq © Roger Hutchings/Katz

PERU

Human rights activist injured by letter bomb

AI has appealed to President Alberto Fujimori for a prompt investigation into a bomb attack on Dr. Augusto Zúñiga, human rights defender and head of the legal department of the Commission for Human Rights. On 15 March 1991 Dr. Zúñiga opened a letter bomb which blew off his left hand and forearm, and caused considerable damage to his office.

At the time, Dr. Zúñiga was working on the case of student Ernesto Castillo Páez, who "disappeared" after he was reportedly detained by police on 21 October 1990 in Lima. The case received wide publicity when a *habeas corpus* petition was upheld by two lower courts (see *AI Newsletter*, March 1991). However, the Supreme Court subsequently annulled the *habeas corpus* on grounds of procedural irregularites. Dr. Zúñiga was warned that the police might seek reprisals against him, but although he informed the authorities of this, no specific measures of protection were apparently offered to him.□

0160

CAMPAIGN FOR PRISONERS OF THE MONTH

Each of the people whose story is told below is a prisoner of conscience. Each has been arrested because of his or her religious or political beliefs, colour, sex, ethnic origin or language. None has used or advocated violence. Their continuing detention is a violation of the United Nations Universal Declaration of Human Rights. International appeals can help to secure the release of these prisoners or to improve their detention conditions. In the interest of the prisoners, letters to the authorities should be worded carefully and courteously. You should stress that your concern for human rights is not in any way politically partisan. In *no* circumstances should communications be sent to the prisoner.

YUGOSLAVIA

Nijazi Beqa: ***an ethnic Albanian from Kosovo, aged 29, he is serving a four-year prison sentence for membership of a group campaigning for Kosovo province to be given the status of a republic within Yugoslavia.***

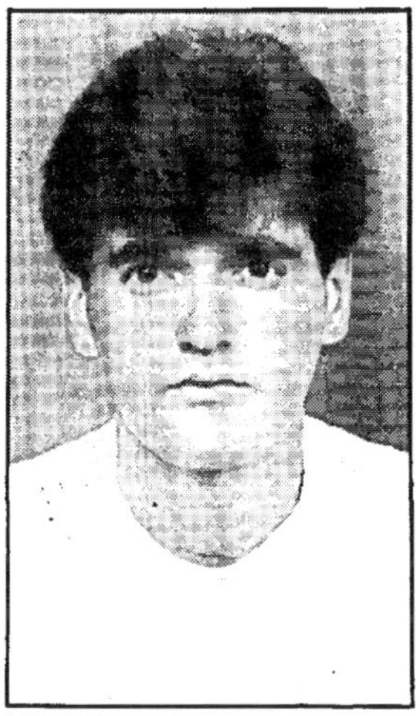

Nijazi Beqa

Nijazi Beqa, a student of physics, married, with one child, was one of 10 ethnic Albanians from the area of Uroševac in Kosovo arrested in September 1988. They were charged with having formed a "hostile" organization, aimed at securing republic status for Kosovo province. Kosovo borders on Albania and most of its population are ethnic Albanians. It is a province of the Yugoslav Republic of Serbia.

Nijazi Beqa and his co-defendants were accused of having joined an illegal organization, distributed "hostile propaganda materials" and of organizing petitions of a "hostile" nature to officials in and outside Yugoslavia. They were not charged with having used or advocated violence. At their trial in Priština in February 1989, all were found guilty and sentenced to imprisonment. Nijazi Beqa received the longest sentence: eight years, later reduced to five years by the Supreme Court of Kosovo.

The Yugoslav federal criminal law was changed in 1990 and many people convicted for similar non-violent political activity were released. However, Nijazi Beqa is still serving his sentence in Dubrav prison near Istok. It is reported that on 22 March he and five other political prisoners there went on a hunger-strike against the conditions under which they are being held.

■Please send courteous letters, appealing for his immediate and unconditional release to: Dr Vlado Kambovski/Federal Minister of Justice/Omladinskih brigada 1/ 11000 Beograd/Yugoslavia.□

PRISONER NEWS

AI learned in March 1991 of the release of 96 prisoners under adoption or investigation. AI took up 118 cases.

MOROCCO

Mohamed Abbad: ***a 37-year-old student and ex-president of the National Union of Moroccan Students (UNEM), he is serving a 15-year prison sentence in Safi Prison.***

Mohamed Abbad is one of 31 people tried in May 1984 in Marrakech following demonstrations in January 1984 against price rises and the imposition of an examination fee for the baccalaureate examination. They were reportedly arrested without warrant several days after the demonstrations, held incommunicado and tortured in *garde à vue* detention.

Mohamed Abbad was sentenced to 15 years' imprisonment on charges including conspiracy to overthrow the government and possessing leaflets aimed at disturbing internal security. The prosecution's evidence consisted of statements which the defendants made to the police in pre-trial custody, allegedly extracted under torture, and confiscated literature. No evidence was produced in court that he had used or advocated violence. He denied all the charges against him except possession of the literature which he said was either on sale in public bookstores or did not advocate violence.

Mohamed Abbad remains in prison with 17 others from this group. Two of the original 31 died during hunger-strikes in 1984 and two others, on hunger-strike since 1985, are isolated and forcibly fed in Averroes Hospital in Casablanca. Mohamed Abbad was originally held in Safi Prison, where he developed diabetes in 1988. He was then transferred to Marrakech where his family lives and could visit him regularly and provide him with the food necessary for his diabetic diet.

On 26 March 1991 he was returned to Safi Prison and in protest he began a hunger-strike which resulted in his falling into a coma, due to his illness, a few days later. He is now held in hospital in Safi.

■Please send courteous letters appealing for his immediate and unconditional release, if possible in French or Arabic to: His Majesty King Hassan II/Palais Royal/ Rabat/Morocco.□

CUBA

Orlando Azcué Rodríguez: ***a 33-year-old cigar factory technician, he is serving a three-year sentence for giving out handwritten leaflets calling for free elections in Cuba.***

Orlando Azcué Rodríguez was arrested on 5 April 1990 in Havana and brought to trial on 12 October on charges of making "enemy propaganda". According to reports of his trial, he was removed from the courtroom because, when asked if he wanted to say anything in his defence, he began to talk about his belief that political change was needed in Cuba. He was found guilty and sentenced to three years' imprisonment.

Orlando Azcué was one of 12 political prisoners in Combinado del Este Prison in Havana who signed a letter dated 1 January 1991 calling for peaceful political change and respect for human rights, that was smuggled out of the prison. The 12 also refused to wear their prison uniform as a way of reinforcing their demands. As a result of their protest, they were transferred to different prisons. Orlando Azcué and two others were taken to "Kilo 7" Maximum Security Prison in Camaguey where, on 17 January, they declared themselves on hunger-strike. They were said to have been forcibly dressed in the prison uniform and held for at least 17 days with their arms chained to the bars of their cells to prevent them from removing the uniform. Orlando Azcué was also said to have been beaten by prison guards on at least three occasions.

In early February he was transferred to Pinar del Río Provincial Prison after agreeing to give up his protest and end his hunger-strike. However, once there he again refused to wear his uniform and was forcibly dressed and handcuffed to the cell bars to prevent him from removing it. On 6 March he was transferred to the prison infirmary suffering from skin problems and a dramatic fall in his blood sugar level resulting from the earlier hunger-strike.

As of mid-April, he remained in the infirmary and was still refusing to wear the prison uniform if returned to his cell.

■Please send appeals requesting his immediate and unconditional release to: Dr. Fidel Castro Ruz/ Presidente del Consejo de Estado/ Ciudad de la Habana/Cuba.□

SWAZILAND

Prisoners freed

FIVE prisoners of conscience held in Swaziland since November 1990 under renewable 60-day administrative detention orders were released on 22 March 1991.

The five were previously imprisoned from June until October 1990 for allegedly organizing a political party — all parties are prohibited. The releases occurred shortly before two AI representatives arrived in Swaziland for talks with the government.□

0161

FOCUS amnesty international

Good news on the front page of *Amnesty (right)*, the movement's first journal: a prisoner is free. Ilker Demir *(far right)*, Turkish prisoner of conscience since 1984, pictured in prison with his daughter. He was released in April 1991 when the Turkish Penal Code was amended. Zikri Hafkhosh *(below)*, one of 315 children who 'disappeared' in Iraq in 1983

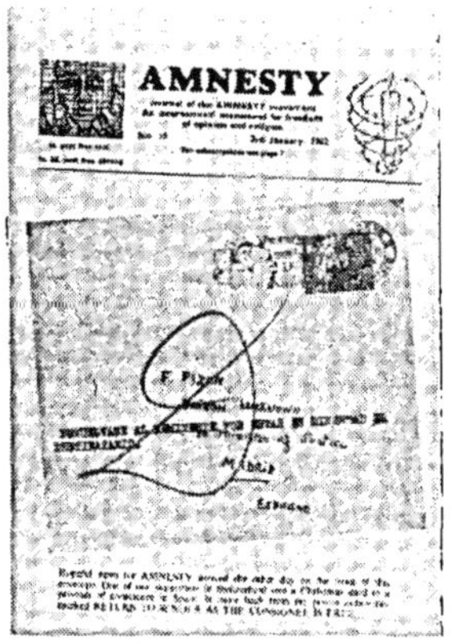

Make tomorrow the day of their freedom

0162

In 1962 *Amnesty*, AI's first journal, had good news on its front page: a prisoner of conscience is free in Spain. A Christmas card sent to him by an AI member in Switzerland had been returned marked "Consignee is free". This is the news AI's members want to hear — that somewhere in the world justice has been done. All too often the bad news dominates the headlines — worldwide human rights violations against a backcloth of war, repression and famine.

AI was founded 30 years ago to campaign for the release of prisoners of conscience around the world. Today the organization continues to focus on their plight. Here we publish the good news. Many of these prisoners are now free. Some have thanked AI, but we take no credit for anyone's freedom

The *Campaign for Prisoners of the Month* in the *Newsletter* has a 26-year history. Every issue has published appeals for the release of prisoners of conscience. The first issue, in January 1971, combined general news about AI's work with the *Postcards for Prisoners Campaign*, a monthly campaign on behalf of three prisoners which began in 1965.

Today the terrible injustice done to those prisoners reaches a mass audience. This *Newsletter*, and the articles in it, are published every month in over 15 languages including Arabic, Brazilian Portuguese, Chinese, English,

This month we review the fate of some of the 92 prisoners of conscience featured in the* Campaign for Prisoners of the Month *in 1989 and 1990

French, Hebrew, Portuguese, Russian, Spanish and Tamil. AI's sections all over the world include the *Prisoner of the Month* cases in the magazines and newssheets they publish in languages, ranging from Faroe to Bangla. In many countries, regional and national newspapers report on the *Prisoner of the Month* cases — the Slovenian Catholic weekly *Druzina*, the French national daily *Le Monde*, and the Pakistani daily *The Muslim*, to name but a few. Year in, year out, the *Campaign for Prisoners of the Month* provides a unique window into the harsh and desperate world of the prisoner of conscience. Hundreds of thousands of people have appealed for their freedom. And the prisoners themselves know that they are not alone, that the world has not forgotten them.

The 1990s began with a dramatic upturn of the fortunes of thousands of prisoners of conscience across eastern and central Europe. In Czechoslovakia former prisoner of conscience Vaclav Havel became President of his country. Others assumed important positions in the government of their countries. In many of these countries the new respect for human rights was embodied in the repeal or revision of laws used to imprison prisoners of conscience.

But there are still prisoners of conscience in Europe, and in every other region of the world.

This month we review the fate of some of the 92 prisoners whose cases were the focus of the *Campaign for Prisoners of the Month* in 1989 and 1990. Thirty-nine of them have been released; about 50 remain in prison. At least one other, Mahmat Abdoulaye, a prisoner of the month in August 1990, will never taste freedom. He was not among the surviving prisoners liberated after the change of government in Chad in December 1990 and is presumed to have died in custody.

None of these people should ever have been prisoners of conscience. They were all arrested for the peaceful expression of their beliefs or opinions or on account of their ethnic origin. Their arrest and detention was not only an assault on their rights but a repudiation of the international standards set by the world community for the protection of everyone's rights. Our task today is to increase the international pressure on behalf of the thousands of prisoners of conscience all over the world, to make tomorrow the day their freedom is restored.□

'I feel glad because I know that there are some people who care about us and about our situation here...thank you from our heart...we can see that many people are trying to help us and we are not alone'

Daniel Xidis, Greece, Prisoner of the Month in November 1990

Free in Africa

Kwame Karikari, Ghana: released December 1988

Akwasi Adu-Amankwah and Yaw Tony Akoto-Ampaw, Ghana: released May 1989

Albert Mukong, Cameroon: released May 1989, rearrested March 1990, acquitted of subversive activities and released April 1990

José Primo Esono Mica, Equatorial Guinea: released February 1990

Oumarou Aman, Cameroon: released from labour camp in January 1991 after being held for more than six years without charge or trial

Peter Chiko Bwalya, Zambia: released April 1989

Thoza Khonje, Malawi: released February 1991, having been detained for two years after making remarks which were interpreted as critical of the Life President

Dr George Mtafu, Malawi: released January 1991. He is Malawi's only neurosurgeon

Wossen-Seged, Michael and Bede-Mariam Mekonnen, Ethiopia: released September 1989

Al-Tijani al-Taïeb, Sudan: released early summer 1990 and then sought refuge in Egypt

Free in the Americas

Manuel González and Lidia González García, Cuba: released on expiry of their sentences, Manuel in January 1990 and Lidia in November 1989

Free in Asia

Syamsu Haji Rauf, Indonesia: released October 1990

Maulavi Abdul Rauf Logari, Afghanistan: released November 1989

Baha bin Mohammed, Brunei: released January 1990 after swearing an oath of allegiance to the Sultan, the Government, and the laws of the state of Brunei-Darussalam — a prerequisite for release

Vincent Cheng and Teo Sho Lung, Singapore: conditionally released in June 1990

Daniel Kokkalis, Greece (*above*), was released in January 1991. Ladji Traoré, Mauritania (*below left*), was released in November 1990. Hiram Abi Cobas Nuñez, Cuba (*below right*), was released in November 1990 on health grounds and served the remainder of his sentence at home. He moved to the United States of America in February 1991.

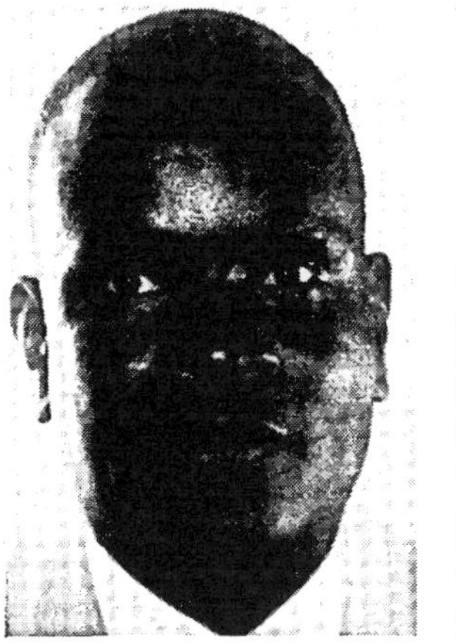

Amos Masondo, South Africa (*above left*), was released under restrictions in February 1989 but was again detained under state of emergency regulations in August 1989. He was released on 19 October 1989 under new restrictions, which were lifted in February 1990. Kevin Desmond de Souza, Singapore (*below*), was released in March 1989. He now works as a legal assistant and is reported to have been admitted to the Singapore Bar.

Over 50 of the *Prisoners of the Month* in 1989 and 1990 have been released. Despite worldwide appeals the remainder are still awaiting freedom. Here we review the fate of the prisoners.

Africa: Francisco Bonifacio Mba Nguema remains in prison in Equatorial Guinea. He is serving a 20-year sentence imposed in 1988 by a military court which found him guilty of attempting to overthrow the government. He was convicted on the basis of confessions he had made under torture and because he had read *The Dogs of War*, a novel about a coup in an imaginary country widely thought to be based on Equatorial Guinea. The only other evidence against him, the testimony of a prosecution witness, was proved to be false in court.

In Kenya Harris Okong'o Arara continues to serve a five-year sentence imposed in 1988 under a law which makes it a criminal offence simply to possess literature critical of the government. After he was convicted, Arara, a former air force officer, said the publications — opposition pamphlets whose contents were kept secret in court — were "honest and truthful", and asked whether it was seditious "to demand fundamental rights and freedoms".

Mulugetta Mosissa, a former civil servant, remains in detention without trial in Ethiopia. He was arrested in 1980, with hundreds of other members of the Oromo ethnic group who were suspected of links with an Oromo guerrilla group. Although many of these detainees were released in 1989, including Mulugetta's wife and son, he is one of about a dozen still held.

The Americas: Three Colombian prisoners of the month remain "disappeared". Dr Alirio de Jesús Pedraza Becerra, a 40-year-old lawyer and human rights worker, was abducted by eight heavily armed men on the night of 4 July 1990 in Bogotá. A judicial inquiry has been initiated into his case but to AI's knowledge no progress has been made. A parallel investigation by the Procurator General's Office has reportedly been impeded by the refusal of the national police to identify the two police agents seen by witnesses as the time of Dr Pedraza's abduction. The police have denied that its agents were present.

Tarcisio Medina Charry, a 21-year-old student, "disappeared" after being arrested in 1988. A judicial investigation into his case ordered the arrest of a member of the national police. However, the case was passed to the military courts who revoked the arrest order. The investigation continues and there is no further information about his fate.

Isidro Caballero, a 33-year-old

0163

Ismail Mehmedov Hyuseyinov, Bulgaria, with his wife. He was released from exile in May 1989 and emigrated to Turkey later that year.

teacher, "disappeared" after being detained on 7 February 1989 by an army patrol. A judicial investigation implicated three members of the Caldas Battalion of the army. The Procurator Delegate for the Armed Forces is conducting a separate investigation, but AI has no information about its progress. Luis Miguel Solís Pajarito was 25 when he "disappeared" in Guatemala on 3 May 1990. He was a leader of the National Council for the Displaced. Despite assurances from government officials that an investigation is in progress, his whereabouts remain unknown.

Elizardo Sánchez Santa Cruz, President of the Cuban Commission of Human Rights and National Reconciliation, who was sentenced to two years' imprisonment in 1989 for "spreading false news with the aim of endangering the prestige or standing of the Cuban state", is still serving his sentence in Agüica Prison: he is due for release in August 1991.

Asia: Alexander Warouw and Manan Effendi have been imprisoned in Indonesia since 1965. Both in their 70s, they continue to serve life sentences imposed in connection with an abortive coup in that year which was blamed on the Communist Party of Indonesia (PKI). Although both were linked to the PKI, when it was still a legal political party, there is no evidence that either of them had knowledge of the events leading to the coup. Their cases were featured in a British Section Christmas card campaign in 1990 and they received 1,704 cards as a result of the appeal. In early 1991 AI received a letter directly from the two men. They had copied out the names and addresses of everyone who wrote to them enclosed with a message of thanks and good wishes, asking that it be sent on.

Also in Indonesia, Agil Riyanto bin Darmowiyoto, a law student, continues to serve a 15-year sentence imposed for subversion in 1987. A prisoner of the month in June 1990, he is one of a group of seven young Muslim activists in Brebes, Central Java, convicted on charges arising from their involvement in Muslim groups known as *usroh*, which aim to deepen awareness of Islamic teachings and Islamic law. He is serving his sentence in an island prison, far from his home and family. Another of the seven students, 20-year-old Wahyudi, a prisoner of the month in 1989, is still serving a seven-year sentence in Cilacap, Central Java.

Kayathiri Vino Sangaralingam was 10 years old when she was arrested in Jaffna District, Sri Lanka, in 1987 with her mother and two older sisters. They all "disappeared" after being taken into custody by members of the Indian Peace Keeping Force. AI has received no further information on their fate since their case was featured in June 1989 and knows of no investigation either by the Indian or the Sri Lankan authorities.

Two prisoners of conscience in Laos have been held for over 15 years for "re-education". Tiao Sisoumang Sisaleumsak and Houmphanh Norasing, both detained since 1975, are among 33 detainees in Laos' northeastern province of Houa Phanh. Their living conditions are harsh with poor provision of housing, food and medicines. Many are in poor health, resulting from years of hard labour and inadequate medical treatment.

The South Korean authorities wrote to AI in response to its appeals for imprisoned artist Hong Song-dam and publisher Chang Ui-gyun. The authorities said that Hong Song-dam, whose case was featured in August 1990, was not imprisoned merely for sending his paintings to North Korea and books to Koreans in Germany, but because his paintings and writings were to promote a Marxist-Leninist revolution. In September 1990 the Supreme Court dismissed the charges of espionage and returned the case to a lower court. In January 1991 Hong Song-dam was sentenced to three years' imprisonment for producing material benefiting North Korea.

Chang Ui-gyun continues to serve an eight-year sentence for espionage. The authorities denied that his arrest in 1987 was solely because he had met pro-North Korean people in Japan and claimed that he had acted on North Korean orders to collect documents on South Korean opposition groups — regarded as state secrets by the courts because they are deemed capable of benefiting North Korea — and to seek to infiltrate dissident groups in order to create social unrest. They also stated that he had received funds from North Korea. AI had found these accusations unsubstantiated.

Father Thadeus Nguyen Van Ly, a Roman Catholic priest in Viet Nam, was arrested in May 1983 after trying to organize an unauthorized pilgrimage. In December 1983 he was sentenced to 10 years' imprisonment for "opposing the revolution". He remains detained at Camp "Three Stars" in Ha Nam Ninh province.

Aung Din, a 26-year-old student leader, was arrested by the martial law authorities in Myanmar on 24 April 1989. Since his case was featured in November 1989, AI has received reports that he was sentenced to four years' imprisonment after an unfair trial by a military tribunal. Nay Min, a lawyer in his 40s, was also arrested under martial law in Myanmar. He continues to serve a 14-year sentence imposed after an unfair trial because of reports he sent to the *British Broadcasting Corporation* and for "possession of anti-government literature".

The four prisoners of the month from China featured in 1989 and 1990 are still in prison. Zhang Jingsheng was sentenced to 13 years' imprisonment in December 1989 for "counter-revolutionary" crimes during the 1989 pro-democracy demonstrations. Xiao Bin, a 42-year-old worker from Dalian, is serving a 10-year sentence for "counter-revolutionary incitement" during the pro-democracy demonstrations. Song Yude, a 36-year-old Protestant evangelist, was sentenced to eight years' imprisonment in 1986 for unofficial religious activities.

In Tibet Ngawang Phulchung, a monk from the Drepung Monastry in Lhasa, is still serving a 19-year sentence imposed at a mass sentencing rally in November 1989. Ngawang Phulchung was one of 10 monks sentenced that month to long terms of imprisonment for their activities in support of Tibetan independence, which included circulating Tibetan translations of the Universal Declaration of Human Rights.

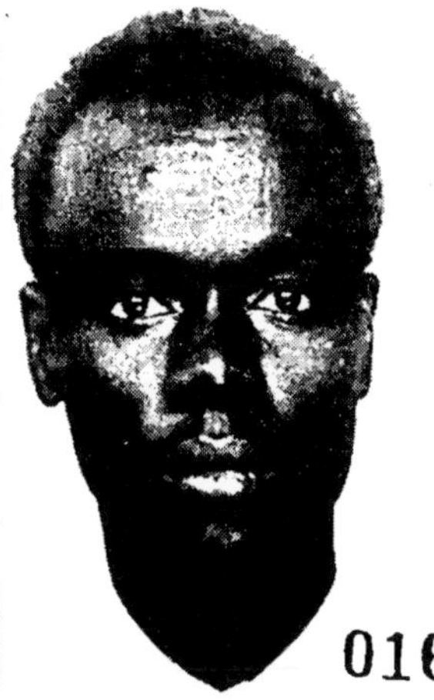

0164

Mahmout Abdoulaye was not among the surviving prisoners liberated after the change of government in Chad in December 1990 and is presumed to have died in custody.

In the Philippines, there have been some encouraging developments in the case of Zosimo Alpino, prisoner of the month in February 1990. He was one of 25 farmers arrested in November 1987 and accused of membership of the New People's Army, the armed wing of the outlawed Communist Party of the Philippines. Zosimo Alpino was released on bail on 13 December 1990. Thirteen of his co-defendants have been acquitted and released unconditionally on the grounds of insufficient evidence for prosecution. The court has yet to rule on the cases of Zosimo Alpino and the remaining 11 defendants.

Mihai Creanga, Romania, was released in May 1989. He was reportedly under house arrest until December of that year

Free in Europe

Branimir Trbojevic, Yugoslavia: released November 1989

Sevinç Tekeli-Öztas, Turkey: released April 1990 after serving the customary 40 per cent of her sentence. Released political prisoners are effectively blacklisted for employment and are denied a passport for travel abroad.

Bohdan Klymchak, USSR: pardoned and released November 1990. He no longer wishes to emigrate and is planning to write his memoirs.

Henrik Gjoka, Albania: released January 1991

Frantisek Starek, Czechoslovakia: released November 1989

Milaim Ziberi, Yugoslavia: released April 1990

Enver Ahmedov Hatibov, Bulgaria: released May 1990

Free in the Middle East

Mubarak 'Abdu Fadhl, Egypt: released April 1990

Sayyid Tahir al-Shimimy, Saudi Arabia: released April 1990

Middle East: Five Saudi Arabian students, prisoners of the month in April 1990, continue to be detained without charge or trial Abdul-'Aziz al-Faris, 'Ali Al-Lail, Salah Nisfan, Hussein Subait and Hatim al-Saddiq are Shi'a Muslims. AI believes they are held because they opposed the government's policy towards the Shi'a community. Shi'a Muslims in Saudi Arabia have long complained of discrimination and denial of their rights to freedom of religious thought and practice.

Three Moroccan prisoners of conscience, serving between them a total of 65 years, remain in prison. Ali Idrissi Kaitouni was given a 15-year sentence for writing poems about social injustice and political oppression in Morocco, deemed by the state to constitute a crime against internal security. Mohamed Srifi, a literature student, was sentenced in 1977 to 30 years' imprisonment for advocating that Morocco become a socialist republic. Assistant teacher Habib Ben Malek was sentenced in the same trial in 1977 to 20 years' imprisonment. They are all held in Kenitra Central Prison.

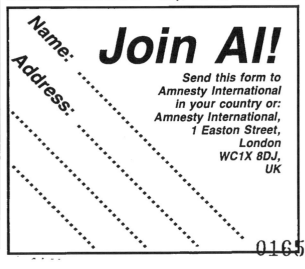

Abdallah Oufkir, (*centre*) Morocco, and other detained members of his family, were reportedly released in February 1990 but are still believed to be subject to restrictions on freedom of movement and association.

In Syria hundreds of prisoners of conscience continue to be detained without charge or trial under state of emergency legislation in force since 1963. Among them are the following who have appeared as prisoners of the month: Hakem Sultan al-Faiz, a 61-year-old Jordanian national and former member of the National Command of the Arab Socialist Ba'th Party, who has been held for almost 20 years; Ahmad 'Abd al-Ra'uf Roummo, a 55-year-old teacher, arrested in 1975; Muhammad Nabil Salem, an engineer, arrested in the wake of a one-day national strike in 1980 and Mahmud Jalbut, a Palestinian arrested in 1980.

AI has received no new information about six members of the Islamic Liberation Party imprisoned in Libya since 1973 for belonging to an illegal organization. 'Ali Muhammad al-Akrami, al-Ajili Muhammad 'Abdul Rahman al-Ashari, 'Ali Muhammad al-Qajiji, Salih Omar al-Qasbi, Muhammad al-Sadiq al-Tarhouni and 'Abdul Qadir Muhammad al-Ya'qubi are believed to be in Abu Salim Prison in Tripoli, although AI received reports that 'Abdul Qadir Muhammad al-Ya'qubi had died at the end of 1988.

In Iran, Mariam Firouz, a writer and translator in her mid-70s, has been imprisoned since 1983 for her non-violent political activities. Although a number of other women prisoners of conscience in related cases have reportedly been freed in recent months, Mariam Firouz remains in prison. Ali Ardalan, a retired civil servant in his mid 70s arrested in June 1990, remains in prison and there is growing concern over his ill-health. His "crime" was to sign an open letter to President Rafsanjani criticizing government failures to uphold rights and freedoms guaranteed by the constitution of Iran.

Zikri Nafkhosh Mustafa, Nabi Muhammad Shukr, Jabbar Rashid Shifki and Ja'far Tamar Mahmud are four of 315 Kurdish children and youths who "disappeared" after being arrested in Iraq in August 1983. AI has received no further information about their fate since their cases were featured in September 1990. Appeals on their behalf have been suspended because of the current situation in Iraq.

Europe: Daniel, Panayiotis and Pavlos Xidis, three brothers, are still serving four-year sentences in Greece for refusing to perform military service. They are not due for release until 1992, and are among some 400 young men held in Greek prisons for their refusal on religious grounds to perform military service. The three brothers are Jehovah's Witnesses, a Christian denomination which does not support the use or advocacy of violence. Their religious beliefs do not allow them to serve in the armed forces in any capacity.

In Turkey Ilker Demir continues to serve his 36-year sentence in Nazilli E-Type Prison for political prisoners. A journalist convicted of making communist propaganda and insulting the authorities, he is reportedly in poor health. The earliest he can expect release is in August 1998. Several initiatives to amend or abolish the articles of the Turkish Penal Code, under which he and most prisoners of conscience were convicted, have so far come to nothing.□

Name:
Address:
Join AI!
Send this form to Amnesty International in your country or: Amnesty International, 1 Easton Street, London WC1X 8DJ, UK

0165

AI visits Sri Lanka

TWO AI delegates were invited as guest speakers to a week-long conference in Colombo on trade unions and human rights. They also met several senior government officials and discussed possibilities for future access by AI to Sri Lanka. AI was last permitted access to the country in 1982.

Among those the delegates met were the Adviser to the President on International Affairs, the Secretary to the Ministry of Defence, the Inspector General of Police, the Commissioner General of Rehabilitation, the Director of the United Nations Division in the Foreign Ministry and the Solicitor General.

Soon after the delegates left, the government announced to the press that "a research visit to Sri Lanka would be considered favourably if a formal request were made" by AI. In April AI submitted such a request.☐

TUNISIA

Torture in prolonged *garde à vue* detention

DOZENS of people are reported to have been tortured while held incommunicado in prolonged *garde à vue* detention by the Tunisian police since January 1991. *Garde à vue* detention allows the police to detain suspects for interrogation for up to 10 days. Recent information from former detainees, lawyers and human rights activists indicates that suspected political opponents of the government, including boys under 18, have been detained in *garde à vue* well beyond the maximum 10-day period and without obtaining further authorization after four days as required by Tunisian law. AI is concerned that the Tunisian Government, by failing to investigate allegations of torture brought to its notice, appears to be condoning its use.

Sadiq Shourou, a lecturer at Tunis University, was arrested on 23 February 1991 and held in *garde à vue* detention for 42 days. When he appeared before an examining magistrate he alleged that he had been tortured. The examining magistrate reportedly ordered a medical examination, but over a week later he had not yet been examined.

AI welcomed the formation by the Tunisian Government of an official human rights council on 9 April 1991, but remained concerned at continuing reports of torture and ill-treatment of political detainees in *garde à vue* detention.☐

MALAWI

Prisoners released

FORMER prisoners of the month Thoza Khonje and George Mtafu were among at least 21 political prisoners released in Malawi between January and March this year — all of them long-term detainees held without charge or trial. It is not yet clear how many of the almost 80 other prisoners freed at the same time were held for political reasons.

Thoza Khonje, a 43-year-old sugar company area manager, was arrested on 28 February 1989, reportedly after being overheard criticizing policy decisions by Life-President Hastings Kamuzu Banda.

George Mtafu, Malawi's only neurosurgeon, was arrested the same month after refusing to apologize for challenging public criticisms of northern Malawians made by Life-President Banda. Other northern Malawians arrested between February and May 1989 are thought to be among those set free. Others freed included William Masiku, detained since 1980, Brown Mpinganjira, detained since 1986, Margaret Marango Banda and Blaise Machira, detained since 1988.

The releases mark the first improvement in the human rights situation in Malawi for several years. However, other prominent prisoners of conscience remain behind bars. For example, Goodluck Mhango, a veterinary surgeon arrested in September 1987, has been rejected for release by a committee established to review the cases of political detainees.☐

BAHRAIN

Torture and unfair trials

ON 9 May AI published *Bahrain: Violations of human rights.** The report describes how in recent years hundreds of political activists or suspected activists, including prisoners of conscience, have been subjected to arbitrary arrest and torture and sentenced after unfair trials.

Many are held for months or years in administrative or pre-trial detention, usually incommunicado, when torture most commonly occurs. A law passed in 1974 allows administrative detention for up to three years, renewable, and some detainees have been held for as long as seven years without charge or trial. Methods of torture include beating, burning with cigarettes, and being forced to stand for many hours without moving.

Political cases are tried by the Supreme Civil Court of Appeal, whose procedures do not meet international standards for fair trial. Defendants may be convicted solely on the basis of confessions, or even on police testimony that a confession was made; they have limited access to defence lawyers and no right of appeal.

AI has repeatedly called on the Bahraini Government to ratify and implement international human rights treaties.☐

**AI Index No. MDE 11/01/91*

GUATEMALA

Police officers convicted of murdering street child

FOUR Guatemalan police officers have been sentenced to prison terms of between 10 and 15 years for the murder of 13-year-old street child Nahamán Carmona López. Nahamán Carmona died in March 1990 as a result of severe beatings by police officers. The judge reportedly increased each sentence by 25 per cent on the grounds that the murder had been committed by state agents acting in an official capacity.

This is the second case in recent years in which Guatemalan government agents are known to have been convicted of human rights violations: the six police officers convicted for the 1987 abduction and murder of two agronomy students were released on appeal in July 1990, despite strong evidence linking them to the crime.

In April AI learned that warrants had been issued for the arrest of two police officers and a civilian in connection with the killing of 17-year-old Anstraum Aman Villagrán Morales, who was shot and killed on 25 June 1990 in Guatemala City by two uniformed police officers.

Thirty-six other criminal lawsuits against 35 National Police officers, three Treasury Police officers, 10 civilians and three judges for abuses against street children are reportedly pending in Guatemalan courts.☐

MAURITANIA

Prisoners killed in custody

IN April AI called on the Mauritanian Government to investigate reports that up to 200 political prisoners had died or been killed in military or police custody — some executed without trial and many others as a result of torture. The victims were among some 3,000 black Mauritanians arrested late last year.

The authorities claimed they were conspiring to overthrow the government, which is dominated by a different community, the Moors, but offered no evidence to substantiate this.

Prisoners released in March 1991 provided AI with information and themselves bore scars from torture. In a few cases prisoners are reported to have been deliberately executed without trial. Most of the reported deaths, however, were due to torture in military barracks and police stations. Detainees were hung upside down and beaten on the soles of their feet, others were buried in sand up to the neck and left to die or were burned all over their bodies. Torture of political detainees in Mauritania has been routine since 1986, but never before on such a scale.

After the March 1991 releases, 64 prisoners were to be tried *in camera* in April. The trial was postponed and the government announced their release at the end of *Ramadan*, in mid-April. It was not known whether other detainees were still held.☐

Death penalty to be abolished

THE death penalty is to be abolished in Anguilla, British Virgin Islands, Cayman Islands, Montserrat and Turks and Caicos Islands, reportedly following discussions between the British Government and the Governors of dependent territories in the Caribbean. The decision was announced by British Secretary of Foreign Affairs Douglas Hurd, on 28 March. He said that the government hoped Bermuda would "decide to follow this example as soon as possible". In a public referendum in 1990, retention of the death penalty was favoured. A debate and a vote in parliament are pending.☐

0166

INDONESIA

Advocates of independence imprisoned

MORE than 130 political prisoners from Irian Jaya are currently serving lengthy prison terms for advocating the province's independence from Indonesia. Most have been convicted since 1988 under Indonesia's sweeping Anti-Subversion Law, accused of attempting to establish an independent state of "West Papua". AI believes that their trials were unfair. The organization has already adopted two of the prisoners as prisoners of conscience and believes that some 80 others may be prisoners of conscience.

Among the possible prisoners of conscience are 37 people sentenced to up to 20 years' imprisonment for their involvement in a peaceful flag-raising ceremony in the town of Jayapura on 14 December 1988. A woman alleged to have sewn the flag was sentenced to eight years in prison and her husband, who led the ceremony, to 20 years. In 1990 a police officer accused of distributing copies of a patriotic song to high-school students was sentenced to 13 years' imprisonment by a military court. Four men who allegedly planned demonstrations in December 1989 to commemorate the 1988 flag-raising, were sentenced to terms of between six and 12 years.

In addition to imprisonment, those believed to have advocated Irian Jaya's independence, whether through peaceful or violent means, continue to be at risk of torture, ill-treatment, "disappearance", and extrajudicial execution by Indonesian security forces. This pattern of human rights violations is described in a recent AI report, *Indonesia: Continuing human rights violations in Irian Jaya (Index No. ASA 21/06/91)*, published in April.□

BRAZIL

Moves to reinstate death penalty

A PROPOSAL for constitutional reform to allow a national plebiscite on the reintroduction of the death penalty in Brazil, for kidnappings, burglaries and rapes resulting in the victim's death, was approved by a Congressional Commission of the House of Deputies in December 1990.

The proposal is to be debated and voted on in Congress during the 1991 parliamentary sessions. If the constitutional amendment is passed by parliament, a binding plebiscite would be held within 18 months. AI has appealed to Brazilian parliamentarians expresssing its concern over the moves to reinstate the death penalty which it believes to be the ultimate cruel, inhuman and degrading punishment.

The death penalty was excluded from the Brazilian Penal Code in 1890 and its abolition is enshrined in the 1988 Constitution.□

AMNESTY INTERNATIONAL NEWSLETTER is published every month in four languages to bring you news of AI's concerns and campaigns worldwide, as well as in-depth reports. Available from Amnesty International (address below)

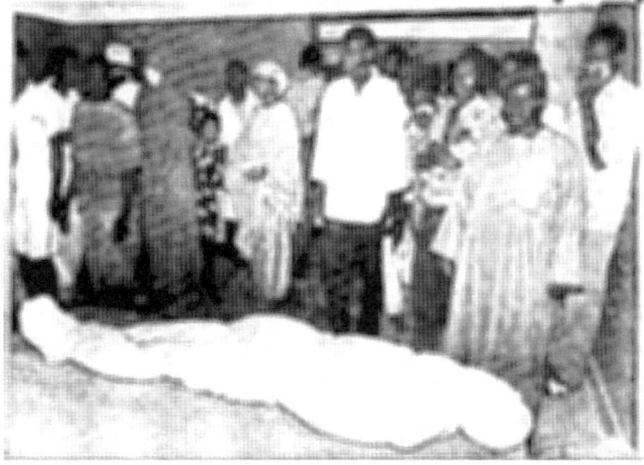

Relatives and friends of a man shot dead during pro-democracy demonstrations in Bamako, the Malian capital, with the body at a hospital morgue © *Reuters*

MALI

Killings precede coup

OVER 150 men, women and children were killed by Mali's security forces in March, after a wave of pro-democracy demonstrations and riots. In the wake of the killings the government led by President Moussa Traoré was overthrown.

At least 40 people were killed in Bamako on 22 March after a student demonstration was stopped by the security forces and rioting broke out. A state of emergency was declared but at least another 40 people were killed the following day. Some were shot dead when thousands of women, protesting against the killings, tried to march on the President's residence. Up to 65 protesters were reported to have been burned to death when security forces set fire to a shopping centre in which they were seeking refuge. Soldiers also shot at mourners burying the dead at two cemeteries in Bamako. AI called on the Malian Government to halt the killings.

Following a general strike and calls for his resignation, the President was arrested on 26 March by fellow army officers.

Some 50 others associated with the former government were also detained. The authorities promised early elections, and said that the former president and others arrested would be brought to trial.□

PEOPLE'S REPUBLIC OF CHINA 0167

A hundred death sentences a month

AS AI launched a campaign in March 1991 against the extensive use of the death penalty in China, a nationwide drive to "sternly crack down" on crime continued unabated. AI has recorded about a hundred death sentences each month since the beginning of 1991. During 1990 AI recorded almost a thousand death sentences, of which at least 750 resulted in executions.

In the official press, Chinese politicians, as well as senior members of the judiciary, have repeatedly urged that instructions to "punish criminals heavily and rapidly" be strictly adhered to. Some prisoners who would not normally have received the death sentence may have fallen victim to political interference in the judicial process. Increased official emphasis on speedy investigation and sentencing in death penalty cases is likely to have further undermined the rights of defendants to a fair trial.

On 14 March 24-year-old Han Weijun was executed. He had been found guilty of setting fire to a car and an armoured personnel carrier commandeered by students during the 1989 pro-democracy demonstrations in Beijing. His was the first reported execution in several months for an offence related to the "counter-revolutionary rebellion". A court notice reported the economic loss of the two vehicles, but did not mention any military casualties. The death penalty is routinely used in China for serious economic crimes which involve no personal violence.□

STOP PRESS

Reverned Lawford Immunde of Kenya, one of the prisoners whose case was featured in the May *Focus*, has been released.

AMNESTY INTERNATIONAL, 1 Easton Street, London WC1X 8DJ, United Kingdom. Printed in Great Britain by Flashprint Enterprises Ltd, London. Available on subscription at £7 (US$12.00) for 12 issues. ISSN 0308 6887

AMNESTY INTERNATIONAL
NEWSLETTER
JULY 1991 VOLUME XXI • NUMBER 6

TURKEY

Mixed outlook for legal reforms

THE Anti-Terror Law passed by the Turkish parliament on 11 April commuted all existing death sentences and brought the release of prisoners of conscience held under the notorious penal code articles 141, 142 and 163, which were at last repealed.

In a letter to the Prime Minister Yıldırım Akbulut, AI welcomed these moves, but expressed grave concern about other provisions of the law which put in question the authorities' will to bring to justice those responsible for torture: alleged torturers will be tried before State Security Courts, whose prosecution service supervised the interrogation from which the torture allegations arose. Moreover, unless the victim actually died in custody, the alleged torturers cannot be tried without the permission of the Interior Minister.

The organization is also concerned that police officers involved in the interrogation of prisoners charged with "terrorist" offences cannot be called into court, making it difficult to challenge the validity of confessions or other statements extracted under torture.

Although tens of thousands of political and criminal prisoners have been conditionally released under the terms of the new law, approximately 2,500 political prisoners, many of whom were sentenced after unfair trials following the 1980 military coup, continue to serve prison sentences of up to 20 years.

AI is recommending that the new provisions relating to the investigation and prosecution of alleged torturers be amended. It also has urged the government to reform or repeal a provision in the new law which would impose a prison term for "making separatist propaganda", even when this contains no advocacy of violence.□

First AI visit to North Korea

FOR the first time ever, an AI delegation visited the Democratic People's Republic of Korea (DPRK). It attended the 85th Inter-Parliamentary Conference in Pyongyang from 29 April to 4 May and also held discussions with legal scholars and government representatives.

Officials of the Supreme People's Assembly and scholars from the Law Faculty of Kim Il Sung University answered the AI delegation's questions on the country's legal system, including the Constitution, criminal procedures, the 1987 Criminal Code and the 1990 Civil Code. Published texts of these codes, which had previously been unobtainable, were given to the delegation.

Academics at the University of National Economy explained various social laws and the system of appeals and petitions against administrative decisions. Aspects of the application of the laws were discussed with a Central Court judge, a member of the Central Lawyers Association and officials of the Ministry of Public Security. The delegates also attended a criminal trial and visited a public security (police) station where they discussed detention and interrogation procedures and inspected cells.

Professors at the Academy of *Juche* Science, officials of the Ministry of Foreign Affairs and others said that the country's state ideology protects human rights, particularly social and economic rights.

Legal scholars stated that the International Covenant on Civil and Political Rights, ratified by the DPRK in 1981, was considered an integral part of the country's law. They said that the 1987 Criminal Code had reduced the penalties for a number of offences. The new code provides for two basic punishments: the death penalty and "re-education through labour" for up to 15 years. AI's delegates were told that the death penalty is imposed rarely and mainly for espionage or sabotage, although they were not given detailed statistics.

Several officials criticized the *Amnesty International Report 1990* which referred to reports that tens of thousands of political prisoners were held at 12 corrective labour camps.

A public security official responsible for "re-education" facilities told the AI delegation that there are about one thousand people in three such camps nationwide. He would not say how many were held for "anti-state" crimes but indicated that all were "outsiders" arrested in connection with the state of war on the Korean peninsula and that these prisoners were held separately from ordinary criminals.

The same official denied knowledge of reports that about 40 staff and students at colleges in Pyongyang had been arrested in 1988 for putting up political posters.□

TOGO

Discovery of 26 bodies leads to investigation of disputed killings

SHORTLY after anti-government demonstrations in Togo's capital, Lome, in mid-April, the bodies of 26 people believed to have been killed by members of the security forces were discovered in a nearby lagoon.

Most had been beaten to death and one had last been seen in the custody of soldiers. This led to allegations that members of the security forces were responsible for the killings and had tried to hide the bodies. Faced with both national and international protests, the government initially denied that soldiers were responsible and blamed ordinary criminals for the killings. It then announced that a commission of inquiry was to investigate the killings.

The body of a suspected victim of a security force killing is dragged from a lagoon, where 25 more bodies were discovered

On 5 April, a week before the discovery of the 26 bodies, Adadoh Kossi and Adjoh Comlan Tintin had been shot dead by soldiers when they tried to topple a statue of President Gnassingbe Eyadema.

In recent months there have been large demonstrations by pro-democracy supporters calling for the President to resign. Since October 1990 several such demonstrations have ended in violence and killings after the security forces attacked initially peaceful demonstrators.□

0168

RELEASED

Jack Mapanje, a Prisoner of the Month in February 1988, has been released. See page 2.

CAMPAIGN FOR PRISONERS OF THE MONTH

Each of the people whose story is told below is a prisoner of conscience. Each has been arrested because of his or her religious or political beliefs, colour, sex, ethnic origin or language. None has used or advocated violence. Their continuing detention is a violation of the United Nations Universal Declaration of Human Rights. International appeals can help to secure the release of these prisoners or to improve their detention conditions. In the interest of the prisoners, letters to the authorities should be worded carefully and courteously. You should stress that your concern for human rights is not in any way politically partisan. In *no* circumstances should communications be sent to the prisoner.

SAUDI ARABIA

Sheikh Samir 'Ali al-Ribeh: *a religious scholar in his late twenties, he was arrested in October 1990 and is currently detained without trial in al-Mabahith al-'Amma (General Intelligence) Prison in Dammam in the Eastern Province.*

Sheikh Samir 'Ali al-Ribeh was arrested at Riyadh airport on his return from Damascus with his wife and two daughters, who were released shortly afterwards. He is suspected of being a sympathizer of the banned *Munadhamat al-Thawra al-Islamiyya fil Jazira al-'Arabiyya*, the Organization of Islamic Revolution in the Arabian Peninsula (OIRAP).

Founded in 1975, the OIRAP is the principal organized Shi'a opposition group in Saudi Arabia. It

Sheikh Samir 'Ali al-Ribeh

has defined its purpose to be primarily that of "educating and enlightening the masses". There is no evidence in its publications of calls to violence or armed action. It has stated that the Shi'a in Saudi Arabia are discriminated against and has urged that they be granted equal rights. Since 1979 hundreds of alleged members or sympathizers of the OIRAP have been detained for prolonged periods without charge or trial.

AI is concerned that Sheikh Samir 'Ali al-Ribeh is being detained solely for the non-violent expression of his political beliefs. The organization has expressed its concern about his case to the Saudi Arabian authorities, but has received no reply.

■Please send courteous appeals for his immediate and unconditional release to: The Custodian of the Two Holy Shrines/King Fahd bin 'Abd al-'Aziz/Office of the Custodian of the Two Holy Shrines/Riyadh/Saudi Arabia.□

RELEASED

Cuba: AI has learned that Edgardo Llompart Martin and Mario Fernandez Mora, who were included in a February 1991 *Prisoner of the Month* article, have been released. Elizardo Sanchez Santa Cruz, Prisoner of the Month in January 1990, has also been released.

VIET NAM

To Thuy Yen: *a writer and poet in his fifties, he was arrested on 13 November 1990 at his home in Ho Chi Minh City, and charged with writing anti-government poetry and making contact with foreign groups deemed "hostile" by the government.*

To Thuy Yen was first arrested in October 1975. He spent five years in a "re-education" camp until 1980 when he was sentenced to 11 years' hard labour in prison. He was released in 1985.

At the time of his arrest in 1990 the police reportedly confiscated anti-government poems and writings, correspondence with foreign "hostile" groups, receipts showing that he had received money from such groups, and tapes of his poetry set to music.

His most recent arrest occured during a crackdown on government critics which began in May and June 1990 and still continues. Among others arrested around this time were academic Doan Viet Hoat and journalist Le Van Tien.

AI believes that To Thuy Yen was arrested for peacefully exercising his right to freedom of opinion and expression. He is currently being detained in a prison in Ho Chi Minh City. To AI's knowledge his case has not been brought to trial. His wife is reportedly allowed to bring food to the prison for him, but not to visit him. Little is known about the conditions of his detention.

■Please send courteous letters appealing for his immediate and unconditional release to: Dô Muoi/Chairperson of the Council of Ministers/Hoi Dong Bo Truong/Ha Noi/Socialist Republic of Viet Nam.□

KENYA

Raila Odinga: *aged 48, a businessman, scientist and son of prominent government critic Oginga Odinga — Vice-President of Kenya from 1964 to 1966 — he was arrested in Nairobi on 5 July 1990. He was immediately detained under Public Security Regulations providing for the indefinite administrative detention, without charge or trial, of anyone held to be endangering the security of the state.*

Raila Odinga has been a prisoner of conscience before, having spent almost seven of the previous eight years in detention. Arrested with him in July were former government ministers Kenneth Matiba, also still detained, and Charles Rubia, who was released in April 1991. They were among businessmen, politicians, lawyers and church leaders calling for multi-party democracy in Kenya, a one-party state since 1982. Raila Odinga had not spoken publicly on political issues but, as in the past, seems to have been arrested because the authorities wished to silence his father, who subsequently announced the formation of a new opposition party, the National Democratic Party, in February 1991. The government has refused to register this party and Oginga Odinga was himself briefly arrested on 7 May.

Raila Odinga is held in permanent solitary confinement in Naivasha maximum security prison 80 kilometres from Nairobi. He is married with three children, but has had only about six short supervised visits from his wife during almost a year's detention.

Raila Odinga

■Please send appeals for his immediate and unconditional release to: His Excellency President Daniel arap Moi/President of the Republic of Kenya/Office of the President/PO Box 30510/Nairobi/Kenya.□

Corrections: May 1991 *Focus*: **Stanza Bopape** "disappeared" in 1988 not 1990. June 1991 *Focus*: **Abdallah Oufkir** was reportedly released in February 1991, not 1990.

0169

Prisoner of conscience released

JACK Mapanje, the internationally renowned poet and a prisoner of conscience in Malawi since 25 September 1987, was released on 10 May after nearly four years in detention without charge or trial.

Under Malawi's Public Security Regulations, the official reason for his detention was never disclosed, but it is widely believed that the increasingly political themes of his poetry had incurred the disapproval of the authorities.

Other prisoners of conscience, including the veteran political leader Orton Chirwa and his wife, Vera Chirwa, a lawyer, remain in prison serving life sentences imposed after a grossly unfair trial in 1983. AI is continuing to urge their immediate and unconditional release.□

FOCUS amnesty international

A worldwide campaign

Maris-Stella Mabitje, a former political detainee in South Africa, meets Swedish AI members who worked on her behalf © Anders Kallersand

'Your letter strengthened me'

0170

When AI first wrote to the parents of Maris-Stella Mabitje, imprisoned under South Africa's emergency laws in 1987, they didn't respond. Maris-Stella wrote back in 1988, after a year in prison.

"I am sorry for the fact that we took such a long time before responding to the letter. The problem is that my parents did not have any idea of who you are and what AI is all about. As a result they were suspicious of the whole business and did not know what to do." The same letter talked about how AI's support helped her at a time when her health was deteriorating.

"I am happy to know that even at trying times such as these there are friends such as you who think of me, my family and are even concerned about the general welfare of all of us behind bars. Your letter strengthened me, I knew that through your help, your prayers, your attempts at urging the authorities to stop being insensitive and act as humanly and reasonably as possible in dealing with all their political opponents, one day we are going to be released and once more be given the opportunity of leading normal lives ... Now I feel that I am not alone at these hard and troubled times. I now feel wanted and I have all the courage to hope on and carry forward with all I am doing."

Soon after receiving this letter, AI learned that Maris-Stella had been transferred to another prison because of her deteriorating health. In March 1989 she was released with restrictions. She had continued to write to AI from prison, and kept doing so after her release.

"... good news, I am free now though not free in the true sense of the word. All I can say is that they released me with restrictions. I am expected to report at the police station daily and not to be out of the yard from six o'clock in the evening until five o'clock in the morning...Well half a loaf is better than no bread. At least I am able to be with my family though I must admit that this is an outside prison...We are still experiencing harassment." Maris-Stella was one of many political detainees who were supporters of the United Democratic Front, a coalition of organizations which, until its disbandment in 1991, was engaged in non-violent opposition to the government's *apartheid* policies. A year after her release, her restrictions were lifted and AI arranged for her and a fellow prisoner to visit Germany, Sweden and Norway to talk about their experiences.□

'You continuously tried to help'

"With that universal love which transcends race and frontier, you continuously tried to rescue and help me during years of imprisonment. Because of your care and love, not only do you have my gratitude, you have caused me to experience that side of humanity characterized by warmth and hope...Eleven years ago, the Taiwanese people, even privately, were not bold enough to receive former political prisoners. Now, though, they dare hold warm welcome parties — openly and publicly. There are many reasons for this change, but the painstaking efforts and influence of Amnesty International may be one of the most important factors."

Taiwan, 1987, prisoner of conscience Huang Hua. Imprisoned for the fourth time in December 1990 for peaceful political activity when he was 52 years old, he has spent a total of more than 21 years in prison.

The site was Chile's National Stadium in Santiago — a place which had been turned into the country's largest detention centre virtually overnight after the 1973 military coup.

Thousands of men and women had been rounded up and held inside — many were tortured, killed or taken away never to be seen again.

That was nearly 20 years ago. In October 1990 the stadium was again packed with thousands of people — but this time, 150,000 who had come to support a concert for human rights held by AI, the worldwide human rights movement.

The concert was a breakthrough for AI's Chilean membership which, 10 years ago, consisted of only two members forced to meet on a park bench because no one would rent them an office. But the membership and campaigning work in Chile expanded and became increasingly diverse over the years as AI tackled more human rights issues and spread its membership to some 70 countries.

Today, over one million AI members, subscribers and donors around the world from all political, religious, racial and age groups are committed to stopping human rights abuses wherever they occur. united by the belief that individual women and men can take effective action.

Campaigning for individuals who are jailed, tortured, "disappeared" or sentenced to death is central to AI's work. The organization works for the release of prisoners of conscience — people detained for peacefully expressing their views — fair trials for political prisoners, opposes the torture of all prisoners and campaigns for the end to the death penalty.

But very often, there is not simply one victim of abuse but hundreds or thousands of them. When individual cases add up to a human rights crisis in a country, AI highlights that country to generate increased international pressure.

The sheer volume of appeals from this global network is a pressure in itself. The President's Office in Colombia is said to have recently received 20,000 letters within a week. And one West African head of state actually complained to an AI delegation that a deluge of letters would arrive as soon as the authorities detained someone for questioning.

Sometimes, AI's work will result in releases or in better treatment. Two Turkish journalists who were tortured in detention in April 1990 said they were treated somewhat better after an urgent appeal had been launched on their behalf. AI's appeals may not always result directly in a prisoner's release, but governments receiving thousands of letters from around the world know that their actions will not go unnoticed. When one Turkish man with a long history of being detained and tortured

0171

'I suffered a lot in prison'

In his first two weeks of freedom, Maina wa Kinyatti of Kenya wrote directly to an AI group in Sweden to give them the news of his release.

"This is to inform you that after six years, four months, 17 days in prison, I am now free. I walked out of the prison gate on Monday 17 October 1988 with my shoulders unbent, with my head unbowed. I feel great to be free again, to walk in the sunshine of freedom. For the first time since 1982 I can touch the green leaves of the trees, I can smell the sweet scent of the flowers; I can share smiles and laughter with the women and children, but I am bitter because those six years of my imprisonment were the best years of my life, the best years of my intellectual development and they were taken away."

Kinyatti was imprisoned in Kenya for expressing his op-

position to the government.

"Allow me to say this: until my dying day I shall never accept a scheme of things in which men and women are imprisoned for their political beliefs, for their writings." Despite the campaigning of AI and other groups, he had to complete a long sentence, much of it spent in solitary confinement.

"I suffered a lot in prison, but I remained strong throughout because I drew my strength and courage from you, from many other international friends. Your collective support and concern kept me going during those days of my imprisonment, during those long days of hunger, boredom and loneliness in solitary confinement. In fact without your support, concern and love, I would not have survived the prison brutality and barbarity."

Like many former prisoners of conscience, Maina also appreciated the letters he received from individual members of AI, and the help they gave him and his wife.

"Please thank those beautiful people in Sweden whose love, concern and understanding sustained me during my imprisonment. I shall always remember them."□

'Our execution was a possibility'

"The continuous pressure which you and other human rights organizations brought to bear upon the Kabul government ultimately resulted in my release...Without such a pressure even our execution at the hands of the Khad was a possibility...In my own case your efforts and support greatly encouraged me and my family, for when I came to know of them I was indeed strengthened by them. I feel strong because it became the proof of the rightness of the cause for which I struggled by lawful means." Afghanistan, 1988, university lecturer Hasan Kaker. A former prisoner of conscience, he was arrested in March 1982 with others apparently for expressing disquiet among students and staff at the increasing number of Russian teachers on campus and earlier widespread arrests of students.

He was released in 1987 and is now in exile in the United States of America.□

was arrested in October 1990 but released the following day, police station officials apparently said, "Oh you're a favourite of Amnesty's, aren't you", as they released him.

AI's work and contact with victims and families can also help overcome their sense of despair and solitude and make them stronger and more determined not to give up.

As part of its campaign work, AI frequently asks for support from doctors, lawyers, trade unionists, and other groups in the community with special interests, skills or influence. There are extensive networks of AI medical and legal groups and a growing number of trade unionists, teachers and journalists who work on behalf of individual prisoners and in general campaigns. These groups may sometimes intervene on behalf of colleagues who are themselves victims of human rights abuses.

In 1989 two Sudanese doctors were arrested and tried for calling a meeting to discuss a doctors' strike at a hospital. Medical groups began an immediate international campaign to publicize their cases and a day before a delegation of scientific and medical organizations was due to arrive in Sudan, the doctors were released.

AI also organizes campaigns or actions about the general human rights situation in a particular country to publicize and combat large-scale human rights violations.

In China the fate of many of the prisoners arrested since the 1989 pro-democracy protests still remains veiled in secrecy. In 1990, as part of a worldwide campaign, AI published the names and details of 700 of the thousands arrested — at that time, the longest list of prisoners in China ever compiled by a human rights organization.

And last year AI launched a campaign on Brazil which drew worldwide attention. Members lobbied embassies, wrote letters and generated publicity in their own countries which resulted in a pledge by the Brazilian President that "we cannot and will not again be a country cited as violent in reports by Amnesty International".

0172

It is this sort of high profile initiative that makes headlines. But the constant, persistent work of AI members around the world still focuses on bringing pressure to bear on behalf of individual victims.

AI members in Japan wrote thousands of letters to the South African authorities about a prisoner of conscience who had gone on hunger-strike in early 1987. No one in the prison could read Japanese so the authorities translated thousands of letters only to discover that they all said "release Dean Farisani". The Reverend Tshenuweni Simon Farisani was released some months later.

In Norway, children from around the country responded to a children's radio show which featured the case of a nine-year-old Ethiopian boy born in prison who had spent his entire life there with his mother. Children sent drawings, cards and letters to the AI office in Oslo and a huge parcel was forwarded to the Ethiopian President with a letter asking for their release. Five weeks later both the boy and his mother were freed.

One Australian group in Hobart decided several years ago to try to speak to the prisoner of conscience in Uruguay on whose behalf they were working after all their letters went unheeded. Undeterred by their inability to speak Spanish, they arranged a telephone hook-up through a translation service in Melbourne 600 kilometres away and telephoned the prison.

"From what we gathered, the impact was absolute panic. We were passed from person to person and they didn't hang up for a long time", one group member said.

The prisoner, a teacher jailed for owning a printing press and accused of distributing subversive literature, was released a few months later.

And in Scotland, the plight of several imprisoned artists was highlighted by a campaign which coincided with Glasgow's year as the cultural city of Europe. Giant banners featuring the artists' work were made for a launch event in the city's main square and over 40,000 signatures were collected.

Human rights emergencies can occur anywhere and at any time and AI has to be prepared to act quickly when it learns that someone is at risk of torture, execution or other human rights violations.

Today, over one million AI members around the world are committed to stopping human rights abuses

When this happens, an Urgent Action network with about 50,000 members in over 60 countries can be mobilized within 48 hours to write, telex or fax immediate appeals to the authorities. One nightwatchman in Ireland writes to every government or authority listed on every Urgent Action — an average of 2,000 letters a year. In France, a network of common-law prisoners who write from their own prisons has developed.

AI's unique worldwide campaigning also extends to the abolition of the death penalty.

In the United Kingdom, as part of a nationwide campaign in 1990 to stop the re-introduction of the death

0173

'The kids never believed they had rights'

"I carry the voice of the street children of Guatemala to thank AI on their behalf for all that you have been doing to help them — the kids never ever believed they had rights. These kids have been exploited by everybody...so when they see something in writing and they see photographs of their friends, they start to think 'Hey, someone cares about us'. When I first wrote to Amnesty, I didn't know who to write to... it was only AI that responded...nobody has given a damn about the kids before and now they realise that people are starting to care...that they as human beings have just as much right to be on this planet as we all do...Things are really moving. Everyone at the highest levels of government are talking about street children — AI has moved mountains."

Guatemala, 1991. Bruce Harris, executive director for Latin America of Covenant House, which works for street children in Guatemala, presents a plaque to AI on their behalf.

penalty for certain crimes, members draped a huge banner over a bridge in London which called on people to "Say no to hanging — Phone your Member of Parliament now".

A comprehensive report on the death penalty was published in 1989 as part of an international campaign for abolition. Petitions were organized and AI members in several countries arranged forums where the mother of a murder victim spoke against executions.

Making the public, and not just governments, aware of human rights is an important part of AI's work and is carried out by members all around the world.

When AI visited Sierre Leone several years ago, its delegation was stopped at five police roadblocks but managed to recruit two new members from among the officers on the way — all the police who stopped the delegation knew of AI.

That in itself shows a significant amount of public awareness which could only have been achieved through the work of members in the country.

In India, more than 5,000 people ran a "race for human rights" in December 1990 carrying banners, which proclaimed that "torture is inhuman" to raise public awareness of human rights. A group in Madras went from village to village explaining the Universal Declaration of Human Rights and collected 15,000 signatures supporting the Declaration.

In an attempt to raise awareness of human rights issues among the army and police in Israel and Brazil, AI members have given lectures on human rights to new recruits. Dutch members have held similar courses for police, business people and Foreign Ministry officials.

Sometimes a visual campaign is most effective, especially in countries where the adult literacy rate is low. In India, one group uses street theatre to present human rights issues to rural communities. The Lahore group in Pakistan also produces plays on human rights themes which tour shanty towns and rural areas. And in Kuwait, AI members organized an exhibition of paintings on the theme of human rights, political repression and free expression.

The strength and success of AI's work is due to its members, who include students, the elderly, tradespeople and professionals.

When governments receive appeals from AI — not just from one country or one group of people but from all around the world — it becomes much harder to dismiss them.

Not every AI campaign or action is going to result in prisoners being freed or detainees being treated better. But at the very least, the organization's continuing campaigns, appeals and publicity remind governments that whatever human rights violations they attempt will be exposed to the harsh glare of international scrutiny. And that's what saves lives.□

'Thanks for keeping my memory alive'

"My nightmare experience is gradually retreating into the past. Please accept my most profound thanks for keeping my memory alive for almost 17 years and for all you continue to do for me."

This message ends Vladimir Balakhonov's letter to AI in May 1989. He had been imprisoned for 17 years from 1973 and enjoyed four months of freedom before being rearrested in 1985 for "anti-Soviet slander". Balakhonov spent another three years in a strict-regime corrective labour camp in Yakutsk before being released in May 1988 after completing his sentence.

"I am writing to thank you from the bottom of my heart for your immense and unceasing efforts over so many years to save my life and free me from imprisonment. No one can tell what would have happened without them.

"I am deeply grateful to you for the humanity, kindness and devotion you have shown towards me...someone who happened to find himself in a situation so desperate that, to an outsider, it must appear more than flesh and blood can bear.

"I am particularly appreciative of the fact that you persisted in your action, irrespective of whether your efforts would culminate in any practical result whatsoever...simply because you were unable to act in any other way. But please be assured that, although — with one exception — your mail did not reach me, I sensed your efforts, care and attention, and this did help me to remain alive and unbroken, despite my uncertainty...or, rather, almost total ignorance...of what was going on beyond the impenetrable barrier of walls and barbed wire surrounding the hell of the gulag."

A year after his release, and having served his whole sentence, Vladimir emigrated to Switzerland, where he was met by local AI members.

"I would also like to express my gratitude for the warm and deeply touching reception I was given at Geneva Airport on 8 April when I finally arrived to resume my life in the Free World... it was a demonstration of the initial stand you had taken so long ago, the noble ideal of protecting someone persecuted for his convictions."□

IRAQ

In the aftermath of the uprising

AI delegations visited Iran and Turkey in May to interview Kurdish, Assyrian, Turcoman and Arab Shi'a refugees about human rights violations committed in Iraq during the March uprising of the Kurds in the north and the Shi'as in the south.

These violations included widespread arrests, torture, and summary and mass extrajudicial executions. Delegates also sought to interview those who had escaped from Iraqi prisons during the uprising, and families of prisoners or the "disappeared", in order to gather information about human rights violations in Iraq over the past decade.

AI had written to the Iraqi Government in April, expressing concern at reports of human rights violations committed against unarmed civilian Iraqi Kurds and Shi'as in the aftermath of the uprising. The Iraqi Government replied in late April, disputing the accuracy of allegations made by AI. Also in April, AI wrote to the Governments of Iran, Kuwait, Syria and Turkey, asking them to allow refugees into their countries and not to send them back to Iraq. AI appealed to the international community to assist these countries in the protection of Iraqi refugees.□

ALBANIA

More than 500 political prisoners freed

MORE than 500 political prisoners, many of them prisoners of conscience, were released in Albania during the first three months of this year. On the eve of multi-party elections on 31 March, the authorities claimed that no more political prisoners were being held. However, a local human rights organization said in May that it believed there were about 40 remaining political prisoners convicted of offences such as "espionage" and "treason". Among those still detained after the elections was prisoner of conscience Edmond Pojani who was arrested in July 1990 and sentenced to two years' imprisonment for "slandering the supreme organs of the State and Party" after he had criticised Enver Hoxha, Albania's former ruler who died in 1985. To AI's knowledge he was still in Bardhor prison camp near Kavajë in May.

After opposition allegations of a cover-up in the investigation of the deaths of four people on 2 April during anti-communist demonstrations in Shkodër, a cross-parliamentary commission was established on 17 April to reinvestigate. The commission found that the security forces were responsible for the deaths; seven people were subsequently arrested, including Shkodër's chief of police. Parliament vetoed the commission's recommendation to dismiss the Interior Minister, but approved the dismissal of the head of the Investigator's Office and the Procurator General.

At the end of April Osman Kazazi, a political prisoner for 38 years until his release in 1989, announced in Tirana that an association of former political prisoners and internees was to be created.

In May President Alia issued a decree establishing a commission to deal with the rehabilitation (including housing and employment) of wrongly sentenced political prisoners or people administratively interned (punished with internal exile). The decree also established the right of the Supreme Court, the Procurator General or the Minister of Justice to issue "certificates of innocence" to those who had been unjustly sentenced. Many former political prisoners have alleged that they were convicted (sometimes repeatedly) on the basis of false evidence obtained under duress from the accused and witnesses.□

NIGER

Tuareg prisoners acquitted

AT a trial before Niger's State Security Court in April, 44 members of the Tuareg minority ethnic group were acquitted and released after a year or more in custody. Many appeared to be prisoners of conscience detained on account of their ethnic origin. Some of the defendants had been accused of attacking government targets in the town of Tchin-Tabaraden in May 1990, but most had been arrested some time before the attack took place.

The trial lasted three days and was attended by several thousand people. An AI observer attended the trial. The court did not examine the allegations of torture made by the defendants, nor have they been adequately investigated by the Niger authorities.□

RWANDA

Thousands of untried detainees released

AT least 3,500 people detained without trial in connection with an armed attack on Rwanda by Uganda-based Rwandese exiles in October 1990 were released by the government in late March and early April.

In all, about 7,000 were arrested in connection with the rebel attack. At least 3,000 of them, all untried detainees, were said by the authorities to have been released between October 1990 and February 1991.

About 50 people arrested in connection with the rebel attack remain in prison. They include 12 people sentenced to prison terms and eight sentenced to death by the State Security Court in January and February after unfair trials. Several dozen others are awaiting trial.

Most of those released were members of the minority Tutsi ethnic group who appeared to have been detained because of their ethnic origin or family relationships with members of the rebel group known as the Rwandese Patriotic Front (FPR) rather than because of any involvement in the fighting.

Others were members of the majority Hutu ethnic group suspected of supporting the FPR because they had criticized the authorities or government policies before the rebel attack. Nearly 300 of those freed were Ugandans who appeared to have been detained on account of their nationality.□

Torture and other abuses persist in Honduras

IN a document published in June AI called on the Government of Honduras to urgently implement measures to protect human rights. The report, *Honduras: persistence of human rights violations*, notes that torture and ill-treatment are still being used during the interrogation of political and criminal suspects. Beatings, the use of the *capucha*, a rubber hood or sheet placed over the face to provoke near-suffocation, and suspension by the wrists were among the methods described.

"They put the *capucha* on my head three times causing asphyxiation and I fainted each time. Then they took it off and one of the policemen pushed down with his foot on my knees causing great pain...I begged them for mercy...shouting at them in despair that I was mother and father to five children..." said a 34-year-old woman detained for five days in February 1991.

A number of people have reportedly been killed by police or military personnel in circumstances suggesting they were extrajudicially executed. There were at least three political killings in 1990 attributed to clandestine groups linked to the armed forces or operating with their acquiescence. These groups were also alleged to be responsible for a pattern of harassment and intimidation directed at members of trade unions and other non-governmental organizations.

AI called on the Government of President Callejas to take steps to protect detainees from torture and to ensure that the perpetrators of human rights violations are brought to justice. The organization said that the authorities have persistently failed to fully investigate human rights abuses, in spite of pledges to do so.□

Stop Press: The Honduras Government has said it will investigate and punish "with the full force of the law" those responsible for killing five peasants in Agua Caliente on 3 May 1991. They were shot dead when military and civilian personnel reportedly attacked a community involved in a land dispute. AI has called for the findings of the investigation to be made public as soon as possible.

CAMEROON

Amnesty for political prisoners

AT the end of March President Paul Biya ordered the release of some 80 political prisoners, including prisoners of conscience, and reduced the sentences of some 20 others. Most had been held for seven years, some without charge or trial, in connection with a coup attempt in 1984.

Demands for democratic reforms and the release of remaining political prisoners continued, however, and demonstrations throughout Cameroon resulted in several deaths. On 22 April the National Assembly granted an amnesty leading to the release of all political prisoners. The authorities also promised early multi-party elections but rejected demands for a national political conference.□

0174

UNITED KINGDOM

Unfair trials, ill-treatment and disputed killings

ON 11 June AI published *United Kingdom: Human rights concerns*. The document outlines long-standing concerns about human rights abuses in the United Kingdom, including the ill-treatment of detainees, unfair trials, killings by security forces in disputed circumstances in Northern Ireland, and the detention of non-British nationals on national security grounds.

Since 1980 hundreds of detainees in Northern Ireland have alleged that they were ill-treated in police custody. Existing procedures and safeguards continue to be inadequate to prevent such ill-treatment. In some trials confessions have been excluded on the basis of allegations of ill-treatment; in civil proceedings former detainees have been awarded compensation for their treatment. However, very few criminal or disciplinary proceedings have been initiated as a result of such cases against the police officers involved. Similar complaints have been made in Great Britain.

In May a former appeal court judge said: "Police standards of behaviour will never improve as long as officers think that those responsible for discipline look the other way when there are accusations of malpractice. The successful prosecution and imprisonment of police officers who are proved to have perverted the course of justice may encourage others not to do likewise."

AI has been concerned about fair trial issues, particularly in cases where detainees were denied legal advice and uncorroborated contested confessions provided the basis for convictions. On several occasions the prosecution service and the police have deliberately withheld crucial evidence from defence lawyers.

Serious allegations about police and army behaviour, particularly in regard to disputed killings, have not been promptly and impartially investigated. Instead there have been internal inquiries and secret reports. A consequence is the frequent allegation that information is suppressed and that the unlawful actions of agents of the state have been deliberately concealed. These issues of concern are of such gravity as to seriously undermine confidence in human rights safeguards in the United Kingdom.□

PERU

Local officials "disappear"

FOUR people from the district of Chuschi, Cangallo province, Ayacucho department "disappeared" after their detention on the night of 14 March. According to reports, some 25 hooded soldiers from the Pampa Cangallo military barracks had entered a peasant community in Chuschi and detained Manual Pacotaype Chaupín, the Mayor of the district, Martín Cayllahua Galindo and Marcelo Cabana Tucno, Secretary and Under-secretary of the Council, and Isaías Huamán Vilca. Relatives went to the Pampa Cangallo military base to ask where the four were being held, but army authorities denied any knowledge of their detention.

On 26 March further inquiries were made at the Pampa Cangallo base by a nine-member delegation from Cangallo which included the Mayor, the Public Ministry's Attorney and Secretary, and four police officers. The delegates were reportedly threatened by soldiers at the base. On 25 April the Mayor of Cangallo, Feliciano Huamaní Quispe, was shot and seriously injured by unidentified assailants. The other members of the delegation are also at risk; human rights defenders have been increasingly targeted over recent years and have suffered arbitrary arrests, death threats, "disappearances" or extrajudicial execution.

AI has called on the government to clarify the legal situation of the four "disappeared" men and to guarantee the safety of those investigating the case.□

AMNESTY INTERNATIONAL NEWSLETTER is published every month in four languages to bring you news of AI's concerns and campaigns worldwide, as well as in-depth reports. Available from Amnesty International (address below)

0175

SYRIA

Eighty released while thousands remain in untried detention

AI welcomed the release on 28 April of 80 political prisoners, including more than 50 prisoners of conscience, who were freed from untried detention in Syria by the Government of President Hafez al-Assad. Reports indicate that all those released had been suspected of membership in the prohibited Party for Communist Action (PCA) or the Communist Party Political Bureau (CPPB).

In a message to the government AI expressed concern, however, about thousands of other suspected opponents of the government, including hundreds of prisoners of conscience, who continue to be detained under state of emergency legislation, in force in Syria since 1963.

Most political prisoners are held without charge or trial, including some who have been held for more than 20 years. Some were tortured during interrogation and held incommunicado for long periods, others remain in prison although sentences imposed by the courts have expired.

Over 700 Palestinians are also reported to have been released from Syrian prisons since 12 March. Hundreds more, including suspected members or supporters of the Palestine Liberation Organization (PLO) and other Palestinian groups, continue to be detained, most without charge or trial. Some have been held since in 1983.□

CHINA

Repression continues

TWO years after the suppression of peaceful pro-democracy protests, which resulted in the massacre of hundreds of civilians in Beijing on 4 June 1989, human rights violations continue to be widespread in China.

Thousands of political prisoners, including prisoners of conscience, remain imprisoned. Some have been sentenced after unfair trials. Others are held without charge or trial under administrative regulations. Thousands of summary executions were carried out during an anti-crime campaign which has continued in 1991. There have been no changes to the laws under which such human rights violations are perpetrated and no attempt to introduce fundamental safeguards.

AI described its concerns in two documents published in June*. One includes a list of over 300 pro-democracy activists and other political prisoners who have been imprisoned since June 1989. For example, Chen Lantao, a prisoner of conscience, was sentenced to 18 years in jail for joining the 1989 protests. The documents also describe AI's concern about unfair trial procedures.

Religious leaders and Tibetan independence activists have also been caught in the sweeping repression. Thousands of Tibetan nationalists have been detained without trial for months at a time since 1987 and at least 200 are still held in Lhasa, the Tibetan capital.

Criminal prisoners have been executed by firing squads in extremely large numbers. During 1990 AI recorded more than 960 death sentences and 750 executions although the organization believes the actual number is in the thousands.□

**Violations of human rights in China - A summary of AI's concerns in 1991* and *China - Trials and Punishments since 1989*

AI visits Ghana

TWO AI delegates visited Ghana in April at the invitation of the Ghanaian authorities to discuss the case of Major Courage Quarshigah and six others accused of conspiring to overthrow the government and held without charge or trial since September 1989 and January 1990. Other issues raised with the government included the long-term administrative detention of at least 50 political prisoners and the continuing use of the death penalty.□

AMNESTY INTERNATIONAL, 1 Easton Street, London WC1X 8DJ, United Kingdom. Printed in Great Britain by Flashprint Enterprises Ltd. London.
Available on subscription at £7 (US$12.00) for 12 issues. ISSN 0308 6887

관리번호	91-640

원본

외 무 부

종 별 :

번 호 : UKW-1280 일 시 : 91 0619 1600

수 신 : 장 관(국연,해기,기정)

발 신 : 주 영 대사

제 목 : A.I. 인사 북한방문

연: UKW(F)-0263

1. 연호, A.I. 인사의 방북에 관한 A.I. NEWSLETTER(7 월) 기사와 관련, 당관에서 6.19(수) 동 일원으로 방북한바 있는 아. 태담당과장 MR.DEREK EVANS 와 접촉한 바, 동인은 하기 언급했음.

가. 7 월판 NEWSLETTER 에 방북활동에 관한 개괄적인 내용을 게재했으나, 상세한 분석이나 평가는 현재 준비중인 연구보고서 (RESEARCH PAPER) 에 수록될 것임. 다만, 동 보고서가 작성되는 대로 자료분석등 절차로 상당기간이 걸릴 것으로 봄.

나. 방북중 북한 관계자들을 다수 면담하고 북한의 법집행 과정에 대한 설명을 청취했으며, 자료를 제공받았으나 수용소 방문등 현장시찰 기회는 없었음.

2. 당관은 상기 NEWSLETTER 기사를 파리주재 연합통신에 제공, 6.19. 자 국내 순환 홍보하였으며, 보다 충실한 내용이 취재 보도되도록 당지 KBS 특파원(정용석)에 의한 MR.EVANS 의 인터뷰 추진(6.25. 예정)에 협조한 바, 결과 추보하겠음. 끝

(대사 이홍구-국장)

예고: 91.12.31 일반

일반문서로 재분류 (1991 .12 .31 .)

검 토 필(1991. 6. 30.)

국기국	장관	차관	1차보	2차보	외연원	외정실	분석관	청와대
안기부	공보처							

0176

PAGE 1 91.06.20 07:10

외신 2과 통제관 BS

[redacted]

정 보 보 고

배부처	법무부 [redacted]	대검	청와대	기 타 기 관
	⊘⊘⊘⊘○○	⊘○	⊘⊘	⊘⊘⊘○○○○
	장차법검 무찰 실국 관관장장	공 안 부 장	사정(법무) 정책조사보좌관	제안외공법 1행 기무보제 조부부처처

A.I 대응활동

1. 제 목

최근 국제사면위원회 동향 보고

2. 출 처

인 권 과

(1991. 6. 21)

3. 내 용

최근 국제사면위원회의 동향중 우리나라와 관련된 부분은 별첨과 같음

첨 부 : 최근 국제사면위원회 동향 보고 1부. 끝.

0177

최근 국제사면위원회 동향 보고

I. AI 뉴스레터 6월호 아국관련 기사

o 주요내용

당부에서 외무부를 통하여 AI측에 기히 전달한바 있는 홍성담, 장의균의 범죄사실 및 정부입장 등이 인용됨

※ 첨부1: 관련기사 사본 (영문)

o 평 가

AI측에 제공한 우리측 반박자료가 AI 정기간행물인 뉴스레터에 인용되고 있는 점등 대응효과가 나타나고 있음

II. AI 뉴스레터 7월호 북한관련 기사

o 주요내용

. 제85차 IPU 평양총회 기간중 최초로 북한을 방문한 AI대표단은 북한의 사법체계 조사활동을 벌였으며 헌법,'87형법,'90민법전을 입수하였음

. 북한 공안당국은 '90년 AI보고서 내용을 반박하면서 현재 3개의 수용소에 천여명의 정치범이 수용되어 있을 뿐이라고 밝힘

. 북한 법학자들은 형법상 사형과 15년까지 부과할 수있는 "노동을 통한 재교육"등 두가지 형벌이 있으며 사형선고는 주로 간첩 및 사보타지에 적용되고 있다고 말함

. 또한 '81년에 비준한바 있는 "시민적 및 정치적 권리에 관한 국제규약(B규약)"이 그들의 법체계에 중요한 일부분이라고 덧붙임

※ 첨부2 : 관련기사 사본 (영문)

o 대응조치

상기자료의 효율적 이용 및 북한법전의 입수방안 등을 외무부와 협의중임

0178

(별첨1)

AMNESTY INTERNATIONAL

NEWSLETTER JUNE 1991 VOLUME XXI • NUMBER 6

The South Korean authorities wrote to AI in response to its appeals for imprisoned artist Hong Song-dam and publisher Chang Ui-gyun. The authorities said that Hong Song-dam, whose case was featured in August 1990, was not imprisoned merely for sending his paintings to North Korea and books to Koreans in Germany, but because his paintings and writings were to promote a Marxist-Leninist revolution. In September 1990 the Supreme Court dismissed the charges of espionage and returned the case to a lower court. In January 1991 Hong Song-dam was sentenced to three years' imprisonment for producing material benefiting North Korea.

Chang Ui-gyun continues to serve an eight-year sentence for espionage. The authorities denied that his arrest in 1987 was solely because he had met pro-North Korean people in Japan and claimed that he had acted on North Korean orders to collect documents on South Korean opposition groups — regarded as state secrets by the courts because they are deemed capable of benefiting North Korea — and to seek to infiltrate dissident groups in order to create social unrest. They also stated that he had received funds from North Korea. AI had found these accusations unsubstantiated.

0179

(별첨 2)

A.I. News Letter July 1991 게재

First AI visit to North Korea

FOR the first time ever, an AI delegation visited the Democratic People's Republic of Korea (DPRK). It attended the 85th Inter-Parliamentary Conference in Pyongyang from 29 April to 4 May and also held discussions with legal scholars and government representatives.

Officials of the Supreme People's Assembly and scholars from the Law Faculty of Kim Il Sung University answered the AI delegation's questions on the country's legal system, including the Constitution, criminal procedures, the 1987 Criminal Code and the 1990 Civil Code. Published texts of these codes, which had previously been unobtainable, were given to the delegation.

Academics at the University of National Economy explained various social laws and the system of appeals and petitions against administrative decisions. Aspects of the application of the laws were discussed with a Central Court judge, a member of the Central Lawyers Association and officials of the Ministry of Public Security. The delegates also attended a criminal trial and visited a public security (police) station where they discussed detention and interrogation procedures and inspected cells.

Professors at the Academy of *Juche Science*, officials of the Ministry of Foreign Affairs and others said that the country's state ideology protects human rights, particularly social and economic rights.

Legal scholars stated that the International Covenant on Civil and Political Rights, ratified by the DPRK in 1981, was considered an integral part of the country's law. They said that the 1987 Criminal Code had reduced the penalties for a number of offences. The new code provides for two basic punishments: the death penalty and "re-education through labour" for up to 15 years. AI's delegates were told that the death penalty is imposed rarely and mainly for espionage or sabotage, although they were not given detailed statistics.

Several officials criticized the *Amnesty International Report 1990* which referred to reports that tens of thousands of political prisoners were held at 12 corrective labour camps.

A public security official responsible for "re-education" facilities told the AI delegation that there are about one thousand people in three such camps nationwide. He would not say how many were held for "anti-state" crimes but indicated that all were "outsiders" arrested in connection with the state of war on the Korean peninsula and that these prisoners were held separately from ordinary criminals.

The same official denied knowledge of reports that about 40 staff and students at colleges in Pyongyang had been arrested in 1988 for putting up political posters.□

0180

1-1

주 영 대 사 관

UKW (F) - 0263　　DATE: 10618 1500

수 신 : 장　관 (국연, 해기, 기정)

발 신 : 주 영 국 대 사

제 목 : A.I. 대표단 북한 방문.

A.I. News Letter July 1991 게재

First AI visit to North Korea

FOR the first time ever, an AI delegation visited the Democratic People's Republic of Korea (DPRK). It attended the 85th Inter-Parliamentary Conference in Pyongyang from 29 April to 4 May and also held discussions with legal scholars and government representatives.

Officials of the Supreme People's Assembly and scholars from the Law Faculty of Kim Il Sung University answered the AI delegation's questions on the country's legal system, including the Constitution, criminal procedures, the 1987 Criminal Code and the 1990 Civil Code. Published texts of these codes, which had previously been unobtainable, were given to the delegation.

Academics at the University of National Economy explained various social laws and the system of appeals and petitions against administrative decisions. Aspects of the application of the laws were discussed with a Central Court judge, a member of the Central Lawyers Association and officials of the Ministry of Public Security. The delegates also attended a criminal trial and visited a public security (police) station where they discussed detention and interrogation procedures and inspected cells.

Professors at the Academy of *Juche* Science, officials of the Ministry of Foreign Affairs and others said that the country's state ideology protects human rights, particularly social and economic rights.

Legal scholars stated that the International Covenant on Civil and Political Rights, ratified by the DPRK in 1981, was considered an integral part of the country's law. They said that the 1987 Criminal Code had reduced the penalties for a number of offences. The new code provides for two basic punishments: the death penalty and "re-education through labour" for up to 15 years. AI's delegates were told that the death penalty is imposed rarely and mainly for espionage or sabotage, although they were not given detailed statistics.

Several officials criticized the *Amnesty International Report 1990* which referred to reports that tens of thousands of political prisoners were held at 12 corrective labour camps.

A public security official responsible for "re-education" facilities told the AI delegation that there are about one thousand people in three such camps nationwide. He would not say how many were held for "anti-state" crimes but indicated that all were "outsiders" arrested in connection with the state of war on the Korean peninsula and that these prisoners were held separately from ordinary criminals.

The same official denied knowledge of reports that about 40 staff and students at colleges in Pyongyang had been arrested in 1988 for putting up political posters.□

연
(북측 입장만 해명하는 내용?)

0181

관리 번호	91-644

	분류번호	보존기간

발 신 전 보

번 호 : WUK-1173 910622 1355 DN 종별 : 지 급

수 신 : 주 영국 대사. 총영사

발 신 : 장 관 (국연)

제 목 : A.I. 대표단 북한방문

대 : UKW-1280 (91-640, 6.21.) 있음 (?)

대호, A.I. 대표단은 방북시 북측으로부터 헌법, 1987년 형법, 1990년 민법, 형사소송법을 입수한 것으로 되어 있는 바, 동 자료의 사본을 입수하여 최선 파편 송부바람. 끝.

(국제기구조약국장 문동석)

일반문서로 재분류 (1991 .12.31.

검 토 필 (1991. 6.30.)

보안 통제	

앙 고 재	91년 6월 22일	UN 과	기안자 성명		과 장		국 장		차 관	장 관
							전결			

외신과통제

0182

기 안 용 지

분류기호 문서번호	국연 2031 - 24521 (전화 :)	시 행 상 특별취급	
보존기간	영구 · 준영구. 10. 5. 3. 1	장	관
수 신 처 보존기간			
시행일자	1991. 7. 3.		

보조기관	국 장	전결	협조기관		문서통제
	과 장				1991. 7. 08
기안책임자		송영완			발 송 인

경 유 수 신 참 조	주영대사	발신명의	1991. 7. 08 외무부
제 목	인권관련자료 송부		

대 : UKW-1168

대호, 법무부에서 작성한 박창수의 사망경위 및 사인에 관한 자료를 별첨 송부하니 A.I.측에 적의 설명후 결과 보고 바랍니다.

첨부 : 상기자료 1부. 끝.

0183

법 무 부

검삼 2031-9350 (503-7055) 1991. 6. 25.

수신 외무부장관

참조 국제기구 조약국장

제목 노조 관련자 사망경위

1. 국연 2031-1555호(91.6.17)와 관련입니다.

2. 박창수의 사망경위 및 사인에 관한 자료를 별첨과 같이 송부합니다.

첨부 : 자료 1부. 끝.

발송 1991. 6. 25 법무부

법 무 부 장 관

결			결재(공람)	
접수일시	1991. 6.26	번호		
처리과	19484			

0184

공　　　　란

공 란

관리 번호 91-4051

원 본

외 무 부

종 별 : 지 급

번 호 : UKW-1373 일 시 : 91 0704 1000

수 신 : 장관(국연,정특,기정)

발 신 : 주 영 대사

제 목 : A.I. 인사면담

대: 국연 2031-22309

연: UKW-1280

7.2(화) 당관 조참사관은 A.I. 아. 태담당과장 MR.DEREK EVANS 와 면담하였는 바, 요지 아래 보고함.

1. EVANS 과장은 지난 5 월 방북과 관련, A.I. 일행은 북한의 법체계 및 운용 파악에 중점을 두었으며, 동 방북을 계기로 북한 당국과의 관계를 발전시켜 북한내 인권개선을 위한 노력을 지속적으로 경주해 나갈 예정이라고 말함.

2. 조참사관은 NEWSLETTER 7 월판을 인용, 대호 북한의 헌법, 형법(87 년),민법(90 년) 형소법의 사본입수 가능성을 타진하였는 바, EVANS 과장은 A.I. 가 북한의 인권문제에 관해 장기적 안목을 가지고 상기 1 항에서 말한 북한 당국과의 관계발전을 중시하고 있는 만큼, 대외 유출할 수 없는 입장임을 이해해 달라고 말함.

3. EVANS 과장은 이어 북한의 인권상황에 관한 보고서는 장차 작성될 것이나 금번 방북결과에 대한 분석이외에도 상당기관 연구검토 과정이 필요할 것으로본다고 말하면서, 이러한 목적을 위해 금후로도 평양의 정부관계 부서는 물론 주 유엔 및 주 제네바 북한대표부와 연락을 유지 발전시켜 나갈 예정이라고 말함.

4. EVANS 과장은 또한 A.I. 의 연례보고서가 오는 7.10(수) 발간될 예정임을 밝히면서 동 보고서가 90 년도 세계각국의 인권상황을 반영하고 있으므로 한국의 보안법 개정이나 A.I. 의 방북 결과등에 관해서는 게재되지 않을 것이라고 말함.(입수되는 대로 보고 예정임)

5. EVANS 과장은 또한 91.9. 중 A.I. 직원이 2 차례 아국을 방문할 예정이라고 말한 바, 제 1 차 방문은 서울에의 국별지부 설치문제를 위한 것이며, 제 2 차 방문은 법무부, 경찰 관계자와 면담을 위한 것이라고함. 상세 내용은 정식요청이 있는대로

국기국 차관 1차보 2차보 구주국 외정실 분석관 청와대 안기부

0187

PAGE 1 91.07.04 18:39

외신 2과 통제관 BA

추보하겠음. 끝

(대사 이홍구-국장)

예고: 91.12.31. 일반

일반문서로 재분류 (1991 .12. 31.)

검 토 필 (1991. 6. 30.)

PAGE 2

0188

원 본

관리 번호	

외 무 부

종 별 :

번 호 : UKW-1401 일 시 : 91 0708 1920

수 신 : 장관(국연,해외,기정)

발 신 : 주 영 대사

제 목 : A.I.연례보고서

연: UKW-1373

연호 91 년도 A.I. 연례보고서(90.1.1.-12.31. 해당) 아국 관련사항을 별첨FAX 송부함.(GMT 91.7.10. 0001 EMBARGO)

첨부: UKW(F)-0284. 끝

(대사 이홍구-국장)

91.12.31. 까지

검 토 필(1991. 6.30.)

국기국	차관	1차보	2차보	외정실	분석관	청와대	안기부	안기부
공보처								

0189

PAGE 1 91.07.09 05:55

외신 2과 통제관 CA

(총 3 매)

3 — 1

주 영 대 사 관

UKW (F) - 0284 DATE: 10708 1930

수 신 : 장 관 (국연, 해외)

발 신 : 주 영 국 대 사

제 목 : 첨부물

첨부 : 2매. 끝

0190

3-2

AMNESTY INTERNATIONAL REPORT

1991

This report covers the period January to December 1990

KOREA
(REPUBLIC OF)

Around 150 people were believed to be prisoners of conscience or possible prisoners of conscience. Thirty prisoners, including several prisoners of conscience held for over 15 years, were released in amnesties. Several prisoners convicted of national security offences complained that they were ill-treated during interrogation. Fourteen people convicted of criminal offences were executed, double the number of executions in 1989.

The National Security Law continued to prohibit contacts with North Korea and activities beneficial to anti-state organizations and North Korea. However, the South–North Exchange and Cooperation Law came into force in August. Under this law, the South Korean Government can authorize its citizens to visit North Korea, to invite North Koreans to the south and to trade and engage in joint ventures with them. Unauthorized contacts with North Koreans continued to result in arrests.

The Constitutional Court made two rulings related to basic freedoms. In January it upheld the constitutionality of Article 13 (2) of the Labour Dispute Mediation Act under which third parties – people not directly connected with the workplace – have been imprisoned for intervening in labour disputes. In April the court ruled that paragraphs (1) and (5) of Article 7 of the National Security Law – which prohibit activities and publications praising anti-state organizations – were constitutional but open to political abuse. Arrests under these provisions continued.

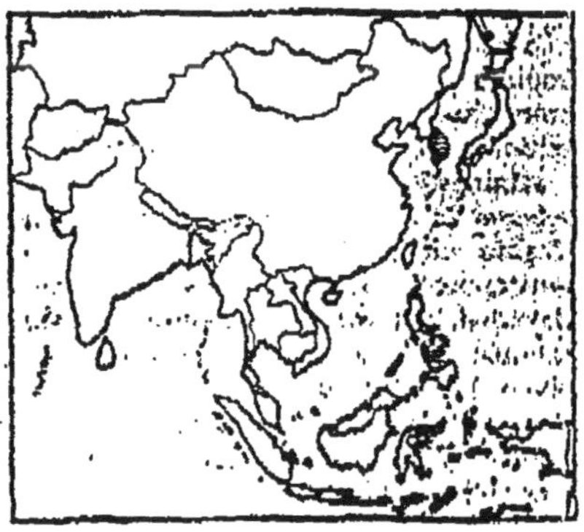

In April the government acceded to the International Covenant on Civil and Political Rights (ICCPR) and its first Optional Protocol. It made reservations on four provisions of the ICCPR, including the right of government employees to organize trade unions. In October the government acceded to the International Covenant on Economic, Social and Cultural Rights.

Over 1,500 people were imprisoned for politically motivated activities. More than half of them were students and workers charged with taking part in illegal demonstrations or committing violent acts. According to a government report to the National Assembly, the number of arrests under the National Security Law increased and 759 people were officially reported to have been charged under this law in the 12 months prior to September 1990. About 250 of them were charged with sympathizing with, or espionage for, North Korea; most of the others were charged with establishing "anti-state" organizations and producing and distributing materials benefiting North Korea.

At least 25 writers and publishers and a number of students were among those tried under the National Security Law for disseminating written or other material said to benefit North Korea. Most received suspended sentences of up to two years' imprisonment. Oh Pong-ok was arrested in February after writing a poem, *Red Mountain, Black Blood*, which the authorities said praised the role played by North Korean leader Kim Il-sung during the Japanese occupation. Oh Pong-ok was released in May with a two-year suspended sentence. Another prisoner of conscience, Kim Song-kyu, was released in April. The President of the student council of Dongguk University, he had been arrested in December 1989 for organizing a student performance of a North Korean revolutionary play.

Over 140 prisoners convicted of espionage continued to serve sentences ranging from five years to life imprisonment. Some had been held since the 1950s but most of those arrested since 1971 had been convicted of visiting North Korea or contacting North Korean agents abroad, notably in Japan. Under the National Security Law, information useful to North Korea, even if it is freely available, is considered a state secret. Many prisoners serving sentences for espionage were believed to have received unfair trials and to have been forced to confess under torture in pre-trial detention. They included prisoners of conscience such as Park Ki-rae, detained since 1974, who served eight years under sentence of death before his sentence was commuted to life imprisonment. Like others he was denied an early release because he refused to write a statement of conversion to "anti-communism".

Unauthorized contact with North Korea continued to be punished by imprisonment. Dissident artist Hong Song-dam was sentenced to seven years' imprisonment in January on charges including sending photographic slides of his painting, *A History of the National Liberation Movement*, to North Korea where they were reproduced for exhibition. He was a prisoner of conscience. In September the Supreme Court upheld sentences of 18 months' imprisonment imposed on four members of *Minjotong*, the Central Council for National Peaceful Reunification. They were arrested in June 1988 because *Minjotong* espoused

0191

AMNESTY INTERNATIONAL REPORT

1991

This report covers the period January to December 1990

certain views on reunification which were similar to those of the North Korean authorities. They too were prisoners of conscience. In November three members of the dissident organization *Chonminnyon*, the National Coalition for a Democratic Movement, were arrested for participating in an unauthorized meeting in Berlin with North Koreans.

Accusations under the National Security Law of organizing or participating in anti-state organizations were brought against members of alleged underground revolutionary socialist or communist groups, composed mostly of students, former students and workers. Around 200 people were believed to have been arrested on such charges in the second half of the year in connection with groups called *Hyukromeng*, the Alliance for the Struggle of the Revolutionary Working Class, *Sanomaeng*, the Socialist Workers League, *Chominiong*, Independent National Unification Group, and *Chonminhongnyon*, the Democratic Students League. The authorities accused them of planning to overthrow the government by force and replace it with a socialist government.

Thirty prisoners who had been convicted on national security charges were released in presidential amnesties in February and May, and it was confirmed that 27 others had been freed in December 1989. Those released included Suh Song, a prisoner of conscience held since 1971, and three other prisoners of conscience – Chin Tu-hyon, Choi Chol-kyo and Paek Ok-kwang – held since 1974 and 1975. Another prisoner of conscience, the Reverend Moon Ik-hwan, was released in October on health grounds after serving one year of his seven-year sentence for an unauthorized visit to North Korea.

Several prisoners complained of beatings and sleep deprivation during interrogation, principally prisoners who were arrested late in the year on suspicion of belonging to "anti-state" organizations. Criminal suspects also alleged that they were beaten, particularly some who were arrested after the government declared a "war on crime" in October. In December the Ministry of Justice told the National Assembly that 53 lawsuits alleging torture and assault had been filed against 115 police officers during the 12 months prior to October 1990. Most such lawsuits were believed to have been unsuccessful.

A former marine officer was sentenced to two years' imprisonment for torturing a marine in military custody in 1983. Compensation was awarded to the relatives of two people who died, in 1986 and 1989, as a result of police ill-treatment.

Some 100 prisoners alleged that they were beaten and tied in painful positions for several hours at a time as a punishment for taking part in a prison protest in August in Seoul Detention Centre. The authorities denied the reports, but the prisoners and their families reportedly filed a complaint with the courts.

Fourteen people who had been convicted of rape, robbery or murder were executed, and two prisoners had their death sentences commuted. Kim Hyun-hui, a North Korean sentenced to death in April 1989 for planting a bomb which blew up a Korean Airlines aircraft, was released under a special amnesty granted by President Roh Tae-woo in April. Suh Sun-taek, sentenced to death in July for spying for North Korea, had his sentence commuted by the Seoul Appeal Court in November.

Amnesty International welcomed the releases of prisoners of conscience and appealed for those still held to be freed. The organization called for the cases of prisoners convicted of espionage to be reviewed to establish whether they had received fair trials. Amnesty International urged the authorities to amend the National Security Law, to enforce safeguards against torture and ill-treatment of prisoners and to abolish the death penalty. In January it published two reports: *South Korea: Return to Repressive Force and Torture?* and *South Korea: Long-term Political Prisoners*. The government responded to these reports and other Amnesty International documents and appeals by reiterating its commitment to human rights and referring to recent prisoner releases and legal reforms in 1989. The government said that they were not holding any prisoners of conscience, arguing that those arrested had "threatened the rule of law and national survival" and were "radical anti-state forces intent on overthrowing our free democratic system". The government also denied that prisoners had been tortured or refused access to their lawyers or relatives.

In October an Amnesty International delegation visited South Korea and discussed human rights concerns with Ministry of Justice officials.

0192

TOTAL P.03

배부처	법무부	대검	청와대	기타기관
	장관, 차관, 법무실장, 검찰국장	공안부장	사정(首席)?, 정무조사보좌관?	제1행조, 안기부, 외무부, 공보처, 법제처

정 보 보 고

1. 제 목

인권문제관련 언론보도

2. 출 처

인 권 과

(1991. 7. 9)

3. 내 용

o 보도요지

. 국제사면위원회는 7.8자로 연례보고서를 발표하면서, 아시아 각국의 인권상황을 거론하였는 바, 그 내용중 아국관련 부분으로 "한국, 인도, 파키스탄, 미얀마 등에서 고문과 가혹행위가 행해지고 있다"는 요지의 언급을 하였다는 것임

. 7.9자 조선(4면 3단), 서울(4면 2단), 국민(5면 1단), 연합통신, 코리아 타임즈(4면), 코리아 헤럴드(4면)

o 대 책

. 국내언론은 외신을 그대로 인용하여 아시아 각국에서 인권침해가 증가하고 있다는 등 막연하게 언급하고 있을 뿐이고 그외 달리 분석이나 대응을 요하는 내용이 포함되어 있지 아니하므로 별도 반박논평을 보도자료로 작성, 배포할 필요성은 없음

. 상기 보고서의 원문은 외무부와 긴밀 협조, 금일중 입수하여 정밀 분석한 뒤 국제사면위 본부에 상세한 대응자료를 작성, 송부하여 정부입장이 충분히 전달될 수 있도록 조치할 계획임

0193

* 조선일보 ('91.7.9. 4면)

"아시아 인권침해 증가"

앰네스티 보고서 고문·불법연행 지속 자행

【런던=AP聯】 국제사면위원회(앰네스티 인터내셔널)는 아시아에서 지난 한햇동안 고문및 불법연행과 불법처형이 늘어나는 등 「아시아는 인권 침해의場」이라고 8일 연례보고서를 통해 밝혔다.

런던에 본부를 둔 국제사면위는 1백41개국에 대한 90년도보고서를 통해 스리랑카에서는 불법처형과 실종이 지속적으로 자행됐으며 중국에서도 사형집행이 늘어났고, 한국·인도·파키스탄·미얀마등에서 고문과 가혹행위가 저질러지는 등 아시아전역에서 인권침해 사례가 보고됐다고 전했다.

이 보고서에 따르면 스리랑카의 바빌롤로아라는 마을의 경우, 지난해 6월파 10월 사이에만도 1천2백명이 실종됐으며 어머니와 아기·어린이들을 비롯, 수천명이 재판을 받지 못한 채 처형됐거나 실종됐다는 것이다.

필리핀에서도 최소 50명이 정부軍에 의해 체포된 뒤 실종됐으며, 부벤 메디나라는 한 남자는 정부軍에 의해 납치된 뒤 온몸에 28군데의 화상을 입고 숨진 채 발견됐다고 보고서는 밝혔다.

* 서울신문('91.7.9.4면)

亞洲 인권침해 여전

앰네스티報告書

【런던AP聯】 국제사면위원회(앰네스티 인터내셔널)는 아시아에서 지난 한햇동안 고문 및 불법연행과 불법처형이 늘어나는 등 「아시아는 인권 침해의 場」이라고 8일 연례보고서를 통해 밝혔다.

0194

* 국민일보 ('91.7.9, 5면)

"아시아 人權침해場 不法연행·처형늘어"

국제사면위

【런던=AP聯】 국제사면위원회(엠네스티 인터내셔널)는 아시아에서 지난 한해동안 고문 및 不法연행과 不法처형이 늘어나는등 「아시아는 인권 침해의 場」이라고 8일 연례보고서를 통해 밝혔다.

0195

국제사면위, "아시아는 인권침해의 場"

(런던 AP=聯合) 국제사면위원회(앰네스티 인터내셔날)는 아시아에서 지난 한햇동안 고문 및 불법연행과 불법처형이 늘어나는 등 "아시아는 인권 침해의 場"이라고 8일 연례보고서를 통해 밝혔다.

런던에 본부를 둔 국제사면위는 1백41개국에 대한 90년도 보고서를 통해 스리랑카에서는 불법처형과 "실종"이 지속적으로 자행됐으며 중국에서도 사형집행이 늘어났고 한국, 인도, 파키스탄, 미얀마 등에서 고문과 가혹행위가 저질러지는 등 아시아 전역에서 인권침해 사례가 보고됐다고 전했다.

이 보고서에 따르면 스리랑카의 바티칼로아라는 마을의 경우 지난해 6월과 10월 사이에만도 1천2백명이 '실종'됐으며 어머니와 아기, 어린이들을 비롯, 수천명이 재판을 받지 못한 채 처형됐거나 실종됐다는 것이다.

스리랑카 정부는 지난 수년간 수천명이 실종됐음에도 불구하고 이들 사건을 조사하기 위한 아무런 조치를 취하지 않았으며 국제사면위의 거듭된 조사단 파견 요청에도 전혀 반응을 보이지 않고 있다고 이 보고서는 덧붙였다.

필리핀에서도 최근 50명이 정부軍에 의해 체포된 뒤 실종됐으며 루벤 메디나라는 한 남자는 정부軍에 의해 납치된 뒤 온 몸에 28군데의 총상을 입고 숨진 채 발견됐다고 보고서는 밝혔다.

또 임산부와 자녀 6명을 포함한 일가족 10명이 정부군에 의해 살해된 것으로 알려졌으며 필리핀 국방장관은 이 사건 관련자들에 대해 일시 구류를 명령했을 뿐 지난해 말까지 아무도 법정에 서지 않았다는 것이다.

한편 인도에서도 분리주의자들에 의한 "폭력과 살인이 전례없이 증가"했으며 정부군이 정치적 동기에 의해 수백명을 살해했다고 보고서는 전했다.

이 보고서는 중국의 경우 지난 89년 체포됐던 민주화 인사들이 아직 재판도 받지 못한 채 억류돼 있으며 지난 1월 천안문사태에 관련된 지도급 민주인사들이 공정치 못한 재판을 받은 뒤 일부는 장기형을 선고받았다고 밝혔다.

보고서는 또 지난해 최소한 3백70명의 중국인들이 불공정한 재판 뒤 사형선고를 받거나 사형당하는등 "89년 이후 최대인" 7백50명이 총살형에 처해졌다고 덧붙였다.

사면위는 이밖에도 미얀마와 아프가니스탄, 캄보디아 등에서 수백명의 정치범이 억류돼 있는 등 아시아 전역에서 불법연행이 자행된 것으로 알려졌다고 전했다.(끝)

(YONHAP) 910708 1849 KST

0196

* 코리아 타임즈 ('91.7.9, 4면)

'Asia-Pacific Gov'ts Still Not Respecting Citizens' Human Rights'

LONDON (AFP) — Governments in Asia and the Pacific continued to resort to torture, "disappearances" and arbitrary arrests of opponents or people expressing their views, Amnesty International said in its 1991 annual report.

Several countries saw an increase in extra-judicial executions while killings carried out or sanctioned by security forces showed no sign of abating in others, according to the report published Wednesday by the London-based human rights group.

Widespread anti-government protests in two countries eventually toppled governments and brought in legal and constitutional reforms.

In Nepal an interim government was set up, political prisoners released and a new constitution drafted following pro-democracy protests, while in Bangladesh similar demonstrations triggered the resignation of the president and the establishment of a caretaker government.

But in some other countries in the region, persecution continued of government opponents and those peacefully expressing their views.

Government forces were involved in thousands of extra-judicial executions either in clashes with armed groups or to suppress protests or calls for greater autonomy, the report said.

In Sri Lanka, where security forces were able to dispose of bodies secretly, thousands of civilians lost their lives in the northeast when conflict erupted again between government forces and armed Tamil separatists.

Some victims were buried alive and others were shot, bayonetted or hacked to death.

Hundreds also died in political killings by government forces in India in response to escalating violence by separatist groups in Jammu and Kashmir.

Scores of suspected government opponents in the Philippines were believed to have been killed by security forces. One man was shot 28 times and his genitals severed, the report said.

Extra-judicial executions were also reported in Burma, Indonesia and Papua New Guinea.

More than half the countries in the region continued to execute or impose death sentences with a dramatic rise in the use of the death penalty in China, where several thousand were believed executed throughout 1990.

Torture or ill-treatment of detainees was widespread throughout the region with deaths resulting in several countries. Methods included beatings, electric shocks, burning with cigarettes, suspension by wrists or ankles, rape and slashing with knives.

Deaths through torture were reported in India and Pakistan, and in Burma civilians were reported forcibly used as human minesweepers.

Torture, ill treatment or poor detention conditions were reported in China, Indonesia, Laos, Malaysia, Papua New Guinea, the Philippines, South Korea and Thailand.

In India at least 10,000 political prisoners were held under preventive detention or "anti-terrorist" laws.

In an "update" to the main report, Amnesty said leading activists in the 1989 Chinese pro-democracy movement had been sentenced in January this year after "unfair" trials, sometimes to long terms in prison.

0197

* 코리아 헤럴드 ('91.7.9, 4면)

Asian gov'ts continue abuses: Amnesty

LONDON (AFP) — Governments in Asia and the Pacific continued to resort to torture, "disappearances" and arbitrary arrests of opponents or people expressing their views, Amnesty International said in its 1991 annual report.

Several countries saw an increase in extra-judicial executions while killings carried out or sanctioned by security forces showed no sign of abating in others, according to the report published Wednesday by the London-based human rights group.

Widespread anti-government protests in two countries eventually toppled governments and brought in legal and constitutional reforms.

In Nepal an interim government was set up, political prisoners released and a new constitution drafted following pro-democracy protests, while in Bangladesh similar demonstrations triggered the resignation of the president and the establishment of a caretaker government.

But in some other countries in the region, persecution continued of government opponents and involved thousands of extra-judicial executions either in clashes with armed groups or to suppress protests or calls for greater autonomy, the report said.

In Sri Lanka, where security forces were able to dispose of bodies secretly, thousands of civilians lost their lives in the northeast when conflict erupted again between government forces and armed Tamil separatists.

Some victims were buried alive and others were shot, bayonetted or hacked to death.

Hundreds also died in political killings by government forces in India in response to escalating violence by separatist groups in Jammu and Kashmir.

Scores of suspected government opponents in the Philippines were believed to have been killed by security forces. One man was shot 28 times and his genitals severed, the report said.

Extra-judicial executions were also reported in Burma, Indonesia and Papua New Guinea.

More than half the countries in the region continued to execute or impose death sentences with a dramatic rise in the use of the death penalty in China, where several thousand were believed to be executed throughout 1990.

Torture or ill-treatment of detainees was widespread throughtout the region with deaths resulting in several countries. Methods included beatings, electric shocks, burning with cigarettes, suspension by wrists or ankles, rape and slashing with knives.

Deaths through torture were reported in India and Pakistan, and in Burma civilians were reported forcibly used as human minesweepers.

Torture, ill treatment or poor detention conditions were reported in China, Indonesia, Laos, Malaysia, Papua New Guinea, the Philippines, South Korea and Thailand.

0198

報 告 畢

長 官 報 告 事 項

1991. 7. 9.
國際機構條約局
國際聯合課 (43)

題 目 : 國際赦免委(A.I.) 91年度 年例報告書

國際赦免委는 91年度 年例報告書(90.1-12월 기간대상)를 7.10. 對外 發表할 豫定인 바, 同 報告書中 미리 入手한 我國關聯 部分要旨 및 이에 대한 對應方案을 아래 報告드립니다.

1. 我國關聯 報告書 要旨

- o 약 150명의 良心囚 또는 의사 良心囚 [redacted] 尙存
- o 良心囚 포함 30명이 大統領 赦免으로 釋放(90.2월 및 5월)
- o 國家保安法 違反 逮捕件數 增加
  - 事前 許可받지않은 北韓과의 接觸, 反國家 革命團體 組織 및 參與, 北韓同調 또는 間諜行爲 關聯 상당수가 服役中
- o 國家保安法 違反者 포함 몇몇 收監者는 本人들이 拷問 및 가혹행위 被害主張
- o 14명의 刑事犯 死刑執行
  - 89년도 보다 倍增
- o 韓國政府는 良心囚가 없다고 主張

앙 고 재	국제연합과	91 년 7 월 9 일	담 당	과 장	국 장	차관보	차 관	장 관
			(서명)	(서명)	(서명)			

0199

2. 評 價

ㅇ 我國關聯 報告書의 일부가 收監者들의 主張 中心으로 記述되어 있어 我國 人權狀況에 대한 均衡잡힌 評價라고 보기는 상when 어려움.

- 동 보고서는 90년도 상황만을 기술, 금년 國家保安法 改正等 현 狀況을 反映한 것은 아님.

ㅇ 특히 北韓人과의 接觸, 北韓을 이롭게하는 行爲에 대한 處罰事例들을 浮刻시킴으로써 國家保安法이 對北韓 關係에 있어 지나치게 엄격히 適用되고 있다는 인상 招來

ㅇ 그러나 90년중 我國의 世界人權規約 加入事實과 良心囚가 없다는 政府의 主張을 揭載함으로써 어느정도 우리당국의 立場을 기술한 것은 그동안 政府가 A.I.측과 緊密한 協議를 持續한 成果로 評價됨.

* 작년도에 비해 報告書 分量도 3페이지에서 2페이지로 줄어듬.

3. 對應方案(案)

ㅇ A.I.는 國際民間機構로서 良心囚 개개인의 釋放을 주목표로 하고 있는 바, 政府次元에서 민감하게 對應하는 것은 不適切

ㅇ 法務部等 關係部處와 協議, 同 報告書에 대한 政府立場을 정하여 이를 駐英大使館을 통해 A.I.側에 傳達

- 年例報告書 발간후 各國別 記述內容 比較後 立場 定立

ㅇ 제네바代表部等 關係公館에 我側立場을 通報, 필요한 경우 적의 活用토록 措置

添附 : 報告書 要旨 飜譯本 1부. 끝.

0200

국제사면위(A.I.) 91년도 연례 보고서중 아국관련 부분

(90.1.1-12.31.해당)

1. 개 요

- 약 150명의 양심수 또는 양심수 후보 상존
- 양심수 포함 30명이 사면으로 석방
- 국가보안법 위반 수감자 일부 학대행위 피해 주장
- 14명의 형사범 사형집행(89년보다 배증)

2. 내 용(요지)

- 국가보안법은 북한과의 접촉 및 반국가단체를 이롭게 하는 행위를 계속 금지하고 있음.
  - 그러나 정부허가하에 북한방문, 북한인 초청 및 북한과의 교역, 합작투자등 가능

- 시민.정치적 권리에 관한 국제인권규약 및 제1선택 의정서 가입(4월) 및 경제.사회.문화적 권리에 관한 국제인권규약 가입(10월)

- 1,500명 이상이 정치적으로 기인된 행동과 관련 구금됨.
  - 이중 반이상이 불법 또는 폭력시위에 가담한 학생 및 노동자

- 국가보안법 위반 체포건수 증가
  - 89.9.-90.9간 758명 구속
  - 이중 250명이 북한동조 또는 간첩행위 관련

0201

o 25명 정도의 작가 및 출판인, 그리고 다수학생이 국가보안법 위반 혐의로 구속

- 대부분이 2년이하 집행유예로 석방
- 양심수인 시인 오봉옥 및 동국대 학생회장 김성규등 포함

o 현재 140명 이상이 간첩혐의로 복역중

- 1971년 이후 체포된 대부분은 북한방문 또는 북한요원 접촉 혐의
- 국가보안법에 의하면 북한에게 유용한 정보는 비록 자유롭게 득할 수 있는 것이라도 국가기밀로 간주
- 간첩혐의로 체포된 많은 죄수들이 불공정한 재판을 받고, 또한 재판전 구금상태에서 고문으로 자백을 강요당한 것으로 믿어짐.
- 박기래등 양심수도 "반공산주의"로의 전향의사를 서면으로 밝히기를 거부하기 때문에 조기석방 대상에서 제외

o 허가받지않은 북한과의 접촉은 불법

- 양심수 홍성담 및 민자통.전민련 관계자들이 북한인과의 접촉 또는 북한과 유사한 견해표명등으로 구속

o 반국가단체 조직 및 참여혐의로 90년 하반기에 약 200명 구속

- 혁노맹, 사노맹, 자민통, 전민학련등 지하혁명단체등과 연루

o 국가보안법 위반 30명이 2월 및 5월 대통령사면으로 석방

- 서승, 진두현, 최철교, 백옥광등 양심수 포함
- 양심수인 문익환 목사 10월에 건강상 이유로 석방

o 몇몇 수감자들은 구타, 잠안재우기등 가혹행위 피해주장

- 반국가단체 가담 혐의자등
- 10월 "범죄에 대한 전쟁" 선포이후 체포된 형사범들
- 89.10-90.10간 고문관련 53건의 소송 접수
- 8월 서울구치소 사건관련 100명의 죄수들이 가혹행위 피해주장

0202

o 강력범 14명 사형집행

- 2명 사형수는 감형(김현희 및 간첩 서순택)

o A.I.는 한국정부의 양심수석방 환영, 추가석방 요망

- 간첩행위 수감자 관련 공정한 재판받았는지 재조사 희망

o A.I.는 국가보안법 개정, 고문방지, 사형제도 폐지 촉구

o 한국정부는 양심수 없음을 주장

- 소위 "양심수"들은 국가존립 및 법질서를 위협하거나 자유민주체제를 전복시키려는 과격분자들이라고 주장

- 수감자에 대한 고문도 부인

o A.I. 대표단이 10월 방한, 법무부 관계자들과 인권상황 협의하였음.

0203

관리번호	91-1704

원 본

외 무 부

종 별 :

번 호 : UKW-1405　　　　일 시 : 91 0709 1700

수 신 : 장관(국연,해외,기정)

발 신 : 주 영 대사

제 목 : A.I.연례보고서

연: UKW-1401

1. 연호 91 년도 A.I. 연례 인권보고서중 북한관련 사항을 별첨 FAX 송부함.

2. 동 보고서 책자 금일 파편 송부함.

첨부: UKW(F)-0286. 끝

(대사 이홍구-국장)

예고: 91.7.31 일반

검 토 필(1991. 6.30.)

국기국　차관　1차보　2차보　분석관　청와대　안기부　공보처

PAGE 1　　　　91.07.10 04:43

외신 2과 통제관 DO

0204

주 영 대 사 관

UKW (F) - 0286 DATE: 10709 1700

수 신 : 장 관 (국연, 해외, 기정)

발 신 : 주 영 국 대 사

제 목 : A.I 연례보고서 (북한관련사항) (첨부물)

Amnesty International Report 1991 발췌

KOREA
(DEMOCRATIC PEOPLE'S REPUBLIC OF)

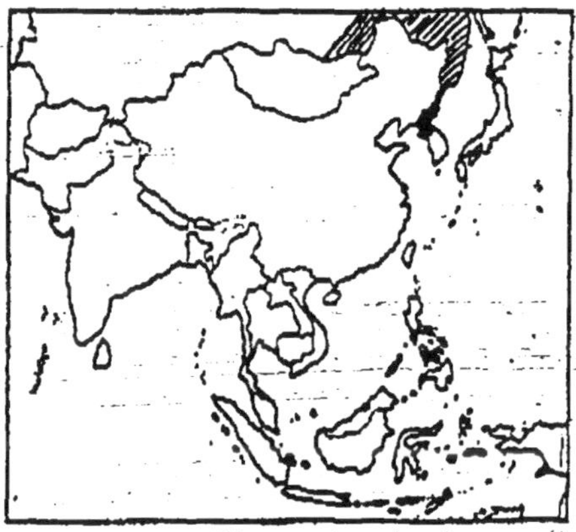

Two Japanese nationals who may have been prisoners of conscience were released after seven years in detention. It was impossible to confirm reports that there were thousands of political prisoners owing to the difficulty of obtaining information about human rights. All news media were controlled by the state and those available to foreigners did not report any political arrests, trials or executions.

Two Japanese seafarers, Beniko Isamu and Kuriura Yoshio, were released in October as a result of an agreement between the Korean Workers' Party and Japan's Liberal Democratic Party and the Japan Socialist Party. Both men had been held since 1983, accused of spying and helping a North Korean soldier defect to Japan aboard their ship. Both denied the accusations. On their return to Japan, Beniko Isamu told reporters that they had neither been formally charged nor tried, although the authorities had previously announced that they had been tried and sentenced to 15 years of "reformation through labour" in December 1987 (see *Amnesty International Report 1989*).

The situation of others reportedly detained in previous years, including about 40 university staff and students said to have been arrested in 1988 (see *Amnesty International Report 1989*), remained unclear. Likewise, it was not possible to confirm other reports that tens of thousands of people might be held for political reasons at corrective camps throughout the country (see *Amnesty International Report 1990*).

There was concern that a number of students who were recalled from their studies in Eastern Europe at the end of 1989 might have been detained on suspicion of criticizing their government while abroad, but this could not be confirmed. On several occasions, however, the ruling Korean Workers' Party called on its members to intensify ideological indoctrination in the advantages of socialism over capitalism, apparently as a reaction to political changes in Eastern Europe, and some sources suggested that returning students were made to attend ideological "re-education" sessions.

Amnesty International welcomed the release of Isamu Beniko and Kuriura Yoshio and sought information from the government about others reportedly detained, but without response. Amnesty International also wrote to the government about its wish to visit the Democratic People's Republic of Korea to discuss human rights with government officials but received no reply.

0205

報 告 畢
(signature)

1991. 7. 10.
國際機構條約局
國際聯合課 (45)

長 官 報 告 事 項

題 目 : 國際赦免委(A.I.) 91年度 年例報告書(北韓)

今 7.10.(水) 對外發表 豫定인 國際赦免委의 91年度 年例報告書 (91.1-12月 기간대상)中 北韓關聯部分 要旨 및 評價를 아래 報告드립니다.

1. 北韓關聯 報告書要旨

o 良心囚로 보이는 2名의 日本人 船員이 北韓勞動黨, 日自民黨, 日社會黨間 合意로 7年만에 釋放됨.

- 北韓當局의 主張과는 달리 釋放된 船員은 裁判받은 적이 없다고 말함.

o 수만명이 政治的 理由로 全國各地에 있는 收容所에 監禁되어 있다고 하나 確認 不可

o 東歐에서 소환된 留學生들이 政府 誹謗嫌疑로 社會主義 "再教育" 過程에 들어가 監禁狀態에 있다고 하나 確認 不可

o 모든 言論이 國家統制下에 있음.

o A.I.는 拘禁者等 관련 北韓當局으로부터 情報수집을 試圖했으나 回信 未接受

- 北韓訪問을 希望하는 書翰을 發送했으나 역시 回信 未接受

0206

2. 評　價

o 基礎資料가 없음으로 詳細하지는 않으나 北韓社會가 철저히 國家 統制下에 있다는 점을 浮刻함으로써 北韓의 劣惡한 人權狀況을 잘 指摘

- 同 報告書는 90年度 狀況만을 記述, 今年 5月 A.I.代表團의 訪北(IPU 총회시) 結果等 最近狀況은 게재되지 않음.

o 北韓當局에 대한 A.I.의 書翰發送에도 불구하고 北韓이 A.I.側에 繼續 非協調的이라는 인상을 강하게 남김.

- A.I. 代表團의 90.10. 韓國訪問 活動과 대조

- 끝 -

0207

국제사면위(A.I.) 91년도 연례보고서중 북한관련 부분

(90.1.1-12.31. 해당)

1. 개 요

- o 양심수로 보이는 2명의 일본인 선원 석방
- o 수천명의 정치범이 있다고 하나 정보입수가 어려워 확인 불가
- o 모든 언론이 국가에 의해 통제상태
  - 외국인이 접하는 뉴스에서는 정치적 구속, 재판등에 대해서는 언급치 않음.

2. 내 용(요지)

- o 북한노동당, 일자민당, 일사회당간의 합의로 양심수로 보이는 2명의 일본인 선원이 7년만에 석방됨. (10월)
  - 그동안 북한당국은 이들이 정식 재판에서 15년간의 "노동을 통한 개혁" 선고를 받았다고 말했으나, 석방된 일선원에 의하면 재판 받은 적이 없다 함.
- o 수만명이 정치적 이유로 전국 각지에 있는 수용소에 감금되어 있다고 하나 확인 불가함.
- o 89년말 동구에서 소환된 유학생들이 해외에서의 정부 비방혐의로 구금되어 있다는 우려가 있으나 확인 불가
  - 북한노동당이 최근 동구의 정치개혁에 대한 대응으로 사회주의 사상교육을 강화하고 있다고 하며, 소식통들은 상기 유학생들이 사상 "재교육" 과정에 들어가 있을 것으로 추측

0208

o A.I.는 2명 일본인 선원의 석방 환영

o A.I.는 구금자들 관련 북한당국으로부터 정보수집을 시도했으나 회신 미접수

- 북한당국과의 인권상황 협의를 위해 북한방문을 희망한다는 내용의 서한 발송 했으나 역시 회신 미접수

0209

배부처	본부	대검	청와대	기타기관
	✓✓✓✓✓○○	✓○	✓✓	✓✓✓○○○○
	장차법검 무찰 실국 관관장장	공 안 부 장	사정비서관 정책조사보좌관	제안외공법 1 기무보제 행 조부부처처

정 보 보 고

1. 제 목 2. 출 처

국제사면위 '91년 연례보고서에 대한 대응 인 권 과

('91. 7. 10)

3. 내 용

○ '91. 7. 9자 정보보고와 관련임.

○ 국제사면위가 발간한 인권보고서를 분석한 결과 그 내용은 예년에 비하여 객관적이고 긍정적 평가에 바탕을 둔 논조이고, 그동안 법무부에서 적극 대응한 결과가 보고서 내용에 상당히 반영되었으나, 국가보안법 위반사범중 일부를 양심수로 분류하는 등 부정적평가는 일부 존재하는 것으로 분석되었음

○ 한편 상기 보고서의 일부내용이 7. 10자 한겨레신문, 중앙일보에 보도된데 대하여는 별첨 반박논평문을 금일중 국내외 언론에 배포할 예정임.

※ 첨 부 : 관련기사 사본 및 논평문 1부. 끝.

0210

* 한겨레신문 ('91.7.10, 6면)

남북한 모두 양심수·정치범 존재

국제사면위 91연례보고서 밝혀

남한 피의자 고문·재소자 부당대우
북한 집단수용·소환유학생 재교육

남한과 북한은 모두 양심수 및 정치범을 수감하고 있는 나라로 국제사면위원회(앰네스티 인터내셔널)에 의해 규정돼 있는 것으로 9일 확인됐다.

국제사면위가 이날 홍콩사무실을 통해 공개한 〈1991년도 연례보고서〉 추가자료에 따르면 남한과 북한은 올 5월말 현재 미얀마·인도·중국·베트남·대만 등과 함께 양심수와 정치범을 가둬놓고 있는 아시아 15개 나라에 들어가 있다.

특히 남한은 중국·필리핀·말레이시아·타이·인도네시아 등과 함께 피의자를 고문하거나 재소자를 부당하게 대우하는 나라로도 규정돼 있다.

국제사면위는 이와 함께 〈91년도 연례보고서〉를 통해 남한에서는 지난 한해 동안 모두 1천5백여명이 정치적 동기에 따른 행위로 수감됐으며, 이 가운데 일부는 조사과정에서 구타 및 잠안재우기 등의 가혹행위를 당했다고 주장했다고 밝혔다.

지난해의 세계인권 상황을 다룬 〈91년도 연례보고서〉 가운데 남·북한 관련 부분의 주요내용은 다음과 같다.

남한 1백50여명의 양심수가 있는 것으로 추정된다. 국가안보를 해친 것으로 판결받은 일부 수감자들은 조사과정에서 부당한 대우를 받았다고 주장하고 있다.

지난해 14명이 형 확정을 거쳐 사형이 집행됐는데 이것은 89년 보다 2배 많은 숫자이다.

정치적 동기에 따른 행위로 수감된 1천5백여명 가운데 절반 이상은 불법시위에 참가하거나 폭력행위 등 처벌에 관한 법률을 위반한 혐의로 기소된 학생과 노동자이다.

이른바 혁명적인 사회주의·공산주의 지하그룹원들을 국가보안법의 반국가단체조직 또는 가담 혐의로 잇달아 기소했다. 이에 따라 90년 하반기에 혁노맹, 사노맹, 자민통, 전민학련과 연계된 약 2백명의 학생·노동자 등이 체포된 것으로 추정된다.

북한 88년 체포된 것으로 알려진 약 40명의 대학관계자와 학생 등을 비롯해 이제까지 억류된 사람들이 어떤 상황에 있는지는 불확실하다.

또한 많은 사람들이 정치적 이유로 북한 전역에 흩어져 있는 집단수용소에 갇혀 있을지도 모른다는 또 다른 보고도 확인할 수 없는 상태다.

89년말 동유럽에서 소환된 상당수 유학생들이 외국에서 정부를 비판했다는 의심에 따라 억류됐을지도 모른다는 우려도 있었지만 이것 역시 확인할 수 없었다. 일부 소식통들은 소환된 유학생들이 이념 '재교육'과정을 밟고 있는 것으로 시사하기도 했다. 〈홍콩=오귀환 특파원〉

0211

* 중앙일보 ('91.7.10, 2면)

韓國 정치범 千5백명 고문등 여전

北韓 수만명 강제수용 사상 재교육

국제사면委 보고서

【파리=裵明復특파원】 韓國에는 정치적인 이유로 수감중인 사람이 1천5백여명에 달하고, 인權에 대한 고문과 부당한 대우가 개선되지 않고 있는등 억압적 인권상황이 계속되고 있다고 국제사면위원회가 10일 발표한 年例보고서에서 밝혔다.

英國 런던에 本部를 둔 국제사면위원회는 이날 내놓은 「91년 人權보고서」에서 이같이 주장하고 투옥중인 양심수에 대한 석방과 국가보안법 개정및 구속자에 대한 고문[illegible] 韓國정부에 촉구했다.

한편 北韓의 인권상황에 대해 이 보고서는 수만명의 정치범이 사상재교육 이유로 집단수용소에 갇혀 강제노동에 시달리고 있는것으로 전해지고 있다며 외부와의 정보차단으로 실제 확인할 길이 없다면서 그동안 수차례에 걸쳐 北韓당국에 인권에 관한 정보제공과 조사단 파견허용을 요청했으나 아무런 응답이 없는 상태라고 밝혔다.

이 보고서는 또 東유럽사태이후 소환된 北韓유학생들의 부모가족들에 깊은 우려를 나타내고 있으며 또한 강제사상재교육대상이 되고 있는 것으로 알려지고 있다고 밝혔다.

'91년도 국제사면위원회 연례인권보고서에 대한 논평

1991. 7. 10

법 무 부

0213

국제사면위원회가 발간한 '91년도 연례보고서중 국내문제에 관한 입장을 밝히고자 함

먼저, 동 보고서가 한국의 인권상황을 거론함에 있어 아국의 국제인권규약 가입사실과 양심수가 없다는 정부의 주장을 게재하는 등 예년에 비하여 객관적이고 긍정적인 시각에서 기술하고 있음을 평가함

그러나 한국정부가 제6공화국 출범이후 자유민주주의 체제를 수호하기 위해 모든 범법자를 적법절차에 따라 처리하고 있음에도 불구하고, 보고서의 일부 내용중 한국에 양심수가 존재하며 범법자에 대한 고문 및 가혹행위가 있었다는 등 일부 구속자 등의 일방적 주장중심으로 기술함으로써 오해의 소지가 생길 수 있음에 우려를 표하는 바임

0214

한국에는 정치적 이유로 부당하게 구속되어 있는 사람은 없으며, 소위 양심수로 거론되고 있는 사람들은 대부분 폭력시위, 방화 등으로 구속된 형사범이거나 사회주의 폭력혁명을 선동한 반국가 사범들일 뿐임

그리고 국가보안법 수감자에 대한 고문 및 가혹행위 사례 주장도 사실과 다르며, 만일 그 같은 사례가 있었다면 적법한 절차에 따라 진행되는 사법절차를 통해 모두 밝혀질 것임

다음, 이 보고서가 북한의 인권상황을 거론하고 있음은 매우 의미있는 일로 평가함

정부는 이와 같이 국제사회에서 북한의 인권상황 개선에 지속적인 관심을 가져 그들이 개방된 국제사회의 일원으로 나올 수 있도록 노력해 줄 것을 기대하는 바임

0215

원 본

외 무 부

종 별 :

번 호 : UKW-1413 일 시 : 91 0710 1720

수 신 : 장 관(국연,해외,기정)

발 신 : 주 영 대사

제 목 : A.I.연례보고서 관련 언론보도

91년도 A.I.연례보고서 발간과 관련한 당지의 언론보도(THE TIMES 지 91.7.10 자제8 면)를 별첨 FAX 송부함.

첨부: UKWF-0287.끝

(대사 이홍구-국장)

국기국 1차보 외정실 분석관 청와대 안기부 공보처

0216

PAGE 1

91.07.11 05:51 FN

외신 1과 통제관

07/10/91 17:38 ☎ 071 589 9134 ROK EMBASSY UK P.01

(총 1 매)

주 영 대 사 관

UKW (F) - 0287 / DATE: 107 10 1720

수 신 : 장 관 (국연, 해외, 기정)

발 신 : 주 영 국 대 사

제 목 : A.I. 연례보고서 관련 언론보도 (첨부물)

The Times (91.7.10, 8면)

신사관	차관실	一차보	二차보	기획실	외정실	분석관	의전장	아주국	미주국	구주국	중아국	국기국	경제국	통상국	문협국	영교국	총무과	감사관	공보관	외연원	청와대	총리실	안기부	공보처

Amnesty condemns human rights abuses

By MICHAEL BINYON, DIPLOMATIC EDITOR

MORE than half the world's governments continued last year to torture, murder and unlawfully imprison tens of thousands of people, despite lip service now paid around the globe to human rights, Amnesty International says.

The annual report of the London-based human rights group found that more than 100 governments tortured or ill-treated prisoners, thousands of people "disappeared" or were executed without legal process in 29 countries, and death sentences were handed down or carried out in 90.

Despite a greater political respect for human rights, symbolised by the release of Nelson Mandela in South Africa and the fall of the Berlin Wall, violations had worsened in 141 countries. Large-scale executions and torture came after Iraq's invasion of Kuwait and highlighted earlier failures by governments to tackle Iraq's poor record.

"We have seen human rights often take a back seat to trade or political concerns and become the casualty of political expediency," Amnesty said. The abuses committed by Iraq made headlines, but serious violations in Burma, Chad, China, Colombia, Mali, Syria, Turkey, Somalia and Morocco did not.

Africa had a dismal record of killings and torture. In Chad the deposed government's final act was to order the killing of at least 300 political prisoners. In Liberia, army and rebel forces executed thousands of people, mostly because of ethnic origin, during the civil war. The greatest number of deaths under torture was reported in Mauritania.

Asia also presented a picture of "disturbing human rights violations", with abuse on a wide scale in India, Sri Lanka, Burma, the Philippines, China and Pakistan. In Sri Lanka the security forces still disposed of bodies secretly, it said. In India, an unprecedented rise in violence and killings by separatist groups was accompanied by politically motivated killings by government forces, Amnesty said. At least 10,000 political prisoners were held, mostly without charge. In the Philippines more than 50 people "disappeared" after being detained, including two women the authorities denied holding but who were found in military custody by visiting Amnesty representatives. In China thousands of pro-democracy protesters arrested in 1989 were still detained without charge. Amnesty recorded 750 executions by firing squad in 1990, the highest number since 1983.

Disappearances and illegal executions were also widespread in Latin America, especially in Colombia and Peru. Children were shot down by death squads in Guatemala and Brazil.

In the Middle East, Amnesty deplored the muted world reaction to hundreds of executions in Iran. In Israel and the occupied territories about 25,000 Palestinians were arrested.

In Europe, Amnesty said, at least 600 political prisoners were still held in Albania at the end of the year. It found evidence of police ill-treatment in Britain, Greece, Austria, France, Italy, Portugal and Spain and the jailing of conscientious objectors in France, Switzerland and Greece. In its campaign against capital punishment, Amnesty said 2,300 people were on death row in more than half of the American states.

0217

정 보 보 고

배부처	법무부	대검	청와대	기타기관
	✓✓✓✓○○ 장차법검 무찰 실국 관관장장	✓○ 공안부장	✓✓ 사정비서관 정책조사보좌관	✓✓✓○○○○ 제안외공법 1행 기무보제 조부부처처

1. 제 목

인권관련 언론보도 (2)

2. 출 처

인 권 과

('91. 7. 11)

3. 내 용

○ '91. 7. 10자 동 제목 정보보고와 관련임.

○ '91 국제사면위 연례보고서에 대한 당부 논평이 7. 10자 AP, Reuter, AFP, UPI 및 7. 11자 한국일보, 경향신문에서 기사로 취급 하였음.

• 인권관련 언론보도 (1)은 연합통신 임

* 첨 부 : 관련기사 사본 1부. 끝.

0218

연합 H1-271.S03 사회(515)

법무부, 국제사면위 보고서 내용 반박

(서울=聯合) 법무부는 10일 국제사면위원회가 최근 발간한 '91년도 연례 인권보고서'와 관련,"우리정부가 6공화국출범이후 자유민주주의 체제를 수호하기위해 모든 범법자를 적법절차에 따라 처리하고있음에도 불구,한국에 양심수가 존재하며 범법자에 대한 고문및 가혹행위가 있었다는등 구속자등의 일방적 주장 중심으로 일부 내용을 기술함으로써 오해의 소지가 생길 수 있음을 우려한다"고 밝혔다.

법무부는 이날 논평을 통해 "한국에는 정치적 이유로 부당하게 구속되있는 사람은 없으며,이른바 양심수로 거론되고 있는 사람들은 대부분 폭력시위,방화등으로 구속된 형사범이거나 사회주의 폭력혁명을 선동한 반국가 사범들 뿐" 이라고 말하고 " 국가보안법 수감자에 대한 고문및 가혹행위사례 주장도 사실과 다르며,만일 그같은 사례가 있었다면 적법절차에 따라 진행되는 사법절차를 통해 모두 밝혀질 것" 이라고 말했다.

법무부는 이어 "이 보고서가 북한의 인권상황을 거론하고 있는 데 대해 매우 의미있는 일로 평가한다"며 " 앞으로도 국제사면위가 북한의 인권상황에 지속적인 관심을 가져 그들이 개방된 국제사회의 일원으로 나올 수 있도록 노력해 주기를 기대한다"고 덧붙였다.(끝)

(YONHAP) 910710 1514 KST

0219

AP-TK-10-07-91 1350GMT<

W1191

r IBX TXA269 10-07 00229

intj 87

^South Korea-Amnesty International

^Seoul Denies Holding Political Prisoners<

SEOUL, South Korea (AP) _ South Korea on Wednesday denied an international human rights group's allegations that it is holding hundreds of political prisoners, and that some prisoners are tortured or harshly treated.

''We want to make it clear once again that no one is being detained in the Republic of Korea because of his political belief,'' the Justice Ministry said in a statement.

The London-based Amnesty International said in its annual report that there are prisoners of conscience, and torture and harsh treatment, in South Korea.

The ministry said the Amnesty report was based on one-sided views of detainees and dissidents and might cause misunderstanding.

''Those who are alleged to be prisoners of conscience are mostly people charged with or convicted of violence during demonstrations, arson or inciting a violent socialist revolution,'' it said.

''The allegations that some of those arrested on charges of violating the National Security Law have been tortured or otherwise harshly treated has no basis in fact, either,'' it said.

''If there had been any such instances, they would all have been brought to light through fair legal proceedings,'' it added.

There are no official figures but dissident groups claim that some 1,500 people have been jailed for anti-government protests or labor activities.

AP-TK-10-07-91 1351GMT<

0220

a6193 BC-LONDON-RAW-SUGAR-NO.6

a6194ALL r
u i BC-KOREA-AMNESTY 07-10 0221
BC-KOREA-AMNESTY
SOUTH KOREA REJECTS ALLEGATIONS OF HUMAN RIGHTS ABUSES

SEOUL, July 10, Reuter - South Korea on Wednesday rejected as baseless allegations by Amnesty International that it is holding "prisoners of conscience" and that some have been tortured and ill-treated.

"The Amnesty International report unquestioningly quotes one-sided allegations by some detainees that there are 'prisoners of conscience' in (South Korea) and that suspects are sometimes tortured and otherwise ill-treated," a statement by the Justice Ministry said.

"Those who are alleged to be 'prisoners of conscience' are mostly people charged with or convicted of violence during demonstrations, arson or inciting a violent socialist revolution," the ministry said.

The Amnesty allegations were contained in the London-based human rights group's latest annual report, released on Tuesday.

The ministry said the allegations were unfounded. "No one is being detained in (South Korea) because of his political belief," the ministry said.

Seoul has said repeatedly it has held no "political prisoners" since President Roh Tae-woo was inaugurated in early 1988.

South Korean dissidents have accused the government of harshly cracking down on protests by using the tough National Security Law that bans pro-communist activities.

REUTER SSW JM ADM
Reut10:54 07-10

0221

GLGL
o0195 ASI/AFP-AV69------
r i SKorea-Amnesty 07-10 0237
Seoul denies torturing political detainees

SEOUL, July 10 (AFP) - South Korea Wednesday rejected Amnesty International's 1991 report that political detainees were being tortured.

The Justice Ministry here said in a statement to the press that the London-based human rights organization "unquestioningly quotes one-sided" allegations by some detainees that there are prisoners of conscience in South Korea and that suspects are sometimes tortured and otherwise ill-treated.

"We are concerned that such passages may cause misunderstandings about the true state of affairs," the statement said, adding that "we want to make it clear once again that no one is being detained in the Republic of Korea because of his political belief."

"Those who are alleged to be 'prisoners of conscience' are mostly people charged with or convicted of violence during demonstrations, arson or inciting a violent socialist revolution," the statement went on.

It also said that the allegation that some of those arrested on charges of violating the National Security Law have been tortured or otherwise harshly treated had "no basis in fact."

The statement called "very significant" that the Amnesty International report discussed the human rights situation in North Korea also.

The report said tens of thousands of political prisoners are interned in forced labor camps in the communist North.

pkm/mb
AFP 100947 GMT JUL 91

0222

ZCZC HKA152 KHA005 NXI
UU HED HUP

R I
#KOREA-COMMENT 7-10
SEOUL TAKES ISSUE WITH AMESTY INTERNATIONAL REPORT
IIGARKO.

SEOUL (UPI) -- THE SOUTH KOREAN GOVERNMENT TOOK ISSUE WITH THE AMENSTY INTERNATIOONAL REPORT 1991 WEDNESDAY AND SAID THERE IS NO ONE IN THE COUNTRY BEING DETAINED BECAUSE OF POLITICAL BELIEF.

THE JUSTICE MINISTRY ISSUED A STATEMENT AND SAID THE AMNESTY INTERNATIONAL HAS TAKEN A MORE OBJECTIVE VIEW OF THE SOUTH KOREAN SITUATION BY NOTING THAT THE COUNTRY HAS JOINED THE INTERNATIONAL HUMAN RIGHTS CONVENTION.

THE STATEMENT, HOWEVER, TOOK ISSUE WITH PART OF THE REPORT AND SAID IT +UNQUESTIONINGLY+ QUOTED ONE-SIDED ALLEGATIONS THAT THERE ARE +PRISONERS OF CONSCIENCE+ IN SOUTH KOREA WHERE DUE PROCESS OF LAW IS STRICTLY BEING ADHERED TO IN HANDLING SUSPECTED CRIMINALS.

+WE WANT TO MAKE IT CLEAR ONCE AGAIN THAT NO ONE IS BEING DETAINED IN THE REPUBLIC BECAUSE OF HIS POLITICAL BELIEF,+ IT SAID. +THOSE WHO ARE ALLEGED TO BE ++PRISONERS OF CONSCIENCE++ ARE MOSTLY PEOPLE CHARGED WITH OR CONVICTED OF VIOLENCE DURING DEMONSTRATIOONS, ARSON OR INCITING A VIOLENT SOCIALIST REVOLSUTION.+

THE MINISTRY STATEMENT FURTHER DENIED ALLEGATIONS THAT SOME OF THOSE ARRESTED ON CHARGES OF VIOLATING THE NATIONAL SECURITY LAW HAVE BEEN TORTURED OR OTHERWISE MALTREATED.

UPI JK
CCCCQQE
=07100949
NNNN

0223

경향신문 ('91.7.11.2면)

정부, "정치범없다"

법무부는 10일 국제사면위원회의 91년도 연례보고서에 대해 논평을 발표, 보고서중 한국에 양심수가 존재한다고 밝힌데 대해 "한국에는 정치적이유로 부당하게 구속돼있는 사람은 없다"고 반박했다.

한국일보 ('91.7.11. 4면)

구속자주장 일방記述
법무부 논평

법무부는 10일 논평을 발표, 국제사면위원회가 「91년 연례보고서」에 한국의 정치범이 1천5백여명에 달하고 고문·가혹행위가 있다는 등 일부 구속자들의 일방적 주장만으로 한국의 인권상황을 기술한 것은 사실과 달라 국제적으로 오해의 소지가 있음을 우려한다고 밝혔다.

0224

報 告 畢

長官報告事項

1991. 7. 16.
國際機構條約局
國際聯合課 (47)

題 目 : 政治犯 및 良心囚의 槪念定義

> 國際赦免委(A.I.)의 7.10. 年例報告書 發表, 我國政府의 "市民的.政治的 權利에 관한 國際人權規約" 加入에 따른 7월말 人權報告書 提出, 그리고 우리의 유엔加入은 我國의 人權狀況에 대한 國內外의 關心을 고조시킬 可能性이 있는 바, 현재까지 政府의 對應時 混用해 왔던 「政治犯」 및 「良心囚」의 槪念을 명확히 구분할 必要性이 있다고 사료되어 아래 報告드립니다.

1. 國際赦免委(A.I.)의 槪念定義

o 政治犯(political prisoner)은 良心囚보다 훨씬 包括的 槪念

- 불법정당 참가등 純粹한 政治的 성격의 法違反은 물론, 犯法 行爲에 政治的 要素 내지는 動機가 조금이라도 있으면 政治犯으로 分類. 즉, 폭력.방화등 명백한 一般刑事犯도 政治犯으로 分類 될수 있음.

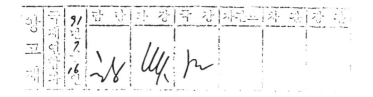

앙 고 재	국제연합과	91년 7월 16일	담 당	과 장	국 장	차관보	차 관	장 관

0225

- 이같이 넓은 槪念을 사용하는 理由는 이들이 政治的 理由때문에 苛酷行爲를 받거나 또는 正常的인 司法節次에서 除外될까봐 우려하는 것임.
- 따라서 A.I.는 政治犯에 대해서 다른 범법자들과 같은 迅速하고 公正한 裁判이 이루어질 것을 要望하는 것이며, 釋放을 요구하는 것은 아님.

o 良心囚(prisoner of conscience)는 정치범과는 뚜렷하게 구별되는 개념인 바, "그들의 政治.宗敎.여타 믿음 또는 人種, 姓別, 言語 때문에" 拘束된 者들을 지칭함.
- 暴力을 사용 또는 옹호한 경우와 같이 一般刑事犯 要素를 내포한 경우는 除外
- A.I.는 良心囚에 대해서는 釋放을 要求함.

2. 人權問題關聯 政府對應時 留意事項

o 政治犯과 良心囚를 區別하여 對應 必要
- 상기 定義에 비추어 政治犯은 人權先進國에도 얼마든지 있을 수 있음을 弘報
- 政治犯에 대해서는 公正한 司法節次를 거치고 있다는 것만 강조하면 됨.
  . "우리나라에 정치범은 없다"라고 强辯하는 것은 오히려 逆效果 招來

o 良心囚가 있다는 주장에 대해서는 그들의 犯法行爲를 구체적으로 밝히면서 그들이 良心囚가 아님을 주장
- 단, 實定法 違反이라고만 하는 것은 說得力 微弱. A.I.등에서는 國家保安法등 實定法 자체를 問題視 하는 경우가 있음.

0226

- 이는 우리의 安保 및 社會狀況 전반에 대한 認識의 부족에서 비롯되는 것이므로 人權團體들의 理解深化를 위한 弘報努力은 필요하지만, 소위 良心囚 개개인의 문제와 관련 지나치게 敏感하게 對應할 필요는 없다고 봄.
- 단, A.I.가 特定人을 나름대로 良心囚라고 결론짓기 전에 對處하는 것이 效果的

※ 최근 아측은 政治犯이란 용어가 誤解의 소지가 크다고 A.I.측에 수차례 지적했는 바, 우리나라에 대하여 政治犯이란 用語 사용을 自制하고 있는 듯함.(91 연례보고서에서는 예년과 달리 "political prisoner"라는 단어 불사용)

3. 其 他

o 상기와 관련 우선 法務部, 靑瓦臺등 關係部處 실무자들과 意見交換할 예정이며, 필요시 여타 關係部處 및 관련 在外公館에 배포 참고토록 할 예정임.

- 끝 -

0227

o 정부내 관계부처 및 본부에도 알리는 것이 좋을듯.

報　告　畢
(서명)

1991. 7. 16.
國際機構條約局
國際聯合課 (47)

長官報告事項

題　目 : 政治犯 및 良心囚의 概念定義

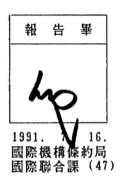

> 國際赦免委(A.I.)의 7.10. 年例報告書 發表, 我國政府의 "市民的·政治的 權利에 관한 國際人權規約" 加入에 따른 7월말 人權報告書 提出, 그리고 우리의 유엔加入은 我國의 人權狀況에 대한 國內外의 關心을 고조시킬 可能性이 있는 바, 현재까지 政府의 對應時 混用해 왔던 「政治犯」 및 「良心囚」의 概念을 명확히 구분할 必要性이 있다고 사료되어 아래 報告드립니다.

1. 國際赦免委(A.I.)의 概念定義

o 政治犯(political prisoner)은 良心囚보다 훨씬 包括的 概念

- 불법정당 참가등 純粹한 政治的 성격의 法違反은 물론, 犯法 行爲에 政治的 要素 내지는 動機가 조금이라도 있으면 政治犯으로 分類. 즉, 폭력.방화등 명백한 一般刑事犯도 政治犯으로 分類될수 있음.

0228

- 이같이 넓은 槪念을 사용하는 理由는 이들이 政治的 理由때문에 苛酷行爲를 받거나 또는 正常的인 司法節次에서 除外될까봐 우려하는 것임.
- 따라서 A.I.는 政治犯에 대해서 다른 범법자들과 같은 迅速하고 公正한 裁判이 이루어질 것을 要望하는 것이며, 釋放을 요구하는 것은 아님.

o 良心囚(prisoner of conscience)는 정치범과는 뚜렷하게 구별되는 개념인 바, "그들의 政治.宗敎.여타 믿음 또는 人種, 姓別, 言語 때문에" 拘束된 者들을 지칭함.
  - 暴力을 사용 또는 옹호한 경우와 같이 一般刑事犯 要素를 내포한 경우는 除外
  - A.I.는 良心囚에 대해서는 釋放을 要求함.

2. 人權問題關聯 政府對應時 留意事項

o 政治犯과 良心囚를 區別하여 對應 必要
  - 상기 定義에 비추어 政治犯은 人權先進國에도 얼마든지 있을 수 있음을 弘報
  - 政治犯에 대해서는 公正한 司法節次를 거치고 있다는 것만 강조하면 됨.
    . "우리나라에 정치범은 없다"라고 强辯하는 것은 오히려 逆效果 招來

o 良心囚가 있다는 주장에 대해서는 그들의 犯法行爲를 구체적으로 밝히면서 그들이 良心囚가 아님을 주장
  - 단, 實定法 違反이라고만 하는 것은 說得力 微弱. A.I.등에서는 國家保安法등 實定法 자체를 問題視 하는 경우가 있음.

0229

- 이는 우리의 安保 및 社會狀況 전반에 대한 認識의 부족에서 비롯되는 것이므로 人權團體들의 理解深化를 위한 弘報努力은 필요하지만, 소위 良心囚 개개인의 문제와 관련 지나치게 敏感하게 對應할 필요는 없다고 봄.
- 단, A.I.가 特定人을 나름대로 良心囚라고 결론짓기 전에 對處하는 것이 效果的

※ 최근 아측은 政治犯이란 용어가 誤解의 소지가 크다고 A.I.측에 수차례 지적했는 바, 우리나라에 대하여 政治犯이란 用語 사용을 自制하고 있는 듯함.(91 연례보고서에서는 예년과 달리 "political prisoner"라는 단어 불사용)

3. 其 他

o 상기와 관련 우선 法務部, 靑瓦臺등 關係部處 실무자들과 意見交換할 예정이며, 필요시 여타 關係部處 및 관련 在外公館에 배포 참고토록 할 예정임.

- 끝 -

0230

Definitions

" 정치범 (political prisoner) 양심수 (prisoner of Conscience) "

Political trials and imprisonment without trial

In many countries, either under the ordinary law or states of emergency, the authorities put people in prison without a trial. In some cases imprisonment lasts for decades. A fair and public hearing within a reasonable time is a basic human right as is the right to freedom from arbitrary arrest and detention. To imprison people for a long period without proving a case against them is a violation of these rights.

Amnesty International opposes the detention of any *political* prisoner without a trial within a reasonable time. It has called on various governments to end administrative internment and other procedures that allow for prolonged political detention without trial.

Amnesty International also opposes trial procedures in political cases that do not conform to internationally agreed standards. For example, secret trials take place. Sometimes they are nominally public, but only those selected by the authorities are allowed to attend. Prisoners are denied a defence lawyer of their choice – or the defence is not allowed to call witnesses or present evidence. Cases are heard by special tribunals and military courts whose composition is incompatible with an impartial hearing or whose procedures fall short of those in ordinary courts.

How does Amnesty International use the term "political prisoner?

Amnesty International uses a broad interpretation of the term "political prisoner" so as to cover all cases with a significant political element. The offence itself may be of a clearly political nature, such as belonging to a banned political party. In other cases, however, a person may be charged with an ordinary crime, but the context in which it is said to have been committed is political, such as a political demonstration. Or it is possible that the accused person may have committed a criminal offence, but for political motives. In other cases, the authorities may be holding a prisoner for political reasons, even though the individual is said to be suspected of a criminal offence. False criminal charges may also be brought against political activists (the charges could be currency offences, for example), when the real reason is to punish them for their political activities – or to deter others from opposing the government. In all such cases there would be a political element to be considered.

It is important to bear in mind that Amnesty International applies this

broad interpretation in assessing political trials and the cases of political prisoners. Apparent contradictions between Amnesty International and governments do arise because each uses such terms in its own way. Some governments say they hold no political prisoners, only criminals or criminal suspects, because all its prisoners are charged or convicted under the normal criminal law. Amnesty International, however, may still speak of "political imprisonment" or "political trials" in such a country if the cases have a political element of any of the sorts described above.

It is important to note that Amnesty International does not oppose political imprisonment *as such* or ask for the release of all political prisoners. Amnesty International needs to establish whether there is a political element in a particular case solely for the purpose of determining whether it falls within the scope of the organization's concern about fair and prompt trials for political prisoners.

The specific category "prisoner of conscience" is distinguished from the general one of "political prisoner" in the following important respects. Prisoners of conscience are precisely defined by Amnesty International's Statute as those held "by reason of their political, religious or other conscientiously-held beliefs or by reason of their ethnic origin, sex, colour or language". The category "prisoner of conscience" does not include those whose imprisonment may reasonably be attributed to their having used or advocated violence.

A crucial difference to bear in mind is that whereas in the case of all political prisoners Amnesty International seeks fair and prompt trials, it is only in the case of prisoners of conscience that Amnesty International says that the individuals should not be in prison at all and asks for their release.

Does Amnesty International call for special status for political prisoners?

Amnesty International does not call for special status for particular groups of prisoners or call on governments to give political prisoners special conditions. Governments are obliged to treat *all* prisoners humanely. Where there are allegations of torture or ill-treatment or where the death sentence has been imposed, the case comes within those concerns of Amnesty International that apply to *all* prisoners: opposition to torture and executions. Where the existence of prisoners of conscience has been confirmed, Amnesty International works for their unqualified, immediate *release*.

0231

What does Amnesty International do in response to political trials and cases of imprisonment without trial?

Amnesty International investigates such cases to determine whether the individuals are prisoners of conscience. It may send observers to trials and examine laws and procedures that permit unfair trials in political cases or

관리번호	91-772

기 안 용 지

분류기호 문서번호	국연 2031 - 1804	(전화:)	시 행 상 특별취급	
보존기간	영구·준영구. 10. 5. 3. 1	장 관		
수 신 처 보존기간				
시행일자	1991. 7. 19.			

보조기관	국 장	전 결	협조기관		문서통제
	심의관				1991. 7. 22
	과 장				
기안책임자		황준국			발 송 인

경 유 수 신 참 조	수신처참조	발신명의		1991. 7. 2 외무부
제 목	정치범 및 양심수의 개념정의			

국제사면위(A.I.)의 7.10. 연례보고서 발표, 아국 정부의 "시민적.정치적 권리에 관한 국제인권규약" 가입에 따른 7월말 인권보고서 제출, 그리고 우리의 유엔가입은 아국의 인권상황에 대한 국내외의 관심을 고조시킬 가능성이 있는 바, 현재까지 정부의 대응시 혼용해 왔던 「정치법」 및 「양심수」의 개념을 명확히 구분할 필요성이 있다고 사료되어 당부자료를 별첨과 같이 송부하오니 귀업무에 참고하시기 바라며, 특별한 의견 있으면 ~~회시해~~ 알려 주시기 바랍니다.

0232

(2)

첨부 : 정치범 및 양심수의 개념정의 1부. 끝.

수신처 : 법무부장관, 공보처장관, 대통령 비서실장,

국무총리 행정조정실장, 안기부장

검 토 필(1991. 6.30.)

0233

政治犯 및 良心囚의 槪念定義

1. 國際赦免委(A.I.)의 槪念定義

o 政治犯(political prisoner)은 良心囚보다 훨씬 包括的 槪念

- 불법정당 참가등 純粹한 政治的 성격의 法違反은 물론, 犯法 行爲에 政治的 要素 내지는 動機가 조금이라도 있으면 政治犯으로 分類. 즉, 폭력.방화등 명백한 一般刑事犯도 政治犯으로 分類 될수 있음.

- 이같이 넓은 槪念을 사용하는 理由는 이들이 政治的 理由때문에 苛酷行爲를 받거나 또는 正常的인 司法節次에서 除外될까봐 우려하는 것임.

- 따라서 A.I.는 政治犯에 대해서 다른 범법자들과 같은 迅速하고 公正한 裁判이 이루어질 것을 要望하는 것이며, 釋放을 요구하는 것은 아님.

o 良心囚(prisoner of conscience)는 정치범과는 뚜렷하게 구별되는 개념인 바, "그들의 政治.宗敎.여타 믿음 또는 人種, 姓別, 言語 때문에" 拘束된 者들을 지칭함.

- 暴力을 사용 또는 옹호한 경우와 같이 一般刑事犯 要素를 내포한 경우는 除外

- A.I.는 良心囚에 대해서는 釋放을 要求함.

0234

2. 人權問題關聯 政府對應時 留意事項

o 政治犯과 良心囚를 區別하여 對應 必要

- 상기 定義에 비추어 政治犯은 人權先進國에도 얼마든지 있을 수 있음을 弘報
- 政治犯에 대해서는 公正한 司法節次를 거치고 있다는 것만 강조하면 됨.
  . "우리나라에 정치범은 없다"라고 强辯하는 것은 오히려 逆效果 招來

o 良心囚가 있다는 주장에 대해서는 그들의 犯法行爲를 구체적으로 밝히면서 그들이 良心囚가 아님을 주장

- 단, 實定法 違反이라고만 하는 것은 說得力 微弱. A.I.등에서는 國家保安法등 實定法 자체를 問題視 하는 경우가 있음.
- 이는 우리의 安保 및 社會狀況 전반에 대한 認識의 부족에서 비롯되는 것이므로 人權團體들의 理解深化를 위한 弘報努力은 필요하지만, 소위 良心囚 개개인의 문제와 관련 지나치게 敏感하게 對應할 필요는 없다고 봄.
- 단, A.I.가 特定人을 나름대로 良心囚라고 결론짓기 전에 對處하는 것이 效果的

※ 최근 아측은 政治犯이란 용어가 誤解의 소지가 크다고 A.I.측에 수차례 지적했는 바, 우리나라에 대하여 政治犯이란 用語 사용을 自制하고 있는 듯함.(91 연례보고서에서는 예년과 달리 "political prisoner"라는 단어 불사용)

- 끝 -

0235

기 안 용 지

분류기호 문서번호	국연 2031 - 27106	(전화:)	시 행 상 특별취급	
보존기간	영구·준영구. 10. 5. 3. 1	장		관
수 신 처 보존기간				
시행일자	1991. 7. 19.			

보조기관	국 장	전 결	협조기관		문서통제
	심의관				1991. 7. 20 통 제 관
	과 장				
기안책임자		송영완			발 송 인

경 유 / 수 신 / 참 조	주영대사	발신명의	발송필 1991. 7. 20 외무부
제 목	A.I. 연례보고서에 대한 논평		

1. 대호, A.I. 연례보고서의 아국관련부분에 대한 법무부 논평을 별첨 송부하니 참고하시기 바랍니다.

2. 한편, 국제민간 인권단체의 아국 인권상황 거론에 대한 대응시 혼용해 왔던 「정치범」 및 「양심수」의 개념을 명백히 구분할 필요가 있는 바, 동 개념을 별첨과 같이 구분 사용키로 하였음을 알려드립니다.

첨 부 : 1. 법무부 논평 1부

2. 「정치범」 및 「양심수」 개념정의 1부. 끝.

0236

기 안 용 지

분류기호 문서번호	국연 2031 -	27107 (전화:)	시 행 상 특별취급	
보존기간	영구·준영구. 10. 5. 3. 1	장		관
수 신 처 보존기간				
시행일자	1991. 7. 19.			

보조기관	국 장	전 결	협조기관		문서통제 (1991. 7. 20 통제관)
	심의관	(서명)			
	과 장	(서명)			
기안책임자		송영완			발송 (1991. 7. 20 외무부)

경 유 수 신 참 조	수신처 참조	발신명의	
제 목	국제사면위 1991년도 연례보고서		

1. 국제사면위(A.I.)는 세계인권상황에 관한 1991년도 연례보고서를 91.7.10. 발표한 바, 동 보고서 내용중 남.북한 관련부분 및 이에 대한 법무부 논평을 별첨 송부하니 업무에 참고하시기 바랍니다.

2. 한편, 국제민간 인권단체의 아국인권상황 거론에 대한 대응시 혼용해 왔던 「정치범」 및 양심수의 개념을 명백히 구분할 필요가 있는 바, 동 개념을 별첨과 같이 구분, 사용키로 하였음을 알려드립니다.

/ 계속 /

0237

첨 부 : 1. A.I. 보고서중 남.북한 관련부분 1부.

2. 법무부 논평 1부.

3. 「정치범」 및 「양심수」 개념 정의 1부. 끝.

수신처 : 주미, 스웨덴, 화란, 노르웨이, 덴마크, 유엔,

제네바, EC, UNESCO 대사, 미국내 총영사관

독일, 호주, 카나다 대사,

뉴욕, 시카고, 마이애미, 상항, 휴스톤, 아틀란타,

시애틀, 라성, 보스톤, 호노루루, 벵쿠버, 몬트리올 총영사

0238

circumstances of Koigi wa Wamwere's arrest and indicated its w[illegible] to send an observer to his trial, but wit[illegible] response.

In November Amnesty International published a report, *Kenya: Silencing Opposition to One-Party Rule.*

KOREA
(DEMOCRATIC PEOPLE'S REPUBLIC OF)

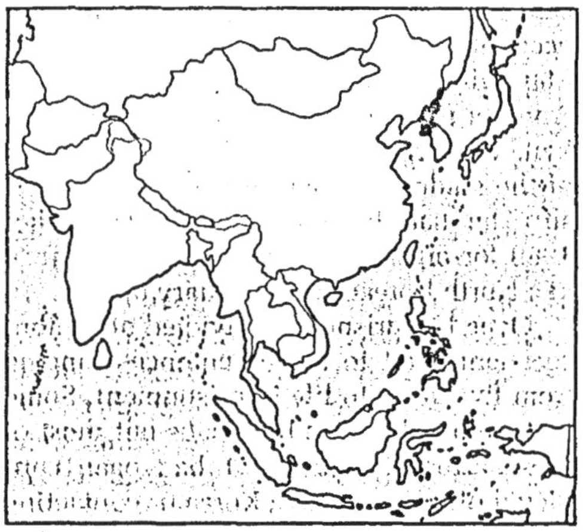

Two Japanese nationals who may have been prisoners of conscience were released after seven years in detention. It was impossible to confirm reports that there were thousands of political prisoners owing to the difficulty of obtaining information about human rights. All news media were controlled by the state and those available to foreigners did not report any political arrests, trials or executions.

Two Japanese seafarers, Beniko Isamu and Kuriura Yoshio, were released in October as a result of an agreement between the Korean Workers' Party and Japan's Liberal Democratic Party and the Japan Socialist Party. Both men had been held since 1983, accused of spying and helping a North Korean soldier defect to Japan aboard their ship. Both denied the accusations. On their return to Japan, Beniko Isamu told reporters that they had neither been formally charged nor tried, although the authorities had previously announced that they had been tried and sentenced to 15 years of "reformation through labour" in December 1987 (see *Amnesty International Report 1989*).

The situation of others reportedly detained in previous years, including about 40 university staff and students said to have been arrested in 1988 (see *Amnesty International Repor*[illegible]*989*), remained unclear. Likewise, it [illegible] not possible to confirm other reports that tens of thousands of people might be held for political reasons at corrective camps throughout the country (see *Amnesty International Report 1990*).

There was concern that a number of students who were recalled from their studies in Eastern Europe at the end of 1989 might have been detained on suspicion of criticizing their government while abroad, but this could not be confirmed. On several occasions, however, the ruling Korean Workers' Party called on its members to intensify ideological indoctrination in the advantages of socialism over capitalism, apparently as a reaction to political changes in Eastern Europe, and some sources suggested that returning students were made to attend ideological "re-education" sessions.

Amnesty International welcomed the release of Isamu Beniko and Kuriura Yoshio and sought information from the government about others reportedly detained, but without response. Amnesty International also wrote to the government about its wish to visit the Democratic People's Republic of Korea to discuss human rights with government officials but received no reply.

0239

KOREA
(REPUBLIC OF)

Around 150 people were believed to be prisoners of conscience or possible prisoners of conscience. Thirty prisoners, including several prisoners of conscience held for over 15 years, were released in amnesties. Several prisoners convicted of national security offences complained that they were ill-treated during interrogation. Fourteen people convicted of criminal offences were executed, double the number of executions in 1989.

The National Security Law continued to prohibit contacts with North Korea and activities beneficial to anti-state organizations and North Korea. However, the South–North Exchange and Cooperation Law came into force in August. Under this law, the South Korean Government can authorize its citizens to visit North Korea, to invite North Koreans to the south and to trade and engage in joint ventures with them. Unauthorized contacts with North Koreans continued to result in arrests.

The Constitutional Court made two rulings related to basic freedoms. In January it upheld the constitutionality of Article 13 (2) of the Labour Dispute Mediation Act under which third parties – people not directly connected with the workplace – have been imprisoned for intervening in labour disputes. In April the court ruled that paragraphs (1) and (5) of Article 7 of the National Security Law – which prohibit activities and publications praising anti-state organizations – were constitutional but open to political abuse. Arrests under these provisions continued.

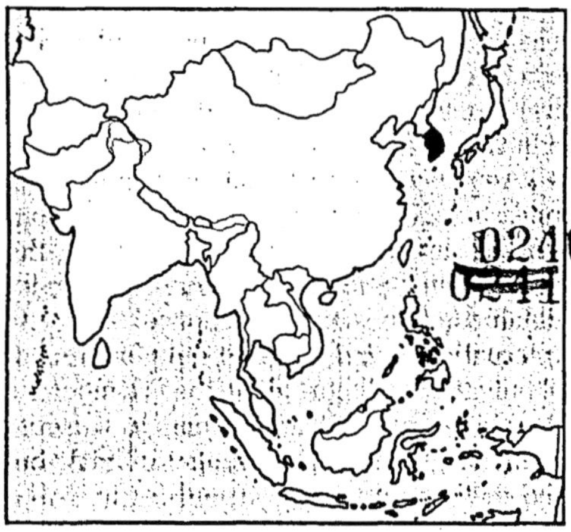

In April the government acceded to the International Covenant on Civil and Political Rights (ICCPR) and its first Optional Protocol. It made reservations on four provisions of the ICCPR, including the right of government employees to organize trade unions. In October the government acceded to the International Covenant on Economic, Social and Cultural Rights.

Over 1,500 people were imprisoned for politically motivated activities. More than half of them were students and workers charged with taking part in illegal demonstrations or committing violent acts. According to a government report to the National Assembly, the number of arrests under the National Security Law increased and 759 people were officially reported to have been charged under this law in the 12 months prior to September 1990. About 250 of them were charged with sympathizing with, or espionage for, North Korea; most of the others were charged with establishing "anti-state" organizations and producing and distributing materials benefiting North Korea.

At least 25 writers and publishers and a number of students were among those tried under the National Security Law for disseminating written or other material said to benefit North Korea. Most received suspended sentences of up to two years' imprisonment. Oh Pong-ok was arrested in February after writing a poem, *Red Mountain, Black Blood*, which the authorities said praised the role played by North Korean leader Kim Il-sung during the Japanese occupation. Oh Pong-ok was released in May with a two-year suspended sentence. Another prisoner of conscience, Kim Song-kyu, was released in April. The President of the student council of Dongguk University, he had been arrested in December 1989 for organizing a student performance of a North Korean revolutionary play.

Over 140 prisoners convicted of espionage continued to serve sentences ranging from five years to life imprisonment. Some had been held since the 1950s but most of those arrested since 1971 had been convicted of visiting North Korea or contacting North Korean agents abroad, notably in Japan. Under the National Security Law, information useful to North Korea, even if it is freely available, is considered a state secret. Many prisoners serving sentences for espionage were believed to have received unfair trials and to have been forced to confess under torture in pre-trial detention. They included prisoners of conscience such as Park Ki-rae, detained since 1974, who served eight years under sentence of death before his sentence was commuted to life imprisonment. Like others, he was denied an early release because he refused to write a statement of conversion to "anti-communism".

Unauthorized contact with North Korea continued to be punished by imprisonment. Dissident artist Hong Song-dam was sentenced to seven years' imprisonment in January on charges including sending photographic slides of his painting, *A History of the National Liberation Movement*, to North Korea where they were reproduced for exhibition. He was a prisoner of conscience. In September the Supreme Court upheld sentences of 18 months' imprisonment imposed on four members of *Minjatong*, the Central Council for National Peaceful Reunification. They were arrested in June 1989 because *Minjatong* espoused

0240

certain views on reunification which were similar to those of the North Korean authorities. They too were prisoners of conscience. In November three members of the dissident organization *Chonminnyon*, the National Coalition for a Democratic Movement, were arrested for participating in an unauthorized meeting in Berlin with North Koreans.

Accusations under the National Security Law of organizing or participating in anti-state organizations were brought against members of alleged underground revolutionary socialist or communist groups, composed mostly of students, former students and workers. Around 200 people were believed to have been arrested on such charges in the second half of the year in connection with groups called *Hyukromeng*, the Alliance for the Struggle of the Revolutionary Working Class, *Sanomaeng*, the Socialist Workers League, *Chamintong*, Independent National Unification Group, and *Chonminhangnyon*, the Democratic Students League. The authorities accused them of planning to overthrow the government by force and replace it with a socialist government.

Thirty prisoners who had been convicted on national security charges were released in presidential amnesties in February and May, and it was confirmed that 27 others had been freed in December 1989. Those released included Suh Song, a prisoner of conscience held since 1971, and three other prisoners of conscience – Chin Tu-hyon, Choi Chol-kyo and Paek Ok-kwang – held since 1974 and 1975. Another prisoner of conscience, the Reverend Moon Ik-hwan, was released in October on health grounds after serving one year of his seven-year sentence for an unauthorized visit to North Korea.

Several prisoners complained of beatings and sleep deprivation during interrogation, principally prisoners who were arrested late in the year on suspicion of belonging to "anti-state" organizations. Criminal suspects also alleged that they were beaten, particularly some who were arrested after the government declared a "war on crime" in October. In December the Ministry of Justice told the National Assembly that 53 lawsuits alleging torture and assault had been filed against 115 police officers during the 12 months prior to October 1990. Most such lawsuits were believed to have been unsuccessful.

A former marine officer was sentenced to two years' imprisonment for torturing a marine in military custody in 1983. Compensation was awarded to the relatives of two people who died, in 1986 and 1989, as a result of police ill-treatment.

Some 100 prisoners alleged that they were beaten and tied in painful positions for several hours at a time as a punishment for taking part in a prison protest in August in Seoul Detention Centre. The authorities denied the reports, but the prisoners and their families reportedly filed a complaint with the courts.

0241

Fourteen people who had been convicted of rape, robbery or murder were executed, and two prisoners had their death sentences commuted. Kim Hyun-hui, a North Korean sentenced to death in April 1989 for planting a bomb which blew up a Korean Airlines aircraft, was released under a special amnesty granted by President Roh Tae-woo in April. Suh Sun-taek, sentenced to death in July for spying for North Korea, had his sentence commuted by the Seoul Appeal Court in November.

Amnesty International welcomed the releases of prisoners of conscience and appealed for those still held to be freed. The organization called for the cases of prisoners convicted of espionage to be reviewed to establish whether they had received fair trials. Amnesty International urged the authorities to amend the National Security Law, to enforce safeguards against torture and ill-treatment of prisoners and to abolish the death penalty. In January it published two reports: *South Korea: Return to Repressive Force and Torture?* and *South Korea: Long-term Political Prisoners*. The government responded to these reports and other Amnesty International documents and appeals by reiterating its commitment to human rights and referring to recent prisoner releases and legal reforms in 1989. The government said that they were not holding any prisoners of conscience, arguing that those arrested had "threatened the rule of law and national survival" and were "radical anti-state forces intent on overthrowing our free democratic system". The government also denied that prisoners had been tortured or refused access to their lawyers or relatives.

In October an Amnesty International delegation visited South Korea and discussed human rights concerns with Ministry of Justice officials.

'91년도 국제사면위원회 연례인권보고서에 대한 논평

1991. 7. 10

법 무 부

0242

국제사면위원회가 발간한 '91년도 연례보고서중 국내문제에 관한 입장을 밝히고자 함

먼저, 이 보고서가 한국의 인권상황을 거론함에 있어 아국의 국제인권규약 가입사실과 양심수가 없다는 정부의 주장을 게재하는 등 예년에 비하여 객관적이고 긍정적인 시각에서 기술하고 있음을 평가함

그러나 한국정부가 제6공화국 출범이후 자유민주주의 체제를 수호하기 위해 모든 범법자를 적법절차에 따라 처리하고 있음에도 불구하고, 보고서의 일부 내용중 한국에 양심수가 존재하며 범법자에 대한 고문 및 가혹행위가 있었다는 등 일부 구속자 등의 일방적 주장중심으로 기술함으로써 오해의 소지가 생길 수 있음에 우려를 표하는 바임

0243

한국에는 정치적 이유로 부당하게 구속되어 있는 사람은 없으며, 소위 양심수로 거론되고 있는 사람들은 대부분 폭력시위, 방화 등으로 구속된 형사범이거나 사회주의 폭력혁명을 선동한 반국가 사범들일 뿐임

그리고 국가보안법 수감자에 대한 고문 및 가혹행위 사례 주장도 사실과 다르며, 만일 그 같은 사례가 있었다면 적법한 절차에 따라 진행되는 사법절차를 통해 모두 밝혀질 것임

다음, 이 보고서가 북한의 인권상황을 거론하고 있음은 매우 의미있는 일로 평가함

정부는 이와 같이 국제사회에서 북한의 인권상황 개선에 지속적인 관심을 가져 그들이 개방된 국제사회의 일원으로 나올 수 있도록 노력해 줄 것을 기대하는 바임

0244

政治犯 및 良心囚의 槪念定義

1. 國際赦免委(A.I.)의 槪念定義

o 政治犯(political prisoner)은 良心囚보다 훨씬 包括的 槪念

- 불법정당 참가등 純粹한 政治的 성격의 法違反은 물론, 犯法行爲에 政治的 要素 내지는 動機가 조금이라도 있으면 政治犯으로 分類. 즉, 폭력.방화등 명백한 一般刑事犯도 政治犯으로 分類될수 있음.
- 이같이 넓은 槪念을 사용하는 理由는 이들이 政治的 理由때문에 苛酷行爲를 받거나 또는 正常的인 司法節次에서 除外될까봐 우려하는 것임.
- 따라서 A.I.는 政治犯에 대해서 다른 범법자들과 같은 迅速하고 公正한 裁判이 이루어질 것을 要望하는 것이며, 釋放을 요구하는 것은 아님.

o 良心囚(prisoner of conscience)는 정치범과는 뚜렷하게 구별되는 개념인 바, "그들의 政治.宗教.여타 믿음 또는 人種, 姓別, 言語 때문에" 拘束된 者들을 지칭함.

- 暴力을 사용 또는 옹호한 경우와 같이 一般刑事犯 要素를 내포한 경우는 除外
- A.I.는 良心囚에 대해서는 釋放을 要求함.

0245

2. 人權問題關聯 政府對應時 留意事項

o 政治犯과 良心囚를 區別하여 對應 必要

- 상기 定義에 비추어 政治犯은 人權先進國에도 얼마든지 있을 수 있음을 弘報

- 政治犯에 대해서는 公正한 司法節次를 거치고 있다는 것만 강조하면 됨.

  . "우리나라에 정치범은 없다"라고 强辯하는 것은 오히려 逆效果 招來

o 良心囚가 있다는 주장에 대해서는 그들의 犯法行爲를 구체적으로 밝히면서 그들이 良心囚가 아님을 주장

- 단, 實定法 違反이라고만 하는 것은 說得力 微弱. A.I.등에서는 國家保安法등 實定法 자체를 問題視 하는 경우가 있음.

- 이는 우리의 安保 및 社會狀況 전반에 대한 認識의 부족에서 비롯되는 것이므로 人權團體들의 理解深化를 위한 弘報努力은 필요하지만, 소위 良心囚 개개인의 문제와 관련 지나치게 敏感하게 對應할 필요는 없다고 봄.

- 단, A.I.가 特定人을 나름대로 良心囚라고 결론짓기 전에 對處하는 것이 效果的

※ 최근 아측은 政治犯이란 용어가 誤解의 소지가 크다고 A.I.측에 수차례 지적했는 바, 우리나라에 대하여 政治犯이란 用語 사용을 自制하고 있는 듯함.(91 연례보고서에서는 예년과 달리 "political prisoner"라는 단어 불사용)

- 끝 -

0246

주 영 대 사 관

영국(정) 723-781 1991. 8. 5.

수신 : 장관

참조 : 국제기구조약국장

제목 : A.I. News Letter 송부

A.I. News Letter 8월관 1부를 별첨 송부합니다.

첨부 : 동 News Letter 1부. 끝.

발송 1991. 8 06 주영국대사관

주 영 대

44223

0247

AMNESTY INTERNATIONAL

NEWSLETTER AUGUST 1991 VOLUME XXI • NUMBER 8

시민사회 보고서

LIBYA

Reforms fail to stop abuses

HUNDREDS of political prisoners, including prisoners of conscience, are believed to be held without trial or after unfair trials in Libya. In a report published in June,* AI cited the cases of 467 prisoners, most of whom have reportedly been held incommunicado since 1989 or early 1990. The majority are held on suspicion of being religious opponents of the government. Five known prisoners of conscience have been held for over 18 years.

The report details the failure of legal reforms introduced or promised in 1988. The reforms fall short of international human rights standards, and in many cases have not been implemented.

AI is particularly concerned that arbitrary arrest and incommunicado detention, which render detainees vulnerable to torture and other ill-treatment, continue to occur and that no legislation or rigorous preventative measures have been introduced to end such abuses. AI has over the past two years repeatedly raised these concerns with the Libyan authorities. The organization has received no response and has publicly called upon the Libyan authorities to act on the recommendations contained in its report. * *Libya: Amnesty International's prisoner concerns in the light of recent legal reforms (AI Index: MDE 19/02/91).*□

AI visits Tunisia

AN AI delegation visited Tunisia in May 1991 and met the Prime Minister and other government officials. The delegation expressed AI's concern about the deterioration of the human rights situation in Tunisia since September 1990 and sought confirmation of the detention and whereabouts of over 70 detainees believed to be held incommunicado. The delegation urged the government to investigate numerous allegations of torture of political detainees, mostly members or suspected members of *Hizb al-Nahda*, the main Islamic opposition group.□

Trade unionists targeted

PHILIPPINES

SCORES of trade unionists in the Philippines have been extrajudicially executed, some have "disappeared" and hundreds have been arrested since the government of President Corazon Aquino came to power in 1986. The majority of the victims have been members of the militant *Kilusang Mayo Uno* (KMU), May First Movement, and its affiliate the National Federation of Sugar Workers. Some KMU members, such as David Borja, have apparently been extrajudicially executed for defending the human rights of fellow trade unionists.

The perpetrators have included members of government security forces, unofficial anti-communist vigilantes and "goons" (hired thugs), acting with the cooperation or support of the official forces.

Human rights violations in the Philippines have occurred within the context of the government's "total approach" counter-insurgency campaign, which aims to end a 22-year armed conflict between government forces and the outlawed New People's Army (NPA) by weakening selected civilian organizations and destroying the armed insurgency movement. The "total approach" has portrayed trade unionists and human rights workers as targets and has served officially to justify serious human rights violations.

AI is aware that violent acts have also been carried out by NPA members. However, AI believes that violence by opposition groups can never be used to justify human rights violations by government or government-backed forces.

AI issued a report entitled *Philippines: Human rights violations and the labour movement (AI Index: ASA 35/16/91)* in June 1991.□

Philippines: Funeral of trade union leader David Borja, killed in July 1990

0248

GUATEMALA

TRADE unionists in Guatemala have reportedly been abducted by heavily armed men, tortured and interrogated about their activities and those of their colleagues. Most were threatened before being released; others have received death threats by telephone.

At least one trade union leader has been killed. Dinora Pérez, aged 28, who was also a member of the Rural Projects Foundation for Guatemala, was shot dead by unidentified men in April 1991.

The circumstances of the abuses suggest the involvement of the security forces, acting in the guise of the "death squads". The recent wave of threats and attacks has forced more than 18 leaders of popular and trade union movements into exile since April 1991. There are fears for the safety of other threatened trade unionists who remain in Guatemala.

Sources in Guatemala link the recent attacks to the decision by unions and popular movements not to participate in the government's proposed "Social Pact". President Serrano publicly accused the unions of being "fronts for the national insurgency movements". In the past such public statements by government officials have led to reprisals against those named in the form of torture, "disappearance" and extrajudicial exectuion.□

CAMPAIGN FOR PRISONERS OF THE MONTH

Each of the people whose story is told below is a prisoner of conscience. Each has been arrested because of his or her religious or political beliefs, colour, sex, ethnic origin or language. None has used or advocated violence. Their continuing detention is a violation of the United Nations Universal Declaration of Human Rights. International appeals can help to secure the release of these prisoners or to improve their detention conditions. In the interest of the prisoners, letters to the authorities should be worded carefully and courteously. You should stress that your concern for human rights is not in any way politically partisan. In *no* circumstances should communications be sent to the prisoner.

SYRIA

Salman 'Abdallah: ***a 61-year-old economist and former member of the National Command of the Ba'th Party in Syria, he has been detained for over 20 years without charge or trial in al-Mezze Military Prison, Damascus.***

Salman 'Abdallah was living in Beirut, Lebanon, when he was abducted by the Syrian security forces in April 1971 and taken to Syria. He is one of dozens of people arrested in 1970 and 1971 following the November 1970 coup which brought President Hafez al-Assad to power.

Eighteen of them remain in detention, all of whom served in, or were closely connected with, the 1966 to 1970 government of the Ba'th Party in Syria.

None of them has been charged or tried and all were reportedly detained for their refusal to cooperate with the present government. They include a former president of Syria, five former cabinet ministers and a former ambassador.

Some of these prisoners were reportedly tortured after their arrest, and have been denied medical treatment in prison. All are said to be in poor health — suffering mainly from stomach ulcers and high blood pressure — due to inadequate medical facilities and prolonged detention in harsh prison conditions. Medicines have to be provided by relatives rather than by the prison administration.

In 1981 some members of the group were reportedly offered release from prison if they agreed to support the government of President Assad but they refused. AI has issued numerous appeals for their release, all of which have remained unanswered by the Syrian authorities.

■Please send courteous appeals for the immediate and unconditional release of Salman 'Abdallah to: His Excellency 'Abd al-Halim Khaddam/Vice-President/Office of the President/Presidential Palace/Damascus/Syrian Arab Republic.□

CHINA

Tamdin Sithar: ***a 45-year-old Tibetan, he is serving a 12-year prison sentence imposed in 1984, apparently for possession of a statement by the Dalai Lama, the Tibetan leader in exile in India. He had previously been detained without trial for several years during the 1970s as a result of a government campaign in 1971 to eradicate "reactionary forces".***

Tamdin Sithar was arrested on 26 August 1983 while working in a labour brigade near Lhasa, capital of the Tibet Autonomous Region of the People's Republic of China (PRC). He had been transferred there after his release in 1975 from a Lhasa prison. He had been held without trial since 1971 because of his alleged membership in a youth group calling for Tibet's independence from China and because of his family background: Tamdin Sithar is a relative of the former junior tutor of the Dalai Lama. He is now believed to be held in Drapchi, Lhasa's main prison, solely because of his family background and his non-violent exercise of his right to freedom of opinion.

Tamdin Sithar is believed to have been tried by the Lhasa Intermediate People's Court in 1984, but the charges against him are unknown. Several other Tibetans detained in 1983, possibly in connection with a wave of arrests during a nationwide "anti-crime campaign", have been accused of "counter-revolutionary crimes" because they advocated Tibetan independence. The charges against Tamdin Sithar may have been similar. The mere possession of texts about Tibetan independence or recorded talks of the Dalai Lama have been grounds for arrest in Tibet since the Dalai Lama's exile in 1959.

■Please send courteous appeals for the immediate and unconditional release of Tamdin Sithar to: GyaltsenNorbu/Chairperson of the Tibet Autonomous Region/ ibet Regional Government/Lhasa/ Tibet Autonomous Region/ People's Republic of China.□

MALAWI

Goodluck Mhango: ***a 34-year-old veterinary surgeon, he has been held in administrative detention without charge or trial since his arrest in the Malawi capital, Lilongwe, in September 1987. He was reportedly badly beaten by police during his arrest and suffered head injuries.***

Goodluck Mhango's arrest followed the publication in a foreign magazine of an article critical of the Malawian Government written by his brother, Mkwapatira Mhango, a journalist in exile in Zambia. Goodluck Mhango was apparently arrested because of his relationship with his brother. Mkwapatira Mhango was a member of the Malawi Freedom Movement (MAFREMO), a clandestine opposition movement. In mid-October 1989 Mkwapatira Mhango and nine members of his family, including his children, died in a firebomb attack on their home in Lusaka. Allegations by Zambian officials that agents of the Malawian Government were responsible have yet to be substantiated.

The Malawian Government has never given any reason for Goodluck Mhango's detention. However, it is believed that the security authorities wished to punish the Mhango family for the 1987 article by his brother.

Since late 1990 the cases of more than a hundred political detainees have been reviewed by government officials and 88 of them have been released. Goodluck Mhango's name is understood to have been considered but rejected.

■Please send courteous letters appealing for his immediate and unconditional release to: H.E. The Life President Ngwazi Dr H. Kamuzu Banda, Life President of the Republic of Malawi/Office of the President and Cabinet/P/Bag 388/Lilongwe 3/Malawi.□

RELEASED

Kenneth Matiba (below), a *Prisoner of the Month* in Kenya in April 1991, was released on medical grounds on 9 June, after suffering a stroke in prison as a result of harsh conditions and inadequate medical treatment.

On 21 June 1991, Raila Odinga (above), who had also been in poor health in a Kenyan prison, was released. He had been designated a *Prisoner of the Month* for July 1991, by which time he was already free.

0249

EUROPE

Birth of a human rights movement

Thirty years ago, an article in a United Kingdom (UK) newspaper launched a campaign called "Appeal for Amnesty, 1961". It was born in outrage at the imprisonment of two Portuguese students who had dared drink a toast to freedom: the event out of which the term "prisoner of conscience" was coined. Eight weeks after the article appeared, delegates from Belgium, France, Ireland, Switzerland, the UK and the United States of America held a meeting in a Luxembourg café. They agreed on two things: the "Appeal for Amnesty, 1961" would become a permanent movement and change its name to Amnesty International. By the end of the year there were AI groups in most western European countries.

Europe was then a very different region. Portugal and Spain were ruled by dictatorships; a junta took power in Greece in 1967. In the year AI was founded Turkey's civilian Prime Minister, Adnan Menderes, was executed on the order of the military generals who had overthrown his government. In 1980 Turkey was again rocked by a military coup.

Political dissent was likewise crushed in eastern and central Europe, symbolized when Warsaw Pact tanks rolled into Czechoslovakia in 1968 and ended the brief "Prague Spring" of liberalization.

AI members in Belgium demonstrate against human rights violations in Sri Lanka

This was the setting for AI's work in its early years. Nearly all of its supporters were then in western Europe, one reason why AI sections in this region are now among the biggest and most effective in the movement; national organizations, with tens of thousands of members, publish their own newspapers and magazines, and mount well-resourced and widely publicized campaigns against human rights violations all over the world. For years, AI drew its most experienced members — its international leadership — from this region, where most of its campaigning techniques evolved.

The AI sections which developed in western Europe during the 1960s and 1970s enjoyed an advantage denied those struggling to develop today. AI was then a relatively unknown organization, with a low public profile, and a limited number of action techniques. Sections were able to develop at their own speed, to devise the campaigning techniques and structures that suited them, without the enormous pressures new sections and groups experience today from the media and the public.

During the 1970s and much of the 1980s official propaganda in eastern and central Europe presented AI in a negative light — in the USSR, as part of the western spy network — and it took courage to be associated with the organization. Government control of the press and the interception of mail from abroad made this difficult to change.

In Bulgaria, the German Democratic Republic (GDR) and Romania people known to be connected with AI were at risk. In the GDR it was illegal to contact organizations abroad without official sanction. Romanian citizens had to report all contacts with foreigners to the local police. Nevertheless, AI occasionally received requests for information from eastern and central Europe. Such requests had to be handled with great care to avoid putting the inquirers at risk.

In the USSR and Poland, however, AI supporters undertook campaigns for human rights. Local human rights activists formed an AI group in Moscow in 1973. They worked for prisoners in Greece, Laos, Mexico, South Africa, Spain, Sri Lanka and Yugoslavia, and in 1976 sent a petition to the Polish Government calling for the release of workers and intellectuals arrested during the mass strikes. Between 1980 and 1983 the group published four newsletters. The Moscow group members were often harassed, and were also isolated from the international movement. By 1986 their number and activities dwindled to the point where the group ceased to function altogether.

There have been active AI supporters in Poland for over 13 years, a long-standing interest which may be partly attributable to AI's campaigns for Polish prisoners. Association with AI often resulted in official harassment. Activists who, in 1977, collected signatures for a petition calling for the release of all the world's prisoners of conscience were tried and fined.

Even after martial law was imposed in December 1981 support for AI in Poland continued. It increased rapidly when, in January 1986, the unofficial "Freedom and Peace Movement" (WiP) decided to publish the *AI Newsletter* in Polish. Apparently because of this, two WiP members were fined and one had a typewriter confiscated. However, WiP members continued to support AI's campaigns, and in 1987 they collected some 800 signatures for a petition to end torture in Afghanistan.

Other Polish organizations also supported AI. In 1986 underground Solidarity used AI's publicity for a *Political Prisoner Week*. That same year an official daily newspaper printed a short report on AI's worldwide *Campaign against Torture*.

The political map of Europe has changed many times since AI was founded, but never as dramatically as in the last three years. The end of the 1980s saw a marked change in official attitudes to AI in eastern and central Europe. State-run newspapers began publishing positive reports on the organization. In 1988 in Hungary a massive public event was organized under the banner of AI for the first time in eastern or central Europe: a concert for *Human Rights Now!* was staged in Budapest during the 1988 world tour held to celebrate the 40th anniversary of the Universal Declaration of Human Rights. Even the Soviet newspaper *Pravda*, for years implacably opposed to AI, suggested a "calmer" approach to the organization. An exception was the GDR which, in February 1989, repeated the old accusation of AI being in "close contact with numerous western secret services". The official news agency asserted that AI's newly published report on the GDR was a work of fiction. The report, *Sweeping Laws, Secret Justice*, documented unfair trials and widespread imprisonment of those who tried to leave the country without permission, or persisted in their efforts to obtain such permission.

A diplomatic breakthrough was not long in coming to the USSR. In March 1989 AI visited Moscow and, for the first time, was well received at the official level. In September AI organized a stall at the Moscow Book Fair, which generated considerable interest. Many people signed the petition against the death penalty and several joined AI.

By the beginning of 1990 AI was receiving a constant stream of letters from people in Poland interested in joining the organization, and forming groups of AI members. Today AI groups in nine towns have formed a "Polish AI Association" which acts as a coordinating body. Its board is elected by the different groups.

1989 saw momentous political change in the GDR, Bulgaria, Czechoslovakia and Romania. The new political freedom had an immediate impact on the possibilities for winning supporters for AI's ongoing campaign against human rights violations.

Most groups of AI members in Hungary, Poland and Slovenia (Yugoslavia) organized their first public campaign during *AI Week* in October 1989. The theme was human rights violations against children.

AI's first public meeting in East Berlin took place in January 1990, and was attended by 150 people. A newspaper report generated a further 500 inquiries from people interested in AI. When Germany unified, the GDR AI association dissolved itself and its members joined the Federal Republic of Germany section.

For the first time in decades the people of most eastern and central European countries have the freedom to join the international human rights movement. Over the last two years AI groups have started up in Bulgaria, the Czech and Slovak Federal Republic, Hungary, Poland, Romania, the Soviet Union and Yugoslavia, and are winning publicity and support for its international work against human rights violations.

José Estuardo Sotz, paralysed by a "death squad" bullet in Guatemala, surrounded by cards and letters from AI members in Europe

The possibilities were highlighted in Hungary, where the new AI group's public appeal for José Estuardo Sotz, a six-year-old boy paralysed by a "death squad" bullet intended for his father, resulted in a major documentary report on Guatemala produced by Hungarian television.

An ambitious translation program to make information about AI widely available is under way. Leaflets about AI have been published in each major eastern and central European language and since December 1990 the *AI Newsletter* has been published in Russian. The 1989 death penalty report *When the State Kills...* was published in Russian and an AI information office has been set up in Moscow. In Hungary and Poland AI members, for the first time, translated the summary of the *1989 Amnesty International Report*. Members of the Slovenia AI group in Yugoslavia met to translate the *1988* and *1989 Amnesty International Reports* and other publications into Slovenian. Selling these publications raised funds to finance other activities such as publishing a monthly newsletter.

In the 1970s and 1980s western European sections were instrumental in trying to develop contacts and avenues for getting AI's information to interested people in eastern and central Europe. Leaflets were translated into the languages of these countries: in Austria they were placed in shops frequented by tourists from Hungary and Yugoslavia; they were handed out to the Soviet sailors who regularly docked in Spain and to the conference delegates and touring performers who visited Finland and the Netherlands.

Despite the serious economic and political problems in central and eastern Europe, the members of these groups are dedicated to campaigning for better human rights all over the world. Appeals from these countries add a new and important dimension of pressure on target governments. By raising human rights awareness in their own societies, these young AI groups can also make a valuable contribution to entrenching the observance of human rights in their own countries.

0251

AI's work with refugees

Since the mid-1980s, many European governments have adopted increasingly strict policies towards asylum-seekers. For example, as part of the process for achieving the single market within the European Community (EC) by the end of 1992, the member states are taking steps to cooperate with one another in imposing visa requirements on nationals of certain countries and sanctions on transport operators that carry people who do not have the required visas or travel documents. AI opposes the forcible return of any person to a country where they risk being imprisoned as a prisoner of conscience, tortured or executed, and is concerned that visa requirements and sanctions may obstruct such people from obtaining access to refugee determination procedures. This concern is intensified when states cooperate in the imposition of such measures.

The threat of fines or sanctions may lead transport operators to prevent asylum-seekers from boarding without visas. Even if airline staff and other transport workers feel compelled to allow some asylum-seekers to board because of the risks they otherwise face, this forces such workers — who are not trained to determine who is a refugee — into making potentially life or death decisions.

In some European states border procedures lack essential safeguards and asylum-seekers have been refused access to the refugee determination procedure and returned directly to their country of origin without any proper examination of their asylum claim.

For example, during May and June 1989, over 3,500 Turkish nationals, mostly Kurds, applied for asylum on arrival in the UK. AI received reports that as many as one hundred Kurds — possibly many more — were returned to Turkey after only a cursory examination by immigration officials at the airport without their applications for asylum being referred to the established refugee determination authority.

The individuals concerned were allegedly refused permission to contact the United Nations High Commissioner for Refugees or other refugee assistance agencies, and their asylum applications were not passed to the UK refugee determination authority for proper examination. Lawyers acting on behalf of 23 of those so expelled obtained a judicial review in the High Court in London; in each of the 23 cases the UK authorities subsequently conceded that the border officials had acted illegally.

In July 1990 over 20 Somalis were refused entry into Italy and returned to Somalia, where they were immediately arrested. Some were beaten at the airport. They were held for several weeks at the National Security Service's regional headquarters in Mogadishu, where there have been many reports of torture of political prisoners in recent years.

These are just some of the many examples which point to the urgent need for European governments to ensure asylum-seekers access to fair and impartial refugee determination procedures. As AI's refugee work has developed, AI sections across Europe have been closely monitoring their government's refugee policies and practices and raising issues of AI concern with their governments and their representatives to the European Community.☐

Human rights violations in Europe

The shifting pattern of events in Europe has been mirrored by a shift in AI's concerns in the region. The most dramatic change in AI's work occurred at the end of the 1980s, as countries which for years had received thousands of appeals for prisoners of conscience opened the doors of their jails.

Throughout the 1970s and 1980s imprisonment on grounds of conscience in eastern and central Europe and the USSR had been a major concern in the region, with AI working on behalf of thousands of prisoners in Bulgaria, Czechoslovakia, the GDR, Hungary, Poland, Romania, the Soviet Union and Yugoslavia. By the end of 1990 most of them had been released, and former prisoners of conscience Vaclav Havel and Lech Walesa had become President of the Czech and Slovak Federal Republic and President of Poland respectively.

By November 1989 the Bulgarian people had won new political freedom. The censorship laws were relaxed and articles in the Penal Code which outlawed freedom of speech were repealed. Many known prisoners of conscience were released and independent political groups emerged. Judicial reforms followed in March 1990 which guaranteed the right to defence in all phases of the legal process. In January 1991 all remaining prisoners sentenced for political offences were released under an amnesty for "crimes against the republic".

Sweeping political changes in Romania followed the overthrow of President Ceausescu in December 1989, but some human rights abuses continued. In June 1990 thousands of workers, many of them miners, were called into Bucharest when violent disturbances followed the eviction of anti-government protesters from University Square. The workers openly attacked those they considered to be government opponents with clubs, pickaxes and other weapons while the security forces stood by. There were many reports of official encouragement and control of these mobs. Over one thousand people were detained, many after being beaten. Most of them were prisoners of conscience held for short periods.

In many countries legislation previously used to imprison prisoners of conscience was amended or repealed. The USSR is publicly committed to bringing its legislation into line with international standards on human rights. In 1989 the Congress of People's Deputies began a program of reform by abolishing laws penalizing peaceful freedom of expression. However, about 20 known or suspected prisoners of conscience are still being held in the USSR. The authorities have increasingly used administrative measures rather than the criminal law to detain prisoners of conscience for short periods; AI received information on over 2,000 such cases in 1989.

As the first year of the new decade ended, Albania became the last country in Europe to end the wholesale suppression of peaceful political dissent. Between January and March 1991 some 700 political prisoners were released. At the end of March 1991 the Albanian authorities claimed that no more political prisoners were being held, but unofficial sources said that at least 40 remained in detention, among them people convicted of offences such as "espionage" and "treason".

Most of the prisoners of conscience in Europe today are young men jailed for their conscientious objection to military service. The United Nations has recognized that conscientious objection to military service is a legitimate exercise of the right of freedom of thought, conscience and religion as laid down in the Universal Declaration of Human Rights. AI has taken up as prisoners of conscience the cases of thousands of conscientious objectors across Europe.

The right to conscientious objection is not recognized in Albania, Bulgaria, Cyprus, Greece, Romania, Switzerland or Turkey, or by the USSR authorities. None of these countries offer alternative civilian service, and those who refuse to perform military service because of their religious or moral objections are routinely imprisoned.

In Cyprus conscientious objectors face multiple prison sentences while at any given time in Greece about 400 Jehovah's Witnesses are serving prison sentences averaging four years for their conscientious objection. Some face the additional punishment of five years' deprivation of their civil rights.

In Switzerland, where a total of 581 people were sentenced to prison terms in 1990 for refusing to perform military service, a national referendum held in June 1991 resulted in a majority vote to amend the penalties for certain categories of conscientious objection.

Over the past three years the Czech and Slovak Federal Republic, Hungary and Poland have all introduced legislation allowing conscientious objectors to perform community service work as an alternative to conscription.

In other countries, such as France, the alternative civilian service is up to twice as long as military service. AI believes that prolonged civilian service may be punitive, and urges governments to introduce civilian alternative service of comparable length to the period of military conscription.

Torture and ill-treatment remain long-standing concerns in Europe, east and west. In Turkey, for instance, thousands of detainees were reportedly subjected to systematic torture in police custody; they were blindfolded, stripped naked, beaten and subjected to electric shocks. At least 10 people have reportedly been tortured to death in Turkey in the last year. In 1990 torture or ill-treatment of those in police or prison custody was reported in Albania, Austria, Denmark, France, Greece, Italy, Portugal, Romania, Spain, Turkey, the USSR, the UK and Yugoslavia.

Albanian refugees arriving in western European countries in 1990, some of whom were recently released political prisoners, spoke of many hundreds of political prisoners being held in labour camps and of political detainees being regularly tortured to obtain confessions. Until then strict official censorship had ensured that little information about opposition to the government reached the outside world.

Allegations of torture and ill-treatment in Austrian police custody have continued into the 1990s. Detainees in police custody were reportedly subjected to deliberate physical violence during interrogation, such as near suffocation and burning with cigarettes. One such victim was an 18-year-old Yugoslav, detained in

Yugoslavia (above): Ethnic Albanians demonstate in Kosovo province, February 1990. Since 1981 ethnic conflict in Kosovo has resulted in widespread violations of human rights © Sipa Press

Romania (above left): Miners attack government opponents in Bucharest, June 1990 © Associated Press

0252

January 1990, who alleged that police officers interrogating him about an attempted theft made him strip, burned him, pushed sharp objects under his fingernails and beat his genitals with a ruler. As a result, he says, he confessed to robberies which he had not committed. The court ordered a medical examination, which confirmed injuries consistent with his allegations. His trial was the first in recent years known to AI in which an Austrian court declined to admit evidence on the grounds that it might have been procured through torture.

Allegations of extrajudicial executions have been a concern in the UK since the early 1980s. Between November 1982 and June 1991, 71 people, mostly Catholics, were killed by UK security forces in Northern Ireland. Many of the victims were unarmed. AI has been concerned by reports that the security forces may have deliberately killed suspected members of armed opposition groups rather than arrest them. Official investigations have failed to res[redacted]hese allegations. Investigati — to the 1982 killings of six unarmed people were obstructed by senior officers of the Royal Ulster Constabulary (RUC) who falsified and concealed crucial information. Although an official inquiry concluded that RUC officers had conspired to pervert the course of justice, the government stated in January 1988 that the officers would not be prosecuted for reasons of "national security" and that the report of the inquiry would not be made public.

United Kingdom: Fergal Caraher, aged 20, was shot dead by British soldiers at a border checkpoint in Northern Ireland in December 1990. His brother Michael, who was also unarmed, was seriously wounded in the same attack © *Pacemaker*

There were reports from Albania that border guards regularly shot without warning people trying to leave the country without official permission. One refugee, Vasilis Mathios, alleged that his son and three others were killed by border guards with bayonets in December 1990 while trying to cross into Greece. However by the beginning of 1991 large numbers of Albanian citizens were leaving the country without hindrance from border guards.

Nationalist and ethnic tensions across the region have provided the context for governments to order or condone human rights abuses. On 19 March 1990 a large crowd of Romanians attacked the headquarters of the Democratic Alliance of Hungarians in Romania in Tirgu Mures. Many of the crowd had been transported from neighbouring villages armed with axes, pitchforks and scythes specifically for this purpose, allegedly with the complicity of local officials. Many ethnic Hungarians were brutally attacked in full view of police and military personnel who reportedly did not intervene to protect them. This incident led to serious intercommunal violence the following day in which five people died and 269 were injured. Those arrested in connection with the events were overwhelmingly members of the Gypsy and Hungarian ethnic minorities.

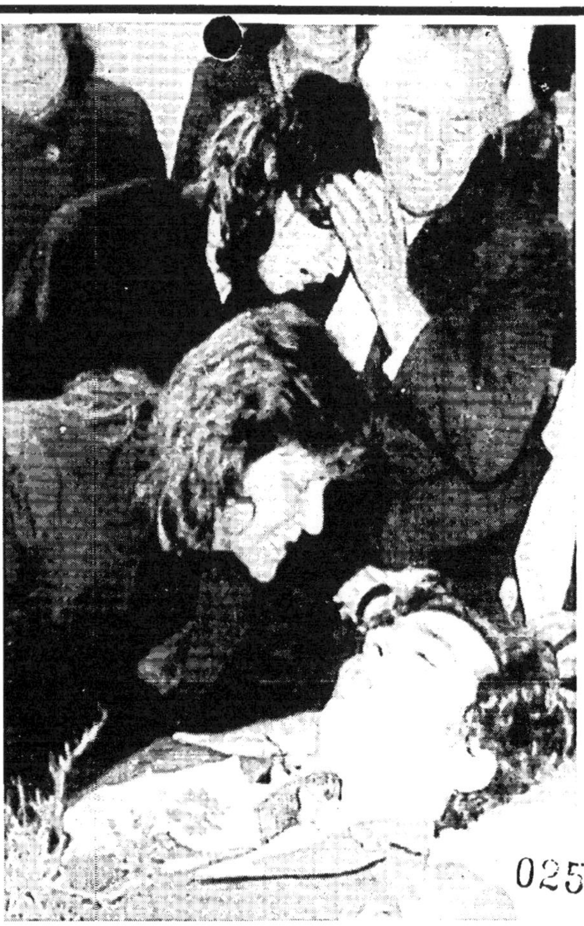
0253
Albania: Mother and fiancée mourn over the body of Arben Broci, killed during demonstrations in April 1991 © *Associated Press*

But some governments have responded to pressure for change. In November 1989 the new Bulgarian administration announced an end to key aspects of the official policy of assimilating ethnic Turks, ending several years of fierce repression of the ethnic Turkish population. They are now permitted to choose their own names, speak Turkish and practice the Islamic religion.

Eastern and central Europe have experienced a revolution in the name of democracy, but some new-found freedoms are vulnerable and without protection in law. Some of these countries face political and economic instability and widespread nationalist tension, circumstances in which governments often resort to human rights violations. And the experience of western Europe shows that wealth and democracy do not always guarantee fundamental rights and freedoms. The cold war may be over, but the war for human rights continues.□

The death penalty

The good news is that Europe is rapidly moving towards the complete abolition of the death penalty. In 1990 alone Andorra, The Czech and Slovak Federal Republic, Hungary and Ireland abolished the death penalty for all crimes; Romania became completely abolitionist on 31 December 1989.

In 1990 and 1991 the Netherlands, Portugal, Romania, Spain and Sweden ratified the Second Optional Protocol to the International Covenant on Civil and Political Rights, the first treaty of worldwide scope aimed at the abolition of the death penalty.

Albania, Poland, Turkey, the USSR and Yugoslavia retain and use the death penalty, but there are positive signs of change in all of these countries. Although Yugoslav courts sentenced four people to death in 1990, no executions were reported. In December the Yugoslav republic of Croatia adopted a new constitution abolishing the death penalty; Slovenia had done so in 1989.

According to the Polish press there have been no executions since April 1988, and the death penalty is abolished in the draft Penal Code currently under discussion in Parliament. Albania reduced the number of capital offences from 34 to 11 in 1990. No executions have been carried out in Turkey since 1984, and under the Anti-Terror Law passed in April 1991 all existing death sentences were commuted to life imprisonment.

In the USSR legislation which would restrict the scope of the death penalty has been deferred since 1988. In 1990, 445 death sentences were passed in the USSR and 195 people executed. However, the first known group seeking abolition of the death penalty was formed in 1990 and in 1991 the government made death penalty statistics public for the first time since 1934.

Mistakes occur in all judicial systems, and states which carry out executions risk killing innocent people. In the UK, the "Guildford Four" were released after 15 years of wrongful imprisonment in October 1989, when the appeal court ruled that the police had lied about their confession statements. When the four were sentenced in 1975 the judge had told them: "had capital punishment been in force, you would have been executed". Only the worldwide abolition of the death penalty can prevent such errors of judgment from becoming lethal.□

SUDAN

Positive steps overshadowed

OVER 200 prisoners of conscience arrested over the past two years have been freed after the Head of State, Lieutenant-General Omar Hassan al-Bashir, announced on 30 April that all political prisoners were to be released. Among those released were Sadiq al-Mahdi, former Prime Minister; Mohamed Ibrahim Nugud, leader of the Sudanese Communist Party; and Dr Ushari Ahmed Mahmoud.

However, AI has learned that at least 60 prisoners of conscience remain in detention. One of them, Gordon Micah Kur, reportedly started a hunger-strike in May.

More suspected government opponents have been arrested since then and there are fears that they might be prosecuted under a penal code introduced in March 1991, based on the government's interpretation of Islamic law (the *Shari'a*). This provides for the imposition of the death penalty on people convicted of apostasy (abandoning Islam), and has raised concern that members of the secular opposition and various religious orders could be brought to trial on this charge.□

USSR

Alternative to military service

ON 14 February 1991 the Soviet news agency TASS announced that the USSR parliament would soon consider a draft law on an alternative to military service. The civilian alternative service would be open to those unable to perform military service because of their "religious or other convictions". The length of alternative service would be three years.

Provisions for an alternative service have already been introduced by several republics, although such provisions are not recognized by the central authorities and are not always accompanied by appropriate enabling legislation. The Russian Republic, for example, has yet to make the necessary legal provisions for an alternative service, although the right to conscientious objection on religious grounds was recognized in October 1990. At present "evading regular call-up to active military service" in the USSR is punishable by up to five years' imprisonment.

In June AI was working for the release of some 14 conscientious objectors imprisoned in the USSR.□

YUGOSLAVIA

Police ill-treatment of ethnic Albanians continues

AI is concerned about continuing allegations of ill-treatment by police in Kosovo of ethnic Albanian citizens under arrest.

On 13 May around 6pm a police patrol on the outskirts of Peć stopped a car and ordered Marjan Vataj, Nduc Kabashi and Tomë Kabashi, all ethnic Albanians, to get out, put their hands up and lie down on the road. After searching them, the police reportedly beat them. They were then taken to the police station, where they were further beaten, until they were released around 11pm, apparently without charge.

Over the last two years, AI has received hundreds of similar allegations of ill-treatment by police in Kosovo. Although it is not possible for AI to assess the veracity of all such reports, their seriousness and frequency indicate a pattern of systematic disregard for elementary human rights in police dealings with ethnic Albanians in Kosovo.

AI has also received reports that police in Croatia have ill-treated ethnic Serbs. AI took action concerning the alleged ill-treatment of 14 Serbs suspected of involvement in shootings in the Plitvice national park on 31 March, and of journalist Predrag Kojović, reportedly beaten by Croatian police when he visited a troubled area on the Croatian border in early May.

AI urged that these allegations be investigated by an independent and impartial body and that the methods and findings of such investigations be made public. AI also urged the authorities to ensure that police are instructed to operate in accordance with internationally established rules, as laid down in the United Nations Code of Conduct for Law Enforcement Officials.□

COLOMBIA

Government urged to dismantle paramilitary forces

A four-member delegation, including AI's Secretary General, Ian Martin, visited Colombia in May to raise continuing concerns about widespread human rights violations.

The delegation held extensive and constructive talks with President César Gaviria and other government officials. AI urged that the paramilitary forces which continue committing human rights violations with impunity be dismantled and that those responsible for extrajudicial executions and "disappearances" be brought to justice.

AI's Secretary General addresses the National Constituent Assembly of Colombia

The National Constituent Assembly, currently in the process of re-writing Colombia's Constitution, invited AI's Secretary General to address it. In his speech Ian Martin said: "In Colombia the need to enshrine clear and unequivocal safeguards in the Constitution clearly acquires particular relevance and urgency in view of the dramatic and escalating levels of human rights violations in recent years... There is compelling evidence that paramilitary forces have formed an integral part of a counter-insurgency program adopted by the Colombian armed forces in which not only members of guerrilla organizations but all those perceived to be sympathizers or supporters of armed opposition groups have become potential targets for human rights violations."

AI called on the Assembly to ensure that the new Constitution contains clear and precise provisions establishing and regulating the accountability of the Colombian armed forces to the constitutionally elected authorities.

The speech, which received widespread media coverage, was rejected by the Colombian Government. Interior Minister Humberto de la Calle Lombana called it "unilateral" and "exaggerated".□

KUWAIT

Appeal to stop unfair trials

IN June AI appealed to the Kuwaiti authorities to stop the trials of those suspected of collaboration with Iraqi forces during their occupation of Kuwait. The proceedings in these trials have been unfair and should be brought into line with international standards.

AI's appeal followed the preliminary report of its delegate to the trials and the imposition of the first death sentence by the Martial Law Court. Twenty-eight more death sentences were subsequently passed; defendants were convicted of offences ranging from joining the Iraqi popular army to running a school during the occupation. On 26 June all death sentences were commuted to life imprisonment.

AI welcomed the commutations but said that extensive human rights violations are continuing in Kuwait and that the authorities have not taken effective steps to end arbitrary arrests, "disappearances", torture or deaths in custody, and possible extrajudicial executions.□

NEPAL 0251

Call for reform

AI is calling on the recently elected Government of Nepal to take steps to prevent the recurrence of the widespread human rights violations which took place before an interim government was appointed in April 1990. In particular, AI is urging the new government to introduce legislation to support the constitution promulgated under the interim government, which provides increased protection for human rights. The organization also recommends that laws and practices relating to arrest and detention be amended to incorporate safeguards provided in international human rights treaties to which Nepal has acceded.□

ETHIOPIA

A new chance for human rights

SEVENTEEN years of brutal repression ended in Ethiopia in May 1991 when President Mengistu Haile-Mariam fled into exile and opposition forces defeated the Ethiopian armed forces. Peace talks in London, chaired by the United States of America, confirmed the Ethiopian People's Revolutionary Democratic Front (EPRDF) as the new interim government in Addis Ababa. The Eritrean People's Liberation Front, allied to the EPRDF, declared itself the provisional government in Eritrea but said that an internationally supervised referendum will be held to decide the future status of Eritrea. It was agreed at the London talks that a broad-based transitional government will soon be formed in Addis Ababa to prepare for multi-party elections.

Hundreds of political prisoners went free, including prisoners of conscience held since 1979. Some were released under a partial amnesty after President Mengistu's departure; others walked out of prison when resistance to the opposition forces collapsed.

An AI report published on 30 May, *Ethiopia: End of an era of brutal repression — a new chance for human rights*, concluded a detailed account of gross human rights violations by the Mengistu government with an appeal to the new authorities to adopt an eight-point human rights agenda.

AI is monitoring the situation of several hundred former officials now detained in Addis Ababa, Asmara and elsewhere. The authorities have said they will receive fair trials in the presence of international observers.□

Palestinian defendants await hearings in the military court in Gaza City

ISRAEL AND THE OCCUPIED TERRITORIES

Military courts in the Occupied Territories

THOUSANDS of Palestinian civilians are tried every year before military courts in the Occupied Territories, most charged with violent offences such as throwing stones. After arrest they are held in prolonged incommunicado detention and are not normally brought before a judge for 18 days. Confessions obtained during this period of incommunicado detention are often the primary evidence against defendants.

Detainees are routinely subjected to torture or ill-treatment, including beatings all over the body, hooding, sleep and food deprivation, and confinement in small dark cells referred to as "closets". Some of these methods may be consistent with secret official guidelines allowing "moderate physical pressure".

Improper pressures are exerted on defendants to plead guilty and enter into a plea bargain with the prosecutors. Confessions cannot be effectively challenged in court and those who contest charges may find their trials delayed for many months. Many defendants thus plead guilty simply because the sentences they are likely to receive are often shorter than the probable period of pre-trial detention. Moreover, those who are convicted after a full trial usually receive much heavier sentences than those who enter into plea bargains. Under such circumstances, the fundamental right to a fair trial is prejudiced.

AI's concerns on these issues are outlined in a paper entitled *Israel and the Occupied Territories: The military justice system in the Occupied Territories: detention, interrogation and trial procedures*, published in July 1991. AI is calling on the Israeli Government to introduce safeguards against torture and ill-treatment and to take steps to ensure that defendants receive a fair trial.□

0255

ARGENTINA

Attacks on government critics

A wave of violent attacks and other forms of harassment has been reported against organizations and individuals who have publicly criticized President Carlos Menem or his government. Hebe de Bonafini, president of the organization Mothers of Plaza de Mayo, began to receive telephone death threats in February 1991, after she attacked President Menem's decision to pardon the former members of the military junta prosecuted for human rights violations. The headquarters of the organization were subsequently broken into four times.

The latest death threat against Hebe de Bonafini was received on 22 May 1991, the same day that film director Fernando Solanas was shot and wounded in both legs by an unknown assailant. The shooting occurred shortly after the publication in the newspaper *Página 12* of an interview with Fernando Solanas in which he publicly criticized President Menem.

No evidence has emerged linking the government or security forces to these incidents. However, AI is concerned that no one has been brought to justice for these abuses and because the victims appear to have been selected because they criticized the government. AI is calling on the authorities to ensure the safety of those threatened, investigate the threats on the life of Hebe de Bonafini and the shooting of Fernando Solanas, and see that those responsible are brought to justice.□

AI visits Haiti

AN AI delegation visited Haiti in May to assess the human rights situation. The delegates had talks with President Jean-Bertrand Aristide, who took office in February 1991, and government officials. They also met victims of human rights abuses, members of human rights groups and church representatives.□

AMNESTY INTERNATIONAL NEWSLETTER is published every month in four languages to bring you news of AI's concerns and campaigns worldwide, as well as in-depth reports. Available from Amnesty International (address below)

AMNESTY INTERNATIONAL, 1 Easton Street, London WC1X 8DJ, United Kingdom. Printed in Great Britain by Flashprint Enterprises Ltd. London. Available on subscription at £7 (US$12.00) for 12 issuse. ISSN 0308 6887

법 무 부

인권 2031-152 503-7045 1991. 8. 8.

수신 외무부장관

참조 국제기구조약국장

제목 정치범 및 양심수 개념 정의에 대한 의견 송부

1. 귀부 국연 2031-1804('91.7.19)와 관련입니다.

2. 위 호로 정치범 및 양심수의 개념 정의에 대한 귀부 자료를 접수하였는 바, 동 자료에 대한 당부의 의견을 별첨과 같이 송부하오니 업무에 참고하시기 바랍니다.

첨 부 : 의견서 1부. 끝.

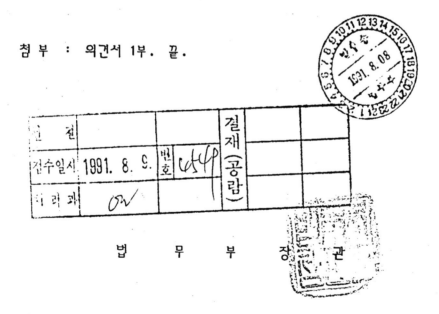

선 결			결재(공람)		
접수일시	1991. 8. 9.	번호	45411		
처 리 과					

법 무 부 장 관

0256

의 견

1. 정치범과 양심수 구별에 대한 문제점

o A.I.가 정치범과 양심수를 구별하여 정치범에 대해서는 석방을 요구하는 것이 아니라 사법절차의 공정성(신속한 공개재판, 가혹 행위 금지등)만을 요구하고있는것이 사실이며, 따라서 정치범의 존재자체는 인권문제가 아니므로 존재자체를 부인하는 것은 적절한 대응방법이 아니라는 점은 일응 수긍할 수 있음

o 그러나, A.I.이외의 인권단체나 미하원의 인권모임등 다른 단체에서는 정치적 동기로 구금된 사람에 대해서도 석방을 요구 하고 있으며(90.10.30.자 미하원의원 연서 서한등 참조), 특히 국내언론이나 국민들이 정치범과 양심수의 개념을 명확히 구별하지 못하고, 정치적인 이유로 부당하게 구금되어 있는 사람이라는 정도로 그 개념을 이해하고 있으므로, 정치범의 존재를 인정하는 것은 A.I.에 대한 대응방법으로는 적절할지 몰라도, 기타 인권단체나 국내 보도용으로는 적절하지 않다고 생각됨

0257

o 따라서 정치범의 개념이 일반에게 명확하게 인식되지 않고있는 현 단계에서는 정치범의 존재를 인정하는 것 보다는 "정치적인 이유로 부당하게 구금되어 있는 사람은 없다"는 입장을 취하는 것이 국내적으로 오해의 소지를 불식시킬 수 있는 방안이라고 생각됨

2. 양심수에 대한 대응방안

o A.I.에서는 양심수로 분류된 사람에 대해서는 즉각적인 석방을 요구하고 있는 바, 아국의 범법행위자가 양심수로 분류되지 않도록 범법행위의 내용을 설명하는 노력이 필요하다는 점에 이견이 없음

o 단, 범법행위의 설명에 있어서는 A.I.가 폭력을 옹호하거나 사용한 경우에는 양심수에서 제외하고 있으므로, 집회와 시위의 폭력성, 이적표현물의 폭력 혁명론, 근로자들의 생산시설 점거, 파괴등의 측면을 중점 설명하는 것이 필요하다고 판단됨

0258

3. 참고사항

o 양심범의 개념

. 사상.신념만의 이유로 투옥, 구금되어 있는 사람

. 확신범.정치범등 유사개념과 혼용되고 있음

o 유사개념

. 확신범 (Überzeugungsverbrechen)

- 도덕적.종교적 또는 정치적 신념을 동기로 하여 현행 법질서에는 위반되더라도 보다 큰 정의와 선을 실현 하는데 이바지 한다는 확신을 가지고 행한 범죄

- 사회변혁기에 빈발하여 형법상의 책임을 어떻게 인정할 것인가가 항상 문제되고 있음. 즉 형법의 범위내에서 해결하기 어려운 정치적 내용을 포함하고 있음

. 정치범 (Political offence, politische Straftat)

- 국가의 실정법에 위반되는 목적 및 수단으로 정치적 활동을 하거나 이에 참가함으로써 성립되는 범죄

- 비합법의 요건은 시대나 정부에 따라 다르고, 실정법의 해석도 주관적.상대적이므로 본인의 자연적 악성보다는 권력의 작용인 인위에 기초하여 성립되는 경우가 많음

0259

o 양심범의 유례

- 중세 정치.종교 일체의 권위주의로부터 인간의 사상적. 윤리적 자유를 추구하는 과정에서 "양심의 자유"를 주창하는 부류를 이단시 하여 "양심범"으로 억압, 처단

- 1922년 독일형법초안에서 금지규범을 인식하고 있음에도 불구하고 양심상의 이유 또는 이와 유사한 윤리적인 동기에서 범행을 할 권리가 있다고 믿도 금지규범을 위반한 자를 "확신범"으로 규정

- 1923년 독일의 "자유형집행의원칙 (Grundsätze über den Vollzug der Freiheitsstrate)" 제52조는 확신범에 대한 형의 집행상의 특전부여규정 설치

- 1933년 나치정권 수립으로 확신범 특별처우원칙은 폐지되고 오히려 정치범으로 개념 수정되어 탄압의 대상

- 1949년 서독 헌법 제4조는 국민이 그 양심에 반하여 병역의무 수행을 강제받지 않을 권리 인정

0260

ㅇ 양심범처벌과 관련된 법적 검토

. 주요 선진제국의 대부분이 양심의 자유를 기본적 인권으로 선언 (프랑스 인권선언, 버지니아 권리장전, 바이마르헌법, 서독, 일본, 스위스, 터어키, 포르투갈, 칠레, 인도, 브라질 등 헌법)

. 양심 (또는 양심상의 결정)에 반하는 행위를 강요받지 아니하는 자유와 관련하여 증언거부. 기자의 취재원에 관한 진술거부. 사죄광고를 명하는 판결. 병역거부 등이 논의되나, 보다 더 큰 정의의 실현 또는 기본적 인권의 내재적 한계 등을 논거로 양심의 자유에 속하지 않는다는 것이 통설

. 양심 (또는 양심상의 결정)이 내심의 작용에 그치는 한 무제한이나 이를 외부에 대하여 표현하거나 실현하려는 경우 이미 양심의 영역을 벗어난 표현의 자유문제가 되어 헌법유보 및 일반적 법률유보에 의한 제한을 받게 된다는 것이 통설 (대법원 및 일본판례 동 취지)

. 야당 및 재야 일부에서 거론하는 양심범(수)의 개념은 순수한 양심 또는 표현의 자유와 결부된 법적개념 이라기 보다 오히려 정치적 행위의 동기, 수사과정에서의 인권 침해 등의 면만을 강조한 투쟁적.정치적 개념이라 할 것이고, 내심을 실현하는 과정에서 다른 국민 및 사회에 끼친 악영향 및 실현결과로서의 실정법위반을 외면한 법적 안정성 및 구체적 타당성을 결한 논리라 할 것임

0261

기안용지

분류기호 문서번호	국연 2031 - 28676 (전화:)	시행상 특별취급	
보존기간	영구·준영구. 10. 5. 3. 1	장	관
수신처 보존기간			
시행일자	1991. 8. 12.		

보조기관	국 장	전 결	협조기관		문서통제 1991. 8. 13 통제관
	심의관				
	과 장				
기안책임자		송영완			발송인 발송 1991. 8. 13 외무부

경 유 수 신 참 조	주영대사	발신명의	
제 목	A.I. 연례보고서에 대한 설명자료		

연 : 국연 2031-27106 (91.7.19)

1. 연호, 91년도 A.I. 연례보고서에 대한 법무부 설명자료를 별첨 송부하오니 A.I. 접촉시 적의 설명하고 결과 보고바랍니다.

2. 91년도 A.I. 연례보고서중 서울구치소 재소자문제 및 고문문제등에 관하여는 "남한의 민족 및 인권을 위한 국제법률가위원회"가 91.1.23. 유엔인권사무국에 제출한 진정서에 대한 아국정부의 답변서(영문, 91.5.6자)를 참고하시기 바랍니다.

0262

(2)

첨 부 : 1. 91년도 A.I. 보고서에 대한 설명자료 1부.

2. 아국정부 답변서(91.5.6자) 1부. 끝.

0263

법 무 부

인권 2031- 11077　　503-7045　　1991. 7. 30

수신 외무부장관

참조 국제기구조약국장

제목 '91 AI 연례 인권보고서에 대한 당부입장

'91 AI 연례 인권보고서에 대한 당부입장을 별첨과 같이 송부하오니 AI 본부측에 적의 설명될 수 있도록 조치하여 주시기 바랍니다.

첨부 : '91 AI 연례 인권보고서에 대한 당부입장. 끝.

1991. 7. 30
법무부

법 무 부 장 관

결재(공람)

1991. 7. 31

24829

0264

'91 국제사면위원회 연례인권보고서에 대한 당부입장

===

양심수 문제에 관하여

o 국제사면위원회는 폭력을 사용하거나 옹호하지 않음에도 신념, 피부색, 성별, 인종적 기원, 언어, 종교를 이유로 구금된 자를 양심수로 정의하는 것으로 알고 있음

o 그러나 그러한 정의도 대상을 판단함에 있어서 명확한 개념이 되고 있지는 아니함. 즉 신념이나 종교를 이유로 구금된 자라고 한다면 어떤 신념이나 종교를 가지고 있다는 사실만으로 구금된 자를 말하는 것인지 아니면 그뿐만 아니라 어떤 신념이나 종교에 입각한 행동이 비폭력적인 경우에도 모두 양심범에 해당한다는 것인지 명백하지 아니함

o 국제사면위원회의 정의가 만약 전자를 의미한다면 대한민국에는 신념, 피부색, 성별, 인종적 기원, 언어, 종교만을 이유로 구금된 자는 없음

o 즉 아국은, 단순히 어떤 사람이 공산주의사상을 가지고 있다는 이유로, 또는 특정종파를 믿는다는 이유로, 피부가 검다는 이유로, 여자라는 이유로 구금을 한 사람은 없음

0265

o 그러나 국제사면위원회의 정의가 후자를 의미한다면, 즉 어떤 사람이 신념이나 종교에 따라 적극적 또는 소극적 행위를 한 경우에 그 행위가 비폭력적인 한 즉각 석방되어야 할 양심수라는 견해에는 전혀 수긍할 수가 없음

o 왜냐하면 어떤 신념이나 종교에 따라 행해진 행위가 비록 비폭력적이라고 할지라도 앞에서 설명한 바와 같이 폭력적 행위에 못지않게 어떤 국가나 사회, 그리고 다른 개인에게 큰 피해와 고통을 줄 수 있기 때문임

o 또한 국제사면위원회의 양심수라는 개념이 어떠한 국가나 사회에 있어서도 적용될 수 있는 인류의 보편적 양심에 기초한 것이라고 믿기 때문에 더욱 후자의 견해는 수긍할 수 없는 것임

o 그리고 어떤 신념이나 종교에 근거하여 행해진 적극적, 소극적 행위에 대해 법적 제재를 가하는 범위는 그 나라의 역사, 환경, 전통, 가치, 윤리 등에 따라 차이가 있을 수 있으며, 결국 그 내용은 그 나라의 국민총의에 바탕을 둔 헌법과 법률로 나타난다고 할 것임

o 지금까지 국제사면위원회에서 양심수로 거론된 사람들을 보면 단순히 그들이 어떤 신념과 의사를 가지고 있다는 이유만으로 구금된 사람은 없음. 그들은 그 신념과 의사를 이유로 적극적 행위에까지 나아간 것이며, 그것이 실정법을 위반하게 된 것임.

0266

즉 북한을 위해 국가기밀을 수집하는 등 간첩행위를 한다거나 몰래 북한을 왕래한다거나 폭력혁명을 선동하는 유인물을 제작, 배포하는 등의 실정법 위반행위를 한 것이며, 이러한 범법행위자에 대하여는 모두 법앞에 평등이라는 차원에서 일반인과 똑같이 사법적 절차에 따라 처리되어야 할 것임

○ 만약 이들도 즉각 석방되어야 할 양심수라고 주장한다면 그것은 각국이 가지고 있는 공산주의자들의 활동에 관한 규제법률, 출입국에 관한 법률, 집회에 관한 규제법률 등에 위반된 사람들이 모두 사상이나 여행, 의사표현의 자유에 대한 신념에 따라 행동을 한 사람들이므로 즉각 석방되어야 한다는 주장과 마찬가지라 할 것이며, 오히려 보편적 양심에 반하는 명백히 부당한 주장이라 할 것임

사형집행된 형사범(14명)이 '89년도의 2배라는 주장에 관하여

○ 1990년중 사형이 집행된 14명은 모두 강도살인 또는 살인범들로서 헌법과 법률에 의한 적법한 재판절차를 거쳐 최종적으로 대법원의 확정판결을 받은 사람들임

0267

고문, 가혹행위 주장에 관하여

o 우리 정부는 국민의 인권을 최대한 보장하고, 특히 부당한 구속과 수사과정에서의 고문행위를 근절하기 위한 나름대로의 노력을 기울여 왔음

o 이에 따라 검사의 구속장소 감찰을 강화하여 월 1회에 한하지 않고 필요할 때마다 수시로 감찰하고, 자체 구속장소가 없는 수사관서에 대하여도 불법사례유무를 조사하여 주사과정상 적법절차가 준수되도록 하고 있으며, 고문, 가혹행위가 발생하는 경우 관련자를 엄중 처벌하여 왔을 뿐 아니라 앞으로도 수사기관에 대한 지휘감독을 보다 철저히 하고 수사요원에 대한 지속적인 인권의식 함양을 통하여 수사과정에서의 인권침해 방지에 만전을 기하도록 함과 아울러 과학적 수사장비와 수사기술을 도입하여 수사를 과학화하도록 노력할 것임

o 최근 사회 일각에서 정부가 고문, 가혹행위로 사건을 조작하였다는 비난을 하고 있으나, 이러한 주장은 사실에 반하는 것으로 부당하다고 아니할 수 없음

0268

국가보안법 문제에 관하여

o 국가보안법은 국가의 안전을 위태롭게 하는 반국가활동을 규제함으로써 우리의 존립기반인 자유민주주의 체제를 수호하고 국민의 자유와 생존권을 보장하기 위하여 제정된 법률로서, 북한의 대남적화통일전략이 변하지 않고 있고 국내 좌익세력의 체제전복위협이 상존하고 있는 이상 여전히 필요한 법률이라 아니할 수 없음

o 정부는 기본권 제한의 최소화 원칙을 선언한 헌법의 정신과 국가보안법의 제정목적에 충실하기 위하여 그동안 법조문을 엄격히 해석, 적용하여 왔으며, 최근 언론. 출판. 예술. 창작의 자유와 관련하여 국가보안법이 적용된 것은 민중폭력혁명 내지 계급투쟁을 선전.선동하거나, 좌익적 시각에서 역사를 왜곡하고 대한민국의 정통성을 부정하거나, 김일성 주체사상을 찬양. 동조하거나 고려연방제 등 대남전략차원의 북한주장을 그대로 대변하는 등 국가의 존립과 안전 및 자유민주적 기본질서에 직접적인 위해를 가하는 행위에 한정된 것이었음

o 정부는 그동안 위와 같은 원칙에 따라 국가보안법을 엄격하게 해석, 운용하여 왔으며, 국제정세의 변화와 남북관계의 진전에 능동적으로 대처하고 국민의 기본적 인권을 보다 광범위하게 보장하기 위해 남북교류협력에관한법률을 제정하고 국가보안법을 개정하는 등 전향적 조치를 취한 바 있음

0269

o 남북교류협력에관한법률은 정부의 승인하에 한 국민이 북한을 방문하거나 북한시민을 한국에 초청하는 것을 허용하였으며, 상호교역과 협력사업에 종사할 수 있도록 하고 있음

o 또한 개정된 국가보안법은

- 국가보안법을 해석, 적용함에 있어서 국민의 기본적 인권을 최대한 보장하여야 한다는 규정을 신설하고

- 간첩죄에 있어서 국가기밀의 행위를 세분하여 국가기밀을 국가의 안전에 중대한 불이익을 회피하기 위하여 한정된 사람만이 접근할 수 있는 것과 그밖의 것에 대하여는 법정형을 완화하였으며

- 금품수수, 잠입.탈출, 찬양.고무, 회합.통신 등 행위는 국가의 존립.안전이나 자유민주적 기본질서를 위태롭게 한다는 정을 알면서 행한 경우에만 처벌하도록 하였고

- 국외공산계열과 관련한 범죄를 삭제하는 한편, 불고지범, 예비.음모죄 등의 범위를 대폭 축소하였음

0270

박기래는 간첩죄로 사형을 선고받은 후 전향을 거부하였다는 이유로 8년간 복역한 후에야 무기징역으로 감형되었으며, 조기석방에서도 배제되었다는 주장에 대하여

o 박기래는 간첩죄 등으로 '74.10.13 구속되어 '76.2.10 대법원에서 사형을 선고받고 복역하던중 '83.8.12 사형에서 무기징역으로 '91.2.25 무기에서 징역 20년으로 2차에 걸쳐 감형되었음

o 박기래는 자신의 범죄행위를 깊이 반성하고 '85.3.29 전향하였으며, 전향후 수형생활이 양호하고 행형성적이 우수하며 일정기간을 복역하는 등 가석방 요건에 해당되어 '91.5.25 사회에 조기 복귀할 수 있도록 가석방 조치하였음

o 국제사면위에서 박기래가 전향을 하지 않아 감형이나 가석방 등의 은전을 받지 못하고 있다는 주장은 사실과 다름

0271

'90.8. 서울구치소에 수용된 재소자 100여명은 소란에 참가하였다는 이유로 체벌 및 폭행을 당하고 수시간동안 시승시갑을 당하였으며 재소자와 그의 가족들이 법원에 고소장을 제출하였다는 주장에 대하여

o 서울구치소 재소자 소란행위의 진상

- '90.8.27 서울구치소는 재소자들에게 반입된 도서 3권을 관계 직원이 규정에 의하여 허가하지 아니하자 재소자 3명이 부당하게 불허된 것이라고 주장하며 소란을 피우는 것을 직원이 만류하여 각자의 방으로 돌려 보냈던 바, 이들은 여러 사동에 수용된 재소자들에게 "교도관들에게 폭행을 당하였다"고 허위 선동하여 많은 재소자들이 근무자의 제지에도 불구하고 불법으로 교무과 사무실과 그 복도로 몰려가서 시설일부를 점거한 채 유리창문 등 기물을 파손하고 책상 등 사무집기로 바리케이트를 설치하며 약 3시간동안 불법 집단난동을 부렸음

- 이들은 해산을 종용하는 교도관들의 설득에도 계속 불응하고 더욱 극렬히 항거하므로 수용된 많은 다른 재소자들의 수용생활의 안정과 구치소 질서의 회복을 위하여 규정에 따라

0272

시승시갑하여 진압하였고, 진압과정에서 일부 직원과 재소자가 재소자들이 휘두른 각목에 맞아 교도관 8명이 사회병원에 이송 되고 재소자 이성우가 비골골절상을 입은 사실이 있었으나 교도관들이 재소자에게 폭행이나 체벌을 가한 사실은 없음

o 관련자 조치

- '90.8.27 서울구치소에서의 재소자 집단소란은 구치소 당국의 엄정한 조사결과 재소자들의 위법 부당한 집단행위로서, 시설 파괴와 직원폭행 등 수용질서를 문란케 하는 범법행위임이 명백하여 주동자 2명을 형사입건하여 현재 1심 재판중에 있으며

- 한편 재소자들의 불법행위를 관계규정에 따라 정당하게 진압한 교정공무원의 행위는 정당한 공무집행행위이며, 재소자를 학대 하거나 사적인 제재를 가한 사실이 없는데도 재소자 이명학 (국보, 삼민동맹사건, 시립대 4년, 22세)의 부 이철이 등은 '90.9.18 구치소장 등을 독직폭행혐의로 고소하여, 사직당국의 조사결과 '90.11.23 무혐의 처분을 받음

0273

기안용지

분류기호 문서번호	국연 2031 32813 (전화:)	시행상 특별취급	
보존기간	영구·준영구. 10. 5. 3. 1	장	관
수신처 보존기간			
시행일자	1991. 9. 3.		

보조기관	국 장	전결	협조기관		문서통제 1991. 9. 04 통제관
	심의관				
	과 장				
기안책임자		송영완			발송인 발송 1991. 9. 04 외무부

경유 수신 참조	주영대사	발신명의	
제 목	국내 인권문제 (A.I. 대책)		

1. 법무부에 의하면, A.I. 회원들이 금년도 2/4분기중 우리정부에 보내온 석방탄원 서한을 검토한 결과, 설명자료를 기송부한 구속자외에 오영식등 19명이 주요 석방요구자로 분석되었다 합니다.

2. 상기 19명에 대한 범죄사실, 처리현황, 정부입장등 법무부가 작성한 설명자료를 별첨 송부하오니 동 내용을 A.I. 측에 적의 설명되도록 조치하여 주시기 바랍니다.

첨 부 : 설명자료 1부. 끝.

0274

법 무 부

인권 2031- 12375 503-7045 1991. 8. 27.

수신 외무부장관

참조 국제기구조약국장

제목 국제사면위원회 관련 협조 요청

1. 국제사면위원회 회원들이 '91. 2/4분기중 각 부처에 보내 온 특정인 석방탄원 편지를 검토한 결과, 귀 부를 통하여 국제사면위에 기히 설명한 자 외에 오영식 등 19명이 주요 석방요구 대상자로 분석되었습니다.

2. 동인들에 대한 범죄사실 및 처리현황, 정부입장 등 설명자료를 별첨과 같이 송부하오니 동 내용이 국제사면위원회 본부 측에 적의 설명될 수 있도록 조치하여 주시기 바랍니다.

첨 부 : 설명자료 1부. 끝.

발송 '91. 8. 27 법무부

법 무 부 장 관

28563

0275

공 란

공 란

공 란

공 란

공 란

공 란

공 란

공 란

공 란

공 란

Uzl/

관리 번호	91 —1036

원 본

외 무 부

종 별 :

번 호 : UKW-1785 일 시 : 91 0903 1120

수 신 : 장관(국연,기정)

발 신 : 주 영 대사

제 목 : A.I. 아국관련 기사

연: UKW-1177

1. A.I. 기관지 NEWSLETTER 91.9. 판에 연호 "서승" 관련 기사가 게재되었는 바, 해당부분 아래와 같이 보고함.

UNFORTUNATELY, THE TIME SPENT WAITING FOR RESULTS CAN SELDOM BE MEASURED IN WEEKS, SOME CAMPAIGNS TAKE DECADES. GROUPS IN GERMANY, NEW ZEALAND AND THE UNITED STATES OF AMERICA KEPT UP THE PRESSURE ON THE SOUTH KOREAN AUTHORITIES FOR 19 YEARS, REPEATEDLY URGING THEM TO RELEASE PRISONER OF CONSCIENCE SOH SUNG. HE FINALLY WENT FREE IN FEBRUARY 1990 AND LATER SAID: "IT IS MY HOPE THAT THOSE WHO WORKED SO HARD ON MY BEHALF WILL NOW CONTINUE TO WORK TO BRING ABOUT THE RELEASE OF ALL THE OTHER POLITICAL PRISONERS INSOUTH KOREA. "SOH SUNG, WHO NOW LIVES IN THE USA, VISITED SEVERAL A.I SECTIONS IN EUROPE DURING A.I'S 30TH ANNIVERSARY MONTH, SPEAKING TO A.I MEMBERS AND PUBLICIZING HUMAN RIGHTS ISSUES THROUGH INTERVIEWS WITH THE LOCAL AND NATIONAL MEDIA.

2. 상기 NEWSLETTER 지 전문은 금파편 송부 예정임.끝

(대사 이홍구-국장)

예고: 91.12.31 일반

일반문서로 재분류 (1991 .12.31. .

국기국 안기부

0286

PAGE 1 91.09.04 22:55

외신 2과 통제관 CH

항

주 영 대 사 관

영국(정) 723-878 1991. 9. 3.

수신 : 장관

참조 : 국제기구국장

제목 : A.I Newsletter 송부

연 : UKW-1785

연호 A.I. Newsletter 91년 9월판 1부를 별첨 송부합니다.

첨부 : Newsletter 91. 9판 1부. 끝.

발송 1991. 9. 03 주영국대사관

주 영 대 사

주영국대한민국대사관인

선 결			결재(공람)		
접수일시	1991. 9.5.				
처리과	01/49324				

0287

AMNESTY INTERNATIONAL
NEWSLETTER SEPTEMBER 1991 VOLUME XXI ● NUMBER 9

UGANDA

Thousands detained without trial

THOUSANDS of civilians have been detained by the army in northern Uganda since late March in counter-insurgency operations. Betty Bigombe, the Minister of State responsible for the north, announced in mid-May that 3,000 "rebels" had been captured in one sub-county alone. Most of them were apparently released uncharged, but hundreds are still imprisoned. At least 600 people have reportedly been convicted of aiding and abetting the insurgents and are being held in prisons near Kampala. Others remain in military custody without charge or trial.

Eighteen prominent northerners arrested in March and April were charged with treason on 7 May. Among them were three members of parliament: Omara Atubo, who was then also Minister of State for Foreign Affairs; Irene Apiu Julu; and Zachary Olum. Some of the accused appeared in court showing signs of beatings and ill-treatment; their lawyers claimed they had been beaten by soldiers only hours before being flown from the north to the Kampala courtroom. The government says it is investigating these allegations.

The treason charges automatically prevent the defendants from applying for bail for 16 months. There is no guarantee that they will be brought to trial within that time. The charges are framed only in general terms and the authorities have so far failed to support them with detailed accusations. AI is concerned that vague treason charges are being used by the authorities to hold the 18, and others similarly charged, when there is little or no evidence on which to bring prosecutions before the courts.

AI has already adopted three of the 18 as prisoners of conscience; all three are community leaders from Gulu, the northern capital, who were arrested after protesting about the ill-treatment of civilians detained by soldiers.☐

MOROCCO

Long-term 'disappeared' released

OVER 200 "disappeared" Western Saharans — "Sahrawis" — held by the Moroccan authorities in secret detention centres for up to 15 years, are reported to have been released since mid-June. Several hundred civilians from the south of Morocco and the Western Sahara reportedly "disappeared" in detention between November 1975, when Morocco first occupied the former colony of the Spanish Sahara, and 1987. They were arrested by Moroccan security forces and imprisoned in secret jails. Until these releases, the Moroccan authorities had consistently denied, to both AI and the United Nations (UN), that they were holding the "disappeared" Sahrawis.

Reports indicate that all Sahrawi detainees have been released from secret detention centres in Laayoune, and from Qal'at M'gouna, where over 200 people are believed to have been held in extremely harsh conditions. Over 40 inmates are said to have died there since 1975. AI is concerned that other "disappeared" may still be detained in other secret centres.

Those released include some of the 88 Sahrawis for whom AI groups have been appealing since the late 1970s; other cases were described in AI's November 1990 report, *Morocco: "Disappearances" of people of Western Saharan origin (AI Index MDE 29/17/90)*. Three of the Mayara brothers, former members of the Royal Moroccan Army, are said to have been released: they were among the first Sahrawis to be arrested and to "disappear" in November 1975. Several people who "disappeared" in 1987 while a UN technical mission was visiting the Western Sahara have also apparently been released, including Sidati Selami ould Lahbib, a blind radio announcer, and his daughter, Atfarah, and Ghalia ment Abdellahi ould Mohamed, an agricultural engineer.

Embarca ment Talab ould Husein, a former radio announcer in Laayoune in the Western Sahara, "disappeared" in September 1979 when she was taken from her home by plainclothes police officers. She is among those reportedly released since mid-June

The releases come in the context of the UN settlement for the Western Sahara, under which a proposed cease-fire on 6 September 1991 is to be followed in early 1992 by a referendum to decide the Western Sahara's future.

AI welcomed the releases of some of the "disappeared" but has urged the Moroccan Government to appoint an impartial commission of inquiry to investigate the fate of all the "disappeared", to bring to justice those responsible for "disappearances" and other human rights violations, and to provide medical treatment and compensation to those now released.☐

SOUTH AFRICA

Internal Security Act amendment fails to provide adequate safeguards

ON 21 June the South African Parliament amended several provisions of the Internal Security Act (1982), including the clauses providing for long-term detention without charge or trial. The Parliament repealed Sections 28 and 50A, which permitted detention without trial for "preventive" reasons. The amended law will be issued as the Internal Security and Intimidation Amendment Act.

Police powers under Section 29 of the 1982 Act, which had permitted them to detain people without charge indefinitely, incommunicado and in solitary confinement for interrogation, were reduced but remain extensive. Under the new law this section, associated in the past with the torture and deaths of detainees, will still enable the police to detain people incommunicado for 10 days, and then apply to a judge to renew the detention for further 10-day periods. Detainees will only have access to a lawyer if the police apply for such an extension, but judges will not be required to call the detainee's legal representative or the detainee to give evidence.

The new law also allows the police discretion not to inform detainees' relatives and lawyers of their detention, and to deny independent medical access to detainees if, in their view, either step would hamper police investigations. The amended Section 29 still falls far short of international standards, and permits conditions where torture or "disappearances" can occur.

In the past, Section 29 detainees were often held for many months without their cases ever being referred to a judge. In July 1991, for example, an inquest court heard evidence regarding the death in June 1990 of a Section 29 detainee, Donald Madisha, who allegedly committed suicide after nearly five months in solitary confinement.☐

0288

CAMPAIGN FOR PRISONERS OF THE MONTH

Each of the people whose story is told below is a prisoner of conscience. Each has been arrested because of his or her religious or political beliefs, colour, sex, ethnic origin or language. None has used or advocated violence. Their continuing detention is a violation of the United Nations Universal Declaration of Human Rights. International appeals can help to secure the release of these prisoners or to improve their detention conditions. In the interest of the prisoners, letters to the authorities should be worded carefully and courteously. You should stress that your concern for human rights is not in any way politically partisan. In *no* circumstances should communications be sent to the prisoner.

USSR

Sergey Osnach: ***aged 21, he was arrested on 13 April 1991 in the Ukrainian town of Shostka and charged with "evasion of regular call-up to active military service" under Article 72 of the Ukrainian Criminal Code.***

Sergey Osnach stood trial on 18 June 1991 for refusing to perform military service in the Soviet army on the grounds that it "does not defend the motherland and the nation, but the 'socialist choice'".

Sergey Osnach

He was sentenced to 18 months' compulsory labour. Known as "building the national economy", this involves working at a site designated by the authorities. Compulsory labour is less severe than imprisonment in a corrective labour colony, but the prisoners are still under surveillance and restricted in their movements. AI believes that restrictions placed on prisoners of conscience while doing compulsory labour are analogous to imprisonment and therefore urges their immediate and unconditional release.

Conscientious objection to military service is recognized by the United Nations as a legitimate exercise of the right of freedom of thought, conscience and religion. AI considers as prisoners of conscience those who for reasons of conscience or profound conviction arising from religious, ethical, moral, humanitarian, philosophical, political or similar motives refuse to perform armed service or undertake any other direct or indirect participation in wars or armed conflicts. AI believes that the true number of detained conscientious objectors in the USSR may be higher than the 13 for whose release the organization was working in July 1991. Of these, most are Jehovah's Witnesses and five were convicted in the Ukraine.

On 14 February 1991 the Soviet news agency TASS announced that the USSR parliament would soon consider a draft law which provides for a civilian alternative service independent of the USSR armed forces. This would be open to those unable to perform military service because of their "religious or other convictions". The length of alternative service would be three years, one year longer than compulsory military service.

■Please send appeals for the immediate and unconditional release of Sergey Osnach, and for the introduction of a civilian alternative to military service to: Leonid Kravchuk, Chairman of the Ukrainian SSR Supreme Soviet/ Verkhovny Soviet UkrSSR/ 9. Kiev/Predsedatelyu KRAVCHUKU L.M./USSR.□

MOROCCO

Kouin Amarouch: ***a 61-year-old former warrant officer, married with six children, he served 10 years in prison for his alleged participation in an attempt on King Hassan II's life. Although he completed his sentence in 1981, he was not released and continues to be held incommunicado, in conditions so harsh as to threaten his life.***

Kouin Amarouch was tried in March 1972, together with 1,080 other members of the Moroccan armed forces, after allegedly participating in an attack on the Royal Palace of Skhirat on 10 July 1971 during celebrations for the King's birthday. Seventy-five of those convicted were sentenced to prison terms, the rest, all cadets, were acquitted. Kouin Amarouch received a 10-year prison sentence.

Following a second coup attempt in 1972, 11 of those held to be responsible were sentenced to death and executed, and 32 others were sentenced to between three years' and life imprisonment.

Those imprisoned after these trials were first held at a prison where they were allowed family visits. However, on 7 August 1973, 61 of the prisoners, apparently those sentenced to three or more years' imprisonment, were transferred to the secret prison of Tazmamert, part of a remote army base in the Atlas mountains in south-eastern Morocco, where Kouin Amarouch and others who have survived the harsh conditions there continue to be held.

Kouin Amarouch is held in total isolation from the outside world, in a small separate cell with little ventilation or light, which becomes extremely cold in winter and extremely hot in summer. The food is poor, and no medical treatment is provided.

Of the 61 prisoners who were transferred to Tazmamert in 1973, at least 29 are said to have died due to the harsh conditions. Of those who have survived, the sentences of all but eight have expired. Kouin Amarouch was due to be released in 1981.

■Please send courteous letters appealing for his release, if possible in French, to: His Majesty King Hassan II/Palais Royal/Rabat/ Morocco.□

BHUTAN

0280

Ratan Gazmere: ***a lecturer in biology at the Institute of Education in Samchi, he was arrested on 8 October 1989 for writing and distributing a booklet entitled*** **Bhutan: We Want Justice,** ***which criticized a government decree he claimed discriminated against Bhutan's ethnic population. He is reportedly being held in untried detention in Wangdi prison in the capital, Thimpu.***

Many Nepali-speaking Bhutanese, who constitute between 20 and 35 per cent of the population in Bhutan, also protested against the April 1989 decree, which required all Bhutanese citizens to wear national dress in public and speak the official language (Dzongkha) or else risk a fine or one week's imprisonment.

Ratan Gazmere's brother, Jogen Gazmere, was arrested in Jhapa, Nepal, in late 1989 along with Sushil Pokhrel and Tek Nath Rizal, a former counsellor to the King of Bhutan who was in exile in Nepal. They were subsequently returned to Bhutan, where they were charged with "anti-national" activities. All three had been active in a Nepal-based organization called the People's Forum for Human Rights, which advocates greater rights for the Nepali-speaking minority in Bhutan. Two students active in the People's Forum, Bakti Prasad Sharma and Biswanath Chhetri, were arrested in Bhutan in late 1989 and charged with "anti-national" activities.

Ratan Gazmere

AI has written to the Government of Bhutan expressing concern and calling for the immediate release of the six men. A reply was received from the government on 9 November 1990 which stated that the King had opposed the bringing to trial of the six men because they are charged with a crime that would carry the death sentence. No further information has been received.

■Please send courteous letters expressing concern and requesting that Ratan Gazmere be immediately and unconditionally released to: His Majesty Druk Gyalpo Jigme Singye Wangchuck/ Thimpu/Bhutan.□

FOCUS amnesty international

0290

No more excuses

AI was founded in outrage at a world in which governments routinely violated the human rights of their people. Thirty years on and the outrage is stronger. Governments which could once plead ignorance have been deprived of that excuse by the strength of the international human rights movement, yet governments around the world continue to sabotage the hopes and dreams that millions of ordinary people have risked their lives and freedom for. The challenge for the 1990s is to build human rights awareness in the broadest sense of the term: to ensure that no government can cloak illegal activities in secrecy; that the rights of even the poorest citizens are upheld; and to build a truly international movement capable of taking action against human rights violations wherever they occur. There are no more excuses.

In Brussels AI members set up 529 life-size silhouettes in the *Grote Markt*; each one described a specific human rights violation

So AI's 30th anniversary — 28 May 1991 — was no cause for celebration. Human rights campaigners around the world were out on the streets, staging demonstrations, raising the public profile of human rights issues through the local or national news media, or simply writing letters of protest to those responsible for torture, "disappearances", the death penalty and executions. It was a day for business as usual. AI's volunteer members — the backbone of its international human rights campaign — share the belief that ordinary people can and should take action in support of the human rights of others. From over 150 countries, members are prepared to write letters, send telegrams and organize campaigns to stop human rights abuses wherever they occur. By the beginning of AI's 30th year, the number of AI members and regular donors surpassed one million — a compelling reminder to all governments of the depth of feeling that exists around the world about human rights.

Many sections used the occasion of the 30th anniversary to organize campaigns aimed at reminding the public that two out of three people are still ruled by governments that torture and kill their citizens; millions of people are still risking their lives simply by peacefully exercising their rights to freedom of thought and expression. The campaigns focused on boosting public support and awareness, and urging more people to join AI and become active in the campaign, write their own letters and take part in wider membership activities.

AI groups around the world campaigned with the slogan "no more excuses". In India, groups in the Madras area made up hand drawn posters urging people to join the fight to stop human rights abuses. Members set up a bookstall in the town centre and displayed publicity material.

Delegates at the annual meeting of the AI section in Abeokuta, Nigeria, one of the longest established sections in Africa

In Pakistan, a concert for human rights featured a group called "Milestones", and brought AI's message to hundreds of people in Karachi. The Karachi group also held a workshop and educational session for new groups-information in Sindh and Baluchistan, and organized a poster competition around the theme of "state and private torture".

Across Europe and North America, AI sections marked the anniversary with seminars, concerts, vigils and walks. Francophone and Flemish members in Belgium used the 30th anniversary to make a special appeal to young people to learn about human rights violations and become active in AI. In Brussels the section arranged 529 life-size silhouettes in the *Grote Markt* in the centre of the city. The silhouettes represented those people suffering human rights abuses who cannot stand up themselves and be seen by the world. The 30th anniversary ceremonies in Ireland included traditional music and poetry readings.

In the Czech and Slovak Federal Republic, former prisoner of conscience Jiri Wolf was involved in a public reading of the poetry of Nguyen Chi Thien, a Vietnamese poet and prisoner of conscience who has spent half his life in jail because of the political nature of his poetry. Many of those who attended the event later wrote letters to the Vietnamese Government, urging the release of Nguyen Chi Thien.n.

The first AI group in Paraguay was officially launched to coincide with AI's 30th anniversary. AI was opened up to the general public at a forum attended by 250 people; there was wide media coverage and support from local non-governmental organizations, political parties, trade unions, the Catholic Church and former prisoners of conscience. Sixty people joined AI on the spot. Week-long activities to mark the 30th anniversary included an art exhibition and a death penalty seminar. A prominent Paraguayan journalist offered to broadcast Urgent Action appeals for the victims of human rights violations, and two priests undertook to contribute to the costs of letters sent by AI members. The potential for AI development seems limitless, even in a country which was virtually closed to the outside world during the 35 years of the Stroessner dictatorship.

AI members confronted the Moroccan ambassador at his home after he refused to receive them at the embassy. This meeting was the first direct contact between a Moroccan Government representative and AI members in an Arab country. In Algeria the AI group in Tizi Ouzou attracted 750 people to a public meeting about human rights violations in Morocco. Many of those attending signed petitions and took away materials which would enable them to write their own letters.

In the Netherlands police officers who are members of AI played a special part in the Morocco action. They sent letters directly to their counterparts in the Moroccan security forces, appealing directly to them about human rights violations.

Peter Benenson, the founder of AI, spent the 30th anniversary in Spain, where he undertook a series of media interviews on behalf of the AI section and a public meeting in Seville. Later in the year, he will tour parts of Europe, Asia and South America. His objective will be to help the AI membership structures in the countries he visits to encourage even more people to care about the human rights of others and to turn that care into action by becoming active in AI. The simple vision he had for AI in 1961 is still intact. If we continue to develop a successful multicultural movement, he said, "our single candle will light the world".

The campaign focused on boosting public support and urging more people to join AI

In Australia, AI members organized an "Australians Who Care" action, designed to publicize AI's work to a broad range of Australians, and to enrol new members. The section devised a special letter-writing program, using the 30th anniversary as a theme.

In Egypt, AI groups organized a public evening event in Cairo which attracted wide media coverage. About 200 people attended the event, which included songs, poetry readings, video shows relating to AI's work, and a photograph exhibition.

AI members also take part in international campaigns to draw attention to human rights abuses in specific countries. During the 30th anniversary month, AI members in 34 countries campaigned against human rights violations in Morocco.

In Denmark, France and the Netherlands, members raised their concerns directly with representatives of the Moroccan Government. In Jordan, a delegation of

But what is it all for? The actions taken by our members can have a positive impact on the lives of women and men around the world. AI's work focuses on individual prisoners: getting them released from prison, calling for fair trial, trying to stop them from being tortured or killed. And while many governments continue to order or condone human rights violations, action brings results. Sometimes getting the simple message to the prisoners that they are not alone, that the world has not forgotten them, gives them the strength to go on. "I will never forget the day AI took up my case", a former prisoner of conscience from Argentina wrote, "because before then we didn't have a real hope to leave the prison alive... somewhere in the world thousands of people knew about me." A woman detained in South Africa wrote: "Your letter strengthened me... Now I feel that I am not alone at these hard and troubled times."

The Madras group in India relaxes after a hectic campaign

Anniversary greetings

AI is by no means the only representative of the international human rights movement. Local, national and international groups devote all or part of their efforts to different aspects of the struggle for social, political and economic rights. AI received dozens of anniversary greetings from such organizations around the world, below are excerpts from just a few.

United Nations: "I wish to congratulate all the members and collaborators of AI on thirty years of work dedicated to the cause of human rights. AI, by its revolutionary approach of mobilizing millions of people all over the world in the fight for respect for human rights, has provided inestimable support to its own work and that of the United Nations." Jan Martenson, Under-Secretary-General for Human Rights

World Confederation of Labour: "We extend our hands to you in warm congratulations and admiration for the great and noble tasks that you have been doing to defend and advance the rights, freedom, respect for and the dignity of man."

Al Haq, the West Bank affiliate of the International Commission of Jurists (Israeli-Occupied Territories): "The work of AI continues to have our deepest respect and admiration. Please accept our best wishes for many more decades of success in defense of human rights around the world."

International Federation of Action of Christians for the Abolition of Torture: "AI...represents a huge hope, hope for the prisoners who are forgotten, tortured, condemned to death; hope for the families and the groups who offer resistance to oppression...Be sure that we remain, in entire independence, side by side with your efforts."

The **Australian Senate** agreed to a resolution, congratulating AI on its 30 years of work on behalf of prisoners around the world, but "noting with regret that the work of AI remains indispensable because of continuing, worldwide human rights abuses, including torture and summary execution of political prisoners."

Twelve former political prisoners from Swaziland: "We would like to congratulate AI for achieving its 30th anniversary of relentless work with a clear record of commitment to Human Dignity worldwide. This is no doubt a very demanding task especially in this our beloved world which is dominated by greed, selfishness and abuse of Human Rights. Today we talk about democratic changes sweeping the world especially our continent Africa and we are proud to give credit to your good organisation AI for consistently having exposed infringements on the dignity of human kind...The pressure you exerted on the government during our trial and the detentions was of great help and no wonder we were released on the eve of the arrival of the delegation you sent here to talk to the government. We thank you very much and urge you to carry on with this good work all over the world."

World Confederation of Organizations of the Teaching Profession: "In the name of more than 13,000,000 teachers, we present our congratulations as well as our thanks for your invaluable service in the cause of human rights... We wish you every success in your future actions but hope that all such action will become less and less necessary."

0291

AMNESTY WORKS

0292

Prisoners of conscience are released every day.

On Thursday 7 February 1991 the Egyptian State Security Intelligence Police arrested Dr Mohammed Mandour, a member of the board of trustees of the Egyptian Organization of Human Rights (EOHR). No reason was given for his arrest; like many others he was told only that he was under administrative detention. He was held incommunicado, raising fears that he would be subjected to physical or psychological torture. Within 24 hours, the AI network was mobilized. Hundreds of members all over the world were asked to send telegrams, letters and faxes to the Egyptian authorities urging the immediate and unconditional release of Dr Mandour. Ten days after his arrest an EOHR representative visited Dr Mandour in prison and reported that he had been subjected to "persistent and savage torture". He had been stripped of his clothes, blindfolded, handcuffed and subjected to electric shocks. Again the membership was notified and again hundreds of appeals flooded the offices of the Egyptian Minister of the Interior. On 26 February, AI received the following message from Dr Mandour:

"I would like to express my deep gratitude for your efforts which resulted in my release February 23 1991... I would also like to relate to you the effect your efforts had upon my morale when I learned of them... I felt I was no longer alone, and the weight of insults, humiliation and physical abuse I had suffered, became much lighter... Your efforts have strengthened my faith in our common movement for human rights and have increased my confidence that our efforts are worthwhile." In May, Dr Mandour travelled to Europe to address the annual meeting of the German Section.

Some long-term prisoners of conscience only regain their freedom when the governments that put them in prison fall from power. In Ethiopia, Mulugetta Mosissa *(right)*, a prisoner of conscience since 1980, walked free when opposition forces defeated the Ethiopian army and took Addis Ababa on 28 May 1991. Here he is seen reunited with his wife, Namat, herself a prisoner of conscience from 1980 to 1989, and his 11-year-old son, Amonsissa, who grew up in prison with his mother and whom Mulugetta Mosissa had never seen

Unfortunately, the time spent waiting for results can seldom be measured in weeks, some campaigns take decades. Groups in Germany, New Zealand and the United States of America kept up the pressure on the South Korean authorities for 19 years, repeatedly urging them to release prisoner of conscience Soh Sung. He finally went free in February 1990 and later said: "It is my hope that those who worked so hard on my behalf will now continue to work to bring about the release of all the other political prisoners in South Korea." Soh Sung, who now lives in the USA, visited several AI sections in Europe during AI's 30th anniversary month, speaking to AI members and publicizing human rights issues through interviews with the local and national media.

Many other former prisoners have been inspired to work on behalf of those who have not yet been released. An ethnic Albanian, whose identity must be kept secret to ensure his safety, served five years in prison for advocating autonomy for the Albanians of Kosovo in Yugoslavia. "My comrades and I were constantly subject to torture", he later wrote. "I shall not describe the details; you know them already through your involvement with political prisoners in every corner of the world. I want to express my respect for AI, for all its activists in all countries...The fight against torture is the fight against the greatest degradation a human being can undergo although I believe that the victims of torture are always morally superior to the torturers. It is because of this that I consider it indispensable to set up an AI group here, too. It seems to me very important to found an association for young people here which will work on human rights violations in other countries: the fate of all political prisoners is very similar."

Not every campaign or action brings about the release of prisoners or better treatment for detainees. But at the very least, continuing campaigns, appeals and publicity remind governments that whatever human rights violations they attempt will be exposed to the harsh glare of inter-

South Korean prisoner of conscience Soh Sung goes free after 19 years in prison

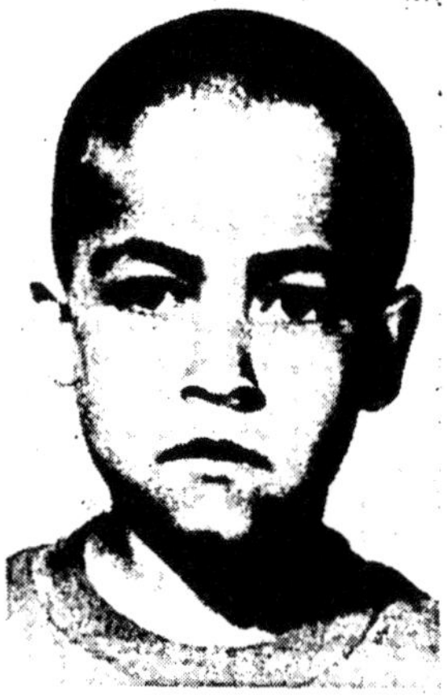

Nahamán Carmona López

Dr Mandour addresses AI's German Section, May 1991

national scrutiny. And that kind of pressure forces changes that might save lives.

Nahamán Carmona López was 13 years' old when he was kicked to death by police officers in Guatemala City. An active campaign of inquiries and publicity by Covenant House — an organization that works with street children in Guatemala — and widespread international outrage led to the arrest and conviction of four policemen in connection with the crime. This was the first known sentencing of official security force agents for human rights violations since the government of President Jorge Serrano Elias came to office in January 1991.

In Morocco, Fatima Oufkir and her six children "disappeared" for 15 years after her husband, General Mohammed Oufkir, died in suspicious circumstances after being implicated in a 1972 plot to assassinate King Hassan II. No one was even sure that the family was still alive until 1987, when four of the children escaped from detention. The four made a radio broadcast and managed to speak with a French lawyer. They described how they had been moved three times during the 15 years, and how they had been kept in virtual isolation in separate windowless cells since 1977. Although the four children were quickly rearrested and returned to detention, they had alerted the outside world to their conditions, which subsequently improved. The family was moved to a farm, and began to receive medical treatment and visits from the children's grandparents. International pressure increased over the next three years, and the family was released in February 1991. Like most former political prisoners, they have not been able to obtain passports, but they appear to enjoy freedom of movement and association within Morocco.

Some long-term prisoners of conscience only regain their freedom when the governments that put them in prison fall from power. In Ethiopia, Mulugetta Mosissa and his pregnant wife, Namat Issa, were arrested in February 1980. Both prisoners of conscience, they were never charged or tried, and were never allowed to see one another, even after the birth of their son, Amonsissa. Namat Issa and Amonsissa, who spent the first nine years of his life in prison, were released in 1989. Mulugetta Mosissa continued to be detained without charge. He had been severely tortured in the first months of his detention, and was subsequently kept in harsh conditions at Maekelawi, Ethiopia's main torture centre. On 28 May 1991 — AI's 30th anniversary — the prison warders fled as forces of the Ethiopian People's Revolutionary Democratic Front advanced on Addis Ababa. Mulugetta Mosissa and hundreds of other political prisoners walked free. Mulugetta Mosissa has now been reunited with his wife, and with the 11-year-old son he had never seen.

In Kenya in 1990 the Reverend Lawford Imunde was sentenced to a six-year prison term for writing, publishing and possessing a "seditious document". The document in question was his own personal diary, which had neither been published nor even shown to anyone else. The diary was said to contain criticisms of the government, but there was no suggestion that it contained any seditious or violent plans. He was released in March 1991, when his sentence was reduced on appeal to one year. In May he wrote to AI: "I cannot thank you enough for your struggles on my behalf...Many may mishandle truth, but for all that they do not do away with it. And it is the only thing that remains when everything perishes!"

These are just a few examples of the hundreds of cases brought to AI's attention every year. In May 1991, the month of our 30th anniversary, AI learned of the release of 101 prisoners under adoption or investigation. Our task today is to increase the international pressure on behalf of the thousands of prisoners of conscience all over the world, to make tomorrow the day their freedom is restored.□

Former prisoner of conscience Vaclev Havel, now President of the Czech and Slovak Federal Republic, celebrates AI's 30th anniversary with the AI group in Denmark that campaigned for his freedom

WHAT YOU CAN DO

AI does more than just talk about human rights violations; it expects its members and supporters to take action, and to encourage others to take action too. Individuals make a difference, and even the most vicious government cannot hold out forever against the massive mobilization of ordinary people.

JOIN

Thousands of people all over the world are crying out for help. You may already sympathize with AI's aims, but we need more than sympathy. We need action. AI has offices in more than 60 capital cities around the world. Get in touch with AI in your country and tell them you want to join us, or write directly to the International Secretariat, 1 Easton Street, London WC1X 8DJ, United Kingdom.

GET ACTIVE

You may already be a member. But whatever your level of involvement, make this the year you increase your commitment, step up your level of activity. If you have not found the time to get involved, use AI's 30th anniversary year as a reason to get busy. Write a monthly letter to help a prisoner; go regularly to your local group's meetings; petition others to support the campaign for human rights.

RECRUIT

Get your friends and colleagues to join the worldwide campaign. There can't be too many people reminding governments that the world is watching when they choose to incarcerate, torture and execute their citizens.

RAISE FUNDS

All of AI's funds are raised by the members, and AI's independence and impartiality is protected by accepting no contributions from governments and by following strict guidelines on financial donations. So run a bookstall, plan a concert, hold an exhibition, organize a sponsored competition or sporting event, or simply rattle a collection tin under people's noses.

JORDAN

Martial law directives repealed

MARTIAL Law Directives giving the government sweeping powers of arrest and detention of security suspects, and providing for their trial by a Martial Law Court, were repealed in July. They had been in force since June 1967 and had facilitated human rights violations. In December 1989 the Jordanian Government had announced that martial law was being "frozen" with a view to lifting it. AI welcomed the decision to repeal the Martial Law Directives and in a message to the Jordanian Government expressed hopes for further speedy progress in human rights reforms.

Martial law, however, has not yet been formally lifted. In addition, wide powers of arrest and detention are still available under the Defence Law, in force since 1939. A draft Defence Law is currently being debated in Parliament.

The Martial Law Court will conclude the trials already initiated before it is abolished. Trials before this court have fallen short of relevant international standards for fair trial, including in capital cases. At least five people tried by this court have been executed since January 1991.□

PRISONER NEWS

AI learned in June 1991 of the release of 140 prisoners under adoption or investigation. AI took up 41 cases.

ORGANIZATION OF AMERICAN STATES

Convention on 'disappearances'

PRESSURE was stepped up within the Organization of American States (OAS) in June for concrete progress on the long delayed Convention on "disappearances".

During the 21st session of the OAS General Assembly in Santiago, Chile, from 3 to 8 June, a number of member states called on the working group studying the draft Convention to have the text ready for examination by the General Assembly in 1992.

AI has attended the OAS General Assembly under a special guest status for the past 10 years and sent a three-member delegation to the Santiago Assembly. The organization had written to all OAS states prior to the General Assembly expressing its concern over the delay in the work on the draft Convention. This Convention seeks to define the crime of enforced disappearance as well as to establish the necessary mechanisms for its prevention and punishment.

Although the main topic of this Assembly was the defence of representative democracy in the Americas, there were also important discussions on some issues within the scope of AI's work. The 1990/91 Annual Report of the Inter-American Commission on Human Rights, which was discussed at the General Assembly, analyses the human rights situation in Cuba, El Salvador, Guatemala, Haiti, Nicaragua, Peru and Suriname and includes resolutions on 86 individual cases — the largest number relating to Peru, and others concerning Argentina, El Salvador, Guatemala, Haiti, Mexico and Uruguay. However, the General Assembly did not pass resolutions on any specific countries.□

PAPUA NEW GUINEA

Military source admits violations

A Papua New Guinea Defence Force officer, Colonel Leo Nuia, confirmed in late June that serious human rights violations had been committed by troops under his command during operations on the island of Bougainville, part of North Solomons Province, in 1990. Among the violations confirmed was the extrajudicial execution of Pastor Raumo Benito and five of his parishioners on 14 February 1990. In an interview with the Australian Broadcasting Corporation, Colonel Nuia also admitted that the bodies of the victims had been dumped at sea from helicopters supplied to the defence forces by the Australian Government. The executions were among dozens of serious violations documented by AI in its report *Papua New Guinea: Human Rights Violations on Bougainville 1989-1990*, published in November 1990.

Following his public revelations, the government recalled Colonel Nuia from active service in North Solomons Province. AI wrote to the government on 28 June welcoming this step but urging it to establish an independent commission of inquiry to investigate all human rights violations reported on Bougainville since early 1989.□

AI visits Rwanda

TWO AI representatives visited Rwanda in early June to discuss the human rights situation in the country and meet government officials and others. The representatives were also allowed to meet 10 political prisoners.

Although most of the 8,000 or more prisoners arrested after a rebel attack on northern Rwanda in October 1990 were released earlier this year, several dozen civilians, about 100 Rwandese soldiers and 15 captured insurgents continue to be held.

Shortly before AI's representatives visited Rwanda, four journalists accused of writing newspaper articles expressing dissenting views were arrested.

The AI representatives expressed concern at the authorities' apparent failure to investigate allegations that members of the security forces had tortured prisoners, sometimes to death, or killed others outright. No efforts have been made to bring those responsible to justice. In many cases the authorities blamed killings on local people rather than the security forces; they admitted that no soldiers or police had been prosecuted for committing abuses since the October 1990 mass arrests.

Eighteen political prisoners convicted in early 1991, many on the basis of statements allegedly made under torture, remain in detention without their torture allegations having been properly investigated. Some of them may be prisoners of conscience.

Secret trials by court martial of government soldiers, some of whom are accused of treason, have reportedly taken place in recent months; few details of the proceedings are available, but they do not appear to meet international standards for fair trial.□

SAUDI ARABIA

Executions resume

0294

ON 24 May a Sudanese national, found guilty of murder, was executed in Saudi Arabia. This was followed by the execution of eight more people on 31 May and of a further seven on 7 June. All those executed, among them Saudi Arabian and foreign nationals, had been found guilty on criminal charges, including rape, murder, robbery and drug-related offences. AI had not recorded any executions in Saudi Arabia since July 1990 and had welcomed this as a positive development. The organization was particularly dismayed to learn of these recent executions.

AI recorded 111 executions in Saudi Arabia in 1989, and 13 between January and July 1990. Executions in Saudi Arabia are public and are usually carried out by beheading with a sword or, in the case of sexual crimes, by stoning to death.

■During the festival of *'Id al Adha* (21 to 25 June), at least 14 political prisoners and detainees, including prisoners of conscience, were released. Among them were seven of the 13 Saudi Arabian nationals who had been sentenced in 1982 in Bahrain with 60 others in connection with an alleged coup attempt in Bahrain in 1981. The 13 had been handed back to Saudi Arabia to serve their sentences in the *Mabahith al-'Amma* (General Intelligence) Prison in Riyadh. Four of them had been released in 1989. The two who remain in prison are brothers: 'Ali and Nadir Muhammad Taqi al-Sayf, who were sentenced to life and 15 years' imprisonment respectively.

Also released during the festival were Sheikh Samir 'Ali al-Ribeh, a former AI *Prisoner of the Month*, and Nasser 'Abdullah al-Yusuf, arrested in April 1988.□

INDIA

AI delegation denied access

AN AI delegation, scheduled to leave for India on 3 July, was not granted entry visas by the Indian Government. The Government informed AI on 3 July that the request for visas was still under consideration and that a decision would be reached by 15 July. As of 22 July, there was still no response from the Indian Government.

In a letter of 23 April to the Foreign Secretary, Muchkund Dubey, AI had proposed that a delegation visit three southern states: Maharashtra, Tamil Nadu and Andra Pradesh. On 11 June AI further specified that a three-member delegation proposed to visit southern India from 3 to 23 July. A Japanese member of the AI delegation was initially granted a visa on 20 June but his visa was withdrawn a few days later.□

PERU

Pattern of violations continues unabated

AN AI delegation, including the Secretary General, visited Peru in July. Meetings were held with President Alberto Fujimori, Prime Minister Carlos Torres y Torres Lara, and with representatives from the Ministries of Defence, Justice and the Interior. The delegation also held talks with the Armed Forces Joint Command and the Director General of the Peruvian National Police. In a meeting with representatives of the Public Ministry, the Attorney General announced that in the 10-year period up to the end of 1990, 5,024 "disappearances" had been registered, of which 1,011 had been clarified.

AI's delegates met these relatives of the "disappeared" in Lima

The AI delegation outlined the organization's concerns, stressing the existence of a continuing and unabated pattern of gross human rights violations — including thousands of "disappearances", torture and extrajudicial executions — as well as threats and attacks against independent and official human rights defenders.

AI pressed for the speedy and effective implementation of recommendations to help reverse the high level of "disappearances" in the zones administered by the military. These included: registers of arrests to be introduced in all military bases; detainees to be released in the presence of a representative from the Public Ministry or a judge; the Public Ministry to be strengthened with increased resources; and the International Committee of the Red Cross to be granted access to detainees in the emergency zones.

The authorities reaffirmed their policy of fully respecting human rights and assured the delegation that all alleged human rights violations would be investigated. However, AI has continued to receive information on cases of grave human rights violations perpetrated by the security forces in the emergency zones during the first 12 months of the new government.

Juan Arnaldo Salomé Adauto, for example, was reportedly tortured by the military after his detention on 24 April. He claimed to have escaped on 10 June from the barracks in Huancayo, Junín, after which he gave a detailed account of his torture to the Special Attorney for Human Rights in Huancayo. But on 22 June the emergency zone Mantaro Front Political-Military Command published an official communiqué, claiming it had investigated the allegations and concluded that Juan Salomé had never been in the custody of the military and was being manipulated by "subversive elements... and other official persons" as part of a campaign to discredit the security forces.□

SENEGAL

Casamance political prisoners released

0295

IN late May the Government of Senegal announced that a political settlement had been reached with the Casamance separatist movement and that all political prisoners from Casamance would be released and legal proceedings against them halted. Some 346 untried prisoners were released. Hundreds of suspected members of the Democratic Forces of Casamance had been arrested in 1990, although none had been tried by the time of the May releases.

From May 1990 onwards there had been an upsurge in violence in Casamance, initially by armed government opponents but subsequently reflected in the response of the security forces. AI learned of the first extrajudicial executions reported in Casamance as well as details of many new cases of torture, which had been reported in Casamance throughout the 1980s. The government has not yet made public the findings of inquiries into reports of extrajudicial killings.□

ROMANIA

Ill-treatment and torture

ALLEGATIONS that police have ill-treated detainees in Romania to induce them to sign confessions continue to be widespread. In Oradea, in the northwest of the country, Ioan Gug alleged that immediately after arresting him on 19 December 1990, following a peaceful public meeting, police officers began to hit him in the abdomen. On arrival at the police station they threw him to the floor and repeatedly hit him until he lost consciousness. When he regained consciousness he was beaten again and witnessed other detainees being similarly treated.

From Tirgu Mureş in the centre of Transylvania, where there is a large Hungarian minority, AI has received reports that detained ethnic Hungarians have been ill-treated. On 9 May, for example, Laszlo Havadtoi was stopped by a plainclothes police officer and compelled to get into a car, where he was beaten. In another case, Endre and Andor Muszka were detained on 23 November 1990 at Tirgu Mureş police station and allegedly handcuffed to a radiator, punched, hit with gun butts, and kicked by the arresting officers until approximately 10 pm, when the officers went home. The relief guard continued to beat them, apparently because they were Hungarian and had not voted for President Iliescu. They were reportedly forced to sing in Hungarian and then punished for doing this. In the morning another police officer threatened that if they did not admit to intending to attack the arresting officer they would remain in detention. After their release AI is informed that the two men received medical certificates attesting to injuries requiring up to 12 days of medical treatment.□

SRI LANKA

Delegation meets human rights groups

IN early June an AI delegation visited Sri Lanka to assess the human rights situation in the country. This was the first time since 1982 that AI has been permitted to visit Sri Lanka for research purposes. During the visit, AI's delegates met government officials and individuals active in the field of human rights. They also interviewed dozens of victims of human rights violations committed by Sri Lankan security forces or by the armed opposition Liberation Tigers of Tamil Eelam (LTTE), which effectively controls parts of the northeast of Sri Lanka.

The delegation also met members of recently established human rights bodies, including the Presidential Commission of Inquiry into Involuntary Removal of Persons, which has been mandated by the government to investigate cases of "disappearances" occurring after 11 January 1991. During the AI delegation's visit, the government announced the creation of a Human Rights Task Force, which will be responsible for registering detainees arrested under emergency regulations or the Prevention of Terrorism Act, and reviewing their treatment in detention.□

AMNESTY INTERNATIONAL NEWSLETTER is published every month in four languages to bring you news of AI's concerns and campaigns worldwide, as well as in-depth reports. Available from Amnesty International (address below)

AMNESTY INTERNATIONAL, 1 Easton Street, London WC1X 8DJ, United Kingdom. Printed in Great Britain by Flashprint Enterprises Ltd. London.

원 본

외 무 부

종 별 :

번 호 : UKW-1841 일 시 : 91 0909 1830

수 신 : 장관(국연,구일,기정)

발 신 : 주 영 대사

제 목 : A.I.활동영역 확대

1. 국제사면위(A.I.)는 9.7.(토) 요꼬하마에서 개최된 GOVERNING COUNCIL 회의후가진 성명에서,정부를 상대로만 인권침해 문제를 제기해왔던 종래의 방침을 변경, 앞으로는 반정부세력(POLITICAL OPPOSITION MOVEMENT)에 의한 살인, 인질억류등의 인권침해도 규탄할 것임을 발표했다고 당지 THE TIMES 가 9.9(월) 동경발 기사로 보도함

2.A.I.는 상기 성명에서 정부에 의한 인권침해의 방지가 여전히 주된 관심사이나스리랑카의 TAMIL TIGERS 나 페루의 SENDERO LUMINOSO와 같은 집단의 잔악한 행위에대하여도 항거해야 한다고 말했다고 전함

3.상기 GOVERNING COUNCIL 회의는 2년에 1번씩 개최되며 A.I.의 각국 국별지부(SECTION)및 국제사무국등 주요기관의 대표가 참석하는 A.I.의 정책 결정회의 임을 참고바람

4.관련 언론보도 별첨 FAX 송부함

첨부: UKWF-0367.끝

(대사 이홍구-국장)

국기국 1차보 구주국 외정실 분석관 안기부

PAGE 1 91.09.10 07:19 DQ

외신 1과 통제관

0296

09/09/91 18:35 ☎ 071 589 9134 ROK EMBASSY UK P.01

(총 1 매)

주 영 대 사 관

UKW(F) - 0367 DATE: 91.9.9.

수 신 : 장 관 (국연, 구일, 기정)

발 신 : 주 영 국 대 사

제 목 : A.I. 활동 영역 확대

(첨부물)

The Times (91.9.9,7면)

Amnesty widens its scope

From REUTER IN TOKYO

AMNESTY International, the scourge of repressive governments, says it now plans to denounce killings, hostage-taking and other human rights abuses committed by political opposition movements.

In a statement issued on Saturday after a meeting of its governing council in Yokohama, the London-based human rights organisation said it hoped this would help thousands more victims of abuse every year. "We continue to hold governments directly responsible for the protection of human rights under international law and violations by governments will remain the focus of our work," it said. "But we must confront the atrocities committed by groups like the Tamil Tigers in Sri Lanka and Sendero Luminoso (the maoist Shining Path guerrillas) in Peru."

Just as it neither supported nor opposed governments, it took no position on the resort to force by opposition groups or on their political agendas, it said. Its "sole concern" was a humanitarian one.

-0297

정 리 보 존 문 서 목 록					
기록물종류	일반공문서철	등록번호	2020020039	등록일자	2020-02-06
분류번호	736.21	국가코드		보존기간	영구
명 칭	A.I.(국제사면위원회) 보고서 및 대응활동, 1991. 전2권				
생 산 과	국제연합과	생산년도	1991~1991	담당그룹	
권 차 명	V.2 10-12월				
내용목차	* 장기수(長期囚) 문제 포함 * 한국 인권관련 보고서				

0001

가

1

주 영 대 사 관

영국(정) 723- 1005 1991. 10.1.

수신 : 장관

참조 : 국제기구국장

제목 : A.I. Newsletter 송부

A.I. Newsletter 91년 10월판 1부를 별첨 송부합니다.

첨부 : Newsletter 91.10판 1부. 끝.

발송 1991. 10. 1 주영국대사관

주 영 대 사

선 결			결재 (공람)		
접수일시	1991.10.4	번호			
처리과	54995				

0002

AMNESTY INTERNATIONAL
NEWSLETTER
OCTOBER 1991 VOLUME XXI • NUMBER 10

UNITED KINGDOM

Ill-treatment and intimidation

AI is urging the UK Government to investigate the reported ill-treatment and threats of further ill-treatment of Damien Austin, a 17-year-old Catholic from West Belfast. AI has long been concerned about the intimidation and ill-treatment of suspects in police custody in Northern Ireland, and believes that existing procedures and safeguards are inadequate to prevent such ill-treatment.

Damien Austin has been detained twice in Castlereagh interrogation centre in Belfast in recent months. He was one of 18 young people arrested in May for questioning after the death of a police officer. Austin was held for three days and alleges that the interrogating officers abused him physically and made death threats. He was released without charge, but reportedly continued to be harassed by the police.

Austin was again arrested and taken to Castlereagh on 17 August. He was examined on arrival by a doctor, who found no marks on his body. He then underwent three interrogation sessions, each lasting up to four and a half hours. He claims to have been beaten during these sessions. A duty doctor examined him the following morning, reportedly noted fresh bruising, and gave him medication for the pain.

Austin maintains that the interrogations continued and the beatings became more severe over the next two days. On the evening of 19 August he was examined by his own doctor, who filed an affidavit in the High Court stating that he found "evidence of severe assaults to his body... Damien Austin is being subjected to severe ill-treatment and the Police Doctor agreed with me on this."

After this examination Austin was allegedly told: "Complain all you want. It's going to get worse." Detectives reportedly threatened Austin with further arrest and told him he would be shot dead by the Ulster Volunteer Force (UVF), a loyalist paramilitary group. On 20 August, after further interrogation sessions, he was released without charge.☐

SRI LANKA

Human rights violations in a context of civil war

On 11 September AI issued a report on human rights violations in northeastern Sri Lanka, where violent conflict between the Sri Lankan security forces and the Liberation Tigers of Tamil Eelam (LTTE) resumed in June 1990.* The LTTE is fighting to establish a separate Tamil state — "Eelam" — in the Northeastern Province.

The report followed a two-week research visit to Sri Lanka in June. The AI team found evidence that thousands of unarmed members of the Tamil community, including women and children, had been killed or had "disappeared" after arbitrary arrest by the Sri Lankan security forces or Muslim or Tamil armed groups operating in conjunction with them. Victims had been shot, bayonetted, stabbed, hacked or beaten to death. Some were reportedly burned alive. Many people were apparently detained or killed simply because they had contact with members of the LTTE — sometimes of the most minimal kind — during the period the LTTE controlled the area.

Sri Lanka: The body of an extrajudicial execution victim was dumped in a crater and burned on tyres, allegedly by the security forces, at Kaluwanchikudy, Batticaloa District, in May 1991. The crater had been caused by an LTTE mortar bomb attack on the local Special Task Force camp in June 1990.

Evidence also emerged of serious abuses by the LTTE, who control a substantial part of the northeast, particularly the Jaffna peninsula. Victims of LTTE abuses included large numbers of Sinhalese and Muslim civilians, among them women and children, as well as Tamil people considered "traitors". The LTTE has taken people into custody, including police officers, those in government service and "dissident" Tamils. Prisoners of the LTTE have been tortured and killed outright; it was the massacre of more than one hundred police officers who had surrendered to the LTTE in June 1990 that marked the opening of the current round of civil war in the northeast.

Most of the human rights violations highlighted in AI's report — extrajudicial executions and "disappearances" — were committed by government forces in the east and in other areas under their control. On 12 June two soldiers were killed in a land-mine explosion at Kokkadichcholai, south of Batticaloa, one of the main eastern towns. In retaliation, soldiers from the local army camp went on the rampage in the nearby villages of Mahiladithivu and Muthalaikuda, killing at least 67 civilians, including women and children. Seventeen villagers from Muthalaikuda, including a 16-year-old boy, were reportedly taken to the site where the land-mine exploded, forced to circle the crater three times and then shot. Their bodies were dumped in the crater and burned.

AI has welcomed the decision by President Ranasinghe Premadasa to institute a commission of inquiry into this incident. The organization is calling for the findings of the inquiry to be made public.

The Sri Lankan Government apparently condones the summary execution of suspected members of the LTTE instead of insisting on their arrest, trial and punishment according to law. AI has submitted a number of recommendations to the government aimed at establishing viable procedures for investigating human rights violations and preventing further such abuses from occurring. The organization has suggested strengthening the work of the Commission of Inquiry into the Illegal Removal of Persons and the Human Rights Task Force, which have recently been established by the government to investigate and respond to evidence of human rights abuses. In particular, AI has urged the government to give people in the northeast greater access to these bodies.

**Sri Lanka: The Northeast — Human rights violations in a context of armed conflict (AI Index No. ASA 37/14/91)*.☐

0003

CAMPAIGN FOR PRISONERS OF THE MONTH

Each of the people whose story is told below is a prisoner of conscience. Each has been arrested because of his or her religious or political beliefs, colour, sex, ethnic origin or language. None has used or advocated violence. Their continuing detention is a violation of the United Nations Universal Declaration of Human Rights. International appeals can help to secure the release of these prisoners or to improve their detention conditions. In the interest of the prisoners, letters to the authorities should be worded carefully and courteously. You should stress that your concern for human rights is not in any way politically partisan. In *no* circumstances should communications be sent to the prisoner.

GREECE

Timotheos Kabourakis: ***aged 20, he is serving a four-year prison sentence in Kassandra Agricultural Prison for refusing to perform military service.***

Timotheos Kabourakis is a Jehovah's Witness whose religious beliefs do not permit him to serve in the armed forces in any capacity. He has been in prison since 14 May 1990, when he appeared at a military camp in Crete in response to call-up instructions. Upon declaring himself opposed on religious grounds to serving in the armed forces he was immediately put in a disciplinary cell where he was held for two months before being transferred to Avlona Military Prison. On 25 June 1990 he was convicted by the Military Court of Crete of "insubordination during a period of general mobilization". In June of this year he was transferred to Kassandra Agricultural Prison.

Timotheos Kabourakis

Some 400 conscientious objectors, nearly all Jehovah's Witnesses, are serving prison sentences in Greek jails. AI considers them all to be prisoners of conscience.

Greek law does not permit conscientious objectors to perform alternative civilian service. They are allowed to carry out four years of unarmed military service, double the length of military service, but for most of them service in the armed forces in any capacity is irreconcilable with their beliefs.

The right to refuse military service for reasons of conscience has been recognized by the United Nations Commission on Human Rights, the Council of Europe and the European Parliament. These bodies have called on states to refrain from imprisoning conscientious objectors and instead to grant them the right to perform alternative civilian service of non-punitive length. A draft law drawn up in 1988 by a former Greek Government which provided for alternative civilian service double the length of military service has still not been passed.

■ Please send courteous appeals for the release of Timotheos Kabourakis and the other 400 imprisoned conscientious objectors and the introduction of alternative civilian service of non-punitive length for conscientious objectors to military service to: Mr Ioannis Varvitsiotis/Minister of National Defence/Ministry of National Defence/Holargos (Pentagono)/Athens/Greece.□

UNITED STATES OF AMERICA

Enrique González: ***a 25-year-old law student and reservist in the US Marine Corps, he was arrested on 26 December 1990 and charged with desertion and "missing movement" (failure to report for active duty). He was sentenced on 25 May 1991 to two-and-a-half years' imprisonment.***

As a result of the invasion of Kuwait by Iraq in August 1990 and the deployment of US troops to the area, Enrique González's unit was called for active duty in November 1990. He is among hundreds — and possibly thousands — of US armed forces members who refused to report for duty and filed application for conscientious objector status.

Enrique González enlisted in the US Marine Corps Reserve in 1984 at the age of 18 without, he said, "ever stopping to think about my feelings towards war. The beliefs which have compelled me to apply for conscientious objector status, at this time, have gradually developed with education and life experience. Today, I am refusing to take arms to kill other human beings and I oppose war because I believe that it is wrong, immoral and unethical to kill another human being."

Although the US armed forces are made up of volunteers, the Military Selective Service Act does allow for the granting of conscientious objector status. The investigating officer acting on Enrique González's application for conscientious objector status recommended that it be granted.

Conscientious objection to military service is recognized by the United Nations as a legitimate exercise of the right to freedom of thought, conscience and religion. AI considers as prisoners of conscience those who for reasons of conscience or profound conviction arising from religious, ethical, moral, humanitarian, philosophical, political or similar motives refuse to perform armed service or undertake any other direct or indirect participation in wars or armed conflict.

■ Please send courteous letters appealing for the immediate and unconditional release of Enrique González to: President George Bush/The White House/1600 Pennsylvania Avenue/Washington DC/20500/USA.□

INDONESIA

Bonar Tigor Naipospos: ***a 29-year-old post-graduate student of political science at Gajah Mada University, Yogyakarta, he was arrested in June 1989 in Jakarta. He was convicted of subversion in October 1990 and sentenced to eight-and-a-half years' imprisonment. In January 1991 the sentence was upheld by the High Court in Yogyakarta.***

Bonar Tigor Naipospos was accused of spreading Marxist ideas and attempting to undermine the Indonesian state ideology, *Pancasila*, through participation in a study club and distribution of banned literature. At his trial, one of the defence witnesses, a lecturer at the Gajah Mada University, testified that informal discussion groups were a common and positive feature of university life, and were encouraged by the professors as an important part of intellectual development.

The charges against Bonar Tigor Naipospos were also related to the conviction of two other students, Bambang Isti Nugroho and Bambang Subono, in 1988. The two were charged with subversion because of their involvement in an informal study group, and with possession of banned books, including some by the renowned Indonesian author Pramoedya Ananta Toer. Bonar Tigor Naipospos was accused of giving books by Pramoedya Ananta Toer to Bambang Subono to sell in 1988, a charge which the latter denied in court.

AI believes that Bonar Tigor Naipospos' imprisonment is a denial of the right to freedom of expression and opinion and the right to impart information to others. Available trial documents and press reports of the proceedings suggest that his trial was intended to intimidate government critics, despite President Suharto's recent calls for greater political openness.

■ Please send courteous letters appealing for Bonar Tigor Naipospos' immediate and unconditional release to: President Suharto/Presiden RI/Istana Negara/Jalan Veteran/Jakarta/Indonesia.□

PRISONER NEWS

AI learned in July 1991 of the release of 57 prisoners under adoption or investigation. AI took up 94 cases.

CORRECTION: On page 8 of the September *AI Newsletter* the Political-Military Command in Peru was incorrectly quoted. The final sentence in the article should have read: The Political-Military Command ... concluded that Juan Salomé had never been in the custody of the military and that he and other official persons were being manipulated by "subversive elements" as part of a campaign to discredit the security forces.

0004

FOCUS amnesty international

According to international law, prisoners whose crimes were committed before their 18th birthday should not suffer the death penalty. Only seven countries worldwide are known to have executed juvenile offenders in the last 10 years; the largest confirmed number of such executions has been carried out in the United States of America. There are more juvenile offenders on death row in the USA than in any other country. Young people on death row in the USA come overwhelmingly from acutely deprived backgrounds, have been physically or sexually abused, and suffer from mental illness or brain damage. Yet in a disturbingly large number of cases, these potentially mitigating factors were never considered by the courts that imposed their death sentences.

USA: Juveniles and the death penalty

On 11 September 1985 the state of Texas executed Charles Rumbaugh for a crime he committed when he was 17 years old. This was the first execution of a juvenile offender in the USA for more than two decades. Since then, three more juvenile offenders have been executed. More than 90 juveniles have been sentenced to death in the USA since the mid-1970s; most have had their death sentences reversed on appeal but at least 31 others remain on death rows in 12 states across the country.

Rumbaugh was convicted and sentenced to death for murdering jewellery store owner Michael Fiorillo in April 1975. Rumbaugh had attempted to rob the jewellery store at gunpoint and Fiorillo, aged 58, reached for his own gun and was fatally shot in the ensuing struggle.

Rumbaugh had spent most of his childhood in a series of reform schools and mental institutions; by the time he reached adulthood, his body was covered in scars from suicide attempts and acts of self-mutilation. In a letter to a penfriend written 18 months before his execution, Rumbaugh said: "I started making mistakes at a very young age and never changed before it was too late. I was 17 years old when I committed the offence for which I was sentenced to die, and I didn't even start thinking and caring about my life until I was at least 20." Rumbaugh was 28 years old when he was executed by lethal injection.

Guy Busby/Mobile Press Register

In 1988 an Alabama jury convicted 15-year-old Clayton Flowers of capital murder and recommended a sentence of life in prison without parole. The judge rejected the recommendation and sentenced Flowers to the electric chair. In July 1991 his conviction and sentence were overturned.

James Terry Roach was electrocuted in South Carolina on 10 January 1986. Roach was convicted and sentenced to death for the rape and murder of a 14-year-old girl, and the murder of her 17-year-old boyfriend. Roach was 17 at the time of the crime. One of his two co-defendants, 22-year-old Joseph Shaw, was also sentenced to death and was executed in 1985. The third defendant, a boy of 16, turned state's evidence and was given a prison sentence.

Roach pleaded guilty, so the case was never heard by a jury. The trial judge agreed that six mitigating circumstances were present in the case, including the fact that Roach had no previous record of violence, was emotionally immature and mentally retarded, and that he was a minor with a passive dependent personality acting under the domination of an adult ringleader (Shaw). Nevertheless, the judge sentenced Roach to death on the grounds that these factors were outweighed by the "heinousness" of the crime. Roach had been represented by a court-appointed attorney, who was later disbarred from practising law. The Governor of South Carolina ignored appeals from Mother Teresa, former President Jimmy Carter and the United Nations (UN) Secretary General, and denied Roach's petition for clemency, despite the mitigating factors and new evidence that Roach was suffering from a degenerative brain disease.

Dalton Prejean was electrocuted in Louisiana on 18 May 1990. Prejean, who was black, was convicted and sentenced to death for the 1977 murder of a white police officer. The 17-year-old offender was tried and sentenced by an all-white jury after the prosecutor used his peremptory challenges (the right to reject potential jurors without explanation) to exclude black people from the jury panel. Prejean was mentally retarded and had a history of mental illness and childhood abuse —factors which were not presented to the jury during the sentencing stage of his trial. The state governor denied clemency, despite a recommendation by the Louisiana Board of Pardons and Paroles that his death sentence should be commuted to life imprisonment without parole.

Twenty-four of the 36 US states with current death penalty statutes allow the death penalty to be imposed on juvenile offenders. The laws of eight states, reinforced by a 1989 Supreme Court decision that the execution of offenders as young as 16 is permitted under the

James Terry Roach, electrocuted in South Carolina in 1986, had been sentenced to death for a crime committed when he was 17 years old. Roach had no previous record of violence and was mentally retarded.

US Constitution, set a minimum age of 16 or 17 in their capital punishment statutes. In eight other states, the minimum age is set between 12 and 15 years. Five states have no minimum at all, although judges and juries are required to consider age a mitigating factor when imposing the death penalty. Three states—Delaware, Oklahoma and South Dakota—specify neither minimum age nor age as a mitigating factor.

AI's research findings

AI has reviewed the cases of 23 juvenile offenders sentenced to death in the USA since 1976, 14 of whom remained on death row as of 1 July 1991. In most of these cases AI obtained information about the crime and background of the defendant from sentencing reports, grounds of appeal filed, court judgments, clemency petitions and psychiatric testimony. The US Supreme Court has recognized the need for particular care and scrutiny in capital cases involving juvenile offenders. The evidence examined by AI demonstrates that these criteria have not been met.

The overwhelming majority of juvenile offenders in AI's study came from acutely deprived or unstable family backgrounds. Many were brought up in the absence of one or both parents, and most of them suffered serious physical or sexual abuse. Joseph Cannon, who was sentenced to death in Texas in 1982, had been so brutally sexually and physically abused as a child that the psychologist reviewing his case concluded that "even in the worst of case histories one seldom encounters traumatization as heinous and extreme as those to which [Cannon] was subjected while growing up." The psychologist noted that Cannon's home environment had been so depraved and oppressive that the conditions on death row represented a significant improvement, leading to progress in his aptitude, self image and IQ during his time in prison.

In 1986 and 1987 a team of psychiatrists and neurologists studied all of the juvenile offenders on death row in Florida, Georgia, Oklahoma and Texas. The team discovered that all 14 of the inmates had sustained serious head injuries in childhood; nine of them had extensive neurological abnormalities, including brain injuries; and seven had been diagnosed as psychotic. Twelve of the 14 had IQ scores well below normal; at least four were borderline mentally retarded. Twelve of the subjects had suffered brutal physical abuse from parents, at least five of them had been sodomized by older male relatives: in one case the sexual abuse started at the age of five. The inmates and many of their parents had histories of alcoholism and drug abuse.

The existence of an acutely deprived background, physical and sexual abuse, brain damage and mental illness, coupled with the youth of the defendants, should have provided compelling mitigating evidence against the death sentence. However, the study found that most of the juvenile offenders on death row lacked the knowledge and experience to realize this; many were ashamed of their poverty and their parents' brutality or sexual abuse, and consequently tried to conceal the very evidence most likely to prevent them from being sentenced to death. The parents were often reluctant to disclose their own abusive behaviour, even when such evidence would be likely to help the defendant. In some cases, family members requested that histories of abuse be minimized, cooperated with the prosecution, testified against their own relatives and urged judges to impose death sentences.

Before the death sentence of William Wayne Thompson, a 15-year-old offender in Oklahoma, was overturned by the Supreme Court, he told a television interviewer:
"A 15-year-old doesn't consider death as happening to them. I mean, ask any 15-year-old would they believe they are gonna die if they did something. They'll tell you no."

Inadequate legal representation

The defence lawyers who should have been relied on to unearth and utilize such information, both in the trial and sentencing phases of the cases, often failed to do so. Virtually all juvenile offenders came from indigent families and so were represented by court-appointed lawyers or public defenders. Despite the complexity of capital trials, many of the young defendants were assigned lawyers with little or no criminal trial experience and severely limited financial resources. Some of the defence lawyers did not investigate their clients' background or psychiatric history, and spent little time preparing their cases for trial. In at least nine of the cases reviewed by AI, lawyers handling later appeals discovered important mitigating evidence which had not been presented at the trial or sentencing hearing.

In Mississippi, the court-appointed lawyer who represented David Tokman, a 17-year-old offender, spent less than seven hours preparing the case for trial and conducted no investigation into Tokman's background. Tokman and two older men were accused of robbing and murdering a taxi driver in August 1980. The prosecution case rested on the testimony of one of Tokman's accomplices, Jerry Fuson, who had not actually witnessed the killing. Tokman's lawyer made no effort to interview Fuson before the trial, or to challenge his testimony in court. Although Tokman was the youngest of the three accused, and had no prior record of violence, his attorney failed to contest the prosecution's assertion that Tokman was more culpable than his accomplices.

The defence counsel had not arranged an independent psychiatric assessment of Tokman, despite evidence suggesting he had a "death wish", had been abusing drugs and had been neglected and physically abused by his father. During the sentencing phase of the trial, no mitigating testimony from Tokman's friends or relatives was presented. During a later appeal hearing, relatives and neighbours testified that despite an abusive and unstable family background, Tokman was widely regarded as hard-working and considerate. Psychiatric experts testified that he had a high potential for rehabilitation. In 1988 a federal circuit court overturned Tokman's death sentence after finding that the conduct of his trial attorney was below reasonable standards and had prejudiced the outcome of the sentencing hearing. Tokman is currently awaiting a new sentencing hearing, scheduled for September 1991, at which he could again be sentenced to death.

In Texas the two court-appointed lawyers who represented Robert Carter, a 17-year-old offender, made only minimal efforts to speak to their client before trial, locate potential witnesses or present mitigating evidence. They failed to request a pre-trial assessment of Carter's mental capacity even though they apparently suspected that he might be retarded. Carter's defence counsel allowed numerous procedural errors on

Sean Sellers, a 16-year-old offender, was sentenced to death in Oklahoma in 1986. At the sentencing phase of the trial the jury was not instructed that Sellers' age at the time of the crime was a mitigating factor. Psychiatrists believe Sellers suffers from severe emotional disturbances. His conviction and death sentence are currently on appeal.

the part of the prosecutor to pass without objection, and some of their remarks to the jury were prejudicial to their own client. During sentencing, they did not invite the jury to consider as mitigating evidence Carter's age at the time of the crime, the fact that he was mentally retarded and had suffered brutal physical abuse as a child, or that he had no previous criminal record.

A post-trial psychiatric examination revealed that Carter was mentally retarded and seriously brain damaged, with limited capacity to understand his own actions or those of others. He was said to be unusually subservient to authority figures, a factor which may have influenced his decision to waive his right to a lawyer and make a full confession at the time of his arrest. Previous employers described him as obedient, hardworking, cooperative and trustworthy. None of them had been asked to testify at his trial.

In Louisiana in 1987, the two inexperienced public defenders representing 15-year-old Troy Dugar offered no defence evidence at all, and their client was found guilty of capital murder. At the sentencing phase of the trial, they neglected to emphasise his age at the time of the crime, which should have been a major mitigating factor. They also failed to mention the defendant's long history of psychiatric illness, his low IQ, a family history of alcoholism and the fact that he himself had started drinking at the age of six and was an alcoholic by the age of 12. The "mitigation" evidence they did manage to produce was damaging to their own client: the testimony of a doctor who claimed that Dugar was "sociopathic" and had no other mental disorder.

The following year, Dr Howard Albrecht examined Dugar and found him to be schizophrenic and mentally retarded. In his opinion Dugar had been incompetent to stand trial. Since he has been on death row, Dugar has reportedly suffered violent fits and hallucinations and has spent long periods under heavy sedation.

In a number of cases, defence lawyers failed to order independent psychiatric examinations because funds to pay for such examinations were not available, and potentially crucial information was thus not presented to the jury. In Georgia a psychologist acting as a witness for the state testified that a defendant, whom he had never interviewed in person, was a "sexual sadist", likely to commit violent sexual acts in the future. The defence was unable to provide any professional rebuttal testimony because their request for funds for a psychiatric evaluation had been denied. The defendant, a 17-year-old offender, spent eight years on death row before her death sentence was vacated by a District Court in 1989. The District Court held that the original trial court should not have denied funds for an independent psychiatric evaluation, and that the testimony of the state psychologist had been unreliable.

Although all death sentences handed down in the USA are automatically appealed to the relevant state supreme court, serious and avoidable errors on the part of defence counsel cannot always be remedied. Failure to object to jury composition, trial venue or other violations of a defendant's constitutional rights are not normally considered on appeal, even though they may have jeopardized the fairness of the proceedings.

Sentencing

US law requires all capital cases to be heard under a two-phase procedure, in which verdict and sentence are determined separately. If a defendant is convicted of capital murder during the trial phase, the court then conducts a separate sentencing hearing, usually before the trial jury. During the sentencing hearing, the defence has the opportunity to present evidence in mitigation —including testimony on the defendant's background, age, and character— aimed at justifying a prison sentence, rather than the death penalty.

The jury that sentenced Dalton Prejean to death was not informed of Prejean's history of childhood abuse, nor about his documented history of mental illness and brain damage. Shortly before Prejean was executed in 1990, one of the original trial jurors appealed to the Governor to grant clemency. The juror had examined information not available at the trial, and had concluded: "I would, if I had another opportunity, vote against the death penalty in favour of institutionalization." Under Louisiana law, the jury must be unanimous in recommending the death penalty; if even one juror dissents, the sentence imposed must be life imprisonment.

In some states juveniles charged with capital crimes are automatically tried in the adult criminal courts, which alone have the power to impose the death sentence. In other states a juvenile court decides whether or not to transfer the case to the jurisdiction of the criminal court. In the cases examined by AI, the juvenile courts did not appear to consider the emotional maturity of the defendant when deciding whether he or she should be tried as an adult. Juveniles charged with capital crimes were commonly sent to the adult criminal court simply because the juvenile system maintains no facilities for long-term incarceration. In one Kentucky case, the juvenile court specifically found that the defendant was "emotionally immature and could be amenable to treatment if properly done on a long-term basis..." However, the court ordered the case to be transferred to the adult court — where the defendant was subsequently sentenced to death — as the state did

In 1986 Paula Cooper was convicted of a murder committed when she was 15 years old. She was sentenced to die in Indiana's electric chair. After three years on death row, her death sentence was set aside by the Indiana Supreme Court, which ruled that because of her age at the time of the crime, the death sentence was a disproportionate punishment.

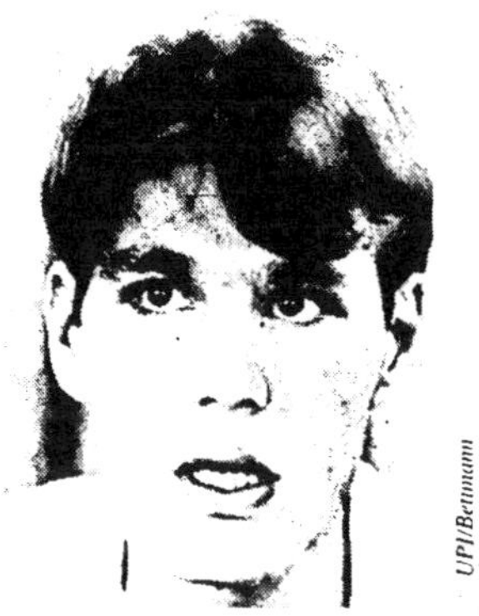

Jay Kelly Pinkerton was sentenced to death in Texas for a murder committed when he was 17 years old. In 1985 the Supreme Court granted a stay of execution 20 minutes before the execution was due to be carried out; a second reprieve came four months later. In May 1986, the Supreme Court rejected his final appeals and Pinkerton was executed by lethal injection.

In 1990 the state of Louisiana electrocuted Dalton Prejean, despite a recommendation by the Pardons and Parole Board that his sentence be commuted to life imprisonment. He had spent nearly 13 years on death row. Prejean, who had once been diagnosed as brain damaged and mentally retarded, said shortly before his execution: "I don't ask to get out of prison. I just ask to live with my mistake...I've changed. There's a whole difference between being 17 and 30."

not provide long-term youth rehabilitation programs.

Conditions on death rows in the USA are generally harsh; most prisoners sentenced to death have no access to prison work, vocational training programs or group educational classes. They are typically confined alone, in small, poorly-equipped cells, with limited opportunities for association with other prisoners and no access to rehabilitative treatment. Such conditions are particularly damaging to juvenile offenders, many of whom eventually have their death sentences overturned on appeal.

International law

International law unanimously prohibits the imposition of the death penalty on juvenile offenders. Article 6(5) of the International Covenant on Civil and Political Rights (ICCPR) states: "Sentence of death shall not be imposed for crimes committed by persons below eighteen years of age and shall not be carried out on pregnant women." Article 4(5) of the American Convention on Human Rights contains a similar provision. The US Government signed both of these treaties in 1977, but has not yet ratified them.

These international standards were developed in recognition of the fact that the death penalty, with its uniquely cruel and irreversible character, is a wholly inappropriate punishment for those who have not attained full physical or emotional maturity and are thus widely recognized as being less responsible for their actions.

The existence of the death penalty undermines the foundations of the criminal justice system by ruling out the possibility of rehabilitation. The execution of young people is particularly abhorrent because their personalities and patterns of behaviour are not fixed and they are more likely than adults to be successfully rehabilitated. Moreover, the young people on death row will not be killed until they have grown to adulthood while appealing their sentences. By the time they are put to death, they may bear little resemblance to the teenagers who committed their crimes.

Supporters of the death penalty often point to its supposed deterrent effect. Detailed research in the USA and other countries has failed to provide evidence that the death penalty deters crime more effectively than other punishments; some studies have found that the "brutalizing" effect of executions actually increases the rate of violent crime. The deterrence argument is even less persuasive when applied to juveniles. Professor Victor Streib of the College of Law at Cleveland State University, who has conducted detailed studies of juvenile offenders, concluded: "It seems clear that few adolescents have any meaningful concept of death. In fact, they seem to be attracted to death-defying behaviour, the threat of a death penalty may actually encourage some juvenile crimes."

US Supreme Court rulings

During the 1980s the US Supreme Court was asked to rule on whether the execution of juveniles was permissible under the Constitution. Lawyers handling these appeals argued that the execution of juvenile offenders constitutes cruel and unusual punishment in violation of the Eighth and Fourteenth Amendments to the Constitution.

In 1982 the Supreme Court vacated the death sentence imposed on Monty Lee Eddings, a 16-year-old offender, on the grounds that the trial judge had refused to consider mitigating evidence at the sentencing hearing. Although the Court failed to rule on the question of whether the death penalty was necessarily cruel and unusual punishment when imposed on a 16-year-old, the Court noted "just as the chronological age of a minor is itself a relevant mitigating factor of great weight, so must the background and mental and emotional development of a youthful defendant be duly considered in sentencing". As AI's findings demonstrate, these principles have been ignored in subsequent cases involving juvenile offenders.

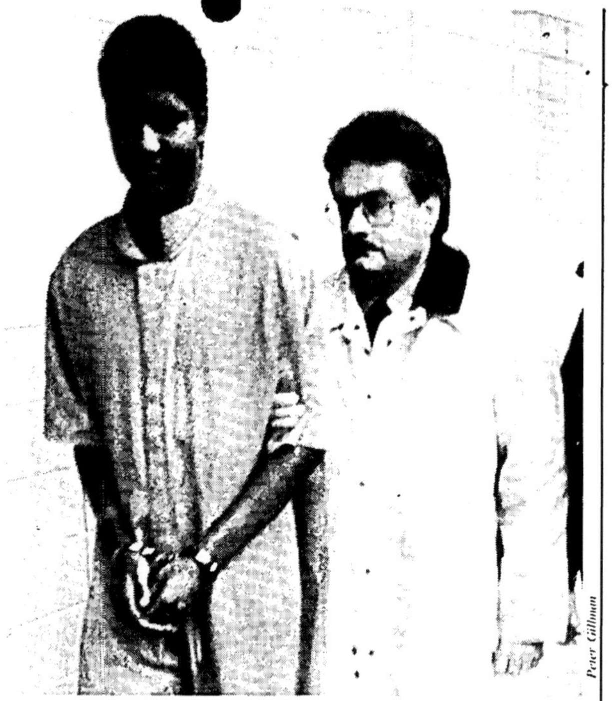

Peter Gillman

Troy Dugar, a 15-year-old offender, was sentenced to death in Louisiana in 1987. Dugar has a long history of psychiatric problems and is borderline mentally retarded — facts which were not presented to the jury during the sentencing phase of his trial. Since the trial he has suffered violent fits and hallucinations. In 1988 the Louisiana Supreme Court ruled that Dugar was "incompetent" to appeal his case, and he was returned to death row to await further proceedings.

"A decent society places certain absolute limits on the punishments that it inflicts —no matter how terrible the crime or how great the desire for retribution. And one of those limits is that it does not execute people for crimes committed while they were children."
New York Times, June 1984

In 1989, by a narrow 5-4 majority, the Supreme Court upheld the death sentences imposed on Kevin Stanford and Heath Wilkins, who were sentenced to death for murders committed when they were 17 and 16 respectively. Writing for the majority, Justice Antonin Scalia said that US society had formed no consensus that such executions constitute "cruel and unusual punishment", and rejected evidence suggesting that the death penalty had no deterrent effect on juveniles. AI described the ruling as "a retrograde step for international human rights". Justice William Brennan, dissenting from the majority, noted that "within the world community, the imposition of the death penalty for juvenile crimes appears to be overwhelmingly disapproved". The execution of juveniles, he said, made no measurable contribution to acceptable goals of punishment.

A significant body of professional opinion in the USA, including the American Bar Association (ABA) and the National Council of Juvenile and Family Court Judges, likewise condemns the imposition of the death penalty on juvenile offenders. In a brief submitted to the US Supreme Court in 1989, the ABA argued that "our society recognizes that minors are less mature, less experienced, less able to exercise good judgment and self-restraint, more susceptible to environmental influence (both positive and negative), and as a result less responsible and less culpable in a moral sense than adults". The ABA acknowledged that some minors charged with serious crimes must be tried and sentenced in the adult criminal courts, but added: "They should not be held to the degree of moral accountability necessary to justify the ultimate sanction of execution."

All of the juvenile offenders on death row were convicted of murder, some committed in particularly brutal circumstances. AI does not argue that juveniles should not be held criminally liable, or subjected to severe punishment where appropriate. However, AI is unconditionally opposed to the death penalty because it is a violation of the fundamental right to life and the right not to be subjected to cruel, inhuman or degrading punishment.

The death penalty is premeditated and cold-blooded murder on the part of the state, and can never be justified as a fitting response to violent crime, however repugnant. There must be restraints on the actions governments can take to punish individuals. As a first step towards the total abolition of the death penalty, and to bring the USA into minimal conformity with international standards, the line must be drawn at the age of 18.□

MYANMAR

Violations against ethnic minorities

FOR decades, armed ethnic minority insurgents in rural Myanmar have been fighting the central authorities. During counter-insurgency activities, the Myanmar armed forces have routinely committed widespread human rights violations against civilians.

In August AI published *Myanmar (Burma): Continuing killings and ill-treatment of minority peoples**, which documents the arbitrary seizure, ill-treatment and extrajudicial execution of members of the Karen, Mon and Indian ethnic minorities by the Myanmar armed forces.

In June and July AI interviewed people along the border between Thailand and Myanmar who had recently fled their homes in Myanmar. Many had been victims of human rights violations or had witnessed such violations against others. The testimonies gathered by AI confirmed that many people seized for work as porters or to clear mines have been deliberately killed or tortured. One 30-year-old epileptic Indian woman was beaten to death by soldiers because she suffered a seizure which made it impossible for her to continue work as a porter.

Other victims included people who were detained and ill-treated, or deliberately killed because soldiers suspected they sympathized with or supported armed ethnic minority groups.

The cases demonstrate that the Myanmar armed forces exercise the *de facto* power to arbitrarily detain, torture or kill people.☐

**AI Index No. ASA 16/05/91*

MAURITANIA

Hundreds of prisoners killed in custody

SOME 339 political prisoners were reportedly killed in Mauritania's prisons, military barracks or police stations between November and March 1991. The victims were among thousands of black Mauritanians arrested in November and December 1990.

Eyewitnesses reported that more than 140 detainees were deliberately executed without trial or tortured to death. A further 200 reportedly died in custody as a direct result of torture or ill-treatment, including extremely harsh prison conditions. Former prisoners have told AI that many detainees were severely beaten, had their genitals tied tightly with a cord or were burned in the eyes with cigarettes.

Most of the detainees were army officers or civil servants belonging to a single black ethnic group from the south, known as the *Hal-Pulaar* or *Fula*. They were rounded up in the country's two largest cities in November and December 1990, following an alleged conspiracy to overthrow the government. However, no independent evidence tying the suspects to a coup plot has emerged and it appears that most were arrested because of their ethnic origin. Black Mauritanians have long been the target of abuses by government forces — who are predominantly of Arab origin — with arrests, torture and extrajudicial executions routine in the south of the country.

In April 1991 AI called on the Mauritanian Government to investigate reports that more than 200 political prisoners had died, but the authorities refused to acknowledge that any deaths had occurred. Since then the organization has received confirmation that 339 named prisoners are missing, and fears that all of them have died or been killed in custody. AI has repeated its demand for an independent public inquiry to ascertain the fate of all those who are still missing, and to establish how many were killed and how they died so that those responsible can be brought to justice.☐

Guide to the African Charter

ON 21 October — African Day of Human and Peoples' Rights — the Organization of African Unity's (OAU) African Charter on Human and Peoples' Rights will have been in force for five years. To mark this anniversary AI has produced an illustrated booklet, *A Guide to the African Charter on Human and Peoples' Rights*, which explains the Charter in non-technical terms. AI members are sending copies of the booklet and the full text of the Charter in Arabic, English, French, Portuguese, Spanish and Swahili to thousands of people throughout Africa.

Another document, *Protecting Human Rights — International Procedures and How to Use Them: the Organization of African Unity and Human Rights*, has been designed for lawyers and human rights workers. It explains the work of the African Commission on Human and Peoples' Rights, which supervises the way governments put the provisions of the Charter into effect.

In June 1991 the OAU Assembly of Heads of State and Government called on the 10 member states which have not yet ratified the Charter to do so and urged other states whose periodic reports are overdue to submit their reports to the Commission. AI members are making similar appeals to governments.☐

SYRIA

Syrian Jews arrested trying to flee country

AT least 23 members of Syria's Jewish community have been arrested since 1987, including women and secondary school students. Most of them were detained without trial, ostensibly after having tried to leave Syria without exit permits, although the authorities have not always specified the charges against them. Several are believed to have been tortured.

Six Syrian Jews — Subhe and Lisa Kastika and their two infant sons, together with Subhe's brother Said and his wife Shafiqua — were arrested on 1 May 1991 in northern Syria and charged with attempting to flee the country. They were held incommunicado for two weeks at a military base and all are alleged to have been severely beaten. Said Kastika is said to have been severely tortured during interrogation because he has a speech impediment which made it difficult for him to answer questions clearly. The two women and the infants were released in Damascus on 21 May. Subhe and Said Kastika are reportedly being held in 'Adra Civil Prison, near Damascus.

AI has recently received reports of the arrest on 25 September 1990 of Ramoun Ibrahim Darwish and his pregnant wife, Gracia; Joseph Rafoul Sabato; Baddur Lalo; Zaki Shaul Sabato and Mair Daoud Pinhas. They were reportedly arrested while trying to leave the country. The two women were released in January 1991 and the four men are reportedly being held in Aleppo Central Prison.

Only two of those detained have been brought to trial. Brothers Eli and Selim Swed, who had been held in untried detention for over three years, were sentenced on 21 May 1991 to six-and-a-half year prison terms, reportedly on charges of treason or espionage. The final hearing of their trial was reportedly held *in camera* on 5 March and lasted only a few minutes; neither the defendants nor their lawyer were allowed to speak. AI has received no response from the Syrian authorities to its request for details of the trial proceedings and of any right of appeal to a higher tribunal.☐

TURKEY

Attacks on human rights activists

DURING June and July a series of attacks was aimed at members of the independent Turkish Human Rights Association in southeast Turkey.

At 2am on 18 June a powerful explosion destroyed the car of Mustafa Özer, a member of the Human Rights Association. At midnight on 25 June an explosion demolished the Human Rights Association office in Diyarbakir. On the morning of 2 July a bomb destroyed the car of Siddik Tan, a board member of the Batman branch of the Human Rights Association. Siddik Tan, his 10-year-old son and a friend were injured in the blast. It is not known who carried out these attacks.

Vedat Aydin, a member of the Human Rights Association, was taken from his house at around midnight on 5 July by several armed men, ostensibly plain-clothes police officers. On the morning of 8 July his dead body was found some 60 kilometres from Diyarbakir with eight bullet wounds, a broken leg and other signs of torture. The body was quickly buried by the police as "unidentifiable" without a full autopsy having been carried out. However, before the family had even identified the body, the Emergency Region Governor reportedly stated that Vedat Aydin had been murdered.

AI has urged the Turkish authorities to initiate thorough, independent and impartial investigations into these incidents and to take all necessary steps to prevent further such attacks.☐

0009

ETHIOPIA

Freed prisoners come to UK

IN July a family of former prisoners of conscience from Ethiopia arrived in the United Kingdom, where they are receiving medical treatment at the Medical Foundation for the Treatment of Torture Victims.

Mulugetta Mosissa and his wife Namat Issa were arrested in 1980 and imprisoned without charge or trial. Their son Amonsissa was born in custody and spent his first nine years in prison; he and his mother were released in September 1989. Mulugetta Mosissa was freed on 28 May 1991 after the fall of the Mengistu government. After his release he told AI: "Many people think we had done a big crime, but we did nothing at all. We were simply talking of democracy, equality, freedom of people, freedom of those who were oppressed."

For nearly 12 years, Mulugetta Mosissa was held in Ethiopia's notorious torture centre in Addis Ababa, *Maikelawi*, where prisoners were repeatedly tortured. "We were tortured until our flesh and bone parted," he said. "I know many people who were disposed of after they died there. Thank you to this organization and all humanitarian organizations who were pressurizing the government to let us free."

Namat Issa told AI: "I had a difficult labour and when my son was born he was already losing consciousness and had difficulty breathing. After 11 days they took me back to prison where I stayed for nearly 10 years... Now we are here for medical treatment and we hope to get a job and live like any other human beings, having human rights in the future."☐

CH[redacted]

Widespread illegal and arbitrary detention

HUNDREDS of thousands of people are detained each year in China under forms of administrative detention which can be imposed by the sole authority of the police or local officials. Although administrative detainees are not charged with any crime and are not afforded any opportunity for trial in a court of law, they can be held for periods of up to four years. The official regulations, decisions and instructions providing for such detention are vague, often unpublished and frequently ignored, resulting in widespread illegal and arbitrary detention.

The number of people currently held under the various forms of administrative detention is believed to be in the millions. Some of the detainees are political or religious dissidents, but the overwhelming majority are simply people of low social status — vagrants, the unemployed and migrants — and those regarded as "social deviants". The torture of detainees and grossly inadequate conditions of detention are reportedly common.

Until 1989 such abuses were reported and openly criticized in the Chinese official press, which denounced the frequent ill-treatment of detainees and the illegal use of administrative detention by the police. Very few such criticisms have been publicly voiced since the June 1989 crackdown on pro-democracy protesters.

In a report released in September AI examined administrative detention through a detailed analysis of Chinese legal texts and commentaries, case histories of prisoners of conscience and the testimonies of former detainees.*

**China: Punishment without crime: administrative detention (AI Index No. ASA 17/27/91).*☐

IRAN

POCs sentenced in unfair trials

NINE prisoners of conscience, including former ministers in the provisional government of the Islamic Republic, were reportedly sentenced to up to three years' imprisonment after unfair trials in May and June. They had been arrested in June 1990 after signing a critical open letter to President Rafsanjani, which called for the implementation of constitutional rights and freedoms.

Some of the prisoners are elderly and in poor health. All are believed to have undergone physical or psychological torture in attempts to make them "confess" on television.

Their trials were summary and conducted in secret, and the defendants were not allowed to have lawyers. Although they had already been held for one year, their prison terms only began the day their sentences were passed.

AI has called repeatedly on the Iranian authorities to release the nine men and sought to send a delegate to observe the trials, but the Iranian Government did not reply to the organization's request.☐

EGYPT

Conflicting reports on missing student

MOSTAFA Muhammad 'Abd al-Hamid 'Othman, a 23-year-old medical student from Qina in Upper Egypt, "disappeared" after his arrest in Zagazig on 17 December 1989. He had been caught up in a wave of mass arrests of suspected supporters and sympathizers of Islamic groups in Egypt following an assassination attempt on the then Minister of the Interior, General Zaki Badr.

Although Mostafa Othman was not known to be a member of any political group, he and a number of other students were arrested and initially taken to Istiqbal Tora Prison, where they were detained under State of Emergency legislation.

Other detainees later confirmed that Mostafa Othman had been held with them at the State Security Intelligence Centre in Lazoghly, Cairo in January 1990, and said that he was complaining of stomach pains. Since his arrest, Mostafa Othman's family have had no contact with him and all attempts to locate him have been in vain.

Inquiries about Mostafa Othman's whereabouts have met with contradictory responses. The Ministry of the Interior claimed that he had been released on 28 December 1989, while the Prisons Administration Department said that he was still being detained in Istiqbal Tora Prison in 1990.☐

PERU

'Disappearance' toll mounts

FIFTEEN people, including five women and seven children, have "disappeared" and may have been extrajudicially executed. Their bodies were reportedly dumped in an abandoned mine, which was subsequently dynamited. The 15, all from Santa Bárbara, Huancavelica, had been detained on 4 July 1991 by soldiers from the Huancavelica and Lircay military bases acting in conjunction with a civil defence patrol.

A six-year-old boy was among the "disappeared". On 11 July his grandfather discovered the boy's body and a number of other half-buried bodies in an abandoned mine. On 14 July a delegation from Santa Bárbara attempted to enter the mine but were stopped by a group of armed men in civilian dress who reportedly identified themselves as military personnel from the San Genaro barracks. Members of the delegation heard a series of explosions coming from the direction of the mine.

Although the provincial prosecutor and an examining magistrate in Huancavelica had been informed on 12 July that bodies had been discovered in the mine, they did not investigate these reports until 18 July, four days after the explosions occurred.

The examining magistrate and the provincial prosecutor entered the mine in the presence of members of the police and armed forces. Although the explosions had damaged the bodies beyond recognition, the examining magistrate discovered human remains, items of clothing and used explosives in the mine. No results of any analysis have been reported and the whereabouts of the "disappeared" remain unclarified.☐

AMNESTY INTERNATIONAL NEWSLETTER is published every month in four languages to bring you news of AI's concerns and campaigns worldwide, as well as in-depth reports. Available from Amnesty International (address below)

AMNESTY INTERNATIONAL, 1 Easton Street, London WC1X 8DJ, United Kingdom. Printed in Great Britain by Flashprint Enterprises Ltd. London.
Available on subscription at £7 (US$12.00) for 12 issues ISSN 0308 6887

0010

공 란

공 란

공 란

공 란

공　　　란

공 란

공　　　란

공 란

공 란

공 란

공 란

공 란

공 란

공　란

공　　　란

공 란

공 란

공 란

공 란

공 란

공 란

공 란

공 란

공 란

대
2 김

주 영 대 사 관

영국(정) 723-54　　　　　　　　　　　　　1991. 10. 7.

수신 : 장관

참조 : 국제기구국장

제목 : A.I. 아국관련보고서

1. 국제사면위원회(A.I.)는 91.10.1.자 당관앞 서한으로 "South Korea; Prisoners Held for National Security Offenses" (A.I.발간 External Document)를 송부하여 왔는바 동 서류를 별첨 보고합니다.

2. 상기 External Document 는 구속자 개별사례를 수록, A.I. 회원이 구속자 석방 탄원서한 작성시 참고토록 하기 위하여 작성된 자료로서 10.1. 자로 A.I. 회원에게 발송되었다고 함을 참고하시기 바랍니다.

첨부 : 1. 서한 사본.
　　　2. 서류 사본. 끝.

발송 1991. 10. 8 주영대사관

일반문서로 재분류 (1991.12.31.)

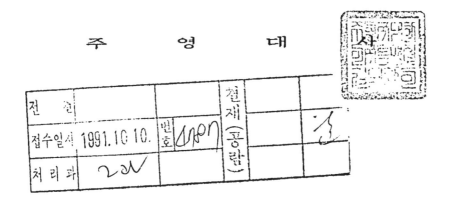

주 영 대 사

전 결			결재(공람)		
접수일시	1991.10.10.	번호 40907			김
처리과	2과				

0035

[EMBARGOED FOR 1 OCTOBER 1991]

amnesty international

SOUTH KOREA

Prisoners Held for National Security Offences

SEPTEMBER 1991 SUMMARY AI INDEX: ASA 25/25/91

DISTR: SC/CO/GR

Amnesty International's concerns about prisoners in South Korea centre around the use of national security legislation. Of the 200 prisoners reported to be currently held on national security grounds Amnesty International believes that some 30 are prisoners of conscience, that is people detained for their non-violent political activities and views. Amnesty International is also concerned about some 30 other prisoners who have been convicted on similar grounds after trials which are believed to have been unfair because the main evidence against them consisted of confessions which the prisoners said had been extracted from them under torture or because of other procedural irregularities.

This document outlines the cases of 35 prisoners and members of two "anti-state" groups who were arrested under national security legislation between 1975 and early 1991. Many were convicted of belonging to "anti-state" organisations, of supporting North Korea or spying for North Korea on the occasion of unauthorized visits to the north or when meeting alleged North Korean agents abroad. Amnesty International has been appealing or making inquiries about these cases with the South Korean authorities for a number of years. The authorities have replied to Amnesty International that the arrests were justified on national security grounds and have provided details on the charges against some prisoners. Amnesty International has taken this information into account in the description of the cases in this document. Some prisoners who had been serving long sentences on national security grounds have been released in amnesties in the last two years; among them were several Amnesty International regarded as prisoners of conscience.

0036

Two laws have been applied in cases of state security : the Anti-Communist Law and the National Security Law. The Anti-Communist Law was abrogated in December 1980 and most of its provisions were then included in the National Security Law. The National Security Law was last amended in May 1991 to restrict its application but there is concern that it could continue to be used to detain people for the non-violent exercise of their rights of freedom of expression or association.

Amnesty International is calling on the South Korean Government to release all prisoners of conscience and to review the cases of other political prisoners who may have been convicted after unfair trials.

KEYWORDS: PRISONERS OF CONSCIENCE1 / LONG-TERM IMPRISONMENT1 / TORTURE/ILL-TREATMENT1 / TRIALS1 / CONFESSIONS / LEGISLATION / INCOMMUNICADO DETENTION / UNLAWFUL DETENTION / ILL-HEALTH / DISABLEMENT / POLITICAL ACTIVISTS1 / STUDENTS1 / SAILORS / TECHNICIANS / FAMILIES / BUSINESS PEOPLE / MILITARY AS VICTIMS / RELIGIOUS GROUP MEMBERS / CHURCH WORKERS / AGED / ACADEMICS / DRIVERS / TEACHERS / ENGINEERS / JOURNALISTS / PUBLISHERS / FARMERS / WOMEN / ARTISTS / TRADE UNIONISTS / POETS / POLITICAL GROUPS / CENSORSHIP / BANNING / RESTRICTION ON MOVEMENT / ESPIONAGE / PRISONERS' LISTS / PRISONERS' TESTIMONIES / COMMUTATION OF DEATH SENTENCE / INVESTIGATION OF ABUSES / PHOTOGRAPHS

This report summarizes a 45-page document (15633 words), *South Korea: Prisoners Held For National Security Offences* (AI Index: ASA 25/25/91), issued by Amnesty International in September 1991. Anyone wanting further details or to take action on this issue should consult the full document.

INTERNATIONAL SECRETARIAT, 1 EASTON STREET, LONDON WC1X 8DJ, UNITED KINGDOM

TABLE OF CONTENTS

1) INTRODUCTION 1
1.1 Division between North and South Korea 2
1.2 The Prospects for Reunification 2

2) NATIONAL SECURITY LEGISLATION 4
2.1 The National Security Law (1980) 5
2.2 May 1991 Amendments to the National Security Law 6

3) PRISONERS HELD UNDER NATIONAL SECURITY LEGISLATION ... 8

4) PRISONER CASES 11
Yu-Chong-sik 11
Cho Sang-nok 11
Shin Kui-yong 12
Lee Hon-chi 13
Park Dong-oon 14
Lee Jang-hyong 15
Ham Ju-myong 15
Prisoner of Conscience: Koh Chang-pyo 17
Park Chan-u 17
Lee Chang-guk 18
Prisoner of Conscience: Kim Song-man 19
Prisoner of Conscience: Hwang Tae-kwon 20
Yang Dong-hwa 21
Kang Yong-ju 22
Lee Joon-ho 23
Kim Yun-su 23
Nah Jon-in 24
Lee Pyong-sol 25
Prisoner of Conscience: Chang Ui-gyun 26
Kang Hui-chol 28
Prisoner of Conscience: Suh Kyung-won 28
Prisoner of Conscience: Pang Yang-kyun 30
Prisoner of Conscience: Yu Won-ho 31
Prisoners of Conscience: Im Su-kyong and Father Moon Kyu-hyun 32
Prisoner of Conscience: Hong Song-dam 34
Prisoner of Conscience: Kim Hyon-jang 36
Oh Tong-yol 37
Prisoner of Conscience: Kim Keun-tae 38

Jang Myung-guk 39
Arrests of "Anti-State" Groups: Reports of Torture and Ill-Treatment . . . 41
Sanomaeng (Socialist Workers' League) 41
Chamintong (Independent National Unification Group) 42
Prisoners of Conscience: Cho Song-woo and Lee Hae-hak 43
Prisoners of Conscience: Lee Chang-bok and Kim Hi-taek 44
Prisoner of Conscience: Reverend Hong Keun-soo 45

SOUTH KOREA

PRISONERS HELD FOR NATIONAL SECURITY OFFENCES

1) INTRODUCTION

Amnesty International's concerns about prisoners in South Korea centre around the use of national security legislation. Of the 200 prisoners reported to be currently held on national security grounds Amnesty International believes that some 30 are prisoners of conscience, that is people detained for their non-violent political activities and views. Amnesty International is also concerned about some 30 other prisoners who have been convicted on similar grounds after trials which are believed to have been unfair because the main evidence against them consisted of confessions which the prisoners said had been extracted from them under torture or because of other procedural irregularities.

This document outlines the cases of 35 prisoners and members of two "anti-state" groups who were arrested under national security legislation between 1975 and early 1991. Many were convicted of belonging to "anti-state" organisations, of supporting North Korea or spying for North Korea on the occasion of unauthorized visits to the north or when meeting alleged North Korean agents abroad. Amnesty International has been appealing or making inquiries about these cases with the South Korean authorities for a number of years. The authorities have replied to Amnesty International that the arrests were justified on national security grounds and have provided details on the charges against some prisoners. Amnesty International has taken this information into account in the description of the cases in this document. Some prisoners who had been serving long sentences on national security grounds have been released in amnesties in the last two years; among them were several Amnesty International regarded as prisoners of conscience.

Two laws have been applied in cases of state security : the Anti-Communist Law and the National Security Law. The Anti-Communist Law was abrogated in December 1980 and most of its provisions were then included in the National Security Law. The

National Security Law was last amended in May 1991 to restrict its application but there is concern that it could continue to be used to detain people for the non-violent exercise of their rights of freedom of expression or association.

1.1 Division between North and South Korea

Korea was a unified state from the seventh century until the imposition of Japanese colonial rule in 1910. At the end of of World War II the country was divided into two military zones at the 38th parallel line, the northern part occupied by the USSR and the southern part occupied by the USA. In 1948 governments were established in the Republic of Korea (South Korea) and the Democratic People's Republic of Korea (North Korea). The Korean war (June 1950 to July 1953) ended with the signing of an armistice agreement which created a four-kilometre-wide demilitarized zone (DMZ) dividing the country near the 38th parallel. Since then the country has remained divided with both sides maintaining large standing armies. Talks involving the various parties to the conflict have continued unsuccessfully since 1953 to bring the war to a formal conclusion through the agreement of a peace treaty. Talks between the two Korean governments aimed at the reunification of the country have been initiated at various times but have made little progress, and contacts between citizens of the North and South have been severely limited.

1.2 The Prospects for Reunification

The prospects for reunification appeared to improve in September 1990 when the Prime Ministers of the two states met for the first time in Seoul. This was followed by two further meetings in October in Pyongyang and December in Seoul but the talks appeared to make little progress. North Korean proposals have included the signing of a non-aggression declaration, the suspension of the annual joint military exercises conducted by the USA and South Korea and the release of South Koreans imprisoned for making illegal visits to the North. South Korea has instead proposed an agreement on inter-Korean relations, including the reopening of communications and trade between the two countries. A fourth round of talks scheduled for February 1991 was cancelled by the North Korean Government to protest the annual "Team Spirit" military exercises but was later rescheduled for August 1991.

Delegates of North and South Korea shake hands prior to first round of prime ministerial talks, 5 September 1990.

(c) Reuters

In August 1990 the South-North Exchange and Cooperation Law came into force in South Korea. Under this new law the government can authorize its citizens, upon application, to visit North Korea, to invite North Koreans to the South and to trade and engage in joint ventures with them.

1991 saw an increased number of contacts between citizens of North and South Korea. In February the sports officials of both countries agreed to form the first unified sports teams to compete in the World Table Tennis Championships in April and the World Youth Soccer Championships in June. In March 1991 two South Korean dissidents were able to meet with North Koreans during a symposium held at Berkeley in the USA and 15 members of the Korea Research Foundation were allowed to meet North Koreans in France when they attended a conference organized by the Association for Korean Studies in Europe. In April 1991 the President of the Korea Travel Trading Corporation was allowed to invite a North Korean to attend the Third Overseas Travel Fair which took place in Seoul in June.

In April 1991 the South Korean Government approved the first direct trade with North Korea, allowing a South Korean company to exchange rice for North Korean coal and cement. Between 29 April and 4 May 1991 a delegation of 25 South Koreans comprising legislators, aides and journalists attended the annual conference of the Interparliamentary Union which was held in Pyongyang. However, talks between the Red Cross societies of both countries, which were broken off in 1985, have not been resumed. It is estimated that ten million Koreans are separated from other immediate family members as a result of the division of the country for more than 45 years.

In June 1991 the National Unification Board said it had approved 500 out of 593 requests from private citizens to contact North Koreans. It added that 172 applications had been approved for South Koreans to meet with their relatives in North Korea. (The National Unification Board is a government appointed body which undertakes research, conducts surveys and provides public information on the issue of reunification).

0042

The South Korean Government insists that it should be the main party to negotiations about reunification with North Korea and it regards initiatives by private citizens or non-governmental organizations, particularly those critical of government policy, to have such discussions with the North as disruptive and liable to favour North Korea. It therefore has refused to grant authorization to people deemed to be dissidents to meet with North Koreans.

In November 1990 the National Unification Board rejected an application for three members of the dissident organization *Chonminnyon* (National Coalition for Democratic Movement) to meet North Koreans during the inaugural meeting of *Pomminnyon* (Pan-National Alliance for the Reunification of Korea). *Pomminnyon* was inaugurated in November 1990 in Berlin at a meeting attended by delegates from North and South Korea and from overseas. The organization has stated as its main objectives the achievement of peaceful national reunification, independence and national unity. Reverend Cho Yong-sul, Cho Song-woo and Lee Hae-hak attended the meeting in Berlin where they met with the Vice-Chairman of the North Korean Committee for the Peaceful Unification of the Fatherland. The three men were arrested upon their return to South Korea.

Reverend Cho Yong-sul is arrested
At Kimpo Airport, 30 November 1991

(c) Reuters

2) NATIONAL SECURITY LEGISLATION

Two laws have been applied in cases of state security: the Anti-Communist Law and the National Security Law.

The Anti-Communist Law, enacted in 1961 and abrogated in December 1980, was intended to "strengthen the anti-communist posture...[and] block the activities of the communist organizations that endanger the national security..." (Article 1). Many of its provisions were similar to those contained in the National Security Law and after its repeal offences concerning pro-communist activities were covered by the National Security Law.

The National Security Law was first enacted in 1960. Its declared purpose is to "control anti-state activities which endanger the national security, so that the safety of the State as well as the existence and freedoms of citizens may be secured" (Article 1). The last two occasions where it was amended were in December 1980 to include provisions formerly in the Anti-Communist Law and more recently in May 1991.

2.1 The National Security Law (1980)

The National Security Law prescribes long sentences of imprisonment or the death penalty for anti-state activities and contacts with anti-state organizations. Over the years the law has been widely used to imprison people who visited North Korea without government authorization, people who met North Koreans or alleged North Korean agents abroad and people who expressed support for North Korea or whose views were similar to positions also taken by the North.

The main provisions of the National Security Law which have been applied to the prisoners whose cases are described in this document are:

Article 2 *(anti-state organization)*: "(1) The term "anti-state organization" as referred to in this Act shall be construed to mean such an association or group within the territory of the Republic of Korea or outside of it, as organized for the purpose of assuming a title of the government or disturbing the State. (2) Such a domestic and foreign association or group that operates along the line of the communists in order to achieve the purpose mentioned in paragraph 1 shall be deemed to be an anti-state organisation."

Article 3 *(formation of anti-state organisation)*: Forming or participating in an "anti-state" organization, or preparing or conspiring to do so. Sentences on conviction range from two years' imprisonment to the death sentence for ringleaders. An "anti-state" organization is defined as an organization whose purpose is to "assume a title of the government or disturb the state". Organizations which have been defined as "anti-state" have included dissident groups or workers, students and political activists. The definition also extends to the North Korean Government.

Article 4 *(acts of treason, espionage or sabotage under instruction from an anti-state organisation)*: "If a component of an anti-state organisation or a person who had been under instruction from such an organisation has committed any acts designed to perform such objectives, he or she shall be punished... [followed by six paragraphs specifying acts of treason, espionage, sabotage, etc]"

Article 6 *(escape and infiltration)*: Illegal travel to North Korea and re-entry into South Korea, or preparing or conspiring to do so, under instructions from North Korea or in order to benefit it. Sentences on conviction range from two to 10 years' imprisonment. Amnesty International considers that the mere fact of travelling to North Korea without evidence either of espionage activities or of the use or advocacy of violence cannot justify imprisonment.

Article 7: *(praise, encouragement, etc.)* Benefiting North Korea by praising it, encouraging it, siding with it or through other means, or preparing or conspiring to commit such an offence. Sentences on conviction range from one to seven years' imprisonment. This provision has been used to imprison people who have written or disseminated material about the North Korean system of government, or which criticized the South Korean Government or the presence of US armed forces in South Korea.

Article 8 *(meetings, communication, etc.)*: Meeting, liaising or communicating with members of an anti-state organization for its benefit, or preparing or conspiring to do so. Sentences on conviction range from one to seven years' imprisonment. This provision has been used against dissidents who have sought to contact North Koreans without the authorization of the South Korean Government.

Article 10 *(failure to inform)*: Failing to inform the authorities about a person who has committed an offence under the National Security Law. The maximum sentence on conviction is five years' imprisonment.

2.2 May 1991 Amendments to the National Security Law

On 10 May 1991 the ruling Democratic Liberal Party unilaterally passed amendments to the National Security Law in spite of protests from opposition National Assembly members. Talks on amending the law had been held among representatives of the main political parties for more than two years without reaching agreement.

A document issued by the government on the amendments highlights the following points:

A new provision (Article 1(2)) was introduced aimed at restricting the use of the law: "The interpretation and application of this law shall be confined to the minimum extent necessary to achieve its purpose. The law shall not be loosely interpreted or otherwise misapplied to unreasonably restrict the basic human rights of citizens."

The definition of "anti-state" organisation in Article 2(1) has been changed to require that it be "equipped with a command and control system".

Article 2 (2) which regarded all communist groups as "anti-state" was withdrawn. The law therefore no longer forbids contact with communist organizations or governments in countries other than North Korea. Provisions of Article 6, 7 and 8 which provided penalties for people praising or communicating with communist parties or governments were also repealed, so that contacts with communist countries are now permitted, except with North Korea.

Article 4 was amended to distinguish between cases where espionage involved "facts, objects or knowledge, access to which is allowed to a limited number of people only in order to prevent grave disadvantages" that their disclosure would "inflict on national security" and cases of espionage involving "lesser secrets". The revised law provides for sentences ranging from a minimum of seven years' imprisonment to the death penalty.

Article 7 was amended so that acts of praising, encouraging or showing sympathy to an anti-state organisation will be punishable only when committed "with the knowledge that it will endanger national security and survival and the free and democratic basic order." The vague expression "or otherwise give aid and comfort to an anti-state organisation" was deleted but the law now specifically makes it an offence to agitate for or incite subversion of the State when this is done knowing that it will "endanger national security and survival and the free and democratic basic order".

Article 2 (2) and Articles 6 and 8 were revised so that acts of giving or receiving goods or money to or from a member of an anti-state organisation, or communicating with a member of an anti-state organisation or someone acting under its instructions, or escaping from or to the territory of an anti-state organisation will be punishable only when committed with "the knowledge that it will endanger national security and survival and the free and democratic basic order."

Under the 1980 law failure to report violations of the law to the authorities was punishable by imprisonment. The 1991 amendments retain failure to report a crime only for violations of Article 3 (formation or affiliation with an antistate organisation), Article 4 (acts of treason, espionage or sabotage by a member of an anti-state organisation) and Article 5 (willing provision of material and assistance to anyone violating Article 4). When this offence is committed by a relative punishment is now to be lessened or waived.

Preparing or conspiring to commit National Security Law offences is now punishable only with respect to some of the offences, while under the 1980 law preparations or conspiracies to commit offences under Article 3 to Article 8 were all punishable.

The 1991 amendments give discretion to a judge to decide whether or not to suspend the civil rights of a person convicted under the NSL; such a suspension (post-imprisonment) was provided in all cases under the previous versions of the law.

Amnesty International welcomes the amendments made to the National Security Law in so far as they define offences more precisely. However, it would appear that the law will continue to allow for the imprisonment of people who support North Korean ideology and seek to contact North Koreans without government permission. Courts trying prisoners under the older versions of the National Security Law have ruled that any information, even if it was available in the public domain, which could be useful to North Korea, qualified as a "state secret". It remains to be seen whether the courts will convict of espionage people accused of passing to North Koreans or (alleged) supporters of North Korea information which is not actually classified as state secrets by the government. The application of the law in actual cases will provide a test of whether it continues to be used to detain government critics merely for the peaceful exercise of their rights of freedom of expression or association.

3) PRISONERS HELD UNDER NATIONAL SECURITY LEGISLATION

Little information is available about prisoners arrested on national security grounds before 1970 although reports suggest that most may have been sent as spies by North Korea or were partisans fighting the US and South Korean forces in the late 1940s or around the time of the Korean War.

The prisoners whose cases are described in this document and whom Amnesty International believes are prisoners of conscience or possible prisoners of conscience or whom it believes may have been convicted after unfair trials were arrested between 1975 and early 1991 and fall into the following categories:

1) South Koreans who visited Japan for study, business or family meetings and who were arrested after returning to South Korea. Some have been accused of having met members or officials of *Chongnyon* (the General Federation of Korean Residents in Japan, a pro-North Korean organisation) and of giving them information on South

Korea. Others are accused of having visited North Korea with the help of *Chongnyon* members. The following prisoners fall into this category:

Yu Chong-sik: arrested in 1975
Cho Sang-nok: arrested in 1978
Shin Kui-yong: arrested in 1980
Lee Jang-hyong: arrested in 1983
Koh Chang-pyo: arrested in 1983
Nah Jon-in: arrested in 1985
Lee Pyong-sol: arrested in 1986
Chang Ui-gyun: arrested in 1987
Kang Hui-chol: arrested 1987

2) South Koreans who did not report visits from relatives who normally live in North Korea and whose clandestine visits to the south were alleged to be for spying purposes. The following prisoners fall into this category:

Park Dong-oon: arrested in 1981
Ham Ju-myong: arrested in 1983
Park Chan-u: arrested in 1984
Lee Chang-guk: arrested in 1984
Lee Joon-ho: arrested in 1985

3) South Korean nationals resident in Japan who were arrested when visiting South Korea and are alleged to have visited North Korea with the help of members of *Chongnyon*. The following prisoner falls into this category:

Lee Hon-chi: arrested in 1981

4) South Koreans who made illegal visits to North Korea or other countries where they are alleged to have met North Korean officials or Korean exiles said to support North Korea and to have passed information to them about the political situation in South Korea. The following prisoners fall into this category:

Kim Song-man: arrested in 1985
Hwang Tae-kwon: arrested in 1985

0048

Kang Yong-ju: arrested in 1985
Yang Dong-hwa: arrested in 1985
Kim Yun-su: arrested in 1985
Suh Kyong-won: arrested in 1989
Pang Yang-kyun: arrested in 1989
Yu Won-ho: arrested in 1989
Im Su-kyong: arrested in 1989
Father Moon Kyu-hyun: arrested in 1989
Cho Song-woo: arrested in 1990
Lee Hae-hak: arrested in 1990

5) South Koreans who were accused of "praising and benefiting" North Korea. Some of these prisoners have been accused of sending information to alleged North Korean sympathizers in other countries. Others were accused of publishing and disseminating pro-North Korean materials in South Korea or of attempting to establish a pro-North Korean organization. Prisoners in this category include:

Hong Song-dam: arrested in 1989
Kim Hyon-jang: arrested in 1989
Oh Tong-yol: arrested in 1989
Kim Keun-tae: arrested in 1990
Jang Myung-guk: arrested in 1990
An estimated 40 members of *Sanomaeng*: arrested in 1990
An estimated 30 members of *Chamintong*: arrested in 1990
Lee Chang-bok: arrested in 1991
Kim Hi-taek: arrested in 1991
Reverend Hong Keun-soo: arrested in 1991

amnesty international

INTERNATIONAL SECRETARIAT,
1 Easton Street, London WC1X 8DJ,
United Kingdom.

TG ASA 25/91.15

Mr K. C. Lee
Embassy of the Republic of Korea
4 Palace Gate
London W8 5NF

1 October 1991

Dear Mr Lee,

I enclose, for your information, a copy of a document Amnesty International issued today to its members South Korea : Prisoners Held for National Security Offences. This document explains Amnesty International's concerns about a number of prisoners serving long sentences of imprisonment under the National Security Law. Most of the cases have been previously publicized by Amnesty International in other documents and this latest document takes into account information supplied by your government on individual cases. Mr Hoffman and Ms McVey gave an advance copy of this document to the officials of the Ministry of Justice they met during their recent visit.

Yours sincerely,

Derek G. Evans
Head of the Asia and Pacific Region
Research Department

☎ (44)(71) 413 5500 Telegrams: Amnesty London WC1 Telex: 28502 FAX: 956 1157

Amnesty International is an independent worldwide movement working impartially for the release of all prisoners of conscience, fair and prompt trials for political prisoners and an end to torture and executions. It is funded by donations from its members and supporters throughout the world. It has formal relations with the United Nations, Unesco, the Council of Europe, the Organization of African Unity and the Organization of American States.

0050

4) PRISONER CASES

Yu-Chong-sik

Arrest: April 1975
Charge: Contacting pro-North Korean organization in Japan
Sentence: Life imprisonment, held in Andong Prison

Yu Chong-sik was born in Seoul around 1940. He was arrested in 1975 and sentenced to life imprisonment. He was accused of having contacted the pro-North Korean organization *Chongnyon* when he was a student in Japan. He claims to have been tortured during his interrogation by the Korean Central Intelligence Agency and is said to be suffering from anxiety and heart problems. Amnesty International does not have any other information about his case. It is seeking further information about the reasons for his arrest and the charges and evidence against him. It is calling on the authorities to investigate the claims that he was tortured and convicted on the basis of a confession obtained under torture.

Cho Sang-nok

Cho Sang-nok

Arrest: 15 January 1978
Charge: Contacting alleged North Korean agent in Japan
Sentence: Life imprisonment, held in Taejon Prison

Cho Sang-nok was born in 1945. He graduated from Chungang University in Seoul and went to Japan in 1976 where he obtained a post-graduate degree in politics. While in Japan he is said to have been outspoken about his political views. He reportedly participated in a campaign calling for the revision of Japanese history books which glossed over atrocities committed by the Japanese military forces in Korea and China during World War II. He is understood to have been opposed to communism but also to have been critical of the government of then President Park Chung-hee. Cho Sang-nok was arrested in January 1978. In 1990 Cho Sang-nok wrote the following in a letter from prison:

> *"They asked me to meet with them outside, and as I was walking toward a driver of a black passenger car, two strangers suddenly poked revolvers into my waist from behind and told me to get in the car quietly. They took me in that car to an unknown location, covering my eyes, and they tortured me in every possible way."*

He was held for interrogation in an unidentified location for 17 days before he was transferred to Seoul Detention Centre. When a relative met him some time after his arrest, he said that he had been beaten and tortured; his ears were bleeding and he appeared very tired. Cho Sang-nok was charged with having contacted a North Korean agent in Japan and receiving money and instructions to set up an underground organization. He is also accused of having sought information on security arrangements at the presidential palace from a neighbour and of having praised North Korea openly on several occasions. In May 1978 he was sentenced to life imprisonment by the Seoul District Court. Amnesty International is seeking further information on the charges and evidence against Cho Sang-nok and is calling on the authorities to conduct an impartial inquiry into the claims that he was tortured and the possibility that he was not given a fair trial.

Shin Kui-yong

Arrest: **February 1980**
Charge: **Meeting his brother (who is said to be a member of a pro-North Korean organization in Japan) and passing information to him on South Korea**
Sentence: **15 years' imprisonment, held in Taejon Prison**

Shin Kui-yong's parents moved from Korea to Japan in 1925 to work as farm labourers and while in Japan gave birth to four sons and two daughters. The whole family, except for one of Shin Kui-yong's brothers, moved back to Korea in 1947 and in 1965 Shin Kui-yong became a merchant seaman. In February 1980 Shi Kui-yong, then aged 43, was arrested and sentenced to 15 years' imprisonment. He was accused of visiting his brother in Japan seven times during his ship's stop-overs in that country. The authorities claim that Shin Kui-yong's brother, who is said to be a member of the pro-North Korean organization *Chongnyon*, recruited him as a spy and gave him money to fund his espionage activities. Shin Kui-yong admitted receiving a small amount of money from his brother on each visit but claimed that this money was passed on to his mother for her upkeep. He also admitted receiving a larger sum of money from his brother after their mother died but claimed that this was to cover funeral expenses. Shin Kui-yong also reportedly confessed to passing his brother information he had learned about the military during his military service some 17 years earlier, but later claimed that he had made this confession under torture. His family say that he was held *incommunicado* for 70 days by an anti-communist intelligence unit. Amnesty International is urging the authorities to investigate the claims that Shin Kui-yong was tortured and unfairly convicted. It is seeking further information about the charges and evidence used to convict him.

Lee Hon-chi

Arrest: 9 October 1981
Charge: Visiting North Korea
Sentence: Death penalty, commuted to life imprisonment, later commuted to 20 years' imprisonment, held in Chonju Prison

Lee Hon-chi, now aged 39, was a Korean resident of Japan. In 1977 he went to work as an electronic technician for a Japanese company in Seoul, and on 9 October he was arrested together with Lee Ju-kwang, a student at Korea University. The two men were charged with leading an espionage ring which had instigated worker unrest and student demonstrations in an attempt to overthrow the government. They were also charged with sending industrial secrets to North Korea. Lee Hon-chi was specifically accused of visiting North Korea in December 1974 where he allegedly received espionage training and joined the North Korean Workers' Party. He is then said to have been assigned to a North Korean agent based in Japan, who instructed him in December 1977 to gain employment in Seoul. The authorities allege that from this date until his arrest he visited Japan on a number of occasions and passed industrial and military information to a North Korean agent. He was also accused of recruiting three other Koreans working for the same company in Seoul with the aim of establishing an espionage network.

Lee Hon-chi was sentenced to death by the courts. His sentence was commuted to life imprisonment (date not known) and commuted to 20 years' imprisonment under a presidential amnesty in December 1988. His wife was also arrested and accused of collaborating with her husband. She was pregnant at the time and gave birth during interrogation. In February 1982 she was given a suspended prison sentence and released. Lee Hon-chi was reportedly denied access to a lawyer and to his family for over four months from his arrest until his first trial in February 1982. In letters to his wife and brother, he claims that the charges of espionage against him were fabricated. He says that he was forced to confess to visiting North Korea and of espionage after ill-treatment and threats from his interrogators. In one of his letters to his wife he says:

"I went through all kinds of abuse, including sleep deprivation, threats, lies, beating. Events in the next few days were a threat to my, your and Sung-o's [their son] life and I gave up everything. I kept telling them from the very beginning that I would cooperate if only they would let me see you. Finally they took me to you at the [army] hospital. Afterwards, I had to cooperate . . ."

Amnesty International is concerned that Lee Hon-chi may have been wrongly convicted after an unfair trial and is seeking further information about the charges and evidence against him. It is calling on the authorities to investigate the claims that he was ill-treated.

Park Dong-oon

Arrest: **March 1981**
Charge: **Visiting North Korea; organizing a pro-North Korean spy ring**
Sentence: **Death, commuted to life imprisonment, held in Kwangju Prison**

Park Dong-oon and several relatives, who have now been released, were convicted of belonging to the "Chindo Permanent Spy Ring" and accused of spying for North Korea. Park Dong-oon was charged with visiting North Korea in 1965 and 1971 where he is alleged to have met members of the Korean Workers' Party and to have received espionage training and instructions to set up a spy ring in South Korea. The authorities also claimed that on several occasions Park Dong-oon met his father who had been missing since the Korean War and is alleged by the authorities to have returned to South Korea as a North Korean spy and to have met with members of his family.

One of Park Dong-oon's uncles, also arrested in this case, claims that they were convicted on the basis of confessions they made under torture. He said:

"My household, which consists of five family members including me was forcefully taken . . . on or about March 9, 1981 without our having committed any crimes and without knowing why. For sixty days, we were illegally detained and went through horrible murderous torture and terror.

It was absolutely impossible to bear the torture both physically and mentally. If there were any way to end my life I would have done so, so that I would not have had to go through all these sufferings".

Witnesses at the trial were reportedly intimidated by intelligence agencies into not supporting Park Dong-oon's alibi for the dates he was accused of travelling to North

0054

Korea and the only evidence of contacts with Park Dong-oon's "father/spy" were the statements made by the defendants during their interrogation.

Park Dong-oon was sentenced to death by the courts. His sentence was later commuted to life imprisonment. Amnesty International is urging the authorities to investigate the claims that Park Dong-oon was tortured to force him to confess to espionage activities. It is seeking further information about the charges and evidence against him and the possibility that he may have been convicted after an unfair trial.

Lee Jang-hyong

Arrest: 15 June 1983
Charge: Meeting his uncle in Japan who is a member of a pro-North Korean group
Sentence: Life imprisonment, held in Chonju Prison

Lee Jang-hyong, now aged 57, is said to have visited Japan on a business trip and while there to have met with his uncle who is a member of the pro-North Korean organization *Chongnyon*. On 15 June 1983 he was arrested and accused of meeting members of *Chongnyon* with the purpose of carrying out espionage on behalf of North Korea. He is reported to have been tortured during interrogation in order to force him to confess to the espionage charges against him. Amnesty International is seeking further information about the charges and evidence against Lee Jang-hyong and is urging the authorities to investigate his claims of torture and the possibility that he was convicted after an unfair trial.

Ham Ju-myong

Arrest: 18 February 1983
Charge: Visiting North Korea and sending information to North Korea
Sentence Life imprisonment, held in Chonju Prison

Ham Ju-myong was born in what is now North Korea. In 1952 he moved to the south and gave himself up to the US forces which were the main component of the United Nations Command which assisted the Republic of Korea during the Korean War. On 18 February 1983 Ham Ju-myong was arrested and accused of passing information to a woman in North Korea whom the authorities said he married between 1950 and 1952. She is said to be the daughter of the manager of the boarding house where he stayed during those two years, and to now be a middle-school teacher. Ham Ju-myong was accused of having sent this alleged wife information about traffic check-points around Kanghwa Island, which is close to the North Korean border, and about Taegu City Airport.

At his trial Ham Ju-myong denied having married in North Korea and spying for the North Korean Government. He admitted visiting Kanghwa Island but said the purpose of his trip was to visit his parents' tomb. Several of his friends who had also come from the north during the Korean War were called to give evidence against him. Before they appeared in court they are said to have been detained for a few days and obliged to write statements testifying that Ham Ju-myong was a communist. In court, one of the witnesses is said to have contradicted his written statement that Ham Ju-myong was not a communist. At that point, the prosecution is reported to have asked for the hearing to be adjourned. At the next hearing, all the witnesses confirmed their written statements, including the witness who had retracted it at the previous hearing. Ham Ju-myong was sentenced to life imprisonment.

Ham Ju-myong claims that he was severely tortured during his three months' interrogation. Although he was arrested in February, his South Korean wife was not allowed to see him until May. At her first visit he was unable to talk because of the pain he said was caused by having been beaten on his chest. He told his wife that electric shocks had been applied on his hands and feet, that he had been repeatedly submerged under water, hung upside-down and strapped to a board and beaten. He commented that he knew when he was to be tortured because he would not be given food that day to stop him from choking during the torture.

Amnesty International is urging the authorities to investigate the claims that Ham Ju-myong was tortured to confess to espionage activities and to review his case in the light of evidence that he was not given a fair trial.

Prisoner of Conscience: Koh Chang-pyo

Arrest: 1 December 1983
Charge: Meeting pro-North Koreans in Japan
Sentence: 15 years' imprisonment, held in Chonju Prison

Koh Chang-pyo, aged 58, served in the military until his retirement in 1979 when he started a business. After his business began to fail he is reported to have come into contact with businessman Kim Byung-ju who lived in the Japanese town of Matsusaka. In 1981 he travelled to Japan at the invitation of Kim Byung-ju to attend a trade fair. In December 1983 Koh Chang-pyo was arrested and accused of being recruited and paid by Kim Byung-ju to carry out espionage activities such as gathering information on members of the military and leading businessmen in his home town, and on military sites along the east coast of the Korean peninsula.

At his trial Koh Chang-pyo stated that he was unaware of Kim Byung-ju's reported pro-North Korean activities. He denied going to Japan to receive espionage training and said that the money he received from Kim Byung-ju was a loan to help his failing business. Koh Chang-pyo alleges that he was tortured in order to make him confess to being a North Korean spy. Koh Chang-pyo's defence lawyers argued that the information he is accused of gathering was openly known to the local community and could not be considered a national secret.

Koh Chang-pyo was sentenced to 15 years' imprisonment. Amnesty International believes there is insufficient evidence that Koh Chang-pyo carried out espionage and is concerned at reports that he was tortured to force him to confess. It has adopted him as a prisoner of conscience and is calling for his immediate and unconditional release.

Park Chan-u

Arrest: July 1984
Charge: Attempting to visit North Korea
Sentence: 15 years' imprisonment, held in Chonju Prison

Park Chan-u was arrested in July 1984 by the Military Security Command on charges under the National Security Law. Sources say that he was arrested after attempting to go to North Korea, although he had no definite plans about what he would do if he got there. Park Chan-u was reportedly separated from his family when he was young and was considered an orphan. He left school early, after his second year at primary school, and earned his living as a labourer. Amnesty International believes that Park Chan-u may be detained solely for his attempt to go to North Korea and is seeking further details of the reasons for his arrest and evidence used to convict him.

Lee Chang-guk

Arrest: **1 May 1984**
Charge: **Visiting North Korea and passing information to a brother, said to be a North Korean spy**
Sentence: **15 years' imprisonment, held in Andong Prison**

Lee Chang-guk was convicted of having been recruited as a spy by his brother who went to North Korea during the Korean war and is said to have come to South Korea on several occasions after.1962 as a North Korean spy. He was also accused of visiting North Korea in 1962 and 1973 where he is alleged to have received espionage training, joined the Korean Workers Party and passed "state secrets".

Lee Chang-guk ran a stationery shop in Inchon and is a devoted Christian. Because his older brother and sister went to North Korea during the Korean war he was under regular police surveillance and his family denied that he ever met his brother after the war or visited North Korea. The main evidence against him was the confession he made during 77 days of interrogation by the Agency for National Security Planning, which he denied in court. Lee Chang-guk is said to have confessed under torture and to have attempted suicide to avoid further torture. He is now 70 years old and is said to be in poor health.

Amnesty International is seeking further information about the charges and evidence against Lee Chang-guk and is urging the authorities to investigate the claims that he was tortured and the possibility that he was convicted after an unfair trial.

Prisoner of Conscience: Kim Song-man

Kim Song-man

Arrest: **6 June 1985**
Charge: **Meeting and passing information to North Koreans**
Sentence: **Death sentence, reduced to life imprisonment, held in Taejon Prison**

Kim Song-man was born in 1957. He comes from a Christian family; his grandfather founded the Evangelical Church in Korea. When a student of physics at Yonsei University in Seoul he was active in the Christian Student Association. In June 1982 he went to the United States and enroled at the Western Illinois University to study political science. During his studies at the Western Illinois University he met Hwang Tae-kwon and Yang Dong-hwa (see below). The three men are said to have been widely read in political science and about the political system in North Korea. The following year Kim Song-man moved to New York and according to some reports contributed articles to *Haeuiminbo* (Overseas Korean News). In June 1983 he visited Europe and stayed at the North Korean embassy in Budapest, Hungary, for three days and discussed the student movement and the political situation in South Korea. He returned to South Korea in July 1983 and is said to have renewed contact with the student movement, formed a group *Chonminjunghoe* (The Entire People Association) and written pamphlets calling for the withdrawal of US troops from South Korea. In November 1984 he visited East Berlin and is said to have given North Korean embassy staff copies of the pamphlets he had written. On 6 June 1985 Kim Song-man was arrested. According to the indictment he was encouraged by the North Koreans he met to engage in anti-government activities and given instructions such as to encourage student activists to enter the Korean Military Academy. Kim Song-man was sentenced to death by the courts, but this sentence was reduced to life imprisonment under a presidential amnesty in December 1988. In his appeal to the Supreme Court in August 1986 Kim Song-man wrote:

> *"I am a person who wishes the independence of our nation and democracy. I think that this ideal can be realized in a socialistic country. I was interrogated and tortured mercilessly at the Agency for National Security Planning. During the interrogation and torture I was even forced to write a suicide letter addressed to my parents in*

order to disguise my possible death as a suicide. The press widely published my forced confession as though it was true. I only long for the day we can enjoy our independence from under slavish submission to a foreign power. Even if all the world does not believe me I know that God knows the truth."

Amnesty International has adopted Kim Song-man as a prisoner of conscience as it believes he is detained solely for his beliefs and that there is no evidence of his having carried out espionage activities or having used or advocated the use of violence.

Prisoner of Conscience: Hwang Tae-kwon

Hwang Tae-kwon

Arrest: **June 1985**
Charge: **Meeting and passing information to pro-North Koreans abroad**
Sentence: **Life imprisonment, reduced to 20 years, held in Andong Prison**

Hwang Tae-kwon, now aged 36, graduated from Seoul National University in agriculture in February 1982 and then joined Western Illinois University. He is believed to have contributed articles on the South Korean student movement or which reflected anti-government and anti-US views to *Haeuiminbo* (Overseas Korean News). In June 1985 he was arrested at Seoul's Kimpo international airport as he returned for a vacation. In appeals to the courts and other documents he has denied knowingly meeting North Koreans or North Korean agents. He admits to having been involved in the student movement and having been critical of the government but rejects the accusation that he is a communist. Hwang Tae-kwon was sentenced to life imprisonment, but this sentence was reduced to 20 years under a presidential amnesty in December 1988. In a letter written from prison in 1988, Hwang Tae-kwon described his interrogation as follows:

". . . after 60 days of torture and beatings in the basement of the Agency for National Security Planning and after three years of imprisonment for a crime I did not commit, having been silenced all those years, I hope my story will expose the crimes that were committed against me by the powers-that-be in order to extract my

'confession'. I am also hoping to restore my own human dignity which has been ruthlessly trampled upon during the interrogation and imprisonment."

Amnesty International has adopted Hwang Tae-kwon as a prisoner of conscience and is calling for his immediate and unconditional release.

Yang Dong-hwa

Yang Dong-hwa

Arrest **June 1985**
Charge: **Meeting and passing information to North Koreans abroad**
Sentence: **Death sentence, commuted to life imprisonment, held in Taejgu Prison**

Yang Dong-hwa was expelled from Chosun University in the southwestern city of Kwangju in May 1980 because of his political activities. He went to the USA and enroled at Western Illinois University in 1983. He did not complete his studies and went to New York where he is said to have been in contact with the publisher of *Haeuiminbo* (Overseas Korean News). Apparently with the help of this publisher he travelled to North Korea where he stayed from 29 August to 8 September 1984. The South Korean authorities accused him of having received political indoctrination there and of having joined the Korean Workers' Party, as well as receiving instructions to infiltrate the South Korean student movement, incite anti-US sentiments and mobilize students to stage a second "Kwangju Incident". On his way back from North Korea Yang Dong-hwa allegedly visited the North Korean embassy in Vienna. He returned to South Korea in September 1984. Amnesty International has no independent information about Yang Dong-hwa's activities between that time and his arrest in mid-1985. He was charged with recruiting a small group of people, mainly students, and giving them instructions. One of those he allegedly recruited was Kang Yong-ju (see below). Yang Dong-hwa is accused of having influenced Kang Yong-ju into giving an anti-US and pro-North Korean slant to students' activities and of having instructed him to recruit other students to bomb the US Cultural Centre in Kwangju. An air stewardess whom Yang Dong-hwa allegedly recruited is said to have taken some anti-government documents produced in South Korea to the publisher of *Haeuiminbo* in New York. Other charges against Yang Dong-hwa are that he obtained information about Kwangju airport - which is partly used by the military - from US soldiers and that he intended to pass this information to North Korea and that he travelled to Seoul to look for information on how to make bombs.

Yang Dong-hwa was sentenced to death by the courts. His sentence was commuted to life imprisonment in December 1988. Amnesty International is concerned that Yang Dong-hwa may have been tortured or ill-treated to force him to falsely admit to charges of inciting others to carry out violent activities. So far it has not been able to collect enough information to show whether these accusations are grounded or false and it is continuing to seek further information on the reasons for Yang Dong-hwa's arrest in order to establish whether he may be a prisoner of conscience.

Kang Yong-ju

Kang Yong-ju

Arrest: 9 June 1985
Charge: Meeting and passing information to a North Korean agent
Sentence: Life imprisonment, held in Taejon Prison

Amnesty International has little information about **Kang Yong-ju**'s political activities prior to his arrest in June 1985. He entered the Medical School of Chonnam National University in Kwangju in 1982 and was expelled from it in February 1985 because of his political activities. He is said to have been involved in activities of the Christian Student's Council and in November 1984 was elected chairman of the student group *Mintu* (People's Struggle). In February 1985 he is reported to have organized student demonstrations on anti-US themes. He is accused of having given information to Yang Dong-hwa about the student movement and of having travelled to Seoul with him to look for books on how to make bombs.

Kang Yong-ju denied these charges in court and some people who knew him thought from his appearance that he had been ill-treated or tortured. Kang Yong-ju, now aged 30, was sentenced to life imprisonment by the courts and did not benefit from a reduction of his sentence under the December 1988 presidential amnesty, as did his co-defendants. Amnesty International has been unable to ascertain whether Kang Yong-ju was involved in organizing or planning acts of political violence and is continuing to seek further information on his case in order to establish whether he may be a prisoner of conscience.

0062

Lee Joon-ho

Arrest: **May 1985**
Charge: **Passing information to North Korea**
Sentence: **Seven years' imprisonment, held in Taejon Prison**

Lee Joon-ho was arrested around May 1985 and sentenced to seven years' imprisonment. The authorities say that he was recruited as a spy for North Korea in 1972 by his uncle, Lee Han-su, who had gone to North Korea after the Korean war. Lee Joon-ho was accused of collecting information on military installations along the west coast of Korea which he passed on to North Korea and of giving the North Korean leader, Kim Il-sung, presents on his 60th birthday. Lee Joon-ho's mother, who was arrested with him, was released in October 1988 after completing her sentence.

Lee Joon-ho, now aged around 40, is said to be a devout Christian and is reported to have refused to sign a statement of conversion to anti-communism, saying that his religion does not allow him to compromise with injustice. Amnesty International is seeking further information about the charges and evidence against Lee Joon-ho.

Kim Yun-su

Arrest: **24 June 1985**
Charge: **Visiting and sending information to North Korea**
Sentence: **15 years' imprisonment, held in Chonju Prison**

Kim Yun-su, now aged around 57, was arrested on 24 June 1985. The authorities accused him of having been recruited as a spy in 1978 by a female colleague when he worked at a driving school in Seoul. He was accused of visiting North Korea via Japan, Austria and Moscow in May 1981 and of allegedly receiving espionage training and orders to set up an underground espionage ring in South Korea. At his trial Kim Yun-su admitted visiting North Korea and Moscow but said that he only did so as a tourist. He is said to have become interested in North Korea and other communist countries after seeing a video of the 1980 "Kwangju Incident" during a visit to Japan. When Kim Yun-su viewed the video information about the incident was only available through underground dissident movements in South Korea or abroad.

Amnesty International is seeking further information about the charges and evidence against Kim Yun-su.

Nah Jong-in

Arrest: 27 April 1985
Charge: Visiting and sending information to North Korea
Sentence: 15 years' imprisonment, held in Taegu Prison

Nah Jong-in, now aged 54, graduated in electronic engineering from Seoul National University. In 1971 he set up the Samhwa Engineering Company and made frequent business trips to Japan. He was arrested on 27 April 1985 and accused of visiting North Korea illegally in 1961 and 1964 and of receiving espionage training while there. The authorities claim that Nah Jong-in was recruited as a spy in 1961 by his sister who had gone to the North around the time of the 1950-1953 Korean War. They allege that he established the Samhwa Engineering Company as a cover for his espionage activities and that he passed military and industrial secrets to a North Korean agent during his business trips to Japan.

Nah Jong-in's wife was questioned about her husband's activities and says she was ordered to confess that she knew that her husband was a spy, something she denied. When she saw her husband after his arrest she noticed that he appeared to be in great pain and appeared unable to walk. He reportedly told her:

> *"They [The Military Security Command] took me and tortured me in all kinds of ways, and I confessed everything. My confession was quite honest and sincere, but they do not take it seriously".*

Nah Jong-in admitted to having visited North Korea in 1961 but denied that he received espionage training while there. He also claimed that the charges that he went to the North in 1964 and that he passed national secrets to an agent in Japan had been fabricated. At his high court appeal hearing the judge accepted Nah Jong-in's claims that he was tortured but upheld his sentence.

Amnesty International is calling on the authorities to investigate the claims that Nah Jong-in was tortured and may have been convicted after an unfair trial.

Lee Pyong-sol

Lee Pyong-sol
(c) Korea Times

Arrest: **7 July 1986**
Charge: **Meeting and passing information to pro-North Koreans in Japan**
Sentence: **15 years' imprisonment, reduced on appeal to 12 years, held in Andong Prison**

Lee Pyong-sol, now aged 53, was a professor at Seoul National University when he was arrested in September 1986 on charges of being the alleged leader of a "spy ring". He was accused of having incited campus and labour unrest and of having organized underground cells among students, workers and teachers.

The authorities claimed that he had been recruited by a North Korean agent based in Tokyo when he was studying there in 1975 and that he became a member of the Korean Workers' Party in February 1976. Lee Pyong-sol was accused of visiting Japan on five occasions between August 1980 and February 1986 in order to report back on his espionage activities to North Korean agents. During these trips he is alleged to have passed on "military and social information" on South Korea collected by his recruits, including over 200 maps. Other sources have told Amnesty International that they believe that Professor Lee Pyong-sol may have been arrested because he is believed to have corresponded with his brother who lives in North Korea.

Lee Pyong-sol denied the accusations against him and claims that he was tortured into making a false confession. In January 1987 he was sentenced by the Seoul District Court to 15 years' imprisonment. In May 1987 his sentence was reduced on appeal to 12 years' imprisonment. Amnesty International is concerned that Professor Lee Pyong-sol may have been convicted after an unfair trial. It is seeking further information about the charges and evidence against him.

Prisoner of Conscience: Chang Ui-gyun

Chang Ui-gyun

Arrest: **5 July 1987**
Charge: **Meeting and passing information to pro-North Koreans in Japan**
Sentence: **15 years imprisonment, reduced on appeal to eight years, held in Taejon Prison**

Chang Ui-gyun, now aged 40, graduated in journalism from Sogang University in 1980 after several interruptions for his military service and to work in order to finance his studies. When at university, he was involved in political and labour issues. After graduating, he set up the *Kaema* publishing company which specialized in books on ancient Korean history. In 1982, his publishing licence was withdrawn after he published a book of poetry which was critical of the government.

In April 1985 he went to Japan and registered as a part-time student of ancient Korean History at Kyoto University. He also used the opportunity of his stay in Japan to learn more about North Korea, as documents from North Korea and books supportive of the north were forbidden in South Korea. He is said, for instance, to have met a journalist working for *Chongnyon* and to have visited the pro-North Korean Choson University, where he borrowed books and attended lectures. Among his other known political activities in Japan was the organization of a meeting in May 1986 on the issue of Korean reunification. The meeting is said to have brought together Korean residents in Japan who supported either North or South Korea.

Chang Ui-gyun returned to South Korea in March 1987 and was arrested on 5 July. He was interrogated for 25 days and was transferred to Seoul Detention Centre on 30 July. Except for a brief encounter with his wife on 11 July, he was not allowed to see anyone until he was indicted on 27 August. He told his wife that he had been subjected to the "tortures everybody knows about". It is believed that he was not allowed to sleep for the first ten days after his arrest and allowed to sleep only two or three hours for the next 15 days.

Chang Ui-gyun was accused of having submitted a sworn statement of loyalty to Kim Il Sung, the North Korean leader, in order to attend a class on North Korean ideology in Japan. The main charges against him were that under instructions from a North Korean agent he passed information on the anti-government movement and opposition parties (considered state secrets by the court because this information is considered useful to North Korea) and sought to infiltrate the dissident movement. Chang Ui-gyun's aim, it was alleged, was to disrupt the Olympic Games and the presidential elections at the end of the year. Chang Ui-gyun's arrest had come a few days after the government had conceded to opposition demands for more democracy following weeks of nationwide protests.

At his trial, which started in November 1987 before Seoul District Court, Chang Ui-gyun admitted meeting a journalist of *Chongnyon* and visiting Choson University, but denied the charges of espionage and of acting under instructions from North Korea and of having received money from North Korea. He admitted reading books on North Korea's *Juche* philosophy but said that he did not support it and had criticized it. When he visited Choson University he had been invited to visit North Korea but he had declined the offer, saying that he would go when the country was reunified.

It would appear that Chang Ui-gyun did pass information on the activities of the main South Korean opposition political parties and dissidents to a South Korean dissident who lives in Japan. This information is said to have included descriptions of political rallies, including one held in Inchon on 3 May 1986 at which many leading dissidents were arrested, and information on the setting up of the National Council for a Democratic Constitution which organized mass demonstrations in support of a revision of the presidential election system in June 1987. Amnesty International was informed that the South Korean dissident was planning to set up a research centre in Japan and that the information passed on by Chang Ui-gyun was to go to this centre.

In December 1987 Chang Ui-gyun was sentenced to 15 years' imprisonment. His sentence was reduced to eight years on appeal in May 1988. Amnesty International has adopted Chang Ui-gyun as a prisoner of conscience as it believes that he was arrested for his political views and activities and that there is no evidence of him being involved in espionage or of using or advocating violence. Amnesty International is also urging the authorities to investigate Chang Ui-gyun's claims that he was tortured during his interrogation.

Kang Hui-chol

Arrest: 1987
Charge: Meeting and passing information to pro-North Koreans in Japan
Sentence: Life imprisonment, held in Taegu Prison

Kang Hui-chol, now aged 34, was arrested in 1987 and sentenced to life imprisonment for spying for North Korea. He is alleged to have travelled illegally to Japan where he enroled in a high-school associated with the pro-North Korean organization *Chongnyon*. Kang Hui-chol claims that he was forced to confess to the carrying out espionage activities under duress. Amnesty International does not have any further details about the case of Kang Hui-chol and is seeking further information about the charges and evidence against him.

Prisoner of Conscience: Suh Kyung-won

Suh Kyung-won
(c) Korea Times

Arrest: 28 June 1989

Charge: Visiting North Korea

Sentence: 15 years' imprisonment reduced on appeal to 10 years, held in Chinju Prison

Suh Kyung-won, now aged 54, an opposition member of the National Assembly, was arrested on 28 June 1989 for making an unauthorized trip to North Korea on 19-21 August 1988. He had travelled to North Korea via Czechoslovakia on the occasion of a visit to Europe. During his stay in Pyongyang he reportedly met the North Korean leader, Kim Il Sung, and Ho Dam, former Minister of Foreign Affairs and Chairman of the Committee on Reunification of the Fatherland. On 20 December 1989 Suh Kyong-won was sentenced to 15 years' imprisonment. His sentence was reduced to ten years' imprisonment following an appeal to the High Court on 25 April 1990.

During the 24 days he was interrogated by the Agency for National Security Planning Suh Kyung-won was prohibited from meeting his lawyers and for one month after his arrest he was not allowed to meet his relatives. When he eventually met his lawyers for the first time on 22 July for 40 minutes, he complained that he had been ill-treated. Press reports quoted him as follows:

> *"ANSP investigators punched me in the face and repeatedly landed crushing blows on my left foot about 10 days after I was taken into custody. The left side of my face was badly swollen and the inside of my mouth began bleeding. They provided me with medical treatment soon thereafter... They forced me to remain awake for the first three nights."*

One of the lawyers who met him on 22 July confirmed that his face was still swollen. Suh Kyung-won met his lawyers for a second time on 20 August for one hour and in the presence of four prison guards. He reportedly reiterated that he had been forced to make a false confession to prosecutors as a result of exhaustion. One of his lawyers quoted him as saying:

> *"For the past 54 days since my arrest, I remember having been allowed to sleep for four days. I slept two or three hours each of these days."*

The senior prosecutor in charge of the case denied Suh's claims: "[The interrogators] never kept Suh from sleeping or exercised any other physical means to make him confess."

At his trial Suh Kyung-won justified his visit to North Korea and his discussion with North Korean officials as motivated by his desire to see Korea reunified. He denied acting as North Korean spy. He is alleged to have received 50,000 US Dollars from the North Korean authorities, which he is said to have used to buy a business, support activities of the farmer's movement and finance his local Party chapter; this has not, however, been independently confirmed.

Suh Kyung-won testified in court to having been ill-treated during his interrogation. According to press reports, when delivering the court's verdict the judge dismissed Suh Kyung-won's claims that he made false statements under duress and allegedly said that "overnight interrogation was inevitable because of the importance of the case". The court found that "the content of Suh Kyung-won's conversation with North Korean leader Kim Il Sung does not appear to have contained what could be called top secrets vital to national security." Because of this and because the government was now promoting reconciliation with North Korea, the judge imposed a lesser sentence of 15 years' imprisonment, although the prosecution had asked for life imprisonment.

Suh Kyung-won was born in 1937 and was a farmer. He has been active in the Catholic Farmers' Association since 1971, was its vice-president in 1982-1984 and its president in 1984-1987. He became famous in the mid-1970s for successfully negotiating compensation from the government for farmers who had switched to producing sweet potatoes on the advice of the authorities but who could not sell their crops as a result of a glut of this product on the market. In the April 1988 parliamentary elections he was elected on the Party for Peace and Democracy ticket for Hampyong-Yonggwang, a district in south-western Korea.

Amnesty International believes that the mere fact of travelling to North Korea without evidence either of espionage activities or of the use or advocacy of violence does not justify imprisonment. It has adopted Suh Kyung-won as a prisoner of conscience and is calling for his immediate release. It is also concerned at reports that he was ill-treated during his interrogation and is calling on the authorities to conduct an investigation into these allegations.

Prisoner of Conscience: Pang Yang-kyun

Arrest:	**2 July 1989**
Charge:	**Failing to report Suh Kyong-won's visit to North Korea and passing information to North Korea**
Sentence:	**Seven years' imprisonment, held in Chonju Prison**

Pang Yang-kyun, now aged 36, and secretary to Suh Kyung-won, was arrested on 2 July 1989 and charged with failing to report Suh Kyung-won's illegal trip to North Korea and passing state secrets to an alleged North Korean agent in Frankfurt in December 1988. On 20 December 1989 Pang Yang-kyun was sentenced to seven years' imprisonment. He is said to be in poor health.

Pang Yang-kyun also claimed that he was ill-treated during his interrogation. A lawyer of the Party for Peace and Democracy who met him on 23 August 1989 said that Pang Yang-kyun's left eye was swollen and that the right side of his face was bruised. During his trial, Pang Yang-kyun alleged that he had been subjected to beatings, death threats and sleep deprivation by the ANSP and the prosecution. He also said that he had been forced under torture to sign a statement agreeing not to disclose his ill-treatment by the ANSP. In its verdict the court conceded that:

"In Pang Yang-kyun's case the court cannot rule out the possibility that he was tortured while being interrogated at the Agency for National Security and Planning. But it cannot be viewed that such duress continued while he confessed to prosecutors."

Pang Yang-kyun was accused of passing national secrets on Suh Kyung-won's behalf to a North Korean agent in West Germany in December 1988. The secrets are said to include a report prepared by Suh Kyung-won and anti-government leaflets. Pang Yang-kyun admitted having collected US $10,000 for Suh Kyung-won but rejected the prosecution's claim that this person was a North Korean agent and that he had passed state secrets to him. He also denied that he had known of Suh Kyung-won's visit to North Korea.

Amnesty International has adopted Pang Yang-kyun as a prisoner of conscience and is calling for his immediate release. It is also calling on the authorities to carry out an investigation into his claims that he was ill-treated during his interrogation.

Prisoner of Conscience: Yu Won-ho

Arrest: 13 April 1989
Charge: Unauthorized visit to North Korea information
Sentence: Ten years' imprisonment, reduced on appeal to seven years, held in Taejon Prison

Businessman **Yu Won-ho**, now aged 61, and Presbyterian minister Moon Ik-hwan were arrested as they returned from a visit to North Korea. Both men were sentenced to ten years' imprisonment on 5 October 1989, reduced to seven years' imprisonment following an appeal to the High Court in February 1990. Reverend Moon Ik-hwan was released on parole in October 1990 but was re-arrested in June 1991.

Yu Won-ho and Reverend Moon Ik-hwan visited North Korea from 25 March to 3 April 1989. They travelled via Japan and China and their arrival in Pyongyang took many people by surprise. Reverend Moon Ik-hwan was the first person to take up an invitation Kim Il Sung, the North Korean leader, had extended in his New Year message to seven South Korean public figures to visit Pyongyang to discuss reunification.

Yu Won-ho was charged under the National Security Law with organizing Reverend Moon Ik-hwan's visit to North Korea and with spying for North Korea. At his trial before Seoul District Court, Yu Won-ho explained that he went to North Korea with

Reverend Moon Ik-hwan to advance reunification and because he did not consider North Korea to be an "anti-state organization" as defined in the National Security Law since President Roh Tae-woo had announced that his government would try to ease tensions with the North. Delivering his judgement the judge acquitted the two men of praising and sympathizing with North Korean leaders. He accepted that their visit had been motivated by their commitment to reunification of the country but said that they had fallen victims to a North Korean propaganda ploy and in so doing had harmed the interests of the South. Yu Won-ho was acquitted of the charges of taking instructions from North Korea and acting in collusion with North Korea.

Amnesty International has adopted Yu Won-ho as a prisoner of conscience and is calling for his immediate and unconditional release.

Prisoners of Conscience: Im Su-kyong and Father Moon Kyu-hyun

Arrest: **15 August 1989**
Charge: **Unauthorized visit to North Korea**
Sentence: **Im Su-kyong: Ten years' imprisonment, reduced on appeal to five years, held in Chongju Prison**

Moon Kyu-hyun: Eight years' imprisonment, reduced on appeal to five years, held in Kongju Prison

Im Su-kyung and Fr Moon-kyun
(c) Popperfoto

Ms Im Su-kyong, now aged 24, and a student of French literature at Hankuk Foreign Languages University, travelled to North Korea via Japan and West Germany to attend the 13th World Festival of Youth and Students which took place in Pyongyang from 1 to 8 July 1989, as a representative of Chondaehyop (The National Council of Students

Representatives). Chondaehyop had been banned by the South Korean authorities from sending a delegate to the festival. The festival has been organized every four years in various locations since World War II by the International Union of Students.

After the festival ended Im Su-kyong joined North Koreans and foreigners in a symbolic "peace march" which she hoped would take her across the length of the peninsula from Mt Paektu in the north to Mt Halla in the south. She announced her determination to return to South Korea on 27 July by crossing the border at the armistice village of Panmunjom.

On 26 July the Catholic Priests Association for Justice announced that they had sent Father Moon Kyu-hyun to North Korea to join Im Su-kyong in her attempt to cross the border. They had made this decision, they explained, because Im Su-kyong is a Roman Catholic and "to show support for the cause of patriotic students yearning for reunification of their Fatherland." Father Moon Kyu-hyun, now aged 46, is the former head of the Education Department of Chongju diocese and was then studying at the Maryknoll seminary in New York, USA. He previously visited Pyongyang in June when he celebrated a mass and discussed reunification with local Christians.

The United Nations Command which controls the armistice village of Panmunjom refused to authorize Im Su-kyong and Father Moon Kyu-hyun to cross the border in the absence of agreement from the South Korean authorities. Im Suh-kyong and Father Moon Kyu-hyun went on hunger-strike from 29 July to 2 August to press their demand to be allowed to cross the demarcation line. On 15 August they were able to cross the border and were immediately taken into custody by the South Korean authorities.

Im Su-kyong, who was suffering from exhaustion, was first sent to Seoul National University Hospital where she stayed until 18 August. She was transferred to the custody of the Agency for National Security Planning. The Agency subsequently told the press that during her interrogation it had arranged for Im Su-kyong to meet several defectors from North Korea in an attempt to have her change her views of North Korea, but said she refused to do so. Her lawyers were denied access to her and on 6 September obtained a court order requiring the Agency to let them meet her. Her family was not allowed to see her until 8 September when her case was transferred from the Agency for National Security Planning to the prosecuting authorities and she was moved to Anyang Prison. She was accused of illegally visiting North Korea, informing North Korean officials about the student movement in the South, praising North Korea and criticizing South Korea's unification policy.

Father Moon Kyu-hyun was interrogated by the National Police Headquarters and was allowed to meet his lawyers and relatives for the first time on 31 August. He was accused of illegally visiting North Korea, praising North Korea and giving speeches blaming the United States and South Korea for the division of the country and saying that South Korea did not want reunification.

Both prisoners were tried before the Seoul District Criminal Court on 13 November 1989. Im Su-kyong denied having praised North Korea and having given speeches that had been written by North Korean officials. She said she had written her own speeches and recalled having been criticized by a North Korean official for expressing the view that North Korea was not making genuine efforts to reunify the country. On 5 February 1990 both were found guilty. Im Su-kyong was given a prison sentence of ten years' imprisonment and Father Moon Kyu-hyun was given a prison sentence of eight years. When delivering the court's verdict, the presiding judge said that "by providing the north with information on the South Korean dissident and opposition movement, they had helped the North militarily". Im Su-kyong and Father Moon Kyu-hyun had their sentences reduced to five years' imprisonment following an appeal to the High Court in June 1990.

Amnesty International considers Im Su-kyong and Father Moon Kyu-hyun to be prisoners of conscience held for their peaceful political views and activities. It is calling for their immediate and unconditional release.

Prisoner of Conscience: Hong Song-dam

Hong Song-dam

Arrest: **31 July 1989**
Charge: **Benefiting North Korea**
Sentence: **Seven years' imprisonment, reduced to three years, held in Anyang Prison**

Dissident artist Hong Song-dam was arrested in July 1989 and accused of praising and benefiting North Korea through his paintings and articles in an art magazine and of spying for North Korea by sending books to an alleged North Korean agent in Germany. The South Korean authorities claim that his paintings support North Korean propaganda.

0074

Hong Song-dam and other artists had created a large mural entitled *History of the People's Liberation Movement* of which he sent photographic slides to North Korea to be displayed at the 13th World Festival of Youth and Students held in Pyongyang in July 1989. The South Korean authorities said that the panel *The Kwangju Struggle*, painted by Hong Song-dam, echoed North Korea's propaganda describing the Kwangju Incident of May 1980 as a people's movement to resist a military dictatorship supported by the USA.

Hong Song-dam was the publisher of an art magazine, *Art Movement*. The South Korean authorities accuse Hong Song-dam of promoting a Marxist-Leninist revolution by the publication of articles which emphasize that artists should contribute to social reforms and must master Marxist-Leninist views on art.

Hong Song-dam had sent books and magazines to a Korean exile in Germany. The authorities claim that the exile is a North Korean agent and that Hong Song-dam's sending of these books amounted to passing state secrets, since knowledge of the political situation in South Korea can help North Korea in its propaganda and other activities.

Hong Song-dam, now aged 36, graduated in Fine Arts in 1980 from Chosun University in Kwangju and is a winner of the Korean National Fine Arts Competition. He is best known for his woodblock prints depicting traditional dance and musicians, scenes of anti-government and anti-United States protest, and images from the 1980 Kwangju Incident in which several hundred people were killed by the military. He is the Director of the Institute of Visual Art in Kwangju and the chairman of the Kwangju chapter of the Korean Nationalistic Artists Federation, an organization of dissident writers, artists, craftspersons, musicians, film-makers, dancers, photographers and architects.

Hong Song-dam was interrogated for three weeks, during which time he was denied access to his lawyer. When he met his lawyer on 24 August he claimed that during his interrogation he had not been allowed to sleep for more than one to three hours a day, that he had been stripped naked and beaten around his head and on his hands to make him confess that he had visited North Korea. Hong Song-dam alleged that his interrogators had stamped on his hands and his lawyer observed during the prison visit that his client's knees were still heavily bruised. During Hong Song-dam's trial before Seoul District Court in September 1989 a forensic pathologist told the court that he had carried out a medical examination of the defendant and had ascertained that he still bore bruises that were the direct results of "battery and kicking".

On 30 January 1990 Hong Song-dam was sentenced to seven years' imprisonment. In September 1990 the Supreme Court dismissed the charges of espionage and returned the case to a lower court. In January 1991 Hong Song-dam was sentenced to three years' imprisonment for producing material benefiting North Korea. Amnesty International has adopted Hong Song-dam as a prisoner of conscience and is calling for his immediate and unconditional release.

Woodcuts by Hong Song-dam

Prisoner of Conscience: Kim Hyon-jang

Kim Hyon-jang and Kim Yong-ae

Arrest: 20 August 1989
Charge: Benefiting North Korean activities
Sentence: Seven years' imprisonment, held in Seoul Prison

Kim Hyon-jang, now aged 41, and his wife Kim Yong-ae, leading members of *Chonminnyon* (National Coalition for Democratic Movement), were arrested on 20 August 1989. Both had been in hiding from police since April 1989 when a number of leading *Chonminnyon* members were arrested for their political activities. They were charged with involvement in the setting up of the "Korea-US Research Institute" (KURI) which was formally established in June 1989. The authorities claimed that KURI's aims were to publish materials which would "incite anti-American sentiment" and support North Korea. Kim Hyon-jang was also accused of sending a facsimile message to the

0076

overseas pro-North Korean group *Hanmintong* and other human rights organizations abroad in June 1989 appealing for support for *Chonminnyon's* campaign for an investigation into the death of student activist Lee Chol-kyu who was found dead in May 1989. In response to this appeal the authorities allege that Kim Hyon-jang received the sum of 176,200 Japanese yen (approximately 1,250 $US) from a pro-North Korean organization. Kim Hyon-jang is also accused of sending information on a *Chonminnyon* meeting to the Council of Korean People in Europe in West Germany, which the authorities regard as a pro-North Korean organization.

In February 1990 Kim Hyon-jang was sentenced to seven years' imprisonment and this sentence was upheld by the Supreme Court in October 1990. Kim Yong-ae was also sentenced to seven years' imprisonment and was freed on bail in June 1990.

Amnesty International has adopted Kim Hyon-jang as a prisoner of conscience and is calling for his immediate and unconditional release.

Oh Tong-yol

Arrest: **15 October 1989**
Charge: **Leading an "anti-state" organization**
Sentence: **Three years' imprisonment, reduced to two-and-a-half years on appeal, held in Anyang Prison**

Oh Tong-yol was arrested on 15 October 1989, along with 14 other members of the dissident labour organization *Inminnoryon (Federation of Democratic Labour Unions in the Inchon area). Inminnoryon* was set up in Inchon in 1987 to provide support for workers in the region. It published two magazines, *The Way of Workers* and *The Socialist*. The organization also ran a counselling service and gave advice to local trade unions.

The 15 prisoners were charged under the National Security Law for membership of an "anti-state" organization and involvement in a number of labour disputes. They were accused of spreading socialist ideas among workers and of advocating the overthrow of the government and the establishment of a "people's government". The charges are believed to be based on articles in the group's magazines and minutes of meetings which were confiscated by the authorities. *Inminnoryon* claims that it merely sought to transform society in a peaceful way through the existing political system. The prisoners were also accused of organizing a number of strikes which became violent. As far as

Amnesty International is aware, the prosecution did not produce any evidence in court to substantiate its claims that the group had used or advocated the use of violence. Minutes of the group's meetings were not made available to defence counsel in court.

In April 1990 the 15 prisoners were tried before Seoul District Court. Seven prisoners were released and the remaining eight received prison terms of between one and three years. Oh Tong-yol was sentenced to three years imprisonment, reduced to two-and-a-half years following an appeal to the High Court in August 1990. Amnesty International is seeking further information about the charges and evidence against Oh Tong-yol as it believes he may be imprisoned for his peaceful political activities.

Prisoner of Conscience: Kim Keun-tae

Kim Keun-tae is arrested, 14 May 1991

(c) Korea Times

Arrest: **14 May 1990**
Charge **Producing and distribution pro-North Korean material, organizing anti-government demonstrations**
Sentence **Three years' imprisonment, reduced on appeal to two years, held in Heongsong Prison**

Kim Keun-tae, a leading dissident and co-chairperson of *Chonminnyon*, (National Coalition for Democratic Movement) was arrested on 14 May 1990. He was charged under the National Security Law with making anti-government statements at a number of public meetings, including the inauguration rally of *Chonminnyon* in January 1989, and with producing and distributing anti-government documents. These statements and documents include the expression of views about the South Korean Government, reunification and relations with foreign states. Although calling for a change of government, none of these statements advocate the use of violence to achieve political changes.

Kim Keun-tae was also charged under the Law on Assemblies and Demonstrations for organizing five demonstrations without informing the police in advance. Two of these demonstrations took place in January and February of 1989, over one year before his arrest. The three other meetings took place in the first half of 1990. Although the charges do appear to be legitimate, Kim Keun-tae was the only leader of *Chonminnyon* prosecuted for organizing these demonstrations. A third charge was made under the Law on Punishment of Violent Acts for the injuries to police officers and damage to property which took place at three demonstrations in 1990. Although many anti-government demonstrations result in violence, many are peaceful and there is no evidence to suggest that Kim Keun-tae organised or incited violence during the three rallies he took part in.

In September 1990 Kim Keun-tae was sentenced to three years' imprisonment. Following an appeal to the High Court in January 1991 his sentence was reduced to two years and this sentence was upheld by the Supreme Court in April 1991. Amnesty International regards Kim Keun-tae as a prisoner of conscience with respect to the charges under the National Security Law and the Law on Punishment of Violent Acts. It urges the authorities to release him after he has served that part of his sentence related to his conviction under the Law on Assemblies and Demonstrations.

Kim Keun-tae, now aged 44, was adopted by Amnesty International as a prisoner of conscience during his detention from 1985 to 1988 for his involvement in the National Youth Alliance for Democracy and for organizing demonstrations against the then president Chun Doo-hwan. On 30 January 1991 four policemen were sentenced to prison terms ranging from two to five years for torturing Kim Keun-tae after his arrest in 1985.

Jang Myung-guk

Arrest: **19 June 1990**
Charge: **Publishing pro-North Korean material;**
Advising third parties in labour disputes
Sentence: **Two years' imprisonment, reduced on appeal to 18 months, held in Anyang Prison**

Jang Myung-guk graduated in economics from Seoul National University in 1970 and has since taken an active interest in the trade union movement. In 1988 he set up the *Suktap* (Stone Pagoda) Labour Counselling Centre and the *Suktap* Publishing Company. At the counselling centre he conducted seminars on subjects such as labour laws, the work of trade unions and their position in Korean society. The *Suktap* Publishing Company published the periodical *Dawn* to which Jang Myung-guk contributed articles on labour issues. Jang Myung-guk's best known publication is *Explanation of Labour Laws*, published in 1982, which is said to have sold over 400,000 copies.

Jang Myung-guk was arrested on 19 June 1990. He was charged under the National Security Law with writing articles benefiting North Korea. These charges are believed to arise from ten articles that he wrote for the periodical *Dawn*. The central ideas in his articles are that South Korea's economy is subordinated to the USA and Japan and that South Korean workers must become a leading force in a movement to realise national independence, set up a democratic government and reunify with North Korea. The prosecution authorities accused Jang Myung-guk of posing a threat to the country's national security by promoting a revolutionary ideology which is similar to North Korean propaganda.

Jang Myung-guk was also charged under Article 13-2 of the Labour Dispute Mediation Act for advice he reportedly gave to workers of the Taxi Drivers Union in Seoul, the Daewoo company, The Seoul Subway Union, Hyundai and Poongsan Heavy Materials Company. Under the Labour Dispute Mediation Act, third parties, that is people who have no direct link with the workplace where a trade dispute is taking place, are banned from intervening in the dispute and may be sentenced to up to five years' imprisonment or a fine. In 1988 Jang Myung-guk is said to have successfully negotiated with the management of a Daewoo company at the request of the trade union, ending a strike after 58 hours. In July 1988 he also advised trade union leaders at Daewoo Defence Industries over the forced resignation of their union president. In 1989 he is reported to have advised leaders of the Seoul Taxi Drivers Union, at their request, on whether they could legally organise a strike, in view of the fact that they are prohibited from doing so because they are regarded as a public service.

In December 1990 Jang Myung-guk was sentenced to two years' imprisonment, reduced to 18 months following an appeal to the High Court in April 1991. Amnesty International is seeking further information about the charges against Jang Myung-guk.

Arrests of "Anti-State" Groups: Reports of Torture and Ill-Treatment

Sanomaeng (Socialist Workers' League)

On 30 October 1990 the South Korean authorities announced the arrests of 40 members of *Sanomaeng* under the National Security Law. At least nine other members of *Sanomaeng* were arrested in March 1991, including its alleged leader Park Ki-pyong, aged 34, a well-known dissident poet.

Sanomaeng was established in November 1989 in Seoul with an initial membership of approximately 400 which grew to over 1,600 members, a large proportion of whom are said to be students and workers. At its inauguration rally in Seoul the organization reportedly claimed to maintain friendly links with the North Korean Workers' Party and the Communist Party of the Soviet Union.

The authorities described *Sanomaeng* as an "anti-state" organization planning to overthrow the government and replace it with a people's democratic government. They say it published and circulated a number of leaflets and documents advocating the establishment of a socialist society and that it advocated the use of violence to achieve political change. Among these are *Eight Tasks of South Korean Socialists in 1990* which sets out eight steps which are needed to achieve a socialist revolution, and several issues of *Wind at Dawn* which discusses the concept of a socialist revolution and the role of the student movement. The prosecution has alleged that 5,000 copies of each issue of *Wind at Dawn* were produced. *Sanomaeng* is also accused of infiltrating a number of trade unions and factories and planning the manufacture of armed weapons. The authorities claimed to have confiscated a number of weapons and publications from the organization.

Several prisoners among those arrested in the *Sanomaeng* case claim to have been ill-treated following their arrest. Families of some of the prisoners and local human rights groups claim that the prisoners were denied visits by family members and lawyers for some time after their arrests. Following protest from the families one visit was permitted after a 20-day period. Lee Song-su, a 27-year-old ex-student of Sung Kyun-kwan University, and Hyon Yon-dok, also aged 27, reportedly told their lawyers that they had been ill-treated. On 23 October 1990 Lee Song-su told his lawyer that he had been beaten by his interrogators because he had refused to answer their questions. On 1 November Hyon Yon-dok reported to his lawyer that he had been kept awake for three consecutive nights, stripped and beaten soon after his arrest. Park Ki-pyong claimed that he too had been beaten and denied sleep for several nights during his interrogation in March 1991.

Amnesty International is seeking further information about the arrests of members of *Sanomaeng* to determine whether any of those arrested are prisoners of conscience. It is calling on the authorities to conduct an investigation into the prisoners' claims that they were tortured and ill-treated.

Chamintong (Independent National Unification Group)

In December 1990 the authorities announced the arrests of some 30 members of *Chamintong*. The authorities allege that *Chamintong* was established in 1988 and supported North Korea's proposals for reunification. It claimed that the organization used and controlled the student body *Chondaehyop* (National Council of Student Representatives) as a "front for revolutionary movement". The group is also accused of instigating a number of violent anti-government demonstrations under orders from the overseas pro-North Korean group *Hanminjun*. Evidence of the connection between *Chamintong* and *Hanminjun* was allegedly found in documents showing that they had a similar structure, used the same radical slogans and had the same aims. *Chondaehyop* representatives have denied the link between the two groups. The authorities claimed to have confiscated 700 items from the organization, including computer disks, recordings of North Korean broadcasts and a detailed program for achieving national reunification under communism by 1995.

Prisoners and their families have claimed that *Chamintong* does not exist and had been fabricated by the authorities and many of the prisoners claim to have been forced to confess to the above accusations. Families of some of the prisoners said that they were stripped and beaten with wooden bars, and kicked and stepped on while made to kneel down on the floor. Kim Yo-sop, a 25-year-old graduate of Hanrim University and another former student, Cho Won-guk, told their lawyers that they had been stripped and beaten. Kim Gi-su, a student at Kyung-hee University, is reported to have written to his family saying that he had been repeatedly slapped and kicked during his interrogation. Kim Dong-kyu, a 24-year-old student, said that he was deprived of sleep for several days after his arrest and was beaten with sticks and kicked. Huh Jung-sook, a 24-year-old female graduate of Kyung-hee University also claimed that she was beaten.

Amnesty International is seeking further information about the arrests of members of *Chamintong*. It is urging the South Korean authorities to conduct an immediate investigation into the claims that some of the prisoners were ill-treated to force them to confess.

Prisoners of Conscience: Cho Song-woo and Lee Hae-hak

Arrest: 30 November 1990
Charge: Unauthorized Meeting with North Koreans
Sentence: 18 months' imprisonment, held in Seoul Prison

Cho Song-woo, aged 40, and Lee Hae-hak, aged 48, staff members of the dissident organization *Chonminnyon* (National Coalition for Democratic Movement) and Reverend Cho Yong-sul were arrested at Kimpo International Airport on 30 November 1990 as they were returning from a trip to Berlin where they had participated in the inaugural meeting of *Pomminnyon* (pan-national conference for the reunification of Korea). They were charged under the National Security Law with making an unauthorized trip to Berlin to meet with North Korean officials. In May 1991 Cho Song-woo and Lee Hae-hak were sentenced to 18 months' imprisonment. Reverend Cho Yong-sul was released on parole.

The three men travelled to Berlin in mid-November to participate in the inaugural meeting of *Pomminnyon,* an organization pledging itself to reunify the country. Participants at the meeting included a North Korean official, Chon Kum-chol, who is Vice-Chairman of the Committee for Peaceful Unification of the Fatherland and also representatives of Koreans living in other countries. At the meeting, *Pomminnyon* made a declaration stating as its main objectives the achievement of peaceful reunification, independence and national unity. It also stated that it aimed to establish a headquarters for the organization in both North and South Korea before the end of January 1991; to achieve the peaceful reunification of North and South Korea by 1995; to replace the current armistice signed in 1953 at the end of the Korean War by a peace agreement; to secure the withdrawal of foreign (US) troops from South Korea and to achieve the abolition of the National Security Law and free travel between North and South Korea.

Amnesty International has adopted Cho Song-woo and Lee Hae-hak as prisoners of conscience, detained for the peaceful exercise of their freedom of expression and association. It is calling for their immediate and unconditional release.

Prisoners of Conscience: Lee Chang-bok and Kim Hi-taek

Arrest: **24 January 1991**
Charge: **Forming a pro-North Korean organization**
Sentence: **Two years' imprisonment**

Lee Chang-bok, aged 54 and **Kim Hi-taek**, aged 40, Co-Chairman and Secretary General of *Chonminnyon* (National Coalition for Democratic Movement), were arrested on 24 January 1991. The government accused them of attempting to form a pro-North Korean organization.

Pomminnyon was inaugurated in Berlin in November 1990, and announced that it aimed to establish regional headquarters in both North and South Korea before the end of January 1991. In South Korea a preparatory committee was formed on 23 January 1991 with the aim of establishing a permanent headquarters. Lee Chang-bok was named as Chairman of its executive committee and Kim Hi-taek was a committee member. On 24 January the two men were arrested and charged with forming a pro-North Korean organization and for contacting the Committee for the Peaceful Unification of the Fatherland in North Korea. The North Korean headquarters of Pomminnyon was established on 25 January 1991.

Amnesty International has adopted Lee Chang-bok and Kim Hi-taek as prisoners of conscience, detained for the peaceful exercise of their freedom of expression and association. It is calling for their immediate and unconditional release.

Prisoner of Conscience: Reverend Hong Keun-soo

Reverend Hong Keun-soo

Arrest: **20 February 1991**

Charge: **Praising North Korea - through published material and speeches**

Reverend Hong Keun-soo lived in the USA from 1978 to 1986 and was at that time an American citizen. He was pastor of the Korean Presbyterian Church of Brooklyn and a member of the Boston Presbytery. He gave up his American citizenship when he returned to South Korea in 1986 and became the pastor of the Hyang Rin Presbyterian Church in Seoul.

Reverend Hong Keun-soo was arrested on 20 February 1991. He was accused of praising North Korea in his sermons; of having spoken in favour of reunification during a television debate on KBS (Korea Broadcasting System) in September 1988 and of publishing a collection of his writings in 1989 entitled *Now is the time to Realize National Reunification*. The writings included an article about Reverend Hong Dong-keun, a lecturer in Christianity at Kim Il Sung University in North Korea. Reverend Hong Dong-keun is reported to have sent a series of lecture notes to Reverend Hong Keun-soo shortly before his arrest. The authorities also accused Reverend Hong Keun-soo of planning to travel to Panmunjom and for his involvement in the establishment of the South Korean headquarters of *Pomminnyon*.

Amnesty International has adopted Reverend Hong Keun-soo as a prisoner of conscience as it believes that he is detained for the peaceful exercise of his rights of freedom of expression and association. It is calling for his immediate and unconditional release.

관리번호	91-33

기 안 용 지

분류기호 문서번호	연이 20352-24PD	(전화:)	시 행 상 특별취급	
보존기간	영구·준영구. 10. 5. 3. 1	장 관		
수 신 처 보존기간				
시행일자	1991.10.15.			

보조기관	국 장	전결	협조기관		문서통제
	심의관				
	과 장				
기안책임자		김종훈			발 송 인

경 유 / 수 신 / 참 조	법무부장관, 국가안전기획부장	발신명의	발송 1991.10.16 외무부
제 목	A.I. 아국 인권관련 보고서		

1. 국제사면위원회(A.I.)는 91.10.1. "South Korea : Prisoners Held for National Security Offences" 제하의 공개문서를 발간한 바, 동문서는 한반도 분단상황 및 국가보안법 개요, 75-91년간 국가보안법 위반으로 수형중인 35건의 사례를 기술한 것입니다.

/계속/

0086

(2)

2. 당부는 상기문서에 대한 아국입장을 주영대사관을 통하여 A.I.본부에 전달하고, 동문서 내용이 언론에 보도될 경우 정부입장을 표명하는 것이 바람직하다는 입장인 바, ~~이에대한 귀부의견 및~~ A.I.측에 대한 정부입장 설명자료를 당부로 송부하여 주시기 바랍니다.

첨부 : A.I. 아국 인권관련 보고서 1부. 끝.

일반문서로 재분류 (1991 .12. 31.)

0087

-ᄀ 1

분류 91
번호 -71

법 무 부

인권 20352-203 503-7045 1991. 10. 30

수신 외무부장관

참조 국제기구조약국장

제목 국제사면위 아국 인권보고서에 대한 당부입장

1. 연이 20352-2490('91.10.15)과 관련입니다.

2. 국제사면위 아국 인권관련 보고서에 대한 당부입장을 별첨과 같이 송부하오니 국제사면위 본부측에 설명될 수 있도록 적의 조치하여 주시기 바랍니다.

첨부 : 국제사면위 인권보고서에 대한 당부입장 및 개인별자료 1부. 끝.

			결재 (공람)		
접수일시	1991. 11. 1.	4374			
처리과	2				

법 무 부 장 관

일반문서로 재분류 (1991.12.31.)

0088

AI의 한국 인권보고서에 관한 당부입장

o 국가보안법 위반행위로 구속된 고창표, 황대권, 서경원, 이창복, 김희택, 김성만, 장의균, 방양균, 유원호, 임수경, 문규현, 홍성담, 김현장, 김근태, 조성우, 이해학, 홍근수는 양심범이므로 즉각 석방되어야 한다는 주장

. 정치범이나 양심범이 무엇인가에 대해서는 말하는 사람마다 그 개념규정을 달리하고 있음

. 그러나 위 개념들을 어떻게 규정하던간에 동 보고서에 언급된 사람들은 간첩행위를 한 사람들이거나 정부의 전복을 기도하는 등 폭력을 사용 또는 옹호한 사람들이며, 재판과정에서 이러한 사실에 대한 충분한 증거가 드러나 모두 유죄판결이 선고된 사람들이므로 양심범이라 할 수 없음

. AI는 일부 국가보안법 위반자들이 폭력을 사용, 옹호하지 아니하였다고 분류하는 오류를 범하고 있는데, 그들에 대한 구체적인

0089

범죄사실을 살펴보면 현 자유민주주의체제 전복과 좌익무장폭력 혁명을 통한 사회주의 국가 건설을 투쟁 목표로하여, 사회 각분야에 침투해서 체제전복 활동을 전개하고 각종 분규의 배후에서 폭력혁명의 이론적 근거를 제시하거나, 이를 조종하여 인명살상, 시설물파괴 및 파출소방화 등을 일삼은 장본인들임

. 그리고 우리는 1953년 한국동란후 40여년동안 세계에서 가장 호전적이고 폐쇄적인 북한과 휴전선 하나를 사이에 두고 대치하여 왔으며, 북한은 UN 에 가입한 후에도 계속하여 우리의 자유민주주의 체제를 파괴하기 위한 대남무력적화통일 노선을 고수하고 있는데, 이러한 위협에 대처하고 우리 국가의 안전과 국민의 생존 및 자유를 확보하기 위하여 자위적이고 방위적인 수단으로 국가보안법이 있는 것임

. 따라서 자유민주주의 체제를 전복하기 위한 반국가활동이나 북한의 대남무력적화통일 전략.전술에 추종하는 국가보안법 위반사범들을 양심범이라는 이름아래 석방해야 한다는 주장은 대한민국의 안전과 한국민의 생존권을 전혀 고려하지 못한 독단적 견해임

0090

o 가혹행위에 의한 자백이 대표적 증거로 채택되어 유죄판결이 선고되었다는 유정식, 신귀영, 임수경, 문규현, 홍성담 등 22명의 주장

. 우리나라 헌법 제12조 제7항에 의하면 피고인의 자백이 고문, 폭행, 협박 등의 방법에 의하여 자의로 진술된 것이 아니라고 인정될 때에는 이를 유죄의 증거로 삼을 수 없도록 되어 있음

. 가사 고문에 의한 자백이 아니라 하더라도, 피고인의 자백이 유일한 유죄증거이고 다른 증거들이 없을 때에는 이를 이유로 유죄판결을 할 수 없도록 되어 있음

. 따라서 피고인의 자백이 유일한 증거일 때는 유죄선고를 할 수 없을 뿐만 아니라, 더 나아가 그 자백이 고문에 의한 것일 때는 유죄선고를 할 수 없음은 말할 것도 없음

. 또한 위 보고서에 언급된 사람들은 검찰에서 피의자 신문조서 작성시 진술거부권을 고지받고 신문이 끝난후 그 기재내용을 확인하여 진술한 대로 적혀 있음을 인정한 다음 조서의 각면에 간인하고 말미에 서명무인까지 하였으며, 조서내용에는 자신들의

0091

범행을 부인하고 변명한 진술부분도 모두 기재되어 있음

. 그리고, 법정에서는 수사기관에서 고문등 부당한 대우를 받았다는 자신들의 주장을 입증할 충분한 기회가 부여되었는데, 그것이 인정될 경우에는 수사서류의 증거능력이 인정되지 않아 유죄판결을 선고할 수 없는 것임

. 그러나 동인들에 대하여는 엄격한 재판과정을 통해 법정에 현출된 충분한 증거들에 의하여 범죄사실이 입증되어 모두 유죄가 인정되었던 것임

o 변호인 접견이 지연되는 등 불공정한 재판을 받았다는 주장

. 헌법 제12조 제4항, 제5항에 의하면 누구든지 체포.구속을 당한 때에는 변호인의 조력을 받을 권리가 있고, 그러한 권리가 있음을 고지받지 아니하고는 체포.구속을 당하지 아니함

. 또한 형사소송법 제34조에 의하여 변호인은 구속당한 피고인 또는 피의자와 접견하고 서류 또는 물건을 수수할 수 있는 등 변호인의 자유로운 접견과 의사소통이 보장되고 있음

0092

. 다만, 단일사건에 수십명의 변호인이 선임되어 다수변호인이 동시에 접견을 요구하거나 혹은 순차로 계속하여 접견을 신청하는 경우 및 피의자에 대하여 극히 중요한 부분을 수사하고 있을 때 의도적으로 접견을 요구하는 등 변호인접견권이 수사를 방해할 목적으로 남용되는 경우에는 불가피하게 접견이 다소 지연되거나 제한될 수 있음

. 요컨대, 변호인접견권은 수사권과 마찬가지로 형사사법의 정의를 실현하는 하나의 수단으로써 그 스스로 내재적 한계가 있다고 할 것이므로, 변호인접견권과 수사권의 관계를 둘러싸고 발생하는 문제점들에 관해서는 계속 연구.검토가 필요하다 할 것임

o 단순히 재일교포를 만나거나 북한을 여행한 사실만으로 구속하는 것은 부당하다는 주장

. 위와 같은 주장을 하는 사람들은 모두 조총련 간부에게 포섭되어 사상 교육과 지령을 받고 간첩행위를 한 사람들이고 심지어는 밀입북하여 간첩밀봉교육을 받은 자도 있으며, 이제까지 단순히

0093

재일교포를 만나거나 북한을 여행한 사실만으로 구속된 사람들은 없음

. 순수한 학술, 경제, 문화 등의 교류를 위한 북한에의 왕래.접촉은 남북교류협력에관한법률 소정의 절차만 밟으면 처벌하지 않으나 자의적으로 밀입북하거나, 북한공작원을 만나 사상교육을 받고 간첩활동을 하는 행위는 국가안보에 위태로운 행위이므로, 군사적 대치 상황에 있는 한반도의 안보여건을 감안할 때 이를 처벌하는 것은 불가피함

0094

공　　　란

공 란

공 란

공 란

공 란

공 란

공 란

공 란

공 란

공　란

공　　　란

공 란

공 란

공 란

공 란

공 란

공 란

공 란

공 란

공 란

공 란

공 란

공 란

공 란

공 란

공 란

공 란

공　　　란

공 란

공 란

공 란

공 란

공 란

공 란

공 란

공 란

공　　란

공 란

공 란

공　　　란

공　　란

공 란

공 란

공 란

공 란

공 란

공 란

공 란

공　　란

공 란

공　　　란

공 란

공 란

공　　란

공 란

공 란

공　　　란

공 란

공 란

공 란

공　　　란

공　　란

공 란

공 란

공 란

공　　　란

공 란

공 란

공 란

공 란

공 란

공 란

공 란

공 란

공 란

공 란

공 란

공 란

공 란

공 란

공 란

공　　　란

공 란

공 란

공 란

공 란

공 란

공 란

공 란

공 란

공 란

공　　　란

공 란

공 란

공 란

공 란

공 란

7h.(예)

주 영 대 사 관

영국(정) 723-1170 1991. 11. 4.

수신 : 장관

참조 : 국제기구국장

제목 : A.I. Newsletter 송부

A.I. Newsletter 91년 11월관 1부를 별첨 송부합니다.

첨부 : News Letter 91년 11월관 1부. 끝.

발송송 1991.11. 6 주 영 국 대사관

주 영 대 사

			결재(공람)		
선 결					
접수일시	1991.11.7	번호			
처리과	2162947				

0192

AMNESTY INTERNATIONAL
NEWSLETTER NOVEMBER 1991 VOLUME XXI • NUMBER 11

EGYPT

Ten years of torture

POLITICAL detainees in Egypt are beaten, suspended in contorted positions, burned with cigarettes and tortured with electric shocks, AI said in a report published in October*.

Torture of political detainees became widespread and systematic after the assassination of President Sadat in October 1981, when a state of emergency was swiftly imposed. Ten years later a state of emergency is still in force, renewed in May 1991 for a further three years, and political detainees held incommunicado under emergency provisions continue to be denied basic protection against torture.

The report includes the Egyptian Government's response to AI's October 1990 report on torture, and comments on specific cases of torture raised by AI.

Mahoud Mohammad Hassan

Since 1981 AI has interviewed former detainees of varying political and social backgrounds who have described their torture. They include Mahmoud Mohammad Hassan, a 38-year-old clerk, who is deaf and mute. He was reportedly tortured over a period of three months in 1981. A medical doctor, Ahmed Isma'il Mahmoud, married with four children, was detained in October 1990. He said he was blindfolded, stripped naked and had his hands bound behind his back. "They put an iron device between my legs to keep them very wide apart, which caused acute pain in my groin muscles. They applied electric shocks to all parts of my body, especially my private parts." Other recent victims include a 17-year-old female student and a 15-year-old boy, both of whom said they were tortured in 1990 to give information on the whereabouts of suspected political opposition activists. Most are alleged members of Islamic groups.

AI's findings are supported by medical reports of examinations of torture victims conducted by forensic doctors working in the Ministry of Justice, and by a number of (Emergency) state security court judgments ruling that confessions were inadmissible as evidence because they were extracted under duress. Many victims have sought and been awarded compensation by the courts.

AI has repeatedly brought its evidence of a consistent pattern of torture of political detainees spanning 10 years to the attention of the Egyptian Government, together with recommendations on how to prevent it. Although Egypt is a party to international human rights treaties which outlaw the use of torture, including the United Nations Convention against Torture, the government has taken no substantive measures to prevent torture.

**Egypt: Ten years of torture (AI Index: MDE 12/18/91).*□

Dr Ahmed Isma'il Mahmoud

YUGOSLAVIA

Violence follows republic's independence

HUNDREDS of people have been killed in the violence following the republic of Croatia's declaration of independence on 25 June 1991. There have been reports of extrajudicial executions, killings and mutilations of civilians or captured members of armed forces and of the torture or ill-treatment of people detained by the various parties to the conflict.

In Cetekovac in eastern Croatia, more than 20 are said to have been killed, including unarmed civilians, by Serbian insurgents who attacked the village on 4 September; an old man described to a visiting journalist how the insurgents had forced him and others to stand in line and shot dead one villager who tried to flee.

Twenty-one Serbian villagers were reported to have been killed on 22 August by Croatian security forces carrying out house-to-house searches in the villages of Kinjacka, Cakle and Trnjani for insurgents believed to have fired mortars at the town of Sisak. A local police chief later denied that the Croatian forces had killed civilians.

Up to 80 Croatian police officers and at least 35 civilians were reported to have died on 1 August in the village of Dalj in Slavonia. According to villagers, Serbian insurgents killed those left wounded after Dalj was occupied by units of the Yugoslav National Army. Autopsies carried out by forensic experts reportedly concluded that some victims had been killed by a bullet in the head after having been wounded.

Civilians and members of security or paramilitary forces are also reported to have been physically ill-treated after being captured or detained. Čedomir Biga, a Serbian who died on 2 September while detained by Croatian police in Dreznik, was said by police to have died from a heart attack. However, a hospital autopsy reportedly found that his back was severely bruised, his ribs were broken and that his death was the result of injuries caused by blows.□

IRAQ

Further UN action needed to protect human rights

IN July AI took the unprecedented step of urging the United Nations (UN) to establish an international on-site human rights monitoring operation in Iraq to prevent torture, killings and other abuses by government forces. AI simultaneously published the findings of its delegates' visits to Iran and Turkey in May to interview Kurds, Arab Shi'a Muslims and others about human rights violations following the uprising in Iraq in March and April this year*.

The report detailed widespread arrests, torture and mass extrajudicial killings of people suspected of participating in the uprising in northern and southern Iraq. Hundreds of civilians were shot dead in the streets by Iraqi forces or executed by firing squads. Countless unarmed civilians fleeing to the borders were killed by helicopter gunships. AI's report confirmed that the human rights violations committed by government forces were brutal in the extreme, and underscored the need for the UN to ensure the long term protection of all those at risk.

AI's proposal, submitted to UN Secretary-General Javier Pérez de Cuéllar and to the Iraqi Government, recommended that the UN operation investigate alleged abuses and be empowered to take action to protect the lives of those endangered. It also said the UN body should work with the Iraqi Government to enforce international standards through strengthening local institutions and structures that would help safeguard human rights in the future.

**Iraq: The need for further UN action to protect human rights (AI Index: MDE 14/05/91)* and *Iraq: Human rights violations since the uprising - Summary of AI's concerns (AI Index: MDE 14/06/91).*□

0193

CAMPAIGN FOR PRISONERS OF THE MONTH

Each of the people whose story is told below is a prisoner of conscience. Each has been arrested because of his or her religious or political beliefs, colour, sex, ethnic origin or language. None has used or advocated violence. Their continuing detention is a violation of the United Nations Universal Declaration of Human Rights. International appeals can help to secure the release of these prisoners or to improve their detention conditions. In the interest of the prisoners, letters to the authorities should be worded carefully and courteously. You should stress that your concern for human rights is not in any way politically partisan. In *no* circumstances should communications be sent to the prisoner.

UGANDA

Daniel Omara Atubo: *a 44-year-old member of the Democratic Party (DP) and Minister of State for Foreign and Regional Affairs, he and 17 other prominent citizens from northern Uganda were charged with treason on 7 May 1991. He is awaiting trial in Luzira Prison, near the capital, Kampala.*

Daniel Omara Atubo was arrested in Kampala on 15 April 1991, at the time of a major counter-insurgency operation by the Ugandan army against rebels who have been active in the northern districts of Gulu, Kitgum, Lira and Apac since 1986.

Hundreds of people were arrested on the grounds that they were suspected of rebel activity. Daniel Omara Atubo and other elected representatives apparently protested at these mass arrests.

After three weeks' detention in a military barracks Daniel Omara Atubo and the 17 others — who include three other DP members who hold government posts — were accused of treason. The government issued statements, before and after the April arrests, criticizing the activities of DP members in northern Uganda and suggesting that they were helping perpetuate the insurgency, although no evidence of this was presented.

The treason charges against Daniel Omara Atubo and the 17 others did not specify the dates, location or nature of the treasonable acts they are alleged to have committed. Under Ugandan law, those charged with treason are not permitted to be granted bail for at least 480 days.

AI is concerned that treason charges have been brought against Daniel Omara Atubo in the absence of evidence against him, on account of his non-violent criticisms of the government.

Daniel Omara Atubo was reportedly badly beaten after his arrest and showed physical signs of ill-treatment when he appeared in court. The government has launched an official inquiry into his alleged ill-treatment but no findings have been made public.

■Please send courteous letters appealing for the immediate and unconditional release of Daniel Omara Atubo to: His Excellency Mr Yoweri Museveni/President of the Republic of Uganda/Office of the President/Parliament Buildings/PO Box 7006/Kampala/Uganda.□

IRAN

Mohammadreza Nezameddin Mohaved: *a 74-year-old retired civil servant, he is serving a three-year sentence for "criticizing the president".*

Mohammadreza Nezameddin Movahed and at least 20 others were arrested in June 1990 after signing a critical open letter to President Hashemi Rafsanjani. The letter called for implementation of constitutional guarantees, freedom and justice, and criticized the government's handling of the economy. Many of the signatories were associates of Mehdi Bazargan, the first Prime Minister of the Islamic Republic or, like Mohammadreza Nezameddin Movahed, members of the Association for the Defence of Freedom and Sovereignty of the Iranian Nation, which was reportedly dissolved on 14 June 1990.

Mohammadreza Nezameddin Mohaved

After their arrest, Mohammadreza Nezameddin Movahed and the others were detained in Evin Prison, Tehran, where they were reportedly put under pressure to sign statements condemning their actions. Some were released; nine were tried and received prison sentences of up to three years and up to 30 lashes.

Mohammadreza Nezameddin Movahed's trial before an Islamic Revolutionary Court was held in June 1991, almost a year after his arrest. He was not allowed legal representation and the proceedings, held *in camera*, reportedly lasted only a few minutes.

Mohammadreza Nezameddin Movahed's health is believed to be deteriorating. He has apparently lost movement in one leg and needs crutches to walk. He also suffers from heart disease.

■Please send appeals requesting his immediate and unconditional release to: President Hojatoleslam Ali Akbar Hashemi Rafsanjani/President of the Islamic Republic of Iran/The Presidency/Palestine Avenue/Tehran/Islamic Republic of Iran.□

LAOS

Thongsouk Saysangkhi: *former Deputy Minister of Science and Technology, he was arrested on 8 October 1990 in the capital, Vientiane, following the circulation of a letter he wrote on 26 August 1990 to the then Prime Minister Kaysone Phomvihan, criticizing the country's political system and asking to resign from his government post and from the ruling Lao People's Revolutionary Party.*

Thongsouk Saysangkhi wrote in his letter that he was opposed to "putrid old regimes that restrict popular liberties and democracy" and "the dictatorial power of personal cliques". He called for "the holding of free elections, the putting into practice of popular liberties and democracy, and the existence of democratic institutions opposed to the maintenance of a system of communist feudalism and Politburo dynasticism." He added, "the history of humankind has now confirmed that a single-party system relying exclusively on coercion and deception is incapable of ever bringing prosperity and happiness to our people." Thongsouk Saysangkhi also reportedly tried to establish a "social democrat club" to promote the idea of multi-party democracy and, with other dissenters, wrote an article supporting such a political system.

On 3 November 1990 the official news media announced that Thongsouk Saysangkhi had "committed propaganda against the policies of the Party and State" and had "conducted activities aimed at overthrowing the regime and creating political disturbances in Vientiane capital". Although it said that he would be "interrogated and tried according to the country's law", to AI's knowledge no formal charges have been brought against him in court. He is reportedly held in "temporary confinement" under administrative detention procedures, probably in Xam Khe prison in Vientiane.

■Please send courteous appeals for his immediate and unconditional release to: President Kaysone Phomvihan/Office of the President/Vientiane/Lao People's Democratic Republic.□

Prisoners released

Orlando Azcué Rodríguez (AI *Prisoner of the Month* in June 1991) was conditionally released from prison in Cuba on 19 July 1991 after serving only 16 months of his three-year sentence for "enemy propaganda".

AI has learned that 'Ali and Nadir Muhammad Taqi al-Sayf were released in Saudi Arabia on 12 August 1991. The September *AI Newsletter* named them as the only two of 13 Saudi Arabian prisoners arrested in Bahrain in 1982 not to have been released.□

0184

THE AMERICAS

Campaigning for human rights

In 1975 Marta Ponce de León fled from political persecution in Uruguay, where her husband Ricardo had been imprisoned for trade union activities. A month later her three children were smuggled out of the country and reunited with their mother in Brazil. The family eventually found refuge in the Netherlands, where they received support and friendship from AI members in the Dutch Section who had adopted Ricardo Vilaró as a prisoner of conscience. Four years later he was freed and joined his family in the Netherlands. When the civilian government was restored in 1985, Marta Ponce de León and her family returned home, where she became one of the founder members of the Uruguayan Section. The new section's slogan reflected the experiences of many of its members: "One doesn't thank solidarity, one repays it."

It is a sentiment which applies across Latin America, where the challenges posed by continuing political repression and economic instability have been met by a flourishing human rights movement. From a handful of sections in the late 1970s, AI membership in the Americas has continued to grow. Today there are sections in Argentina, Barbados, Bermuda, Brazil, Canada, Chile, Ecuador, Guyana, Mexico, Peru, Puerto Rico, the United States of America (USA), Uruguay and Venezuela. There are AI groups in Aruba, Colombia, Costa Rica, Curaçao, the Dominican Republic and Paraguay and groups-in-formation in the Bahamas, Bolivia and Grenada, all with members actively campaigning to secure the release of prisoners of conscience, ensure fair and prompt trials for political prisoners and abolish torture and executions. To ensure impartiality no AI group ever works on the case of a prisoner in its own country.

AI is by no means the only representative of the broader human rights movement in the region. A long legacy of political repression has led to the creation of networks which provide information, support and direct assistance to victims of human rights violations. The people of Latin America have organized on a number of fronts to combat the excesses of the military dictatorships, and the structures they built provide the basis for an active human rights movement today. The experience of military dictatorships and civil wars has given the people of the region a profound understanding of the everyday relevance of human rights, and of the suffering inflicted by governments that persistently ignore the human rights of their citizens.

In the 1960s and 1970s international interest in human rights focused mainly on political prisoners. The challenge to AI development in those years was to provide an agenda relevant to the people of the Americas. AI's first worldwide Campaign Against Torture (CAT), launched in late 1972, generated enormous interest and support in Brazil, where brutal torture was an everyday fact of life. A second CAT was launched in 1984. Although AI members do not campaign against abuses in their own countries, activists were able to take to the streets in support of AI's 12-point plan for the worldwide abolition of torture. By the end of 1990, the United Nations Convention against Torture and Other Cruel, Inhuman or Degrading Treatment or Punishment had been ratified by countries across the region, including Argentina, Bolivia, Brazil, Chile, Colombia, Guatemala and Mexico.

In Brazil AI groups began to form in the early 1980s while the country was still under military rule. In 1983 AI launched a campaign to expose unlawful political killings by government forces or officially sanctioned "death squads" throughout the world. The newly-formed Brazilian groups used letters, petitions and visits to embassies to publicize the campaign. In 1984 the São Paulo group's offices were damaged in an arson attack and a letter bomb was delivered to the home of an AI member. Until 1986 it was illegal to mention AI in the press. But the Brazilian members persevered and their numbers continued to grow. In 1985 the Brazilian Section was established. In 1986 they persuaded the national mint house to produce commemorative medals and stamps for AI's 25th anniversary and by 1987 the Brazilian Section was playing host to AI's International Council Meeting, attended by AI members from more than 60 countries.

The first two members of AI's Chilean Section used to meet on a park bench because no one would rent them an office. Membership development was slow but committed individuals continued working to promote the human rights of others. By 1985 the newly-formed Chilean Section was holding its first Annual General Meeting (AGM), which was attended by nearly 200 people. This AGM provided many of the new members with their first experience of voting; at a time when large public gatherings were strictly outlawed, the meeting provided a unique opportunity to discuss policy and action. By October 1990 the section was hosting a concert for human rights, called "From Chile an embrace of hope". The event, which drew 150,000 people, was symbolically staged at Chile's notorious National Stadium—the site where many hundreds of men and women had been brutally tortured, murdered or "disappeared" after the 1973 military coup.

New AI groups and sections continue to prosper and to have a considerable regional impact in promoting and publicizing human rights issues. But the success of AI development in Latin America cannot be measured so much in the size of the membership, which is still relatively small, but by the fact that it exists at all. Across the region, human rights activists and investigators have themselves become victims of human rights violations. In Peru, for instance, the offices of at least two human rights organizations, including AI, were extensively damaged in bomb attacks in 1990, and several prominent Peruvian human rights activists were repeatedly threatened with death.

In much of the region, endemic poverty and crippling inflation force most people to devote their energies to simple survival. The cost of postage is high and funds for the local production of campaign materials are limited. Campaign techniques have to be evaluated for both cost and impact. Groups have demonstrated considerable ingenuity and resourcefulness in overcoming this challenge. In Brazil, Mexico and Peru groups have staged street theatre productions aimed at raising public awareness of human rights issues. In Ecuador, Mexico and Paraguay, AI members persuaded national artists to donate pictures and sculptures for exhibitions which generated publicity and income for local groups.

Local groups were the driving force behind AI's 1988 "Human Rights Now!" campaign, which commemorated the 40th anniversary of the Universal Declaration of Human Rights. The goal of the campaign was to increase AI membership and show the world's governments that individual people are watching what they do and are willing to mobilize whenever and wherever human rights violations occur. AI members around the world circulated petitions, urging governments to ratify international human rights treaties and to act for worldwide human rights protection. In Colombia the AI group in Barranquilla alone collected nearly 40,000 signatures.

International rock musicians supported the campaign goal of increasing worldwide human rights awareness, performing for

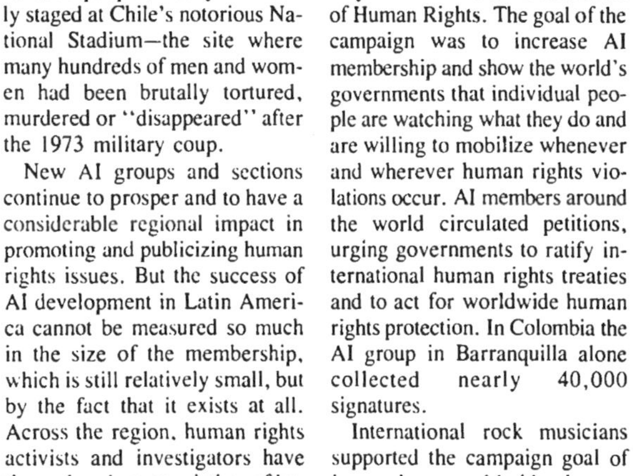

Guyana: Viv Richards, Captain of the West Indies Cricket Team, with young AI members during "AI Week", March 1990

0195

Marta Ponce de León, a founder member of the Uruguayan Section

more than a million people in 19 countries across the world during the "Human Rights Now!" concert tour. The penultimate concert, attended by over 35,000 people, was held in Mendoza, Argentina, on the Argentina/Chile border, to enable Chileans to attend. The concert's organizer explained that the site was symbolic: "The artists would sing from a country that had terrible human rights violations to a country where abuses are still occurring. It would be a peaceful army of voices crossing the Andes." In a powerful and moving expression of the human rights message, rock musician Sting sang "They dance alone", written as a tribute to the mothers of the thousands of people who "disappeared" in Chile under the Pinochet government.

AI development in Latin America has been reinforced by an extensive translation program. The Spanish edition of the *AI Newsletter Prisoner of the Month Campa*[redacted]d the CAT appeals were l [redacted]ed in 1976. The monthly *AI Newsletter* is now published in Spanish; volunteer activists in Brazil have made a Portuguese translation regularly available. The establishment of AI's Spanish language translation program, *Editorial Amnistía Internacional*, based in Madrid, has helped Spanish-speaking members in their campaigning.

In 1990 AI groups and sections in the Caribbean launched an "AI Week" to highlight AI's concerns on young people and encourage new members to join. In May 1991 members from across the Caribbean and an observer from Jamaica gathered to discuss and plan actions for a campaign at the time of AI's 30th anniversary. AI's 30th birthday was marked at a regional press conference in Georgetown, Guyana, which was shown on local television stations.

In Venezuela, following the section's effective work with the home government, the Chamber of Deputies published a resolution congratulating AI on its 30th anniversary in recognition of "the Venezuelan peoples' committment to the noble principles of the organization".

Campaigning for the abolition of the death penalty is an issue on which AI members are allowed to address their own governments. In Argentina in 1990 a presidential initiative to reintroduce the death penalty for comm[redacted]w crimes was withdrawn in [redacted]e of public and political opposition. AI members had mobilized to lobby politicians, publicize arguments against the death penalty in the press and enlist the support of non-governmental organizations. In response to moves to reintroduce the death penalty for common-law crimes in Brazil in 1988, the section produced a special booklet outlining the arguments against the death penalty which was distributed to politicians and received wide media coverage. The proposal was subsequently defeated in the Constituent Assembly.

Human rights education plays an indispensable role in mobilizing people to participate in the worldwide movement. Most sections in the region take part in regular discussions with school and university students. The Porto Alegre groups in Brazil have successfully lobbied to introduce human rights education into the state schools curriculum, with AI members serving as special advisers. In Mexico the section is coordinating an extensive human rights education program in schools and local communities. The Brazilian Section has started a program of lectures on human rights in police academies, and in 1990 persuaded a Brazilian police academy to stage an exhibition of AI's work against torture. Every section in the Caribbean has developed some direct link to school students, either through the Urgent Action system or by involving them in special campaigns. The Guyanese Section conducts a formal human rights education course for the Mining and Amerindian communities.

Although the US and Canadian Sections have large and long-established memberships, the orientation of AIUSA has shifted dramatically over the last five years. A burgeoning youth wing now has about 2,700 student groups in secondary schools, colleges and universities. In 1986, when the youth program consisted of about 150 groups, a concert tour entitled "Amnesty International: the Conspiracy of Hope" alerted hundreds of thousands of young people to worldwide human rights issues. The concert tour provided a tremendous membership boost, many of those who joined remain active in AI, and growth in youth membership continues. The Canadian youth campus program got off the ground in 1987, and now comprises nearly 500 groups in the English-speaking and francophone branches. The Canadian Section supports a similar youth program at the University of Georgetown in Guyana, and has provided them with resource materials, including scripts of plays and skits based on human rights themes.

Impunity: sabotaging the rule of law

Many countries in Latin America are bringing their legislation into conformity with international human rights standards, or are promising to do so, while others are establishing institutions aimed at promoting and protecting these rights. But promises have not been enough to end a pattern of gross human rights violations across the region. In 1990 alone thousands of men, women and children "disappeared", were murdered by "death squads" or brutally tortured in police or military custody, sometimes to death.

AI believes that the phenomenon of impunity encourages this continuing pattern of violations. Impunity — literally the exemption from punishment — undermines public confidence and faith in the rule of law. Without such confidence, no judicial system can operate effectively. The Guatemalan Human Rights Procurator, examining the situation in his own country, concluded that: "Impunity is nothing else but the institutionalization of crime."

International standards require governments to investigate human rights violations thoroughly and impartially and to ensure that those responsible are brought to justice. Victims, their relatives and society have a vital interest in knowing the truth about past abuses and in the clarification of unresolved human rights crimes. Bringing the perpetrators to justice sends a clear message that violations of human rights will not be tolerated and that those who commit, permit or condone such acts will be held fully accountable. When investigations are not pursued and the perpetrators are not held to account, the self-perpetuating cycle of violence results in continuing violations of human rights cloaked by impunity.

Colombia: Bodies of members of a judicial inquiry investigating killings and "disappearances", shot dead by paramilitary "death squads" in the Magdalena Medio region in January 1989

Amnesty laws which prevent prosecution or terminate pending investigations also contribute to impunity. In 1989, for example, President Carlos Menem of Argentina pardoned 39 senior military officers who were to be tried for violations perpetrated by the Argentine armed forces during the "Dirty War" from 1976 to 1983. This decree, combined with the 1978 Amnesty Law, effectively closed investigations into past human rights violations. Some 9,000 documented cases of "disappearance" remain unresolved. In 1990 the president pardoned and released the leaders of the military government and other high-ranking officers jailed for crimes committed during the "Dirty War".

Impunity erodes respect for law and justice, leading to the occurrence of further violations. If this cycle is ever to be broken, AI believes that all governments must assume responsibility for ensuring that thorough and impartial investigations of human rights violations proceed and are made public; that those responsible for human rights violations be brought to justice and given appropriate punishment; and that amnesty laws should never be used to enable perpetrators to evade accountability before the law.

0196

Human rights violations in the Americas

AI has serious and long-term concerns about human rights violations in the Americas region, but increasingly they do not reflect the organization's traditional focus on prisoners of conscience. The practice of detaining such prisoners is no longer prevalent in Latin America, but this change has coincided with a dramatic increase in extrajudicial executions and "disappearances". Torture remains widespread. The only countries in the region holding people adopted by AI as prisoners of conscience are Cuba, Peru, and the USA.

AI groups worldwide campaigned strongly on behalf of Latin American prisoners of conscience in the 1960s and early 1970s, when the only action techniques used by the organization were work by groups on individual prisoners of conscience or investigation of prisoners thought probably to be prisoners of conscience. But from the early 1970s, when thousands of victims of torture or "disappearance" were reported each year from Brazil, Chile, Paraguay and Uruguay, the techniques were too slow. By the time letters started reaching the authorities, the prisoner was often dead or "disappeared".

To meet the critical need for rapid response, AI's first-ever Urgent Action was launched in 1975 on behalf of Luís Basílio Rossi, a Brazilian prisoner of conscience who was being tortured in custody. Several weeks after the action began, AI received a letter from Luís Basílio Rossi saying that he was no longer being tortured. His captors had been so disturbed by the level of publicity generated by the action that they had forced him to write to AI in an effort to make the publicity stop.

Brazil: A military police officer forces his gun into a street child's mouth, December 1990. Street children in Brazil are frequently the victims of arbitrary arrest, torture and extrajudicial executions by police officers © *Folha de Sao Paulo*

The first report AI ever issued on torture was on Brazil in 1972. Since the end of Brazil's military dictatorship in 1985, political arrests and killings have ceased. But despite promises by the newly-elected civilian government, torture in custody continues to be widespread in Brazil and endemic across the region.

In Mexico, for instance, although the government has publicly prohibited torture, almost anyone arrested is at risk, including those detained for political reasons or in land disputes, human rights activists and criminal suspects. Methods of torture — sometimes fatal — range from beatings, near-asphyxiation and sexual abuse, to electric shocks applied to genitals and other sensitive parts of the body. Women and children are not exempt; one teenager had been so savagely beaten that he scarcely reacted when two of his toenails were pulled out.

In countries including Colombia, El Salvador, Guatemala and Peru, torture commonly occurs in the context of counter-insurgency operations and is used by the armed forces both as a means of interrogation and as a form of punishment. Peasants have been brutally tortured to death; other victims are threatened with death should they report their experiences. Systematic beatings, near drowning, electric shocks, hanging by the arms for prolonged periods and threats of mutilation or death are the forms of torture most commonly reported. In June 1991 a group of *campesinos* (peasant farmers) were arrested in the department of Morazán, El Salvador. After their release, they described to human rights groups how they were beaten and subjected repeatedly to the *capucha* (a lime-filled hood placed over their heads) while being held by soldiers who tried to force them to admit to possessing weapons and to links with an armed opposition group. One man said he was left hanging upside-down overnight and beaten repeatedly.

Enforced "disappearance" continues to be widely used or tolerated by governments in Latin America as a means of eliminating dissent or of terrorizing the community. "Disappearances" are no longer associated primarily with military dictatorships. "Disappearances" are increasingly prevalent in countries with elected civilian governments where a wide range of legal remedies are theoretically available to victims and relatives. Yet as a result of the clandestine nature of this method of repression, and the failure of the authorities to ensure that legal remedies are implemented, mechanisms intended to protect the individual have rarely proved to be effective against a practice specifically designed to flout the rule of law and to ensure the impunity of the perpetrators.

Peru: Wife of one of the thousands of victims of "disappearances" © *La Republica*

The term *"desaparecido"* ("disappeared") first entered the human rights lexicon from Guatemala, where it has been used since 1966 to describe the government practice of disposing of political opponents while evading accountability by making them "disappear". Since then, the phenomenon has spread throughout Latin America and continues to occur in Guatemala on a massive scale. Under a series of governments over the last two decades, many thousands of people from all sectors of Guatemalan society have gone missing after abduction by heavily armed men in plain clothes. Many of the victims are never seen again. In other cases, bodies which have been mutilated to prevent identification have been dumped on far-away roads or buried in clandestine cemeteries. Hundreds of children are among Guatemala's "disappeared".

In Peru the practice of "disappearance" started in early 1983 and has assumed such proportions that from 1989 onwards, more cases of "disappearance" have been reported to the United Nations Working Group on Enforced or Involuntary Disappearances from Peru than from any other country. Over the last nine years AI has received details of over 3,700 people who have "disappeared" after detention or abduction by the security forces. The real number is believed to be far higher.

Over 1,500 people have reportedly "disappeared" in Colombia in the last 10 years. Victims include teachers, trade unionists and human rights workers, although the majority are peasant farmers. In Valle del Cauca department 16 people from the town of Trujillo and surrounding communities "disappeared" in April 1990. According to the Procurator General, an army major attached to the Third Infantry Battalion ordered the illegal detention and participated in the torture and "disappearance" of the 16 people. A local priest who had been assisting the relatives of the "disappeared" was later abducted and killed.

In countries including Colombia, El Salvador and Guatemala "death squads" made up of members of the military and security forces acting in civilian guise and civilians working with them murder thousands of unarmed

0197

civilians each year. Some target real or perceived political opponents, others kill members of peasant or indigenous communities in zones of conflict between government forces and opposition groups. Governments and their armed forces are able to use the fiction of "death squads" to evade accountability by attributing politically motivated murders to these shadowy and supposedly uncontrollable groups. In a number of countries, however, compelling evidence linking "death squads" to the police and military forces has emerged. In Colombia and El Salvador such evidence includes the testimonies of former members of the military. In Brazil the Rio de Janeiro police department admitted in April 1990 that half the city's identified death squad members were police officers. In 1989, 10 members of the National Federation of Salvadorian Trade Unions were killed when a bomb exploded at the union headquarters in circumstances suggesting the involvement of the security forces. In Colombia the national trade union confederation estimated that between 1986 and 1990, more than 300 of its members were killed by the security forces or civilians working with them in the guise of the "death squads".

Hundreds of street children in Brazil, Colombia, Guatemala and Mexico have been tortured or killed by "death squads" or uniformed law enforcement officials. As extreme poverty, political upheaval or loss of their parents force more and more children to fend for themselves, they become increasingly vulnerable to abuse or "elimination". An estimated seven million children live and work on the streets of Brazil alone. Some are involved in petty theft, others make a meagre living begging or scavenging on rubbish tips. Such children have become "suspected criminals" in the ey[redacted]many civil and military p officers. Brazilian human rights organizations believe that at least one child a day is killed by death squads; many hundreds of others suffer brutal torture.

Hundreds of Brazilian Indians, peasants and rural trade unionists trying to defend their land and communities from incursions by ranchers and mining and timber companies have been killed, often with the acquiescence or collusion of local government authorities. Many others have been threatened or attacked, but the authorities have persistently failed to guarantee the legal rights of indigenous peoples or to investigate violent assaults on them. No progress has been made in bringing to trial non-Indian settlers accused of ambushing and killing 14 members of the Ticuna tribe, five of them children, in 1988.

Many civilians have been murdered in military operations by uniformed regular armed forces. In El Salvador, for instance, six Jesuit priests, their housekeeper and her daughter were shot dead in 1989 by a group of about 30 uniformed men, whom the government later admitted were members of the armed forces.

In the early hours of the morning of 18 August 1991, about 30 men in military uniform entered the home of Antonio Palacios Urrea in Fusugasugá, Colombia, and shot dead five occupants of the house. Antonio Palacios, said to be a sympathizer of a legal left-wing political party, was killed along with three of his children and his son-in-law.

In mid-October 1990 villagers in Peru discovered three mass graves — the gruesome evidence of a recent massacre. A few weeks earlier, nearly 40 people from peasant communities had been detained by a patrol from the Castropampa military base in Huanta, in a joint operation with civil defence patrol members *(montoneros)*. The patrol released several prisoners but took 18 of them to a ravine and apparently beat and then shot them. The massacre was investigated by the Public Ministry and a Senate Commission of inquiry. The Senate Commission published its report in May 1991, which attributed the killings to a combined force of soldiers and *montoneros*. At least three other massacres by the security forces have taken place in Peru since the new government took office.

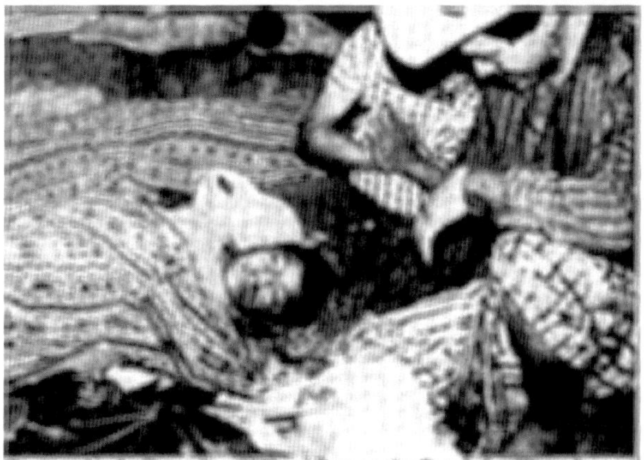

© Peter Barwick/Americas Watch

Guatemala: In December 1990 soldiers at the Panabaj military base of Santiago Atitlán opened fire on a peaceful crowd of unarmed people, killing at least 15 indigenous Indian villagers, including three children, and wounding 19 others. Above, relatives grieve over the dead

El Salvador: Members of the Committee of Relatives for the Release of the Disappeared and Political Prisoners of El Salvador examine photographs of alleged "death squad" victims in their search for their missing loved ones

© *Magnum*

It is not only in the course of counter-insurgency operations that extrajudicial executions take place. There were reports that following the US military invasion of Panama in 1989, US troops did not take adequate care during military operations, leading to the unwarranted deaths of non-combatant civilians. Victims were allegedly buried in mass unmarked graves to conceal the number of civilian casualties; some of the victims may have been extrajudicially executed.

AI has become increasingly concerned over the escalating incidence of attacks and threats on human rights activists and investigators. In July 1990, for instance, eye-witnesses in Colombia reported that eight heavily-armed men seized Dr Alirio de Jesús Pedraza Becerra, a lawyer and human rights worker, and pushed him into a waiting car. He was never seen again. Dr Pedraza, an active member of the Political Prisoners Solidarity Committee, was pursuing investigations into the alleged torture of a number of trade unionists who had been detained by soldiers of the army's Third Brigade. Other members of the Committee have since received death threats.

In August of 1991 José Miguel Mérida Escobar, head of the Homicide Section in the Department of Criminal Investigation of the Guatemalan National Police, was shot at point-blank range in the street outside the National Police Building. The killing is believed to be linked to his role in investigating previous extrajudicial executions and his reported allegations that high-ranking military officials were involved in the 1990 murder of anthropologist Myrna Mack Chang.

The magnitude of the widespread human rights violations afflicting the Americas is also demonstrated by the fact that tens of thousands of refugees have fled their homes seeking asylum in other countries. Although international law prohibits the forcible return of refugees to countries where they risk serious human rights violations, countries in the region have not always been willing to provide asylum-seekers with protection against forcible return.

Judicial executions continue to take place in the USA and in several Caribbean countries. There are over 2,300 people on death row in the USA, including at least 30 juvenile offenders, four of whom have been executed since 1976. In 1989 St Vincent and the Grenadines introduced the death penalty for juvenile offenders over the age of 16. In Chile a government bill to abolish the death penalty was rejected by the Senate in late 1990.

Many countries in the Americas have passed through the bitter experience of military dictatorships to an almost universal return to elected civilian governments. Yet across the region, elected governments with a stated commitment to human rights have failed to guarantee that those rights are respected in practice. Many civilian governments continue to be unwilling or unable to control their police and armed forces or to defend the human rights of even the most defenceless sectors of society — street children, indigenous peoples and the poor.□

0198

ZAIRE

Opposition party supporters targeted

THE Zairian security forces have killed more than 50 unarmed opposition party supporters since April 1991, despite the end in 1990 of a 25-year ban on opposition parties and official recognition of several dozen political parties. Most of the killings have occurred during demonstrations, but individuals have also been targeted.

The worst incident occurred in April, in the southern provincial town of Mbuji-Mayi, when troops opened fire on supporters of the Union for Democracy and Social Progress party, who were protesting at arrests and seizure of property by soldiers. The authorities said nine people had died: unofficial sources estimated the number to be more than 40.

In September there were two incidents in the capital, Kinshasa. On 2 September, troops opened fire when barricades were erected by a group protesting against a sharp increase in the cost of living and the government's failure to convene a national conference to discuss the country's political future. Two days later, at least three people were killed when members of the paramilitary Civil Guard and supporters of the ruling party attacked the offices of two opposition parties.

AI has called for an independent inquiry into the killings and repeatedly called for a curb on the use of firearms by the security forces.□

CUBA

Crackdown on government critics

TOUGHER measures have recently been introduced by the Cuban authorities to quash dissent.

"Rapid response brigades", comprising ordinary citizens, security officials and Communist Party activists, have carried out several so-called "acts of repudiation", including verbal and physical abuse and short-term detention, against known political and religious dissenters.

For example, on 19 July some 20 people demonstrated outside the home of Roberto Luque Escalona, the author of a book criticizing President Fidel Castro, which has been published abroad. The crowd shouted insults and wrote pro-government slogans on the walls of his house. Three days earlier Roberto Luque Escalona had begun a hunger-strike, in protest at what he said was the lack of political freedom in Cuba, to coincide with the Pan-American Games, then about to take place in Cuba. He was arrested by two police officers who arrived during the demonstration at his home, and held at the headquarters of the Technical Investigations Department until 21 August when he was released pending trial on a charge of "disrespect", which carries a maximum prison sentence of three years.

In another incident State Security police arrested Yndamiro Restano, president of the unofficial Harmony Movement (MAR), and at least seven other MAR members, after confiscating documents from his house. All were released after 24 hours with an official warning that they would be charged with "illegal association", "enemy propaganda" and "incitement to rebel" if they did not stop their political activities.□

BANGLADESH

Members of tribal groups tortured and killed

AN AI report published in August* describes torture and extrajudicial executions of non-combatant tribal inhabitants of the Chittagong Hill Tracts by security forces during 1989 and 1990. These violations have occurred in the context of a continuing conflict since the mid-1970s between the security forces and armed tribal groups seeking regional autonomy.

Reports of rape of tribal women by security force members continue to be received by AI. In October 1990, 14 young women returning home from a Buddhist festival were reportedly held at gunpoint and repeatedly raped by soldiers. According to unofficial sources the incident was investigated and at least two security force members were disciplined. However, it is not clear if criminal procedures have been initiated.

Non-combatant tribal members were also subjected to other forms of torture during 1989 and 1990. These included beatings with clubs and rifle butts, administration of electric shocks and having chili water forced in their nostrils while hanging upside-down. Some refugees from the area have reported that soldiers urinated and poured hot water on them while they were held in pits in the ground.

AI submitted its report to the new Government of Bangladesh, urging it to end these human rights violations but to date has received no response.

**Bangladesh: Human rights in the Chittagong Hill Tracts, 1989-1990 (AI Index: ASA 13/04/91).*□

GRENADA

Death sentences commuted

FOURTEEN people, including members of the former People's Revolutionary Government, sentenced to death in 1986 for the murder of Prime Minister Maurice Bishop and others in 1983, had their death sentences commuted to life imprisonment on 14 August 1991.

In an address to the nation on 14 August announcing the Mercy Committee's recommendation that the sentences be commuted, Prime Minister Nicholas Brathwaite acknowledged that there were "many persons, groups and organisations at home and abroad who pleaded for clemency". In letters to the Prime Minister and the Mercy Committee on 29 July AI had urged that the sentences be commuted and stressed that the resumption of executions in Grenada after 13 years would be a retrograde step for human rights. The organization also drew attention to additional grounds for granting clemency, including evidence suggesting bias on the part of the trial jury. AI had also been concerned that some of the prisoners might be executed for reasons of political expediency: before the announcement of commutations, executions of some of the prisoners had been scheduled to take place before 1 August when Grenada was due to re-enter the Eastern Caribbean states court system, which would provide right of final appeal to the Judicial Committee of the Privy Council in London, England.

Prime Minister Brathwaite also announced on 14 August that a similar recommendation by the Mercy Committee would soon be made on behalf of the other nine prisoners currently on death row in Grenada.□

ALGERIA

AI raises concerns with new Human Rights Minister

ON 4 June, following a general strike call made on 25 May by the Islamic Salvation Front (FIS), a legal political party, and subsequent mass demonstrations by FIS supporters, the Government of Algeria declared a state of siege. In August, an AI delegation visited the country to investigate the killings of at least 55 demonstrators and bystanders by security forces; the detention without trial of over 1,000 people in internment camps; the use of military courts; and the reported ill-treatment of at least 40 detainees, particularly in Alger, Mostaganem, and Msila.

In September, AI raised its concerns with the newly-appointed Minister for Human Rights, Ali Haroun, when he visited the International Secretariat in London. He said that the internment camps had been closed and their inmates released. AI welcomed this but urged that a public inquiry be held into the alleged ill-treatment of detainees and the killings of demonstrators by the security forces since 25 May.

AI also discussed with the Minister cooperation on human rights education in Algeria.□

BRAZIL

Death penalty debate deferred

ON 27 August a proposal by Congressman Amaral Netto to reintroduce the death penalty in Brazil was returned to the Constitution and Justice Commission for further study following serious questions by parliamentarians regarding its constitutionality.

The parliamentary debate has been deferred.□

GUATEMALA

Police investigator killed

THE head of the Homicide Section of the Guatemalan National Police Department of Criminal Investigation was shot dead on the morning of 5 August 1991 while walking with his wife and child 70 metres from the National Police headquarters in Guatemala City. A former member of the élite corps of the National Police was reportedly arrested the following day in connection with the murder.

José Miguel Mérida Escobar led the investigation into the stabbing death, in September 1990, of anthropologist Myrna Mack Chang and wrote the police report which named an officer of the intelligence branch of the army as one of those responsible for the killing. In July 1991 a warrant was issued for the officer's arrest but to date he has not been apprehended.

A few days before he was killed, José Miguel Mérida Escobar had reported to the Office of the Human Rights Procurator that, since the findings of his report became publicly known, he had been followed by unidentified armed men. Foreign and Guatemalan journalists later reported receiving warnings from anonymous sources not to publish any information on Myrna Mack Chang's killing.

At the time of his murder, José Miguel Mérida Escobar was reportedly preparing to testify about the killing of Myrna Mack Chang before the Inter-American Human Rights Commission of the Organization of American States meeting in the United States of America.□

HONG KONG

Unfair treatment for asylum-seekers

AI continues to be concerned at the long-term detention in Hong Kong of thousands of Vietnamese asylum-seekers. The organization has called for a review of Hong Kong's detention policy for asylum-seekers.

Over 50,000 Vietnamese asylum-seekers are stranded in detention centres in Hong Kong, most of them awaiting "screening" to determine whether they are considered refugees. The rest have been "screened out" — denied refugee status — and if they choose not to return to Viet Nam under a "voluntary repatriation program" they may face indefinite detention in Hong Kong, or an increasing threat of forcible return to Viet Nam.

In a report in January 1990 AI expressed concern that the screening process in Hong Kong was critically flawed and that asylum-seekers at risk of human rights violations might be denied refugee status and returned to Viet Nam. Some of the report's recommendations have since been implemented by the Hong Kong authorities but AI continues to call for each asylum-seeker to receive legal advice at all stages of the process and to receive an oral hearing when appealing against refusal of refugee status. Also, asylum-seekers who were "screened out" prior to recent changes in the screening process should have their cases fully reviewed.

The screening procedures currently in effect in Hong Kong are part of the Comprehensive Plan of Action (CPA), an international agreement covering the treatment of Vietnamese asylum-seekers in the countries of "first asylum" in southeast Asia, including Indonesia, Malaysia and Thailand. In August 1991 a meeting of non-governmental organizations, including AI, and the Office of the United Nations High Commissioner for Refugees, was held in Singapore. It noted discrepancies in screening procedures and the treatment of asylum-seekers among CPA countries and proposed concrete improvements. AI continues to monitor the procedures.□

Vietnamese asylum-seekers arrive in Hong Kong, where over 50,000 are stranded in detention centres, most of them awaiting "screening" to determine whether they are considered refugees.

PRISONER NEWS

AI learned in August 1991 of the release of 95 prisoners under adoption or investigation. AI took up 105 cases.

ANGOLA

Prisoners released but fate of many hundreds still unknown

SEVERAL hundred prisoners have been released in Angola, following a peace agreement in May between the government and the National Union for the Total Independence of Angola (UNITA). However, the fate of hundreds of others remains unknown.

The first releases occurred in mid-July when the government commuted all death sentences and proclaimed an amnesty for all political and some criminal prisoners. Those released include Moisés André Lina, the leader of a political group who was arrested in 1983 and sentenced to death in 1987 on charges of attempting to overthrow the government.

The releases were temporarily suspended in late July when each side accused the other of failing to respect the terms of their agreement. UNITA complained that the government amnesty fell outside the legal framework of the agreement and some released prisoners who had been held by UNITA alleged that other prisoners had been forced to remain in Jamba, UNITA's headquarters in southeastern Angola.

AI welcomed the releases and the commutation of death sentences but is concerned that many hundreds of prisoners, arrested or captured in the context of the civil war which began in 1975, remain unaccounted for. The Angolan Government and UNITA admit to holding a total of less than 2,000 prisoners. The government has also failed to account for many hundreds who "disappeared" in custody after an unsuccessful coup attempt in 1977.□

AMNESTY INTERNATIONAL NEWSLETTER is published every month in four languages to bring you news of AI's concerns and campaigns worldwide, as well as in-depth reports. Available from Amnesty International (address below)

0200

AMNESTY INTERNATIONAL, 1 Easton Street, London WC1X 8DJ, United Kingdom. Printed in Great Britain by Flashprint Enterprises Ltd. London. Available on subscri tion at £7 (US$12.00) for 12 issuse. ISSN 0308 6887

관리 번호	91 —108

외 무 부

110-760 서울 종로구 세종로 77번지 / (02) 723-8934 / (02) 723-3505

문서번호 연이 20314-2114

시행일자 1991.11.4.

(경유)

수신 주영대사

참조

취급		장 관
보존		
국 장	전결	
심의관		
과 장		
기안	김종훈	협조

제목 AI 아국관련 보고서

대 : 영국(정) 723-54(91.10.17)

대호, AI가 발간한 "South Korea : Prisoners Held for National Security Offences"에 대한 법무부 입장자료를 별첨 송부하오니 귀관 업무에 활용바라며, 필요한 경우 AI측에 우리 입장을 적의 설명하여 주시기 바랍니다.

첨부 : 법무부 입장자료 1부. 끝.

예고문에 의한 일반문서로 재분류 (1991 . 12. 31.)

0201

관리번호	91-88

외 무 부

110-760 서울 종로구 세종로 77번지 / (02) 723-8934 / (02) 723-3505

문서번호 연이 20314-2776
시행일자 1991.11.6.
(경유)
수신 수신처참조
참조

취급		장 관
보존		(서명)
국 장	전결	
심의관	(서명)	
과 장	(서명)	
기안	김종훈	협조

제목 AI 아국 인권관련 보고서

1. 국제사면위원회(AI)는 91.10.1. "South Korea : Prisoners Held for National Security Offences" 제하의 공개문서를 발간한 바, 동 문서는 한반도 분단상황 및 국가보안법 개요, 75-91년간 국가보안법 위반으로 수형중인 35건의 사례를 기술한 것입니다.

2. 상기와 관련, 법무부에서 작성한 사례별 설명자료를 별첨 송부하오니 귀관 업무에 활용하시기 바랍니다.

일반문서로 재분류 (1991.12.31.)

첨부 : 1. AI문서(개요) 1부.
2. 법무부 작성자료 1부. 끝.

수신처 : 주호주, 오지리, 벨지움, 카나다, 덴마크, 펀란드, 불란서, 독일, 그리스, 아일랜드, 이태리, 화란, 뉴질랜드, 놀웨이, 폴투갈, 스페인, 스웨덴, 스위스, 미국, 유엔대표부, 제네바대표부, EC대표부, 유네스코대표부 대사

문서로 재분류 (.99 . . .

0202

외 무 부

110-760 서울 종로구 세종로 77번지 / (02) 723-8934 / (02) 723-3505

44095

문서번호 연이 20314-
시행일자 1991.11.25.
(경유)
수신 주영대사
참조

취급		장 관
보존		
국 장	전결	
심의관		
과 장		
기안	여승배	협조

제목 A.I. 아국관련 설명자료

연 : 연이 20314-2668

91. 3/4분기중 A.I. 회원들이 각부처에 보내온 특정인 석방탄원 진정서중 연호 기송부한 법무부 자료에서 설명된자들~~을 제외한~~ 에 추가하여 김동균등 13인에 대한 법무부 입장자료를 별첨 송부하오니 귀관업무에 활용바라며, 필요시 A.I.측에 우리입장을 적의 설명하기 바랍니다.

첨부 : 법무부 입장자료 1부. 끝.

0203

법 무 부

인권 2031- 16395 503-7045 1991. 11. 21.

수신 외무부장관

참조 국제기구조약국장

제목 국제사면위원회 관련 협조 요청

1. 국제사면위원회 회원들이 '91. 3/4분기중 각 부처에 보내온 특정인 석방탄원 편지를 검토한 결과, 귀부를 통하여 국제사면위에 기히 설명한 자 외에 김동균 등 13명이 주요 석방요구 대상자로 분석되었습니다.

2. 동인들에 대한 범죄사실 및 처리현황, 당부입장 등 설명자료를 별첨과 같이 송부하오니, 동 내용이 국제사면위원회 본부측에 적의 설명될 수 있도록 조치하여 주시기 바랍니다.

첨부 : 설명자료 1부. 끝.

법 무 부 장 관

2 39108

0204

공 란

공 란

공 란

공 란

공 란

공 란

공 란

공 란

공 란

공 란

7ㅎ

주 영 대 사 관

영국(정) 723-1302 1991.12.3

수신 : 장관

참조 : 국제기구국장

제목 : A.I. Newsletter 송부

A.I. Newsletter 91년 12월판 1부를 별첨 송부합니다.

첨부 : Newsletter 91년 12월판 1부. 끝.

발송 1991.12.3 주영국 대사관

주 영 대 사

선 결		결재		
접수일시	1991.12.5	68918		
처리과				

0215

AMNESTY INTERNATIONAL

NEWSLETTER DECEMBER 1991 VOLUME XXI • NUMBER 12

HAITI

Human rights abuses follow coup

ON Monday 30 September troops overthrew the elected government of President Jean-Bertrand Aristide, who had taken office on 7 February 1991. In the aftermath of the coup, AI learned of widespread human rights violations by the security forces. These included extrajudicial executions, beatings and illegal arrests of President Aristide's supporters.

In the days following the coup soldiers opened fire on hundreds of civilians in different sectors of Port-au-Prince, including Cité Soleil and Lamentin 54, and in other parts of the country, leaving hundreds dead and wounded. Among those extrajudicially executed was Jacky Caraïbe, director of Radio Caraïbe, who was seized on 30 September by soldiers, beaten in front of his family and taken away. His severely tortured body was found shortly afterwards.

Several supporters of President Aristide were arrested and beaten. On 7 October, Port-au-Prince Mayor Evans Paul was severely beaten following his arrest by soldiers at Port-au-Prince airport. He was released hours later. Other supporters of President Aristide, including an employee at the Port-au-Prince town hall, the administrator of a day care centre, a businessman and a well-known singer were among the scores arrested without warrant in the days following the coup. At the time of writing, AI was investigating their legal situation.

Members of President Aristide's cabinet, who went into hiding when the coup started, said that soldiers entered their homes looking for them, and then damaged their homes.

Radio stations were attacked and damaged by soldiers, and most of them subsequently stopped broadcasting.

Grassroots organizations reported harassment of their members, and priests close to President Aristide went into hiding, in fear for their safety. Two Christian activists, Sénatus and Fritzner Nosther, were detained without warrant on 4 October by soldiers in the southern city of Jacmel.□

TUNISIA

Executions resume in Tunisia

FIVE men were executed on 9 October 1991 in Tunisia, despite President Ben Ali's repeatedly stated personal opposition to the death penalty.

Three of those executed, all suspected sympathizers of the illegal Tunisian Islamic movement *Hizb al-Nahda*, had originally been sentenced in May 1991 to prison terms ranging from 20 years to life imprisonment for murder and arson against an office of the ruling party; these sentences were raised to the death penalty by the Court of Appeal in June. The others were convicted of rape and murder.

In November 1990, a man convicted of multiple rape and murder became the first person in Tunisia to be executed since the President came to power in 1987. At the time the Tunisian Government stated that this execution was an exception, carried out because of the particularly heinous nature of the crime.

AI has written to President Ben Ali expressing its deep regret at this resumption of executions, and urging him to commute all outstanding death sentences as a first step towards the abolition of the death penalty.□

A mock-up of the Astra car in which the army shot and killed the two is displayed in an army canteen. The text to the left says: "Vauxhall Astra, Built by Robots, Driven by Joyriders, Stopped by A COY!" [Meaning A Company of the Parachute Regiment].

© Pacemaker Press

UNITED KINGDOM

Soldier charged with murder

KAREN Reilly, 18, and Martin Peake, 17, were shot dead in Northern Ireland in September 1990 while driving a stolen car. They were killed by soldiers from the Parachute Regiment. Soldiers initially alleged that they fired at the car after it had driven through an army checkpoint and hit a soldier. However, eye-witnesses stated that they saw soldiers simulating a leg injury in order to corroborate the above statement.

In July 1991 six soldiers were charged in connection with the deaths of Karen Reilly and Martin Peake: one with murder, two with attempted murder, and all six with attempting to pervert the course of justice and obstructing the police investigation.

For many years AI has been calling for an independent judicial inquiry to investigate the pattern of disputed killings by security forces in Northern Ireland in order to help prevent unlawful killings.□

CHAD

Four killed by firing squad

FOUR people, three of them soldiers, were publicly executed by firing squad on 7 October 1991 in the capital, N'Djamena. They were convicted of criminal offences and sentenced to death in recent months, with no right of appeal, by a military court set up in April 1991.

These were the first court-ordered executions to take place in Chad for many years.□

0216

CAMPAIGN FOR PRISONERS OF THE MONTH

Each of the people whose story is told below is a prisoner of conscience. Each has been arrested because of his or her religious or political beliefs, colour, sex, ethnic origin or language. None has used or advocated violence. Their continuing detention is a violation of the United Nations Universal Declaration of Human Rights. International appeals can help to secure the release of these prisoners or to improve their detention conditions. In the interest of the prisoners, letters to the authorities should be worded carefully and courteously. You should stress that your concern for human rights is not in any way politically partisan. In *no* circumstances should communications be sent to the prisoner.

ISRAEL/OCCUPIED TERRITORIES

Abie Nathan: ***an Israeli peace campaigner aged 64, he began an 18-month prison sentence on 10 October 1991. He was convicted of breaking a 1986 law forbidding unauthorized contacts between Israeli citizens and groups designated as "terrorist" by the Israeli authorities.***

Abie Nathan was charged with having met Palestine Liberation Organization (PLO) Chairman Yasser Arafat in Tunis on 10 and 16 March 1990. During these meetings they reportedly discussed the development of the Middle East peace process, direct talks between the PLO and Israel, the Palestinian *intifada* (uprising) and the fate of Israeli soldiers missing in Lebanon.

"It's a sad day for democracy, for human rights and for peace," Abie Nathan reportedly said after he was sentenced. He has decided not to appeal against his conviction and sentence and has pledged to renew his contacts with the PLO immediately upon his release from prison.

© Associated Press

Abie Nathan

Abie Nathan spent four months in prison in 1989 and 1990 for having met Chairman Arafat and other senior PLO leaders in September 1988. AI at that time called for his release. Abie Nathan also served a 40-day prison sentence in 1966 for flying a plane to Egypt carrying a petition for peace in the Middle East signed by 100,000 Israelis.

Amnesty International believes that Abie Nathan is once again a prisoner of conscience. The Israeli Government maintains that Abie Nathan was prosecuted "not ... because of his political views or his expression of them, but as a consequence of his actions". However, the internationally recognized rights to freedom of expression and to peaceful association fully encompass peaceful actions such as those carried out by Abie Nathan.

AI believes that the 1986 law should be reviewed to ensure that it does not lead to the imprisonment of prisoners of conscience.

■Please send courteous letters appealing for the immediate and unconditional release of Abie Nathan to: President Chaim Herzog/ Office of the President/Beit Hanasi/3 Hakeset Street/Jerusalem 92188/Israel.□

© Caroline Austin

Vic Williams

PEOPLE'S REPUBLIC OF CHINA

Jampa Ngodrup: ***a 46-year-old Tibetan medical doctor in Lhasa, capital of the Tibet Autonomous Region of China, he was sentenced on 24 December 1990 to 13 years' imprisonment on charges of spying.***

A doctor at Lhasa's City Barkor Clinic, Jampa Ngodrup was apparently detained on 20 October 1989 and formally charged on 13 August 1990. He was accused of having, "with counter-revolutionary aims, collected lists of people detained in the disturbances and passed them on to others, thus undermining the law and violating the [laws of] secrecy". The "disturbances" refer to activities by supporters of Tibetan independence in Lhasa in 1988.

The court's verdict on Jampa Ngodrup's case said he had asked a young monk working at the Barkor Clinic to compile a list of people detained as a result of violent clashes between police forces and demonstrators on 5 March 1988. Jampa Ngodrup is said to have passed the list on to a foreign resident who in turn gave Jampa Ngodrup a list of people injured and detained in a pro-independence demonstration on 10 December 1988. Jampa Ngodrup apparently confessed to all charges.

The court ruled that Jampa Ngodrup be deprived of his political rights for a further four years after he has served his 13-year sentence.

Amnesty International considers Jampa Ngodrup to be a prisoner of conscience, detained and sentenced solely for the peaceful exercise of his right freely to receive and impart information.

■Please send courteous letters appealing for the immediate and unconditional release of Jampa Ngodrup to: Gyaltsen Norbu/ Chairperson of the Tibet Autonomous Region/Tibet Regional Government/Lhasa/Tibet Autonomous Region/People's Republic of China.□

© Tibet Information Network

Jampa Ngodrup

UNITED KINGDOM

Vic Williams: ***a 28-year-old soldier in the British Army's Royal Artillery, he has been sentenced to 14 months' imprisonment for desertion and "conduct prejudicial to good order and military discipline".***

On 11 September 1991 a court martial found Vic Williams guilty on three charges relating to deserting his regiment and speaking out against the Gulf War. He went absent without leave from his regiment in December 1990, the day before he was due to be sent to Saudi Arabia. He left because he had decided that his conscience could not allow him to take part in military action arising from the Gulf crisis.

Vic Williams has said that he left his regiment only after concluding that he had no other option remaining (at no time prior to his decision to leave was he made aware of his rights as a soldier to register a conscientious objection to military service). The regulations setting out the procedure whereby a soldier in the British Army can apply for conscientious objector status are classified as a "restricted" document — to which only Army officers have access.

Evidence given by officers at the court martial and the statement made by the judge advocate at the close of the proceedings supported Amnesty International's concern that Vic Williams was not guaranteed reasonable access to information about procedures for registering his conscientious objection to military service in the Gulf War.

■Please write courteous appeals for the immediate and unconditional release of Vic Williams to: The Right Honourable John Major MP/Prime Minister/ 10 Downing Street/London SW1 2AA.□

PRISONER NEWS

AI learned in September 1991 of the release of 59 prisoners under adoption or investigation. AI took up 15 cases.

0217

FOCUS amnesty international

Gross and widespread human rights violations have afflicted Peru for almost a decade. Since 1983 large areas of the country have been progressively designated emergency zones and placed under military control as part of counter-insurgency operations against the armed opposition groups, principally *Sendero Luminoso* which has been responsible for widespread atrocities.

Thousands of people have "disappeared" or been extrajudicially executed after being abducted by members of the security forces. Most of those who were killed had been brutally tortured, as were the few who survived abduction or "disappearance".

Most of the victims have come from towns and isolated peasant communities in remote rural areas. Often they were targeted simply because they lived in zones of armed conflict between government forces and opposition groups. In recent years, "disappearances" have increased in urban areas. Human rights defenders, often the only hope for victims seeking help for themselves or their relatives, have been threatened, tortured, killed and "disappeared".

By July 1990 nearly half of the country was under emergency regulations. In most emergency zones, headed by political-military commands, the armed forces, in practice, have not been accountable to the civilian authorities. It is within these emergency zones that the vast majority of human rights violations by military forces and abuses by opposition groups have been committed.

This was the legacy inherited by the new government of President Alberto Fujimori which took office in Peru on 28 July 1990.

The promise

In his inaugural speech on 28 July, President Fujimori promised to respect human rights fully: "The terrorist violence our fledgling democracy currently faces cannot justify the occasional or systematic violation of human rights."

The "central element" of the new government's policy was to be the creation of a national human rights commission. During the government's first year in office further measures to

© Vera Alentz

Widows in formation for civil defence patrol

Peru: The suffering continues

reinforce these pledges were promised. In February 1991, for example, the government stated that it was adopting measures to "make available registers of detention...(and) promptly and objectively to establish the fate of those whose 'disappearance' is claimed as certain".

In May 1991 the government outlined a new set of proposals on human rights and referred to the need "to eliminate every form of excess by the security forces in fulfilment of their duties, and to punish those responsible".

The reality

Despite these promises there was no significant improvement in Peru's human rights record in the first year of the new government. The pattern of endemic human rights violations arising from *Sendero Luminoso*'s armed actions against government forces and the civilian population continued.

Between 28 July 1990 and 27 July 1991, AI received reports of 179 "disappearances" and 58 extrajudicial executions perpetrated by members of the security services. Most of these violations were committed in the emergency zones under military control. The difficulty of obtaining information in these zones means that the true total of violations may be significantly greater. Human rights defenders and their organizations are still under attack.

In September 1991 the government announced new measures on human rights, including giving Public Ministry prosecutors full authority to enter all detention centres, including military installations in the emergency zones, to investigate the condition of detainees and alleged "disappearances". On 13 September the government announced that President Fujimori had ordered all members of the armed forces to respect human rights. He stated that those who disobeyed this order "will be severely punished".

Whether these measures will succeed in ending the pattern of gross human rights violations in Peru remains to be seen. In addition, the government has yet to indicate whether it intends to investigate past human rights violations and bring those responsible to justice, a measure that AI considers an essential element of a policy to end human rights violations.

The armed opposition

Sendero Luminoso is the main armed opposition group in Peru. Since 1980 it has repeatedly engaged in operations which have included the torture and execution-like killing of captive civilians, local authorities and members of the security forces.

Among the civilian victims have been members of peasant communities and rural cooperatives who refused to join or support *Sendero Luminoso*. Often they have been killed or tortured following mock trials.

Sendero Luminoso has also engaged in a protracted strategy of sabotaging public utilities and destroying the livestock and produce of peasant communities.

In the run-up to the 1990 presidential elections *Sendero Luminoso* reportedly assassinated several parliamentary candidates and bombs were planted in public places, causing several casualties. *Sendero Luminoso* has been accused of murdering some 90 mayors in the emergency zones

0218

since 1982. Its attacks have left some areas without any civilian authorities: the latter have either fled or been killed.

In the past year, AI has continued to receive numerous reports of *Sendero Luminoso* atrocities. For example, in May 1991 its members reportedly carried out the execution-style killing of a former prisoner of conscience, Porfirio Suni Quispe, who had been elected a regional deputy.

The other main armed opposition group in Peru is the Túpac Amaru Revolutionary Movement (MRTA), which began to launch armed attacks in June 1984. By 1991 the group had extended its sphere of operations to rural as well as urban areas.

The MRTA engages in sabotage, political killings, the occupation of towns, villages and public buildings, and armed attacks on police and army patrols. According to reports, MRTA members have been known occasionally to kill their captives.

AI, as a matter of principle, condemns the killing or torture of prisoners, other deliberate and arbitrary killings and the taking of hostages by political opposition groups. It does not treat such groups as if they had the status of governments. It is governments which are obliged to uphold international human rights standards. However, any opposition group should abide by minimum international standards of humane behaviour, such as the principles contained in humanitarian law.

Impunity

The central issue which underlies the continuing pattern of human rights violations is that members of the armed forces are rarely brought to justice for the crimes they commit and therefore act with impunity.

Human rights violations have continued despite the legal safeguards enshrined in the Constitution and in international human rights standards which Peru has pledged to uphold.

Although thousands of civilians have been reported extrajudicially executed or "disappeared" in the emergency zones during the past decade, no members of the armed forces are known to have been convicted for their part in these violations.

To AI's knowledge, judicial proceedings have been initiated in only four of the hundreds of cases of "disappearance", extrajudicial execution and torture reported to the organization since President Fujimori took office.

Public prosecutors attached to the Public Ministry, the official

Army tank patrolling Lima, 1990 © *Alejandro Balaguer*

body responsible for upholding human rights, and the judiciary have attempted to investigate the violations. However, they have been repeatedly obstructed and sometimes threatened by the military. AI, therefore, welcomed new legislation passed on 2 September which gave public prosecutors full powers to enter all detention centres in Peru, including military bases in the emergency zones, to investigate reports of "disappearance".

In most cases of human rights violations, witnesses have testified that members of the armed forces were responsible. In most instances, the military either deny their involvement or claim the detainee has been released, in the case of "disappearances", or else attribute the abuses to the armed opposition. Further action is rarely taken.

A major obstacle to bringing to justice those involved in perpetrating human rights violations in the emergency zones has been the role of military courts which, under current Peruvian law, have sole jurisdiction over members of the armed forces accused of human rights violations committed while on duty. These courts, which are presided over by military officers

Detention by the security forces near Uchiza, San Martín department; many of those detained by the military later "disappear" © *Alejandro Balaguer*

and exclude members of the public from their proceedings, have routinely closed cases of military involvement in human rights violations, and exonerated the defendants.

Unless the present government breaks the pattern and brings the perpetrators of human rights violations to justice before civilian courts, and ensures that basic preventive measures are effectively implemented, there is little hope for the future.

The government must enforce the measures it takes to make the armed forces accountable for their actions and ensure that those responsible for human rights violations are brought to justice.

'Disappearance'

Twenty-two-year-old student Ernesto Castillo Páez was last seen on 21 October 1990. He was in the custody of police officers who detained him as he was walking through the Central Park in the Villa El Salvador neighbourhood of Lima. Eye-witnesses saw him handcuffed, forced into the boot of a patrol car, and driven away.

In an historic ruling, Judge Elva Greta Minaya Callo upheld a *habeas corpus* petition on his behalf, saying there were serious irregularities in police procedure.

However, the Supreme Court annulled the *habeas corpus* writ on the grounds of procedural irregularities.

The lawyer for Ernesto Castillo Páez' family, Dr Augusto Zúñiga Paz, who is also head of the legal office of the independent Commission for Human Rights, received death threats as a result of his work on the case. He informed the Supreme Court of the threats in February 1991 but apparently received no form of protection.

On 15 March a large envelope was delivered to Dr Zúñiga's office. It was a letter bomb; it exploded when he opened it and severed his left forearm. According to the Defence Ministry, the package contained explosive of a type used only by the Navy.

Torture

Fidel Intusca, a mine worker, was detained in August 1990 and taken to the military base at Puquio, Ayacucho department. There, he said, he was severely tortured. He escaped shortly afterwards.

"They stripped me down to my underpants and socks. They tightened the gag and the blindfold. They chained my wrists behind my back and tied my ankles so tightly that it felt like steel. Then...they beat me in the most sensitive areas...I was tortured for

0219

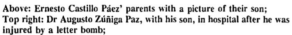

Above: Ernesto Castillo Páez' parents with a picture of their son;
Top right: Dr Augusto Zúñiga Paz, with his son, in hospital after he was injured by a letter bomb;
Bottom right: Fidel Intusca with photographs showing the injuries he sustained under torture.

more than four hours. They beat me and put me into a vat full of water until I was half dead."

Fidel Intusca was tortured because the military suspected he was involved with *Sendero Luminoso*.

The independent Association of Human Rights (APRODEH) and a senator denounced his torture and demanded guarantees for his safety. APRODEH director Francisco Soberón received death threats after publicizing this case. The senator, Javier Diez Canesco, also received death threats and on 16 November 1990 a bomb was thrown at his house. Although the blast caused material damage, no one was hurt.

Massacre

In mid-October 1990 villagers from Huamanga province discovered three mass graves — the gruesome evidence of a recent massacre. One witness described the scene as they uncovered 18 bodies: "Everyone starts digging frantically, some with spades, others with pick-axes, and others with their bare hands. Nearly all of them are crying and the stench is increasing. The weeping aloud of the relatives turns to melancholic songs in the local Quechua dialect. Zacarías Cconocc Huayhua...sings words of grief to his wife whom he has just recognized."

A few weeks earlier, on 21 and 22 September, nearly 40 people from peasant communities were detained by a military patrol from the Castropampa military base in Huanta, in a joint operation with civil defence patrol members (*montoneros*). The joint force entered the districts of Santiago de Pischa and San José de Ticllas, Huamanga province, following a *Sendero Luminoso* attack in the locality.

The patrol released several prisoners but took 18 of them to a ravine named Chilcahuaycco

> ***"The weeping aloud of the relatives turns to melancholic songs in the local Quechua dialect"***

and apparently beat and then shot them. On 18 October their bodies were exhumed from three mass graves in the presence of a provincial prosecutor, a judge, police officers and two doctors. Seventeen of the bodies were identified.

The massacre was investigated by the Public Ministry and a senate commission of inquiry. In February 1991 the Public Ministry's Special Attorney for Human Rights announced that an army sergeant was to be charged with homicide. The Senate Commission published its report in May 1991. It attributed the killings to a combined force of soldiers and *montoneros*.

At least three other massacres by the security forces have taken place since the new government took office.

Protect human rights

AI urges the Government of Peru to take the following steps to ensure that human rights are upheld and maintained.

1. Prevent human rights violations

- The President, as Commander-in-Chief of the Armed Forces, should ensure that the security forces obey orders that counter-insurgency operations must be carried out within the framework of national and international law, and that human rights violations are not tolerated.
- The political-military commands should rigorously ensure the protection of human rights in the emergency zones.
- Up-to-date registers of detention should be maintained in recognized detention centres throughout Peru and in armed forces installations in the emergency zones. These registers should be made

0220

Funeral of Thomas Quispe Sayhua, a peasant leader

available on request to relatives, Public Ministry officials, judges, lawyers and representatives of human rights organizations.

- International human rights organizations which monitor the conditions of political detainees should be granted unrestricted access to all places where detainees are held.
- A Public Ministry official or a judge should be notified promptly of all arrests.
- Judges, doctors, lawyers and relatives should be given prompt and regular access to detainees.
- Detainees should be released before a public prosecutor or a judge, in order to verify that the release occurred.
- The government should seek to prevent extrajudicial executions by ensuring strict control over all security force personnel engaged in counter-insurgency operations.
- The government should explicitly prohibit and take measures to prevent rape and sexual abuse by soldiers.

2. Investigate human rights violations

- All reports of "disappearances", extrajudicial executions and torture should be immediately and thoroughly investigated by impartial and independent teams, headed by special prosecutors appointed by the Public Ministry, with powers to require members of the security forces to submit evidence.
- The Public Ministry and the judiciary should receive the political support and resources necessary to carry out their duties.
- All investigations of extrajudicial executions should include adequate autopsy procedures, and the collection and analysis of all physical and documentary evidence and statements from witnesses.
- Victims and witnesses who wish to give evidence of human rights violations should receive official protection on request, as should journalists and human rights monitors investigating such abuses.

3. Bring the perpetrators to justice

- All members of the security forces against whom there is evidence that they ordered, committed or concealed human rights violations, should be brought to justice before the civilian courts.
- Individual officers against whom there is evidence of involvement in human rights violations should be suspended from active service during investigation and judicial proceedings.

4. Compensate the victims

- The victims of human rights violations, including families and dependants of victims of "disappearance" and extrajudicial execution, should receive full compensation and, where necessary, medical treatment and rehabilitation.

What you can do

Involve any organizations you know of, such as your church, trade union, professional body, social club, business, local council, women's group, law firm or political party. Ask them to write to the President of Peru, calling on him to:

- uphold human rights;
- investigate all reports of human rights violations;
- bring the perpetrators to justice;
- compensate the victims.

Human rights experts are convinced that organizations like these are influential upon the Peruvian Government. That is why we are asking people to approach all sorts of organizations and ask them to write letters to Peru.

- If you want to know more about our concerns in Peru, contact the AI office in your country and ask for the 1991 Peru Report: *Human rights in a climate of terror.*
- If you want to get more involved — join AI
- If you don't have the time to get involved — make a donation to AI.

Defend the defenders

Organizations working on the defence of human rights in Peru are under attack by *Sendero Luminoso* and the government. In July 1991 the *Sendero Luminoso* newspaper *El Diario* accused human rights defenders of "spilling crocodile tears" in denouncing human rights violations perpetrated by the security forces. At the end of September the official government newspaper *El Peruano* reported a speech by President Fujimori to the armed forces. He charged human rights defenders with being "useful sops" and of collaborating with subversion.

Human rights defenders in Peru are under attack and need your help. You can help them by copying your letters (see above) to the coordinating body of human rights organizations in Peru. In this way human rights organizations there will know how concerned people outside Peru are about the human rights situation in that country.

Send copies to:

Coordinadora Nacional de Derechos Humanos, Capac Yupanqui 2151, Depto. 204, Lima, Peru.☐

JORDAN/SAUDI ARABIA

Saudi Arabian at risk after *refoulement* by Jordan

ON 2 October 1991 Jordanian security forces arrested Muhammad al-Fasi, a Saudi Arabian businessman, and reportedly handed him to Saudi Arabian authorities at the al-Haditha crossing point on the Saudi-Jordanian frontier.

Muhammad al-Fasi had been publicly critical of the Saudi Arabian Government during the Gulf crisis and its aftermath. He is allegedly being held in a secret location in Riyadh where it is feared he is at risk of torture and execution.

AI issued urgent appeals calling on the Saudi Arabian authorities to clarify his fate and whereabouts, and to provide assurances that he will not be ill-treated or executed. AI also sought clarifications from the Jordanian authorities as to their reason for expelling Muhammad al-Fasi, and any assurances they may have sought or obtained from the Saudi Arabian Government that his human rights would not be violated.□

Muhammad al-Fasi

PAKISTAN

Ahmadis imprisoned for practicing their religion

POLICIES pursued by the government of President Zia (1977 to 1988) and the present government of Nawaz Sharif, in office since November 1990, have violated the right to freedom of religion, particularly for the Ahmadis of Pakistan. The Ahmadiyya community, numbering over three million members in Pakistan, considers itself Muslim but is regarded as heretical by orthodox Muslims.

Changes in the Pakistan Penal Code introduced in recent years make it a criminal offence for Ahmadis to profess, practice and propagate their faith. In the most recent such amendment the death penalty has become the mandatory punishment for the offence of defiling the name of the Prophet Mohammad. Orthodox Muslims consider that an Ahmadi defiles the Prophet's name by speaking or writing it.

Amnesty International is concerned that Ahmadis continue to be charged, convicted and given prison terms solely for the peaceful exercise of their religious beliefs. For instance, in November 1990 two brothers in Abbotabad were each sentenced to six years' imprisonment and given a heavy fine for having preached about their faith. Several Ahmadis are known currently to be serving prison sentences for using Muslim phrases of greeting.

Amnesty International published a document in September 1991 describing human rights violations and abuses reportedly suffered by Ahmadis in 1990 and 1991.* It urged the Pakistan Government to release all Ahmadi prisoners of conscience unconditionally and immediately, and to bring the country's legislation in line with international human rights standards.

* *Pakistan: Violations of human rights of Ahmadis (AI Index: ASA 33/15/91).*□

MACAO

Basic Law fails to protect human rights

Macao, the Portuguese territory on the southern coast of China, will revert to Chinese sovereignty in 1999. The draft of the Basic Law, which will govern the Macao Special Administrative Region (MSAR) after 1999, was published in July. In a memorandum submitted to the Macao Basic Law Drafting Committee in November, Amnesty International said the draft Basic Law did not adequately protect fundamental human rights. It failed in particular to include safeguards against the reintroduction of the death penalty, which was abolished in Macao in the 19th century.

AI also expressed concern that the United Nations International Covenant on Civil and Political Rights, currently in force in Macao by virtue of Portugal's ratification, should continue to apply to the MSAR beyond 1999.□

COLOMBIA

Lawyer threatened

Dr Eduardo Umaña Mendoza, law professor and human rights lawyer, has been repeatedly threatened with death over a number of months, apparently as a result of his activities in defence of human rights. Although no specific motive was given, the threats may be connected to Dr Umaña's role in representing the surviving members of a peasant family whose relatives were allegedly killed by members of the Colombian army

On 18 August Antonio Palacios Urrea, three of his children and his son-in-law were shot dead by soldiers in their home on the outskirts of Fusagasugá, Cundinamarca department. Two men, whose identity is not yet clear, were also found dead at the entrance to the house. A statement issued by the Commander of the XIII Brigade of the Colombian army alleged that those killed were members of a guerrilla group who had died during an armed confrontation with soldiers. This version of events was contradicted by eye-witness reports and the findings of police and journalists who visited the scene shortly afterwards who reportedly found no evidence that the people inside the house had fired on their attackers. The only adult survivor of the attack testified to the military court investigating the killings that her relatives were shot through the back of the head after being made to lie face down on the floor. At the end of September, military investigating court No. 115 issued arrest warrants against a second-lieutenant, a sergeant and five privates, in connection with the killings.

On learning of the threats against Dr Umaña, the Colombian authorities took steps to safeguard his immediate physical integrity. However, AI remains concerned about the long-term safety of Dr Umaña.□

SOUTH AFRICA

Black Sash members detained in 'homeland'

IN October 1991 Amnesty International called for the release of 11 members of the South African human rights organization Black Sash, detained in the nominally independent "homeland" of Bophuthatswana. They were arrested on 5 October while staging a peaceful protest to highlight repression in Bophuthatswana. After three days' imprisonment they were convicted of attending an illegal gathering under the terms of Bophuthatswana's Internal Security Act, fined, and released from custody.

The police action against the members of Black Sash, which, although legal elsewhere in South Africa, remains banned in Bophuthatswana, underscored the extremely restrictive conditions confronting human rights as well as political activists in Bophuthatswana.

The "homeland's" Internal Security Act effectively prohibits the holding of any public meeting or demonstration unless official permission has been granted. Officials rarely agree to or even respond to requests to hold meetings. This provides the security forces with broad scope to disperse any meeting, and has imposed severe constraints on political activists who have frequently been arrested and charged. On 7 April 1991 a group of over 60 people were arrested at an African National Congress (ANC) workshop in Itsoseng and charged with attending an illegal gathering.

Human rights activists have also been affected. Members of the Mafikeng Anti-Repression Forum (MAREF) have been repeatedly detained since MAREF's formation in mid-1990, and MAREF's chairperson was one of five observers arrested at the Black Sash protest on 5 October. She was released uncharged.

In addition to detaining and charging activists under the Internal Security Act, on various occasions over the past year the police have dispersed non-violent gatherings with gunfire, resulting in injuries or deaths. A young man, Johannes Mafatshe, was shot dead on 21 March 1991 when police opened fire to disperse peaceful demonstrators in Phokeng.□

0222

BURUNDI

Arrests by security forces

ABOUT 100 members of the majority Hutu ethnic group were arrested between July and November 1991 by members of the Burundi security forces in various parts of the country. Virtually all those arrested were accused of being supporters of the opposition *Parti pour la libération du peuple hutu* (PALIPEHUTU), Hutu People's Liberation Party, which the government accuses of seeking political change through violence against the minority but dominant Tutsi ethnic group. These were the first large-scale arrests of government opponents since a program of political reforms started in 1989.

Arrests were particularly numerous in September, when members of the Burundi refugee community in Tanzania, which had previously provided support for PALIPEHUTU, returned to Burundi as part of a voluntary repatriation scheme. Returnees were among 40 people detained in Muyinga province, in the northeast.

Some detainees were subjected to severe beatings while in police custody, for example at the *Brigade spéciale de recherche* (BSR), Special Investigation Brigade, in Bujumbura. By October most had been transferred to ordinary prisons but had not been tried. They were accused variously of circulating tracts, receiving foreign assistance to endanger the security of the state and engaging in activities which might disturb the peace. Five of those arrested in July were apparently meeting to plan a commemoration of the anniversary of the death of the PALIPEHUTU leader, Remy Gahu[illegible]n prison in Tanzania in August 1990.

The arrests coincide with the publication in September of the recommendations of a Constitutional Commission. This called for the establishment of a multi-party political system in place of the present one-party state, with a ban on parties based on just one ethnic group.□

USSR: Allegations of ill-treatment

AI is concerned about numerous reports of ill-treatment of ethnic Armenians during an operation by Soviet troops and Azerbaydzhani special police units (OMON) in April and May this year in areas of the Republic of Azerbaydzhan which have been the scene of ethnic violence.

Many men detained, both briefly by the OMON and in Azerbaydzhani prisons, claim they were beaten and otherwise ill-treated: allegations refer to regular daily beatings with truncheons, often to the point of unconsciousness; rape and insertion of bottles into the anus; and deprivation of food and water. At least two men reportedly died in prison from injuries inflicted. One, a police officer, is said to have been tortured and his cries relayed by radio to other ethnic-Armenian officers as a warning. The other reportedly had his skull fractured in 15 places, broken fingers and numerous stab wounds. The official cause of death was given as suicide by hanging and internal haemorrhaging respectively.

AI is also concerned that in other instances, during the operation some unarmed civilians were reportedly killed deliberately by law-enforcement officials without warning or attempts to apprehend them, and that some people are said to have been detained for short periods solely on grounds of their ethnic origin.

AI recognizes that law-enforcement officials in the area are charged with keeping order in a situation in which they and the civilian population are subject to attacks from armed bands. However, it is urging that all law-enforcement officials be made aware of, and conform to, the United Nations Code of Conduct for Law Enforcement Officials and other international human rights standards. It is also urging the authorities to initiate a full and prompt inquiry into allegations of ill-treatment; that the findings be made public; and the perpetrators brought to justice.□

AMNESTY INTERNATIONAL NEWSLETTER is published every month in four languages to bring you news of AI's concerns and campaigns worldwide, as well as in-depth reports. Available from Amnesty International (address below)

GUATEMALA

Reports of police brutality

EXEQUIEL Trujillo Hernández, Francisco Castillo García and Carlos Geovanny Rosales Chávez were arrested in Guatemala City on 25 August 1991, accused of murdering nine people, including two police officers and two university students. The photos of the three accused, who appeared scarred and bruised, were shown on the national press. Several days later, relatives of the men claimed that the detainees had been tortured.

According to the men's testimonies, moments after their arrest they overheard police say "With these, we wash our hands". They were taken to the 6th Police Precinct and beaten. Then they were handcuffed, blindfolded and taken to the National Police headquarters, where they were separated. They said each was taken to a room in the Criminal Investigation Department (DIC), where they were again beaten with fists and sticks and kicked while interrogated. Two of them claimed they had sticks introduced in the anus. Police also threatened to kill them and their families.

Two of the men said they were then taken to an open space, given a gun and made to shoot. Back in the DIC, police agents applied the paraffin test (to assess whether firearms had been used), resulting in severe burns to the men's hands. Finally, they were transferred to the Preventive Detention Centre in Zone 18 of Guatemala City. Sources inside Guatemala, including Congressmen and the University Students Association, have expressed doubt whether, despite police statements, the men did commit all the killings attributed to them. AI is concerned that Guatemalan police reportedly used torture and threats in order to obtain evidence to prosecute the three men.□

YEMEN

Executions carried out

ON 13 August 1991 five executions and five amputations took place in public in the northern provinces of the Republic of Yemen. Those executed were convicted of murder, while those whose right hands were amputated were convicted of repeated theft. According to eye-witnesses, the severed hands were displayed in the town centre. The amputations were the first reported since unification in May 1990.

Before unification, executions and amputations took place in the former Yemen Arab Republic (YAR) in accordance with interpretation of the shari'a. The Unity Agreement between the YAR and the People's Democratic Republic of Yemen stipulated that separate legislation would remain in force during a 36-month transitional period, during which time a common penal code and other relevant legislation would be agreed upon.□

MOROCCO

Detention centre demolished

THE secret detention centre of Tazmamert in southeastern Morocco is said to have been demolished in mid-September 1991 and its inmates moved to an undisclosed location. Only one of the Tazmamert detainees, M'Barek Touil, who is married to a US citizen, was released on 23 September 1991; the fate of the others remains unknown.

Of the 61 former military personnel moved from Kenitra Military Prison to Tazmamert in 1973, 29 are said to have since died, almost certainly due to the harsh conditions of detention. These detainees, convicted of taking part in attempted coups against King Hassan II in 1971 and 1972, were held incommunicado, completely cut off from the outside world for 19 years; the only news from them was in rare letters smuggled out. The sentences of many of them had expired 17 years ago.

The Moroccan authorities have never given any reason for continuing to hold these prisoners and have repeatedly denied the existence of this secret detention centre.□

0223

AMNESTY INTERNATIONAL, 1 Easton Street, London WC1X 8DJ, United Kingdom. Printed in Great Britain by Flashprint Enterprises Ltd, London. Available on subscri tion at £7 US$12.00 for 12 issues. ISSN 0308 6887

관리 번호	91-222

주 영 대 사 관

영국(정) 723-62 1991.12.9

수신 : 장관

참조 : 국제기구국장

제목 : A.I. 인권보고서

연호 A.I 발간 아국관련 인권보고서(South Korea: Arrests of Political Prisoners in 1991) 및 A.I측 서한(사본)을 별첨 송부합니다.

첨부 : 1. 인권보고서

2. 서한 사본. 끝 .

예고: 92.6.30 일반

일반문서로 재분류 (1992 .6 .30.)

주 영 대 사

0224

amnesty international

SOUTH KOREA

Arrests of Political Prisoners During 1991

NOVEMBER 1991 SUMMARY AI INDEX: ASA 25/34/91

DISTR: SC/CO/GR

Amnesty International is concerned about some 50 political prisoners who were arrested during 1991. It considers many of them to be prisoners as prisoners of conscience, detained for the peaceful exercise of their rights to freedom of expression and association. Amnesty International is asking for the immediate and unconditional release of all prisoners of conscience, and is seeking further information about others whom it believes may be prisoners of conscience.

This document gives a brief outline of some of these 1991 arrests and a statement of Amnesty International's concern in each case.

Information about other prisoners of concern to Amnesty International arrested in previous years can be found in the document *South Korea: Prisoners Held for National Security Offences* (ASA 25/25/91).

KEYWORDS: PRISONERS OF CONSCIENCE1 / POLITICAL GROUPS1 / BANNING1 / RESTRICTION ON MOVEMENT / TRADE UNIONISTS1 / CHURCH WORKERS / AGED / WOMEN / ACADEMICS / ARTISTS1 / WRITERS / DIRECTORS / STUDENTS1 / MILITARY AS VICTIMS / TEACHERS / REARREST / DEMONSTRATIONS / MASS ARREST / INCOMMUNICADO DETENTION / TORTURE/ILL-TREATMENT / POLICE / EXTRAJUDICIAL EXECUTION / CONTINUED DETENTION / STRIKES / POLITICALLY MOTIVATED CRIMINAL CHARGES / DEATH IN CUSTODY / POST MORTEMS / LEGISLATION / PHOTOGRAPHS /

This report summarizes a 20-page document (7681 words), *South Korea: Arrests of Political Prisoners During 1991* (AI Index: ASA 25/34/91), issued by Amnesty International in November 1991. Anyone wanting further details or to take action on this issue should consult the full document.

INTERNATIONAL SECRETARIAT, 1 EASTON STREET, LONDON WC1X 8DJ, UNITED KINGDOM

0225

amnesty international

SOUTH KOREA

ARRESTS OF POLITICAL PRISONERS DURING 1991

November 1991
AI Index: ASA 25/34/91
Distr: SC/CO/GR

INTERNATIONAL SECRETARIAT, 1 EASTON STREET, LONDON WC1X 8DJ, UNITED KINGDOM

0226

TABLE OF CONTENTS

1) INTRODUCTION 1

2) LAWS USED TO DETAIN POLITICAL PRISONERS 1
The National Security Law 1
The Law on Assemblies and Demonstrations 2
The Labour Dispute Mediation Act 2

3) POMMINNYON ARRESTS 3

4) IMPRISONED ARTISTS 6
The arrests of Chong Son-hee, Choi Ik-kyun and Oh Chin-hee 6
The arrests of Cha Il-hwan, Park Yong-kyun and Lee Chin-woo 8
The case of Park In-bae 8

5) ARRESTS OF RESEARCH STUDENTS 9

6) ARRESTS RELATING TO DEMONSTRATIONS IN MAY AND JUNE . . 11
The Death of Kang Kyung-dae 11
Arrests of Dissident Leaders 11
The Arrest of Kang Ki-hun 13
The Arrest of Suh Jun-shik 13

7) IMPRISONED TRADE UNIONISTS 14
Arrests for Third Party Intervention 14
The Death of Park Chang-su 16
The Arrests of Chonkyojo Members 16
The Arrest of Choi Jae-ho 18

8) ARRESTS OF MEMBERS OF THE ARMED FORCES 18

9) FURTHER ARRESTS OF MEMBERS OF SANOMAENG 19
The case of Park Noh-hae 19

0227

SOUTH KOREA: ARRESTS OF POLITICAL PRISONERS DURING 1991

1) INTRODUCTION

Amnesty International is concerned about some 50 political prisoners arrested during 1991. It considers many of them to be prisoners of conscience, detained for the peaceful exercise of their rights to freedom of expression and association. Amnesty International is asking for the immediate and unconditional release of all prisoners of conscience, and is seeking further information about others whom it believes may be prisoners of conscience.

This document gives a brief outline of some of these 1991 arrests and a statement of Amnesty International's concern in each case.

Information about other prisoners of concern to Amnesty International arrested in previous years can be found in the document *South Korea: Prisoners Held for National Security Offences* (ASA 25/25/91).

2) LAWS USED TO DETAIN POLITICAL PRISONERS

The National Security Law

The National Security Law prohibits anti-state activities and contacts with anti-state organizations. During 1991 the National Security Law was widely used to imprison people who met North Koreans or alleged North Korean agents abroad without government authorization, people who established or belonged to an alleged anti-state organization, and people accused of praising or benefiting North Korea.

On 10 May 1991 the ruling Democratic Liberal Party unilaterally passed amendments to the National Security Law, in spite of protests from opposition National Assembly members. Talks on amending the law had been held among representatives of the main political parties for more than two years without reaching agreement. Under the new law "anti-state organizations" include only groups with a "command and control system which aim to disturb the state". Contacts with communist organizations are now permitted, with the exception of those allegedly linked to North Korea. The offence of "praising, encouraging or showing sympathy" to North Korea will be punishable only when committed "with the knowledge that it will endanger national security and survival of the free and democratic basic order". The offence of espionage was redefined. Amnesty International welcomed the amendments in so far as they define offences more precisely but expressed concern that the law will continue to allow for the imprisonment of people who support North Korean ideology and seek to contact North Koreans without government permission.

The Law on Assemblies and Demonstrations

The Law on Assemblies and Demonstrations authorizes anti-government demonstrations so long as public order and security are protected. Under the law, those who are planning to hold a demonstration must obtain prior permission from the police at least 48 hours beforehand. Permission to hold a demonstration may be denied if it would be a direct threat to the public peace. During 1991 many trade union and dissident leaders were imprisoned under the Law on Assemblies and Demonstrations for organizing demonstrations without obtaining police approval. Some trade union and dissident groups said that their applications were irrelevant because they are never granted permission to hold demonstrations, apparently because of political considerations.

The Labour Dispute Mediation Act

Article 13(2) of the Labour Dispute Mediation Act prohibits a third party, that is somebody who has no immediate connection with a workplace where a dispute is taking place, from intervening in the dispute. In March 1990 President Roh Tae-woo vetoed an amendment of the law passed by the National Assembly to delete this provision. In January 1990 the Constitutional Court ruled that the ban on third party intervention was not unconstitutional. The authorities regard as third party intervention the distribution of leaflets and other documents giving advice to trade union members about their labour rights and about the conduct of wage negotiations. During 1991 a number of trade union leaders where charged with third party intervention in labour disputes.

3) POMMINNYON ARRESTS

The South-North Exchange and Cooperation Law, enacted in 1990, enables South Koreans to apply to the government for permission to meet with North Koreans. In 1991 there were many contacts between citizens of North and South Korea. For example, in February the two countries formed unified sports teams to compete in the World Table Tennis Championships in April and the World Youth Soccer Championships in June. Academics, politicians, members of the religious community, students, scientists and others from both countries were permitted to meet. However, the South Korean authorities continued to ban unauthorized contacts and insisted that it be the only channel to discuss reunification. Amnesty International is calling for the release of 12 members or alleged members of *Pomminnyon* (Pan-National Alliance for Reunification of Korea) who it believes to have been imprisoned for the peaceful exercise of their freedom of expression and association, and for having unauthorized contacts with North Koreans, in some cases only indirectly.

Pomminnyon was inaugurated in Berlin in November 1990. Its objectives include the achievement of peaceful national reunification by 1995, independence and national unity. The organization aimed to establish a headquarters for the organization in North and South Korea in 1991, to replace the current armistice (signed in 1953 at the end of the Korean War) by a peace agreement, to secure the withdrawal of foreign (US) troops from South Korea, the abolition of the National Security Law and free travel between North and South Korea.

Three staff members of *Chonminnyon* (National Democratic Alliance of Korea), **Cho Song-woo**, **Lee Hae-hak** and Reverend **Cho Yong-sul**, travelled to the inaugural meeting of *Pomminnyon* in Berlin where they met a North Korean official and Koreans from other countries. The three had applied to the South Korean authorities for permission to attend the meeting but this had been denied. They were arrested at Seoul's Kimpo International Airport on 30 November 1990 as they returned from Berlin and were charged under the National Security Law with making unauthorized contact with North Korean officials. In May 1991 Cho Song-woo and Lee Hae-hak were sentenced to 18 months' imprisonment. Reverend Cho Yong-sul, aged 70, was given a suspended sentence of one year's imprisonment and released. Amnesty International has adopted Cho Song-woo and Lee Hae-hak as prisoners of conscience and is calling for their release.

On 25 January 1991 the North Korean headquarters of *Pomminnyon* was established. In South Korea a preparatory committee was organized on 23 January 1991 at Hyang Rin church in Seoul. Over 80 committee members attended this meeting which decided

0230 ~~0229~~

to form the South Korean headquarters of *Pomminnyon* and to organize a pan-national rally in August 1991 in Seoul. On 24 January two of the preparatory committee's leading members, **Lee Chang-bok** and **Kim Hi-taek**, both staff members of *Chonminnyon*, were arrested and charged under the National Security Law with forming an anti-state organization and making illegal contact with North Koreans. In July 1991 Lee Chang-bok and Kim Hi-taek were each sentenced to two-and-a-half years' imprisonment. **Kwon Hyong-taek**, also a member of *Pomminnyon's* preparatory committee, was arrested on 19 April 1991 on the same charges. He was later sentenced to one-and-a-half years' imprisonment. Amnesty International has adopted Lee Chang-bok, Kim Hi-taek and Kwon Hyong-taek as prisoners of conscience and is calling for their release.

Reverend Hong Keun-soo, 54-year-old pastor of Hyang Rin Presbyterian Church in Seoul, was arrested on 20 February 1991. He was accused of praising North Korea in his sermons, of having spoken in favour of reunification during a television debate on KBS (Korea Broadcasting System) in September 1988, and of publishing a collection of his writings in 1989 which included an article about Reverend Hong Dong-keun, a lecturer in Christianity at Kim Il-sung University in North Korea. The authorities also accused Reverend Hong Keun-soo of planning to travel to Panmunjom and for his involvement in the establishment of the South Korean headquarters of *Pomminnyon*. In August 1991 Reverend Hong Keun-soo was sentenced to two years' imprisonment.

The Chairperson of *Pomminnyon's* preparatory committee, **Reverend Moon Ik-hwan**, was re-arrested on 6 June 1991. Moon Ik-hwan, a 72-year-old Presbyterian Minister, had been arrested in April 1989 for making an unauthorized visit to North Korea and meeting North Korean government officials. He was sentenced to seven years' imprisonment but was released in October 1990 on grounds of ill-health.

The authorities are reported to have re-arrested Reverend Moon Ik-hwan because he violated the terms of his parole by again becoming involved in political activities. Since his release, Reverend Moon Ik-hwan is reported to have delivered speeches at least 100 meetings of students and dissidents and to have participated in other political

0231

activities. State prosecutors are reported to have warned Reverend Moon Ik-hwan on several occasions that he might be reimprisoned if he did not curtail his activities. On 6 June Reverend Moon Ik-hwan was rearrested on the grounds that he had violated the terms of his parole by engaging in political activities and that his health had improved. Amnesty International has readopted Reverend Moon Ik-hwan as a prisoner of conscience and is calling for his release.

From 29 to 30 June 1991 a second *Pomminnyon* meeting was held in Berlin. Topics of discussion at this meeting included the organization of a pan-national conference to be held in Seoul around 15 August (National Liberation Day). Two student delegates belonging to *Chondaehyop* (National Council of Student Representatives) made an unauthorized visit to Berlin to attend this meeting. On the evening of 30 June the *Pomminnyon* headquarters in Berlin are reported to have sent a facsimile message to *Chonminnyon* with the request that it be forwarded to *Chondaehyop*. The message was intercepted by the authorities and two staff members of *Chonminnyon*, **Kim Hyong-min** and **Chung Yoon-so**, who were working in the office were arrested and charged under the National Security Law for being in communication with an anti-state organization. On 8 July 1991 two other members of *Pomninnyon's* preparatory committee, **Kim Kwe-sang** and **Lee Kwan-bok**, were arrested on the grounds that they had been involved in the organization of the planned pan-national conference. These four prisoners are currently on trial. Amnesty International has adopted them as prisoners of conscience and is calling for their release.

RELEASED

Park Soon-kyung, a 68-year-old theologian was arrested on 13 August 1991 for involvement in the formation of the South Korean headquarters of *Pomminnyon*. Park Soon-kyung is also accused of delivering a lecture at a Christian meeting in Japan in which she is reported to have made a comparison between the *Juche* ideology of North Korea and Christian theology and to have said that it is necessary for South Koreans to understand the *Juche* ideology in order to bring about reunification between the two countries.

RELEASED

4) IMPRISONED ARTISTS

The arrests of Chong Son-hee, Choi Ik-kyun and Oh Chin-hee

On 18 and 19 March 1991 eleven members of *Somiryon* were arrested and charged under the National Security Law with activities benefiting North Korea. In July three of them, Chong Son-hee, Choi Ik-kyun and Oh Chin-hee, were given sentences of imprisonment ranging from eighteen months to two years; the others were given shorter sentences and have now been released. Amnesty International believes that Chong Son-hee, Choi Ik-kyun and Oh Chin-hee have been detained in violation of their rights to freedom of expression and association and is calling for their release.

Somiryon is affiliated to the National Minjung Arts Movement (*Minmiryon*). The aims of these artists' groups is to practice and promote realism in art. The works of their members depict scenes of the life of ordinary or working people and often contain political messages, in particular in support of Korean reunification. They also campaign for freedom of artistic expression. In 1989 they arranged for a photographic slide of a painting entitled *History of the National Liberation Movement* to be sent to North Korea where it was reproduced and exhibited. Artist Hong Song-dam who designed the painting is currently serving a three-year prison sentence for sending the slide to North Korea.

Chong Son-hee (Ms), aged 32, was the representative of *Somiryon*, the Seoul region chapter of *Minmiryon* and a member of the Central Committee of *Minmiryon*. She is a painter and worked with others on the production of the section entitled *Fatherland Reunification Movement* of the painting *History of the National Liberation Movement*. She also contributed to the exhibitions *National Independence* and *Power of the People* in 1990 and 1991. Chong Son-hee was arrested on 18 March 1991 and has been sentenced to two years' imprisonment. She was accused of various activities as the representative of *Somiryon*, such as convening its several general meetings since April 1990, organizing and attending lectures on popular art theory and on the North Korean *Juche* ideology. She was held responsible for painting a banner on the theme of Korean reunification for the Student Council of Yonsei University and the painting of a mural about Im Su-kyong, a student detained for illegally visiting North Korea in 1989. Chong Son-hee was also charged for her active involvement in the Workers' Fine Arts School set up in the Kuro industrial zone in Seoul and for receiving and keeping various art publications, including copies of *Fine Arts Movement* published by *Minmiryon*. Amnesty International has adopted Chong Son-hee as a prisoner of conscience and is calling for her release.

Choi Ik-kyun (pen-name Choi Yol), aged 35, is an art critic who has published numerous articles as well as books, such as *A History of the Contemporary Art Movement in Korea* and *Theory and Practice of Minjok (National) Art*. He was the chairperson of the Art Criticism Group of *Somiryon* and the chairperson of *Minmiryon*. Choi Ik-kyun was arrested on 18 March 1991 and sentenced to 18 months' imprisonment. He was accused of drafting the platform of *Minmiryon* in April 1990, and of actively supporting the formation of *Somiryon*. He was also accused of giving lectures at meetings organised by the two groups.

Another charge against Choi Ik-kyun relates to the contents of seven editions of *Minmiryon*'s publication *Fine Arts Movement* of which he was the publisher. The authorities claim that the magazine advocated socialist realism and reflected marxist-leninist views, praised North Korean art and agitated for class struggle. Choi Ik-kyun was in particular charged with reproducing in the magazine's fifth issue a statement of appeal written in prison by Hong Song-dam in which Hong expressed political beliefs which the authorities regard as pro-North Korean. Choi Ik-kyun is also accused of having in his possession various books and documents on socialism and North Korea. Amnesty International has adopted Choi Ik-kyun as a prisoner of conscience and is calling for his release.

Oh Chin-hee (Ms), aged 24, was arrested on 18 March 1991 and sentenced to 18 months' imprisonment. She was a member of the Central Committee of *Somiryon* and participated in various exhibitions, including the exhibitions *Spring in the Fatherland* and *National Independence*, both held in 1990. Amnesty International believes that Oh Chin-hee has been charged for her activities as a leading member of *Somiryon*. It has adopted her as a prisoner of conscience and is calling for her release.

The arrests of Cha Il-hwan, Park Yong-kyun and Lee Chin-woo

Three other members of *Somiryon* have been arrested in recent months. **Lee Chin-woo** was arrested on 29 June 1991, **Park Yong-kyun** was arrested on 5 September 1991 and **Cha Il-hwan** was arrested on 12 September 1991. Cha Il-hwan, aged 32, was previously arrested in August 1989 along with artist Hong Song-dam on charges of sending a photographic slide of the painting *History of the National Liberation Movement* to North Korea. He is reported to have been beaten and deprived of sleep during his interrogation and to have been denied access to his family for 14 days after his arrest. In December 1989 he was given an 18-month suspended sentence and released. After his release Cha Il-hwan left the artists movement and went to work on a farm in North Kyongsangbuk province, the area where he grew up.

Amnesty International believes that Cha Il-hwan, Lee Chin-woo and Park Yong-kyun may be prisoners of conscience. It is seeking further information about the reasons for their arrest and the charges against them.

The case of Park In-bae

Park In-bae, a 38-year-old stage director, was arrested in April 1991 and sentenced to two years' imprisonment. Park In-bae is Chairperson of the Seoul Labourers' Cultural Federation which is affiliated to the Korean National Artists Federation. He was accused of distributing four illegal tape recordings between 1989 and April 1991, the date of his arrest. The tape recordings were produced and distributed by small groups of people belonging to the Seoul Labourers' Cultural Federation and mainly consisted of songs written for the labour movement and performed by a variety of artists. Around 50,000 copies of the tapes were produced and sold. Under the law concerning the production of audio and video recordings, anyone who wishes to produce such a recording must submit an advance copy to the authorities.

The police are reported to have searched the offices of the Seoul Labourers' Cultural Federation and to have confiscated a number of the Federation's documents. They did not arrest any of the people involved in the manufacture of the tapes, or any of the other people involved in their distribution. Neither did they arrest any of the singers or song writers whose work was featured on the tapes.

Park In-bae was also accused of keeping the profits from the sale of the tapes for his own personal use. The Federation has denied this, saying that profits were minimal and were kept by the small groups of people who made the tapes.

Amnesty International adopted Park In-bae as a prisoner of conscience and called for his immediate release. It was also concerned at reports that he was suffering from diabetes and tuberculosis. On 24 September 1991 a doctor who examined Park In-bae in prison stated that he needed immediate hospitalization. On 9 October Park In-bae was transferred to a hospital and on 25 October he was released.

5) ARRESTS OF RESEARCH STUDENTS

In late June 1991 six research students belonging to Seoul Social Science Institute were arrested under the recently amended National Security Law. Two of the researchers were released and the other four were charged under Article 7 of the law for possessing and publishing articles and books praising North Korea. These publications are said to have espoused a theory of neo-colonial, national, monopolistic capitalism and to have thereby agreed with the activities of North Korea. Some of the publications are said to reflect the prisoners' beliefs in the cause of socialist revolution. Shortly after the arrests, several lawyers are reported to have commented that the arrests had been carried out without taking into account the spirit of the recent revision of the National Security Law.
Amnesty International believes that these prisoners have been detained for the peaceful exercise of their freedom of expression.

Shin Hyon-jun, aged 29, was studying for a doctorate in economics at the time of his arrest. He was accused of contributing articles to a number of publications including a thesis about the transformation of capitalist society, a methodological study about the history of socialism and a number of other theses which had been formally submitted to Seoul National University. He was held responsible for the entire contents of several books including *Socialism: It's Theory, History and Reality* to which he contributed one essay. Shin Hyon-jun is also alleged to have written leaflets entitled *The Socialist Reforms* and *The Korean Peninsula* for distribution at a symposium organized by *Haktanhyop* (association of scholars) and to have submitted a thesis entitled *Socialism and Communism* to a seminar on socialism organized by the Association of Scholars for Korean Social Economics. Amnesty International has adopted Shin Hyon-jun as a prisoner of conscience and is calling for his release.

Kwon Hyon-jong, aged 26, was studying for a master's degree in economics at the time of his arrest. He was accused of contributing to various publications including a book entitled *The Development of Korean Capitalism*, and for the contents of several theses he submitted to Seoul National University and a book entitled *Korean Capitalism in the 1980s*. As in the case of Shin Hyon-jun, he was held responsible for the entire contents of some books to which he had only contributed one essay. Kwon Hyon-jun was also accused of possessing pamphlets published by various democratic groups. Amnesty International has adopted Kwon Hyon-jong as a prisoner of conscience and is calling for his release.

Lee Chang-hui, aged 28, is studying for a doctorate in politics and was completing his term of military service at the time of his arrest. He was accused of writing a number of articles for journals and magazines, including contributions to the quarterly journal *Reality and Science*; an essay which was published in three university magazines and a study of democratic revolutions. He was additionally charged with the translation of a book written by Lenin and the possession of a number of pamphlets published by democratic groups and two books entitled *The Literature for Workers Liberation* and *History of World Philosophy*. Amnesty International has adopted Lee Chang-hui as a prisoner of conscience and is calling for his release.

Song Ju-myong, aged 28, is studying for a doctorate in politics and was completing his term of military service at the time of his arrest. He was suspected of writing several theses and articles, one of which was published by *Haktanhyop* and one which dealt with the situation and controversy surrounding the democratic (people's) movement and the characteristics of the 6th republic. Son Ju-myong was also accused of possessing a book by Y Krasin entitled *The Theory of Socialist Revolution*. Amnesty International has adopted Song Ju-myong as a prisoner of conscience and is calling for his release.

Song Ju-myong and Lee Chang-hui were serving in the military at the time of their arrest and are being held in a military prison. They were interrogated by the military security police. Lawyers working on behalf of Song Ju-myong and Lee Chang-hwi said they were denied access to their clients on 23 July. The lawyers filed an appeal to the military court. On 1 August they were given permission to see the two prisoners.

The Seoul Social Science Institute consists of some 70 scholars and graduate students of political science, sociology and economics. The Institute has viewed the arrests as a serious encroachment upon academic freedom and has pointed out that its members have consistently disagreed with the North Korean interpretation of *Perestroika* and its analysis of South Korean society.

Shortly after the arrests members of 25 different research associations established a "Committee to work against the oppression of freedom of thought and scholarship". Members of this committee have pointed out that the books and journals in question are still widely available in university bookshops and the theses had already been examined by a board of professors. On 1 July the committee issued a press statement protesting at the arrests as a violation of freedom of expression. They said that theories on socialism and revolution are widely studied throughout the world and cannot be ignored by social scientists. On 4 July the Ministry of Justice issued a statement saying that the books and pamphlets in question contained "provocative and threatening" ideas.

6) ARRESTS RELATING TO DEMONSTRATIONS IN MAY AND JUNE

The Death of Kang Kyung-dae

On 26 April 1991 student Kang Kyung-dae was beaten to death by riot police during an anti-government demonstration. His death provoked violent demonstrations throughout South Korea by students, workers and dissident groups and led to the arrests of five riot policemen on charges of murder. On 19 August four of the policemen were sentenced to prison terms of between two and three-and-a-half years. The fifth was given a suspended sentence and released.

Soon after the death of Kang Kyung-dae students, trade union leaders and dissident leaders established a committee to make arrangements for his funeral. After the funeral had taken place, a task force was established as a means of continuing to protest against the death of Kang Kyung-dae and the government's policies in general. The task force is said to have included representatives from around 55 dissident groups from political, labour and academic circles.

During the following weeks many protests and demonstrations were organized throughout the country. A number of people committed self-immolation as a gesture of protest against the death of Kang Kyung-dae and on 25 May a women student named Kim Kwi-jong was killed during a demonstration. Dissidents and students say that she was either beaten by riot police or suffocated by tear gas while the authorities claim that she was trampled to death by fellow protesters.

Arrests of Dissident Leaders

Following the protests and demonstrations the authorities announced a crackdown on dissidents and students . In early June the National Police Headquarters (NPH) were reported to have established special task forces throughout the country to arrest some 90 students and activists in connection with the anti-government demonstrations. Arrest warrants were issued for several dissident leaders who were staging a sit-in protest in Myongdong Cathedral. In June and July a number of dissident and trade union leaders, including those listed below, were arrested because of their alleged involvement in anti-government protests. Amnesty International is seeking further information about the arrests of the following people, whom it believes to have been charged under the Law on Assemblies and Demonstrations for organizing demonstrations without obtaining a permit and under the Law on the Punishment of Violent Acts for the violence which occurred at some of these demonstrations.

- **Hyon Ju-ok**, acting Chairman of *Chonnohyop* (National Council of Labour Unions) was arrested as he left Myongdong Cathedral on 14 June to attend an important union meeting. Hyon Ju-ok was also charged under the Labour Dispute Mediation Act for giving advice to member unions.

- **Lee Su-ho**, Vice-President of *Chonkyojo* (Korean Teachers and Educational Workers Union), was arrested on 25 June.

- Four people were arrested on 29 June as they left Myongdong Cathedral. They are **Choi Jong-jin**, a member of *Chonnong* (National Farmers' Union); **Lee Dong-chin**, a member of *Chonkyojo*; **Lee Sun-hyong**, acting Chairperson of Seoul Labour Union and **Suh Jun-shik**, Director of the Human Rights Committee of *Chonminnyon* (National Democratic Alliance of Korea). Suh Jun-shik was also charged under the Social Surveillance Law and further information about his case is given below.

- **Im Mu-yong**, a staff member of *Chonminnyon*, and **Reverend Han Sang-yol**, were arrested on 6 July. Reverend Han Sang-yol is also believed to have been charged under the National Security Law.

- Two members of *Chonkyojo* were arrested on 2 July. They are **Chang In-kwon**, Chairman of the Ulsan branch and **Yu Sang-dok**, Director of Policy and Planning. Further details about Yu Sang-dok are given in Section 7, on imprisoned trade unionists.

Many dissident and human rights groups have expressed concern that these leaders were imprisoned to curtail their political activities and to put an end to a series of anti-government protests.

Amnesty International is concerned that these prisoners may have been imprisoned for their peaceful activities as the leaders of dissident political and trade union groups. It is urging the authorities to ensure that they receive a fair trial and to release them if they have been imprisoned for the peaceful exercise of their rights to freedom of expression and association.

The Arrest of Kang Ki-hun

Kang Ki-hun, aged 27, is a staff member of *Chonminnyon*. He was arrested on 24 June and charged under the Criminal Code with aiding and abetting the suicide of Kim Ki-sol, also a staff member of *Chonminnyon*, who committed self-immolation on 8 May in protest at the killing of Kang Kyung-dae. Dissident groups have suggested that the police fabricated a case against Kang Ki-hun in order to discredit *Chonminnyon* and other groups at a time when they were at the centre of anti-government protests.

The evidence in this case consists of the analysis of Kim Ki-sol's handwriting carried out by the National Scientific Institute who claimed that entries in Kim Ki-sol's diary had been made by Kang Ki-hun, thus implicating him in the suicide. The Korean National Council of Churches commissioned an independent analysis which found that the entries in Kim Ki-sol's diary were made by himself. According to press reports, Kim Ki-sol's girlfriend, Hong Song-un, said that Kang Ki-hun may have been involved in the suicide. However, there is concern that she was interrogated for long periods by the police and held *incommunicado*, although she was later released.

Kang Ki-hun faces an additional charge under the National Security Law. He is accused of belonging to of *Hyuknomaeng* (Revolutionary Workers' Federation) which is considered by the authorities to be an "anti-state" group. When searching his house police are reported to have found the minutes of a *Hyuknomaeng* meeting.

Amnesty International is urging the authorities to ensure that Kang Ki-hun is given a fair trial and is released if he has been imprisoned for his peaceful political activities.

The Arrest of Suh Jun-shik

Suh Jun-shik was born in 1948 in Japan. He was adopted by Amnesty International as a prisoner of conscience during his previous imprisonment from 1971 to 1988. When his sentence for alleged espionage expired in 1978 he remained in detention under the Public Security Law until his release in 1988 because he refused to "convert to anti-communism". He was rearrested on 29 June 1991 and charged under the Law on

Assemblies and Demonstrations with organizing illegal anti-government demonstrations and under the Law on the Punishment of Violent Acts for the violence which broke out at some of these demonstrations.

In addition to the charges mentioned above, Suh Jun-shik is charged under the Social Surveillance Law with failing to report to the police over the three year period since his release in 1988. The Social Surveillance Law was enacted in 1989 and under its terms certain released political prisoners are required to report to the authorities about their meetings, political activities, travel etc. Some 300 former prisoners are subject to this law and face prison terms of up to one year for failure to comply with its terms. Amnesty International adopted Suh Jun-shik as a prisoner of conscience during his imprisonment from 1971 to 1988 and considers the reporting requirements under the Social Surveillance Law to be a violation of his rights to freedom of expression and association.

During the first hearing of his trial in September Suh Jun-shik denied responsibility for the organization of anti-government demonstrations and for the violence which occurred at some of them. Amnesty International believes that Suh Jun-shik may be a prisoner of conscience, detained for the peaceful exercise of his rights to freedom of expression and association. It has urged the authorities to ensure that he receives a fair trial and to release him if he has been detained for his peaceful political activities.

7) IMPRISONED TRADE UNIONISTS

Arrests for Third Party Intervention

In February 1991 seven trade union leaders belonging to the Association of Large Factory Trade Unions were arrested and charged with third party intervention in a labour dispute. The seven men were arrested as they left a meeting of the Association of Large Factory Trade Unions which had discussed plans for spring wage negotiations and solidarity with workers at the Daewoo Shipbuilding and Heavy Machinery Company who had gone on strike the previous day. They were accused of distributing leaflets urging workers at Daewoo to go on strike. **Lee Eun-ku**, President of the Daewoo Motor

Company trade union, **Chong Yoon-kwang,** President of Seoul Subway company trade union and **Hong Young-pyo,** Secretary of the Conference of Large Faction Trade Unions, were each sentenced to one-and-a-half years' imprisonment. **Yoon Myong-won,** President of Daewoo Precision trade union, was sentenced to one year's imprisonment. Two others were given suspended prison sentences and released. Amnesty International believes that these men are prisoners of conscience if they are detained for giving advice about peaceful trade union activities. The seventh prisoner, Park Chang-su, died in early May after falling from the roof of a prison hospital. Further information about Park Chang-su is given below.

Kim Yong-dae, acting President of Chonnohyop (National Council of Labour Unions), was arrested on 21 December 1990 and charged under the Labour Dispute Mediation Act for advising around 70 union affiliates to reject inspection of union documents by the Ministry of Labour. He is also accused of inciting around 100 illegal strikes by distributing *Chonnohyop* propaganda including a set of guidelines for unions to use in wage negotiations. Kim Yong-dae is also charged under the law on Assemblies and Demonstrations for the organization of several gatherings and demonstrations which took place in late 1989. In May 1991 he was sentenced to 18 months' imprisonment. Amnesty International believes that Kim Yong-dae may have been imprisoned solely for the organization of peaceful demonstrations and the distribution of advice to trade union members about legitimate trade union activities. It is seeking further information about the charges used to convict him.

Hyon Ju-ok, aged 36, acting President of Chonnohyop, was arrested in June 1991 and charged with third party intervention for the advice sent to member unions during his term as union president. Amnesty International is seeking further information about the charges against Hyon Ju-ok as it believes these may relate to the distribution of advice about peaceful and legitimate trade union activities. Hyon Ju-ok has also been charged under the Law on Assemblies and Demonstrations and the Law on the Punishment of Violent Acts for organizing several demonstrations in May and June 1991.

In June 1991 **Cha Su-ryun,** a leader of the Korean Federation of Hospital Workers' Unions, was arrested on charges of violating the prohibition of third party intervention. The accusations are based on advice given out to members and a number of speeches she had made in solidarity with other trade unions. Amnesty International was concerned that she may have been detained for her peaceful political activities. Cha Su-ryun was sentenced to one years' imprisonment, suspended for two years, and released.

The Death of Park Chang-su

On 6 May 1991 trade union leader Park Chang-su died after allegedly committing suicide by jumping from the window of Anyang prison hospital. Park Chang-su, President of Hanjin Heavy Industry trade union, was arrested in February 1991 along with six other trade union leaders who were attending a regular meeting of the Association of Large Factory Trade Unions (see above). Park Chang-su is alleged to have committed suicide as a protest at the death of Kang Kyung-dae who was beaten to death by riot police in a demonstration on 26 April. Kang Kyung-dae's death provoked mass demonstrations throughout South Korea in May and June and prompted several people to commit suicide in a gesture of protest.

The official autopsy report on Park Chang-su's death made no mention of any suspicious circumstances surrounding the death. This has been disputed by trade unions and human rights groups who have suggested that Park Chang-su's death was not a result of suicide. To Amnesty International's knowledge the authorities have not ordered an independent inquiry into the death of Park Chang-su.

The Arrests of Chonkyojo Members

Chonkyojo (Korean Teachers' and Educational Workers' Union) was inaugurated in May 1989 and was immediately declared to be illegal by the authorities. The Constitution guarantees trade union rights, except for public employees, and the Civil Service Law prohibits teachers in state-run schools from establishing or joining unions. Similar restrictions apply to teachers in private schools under the Private School Law. When it ratified the International Covenant on Civil and Political Rights in April 1990, the government made a reservation to Article 22 which guarantees the right to form and join trade unions. *Chonkyojo* has declared its aims to be the realization of a "nationalistic, democratic and humane" education, including broad educational reforms and the recognition of teachers' rights to form a union. The union has been accused by the authorities of trying to introduce "leftist" ideology into schools and attempting to alter the country's democratic system. *Chonkyojo* has around 15,000 members, most of whom have had to take out secret membership. Since 1989 around 1,500 teachers have been dismissed from their posts because of their membership of the union.

The Arrest of Lee Pu-yong: Because *Chonkyojo* is regarded as illegal it never receives police permission to hold demonstrations. Over the past two years several thousand teachers are reported to have been briefly detained for taking part in demonstration rallies in support of the union's aims and of these over 100 have been tried and sentenced. Most received suspended prison sentences and were released. In May 1990 *Chonkyojo* held a rally to celebrate its first anniversary. At that time **Lee Pu-yong** was acting president of the union. After the rally an arrest warrant was issued for Lee Pu-yong and he went into hiding. He was arrested in June 1991 and charged with holding an illegal demonstration. The rally was reported to have been peaceful and Lee Pu-yong was not charged with violence. Amnesty International has adopted Lee Pu-yong as a prisoner of conscience, detained for the peaceful exercise of his freedom of expression and association, and is calling for his release. Lee Pu-yong was also adopted as a prisoner of conscience during his previous imprisonment, from July to November 1989 when he was charged in connection with his activities on behalf of *Chonkyojo*. In November 1989 he was sentenced to 18 months' imprisonment, suspended for two years, and released.

The Arrest of Yu Sang-dok: Yu Sang-dok, Director of Policy and Planning of *Chonkyojo*, was arrested on 2 July 1991 on charges under the National Security Law and the Law on Assemblies and Demonstrations. The charges under the National Security Law relate to an article which Yu Sang-dok published in *Chonkyojo*'s newsletter *Education Movement* in March 1991. The article, entitled *Teachers' Role in Establishing a Democratic Government*, is alleged to have benefited North Korea by advocating that workers and others should work together to establish a "democratic government". It also criticised the current educational system and advocated the abolition of anti-communist education. To Amnesty International's knowledge, the article did not use or advocate the use of violence. The author of the article was not arrested.

Yu Sang-dok is also charged under the Law on Assemblies and Demonstrations with planning and participating in two demonstrations organized by *Chonkyojo*. One was held on 18 November 1990 and the other, *Chonkyojo*'s anniversary rally, was held on 26 May 1991. To Amnesty International's knowledge the demonstrations were peaceful and Yu Sang-dok was not charged with violence. Another charge against Yu Sang-dok relates to two demonstrations which took place in May 1991 following the death of Kang Kyung-dae who was beaten to death by riot police on 26 April 1991. Yu Sang-dok is accused of participating in a demonstration on 14 May and with helping to plan Kang Kyung-dae's funeral procession which took place on 18 May and is said by the authorities to have posed a threat to "public peace and order". Some 20 other people are alleged to have been involved in planning the funeral procession but most were not indicted. Yu Sang-dok was not charged with violence.

Amnesty International believes that Yu Sang-dok may be a prisoner of conscience, detained for the peaceful exercise of his freedom of expression and association.

The Arrest of Choi Jae-ho

Local elections were held in South Korea in 1991. The elections were held on 26 March, for local councils in cities, counties and municipal wards and on 20 June for local councils in large cities and provinces.

Choi Jae-ho, 42-year-old President of the Korean Federation of Clerical and Financial Workers' Unions (*Samokomyung*), was arrested on 10 August 1991 and charged under the Local Election Law for advising union members not to vote for candidates from the ruling party on account of its suppression of trade union activities. The Korean Federation of Clerical and Financial Workers' Unions has 126 member unions throughout South Korea and is affiliated to the International Federation of Commercial, Clerical, Professional and Technical Employees (FIET) which has member unions in over 100 countries throughout the world.

Amnesty International adopted Choi Jae-ho as a prisoner of conscience, detained for the peaceful exercise of his freedom of expression. In September Choi Jae-ho was sentenced to one year's imprisonment, suspended for two years and released.

8) ARRESTS OF MEMBERS OF THE ARMED FORCES

In September 1991 the Defense Ministry announced the arrests of 34 military conscripts between the months of January and August. Most had been charged under the National Security Law with instigating left-wing activities in the military by distributing revolutionary material and attempting to indoctrinate fellow draftees with Communist ideology. The report said that these prisoners had joined left-wing organizations before enlisting in the army and had continued their activities on behalf of these organizations while doing their military service.

In April 1991 the Defense Security Command (DSC) announced the arrests of a number of soldiers from the army and navy bases in Pusan. The soldiers were accused of belonging to two "seditious rings" which spread North Korean propaganda and were said to have tried to indoctrinate soldiers with communist literature. They are reported to have produced five issues of a pamphlet entitled *Patriotic Soldier* which they then distributed to students, dissident organizations and labour unions in Pusan. The pamphlets are said to have called for the withdrawal of US forces from Korea (US forces have been stationed in South Korea since the end of World War II), democratisation of the armed forces and an end to the annual "Team Spirit" Korea/US military exercises. Some of the soldiers are alleged to have formed a "reading circle" and invited workers and students to belong. The DSC claimed that this reading circle was a leftist study group and that its members read pro-North Korean books such as *Workers Economics* in order to "arm themselves with revolutionary ideas". In September Amnesty International learned that at least three of these prisoners had been tried and sentenced. **Kang Sang-min** was sentenced to eight months' imprisonment, **Chong Ki-ho** was sentenced to one year's imprisonment and **Suh Jae-ho** was sentenced to three years' imprisonment.

On 27 June the DSC reported that five soldiers and five students had been charged under the National Security Law with engaging in "pro-North Korean" and "anti government" activities in an attempt to demoralize and destabilize the military. Those arrested included soldiers **Song Chae-bong** and **Chong Chun-tae.** The two men were accused of belonging to a left-wing ring called *Chajudaeo* which aimed to bring about reunification through a socialist revolution. They are said to have tried to indoctrinate other soldiers and to have distributed pro-North Korean propaganda in the military.

Amnesty International believes that Suh Jae-ho, Chong Ki-ho, Kang Sang-min, Chong Chun-tae and Song Chae-bong may be prisoners of conscience, detained solely for their peaceful political activities. It is seeking further information about the charges and evidence against them.

9) FURTHER ARRESTS OF MEMBERS OF SANOMAENG

Around 100 members of *Sanomaeng* (Socialist Workers' League) are reported to have been arrested between September 1990 and March 1991 under the National Security Law for membership of an anti-state organization which was allegedly planning to overthrow the government and replace it with a socialist or communist government. Shortly after the arrests of some 40 members, in September 1990, Amnesty International received reports that several of the prisoners had been beaten and deprived of sleep during their interrogation. By September 1991 around 50 *Sanomaeng* members had been sentenced to prison terms ranging from 18 months to life imprisonment. Amnesty International is concerned that some may be prisoners of conscience, detained for the peaceful exercise of their freedom of expression and association. It is seeking further information about the charges used to convict them.

The case of Park Noh-hae

Sanomaeng leader, **Park Noh-hae** was arrested in March 1991. Park Noh-hae, aged 33, is a well-known poet and political activist whose first book of poems, *The Dawn of Labour*, was published in 1984. Park Noh-hae told his lawyers that during his interrogation by the Agency for National Security Planning he had only been allowed to sleep for two to four hours each night during the first 25 days of his imprisonment and that he had been beaten on three occasions by a group of around 13 interrogators. He is said to have attempted suicide as a result of the beatings and sleep deprivation. In September 1991 Park Noh-hae was sentenced to life imprisonment; the prosecution had requested that he be sentenced to death. Amnesty International is seeking further information about the charges against Park Noh-hae and is concerned at reports that he and other members of *Sanomaeng* were ill-treated during interrogation.

amnesty international

INTERNATIONAL SECRETARIAT,
1 Easton Street, London WC1X 8DJ,
United Kingdom.

Ref.: TG ASA 25/91.16

Mr K C Lee
Embassy of the Republic of Korea
4 Palace Gate
London W8 5NF

4 December 1991

Dear Mr Lee,

I enclose two copies of a document Amnesty International has recently issued to its members South Korea : Arrests of Political Prisoners During 1991. I would be grateful if you could forward a copy to your Government.

We would be pleased to receive your Government's comments on the cases mentioned in the document. We would in particular appreciate detailed information on the charges and evidence against the prisoners arrested for the demonstrations that took place in the aftermath of the death of student Kang Kyung-dae. These cases are outlined on pages 11 to 14.

We would also like to receive your Government's comments on the arrest of 34 military conscripts during the year, as announced by the Defense Ministry in September. The cases of five of them are described on pages 18 and 19.

We believe that there have been no executions of prisoners in your country so far this year. Could you obtain a confirmation of this from your Government?

We were pleased to read press reports that the Ministry of Justice is reviewing the cases of prisoners with a view to releasing a number of them in mid-December. Amnesty International hopes that all the prisoners currently detained for the peaceful exercise of their rights of freedom of expression and association will benefit from this measure of clemency.

Yours sincerely,

Derek G. Evans
Head of the Asia and Pacific Region
Research Department

☎ (44)(71) 413 5500 Telegrams: Amnesty London WC1 Telex: 28502 FAX: 956 1157

Amnesty International is an independent worldwide movement working impartially for the release of all prisoners of conscience, fair and prompt trials for political prisoners and an end to torture and executions. It is funded by donations from its members and supporters throughout the world. It has formal relations with the United Nations, Unesco, the Council of Europe, the Organization of African Unity and the Organization of American States.

0248

국제사면위원회 한국 보고서

보안법관련 양심수 석방 촉구

앰네스티 인터내셔널(국제사면위원회)는 최근 국가보안법으로 구속된 2백여명 가운데 최소한 30여명이 비폭력적 정치활동과 정치적 견해 때문에 구금된 '양심수'라는 요지의 보고서를 '한국, 국가보안법 위반 구속자들'이라는 제목으로 〈한겨레신문〉에 보내왔다.

국제사면위원회는 이 보고서에서 "이들은 고문에 의하거나 절차상의 잘못으로 인해 공정하지 못한 재판에서 유죄판결을 받았다"고 주장하며 이들의 석방을 촉구했다. 보고서를 요약해 싣는다. 〈편집자〉

최근 한국에서는 국가보안법 개정이 활발히 논의되고 있다. 국제사면위는 이번 개정 논의들이 위법사항들을 더욱 엄밀히 규정하고 있다는 점에서 이를 환영한다.

그러나 이 법은 북한의 이념을 지지하고 정부의 허가없이 북한 사람들을 접촉하려는 자람들을 여전히 구속할 수 있도록 하는 것으로 여겨져 안타깝다.

따라서 국가보안법 개정 노력이 좀더 개방적인 가운데 빠른 속도로 이뤄져야 하며 앞으로 정부의 비판자들이 단지 신념, 표현 또는 결사의 자유에 관한 권리를 평화적으로 행사했다는 이유로 구속되지 않는 방향으로 법 개정이 이뤄지기를 바란다.

이와 함께 75~91년에 구속된 다음의 양심수들은 하루빨리 석방돼야 한다.

우선 남한 출신으로 유학 또는 업무를 위해 일본에 갔다 구속된 사람들로, 유종식(75년 구속), 조상록(〃), 신귀용(80년), 이장형(83년), 나전인(85년), 이평설(86년), 강휘철(87년)씨 등이다.

또 북한에 살고 있는 친지들이 방문해온 것을 신고하지 않았다는 이유로 구속된 박동운(81년), 함주명(83년)씨 등 5명도 석방돼야 한다고 본다.

특히 북한을 방문하거나 남한의 정치상황에 관한 정보를 북한 쪽에 건네주었다는 혐의로 구속된 다음 사람들은 우선적으로 석방돼야 한다. 김성만(85년), 황태권(〃), 서경원(89년), 방양균(〃), 유원호(〃), 임수경(〃), 문규현(〃), 조성우(90년), 이해학(〃)씨 등이 이 범주에 속한다.

마지막으로 북한을 '찬양'하거나 북한에 '이익을 준' 혐의로 기소된 남한 사람들의 석방도 촉구한다. 홍성담(89년), 김현장(〃), 김근태(90년), 이창복(91년), 김희택(〃), 홍근수(〃)씨 등과 사노맹 및 자민통 관련 구속자들이 바로 그들이다.

국제사면위는 이들이 양심수라고 믿으며, 이들 가운데 일부가 주장하는 고문이나 불공정 재판에 의한 유죄판결에 대한 관계당국의 공정한 조사가 뒤따르기를 촉구한다.

전향간첩 최인정씨 21일 숨져

북녘가족 그리다 남녘땅 묻혀

북한주민 접촉 신청서 내기 하루전
KNCC인권위 유해 북한송환 추진

불치병에 시달리며 북녘에 두고온 가족들을 애타게 그리워하던 한 전향간첩이 정부에 북한주민접촉신청서를 내기 하루 전날 끝내 숨을 거뒀다.

지난 64년 공작원으로 남파됐다 이틀 만에 체포돼 23년 동안 옥살이를 한 뒤 출소한 최인정(64·사진)씨가 21일 오후 10시께 투병중이던 대전시 충남대병원 6215호 병실에서 숨졌다.

최씨는 22일 한국기독교교회협의회(KNCC) 인권위원회 주선으로 서울에 올라와 북녘의 가족들을 만나기 위한 북한주민접촉신청서를 통일원에 낼 예정이었다.

최씨는 88년 12월 교계의 신원보증으로 가석방된 뒤 감옥에서 취득한 열관리자격증으로 대전의 한 회사에 취직해 보일러기사로 일하던 중 지난해 11월 간암3기 선고를 받고 충남대병원에서 시한부 삶을 살아왔다.

최씨는 지난달 4일 병상에서 북녘의 아내에게 보내는 애절한 내용의 편지를 쓰기도 했다.(〈한겨레신문〉 10월6일자)

교회협의회 인권위 신승민 목사는 "의학상 사형선고를 받은 최씨에게 북의 가족들을 만날 수 있도록 해야겠다는 인도주의적인 생각에서 북한주민접촉신청서 제출을 주선해왔다"면서 "21일 오후 최씨와 가진 전화통화에서 최씨는 '내일(22일) 아침 서울에 올라오기 위해 새마을호 열차표까지 끊어놨다'면서 죽기 전에 가족들을 만날 수 있으리라는 한가닥 희망에 몹시 기뻐했었다"고 안타까워했다.

최씨는 죽기 전에 작성한 북한주민접촉신청서에 '접촉일정과 장소'를 "1991년 12월31일 판문점 공동경비구역 회의장"으로, '접촉방법'을 "공동경비구역 회의장에서 북한의 가족과 함께 다과와 음료수를 나눠 먹으며 가족의 소식을 묻고 현주소(충남대병원)로 귀향함"이라고 적어 놓았다.

교회협의회 인권위원회는 최씨가 병상에서 쓴 편지를 세계교회협의회를 통해 북쪽에 전달하는 방안을 적극 모색키로 하는 한편 앞으로 최씨 유해의 북한송환도 추진해 나가겠다고 밝혔다. 〈박찬수 기자〉

0249

관리 번호	91-198

원 본

외 무 부

종 별 :

번 호 : UKW-2436 일 시 : 91 1209 1810

수 신 : 장관(연일)

발 신 : 주 영 대사

제 목 : A.I.아국관련 보고서

대: 국연 2031-32814, 연이 20314-2668

연: UKW-1944

1. 당지 A.I. 는 91.11. 아국관련 인권보고서(SOUTH KOREA: ARRESTS OF POLITICAL PRISONERS DURING 1991)를 발간, A.I. 회원에게 배포하였음을 12.4. 자 A.I. 아태담당과장 DEREK EVANS 명의의 서한으로 알려왔음.(동 보고서 동봉)

2. 동 보고서는 1991 년동안 아국에서 체포된 약 50 명의 정치범에 대하여 우려를 표하며, 그중 상당수가 양심수라고 보고 있다면서, 이들 양심수를 무조건조속한 시일내에 석방할 것을 요청하고 있음

3. 또한 EVANS 과장은 상기 서한에서, A.I. 는 특히 아래사항에 대하여 관심을 가지고 있다고 하면서 이에대한 정부의 의견을 요청한바, 본부지침 및 관련사항 회시바람

. 강경대 사망과 관련된 시위에서 체포된 자들의 혐의사실 및 증거

. 지난 9 월 국군사병 34 명의 체포

. 금년중 죄수의 사형 집행 사례 유무 여부

. 금년 12 월 중순 사면(설)에 대한 환영 및 확대실시 희망

4. 당관 이서기관은 12.9. A.I. 한국담당연구관 MS VANDALE 에게, 동 보고서에는 대호관련 이미 당관에서 구체적인 범죄사실 등 제반사항을 설명한 바 있는 김영대, 김희택, 이은구, 이창복등 10 여명이 포함되어 있음을 지적하였는바,동 연구관은 상기인들에 대한 아측의 설명이 A.I. 가 이미 알고 있는 사실과 다를바 없거나 설득력이 없는 경우에는, 다시 A.I. 회원들이 석방 탄원 서한을 발송토록 이들을 동 보고서에 포함시켰다고 말함

5. 상기 서한 및 보고서는 12.10(화) 파편 송부예정임.끝

국기국 장관 차관 1차보 외정실 청와대 안기부

PAGE 1

91.12.10 05:30

외신 2과 통제관 FM

0250

(대사 이홍구-국장)
92.6.30 일반

일반문서로 재분류 (1992.6.30.)

PAGE 2

0251

報 告 畢
(signature)

長官報告事項

1991. 12. 16.
國 際 機 構 局
國際聯合2課(12)

題 目 : AI 我國 人權狀況 報告書 配布

> 91.12월 國際赦免委(AI)는 我國 人權狀況과 관련, "South Korea : Arrests of Political Prisoners During 1991" 題下의 報告書를 配布하고, 同報告書에 대한 우리政府 立場을 問議하여 온바, 關聯內容을 아래 報告드립니다.

1. 報告書 內容 및 AI 要請事項

o 91년중 國家保安法, 集示法等 違反으로 逮捕된 "政治犯" 50여명의 事件概要를 중심으로 作成된 AI 會員用 報告書(총 20면)임.

* AI는 91.10월에도 "South Korea : Prisoners Held for National Security Offences" 題下의 報告書 配布

o 駐英大使館 앞 書翰에서 아래 事項에 대한 政府立場 要請

- 강경대 事件관련 示威時 逮捕人士의 嫌疑內容
- 91.9월 國軍士兵 34명 逮捕
- 91년중 死刑執行 實積
- 91.12월중 特別赦免報道 관련 赦免時 "政治犯" 포함 希望

2. 向後 對策

o 法務部에서 回報를 받는대로 금번 報告書에 대한 政府立場을 AI에 通報

3. 言論對策 : 해당없음. 끝.

0252

관리 번호	91 -244

외 무 부

110-760 서울 종로구 세종로 77번지 / (02) 723-8934 / (02) 723-3505

문서번호 연이 20314-3060
시행일자 1991.12.14.
(경유)
수신 법무부장관
참조

취급		장 관
보존		
국 장	전결	
심의관		
과 장		
기안	김종훈	협조

제목 AI 아국 인권관련 보고서 배포

1. 주영대사 전문 UKW-2436(91.12.9)와 관련입니다.

2. AI는 아국 인권상황과 관련, 91.11월 배포한 보고서, "South Korea : Arrests of Political Prisoners During 1991"를 12.9. 주영대사관에 전달하고, 동 보고서에 대한 아국정부 의견, 특히 아래 사항에 대한 정부입장을 문의하여 왔습니다.

- o 강경대 사망 관련 시위에서 체포된 인사들의 범죄혐의 및 증거
- o 91.9월 국방부가 발표한 91년중 군인 34명의 체포 문제
- o 91년중 사형집행 실적
- o 91.12월중 예정된 것으로 보도된 특별사면 조치시 양심수 포함희망

3. 상기관련, 동 보고서에 대한 귀부 입장 및 사례별 설명자료(영문)을 가급적 조속히 당부에 송부하여 주시기 바랍니다.

일반문서로 재분류(1992.6.30)

첨부 : 1. AI의 주영대사관앞 서한 사본
2. AI 보고서 1부. 끝.

0253

報 告 畢

長官報告事項

1991. 12. 16.
國 際 機 構 局
國際聯合2課(12)

題 目 : AI 我國 人權狀況 報告書 配布

> 91.12월 國際赦免委(AI)는 我國 人權狀況과 관련, "South Korea : Arrests of Political Prisoners During 1991" 題下의 報告書를 配布하고, 同報告書에 대한 우리政府 立場을 問議하여 온바, 關聯內容을 아래 報告드립니다.

1. 報告書 內容 및 AI 要請事項

- 91년중 國家保安法, 집시法等 違反으로 逮捕된 "政治犯" 50여명의 事件概要를 중심으로 作成된 AI 會員用 報告書(총 20면)임.
  - * AI는 91.10월에도 "South Korea : Prisoners Held for National Security Offences" 題下의 報告書 配布
- 駐英大使館 앞 書翰에서 아래 事項에 대한 政府立場 要請
  - 강경대 事件관련 示威時 逮捕人士의 嫌疑內容
  - 91.9월 國軍士兵 34명 逮捕
  - 91년중 死刑執行 實積
  - 91.12월중 特別赦免報道 관련 赦免時 "政治犯" 포함 希望

2. 向後 對策

- 法務部~~와 協議~~에서 회보를 받는대로, 금번 報告書에 대한 政府立場을 AI에 通報

3. 言論對策 : 해당없음. 끝.

91 12 16

0254

주 스 페 인 대 사 관

3신

주스페인(총)1211-519　　　　1991. 12. 18. 미주기구협조

수신 : 장관

참조 : 구주국장

제목 : 석방 탄원서 보고

AMNESTY INTERNATIONAL 스페인지부 명의의 김성만(KIM SONG-MAN)에 대한 석방탄원서를 접수하였기 별첨 송부합니다.

첨부 : 동 탄원서 1부.끝.

발송 91.12.20 주스페인 대사관

주 스 페 인 대 사

선 결		결 재	
접수일시	1991.12.26		
처리과	73213		

0255

amnesty international

UNIDAD TERRITORIAL

PLAZA DEL OBISPO, 1-1.°
TELEFONO 21 07 53
MALAGA-15

5 de diciembre de 1991

Sr. Myung-Kwan Chang
Embajador
Embajada de la República de Corea
Miguel Ángel, 23
Madrid

Muy señor nuestro:

Adjunto nos permitimos enviarle varias listas con firmas de distintas personas, las cuales hacen una petición al presidente de Corea para que libere a KIM SONG-MAN, el cual lleva preso mucho tiempo por oponerse a la política del gobierno de una forma no violenta.

Le rogamos haga llegar al presidente Roh Tae-woo estas lista. También incluímos foto del mencionado preso.

Dándole las gracias le saludamos atentamente

Maribel Repullo Picasso
Coordinadora de Campañas

Amnesty International es un movimiento mundial pro derechos humanos que trabaja imparcialmente por la liberación de los presos de conciencia: hombres y mujeres detenidos en todo el mundo por sus convicciones, color, origen étnico, sexo, religión o idioma, siempre y cuando no hayan recurrido a la violencia o abogado por ella. Amnesty Internacional se opone sin excepciones a la imposición de la pena de muerte y la tortura y propugna la realización de juicios expeditos e imparciales para todos los presos políticos. Es independiente de todo gobierno, partido político, ideología, interés económico o credo religioso. Se financia con suscripciones y donaciones de sus afiliados en todo el mundo. Tiene caterorfa consultiva con las Naciones Unidas (ECOSOC), UNESCO y el Consejo de Europa: mantiene relaciones de trabajo con la Comisión Interamericana de Derechos Humanos de la Organización de Estados Americanos, y es miembro del Comité Coordinador de la Oficina para la Ubicación y Educación de Refugiados Africanos (BPEAR) de la Organización de Unidad Africana.

0256

amnesty internatior de España
unidad territorial de Madrid

Donoso Cortés, 22-1.°
Teléfono 593 02 33
28015 MADRID

His Excellency President ROH Tae-Woo,
The Blue House,
1 Sejong-no,
Chogno-gu,
Seoul,
Republic of Korea.

Su Excellencia:

Quiero expresarle mi más profunda indignación respecto del caso de **Kim Song-Man**, hecho prisionero por oponerse a la política del Gobierno. No hay evidencia de que estuviera involucrado en ninguna actividad violenta y es muy probable que su confesión se obtuviese mediante tortura.

Le insto, respetuosamente, a que sea liberado inmediatamente.

NOMBRE	CIUDAD	FIRMA
GEORGES BERKOWITSCH	- MADRID -	
ALFONSO MARIN	- MADRID	
JULIO SERRANO SERRANO	- MADRID	
Andrés Moncó Pérez	Madrid	
José Gª Rama Alonso	Madrid	
AGUSTIN MILLAN PONCELA	MADRID	
ERNESTO HERRERO CAMBERO	MADRID	
MOINELO CAMPORRO ANTONIO	MADRID	
MARTA GONZALEZ PARIENTE		Marta González
SARA BARCELÓ CORDÓN	- MADRID -	
JESUS Paramés Cashera	MADRID	

Secretariado Internacional - 1 Easton Street - London WC1X 8DJ.

Amnesty International es un movimiento pro derechos humanos que trabaja imparcialmente por la liberación de los presos de conciencia: hombres y mujeres detenidos en todo el mundo por sus convicciones, color, origen étnico, sexo, religión o idioma, siempre y cuando no hayan recurrido a la violencia o abogado por ella. Amnesty International se opone sin excepciones a la imposición de la pena de muerte y la tortura y propugna la realización de juicios expeditos e imparciales para todos los presos políticos. Es independiente de todo gobierno, partido político, ideología, interés económico o credo religioso. Se financia con suscripciones y donaciones de sus afiliados en todo el mundo. Tiene categoría consultiva con las Naciones Unidas (ECOSOC), UNESCO y el Consejo de Europa; mantiene relaciones de trabajo con la Comisión Interamericana de Derechos Humanos de la Organización de Estados Americanos, y es miembro del Comité Coordinador de la Oficina para la Ubicación y Educación de Refugiados Africanos (BPEAR) de la Organización de Unidad Africana. Premio Nobel de la Paz 1977.

0259

amnesty internatio de España
unidad territorial de Madrid

Donoso Cortés, 22-1.º
Teléfono 593 02 33
28015 MADRID

His Excellency President ROH Tae-Woo,
The Blue House,
1 Sejong-no,
Chogno-gu,
Seoul,
Republic of Korea.

Su Excellencia:

Quiero expresarle mi más profunda indignación respecto del caso de **Kim Song-Man**, hecho prisionero por oponerse a la política del Gobierno. No hay evidencia de que estuviera involucrado en ninguna actividad violenta y es muy probable que su confesión se obtuviese mediante tortura.

Le insto, respetuosamente, a que sea liberado inmediatamente.

NOMBRE	CIUDAD	FIRMA
AGUSTIN CAVERO	MADRID	[signature]
Falo Marcos Velasco	Xixón	[signature]
Fco Segura Corto	Madrid	[signature]
Susana Mulas	MADRID	[signature]
Mª R. POYATOS	CUENCA	[signature]
JAUME FREIXES	LLEIDA	[signature]
JAVIER ARIAS BONEL	MADRID	[signature]
ESTHER SANCHEZ	GUADALAJARA	[signature]
M. Mendizábal	Madrid	[signature]
Mª Isabel Sanchez	Guadalajara	[signature]
DAVID IREZANI	MADRID	[signature]

Secretariado Internacional - 1 Easton Street - London WC1X 8DJ.

Amnesty International es un movimiento pro derechos humanos que trabaja imparcialmente por la liberación de los presos de conciencia: hombres y mujeres detenidos en todo el mundo por sus convicciones, color, origen étnico, sexo, religión o idioma, siempre y cuando no hayan recurrido a la violencia o abogado por ella. Amnesty International se opone sin excepciones a la imposición de la pena de muerte y la tortura y propugna la realización de juicios expeditos e imparciales para todos los presos políticos. Es independiente de todo gobierno, partido político, ideología, interés económico o credo religioso. Se financia con suscripciones y donaciones de sus afiliados en todo el mundo. Tiene categoría consultiva con las Naciones Unidas (ECOSOC), UNESCO y el Consejo de Europa; mantiene relaciones de trabajo con la Comisión Interamericana de Derechos Humanos de la Organización de Estados Americanos, y es miembro del Comité Coordinador de la Oficina para la Ubicación y Educación de Refugiados Africanos (BPEAR) de la Organización de Unidad Africana. Premio Nobel de la Paz 1977.

026

amnesty internatio■■—de España
unidad territorial de Madrid

Donoso Cortés, 22-1.º
Teléfono 593 02 33
28015 MADRID

His Excellency President ROH Tae-Woo,
The Blue House,
1 Sejong-no,
Chogno-gu,
Seoul,
Republic of Korea.

Su Excellencia:

Quiero expresarle mi más profunda indignación respecto del caso de **Kim Song-Man**, hecho prisionero por oponerse a la política del Gobierno. No hay evidencia de que estuviera involucrado en ninguna actividad violenta y es muy probable que su confesión se obtuviese mediante tortura.

Le insto, respetuosamente, a que sea liberado inmediatamente.

NOMBRE	CIUDAD	FIRMA
BEGOÑA ASENJO LORENZO	MADRID	
Alvaro Fernández Garín	MADRID	
Víctor Cuevas Barbadillo	MADRID	
Jesús Pastor de Dompablo	MADRID	
ANDRES LARRINAGA ARECHAGA	MADRID	
ALFREDO MARTINEZ MECHA	"	
[illegible]	Madrid	
Fernanda Egido Arteaga	Madrid	
J. Antonio Garzo.	"	
CARMEN RAMIREZ GLEZ	MADRID	
Catherine Urwitz	Madrid	

Secretariado Internacional - 1 Easton Street - London WC1X 8DJ.

Amnesty International es un movimiento pro derechos humanos que trabaja imparcialmente por la liberación de los presos de conciencia: hombres y mujeres detenidos en todo el mundo por sus convicciones, color, origen étnico, sexo, religión o idioma, siempre y cuando no hayan recurrido a la violencia o abogado por ella. Amnesty International se opone sin excepciones a la imposición de la pena de muerte y la tortura y propugna la realización de juicios expeditos e imparciales para todos los presos políticos. Es independiente de todo gobierno, partido político, ideología, interés económico o credo religioso. Se financia con suscripciones y donaciones de sus afiliados en todo el mundo. Tiene categoría consultiva con las Naciones Unidas (ECOSOC), UNESCO y el Consejo de Europa; mantiene relaciones de trabajo con la Comisión Interamericana de Derechos Humanos de la Organización de Estados Americanos, y es miembro del Comité Coordinador de la Oficina para la Ubicación y Educación de Refugiados Africanos (BPEAR) de la Organización de Unidad Africana. Premio Nobel de la Paz 1977.

0261

amnesty internation de España
unidad territorial de Madrid

Donoso Cortés, 22-1.º
Teléfono 593 02 33
28015 MADRID

His Excellency President ROH Tae-Woo,
The Blue House,
1 Sejong-no,
Chogno-gu,
Seoul,
Republic of Korea.

Su Excellencia:

Quiero expresarle mi más profunda indignación respecto del caso de **Kim Song-Man**, hecho prisionero por oponerse a la política del Gobierno. No hay evidencia de que estuviera involucrado en ninguna actividad violenta y es muy probable que su confesión se obtuviese mediante tortura.

Le insto, respetuosamente, a que sea liberado inmediatamente.

NOMBRE	CIUDAD	FIRMA
Javier Zapater	MADRID	
ANA ISABEL LUCAS TORRES	Madrid	
MARTIN VALMASEDA	Madrid	
VIRGINIA SOBRINO	MADRID	
SONIA ACAL REY	MADRID	
Ignacio Alvarez Sánchez	Madrid	
Alfredo Quitián	Madrid	
Lourdes Barroso	Madrid	
Fernando Bort Misol	Madrid	
Mª Angeles Meleiro Tabal	Santander	
BEGOÑA ASENJO LORENZO	MADRID	

Secretariado Internacional - 1 Easton Street - London WC1X 8DJ.

Amnesty International es un movimiento pro derechos humanos que trabaja imparcialmente por la liberación de los presos de conciencia: hombres y mujeres detenidos en todo el mundo por sus convicciones, color, origen étnico, sexo, religión o idioma, siempre y cuando no hayan recurrido a la violencia o abogado por ella. Amnesty International se opone sin excepciones a la imposición de la pena de muerte y la tortura y propugna la realización de juicios expeditos e imparciales para todos los presos políticos. Es independiente de todo gobierno, partido político, ideología, interés económico o credo religioso. Se financia con suscripciones y donaciones de sus afiliados en todo el mundo. Tiene categoría consultiva con las Naciones Unidas (ECOSOC), UNESCO y el Consejo de Europa; mantiene relaciones de trabajo con la Comisión Interamericana de Derechos Humanos de la Organización de Estados Americanos, y es miembro del Comité Coordinador de la Oficina para la Ubicación y Educación de Refugiados Africanos (BPEAR) de la Organización de Unidad Africana. Premio Nobel de la Paz 1977.

0262

His Excellency
President ROH Tae-woo
The Blue House
1 Sejong-no
Chongno-gu
Seoul
Republic of Korea

Your Excellency,

The undersigned wish to express their deep concern at the case of KIM SONG-MAN who is serving a term of life imprisonment for expressing his opposition to government policy, and as he was not involved in violent activities, they urge you to release him immediately.

NOMBRE	DIRECCION	FIRMA
MARIA ISABEL REPULLO PICASSO	VICENTE ESPINEL, 25 - MÁLAGA	[signature]
MARIA ANGELES GUTIERREZ REPULLO	URB. EL CANTAL, 55 - RINCÓN DE LA VICTORIA	[signature]
CRISTÓBAL ESPAÑA ANGEL	MARQUÉS, 5 - MÁLAGA	[signature]
Eduardo GIL SAENZ	Maestranza, 8 MALAGA	[signature]
Mª CARMEN ARIZA GONZÁLEZ	AVDA LAS POSTAS, 24 MÁLAGA	[signature]
Mª DOLORES MORENO MORALES	C/ DEL RÍO 28, VÉLEZ	[signature]
JAIME LOPEZ RAMIREZ	C/ SONDALEZAS, 6 6º D MALAGA	[signature]
CARMEN GOMEZ VARO	AVDA) PINTOR SOROLLA 54 MALAGA	[signature]
Manuel Pérez Cantarero	C/ Reimundo Lulio 7 Málaga	[signature]
Mª MARCELA GODÍNEZ MORENO	C/ HERNAN CORTES, 15 MALAGA	[signature]
ELENA Mª MARTÍNEZ RODRIGUEZ	C/ VIRGEN DE LA CABEZA, 10 MALAGA	[signature]
ANA PEREA RODRIGUEZ	C/ BARON DE LES, 14, MALAGA	[signature]
Mª BEATRIZ BLETA CANTERO	C/ ALCARAVEA 55, 5ºD - MÁLAGA	[signature]
Pepi Fdez Kioboo	Alameda Barceló, 66, 1ºC	[signature]
Mª del Mar Casado Rodríguez	Tº Cortes	[signature]
Manolo Murillo Trujillo	Avd. Pres XXIII	[signature]

(TRADUCCION: Los abajo firmantes quieren expresar su preocupación por el caso de KIM SONG-MAN que está cumpliendo una condena de cadena perpetua por expresar su oposición a la política del gobierno, y como no estaba involucrado en actividades violentas, le instan a que sea liberado inmediatamente.)

0263

His Excellency
President ROH Tae-woo
The Blue House
1 Sejong-no
Chongno-gu
Seoul
Republic of Korea

Your Excellency,

The undersigned wish to express their deep concern at the case of KIM SONG-MAN who is serving a term of life imprisonment for expressing his opposition to government policy, and as he was not involved in violent activities, they urge you to release him immediately.

NOMBRE	DIRECCION	FIRMA
Andrés M. Sánchez S.	Los Negros 19, 2 P. 29013-MÁLAGA (SPAIN)	Andrés M. Sánchez
María José Sánchez Santamaría	Los Negros 19 1º P 29013 MÁLAGA	María J. Sánchez
Elisa Santamaría G.	Los Negros 19 2º P 29013 Málaga	E. Santamaría
Ana B. Cintas	S. Grazalema 26 1 2º C	[illegible]
Francisco José Sánchez Santamaría	Los Negros 19 2P 29013 Málaga (SPAIN)	Francisco José S. S.
MARIA VICTORIA GONZALEZ	LOS NEGROS 19 1º P	María José Victoria
ELISA SANCHEZ SANTAMARIA	LOS NEGROS 19, 2º D 29013 MALAGA (ESPAÑA)	Elisa Sánchez
MIGUEL CAMPOS COBOS	CRISTO DE LA EPIDEMIA 37 29013 Málaga (España)	Miguel Campos
REMEDIOS CUEVAS FDEZ-GALLEGO	GORDON, 18, 12-C	R. Cuevas
DOMINGO SANCHEZ MARTINEZ	C/Alameda de Capuchinos nº 23 3º B	Domingo Sánchez M.
BELEN MORENO ORTA	C/ CRISTO DE LA EPIDEMIA Nº 93 4ºA CP 29013	[illegible]
Charo Ramos Andrades	C/Maestro Navas nº 4. 1º D. 29014 Málaga (España)	[illegible]
Mª Eugenia Fernández Quijano	Parque del Sur Bq Dr 14º-4 29014 Málaga (ESPAÑA)	Mª Eugenia
Mª Teresa Espinosa Cuevas	C/Ayala nº 7, 8ºC	M. T. Espinosa
Teresa Perelló Pérez	Los Negros 19-6º-R	Teresa Perelló
Mª José Bretones Pérez	C/El Concejo 99 (Fuengirola)	Mª José Bretones
Pori Noguera Navas	D.N.I 24256018	P. Noguera
Mª Carmen Ramos Díez	D.N.I 25.540.286	[illegible]

(TRADUCCION: Los abajo firmantes quieren expresar su preocupación por el caso de KIM SONG-MAN que está cumpliendo una condena de cadena perpetua por expresar su oposición a la política del gobierno, y como no estaba involucrado en actividades violentas, le instan a que sea liberado inmediatamente.)

0264

His Excellency
President ROH Tae-woo
The Blue House
1 Sejong-no
Chongno-gu
Seoul
Republic of Korea

Your Excellency,

The undersigned wish to express their deep concern at the case of KIM SONG-MAN who is serving a term of life imprisonment for expressing his opposition to government policy, and as he was not involved in violent activities, they urge you to release him immediately.

NOMBRE	DIRECCION	FIRMA
Rafael Arjona Gómez	C/ Alcalde J. Mª Corona Nº 4 2-G	
RAFAEL LOZA GOMEZ	C/ AVDA LA LUZ 6-1-1	
Fco. Javier Alcántara Benitez	C/ Martidanca 7.9.	
Manuel García López	C/ Juan Juliani 9	Manuel Gª López
Salvador Godoid Reina	C/ Antonio Gaudio pl 8 1ª	Salvador
JUAN Fco COCA GONZÁLEZ	C/ CORREO DE ANDALUCIA, 15 1ºC	
Felipe Muñoz Brieva	Avda. Velázquez Nº 8-10C	
Mercedes Vargas Jimenez	C/ Al. Gos. Mª B9-2.9	Mercedes
Virginia Pariente Valero	Manes Bernateu 3 3º A	
Belén Sánchez Camacho	Carnicerito 1, 4º D	
Belén Sierra Sierra	Ingeniero La Cierva 16	B. Sierra
Juan Antonio Gómez Mayo	Ingeniero La Cierva 9-4	
Mª Inmaculada Aparicio Cañete	Avda. La Luz, Bl. 37-5º1	
Antonio Jesús Sánchez Gordillo	C/ Salcillo Nº 1-5º-4	J. Jesús Sánchez
Fernando González Martín	Plaza La Luz 3 3º2	
CARMEN SIERRA SIERRA	C/ ING. LA CIERVA 16, 3º 1ª	CARMEN
ISABEL RIVAS LOPEZ	C/ DECANO ANTº SEDANO 5y7	Isabel Rivas
Antonio Ruiz Cordoba	C/ INGENIERO LA CIERVA 10 6º 3	

(TRADUCCION: Los abajo firmantes quieren expresar su preocupación por el caso de KIM SONG-MAN que está cumpliendo una condena de cadena perpetua por expresar su oposición a la política del gobierno, y como no estaba involucrado en actividades violentas, le instan a que sea liberado inmediatamente.)

0265

His Excellency
President ROH Tae-woo
The Blue House
1 Sejong-no
Chongno-gu
Seoul
Republic of Korea

Your Excellency,

The undersigned wish to express their deep concern at the case of KIM SONG-MAN who is serving a term of life imprisonment for expressing his opposition to government policy, and as he was not involved in violent activities, they urge you to release him immediately.

NOMBRE	DIRECCION	FIRMA
Aurora Madrid Rodríguez	C/ Alcalá [illegible] 2, 8°D CP 29003	
Ana Mª Pedraza Moreno	P. Virgen de Belén [illegible] 5°B	
Jose A. Gallego Jimenez	C/ ING. LA CIERVA 30-5-4	
JUANA ALBA MARÍN	TRAVESÍA LA LUZ, 24-8°-1	
José Antonio Recio Martín	C/ EDUARDO TORROJA Nº 5-4-1	
Mª JOSÉ ARROCHA JIMÉNEZ	C/ JOAQUÍN ALONSO Nº 15-2-D	
Fco. Javier Becerra Durán	P. Virgen de Belén nº 6 8°c	
Mª ANGELES RECIO MARTIN	C/ EDUARDO TORROJA 5-4-1	
DAVID FERNANDEZ GAMBERO	C/ ALVAREZ CURIEL Nº 14	
EVA PALMA CABRERA	C/ Pajarete 124. 3ª Fase. El Lagar. Alh. Torre	
Antonio Caro López	[illegible] 3 [illegible]	
Pilar [illegible]	C/ [illegible] 16 3-1	
[illegible] Valadez Clavijo	C/ Stravinsky 8, 5°A	
MIGUEL A. VARGAS JIMÉNEZ	C/ ALC. JOSÉ Mª CORONA Nº 4	
MARCOS ANTONIO MUÑOZ CARRASCO	C/ CARNICERITO 18°A	
Fco Jose López de las Heras	C/ Juan Sebastián Bach 1, 6°C	
Jesús Muñoz Bricva	AVDA. VELAZQUEZ 8-10°C	
Mª Nieves Arjona Gómez	C/ Alcalde José Mª Corona nº 4 2°G	

(TRADUCCION: Los abajo firmantes quieren expresar su preocupación por el caso de KIM SONG-MAN que está cumpliendo una condena de cadena perpetua por expresar su oposición a la política del gobierno, y como no estaba involucrado en actividades violentas, le instan a que sea liberado inmediatamente.)

0266

His Excellency
President ROH Tae-woo
The Blue House
1 Sejong-no
Chongno-gu
Seoul
Republic of Korea

Your Excellency,

The undersigned wish to express their deep concern at the case of KIM SONG-MAN who is serving a term of life imprisonment for expressing his opposition to government policy, and as he was not involved in violent activities, they urge you to release him immediately.

NOMBRE	DIRECCION	FIRMA
Mª de la Cruz Segura Molina	C/ Torcal, 2 7ºC-2	Mª de la Cruz
Aurora Rodríguez	C/ Alcalareño 2-8-D	Aurora Rodríguez
María José Alcántara Leiva	C/ Alcalareño 2, 8ºC	[illegible]
Cecilia Madrid Díaz	C/ Alcalareño 2 8 D	Cecilia Madrid
Rosa Mª Becerro	C/ Torcal 2-8-C-2	Rosa Mª B.
Francisco Vázquez Sáez	C/ Torcal 2-8ºC-2	F. Vázquez
Antonio Zaragoza Rodríguez	C/ Alcald. Joaquín Alonso Nº 30	A. Zaragoza Rodríguez
Juan Mª Montes	C/ [illegible]	[illegible]
Débora M. Perino Fdez	La Fresneda, s/n Campanillas	D. M. Perino
F. J. Garro Pérez	C/ Na Almería Nº 1 Adra (Almería)	Javier Garro
José David Montes	Toledo C/ Salino, 43	José Montes
Rafael Montes Merino	C/ Salino, 43	[illegible]
Antonio Somodevilla Mangas		Antonio
Juan Urbano Segui	C/ Begoñana Nº 8 1º Dcha	J. Urbano
María José Aguilar	C/ Hoyo Higuerón, Nº 14	Mª José Aguilar
Gabriel Abad Fernández	Avda. Europa, 51, 5º D	[illegible]
Rafael Serrano Marcilla	Bda. las Bellas [illegible]	[illegible]
Isabel Escalante Sánchez	C/ M. Falla B. 9 P. 1 1º B	I. Escalante

(TRADUCCION: Los abajo firmantes quieren expresar su preocupación por el caso de KIM SONG-MAN que está cumpliendo una condena de cadena perpetua por expresar su oposición a la política del gobierno, y como no estaba involucrado en actividades violentas, le instan a que sea liberado inmediatamente.)

0267

His Excellency
President ROH Tae-woo
The Blue House
1 Sejong-no
Chongno-gu
Seoul
Republic of Korea

Your Excellency,

The undersigned wish to express their deep concern at the case of KIM SONG-MAN who is serving a term of life imprisonment for expressing his opposition to government policy, and as he was not involved in violent activities, they urge you to release him immediately.

NOMBRE	DIRECCION	FIRMA
MARIA LUISA MERINO CORDOBA	JUAN SEBASTIAN ELCANO Nº 52	
Rafael Torres Pacheco	Peinado nº 15 2º 1ª	
Francisco J. Barrionuevo Jiménez	Rafael Arrabuca, 19	
José A. Alcántara Molina	Camino del Pato, 23	
EVA DE PEDRO MELERO	C/ REINA JULIANA, 17	
ALICIA SALAZAR BURGUEÑO	C/ ARAGÓN Nº 6	Alicia Salazar
M. ALBERTO MUÑOZ ROMERO	C/ ARROYEROS 13 NERJA	
ANTONIO LUIS JIMÉNEZ DÍAZ	C/ ISAAC PERAL 6-9º-B	
Carmen Quiñones Torres	C/ P.M. del Palo nº 10 8º A	
Natalia Galán Gutiérrez	C/ Casas de Campos 18 3º 2	
Elena Frade Piano	C/ Mayoral 2 12-2	Elena Frade
SERGIO COÑETE HIDALGO	C/ MIRAFLORES UNIDOS 2 9º	
Carolina Enríquez Gómez	C/ DEL PATO nº 2	
Yolanda Rubio Moreno	Pasaje Luis de Pablo R 2	
MANUEL ALGARRA GLEZ	MUÑOZ TORRERO 7. 1º E	
OLGA NEGRI ARJONA	C/ CONCEJAL E HEREDIA 2	Olga Negri

(TRADUCCION: Los abajo firmantes quieren expresar su preocupación por el caso de KIM SONG-MAN que está cumpliendo una condena de cadena perpetua por expresar su oposición a la política del gobierno, y como no estaba involucrado en actividades violentas, le instan a que sea liberado inmediatamente.)

0268

His Excellency
President ROH Tae-woo
The Blue House
1 Sejong-no
Chongno-gu
Seoul
Republic of Korea

Your Excellency,

The undersigned wish to express their deep concern at the case of KIM SONG-MAN who is serving a term of life imprisonment for expressing his opposition to government policy, and as he was not involved in violent activities, they urge you to release him immediately.

NOMBRE	DIRECCION	FIRMA
Hª Juque	Canclus Perez 14	[signature]

(TRADUCCION: Los abajo firmantes quieren expresar su preocupación por el caso de KIM SONG-MAN que está cumpliendo una condena de cadena perpetua por expresar su oposición a la política del gobierno, y como no estaba involucrado en actividades violentas, le instan a que sea liberado inmediatamente.)

0269

His Excellency
President ROH Tae-woo
The Blue House
1 Sejong-no
Chongno-gu
Seoul
Republic of Korea

Your Excellency,

The undersigned wish to express their deep concern at the case of KIM SONG-MAN who is serving a term of life imprisonment for expressing his opposition to government policy, and as he was not involved in violent activities, they urge you to release him immediately.

NOMBRE	DIRECCION	FIRMA
Mª Pilar Arcas Barrientos	S. Millan 11 1º A Málaga	[signature]
Karl M. Türk	S. Millan 11 1º A Malaga (E)	[signature]
Andrés Pérez López	C/ Pico de las palomas Nº 3	[signature]
Mª del Carmen Ramos Luque	C/ Antonio Cabezón nº 28 Colomera [illegible]	[signature]
Dolores Salve Martín	Huelva 3 5º B Fuengirola	[signature]
Fco José Villanueva Benítez	Avda Mayorazgo Nº 9 2º 1	[signature]
[illegible]	[illegible]	[signature]
Mª Teresa Delgado Claros	C/ Axarquía-Florida Blanca P03-1º H	[signature]
Beni Medina Alcántara	C/ Francisco Correa BL-5 3-K	[signature]
Mª Fernanda Mejías Rosado	[illegible]	[signature]
Mª del Pilar Luque Blanco	Abogado F. Orellana 14-3º2	[signature]
Mª Victoria Santiesteban de la Rubia	Poeta Jiménez Molina 24 D-1º C	[signature]
Dolores Alarcón	La Unión 7 3	[signature]
Mª José Romero Hermoso	Martínez Maldonado 70 5º L	[signature]
Mª Carmen Luque Segovia	C/ Escultor Expósito 3	[signature]
Justino Díez	C/ Obispo Pedro de Moya Nº 3-4-C Málaga	[signature]
Ana Elena Martín	C/ Pto Moreno Villa 2. 7º 4 Málaga	[signature]

(TRADUCCION: Los abajo firmantes quieren expresar su preocupación por el caso de KIM SONG-MAN que está cumpliendo una condena de cadena perpetua por expresar su oposición a la política del gobierno, y como no estaba involucrado en actividades violentas, le instan a que sea liberado inmediatamente.)

0270

His Excellency
President ROH Tae-woo
The Blue House
1 Sejong-no
Chongno-gu
Seoul
Republic of Korea

Your Excellency,

The undersigned wish to express their deep concern at the case of KIM SONG-MAN who is serving a term of life imprisonment for expressing his opposition to government policy, and as he was not involved in violent activities, they urge you to release him immediately.

NOMBRE	DIRECCION	FIRMA
ANTONIO JESÚS CORONADO MORÁN	C/TOQUERO, 20 (29013) - MALAGA	[signature]
Antonio Jesús Carrasco Bootello	C/Toquero, 20 (29013 - Málaga)	[signature]
ANDRÉS MERINO MATEO	C/ Toquero, 20 / 29013 - Málaga.	[signature]
DANIEL GUERRERO GARCÍA	C/Toquero, 20/29013 - Málaga	[signature]
Juan Abel García Castaño	C/Toquero 20/29013 - Málaga	[signature]
Fco Baquero Vargas 33388678	C/ Toquero 20/29013 - Málaga	[signature]
José Vega Aguilar	C/Toquero 20/29013 Málaga	[signature]
Benito García	C/ Toquero 20/29013 Málaga	[signature]
JUAN JESÚS JOYERA	C/Toquero, 20 29013 Málaga	[signature] DNI 25.326.48
JUAN A. BRAVO	C/Toquero 20/29013 Málaga	[signature]
Félix Mediavilla Esteban	C/Toquero 20/29013 Málaga	[signature]
Fermín Negre Moreno	C/ Larga 8 29640 Fuengirola	[signature]
JUAN JOSÉ LOZA GÓMEZ	C/ Toquero Nº 20, 29013 MÁLAGA	[signature]
Cristóbal Bueno Pérez	C/ Toquero 20, 29013 MALAGA	JC Bueno
Alvaro Carrasco Vergara	C/ Antº Trueba 14 29017 Málaga	[signature]
ANTONIO DOMINGUEZ RODRIGUEZ	C/ Alcazaba 18 29006 Malaga	[signature]
Mª CLARA GARCERÁN ORTEGA	C/ CÓMICO RIQUELME 17, MALAGA	[signature]
REINALDO AGUILERA AGUILERA	C/TOQUERO, 20. 29013, MÁLAGA	[signature]
Francisco M. Ortega Carpio	C/TOQUERO, 20 29013 MALAGA	Francisco M. Ortega

(TRADUCCION: Los abajo firmantes quieren expresar su preocupación por el caso de KIM SONG-MAN que está cumpliendo una condena de cadena perpetua por expresar su oposición a la política del gobierno, y como no estaba involucrado en actividades violentas, le instan a que sea liberado inmediatamente.)

0271

His Excellency
President ROH Tae-woo
The Blue House
1 Sejong-no
Chongno-gu
Seoul
Republic of Korea

Your Excellency,

The undersigned wish to express their deep concern at the case of KIM SONG-MAN who is serving a term of life imprisonment for expressing his opposition to government policy, and as he was not involved in violent activities, they urge you to release him immediately.

NOMBRE	DIRECCION	FIRMA
Francisco Burgos Garcia	Camino de Vilchez, P.3 1ºE Alhaurin el Grande (Malaga	[signature]
J. SATURNINO GONZALEZ ROSON	C/ RIO Rocio Nº1 - 6º3 Málaga	[signature]
ANTONIO ZARO VERA	Alameda de Capuchinos, 8. 3ºF 29014 MALAGA	[signature]
Enrique Enriquez Bravo	Rocio, 64 MALAGA	[signature]
LORENZA TORRES ARDOY	C/LEOPOLDO ALAS CLARIN Nº1-3º-C 29002-MALAGA	[signature]
SALVADOR VERDUGO MORTÍN	Avda. PLUTARCO, 2-4º-2 29010 MALAGA	[signature]
Piedad Pacheco Pino.	C/ Leopoldo Alas Clarín, nº 5. 2ºA. 29002-Málaga	[signature]
Alicia Arteta Vico	C/Pintor [illegible] 29017 Málaga	[signature]
Mª Victoria Alonso Martinez	C/ Eugenio Sellés, 6-Málaga	[signature]
Luis López-Cózar Martinez	Eugenio Selles C Malaga	[signature]
Ana Rosas Pérez	Avda. del Carmen, 8-Málaga	[signature]
Carmen Camacho Sanchez	Avda Andalucia nº2-Malaga	[signature]
Elvira garcia Chacon	Eugenio Selles 32-Malaga	[signature]
Araceli Soler Checa	Salitre 40, MALAGA	[signature]
Yolanda Mendoza López	Avda Caballerizas 2 MALAGA	[signature]
Agustin Pacheco Pino	C/N. Sra Candelaria 23, 6ºC	[signature]
Dª CARMEN ELIAS NUÑEZ	Pje Virgen de Belen nº6	[signature]
Miguel Fco. Garcia Rueda	C/ Beguñanc 4-2ºJ	[signature]

(TRADUCCION: Los abajo firmantes quieren expresar su preocupación por el caso de KIM SONG-MAN que está cumpliendo una condena de cadena perpetua por expresar su oposición a la política del gobierno, y como no estaba involucrado en actividades violentas, le instan a que sea liberado inmediatamente.)

0272

His Excellency
President ROH Tae-woo
The Blue House
1 Sejong-no
Chongno-gu
Seoul
Republic of Korea

Your Excellency,

The undersigned wish to express their deep concern at the case of KIM SONG-MAN who is serving a term of life imprisonment for expressing his opposition to government policy, and as he was not involved in violent activities, they urge you to release him immediately.

NOMBRE	DIRECCION	FIRMA
Juan R. Díaz Robledo	Av. Andalucía, 25, 13º B 29006 Málaga (SPAIN)	[signature]
JESÚS IGNACIO DÍAZ ROBLEDO	IDEM	[signature]
Pedro Díaz Calero	IDEM	[signature]
Mª Rosa Bocanegra Hidalgo	Avd Andalucía 25 11º B 29006 Málaga (SPAIN)	[signature]
LOURDES DÍAZ ROBLEDO	AVDA ANDALUCÍA Nº 25 (SPAIN)	[signature]
Mª Carmen Herrera	Marta Escobar nº 35 (spain)	[signature]
José P. Pérez Correa	C/SOMERA 10·3º DCHA MÁLAGA (")	[signature]
VIRTUDES HIDALGO PACHECO	MALAGA 29002	[signature]
Dolores Martín Castillo	29240 (Malaga)	[signature]
Socorro Ruiz Mora	Antequera 29200	[signature]
Mª Angeles Torres Picón	Antequera 29200	[signature]
Isabel Mª Pérez Vegas	Antequera 29200	[signature]
Dolores Cañete Ariza	Cuevas de S. Marcos 29210	[signature]
Sandrine Sánchez [illegible]	Avda/Salvador Allende nº21 6A	[signature]

(TRADUCCION: Los abajo firmantes quieren expresar su preocupación por el caso de KIM SONG-MAN que está cumpliendo una condena de cadena perpetua por expresar su oposición a la política del gobierno, y como no estaba involucrado en actividades violentas, le instan a que sea liberado inmediatamente.)

0273

His Excellency
President ROH Tae Woo
The Blue House
1 Sejong-no
Chongno-gu
Seoul
Republic of Korea

Your Excellency,

The undersigned wish to express their deep concern at the case of KIM SONG-MAN who is serving a term of life imprisonment for expressing his opposition to government policy, and as he was not involved in violent activities, they urge you to release him immediately.

NOMBRE	DIRECCION	FIRMA
Mª Isabel Castañeda Gorhón	C/ Obispo Calvo y Valero, 41	[signature]
José Ramón Solís Moreno	El Torno - Jerez	[signature] DNI 3164[illegible]
Mª Dolores Matas Matas	C/ Corredera 38 Arcos Fra	[signature] DNI 74624030
Manuel Castro Álvarez	Avd. Solís [illegible] 34 Ubrique (Cádiz)	[signature] 25572669
Mª Jesús Navarro Franco	C/ [illegible] la Giralda, Bornos	[signature] DNI 27474687
Pedro Cabrera Ruiz	C/ Clavo s/n La Barca Florida	[signature] 26182610
Mª Inmaculada Rodríguez Alonso	Bornos	[signature] 31645947
Felipe Sánchez Villalba	Cadena 2 Arcos	31664761
Pedro Hernández Benito		[signature] 24164198
Luis Camagnilla Bermúdez		[signature] 30.470.765
Maribel Ruiz Ortiz	Arcos de la Frontera	[signature] 25.570.411
Juan Gómez Márquez		[signature] 25569385

(TRADUCCION: Los abajo firmantes quieren expresar su preocupación por el caso de KIM SONG-MAN que está cumpliendo una condena de cadena perpetua por expresar su oposición a la política del gobierno, y como no estaba involucrado en actividades violentas, le instan a que sea liberado inmediatamente.)

0271

His Excellency
President ROH Tae-Woo
The Blue House
1 Sejong-no
Chongno-gu
Seoul
Republic of Korea

Your Excellency,

The undersigned wish to express their deep concern at the case of KIM SONG-MAN who is serving a term of life imprisonment for expressing his opposition to government policy, and as he was not involved in violent activities, they urge you to release him immediately.

NOMBRE	DIRECCION	FIRMA
Mª DOLORES LUNA ADAME	C/ CHILE 25 ARCOS FRA.	26.203.886.
Antonio José Cano Alcázar	Jerez Frontera	30508734
Mª Dolores Cantero Ahumada	Sanlúcar Bda	52.324.461
J.A. Bautista Lamilla	Sevilla	27.277.374
María Antonia [illegible] Valenzuela	Arcos de la Fra	29.731.046
Patro Ordóñez Moreno	Ubrique	25575821
Jesús-R. Taranilla Alonso	Jerez de la Fra.	9.748.501
[illegible]	Arcos	25981062

(TRADUCCIÓN: Los abajo firmantes quieren expresar su preocupación por el caso de KIM SONG-MAN que está cumpliendo una condena de cadena perpetua por expresar su oposición a la politica del gobierno, y como no estaba involucrado en actividades violentas; le instan a que sea liberado inmediatamente.)

0275

His Excellency
President ROH Tae Woo
The Blue House
1 Sejong-no
Chongno-gu
Seoul
Republic of Korea

Your Excellency,

The undersigned wish to express their deep concern at the case of KIM SONG-MAN who is serving a term of life imprisonment for expressing his opposition to government policy, and as he was not involved in violent activities, they urge you to release him immediately.

NOMBRE	DIRECCION	FIRMA
Juan Luis Garrido	Bornos	Juan Luis Garrido
Oliver Redondo Jimenez	Bornos	
Moisés Baños Ramírez	Bornos	
José Antonio Ramos Ramírez	Bornos	
Manuel Roldan	Arcos	
José Antº Venegas	Villamartin	José Antº Venegas
Jacinto Marquez	Bornos	Jacinto
Juan Manuel Jimenez	Coto de Bornos	
Juan de Dios Bautista Martínez	Arcos	79251823
Amparo Gutierrez Lora	Algar	
Guadalupe Guerrero Albertos	Arcos	Guadalupe
Alicia Díaz Bernal	Arcos	Alicia Díaz Bernal
José Manuel Hervás Bautista	Arcos	31688445
Antonio Manuel Gordillo	Arcos	A. M. Gordillo 75.867.965
Marisa Jiménez Barrera	Arcos	Marisa Jiménez
Rocío Fuénes Montero	Coto de Bornos	Rocío Fuénes 31685595
Montaña Hurtado Labrador	Coto de Bornos	Montaña 758666
Juan de Dios Gallardo Ríos	ARCOS	

(TRADUCCION: Los abajo firmantes quieren expresar su preocupación por el caso de KIM SONG-MAN que está cumpliendo una condena de cadena perpetua por expresar su oposición a la política del gobierno, y como no estaba involucrado en actividades violentas, le instan a que sea liberado inmediatamente.)

0276

His Excellency
President ROH Ta[redacted]o
The Blue House
1 Sejong-no
Chongno-gu
Seoul
Republic of Korea

Your Excellency,

The undersigned wish to express their deep concern at the case of KIM SONG-MAN who is serving a term of life imprisonment for expressing his opposition to government policy, and as he was not involved in violent activities, they urge you to release him immediately.

NOMBRE	DIRECCION	FIRMA
Pagui Chacón Mancheño	Espera	31699880
Carmen Mª Bueno Barrera	Arcos	
Manoli García Hernandez	Jedula (Cadiz)	
Rocío Garrido Durán	(Arcos)	
Mª Angeles González Sanchez	(Arcos)	
Antonia Vega Mancera	(Arcos)	25869469-W
Jose González Lopez	(Villamartin)	
Genoveva Cadillo Quiñones		Genoveva Cadillo 31700749
Pilar González Regordán	(Arcos)	
Natalia Bernal Morato	Villamartín	
Mª del Carmen Carrera Jurado	(Bornos)	Mª Carmen 31703477
Inmaculada Barrego Rodríguez	Prado del Rey	Inmaculada
Enrique Holgado Holgado		Enrique
Maria José González Bornos		Maria José

([illegible] preocupación por el caso de KIM SONG-MAN que está cumpliendo una condena de cadena perpetua por expresar su oposición a la política del gobierno, y como no estaba involucrado en actividades violentas, le instan a que sea liberado inmediatamente.)

0277

His Excellency
President ROH Tae-Woo
The Blue House
1 Sejong-no
Chongno-gu
Seoul
Republic of Korea

Your Excellency,

The undersigned wish to express their deep concern at the case of KIM SONG-MAN who is serving a term of life imprisonment for expressing his opposition to government policy, and as he was not involved in violent activities, they urge you to release him immediately.

NOMBRE	DIRECCION	FIRMA
José Luis Jaime García	C/Chile, 25 Arcos Fra - Cádiz	[signature] DNI 25.059.371
Juan Pedro Raya Molero	C/ B. Combao nº 13-4º / 11630 - Arcos Fª (Cádiz)	[signature] D.N.I. 31.637.488
José María Torres Barranco	C/Molino, 16. Utrera (Sevilla)	[signature] 34021120
Manuel Marcelo Perez	C/ Cordilla 45 Osuna (Sevilla)	[signature] 75405272
Antonio Domínguez Ojeda	C/ Los Soles Bloque 2 2º Dcha.	[signature] 29733346
José Antº Sánchez García	C/ Vera-[illegible], 34 (Villamartín)	[signature] 75.847.926
Juan Antº Rubiales Bernabé	C/ Cava Nº 3	[signature] 79251468
Fco. Javier Luque Jurado	La Pedrosa Nº 6	[signature] 31690238
J. Carlos Soria Tenorio	C/ Gardenia Nº 2-2B	[signature] 75865860
Fco Javier Fernández Garrucho	Espera (Cádiz)	[signature] 79252159
Manuel Jesús García Vega	Arcos de la Fra (Cádiz)	[signature] 31686932
Antonio Javier Sanchez Bautista	Arcos de la FRA (Cádiz)	31686493
Manuel Muñoz Moreno	Arcos de la Fra (Cádiz)	[signature]
Juan Luis Garrido Córdoba	Arcos de la Fra (Cádiz)	[signature]
José Luis Navarro Rodríguez	Algar (Cádiz)	[signature]
José A. Nieto Salguero	CRA Algar Km 8	[signature] 31.690.719
David Calle Rey	Arcos de la Fra (Cádiz)	[signature]
Mª Elena Perez Carrasco	Villamartín (Cádiz)	52282630

(TRADUCCIÓN: Los abajo firmantes quieren expresar su preocupación por el caso de KIM SONG-MAN que está cumpliendo una condena de cadena perpetua por expresar su oposición a la política del gobierno, y como no estaba involucrado en actividades violentas, le instan a que sea liberado inmediatamente.)

0278

His Excellency
President ROH Tae-woo
The Blue House
1 Sejong-no
Chongno-gu
Seoul
Republic of Korea

Your Excellency,

The undersigned wish to express their deep concern at the case of KIM SONG-MAN who is serving a term of life imprisonment for expressing his opposition to government policy, and as he was not involved in violent activities, they urge you to release him immediately.

NOMBRE	DIRECCION	FIRMA
Antonio Perez Calvillo	La palma 43 Villamartin	[signature] 75864040
Juan Sales Temblador Delgado	Arcos	[signature]
Jose Mª Arocha Friaza	Villamartin	Jose Mª Arocha
José Vte Dávier Gil	Villamartin.	[signature] 75864858
Antonio Mariscal Pérez	Prado del Rey	[signature]
José Antonio Tamayo Aguilera	Prado del Rey	Antonio
José Carlos Lobo Gonzalez	Bornos	[signature]
Antonio José Serrano García	Arcos	[signature]
Víctor Manuel López Marchán	San Jerónimo Nº 29	Víctor M.
Juan Antonio Rosado Bernal	(ARCOS)	[signature]
Miguel Vázquez Bernabé	Espera (Cádiz)	Miguel
Gabriel Baños Carrera	Bornos (Cádiz)	Gabriel Baños
Daniel Valle Rodriguez	(Espera Cadiz)	Daniel Valle
Antonio José Galindo	Bornos (Cadiz)	Antonio José Galindo
Fco. Manuel Sánchez Rodríguez	PRADO DEL REY	[signature]
Cristóbal Jiménez Aguilera	(Villamartin) (CÁDIZ)	[signature]
Juan Medina Diaz	(Cadiz)	[signature]
Jose Angel López Sierra	Bornos Cádiz	Jose Angel López

(TRADUCCION: Los abajo firmantes quieren expresar su preocupación por el caso de KIM SONG-MAN que está cumpliendo una condena de cadena perpetua por expresar su oposición a la política del gobierno, y como no estaba involucrado en actividades violentas, le instan a que sea liberado inmediatamente.)

0279

His Excellency
President ROH Tae-woo
The Blue House
1 Sejong-no
Chongno-gu
Seoul
Republic of Korea

Your Excellency,

The undersigned wish to express their deep concern at the case of KIM SONG-MAN who is serving a term of life imprisonment for expressing his opposition to government policy, and as he was not involved in violent activities, they urge you to release him immediately.

NOMBRE	DIRECCION	FIRMA
Ana Casanova Lienzo	Barranquilla de Colombia, 4	[illegible]
Emilia Fernández Fernández	Pasaje Cantarero 3	[illegible]
Yolanda Yáñez	Edificio Ingenio, 2	[illegible]
Adolfo García	C/ San Pedro, 12	[illegible]
Ofelia Bueno Ávila	27 Marzo, 137	[illegible]
José J. Guerra Mena	C/ Carrera Teral de Almería S/N	[illegible]
M. Dolores Guerra Mena	C/ Carrera Almería S/N	[illegible]
ARANTXA GONZALEZ	SAN JOSE, C/ LABRAKO TORRE N.8.B Bilbao	Arantxa

(TRADUCCION: Los abajo firmantes quieren expresar su preocupación por el caso de KIM SONG-MAN que está cumpliendo una condena de cadena perpetua por expresar su oposición a la política del gobierno, y como no estaba involucrado en actividades violentas, le instan a que sea liberado inmediatamente.)

0280

His Excellency
President ROH Tae-woo
The Blue House
1 Sejong-no
Chongno-gu
Seoul
Republic of Korea

Your Excellency,

The undersigned wish to express their deep concern at the case of KIM SONG-MAN who is serving a term of life imprisonment for expressing his opposition to government policy, and as he was not involved in violent activities, they urge you to release him immediately.

NOMBRE	DIRECCION	FIRMA
PEDRO OSORIO CARRETERO	C/TOQUERO, 20 - 29013 (MALAGA)	
Antonio Anaya González	c/ Toquero 20	
Juan R. Pérez Rosa	c/ Toquero, 20	
Francisco Sánchez Sánchez	c/ Toquero 20	
Emilio Miguel de los Santos Bancalero	c/ Concejal Fernández Bermudo nº 4-1ºA	
Daniel Haricllo García	c/ Toquero 20	
Rafael Enrique Torres García	Av. de José Ortega y Gasset 7	
Leandro José Carrasco Bootello	c/ Toquero 20	
Antonio J. Sosa Mateos	c/ Toquero, 20 29013 Málaga	
JOSE BERNARDO LOPEZ DE URALDE	C/PEDRO DE CONTRERAS, 1, 1ºB	
JOSE A. NARBONA	C/TOQUERO 20, 29013 MALAGA	
Francisco José Berrocal Fraiz	C/ de Aceras 2, 29012	
Rafael Carrión Barragán	c/ Toquero, 20 (29013 Málaga)	
Emilio J. Martín Gómez	C/ TOQUERO, 20 (29013 MALAGA)	
ANGEL ANTONIO CHACON LOPEZ	C/ Toquero, 20	
SALVADOR MARISCAL LOPEZ	C/TOQUERO Nº 20	
José Francisco Luna Rojas	C/ Toquero, 20	
Agustín Clavijo Pendón	C/Toquero 20	

(TRADUCCION: Los abajo firmantes quieren expresar su preocupación por el caso de KIM SONG-MAN que está cumpliendo una condena de cadena perpetua por expresar su oposición a la política del gobierno, y como no estaba involucrado en actividades violentas, le instan a que sea liberado inmediatamente.)

0281

His Excellency
President ROH Tae-woo
The Blue House
1 Sejong-no
Chongno-gu
Seoul
Republic of Korea

Your Excellency,

The undersigned wish to express their deep concern at the case of KIM SONG-MAN who is serving a term of life imprisonment for expressing his opposition to government policy, and as he was not involved in violent activities, they urge you to release him immediately.

NOMBRE	DIRECCION	FIRMA
Antonio César Muñoz	Malaga C. Mariblanca, 4	Antonio César
Antonio Garrido García	Avda Imperial Nº8 Apto 608 Torremolinos	Garrido
Pablo Palomino	Violetas 16	Pablo Pal[illegible]
Antonio Jimenez	Pza Mirajuna 3 Málaga	[illegible]
Jose Abreu Torres	Juan de Torres 4, 1º	[illegible]
Teresa de Jesús Mefina	" " "	[illegible]
Jose Jurado Priego	C/ Pasillo del Matadero Nº6 - 1º Dcha	[illegible]
Maria Albo Martin	C/ Victoria 110 3º C.P. 29012	[illegible]
Javier García Muñoz	Arroyo 7 29007 Málaga	Javier
Juan J. Franco	Tejares 27 Málaga	[illegible]
Miguel Angel Pace Zaragoza	C/ Palo Mayor 29010 Avda Andalucía 4-4ºB Málaga	[illegible]
Rafael Vadillo Martín	26 Febrero 8-2-2	[illegible]
Rosa Lopez Perna	Mariblanca Nº4	Rosa
Alicia Cueto Granados	C/ Av. García Villegas 8 1º 29007	Alicia
Carmen Gomez Huelgas	C/ Granados 82, 1º Int	[illegible]
José Mañu Muñoz	C/ Juan XXIII 22	[illegible]
Dionisio Salvador Sanchez Gonzalez	Checa Salcedo Nº 19	[illegible]

(TRADUCCION: Los abajo firmantes quieren expresar su preocupación por el caso de KIM SONG-MAN que está cumpliendo una condena de cadena perpetua por expresar su oposición a la política del gobierno, y como no estaba involucrado en actividades violentas, le instan a que sea liberado inmediatamente.)

0282

His Excellency
President ROH Tae-woo
The Blue House
1 Sejong-no
Chongno-gu
Seoul
Republic of Korea

Your Excellency,

 The undersigned wish to express their deep concern at the case of
KIM SONG-MAN who is serving a term of life imprisonment for expressing his opposition to government policy, and as he was not involved in violent activities, they
urge you to release him immediately.

NOMBRE	DIRECCION	FIRMA
J. Enrique Laíño Sánchez	C/ Joaquin Costa 10 2:B Málaga	
Maria Fernandez Boza	C/ San Sebastian II Cañillas de Aceituno	
Daniel Castillo Cañellas	C/ Juan Díaz del Moral nº 27	
José Luis Matoso Aguilar	C/ Santa Ana 13 Bis	
A. Antonio Quirós Traura	C/ La Córdoba 29	
Sebastián Mª Gbo Berenz	C/ Alozaina, 32, 5º A	
Mª José Bautista García	C/ Alozaina, 32, 5ºA	
Manuel Tinoco Pérez	Benaque S/n.	
Paloma González Lamothe	A Bailac 6.	
Raúl Romera Valderal	C/ Conde de Cienfuegos nº 8. 1ºI	
Isabel Mª Mate	C/ camino de suarez N 27	
Silvia Mate Moreno	C/ Cno. Suarez 27	
Victor Frias Jiménez	Cno. Suarez 74	
Mª Adoración Saavedra	C/ Armenqual de la Mota 21	
Juan Luna Martín	Fresnua 5	
NURIA KÜSTNER ROSELL	25104546	
Yolanda Küstner Rosell	C/ Doña Tolosa 2, 5E DNI 25098287	
V. M. Bartitt. Fernandez	Vidrera 25079990	

(TRADUCCION: Los abajo firmantes quieren expresar su preocupación por el caso de KIM
SONG-MAN que está cumpliendo una condena de cadena perpetua por expresar su oposición
a la política del gobierno, y como no estaba involucrado en actividades violentas,
le instan a que sea liberado inmediatamente.)

0283

His Excellency
President ROH Tae-woo
The Blue House
1 Sejong-no
Chongno-gu
Seoul
Republic of Korea

Your Excellency,

The undersigned wish to express their deep concern at the case of KIM SONG-MAN who is serving a term of life imprisonment for expressing his opposition to government policy, and as he was not involved in violent activities, they urge you to release him immediately.

NOMBRE	DIRECCION	FIRMA
EMILIO JIMENEZ MARQUEZ	C/ MAURICIO MORO - 5.	Jiménez
Alejandro Lorca [illegible]	[illegible]	[illegible]
EVA MARTÍNEZ SÁNCHEZ-MORALES		[illegible]
Mª TERESA MONTILLA [illegible]		[illegible]
PILAR CARRIZO GARCIA		[illegible]
Mª DEL MAR PÉREZ SOLÍS		[illegible]
José A. Romero Rico		[illegible]
Mª Jesús Zea Montero		[illegible]
Mª Isabel Fernández Calvo		[illegible]
Carlos Alcalá Parejo		[illegible]
José Antº Araujo García	31836378	José Araujo
Sandra Hernández Arroyo	33397377	[illegible]
MANUEL FERIA GARCIA	3336900?	[illegible]
PEDRO ANTONIO ORTEGA MARTINEZ	MARTINEZ BARRIONUEVO 5 2510224	[illegible]
ANA CHACON LOPEZ-MUÑIZ	5409575	[illegible]
BEATI MORATA PEREZ	24.291.692	[illegible]
ADELA CIFUENTES MELCHOR	24.904.357	[illegible]
Guillermo [illegible] Parejo	33363392	Guillermo [illegible]

(TRADUCCION: Los abajo firmantes quieren expresar su preocupación por el caso de KIM SONG-MAN que está cumpliendo una condena de cadena perpetua por expresar su oposición a la política del gobierno, y como no estaba involucrado en actividades violentas, le instan a que sea liberado inmediatamente.)

0284

His Excellency
President ROH Tae-woo
The Blue House
1 Sejong-no
Chongno-gu
Seoul
Republic of Korea

Your Excellency,

The undersigned wish to express their deep concern at the case of KIM SONG-MAN who is serving a term of life imprisonment for expressing his opposition to government policy, and as he was not involved in violent activities, they urge you to release him immediately.

NOMBRE	DIRECCION D.N.I.	FIRMA
VICTOR M. BRAVO ETELVINA	27102385	
Fº MOLINA DELGADO	25704729	
Ana Ballarene Villalba	27375458	
Francisca García	24868688.	
LAZARA BARRANQUERO	27377137	
Fco. J. Martín Santos	24849424	
ANTONIO SALAZAR LUQUE	25314629	
GABRIEL W. ORTIZ SEGURA	33367300	
Susana Duran Martín	33387970	
MANUEL LLORET TENLLADO	24869373	
JOSE ANTONIO OLMEDO JIMENEZ	33343628	
Mª ANGELES RODRIGUEZ	25686379	
MANUEL J. FDEZ MEDINA	33387789	
Francisco Nuñez Ramírez	25679073	
Yolanda González Gaitán	33397079	
MIGUEL BORREGO DOMINGUEZ	25687572	
PABLO MARILLO AGUIRRE	25.586.018	
EVELIO VALDERAS FARFANTE	791997	

(TRADUCCION: Los abajo firmantes quieren expresar su preocupación por el caso de KIM SONG-MAN que está cumpliendo una condena de cadena perpetua por expresar su oposición a la política del gobierno, y como no estaba involucrado en actividades violentas, le instan a que sea liberado inmediatamente.)

0285

His Excellency
President ROH Tae-woo
The Blue House
1 Sejong-no
Chongno-gu
Seoul
Republic of Korea

Your Excellency,

The undersigned wish to express their deep concern at the case of KIM SONG-MAN who is serving a term of life imprisonment for expressing his opposition to government policy, and as he was not involved in violent activities, they urge you to release him immediately.

NOMBRE	DIRECCION	FIRMA
Fco. Javier Ojea Perez	C/Obispo Juan de Torres 1-4ºD	
Marta Gonzalez de Castro	C/Obispo Juan de Torres 1-4ºD	
Francisco Roper Morante	25326262	
Joly Rodriguez Perez	c/ Larios 7	
Mª José García	Ciudad Jardín	
Francisco Rivera	Los Gindes	
Fernando Cebrian de la Serna	25085936	
Ana Zayas Castilla	25098525	
Ildefonso José López Martín	25101.196	
Asuncion Arteaga Gimenez	27855586	
Ascension Castaño Jorge	25.084.179	
Pilar Alonso Sanchez	7.798.769	
Carlos Pinto Jimenez	30-576-180	
Francisco Rio	C/ Ciudad Rezuelo 15 - 33365134	
Luzipaz López Requena	33352.372.	
Antonio Delgado Duarte	33355062	
Elisabet Rodriguez Zurita	33369863	
Miguel Gómez Martínez	25.703.381	

(TRADUCCION: Los abajo firmantes quieren expresar su preocupación por el caso de KIM SONG-MAN que está cumpliendo una condena de cadena perpetua por expresar su oposición a la política del gobierno, y como no estaba involucrado en actividades violentas, le instan a que sea liberado inmediatamente.)

0286

His Excellency
President ROH Tae-
The Blue House
1 Sejong-no
Chongno-gu
Seoul
Republic of Korea

Your Excellency,

The undersigned wish to express their deep concern at the case of KIM SONG-MAN who is serving a term of life imprisonment for expressing his opposition to government policy, and as he was not involved in violent activities, they urge you to release him immediately.

NOMBRE	DIRECCION	FIRMA
José Pascual Madrona	Sánchez Albarrán, 15, 3º D 29014 - Málaga	
Luisa María Romero Chamorro.	C/ José Antonio Aragonés, Nº8, 29010. Málaga	
Mª Isabel Blanco Cueto	Avda Andalucía 13-3º-H 29002 Málaga	
Jesús Jiménez Clavero	" " " " "	
Dolores López Cebrián	C/ Las Suindas, 9, 1º 29014 Málaga	
Juan Manuel Alonso	Alameda Capuchinos 8. _29014 - Málaga	
Consuelo Domínguez	Almda. Cpchinos 21-29014 Málaga	
M. Ángeles Ariza Serna	C/ Victoria, 100, 3ºB. 29012. Málaga	
Gloria Velasco Castillo	C/ Rio 16 Antequera - Malaga	
Andrés Santamaría González	San Millán 7. -1ºB.- 29013	
Mª Auxiliadora Corcelles	San Nicolás nº 17-4º A - 29016	
Ana María López Cebrián	Plaza de Narvaez, 9, 9ºA-29014 Málaga	
Francisco Javier Ruiz Leal	"Parque del Sur", Bl. 9, 9º - 29014 - Málaga	

(TRADUCCION: Los abajo firmantes quieren expresar su preocupación por el caso de KIM SONG-MAN que está cumpliendo una condena de cadena perpetua por expresar su oposición a la política del gobierno, y como no estaba involucrado en actividades violentas, le instan a que sea liberado inmediatamente.)

0287

His Excellency
President ROH Tae-woo
The Blue House
1 Sejong-no
Chongno-gu
Seoul
Republic of Korea

Your Excellency,

The undersigned wish to express their deep concern at the case of KIM SONG-MAN who is serving a term of life imprisonment for expressing his opposition to government policy, and as he was not involved in violent activities, they urge you to release him immediately.

NOMBRE	DIRECCION	FIRMA
Pedro Leiva Béjar	Avda Bonaire 4 3ºC 29004 Málaga España	P. Leiva
María Isabel Leiva Béjar	Avd. Bonaire 4 3ºC 29004 Málaga	[illegible]
José Manuel Leiva Béjar	Avd. Bonaire 4-3ºC 29.004 Málaga	[illegible]
Ruben Aguilar Guerrero	Avd. Juan XXIII 29006 - Malaga	[illegible]
Friedrich v. Maltzahn	C/Beatas 6, 4 29008 - Malaga	v. Maltzahn
Juan Fco Gutierrez Lozano	C/[illegible] 1, 29011	[illegible]
Antonio J. Pelaez Tortosa, Avda Mijas, Nº 15, 1º		[illegible]
Mª del Mar Cordero de Mesa	[illegible] 28 29018 Malaga	[illegible]
Elena Mayorga Toledano, camino de la desviación nº 46		Elena Mayorga
Alicia Martin Bjerklund	C/Pozos blancos nº 11	[illegible]
Fco Escoriza Doblas	Herrera Oria El Carmen I P2	[illegible]
Mª José Chamorro Portillo	VAB Barceló	[illegible]
Mª Jose Galvez Imaz	Mirador Palmeras III B Nº 58 A	[illegible]
Antonio Ruiz Barba	C/Montes de Oca nº 12	Antonio Ruiz
Mª Angeles Sánchez García	Avda Pio XII, Nº 3	[illegible]
Jose Luis Yuste Delgado	C/[illegible] Nº 4 [illegible]	[illegible]
Diego Palomo Molis	C/Los Almendros Nº 3 Ach. El Grande	[illegible]
Adelaida Bejar Corrabal	Avd. Bonaire 4 3ºC 29004 Malaga	Adelaida Bejar

(TRADUCCION: Los abajo firmantes quieren expresar su preocupación por el caso de KIM SONG-MAN que está cumpliendo una condena de cadena perpetua por expresar su oposición a la política del gobierno, y como no estaba involucrado en actividades violentas, le instan a que sea liberado inmediatamente.)

0288

His Excellency
President ROH Tae-woo
The Blue House
1 Sejong-no
Chongno-gu
Seoul
Republic of Korea

Your Excellency,

The undersigned wish to express their deep concern at the case of KIM SONG-MAN who is serving a term of life imprisonment for expressing his opposition to government policy, and as he was not involved in violent activities, they urge you to release him immediately.

NOMBRE	DIRECCION	FIRMA
FRANCISCO LÓPEZ CARMONA	C/ MARQUÉS DE VIANA 77, 3°C 28039 MADRID	[signature]
CONCEPCIÓN CARMONA JIMÉNEZ	C/ BLANCO CORIS 10. 4°A 29007 MALAGA	[signature]
JOSE. A. LOPEZ VILLEGAS	C/ BLANCO CORIS, 10-4°A 29007 MALAGA	[signature]
JOSE ANTONIO LOPEZ CARMONA	C/ BLANCO CORIS 10 4° A 29007 MALAGA	[signature]
JUAN ANTONIO CHAVES MARTIN	C/ EMILIO PRADOS 26-6°-2 29003 MALAGA	[signature]
INES FUERTES AMPUDIA	C/ RIBERA MANZANARES 97 2° D 28008 MADRID	[signature]
ANTONIO CEBREIRO GARCIA	C/ MARQUES DE VIANA 77, 3°C 28039 MADRID	[signature]
Miguel Ángel López García	C/ Marqués de Viana, 77 3°C 28039 MADRID	[signature]
SOFIA FUERTES AMPUDIA	RIBERA DEL MANZANARES 97-2°D 28008 MADRID	[signature]
MANUELA GOMEZ MARIA	Gta S. Antonio de la Florida, 2. 3°A	[signature]
JOSE A. BLANCO DE LARA	PRINCESA 3 DUP. B 17	[signature]
JUAN C. GARCIA-SAMPEDRO	C/ Marquez 4 4°C-1 28009 MADRID	[signature]
Elena Fuertes Ampudia	AV. de Valladolid nº 57-59 P. 5-3°A.	[signature]
Marta Fuertes Ampudia	Trva. de Caballeros nº 5	[signature]
Mª Inés Sánchez Marta	C/ Arzobispo [illegible] nº 21	[signature]

(TRADUCCION: Los abajo firmantes quieren expresar su preocupación por el caso de KIM SONG-MAN que está cumpliendo una condena de cadena perpetua por expresar su oposición a la política del gobierno, y como no estaba involucrado en actividades violentas, le instan a que sea liberado inmediatamente.)

0289

His Excellency
President ROH Tae-WUU
The Blue House
1 Sejong-no
Chongno-gu
Seoul
Republic of Korea

Your Excellency,

The undersigned wish to express their deep concern at the case of KIM SONG-MAN who is serving a term of life imprisonment for expressing his opposition to government policy, and as he was not involved in violent activities, they urge you to release him immediately.

NOMBRE DIRECCION FIRMA

Juan Fco Pérez Gómez ; C/ ALTA-136 ; 29480 Gaucín (Málaga)

Mª Dolores Sanjuán Salas; C/ Cañamaque Nº33 Gaucín 29480 (Málaga)

Eladio Ocaña Serrano / Cañamaque 114 - Gaucín (29480) Málaga

Pedro Martín Vázquez C/ cañamaque 55 — Gaucín - Málaga

Enrique Domínguez Martínez C/ cañamaque

Pedro Juan Márquez Hidalgo c/ Jose Antonio Nº B — GAUCÍN - MÁLAGA

Petra Medina Godino C/ Piedras nº 50 Gaucín

Mª Angeles Prieto Moya c/ Arrabalete Nº 62 Gaucín.

ana Medina C/ Alta Nº 53

Mª Isabel Casas Galdeano Casares Nº 40 Gaucín

Antonia Vázquez Domínguez C/ Luis Domínguez 46 Gaucín

MARÍA JOSÉ LERMOS RUIZ C/ ALTA Nº 114 29480. GAUCÍN (MÁLAGA)

Virginia Ramos Martín c/ cañamaque Nº 132. Gaucín (Málaga)

Bernardina Martín C/ Piedras 81 Gaucín Málaga

Mónica Martín Vázquez / C/ Cañamaque Nº 55. GAUCÍN

SÁNCHEZ ANDRADES MARI CARMEN / CASARES, 34 GAUCÍN

PILAR MEDINA CANTUDO / Alta, 69, GAUCÍN

(TRADUCCION: Los abajo firmantes quieren expresar su preocupación por el caso de KIM SONG-MAN que está cumpliendo una condena de cadena perpetua por expresar su oposición a la política del gobierno, y como no estaba involucrado en actividades violentas, le instan a que sea liberado inmediatamente.)

0290

Inés Mena Gil B/ ALTO 118 Gayimu
Josefa torres Hidalgo C/ Cañamaque nº 4

0291

His Excellency
President ROH Tae-woo
The Blue House
1 Sejong-no
Chongno-gu
Seoul
Republic of Korea

Your Excellency,

The undersigned wish to express their deep concern at the case of KIM SONG-MAN who is serving a term of life imprisonment for expressing his opposition to government policy, and as he was not involved in violent activities, they urge you to release him immediately.

NOMBRE	DIRECCION		FIRMA
ENRIQUE LLOVET	SEGRE, 20	MADRID	Enrique Llovet

(TRADUCCION: Los abajo firmantes quieren expresar su preocupación por el caso de KIM SONG-MAN que está cumpliendo una condena de cadena perpetua por expresar su oposición a la política del gobierno, y como no estaba involucrado en actividades violentas, le instan a que sea liberado inmediatamente.)

0292

His Excellency
President ROH Tae-woo
The Blue House
1 Sejong-no
Chongno-gu
Seoul
Republic of Korea

Your Excellency,

The undersigned wish to express their deep concern at the case of KIM SONG-MAN who is serving a term of life imprisonment for expressing his opposition to government policy, and as he was not involved in violent activities, they urge you to release him immediately.

NOMBRE	DIRECCION	FIRMA
FDEZ. PARADAS MERCEDES	C/LOS MARTINEZ, 36 CAMPANILLAS - MALAGA	[signature]
ORTEGA HURTADO, FERNANDO	KUDA/ ANDALUCÍA 25	[signature]
HEREDIA FLORES, V. M.	c/ Comandante, 1	[signature]
PARADAS PARADAS MERCEDES	C/ LOS MARTINEZ, 36 CAMPANILLAS - MALAGA	[signature]
PELÁEZ SANTAMARÍA, SALVADOR	C/ DIPUTACIÓN, 25 4°C 29780 NERJA	[signature]
FDEZ. PARADAS FCO. JAVIER	C/ LOS MARTINEZ, 36 CAMPANILLAS	[signature]

(TRADUCCION: Los abajo firmantes quieren expresar su preocupación por el caso de KIM SONG-MAN que está cumpliendo una condena de cadena perpetua por expresar su oposición a la política del gobierno, y como no estaba involucrado en actividades violentas, le instan a que sea liberado inmediatamente.)

0293

His Excellency
President ROH Tae-woo
The Blue House
1 Sejong-no
Chongno-gu
Seoul
Republic of Korea

Your Excellency,

The undersigned wish to express their deep concern at the case of KIM SONG-MAN who is serving a term of life imprisonment for expressing his opposition to government policy, and as he was not involved in violent activities, they urge you to release him immediately.

NOMBRE	DIRECCION	FIRMA
TOMAS PEREZ BENZ	ESPERANTO, 18	[illegible]
Cristina Perez B.	Esperanto 18	[illegible]
Hannelore Benz	Esperanto	[illegible]
José Pérez Palmis	Esperanto 18	[illegible]
Nina Ramos Espildora	Juan de Austria 1	[illegible]
Sonia Sierra Ortega	Esperanto 13	[illegible]
Trinidad Ortega	Esperanto 13	[illegible]
Susana Moreno	Esperanto 13	[illegible]
M-Angel Sierra	Esperanto 13	[illegible]
E. Sierra Valle	Esperanto 13	[illegible]
Marina González Fndez.	C/ Fndo El Católico, 13	[illegible]
Begoña Martín Torres	Plza Conde de Peñalver, 10	[illegible]
Antoni Molins Morin	C/ Deus 31 4º 5	[illegible]
Gustavo Molinari	C/ S. Rueda nº 5	[illegible]
MANRIQUE BUSTO	POLA MONTICULO, 4	[illegible]
ÓSCAR GONZALEZ	C/ Mª BARRANCO	[illegible]

(TRADUCCION: Los abajo firmantes quieren expresar su preocupación por el caso de KIM SONG-MAN que está cumpliendo una condena de cadena perpetua por expresar su oposición a la política del gobierno, y como no estaba involucrado en actividades violentas, le instan a que sea liberado inmediatamente.)

0294

His Excellency
President ROH Tae-woo
The Blue House
1 Sejong-no
Chongno-gu
Seoul
Republic of Korea

Your Excellency,

The undersigned wish to express their deep concern at the case of KIM SONG-MAN who is serving a term of life imprisonment for expressing his opposition to government policy, and as he was not involved in violent activities, they urge you to release him immediately.

NOMBRE	DIRECCION	FIRMA
JULIAN GOMEZ DEL CASTILLO	Avenida Betanzos 2-10º 28029 Madrid	
Angel Ballesteros Castañeda	C/Conde Benavente 2-5ºC 47003 VALLADOLID	
RAFAEL DELGADO CHECA	C/GORDON, 18 11-E MALAGA	
Mª Antonia Alcaide Lastre	Sor Lucía 4 - Málaga	
Pepa Ruiz	C/BALAZÓN 2-6º	
Mª Carmen Ramos Díaz	c/ca-Soledad nº 8 Benarrabá (Málaga)	

(TRADUCCION: Los abajo firmantes quieren expresar su preocupación por el caso de KIM SONG-MAN que está cumpliendo una condena de cadena perpetua por expresar su oposición a la política del gobierno, y como no estaba involucrado en actividades violentas, le instan a que sea liberado inmediatamente.)

0295

His Excellency
President ROH Tae-woo
The Blue House
1 Sejong-no
Chongno-gu
Seoul
Republic of Korea

Your Excellency,

The undersigned wish to express their deep concern at the case of KIM SONG-MAN who is serving a term of life imprisonment for expressing his opposition to government policy, and as he was not involved in violent activities, they urge you to release him immediately.

NOMBRE	DIRECCION	FIRMA
Jose Contreras Domingo	C/. Lirios, 3, 29013-Malaga	[signature]
Francisco J. Cortas Rivera	A. Capuchinos -35/29013 Malaga	[signature]
Jesus Miranda Sánchez	Edificio Heroe Bermeja-6 29680 Estepona (Malaga)	[signature]
J. Fco Murillo Mas	Urban. El Consul Bl-3 8º2 29610 Malaga	[signature]
A. Félix Martín Bellido	Fco. Quevedo, 14-16 Torremolinos (Málaga)	[signature]
Fco J. González García	C/ Zaragüeta, nº 11, Blq 3, 3º Izq. (Málaga)	[signature]
Juan Prado Romero	Pza Mateo Luzon 3-6º D	[signature]

(TRADUCCION: Los abajo firmantes quieren expresar su preocupación por el caso de KIM SONG-MAN que está cumpliendo una condena de cadena perpetua por expresar su oposición a la política del gobierno, y como no estaba involucrado en actividades violentas, le instan a que sea liberado inmediatamente.)

0296

His Excellency
President ROH Tae-woo
The Blue House
1 Sejong-no
Chongno-gu
Seoul
Republic of Korea

Your Excellency,

The undersigned wish to express their deep concern at the case of KIM SONG-MAN who is serving a term of life imprisonment for expressing his opposition to government policy, and as he was not involved in violent activities, they urge you to release him immediately.

NOMBRE	DIRECCION	FIRMA
José Ramírez Parra	Fuengirola	
Arantxa García Gozena	Mijas	
Jesús Fco Aguilera Moreno	Mijas-Pueblo	
Santiago Martín Villamor	Mijas-Pueblo	
Patricia Marín Rodríguez	Mijas-Pueblo	
Esther Verdugo Martín	(Mijas-Costa)	
Guadalupe Rodríguez Peinado	Mijas	
María Belén Cruz Tamayo		
Elena Mayo Rueda		
Susana González Márquez	Mijas	
Soraya Fdez. Grgato		
Cristina de la Torre.		
Christina Reina Suole		
Cristina Navas Jiménez	(Mijas-Costa)	
Ana María Portillo López	(Mijas-Costa)	
EVA SERRANO	FUENGIROLA	
Rocío Olmedo García		
ALICIA GONZALEZ PERICET		

(TRADUCCION: Los abajo firmantes quieren expresar su preocupación por el caso de KIM SONG-MAN que está cumpliendo una condena de cadena perpetua por expresar su oposición a la política del gobierno, y como no estaba involucrado en actividades violentas, le instan a que sea liberado inmediatamente.)

0297

His Excellency
President ROH Tae-woo
The Blue House
1 Sejong-no
Chongno-gu
Seoul
Republic of Korea

Your Excellency,

The undersigned wish to express their deep concern at the case of
KIM SONG-MAN who is serving a term of life imprisonment for expressing his opposition to government policy, and as he was not involved in violent activities, they
urge you to release him immediately.

NOMBRE	DIRECCION	FIRMA
Crescencio Aguado Orteja	C/ Cervantes 8-5°1 Málaga	
Encarnación Gil Río de Rivera	C/ Cervantes 8-4°1 Málaga	
NURIA AGUADO GIL	C/ Cervantes, 8, 4°1	
Manuela fernandez cortes		
Auxiliadora Duarte Casesnovas		Casanovas
RICARDO RUIZ MERIDA		
INMACULADA CUEVAS MILLAN		
ENCARNACION AGUADO GIL	LOS FLAMENCOS 10	
Isabel Auza Planchuelo	avda San Isidro 3	
TOMAS CAMPOS GARRIGUES	C/ MORENO MONROY N° 6	
ROCIO AGUADO GIL	C/ CERVANTES N° 8 4° 1	Rocio Aguado
M° del Carmen Becerra Castaño	C/ Beethoven 4 3°1	
M° Teresa Martin de Jordes	Del Pastor, 15 7°c	
Ana Reyes Galán Palmero	C/ ISAAC PERAL N° 23 Y	33368749
Purificación Noguera Navas	D.N.I. 24256018	

(TRADUCCION: Los abajo firmantes quieren expresar su preocupación por el caso de KIM
SONG-MAN que está cumpliendo una condena de cadena perpetua por expresar su oposición
a la política del gobierno, y como no estaba involucrado en actividades violentas,
le instan a que sea liberado inmediatamente.)

0298

His Excellency
President ROH Tae-woo
The Blue House
1 Sejong-no
Chongno-gu
Seoul
Republic of Korea

Your Excellency,

The undersigned wish to express their deep concern at the case of KIM SONG-MAN who is serving a term of life imprisonment for expressing his opposition to government policy, and as he was not involved in violent activities, they urge you to release him immediately.

NOMBRE	DIRECCION	FIRMA
Antonio Clavero Barranquero	EUTS Málaga	[signature]
ISABEL MARTÍNEZ	EUTS Málaga	[signature]
José C. Medina	EUTS Málaga	[signature]
ASUNCION CARRETERO JUMILLA	EUTS Málaga	[signature]
VERONICA GZLEZ TAGLE	EUTS Málaga.	[signature]
TRINI LOPEZ	EUTS Málaga	Trini López
Ana Kaundo	EUTS / Málaga	Ana Kaundo
Francisco Cosano Rivas	EUTS/Málaga	F. Cosano 25-09-1991
Diego Montero Carrión	EUTS MALAGA	[signature]
CARLOS GALLEGO FORTALVA	EUTS. MALAGA	[signature]
LUISA BARRIONUEVO PASTOR	E.U.T.S / Málaga	[signature]
CLARISSE Ana	c/ Conde Lucanor 1. GUADALMAR / Málaga	[signature]

(TRADUCCION: Los abajo firmantes quieren expresar su preocupación por el caso de KIM SONG-MAN que está cumpliendo una condena de cadena perpetua por expresar su oposición a la política del gobierno, y como no estaba involucrado en actividades violentas, le instan a que sea liberado inmediatamente.)

0299

His Excellency
President ROH Tae-woo
The Blue House
1 Sejong-no
Chongno-gu
Seoul
Republic of Korea

Your Excellency,

The undersigned wish to express their deep concern at the case of KIM SONG-MAN who is serving a term of life imprisonment for expressing his opposition to government policy, and as he was not involved in violent activities, they urge you to release him immediately.

NOMBRE	DIRECCION	FIRMA
Francisco Gómez Aracil	c/ Mauras de Tolosa, 2-33 Malaga	[signature]
Alejandro Vergara	C. Jorañez 21 Cártama Málaga	[signature]
Enrique Gomez Aracil	Pº Marítimo 15 - Malaga - 25033998	[signature]
Nieves Casares Merelo	Pº Marítimo 15 Malaga - 12682305	Nieves Casares
José Mª Gomez Aracil	c/ Eugenio Selles nº 1 Malaga - 24666116	[signature]
Benita Calderon Caro	c/ Mauras de Tolosa 2-33-28-106-601 Malaga	Benita Calderón
Mª Eluisa Rubio Aracil	c/ Gral. Ibañes nº 21 Málaga DNI 25.262327	[signature]
Mª Luisa Aracil Diaz	c/ Granada 82 - Malaga	M. L. Aracil
Maria del Carmen Aracil Diaz	c/ Pinto Ejidos 75, 2º Malaga	[signature]
P. Aracil	(Victoria 75, 2º A) 24574275	P. Aracil
Isabel Aracil Dias	Victoria 75 2º 24639012	Isabel Aracil
Mª Dolores Pretel	Eugenio Selles 1 - 24767751	[signature]
Carlos Gomez Aracil	c/ Granada 4-82 - 29015 Malaga 25.011.941	[signature]
Victoria Abril Sanchez	c/ Granada nº 82 29015 Malaga 24724613	[signature]
F. German Garcia Robles	c/ Canovas del Castillo 5 Malaga 36865914	[signature]
Mª Luisa Gomez Aracil	c/ Canovas del Castillo Malaga 24666117	Mª Luisa Gomez
Ricardo Gómez Hueljas	c/ Granada 82 Málaga 24852313	
Germán García Gómez	c/ Cánovas del Castillo 5 - 25062878	[signature]

(TRADUCCION: Los abajo firmantes quieren expresar su preocupación por el caso de KIM SONG-MAN que está cumpliendo una condena de cadena perpetua por expresar su oposición a la política del gobierno, y como no estaba involucrado en actividades violentas, le instan a que sea liberado inmediatamente.)

0300

3인

관리 번호	91-249

외 무 부

종 별 :

번 호 : UKW-2545 일 시 : 91 1223 1600

수 신 : 장관(연이,기정)

발 신 : 주 영 대사

제 목 : A.I. 서한

A.I. 사무총장 IAN MARTIN 은 12.18. 아국정부의 사형집행에 대하여 아래와같은 내용의 12.20 자 서한을 법무부장관 앞으로 보내왔음을 보고함.

-A.I. 는 12.18. 9 명의 죄수에 대한 한국정부의 사형집행에 대하여 유감을표시함.

-사형은 지극히 잔인하며, 비인간적인 처벌임. 사형이 종신형보다 범죄예방에 더효과있다는 증거가 없음이 유엔 조사결과 밝혔졌음. 또한 사형제도가 없는 국가의 경험에 따르면, 흉악범의 경우 처형하지 않고도 사회와 격리시키는 것이 가능하다고함.

-이러한 이유로 A.I. 는 한국정부가 더이상의 사형집행을 중지하고 사형제도의 폐지를 고려할 것을 요청함.

첨부: 서한사본 (UKWF-674). 끝

(대사 이홍구-국장)

예고: 92.6.30 일반

일반문서로 재분류 (1992.6.30.)

— 1억 10본부와 협조,
우리측 설명자료를 주영대사에게 타경로록 고려할것
12/26

국기국 장관 차관 1차보 분석관 청와대 안기부

PAGE 1

91.12.24 05:40

외신 2과 통제관 BW

0301

주 영 국 대 사 관

UKW(F) : 0674 년월일 : 11223 시간 : 1600

수 신 : 장 관 (연이, 기정) 사본: 법무부장관

발 신 : 주 영 대 사

제 목 : 청부

보 안 통 제	필

(출처 :)

Page

(674 - 7 - 1)

외신 1과 통 제	

0302

amnesty international

INTERNATIONAL SECRETARIAT,
1 Easton Street, London WC1X 8DJ,
United Kingdom.

Fax: 071-956 1157

Tel: 071-413 5500

FACSIMILE COVER SHEET

TO: Mr K C Lee, Second Secretary, Embassy of the Republic of Korea, London

FROM: Derek Evans

DATE: 20 December 1991

DESTINATION FAX NO.: 5891326

TOTAL NUMBER OF PAGES INCLUDING THIS COVER SHEET: two

If you do not receive all of the pages, or they are not fully legible, please call us as soon as possible on (71)4135664.

COMMENTS/MESSAGES

Our ref.: TG ASA 25/91.18

Dear Mr Lee,

Attached is a copy of the message Mr Ian Martin sent today to Mr Kim Ki-choon, Minister of Justice of the Republic of Korea, expressing our regret at the execution of nine prisoners on 18 December.

Yours sincerely,

Derek G. Evans
Head of the Asia and Pacific Region
Research Department

674
(3-2)

☎ (44)(71) 413 5500 Telegrams: Amnesty London WC1 Telex: 28502 FAX: 956 1157

0303

Amnesty International is an independent worldwide movement working impartially for the release of all prisoners of conscience, fair and prompt trials for political prisoners and an end to torture and executions. It is funded by donations from its members and supporters throughout the world. It has formal relations with the United Nations, Unesco, the Council of ...

amnesty international

INTERNATIONAL SECRETARIAT,
1 Easton Street, London WC1X 8DJ,
United Kingdom.

Fax: 071-956 1157

Tel: 071-413 5500

FACSIMILE COVER SHEET

TO: Mr Kim Ki-chon, Minister of Justice of the Republic of Korea

FROM: Ian Martin, Secretary General, Amnesty International

DATE: 20 December 1991

DESTINATION FAX NO.: Ministry of Foreign Affairs 010 82 2 720-2686
Please forward to Mr Kim Ki-chon, Minister of Justice

TOTAL NUMBER OF PAGES INCLUDING THIS COVER SHEET: one

If you do not receive all of the pages, or they are not fully legible, please call us as soon as possible on (44)(71)4135664.

COMMENTS/MESSAGES

Our ref.: TG ASA 25/91.17

Dear Mr Kim Ki-chon,

Amnesty International regrets the decision of your government to order the execution of nine convicted prisoners on 18 December.

Executions are the ultimate cruel, inhuman and degrading punishment. Studies conducted for the United Nations have found that there is no evidence that executions have a greater deterrent on crime than life imprisonment. The experience of abolitionist countries shows that dangerous offenders can be kept safely away from the public without resorting to executions. For these reasons, Amnesty International calls on your government to stop further executions and consider the abolition of this punishment.

Yours sincerely,

Ian Martin
Secretary General
Amnesty International

674-
(3-3)

0304

관리 번호	91-256

법 무 부

인권 2545-329 503-7045 1991. 12. 30

수신 외무부장관

참조 국제기구조약국장

제목 국제사면위 서한관련 설명자료 송부

1. UKW-2545 ('91.12.23)과 관련입니다.

2. 귀부에서 요청한 국제사면위 '91.12.18 사형집행과 관련한 서한에 대한 설명자료를 별첨과 같이 송부하오니, 동 단체에 적의 설명될 수 있도록 조치하여 주시기 바랍니다.

첨부 : 사형집행에 대한 설명자료 1부. 끝.

법 무 부 장 관

일반문서로 재분류 (1992. 6. 30.)

0305

사형집행에 관한 설명자료

====================

1. 사형집행 일시.장소

   ○ 91.12.18. 10:00-16:05 서울구치소, 광주교도소

2. 사형집행 배경

   ○ 이번 사형집행은 사형확정자에 대한 통상적 형집행의 일환임

   ○ 집행대상자 9명은 모두 사람으로서 도저히 범할 수 없는 잔인한 방법으로 살인을 하는등 반인륜적, 반사회적인 강력범죄를 범한 자들로서 법원의 확정판결에 따라 사형이 집행된 것임

공　　　란

공 란

공 란

공　　란

5. 참고사항

ㅇ 근래 실시된 한 연구기관의 국민여론조사에 의하면 대다수 우리나라 국민들(조사대상인원중 71.6%)은 범죄인에 대한 현행 처벌방식이 너무 가볍다고 불만을 표시하고 검거된 범인에 대한 엄중처벌에 역점을 두어야 한다는 의견이 다수를 차지하였음. (1990.12.10.부터 13일 사이에 실시된 한국형사정책연구원의 국민여론조사 결과 참조)

ㅇ 이러한 여론조사결과를 보더라도 우리나라 국민들은 현행 사형제도의 존치를 원하고 있다는 것을 알 수 있음

ㅇ 형벌 제도는 각 나라의 문화적전통과 배경, 국민들의 법감정, 사회구조등에 따라 달라질 수 있는 것이므로 외국의 예를 우리나라에 획일적으로 적용하는 것은 부당하다고 사료됨

외교문서 비밀해제: 한국 인권문제 4

한국 인권문제 국제사면위원회 방한 및 대응 2

초판인쇄 2024년 03월 15일
초판발행 2024년 03월 15일

지은이 한국학술정보(주)
펴낸이 채종준
펴낸곳 한국학술정보(주)
주 소 경기도 파주시 회동길 230(문발동)
전 화 031-908-3181(대표)
팩 스 031-908-3189
홈페이지 http://ebook.kstudy.com
E-mail 출판사업부 publish@kstudy.com
등 록 제일산-115호(2000. 6. 19)

ISBN 979-11-7217-058-5 94340
979-11-7217-054-7 94340 (set)

이 책은 한국학술정보(주)와 저작자의 지적 재산으로서 무단 전재와 복제를 금합니다.
책에 대한 더 나은 생각, 끊임없는 고민, 독자를 생각하는 마음으로 보다 좋은 책을 만들어갑니다.